14

CULTURAL SCIENCES

UNIVERSITY OF ILLINOIS PRESS, URBANA, 1963

CULTURAL SCIENCES

THEIR ORIGIN AND DEVELOPMENT

BY FLORIAN ZNANIECKI

Originally published in a clothbound edition, 1952. Copyright 1952 by the
Board of Trustees of the University of Illinois. Manufactured in the United
States of America. Library of Congress Catalog Card No. 52-7838.

Twelve years ago, I planned to write a relatively short introduction to the *future* of sociology, including a survey of the sociological problems awaiting solution and an anticipation of new problems. I realized soon, however, that we cannot foresee the future of a science without taking into consideration not only its present, but also its past. For every science is evolving gradually, and its achievements and problems at any time originate in past achievements and problems.

I decided therefore to prepare an outline of the historical evolution of sociology. But this evolution proved to be inseparably connected with the whole development of philosophic and scientific knowledge, and historians have traced the origin of this development as far back as three thousand years ago. This explains why I begin my outline with the period preceding the growth of Greek theoretic thought, and survey briefly the persistence of certain old philosophic theories and the progress of new scientific theories.

It does not explain, however, the main content of this work, as indicated by its title. Why the term "sciences" in the plural? It conflicts with the ideal of the unity of scientific knowledge, in which many scientists believe. Why the adjective "cultural"? It contradicts the current theory according to which, even if there are several sciences, each of them (including sociology) is a "natural" science.

Well, in my younger days when I was a philosopher, like most other philosophers, I believed in the future unification of all valid knowledge. I did not base this belief, however, on the prevalent doctrine that all valid knowledge will become united because it is scientific knowledge of nature, and the natural universe will prove to be united. I relied, instead, on the doctrine that all valid knowledge is knowledge of culture, since even human observations and theories of nature are cultural products; and it will become united because the entire world of culture, when studied in historical perspective, will prove to be united.

But, contrary to both doctrines, the development of scientific knowledge of nature as well as of culture has resulted in a growing functional differentiation and multiplication of sciences. I see no reason to regret this historical trend or to hope that it will be reversed. It continually broadens the scientific horizon and enriches the intellectual life of mankind. The main objection against it is the excessive specialization of individual scientists, who know nothing beyond their own fields of research. But this is a practical problem which can be solved by new education and new creative cooperation among specialists.

Are we justified, however, in assuming, as the title of this book suggests, that there is a definite class of *cultural* sciences, different from those sciences which are popularly called *natural,* and that sociology belongs to this class? Here, again, we refer to historical evidence. The more objective, thorough, and methodical the scientific research in the world of culture, the more manifest the essential difference of this world from the natural universe. Many admirers of natural sciences, epistemologists, and metaphysicians do not like this result of scientific progress. But they cannot stop it.

Like every author, I am aware that I have many personal obligations to others. As far as this book is concerned, it would have taken me nearly twice as much time without the collaboration of my wife, Eileen Markley Znaniecki, and some parts of it might be more difficult to understand. J. William Albig did everything possible to encourage and help me complete the work. Robert Bierstedt, who read the manuscript as it was being written, gave me stimulating appreciation, constructive criticism, and significant suggestions.

But some of my obligations began long before this book was started. If William I. Thomas had not asked me to collaborate with him on *The Polish Peasant,* I would probably have remained all my life a philosopher, and never have turned to sociology as an inductive science. I owe to Robert M. MacIver and Theodore Abel an invitation from Dean (now President) William F. Russell of Teachers College which brought me to Columbia University for two years, from 1931 to 1933. Thanks again to Robert MacIver, I lectured at Columbia University in the summer and fall of 1939, and thus escaped a Nazi concentration camp and could join the University of Illinois faculty in 1940.

Contents

Knowledge and the concept of order

In our historical period, knowledge is considered more important than ever before. Never were so many institutions devoted to the maintenance and development of knowledge. Never was so much knowledge imparted by those who have it to those who lack it. But there are different conceptions of knowledge and many controversies as to what knowledge is true.

Most widely spread, indeed almost universal, is the conception that knowledge means knowing how to do what one wants or has to do: how to plant or harvest a crop, how to cook a meal, how to paint a house, how to drive a car, how to perform a certain job in a factory, how to manage a business, how to speak or write, how to accumulate money, how to train a child, how to make friends, how to win an election, how to lead an army to victory. In this sense, it is always somebody's knowledge; somebody proves that he knows how by achieving the results which he intended to achieve, and the final test is success.

We shall call this *pragmatic* knowledge. The proof of its truth does not show how the knower obtained it; he may have learned it from somebody else or reached it by trial and error or derived it from scientific sources. The diversity of this kind of knowledge is very great, and its innumerable varieties are not systematically integrated. Although controversies as to its effectiveness can be easily solved, controversies as to its usefulness often remain unsolved. For knowledge which is useful to the one who has it may be harmful to others; knowing how to win an election or a battle, how to gain money by speculation or by competitive salesmanship is useful to the winner, but harmful to the loser.

A different type is knowledge of good and bad, or, in modern terms, of right and wrong. The test of its truth is the agreement of thinkers who are considered authoritative judges. It has several varieties. The most popular and the most important, according to general opinion, is knowledge of what is *morally* good and bad. It is now being applied by thinkers all over the world to everything men do individually or collectively, especially in dealing with other men. Their judgments are expressed in many thousands of books and articles and are, of course, highly controversial. Not so much importance is ascribed to the knowledge of what is aesthetically good and bad, although it is also very controversial. It is manifested in judgments about literature, music, painting, sculpture, architecture, clothes, etc.

More inclusive and extremely important from the point of view of those who share it is *religious* knowledge, revealed to men by gods, mostly through the medium of prophets and priests. Divine revelation is the absolute test of its truth. But many different revelations have occurred, and what is true according to one of them may be false according to others.

Relatively few people are acquainted with *philosophic* knowledge. It ranges from inclusive systematic theories about the ultimate essence of everything, through more limited theories about the essence of nature, culture, goodness, beauty, knowledge in general, down to methodical criticism of certain kinds of knowledge—pragmatic, moral, religious, philosophic, scientific—which may or may not lead to special systematic theories. Its truth is judged by principles of logical reasoning, sometimes supplemented by direct intuition. Those who share it consider that it has supremacy over all other kinds of knowledge. But many different philosophic theories have been formulated, and numerous contradictions can be found among them.

Finally, most of the knowledge which is being imparted to youth on higher educational levels is *scientific* knowledge. The recognized test of its truth is, generally speaking, a combination of logical reasoning and empirical or factual evidence. But we find quite a few controversies as to what empirical evidence is and what it proves. In American colleges and universities, we usually discover four divisions of scientific knowledge: mathematics, natural science(s), humanities or humanistic studies, and social science(s). Mathematics is the most exact logically. Though it does not use empirical evidence to test the truth of its own theories, yet it is considered by mathematicians and some philosophers as the foundation of all true knowledge, for it can be applied to various realms of knowledge, and its applications can be tested. Natural science is also now quite uniformly standardized, so far as tests of truth are concerned. Unlike moral, religious, or philosophic knowledge, it has no controversial issues that cannot be solved sooner or later by new scientific tests. And, unlike pragmatic knowledge, it manifests considerable integration, though perhaps not enough to justify the use of a single noun. The humanities have little integration, and much of the knowledge imparted under this rubric is moral, aesthetic, philosophic. That part of it which is considered scientific has standards which differ from those of the natural sciences, but they are sufficiently uniform to prevent insolvable controversies. The division of social sciences lies somewhere between the natural and the humanistic, in some measure overlapping both, as when psychology and human geography are listed under both natural and social sciences, and history under both social sciences and humanities. It uses sometimes standards of natural science, sometimes standards of the humanities; it strives sometimes for integration, sometimes for separation; and within it are waged continuous controversies as to what is scientific knowledge.

As one who imparts knowledge to the younger generation, I have been puzzled for a long time by the coexistence of those diverse types of knowledge in the modern world, and by the numerous controversies among their adherents. Do they have anything in common? If so, why do they differ so widely? What is the connection, if any, between them, particularly between the four divisions of scientific knowledge, and between scientific knowledge in general and other types of knowledge? What is the significance of the controversies between thinkers, and why are they so prominent in certain types of knowledge, but not in others? And, finally, is it possible to anticipate what will be the future of knowledge?

The answers to these questions might be sought in a philosophy of knowledge. Philosophers—epistemologists, logicians, methodologists—have been investigating knowledge for centuries. From their point of view, only those results of human thinking which can be proved true by universal standards of truth constitute knowledge. According to this principle, most of what is popularly called knowledge is not knowledge at all; it is subjective illusions, imaginations, beliefs, prejudices, wishful thoughts, which are either false or unprovable.

The philosophic approach, however, has certain limitations. First, it does not explain why so many thinkers have continuously and consistently assumed, sometimes for centuries, that what they know is true, in spite of the fact that it conflicts with universal principles of truth. The explanation of this must be sought not in epistemology, logic, or methodology, but in some other realm of knowledge. Second, many judgments of philosophers as to what constitutes true knowledge are controversial, and some of these controversies seem insolvable. Third, many philosophers leave out of consideration the fact that modern knowledge, especially scientific knowledge, is continually growing and changing; some epistemological, logical, methodological principles which were or seemed to be applicable to all knowledge a century ago are inapplicable to the new knowledge which has emerged since then. Thus, as we shall see later on, several philosophers ignore altogether the existence of "social sciences," with their new epistemological and methodological standards, and treat them as if their basic standards were moral. And only half a century ago did philosophers fully realize that the principles of

Aristotelian logic had to be supplemented and modified in consequence of new developments in mathematics and physical science.

Another way of solving these problems is to investigate various types of knowledge not as they are judged by philosophers, but as they are conceived by the thinkers themselves who assume that what they know is true. This is the approach which has been used by historians and ethnologists. Historians have investigated many theories or doctrines which have appeared in writing, and contain various kinds of judgments that the authors claimed to be true— mostly philosophic, but also religious, moral, pragmatic, scientific. They usually refrain from judging these doctrines, as philosophers do, by some universal standards of truth. Instead, their main task is to reconstruct them as thoroughly as possible from written documents and to trace whatever connections may be found between contemporary and successive doctrines. Ethnologists have studied various types of knowledge orally expressed in contemporary nonliterate societies. From a comparative survey of this historical and ethnological material, tentative hypotheses concerning knowledge in general may be drawn.

In the first place, briefly and popularly speaking, every kind of knowledge which its bearers believe to be true is supposed to be knowledge of some intelligible *order* which exists among the vast multiplicity and diversity of objects and events in the midst of which men live. Knowledge of such order is considered indispensable for men to discover what certain objects are and how they differ from other objects, to explain why certain events occurred, and to foresee certain events which will occur. If they are guided by this knowledge in their actions, it is expected to help them achieve satisfactory results and to avoid events detrimental to them.

Second, the diversity of knowledge found in the modern world is due to different conceptions of order. The primary difference is that between the evaluative and the nonevaluative conception. The former is almost universal among religious and moral thinkers, predominates among pragmatic thinkers, and is accepted by quite a few philosophers. They conceive order as that which conforms with their standards of right; what is wrong is that which interferes with order, disturbs it, or even destroys it. This explains the numerous insolvable controversies between them; for, inasmuch as their conceptions of right differ, what is order in the judgment of some is disturbance of order in the judgment of others. According to the nonevaluative conception, almost unanimously accepted and applied by natural scientists, order includes all regularities which scientists discover by investigating methodically the factual relationships between empirical data, no matter how these relationships are evaluated by thinkers.

Finally, the historians who investigated past knowledge reached certain conclusions of great significance for contemporary knowledge. They found that some of the pragmatic and moral conceptions now in use already existed at the time writing was invented, and must have existed long before that. The basic conceptions which predominate in present religious knowledge, judging from the evidence contained in "sacred books," were developed four or five thousand years ago, although their development probably began earlier. The basic conceptions of philosophic knowledge were developed in the classical period of ancient Greece. The basic conceptions used by present scientists also began to develop in classical antiquity, but they reached full development only in the course of the last four centuries. Thus, according to historical evidence, new species of knowledge emerged from those which existed before. (We use the word "species" instead of "type" or "class" in order to avoid certain logical controversies.) This is what biologists call "evolution." The term does not imply that with the appearance of new species the old species necessarily disappear; they may continue to exist, and still other species may emerge from them later. Nor does it mean that a new species necessarily continues to exist and remains essentially changeless; it may disappear completely or, if it lasts, other new species may later emerge from it.

Neither the continued existence of earlier species of knowledge nor the evolution of new species can be explained, unless we take into consideration the fact that knowledge is produced and maintained by thinkers. And in the past, as well as in the present, thinkers have manifested conflicting tendencies. The great majority of thinkers to whom knowledge has been imparted by their predecessors and who in turn impart it to their successors are inclined to believe that they truly know everything that is essential about the order to which this knowledge refers. We find this belief in every historical period among bearers and transmitters of traditional pragmatic knowledge, moral knowledge, religious knowledge. Even philosophers, who were the first to assume the function of critics of established knowledge, as soon as they developed systematic theories of their own, were inclined to consider their knowledge as absolutely true and complete.

If these beliefs had been shared by all thinkers, the evolution of knowledge would obviously be inexplicable. But throughout history some thinkers have been searching for and have sometimes discovered various kinds of order previously unknown. They usually met opposition from the bearers of established knowledge who were sure that it was complete; nonetheless, the search went on, though sometimes with long interruptions, and gradually resulted in the development of new varieties of knowledge.

Modern scientific knowledge, the latest result of this slow, agelong evolution may represent the final result. This is not because scientists know everything that is to be known, but because search for the unknown, which was incompatible with older forms of knowledge, has been recognized by scientists as one of their main functions. Consequently, whatever new knowledge may emerge from this search will remain an integral part of scientific knowledge.

The history of the natural sciences after their basic principles were fully developed and accepted clearly indicates how radically scientific knowledge differs in this respect from older species of knowledge. The continual search of many scientists for various kinds of natural order previously unknown results in new discoveries leading to more research and more discoveries. The range of scientific knowledge about nature is expanding, and its wealth of content is increasing with an unprecedented rapidity. And as it expands and increases, innumerable new varieties of pragmatic knowledge, more efficient and more complex than ever before, are derived from it.

In view of the tremendous dynamic growth of natural sciences and their technical applications, these sciences, taken together, dominate all modern knowledge. This is recognized not only by those who extol their growth as the greatest human achievement, but also by others who resent their power and wish that scientific knowledge of nature could be subordinated to other kinds of knowledge. Ideologists who realize that the pragmatic power derived from natural sciences can be as effectively used for purposes which conflict as for those which harmonize with their ideas of right and wrong want scientists to be guided in their research by "higher" moral authorities. Religious thinkers deplore the skeptical attitude of most natural scientists toward the assumption that the divine origin of natural order can be proved by scientific research. They reciprocate by maintaining a skeptical attitude toward natural sciences, claiming that, because scientific theories are continually changing, their truth is always doubtful; whereas divine knowledge is eternal and absolutely true. Philosophers of culture object to the exaltation of natural sciences to the detriment of other human achievements—art, literature, religion, morality, law, social organization, and of course philosophy itself.

But it is hard to reverse evolutionary trends without destroying their results. Natural sciences gained their independence from older disciplines during a period when their growth was much slower and their practical influence much weaker than it is now. The main reason why they succeeded was that they eliminated the insolvable controversial issues springing from evaluative conceptions of order, rejected dogmatic adherence to established doctrines, and accepted common methodical principles which enabled scientists to cooperate in their search for the unknown as no thinkers had ever done before. How can we expect that two hundred years later, after their cooperation has yielded such historically unprecedented results, they could be induced to submit again to the guidance of authoritative exponents of various conflicting moral, religious, or philosophic doctrines; to become involved in nonscientific controversial issues which would make cooperation difficult, if not impossible; and to stop their search for the unknown whenever it might result in discoveries which would invalidate rather than confirm some established theory?

And yet, in spite of the marvelous development of natural sciences, wide areas of human knowledge still remain beyond their reach. Natural scientists cannot adequately investigate the content of many varieties of pragmatic knowledge—political, educational, economic, linguistic, etc. Nor can they include in their research that realm to which moral and aesthetic thinkers refer. They obviously cannot study gods and their activities, divine revelations, and mythical events. The very existence of natural sciences raises problems which natural scientists cannot solve, for science itself is not a part of the natural order which scientists investigate. The history of knowledge in general and of natural sciences in particular is not a natural science. The process in the course of which an individual becomes a natural scientist, by learning through communication with others the agglomerated results of previous scientific research and the use of scientific methods, is entirely different from those natural processes which he learns to investigate. The economic and social conditions upon which the existence and development of scientific knowledge depend differ very much from the physical, chemical, and biological conditions under which scientists work; and they are not being studied by physicists, chemists, or biologists. The present impact of political groups upon the practical application of the results of physics and chemistry by scientists is certainly not a physical, chemical, or biological fact.

Of course, all the areas which are not included within the realm of natural science are considered by pragmatic, religious, moral, aesthetic, philosophic thinkers as their own. Many of them still claim that they know all that is essential about these areas. Four hundred or even three hundred years ago, almost the only challenge to their claims was given by skeptics and critics who pointed out the numerous insolvable controversies among them and their inability to reach any general agreement whatsoever.

But, as we know, certain important changes have occurred since then. During the last two and a half centuries an increasing number of students began to apply an approach, partly modeled on that of natural sciences, to those areas of knowledge which natural sciences left out. They ceased to evaluate positively or negatively that which they studied, began to question the ultimate truth of established knowledge, assumed the function of searching for new knowledge, and accepted the principle of factual evidence in testing their conclusions. This is how the present humanistic and social sciences gradually developed. The progressive use of historical evidence during the last hundred years in studying the evolution of knowledge itself is one of the results of this development.

However, the use of the scientific approach in these areas of knowledge has apparently been less successful than in the natural domain. Many epistemologists, logicians, and methodologists who compare the results of this approach with those of contemporary natural sciences doubt whether these new studies can ever become "sciences," in the sense in which this term is applied to the methodical investigation of nature, and sometimes even explicitly deny this possibility. In surveying works of historians, cultural anthropologists, political scientists, economists, sociologists, and studies of literature, art, religion, law, those critics emphasize how defective such works are from the scientific point of view. And indeed many of them are still full of evaluative judgments implying the age-old antithesis between good and bad, right and wrong, and resulting in insolvable controversies. Quite a few of them are dogmatic, contain only that empirical evidence which confirms the theories of the authors, and omit any evidence which might invalidate their theories. Some of the most famous works include speculative doctrines which can be neither proved nor disproved by empirical evidence. And numerous monographic works which do conform with the elementary principles of scientific research are mere descriptions of particular empirical complexes, unconnected with other descriptions and opening no way for new general hypotheses to be tested by comparative research.

All this seems to justify the pessimistic attitude of the critics and leads some of them to assert that social and humanistic studies can reach the scientific level only if and insofar as they become integral parts of natural sciences. Whatever cannot be incorporated into the latter is not science at all; its most respectable designation is "art." This distinction is expressed in the term "College of Liberal Arts and Sciences." But if these same critics had lived two and a half centuries ago and surveyed the chemical, botanical, zoological, even the physical and astronomical works published at that time, they would have found that many, perhaps the majority, of them had similar defects. By now, of course, such works have either been destroyed except for brief summaries or are buried in libraries, where they are occasionally dug up by historians; only those are remembered which made some contributions to later scientific developments. If the achievements of natural sciences are dynamic, not static, and can be fully appreciated only if considered in their historical growth, should not the newer "sciences" be also viewed in historical perspective? If their present condition is no better than that of chemistry or biology some centuries ago, it may simply be because their development began later; and this late beginning, in turn, may be explained by methodical difficulties greater than those which natural scientists had to overcome. A study of their development may prove that the pessimists are wrong, that these "sciences" are on the way to becoming sciences in the full sense of the term.

Recent historical surveys of some of these sciences already provide considerable evidence in favor of this supposition. Thus, during the last twenty-five years, a number of works, individual or collective, dealing with the development of sociology have been published. Although some disagreement appears as to the range of sociological research and the relative effectiveness of methods used in this research, the agglomerated results of these studies leave no doubt that sociology has achieved considerable scientific progress since Comte's first attempt to lay its foundations as a new systematic science.[1] Historical surveys by specialists in several other divisions of social and humanistic studies show that a parallel development has been going on in their respective realms. And, significantly, most of this scientific progress seems to be due not to a gradual absorption of these studies by natural sciences, but, on the contrary, to their increasing independence of natural sciences, on which some of them (particularly sociology, economics, and anthropology) were originally dependent to a considerable degree.[2]

This apparently indicates that the scientists who contribute to this progress are searching for and discovering among the specific data and facts which they study some kinds of objectively ascertainable order, different from those kinds of order which natural scientists have been discovering in their research. Is this search going on, or at least beginning, in *all* the areas of study which are included under the concepts of social sciences and humanities? If so, what, if anything, do the various kinds of order which they are discovering have in common?

Nowadays, the data which social scientists and humanists are studying and which natural scientists—astronomers, physicists, chemists, biologists, geologists—ignore are designated by the general term "culture." The concept which this term symbolizes includes religion, language, literature, art, customs, mores, laws, social organization, technical production, economic exchange, and also philosophy and science. Suppose we call all these special divisions "cultural studies" or, insofar as they become scientific, "cultural sciences."

But what's in a name? The name "natural sciences" is meaningful, for its use postulates a universal category of natural order including all specific orders or regularities which students of nature—astronomers, physicists,

[1] The best general survey of the history of social thought is given by Harry E. Barnes and Howard Becker, *Social Thought from Lore to Science*, 2 vols. (Boston: Heath, 1938). I owe much to this work. A brief but excellent outline of the history of sociology is that of Floyd N. House, *The Development of Sociology* (New York: McGraw, 1936).

Pitirim Sorokin's *Contemporary Sociological Theories* (New York: Harper, 1928) is much more inclusive than the title suggests, and the approach is predominantly critical, from the point of view of the author's own theory.

[2] Quite a few cooperative works on recent developments in the social sciences in general and especially in sociology have been written since 1930: *Fields and Methods of Sociology*, ed. L. L. Bernard (New York: Farrar, 1934); *Contemporary Social Theory*, eds. Harry E. Barnes, Howard Becker, and Frances B. Becker (New York: Appleton, 1940); *Twentieth Century Sociology*, eds. Georges Gurvitch and Wilbert Moore (New York: Philosophical Library, 1945).

chemists, biologists—have discovered or will discover in their special realms of research. This postulate has been continuously validated, though the conception of the universal order changed somewhat during the last century. The name "cultural sciences" will be meaningful only if we postulate the existence of a universal category of *cultural order* including all specific orders which students of culture have discovered or will discover.

I believe that such a postulate is necessary for continuous scientific progress in the whole domain of cultural studies. As a student of sociology, I came to the conclusion some time ago that sociologists already have a workable conception of cultural order in their own realm of research; it is an order of relationships among that kind of human actions which are called "social."[3] About the same time a somewhat similar conclusion was reached, though in a different way, by Talcott Parsons.[4] This led me to the tentative hypothesis that cultural order in general is an order of relationships among all kinds of human actions.

But what is the significance of this hypothesis from the scientific point of view? One does not need to be a scientist to know that some order exists among human actions. Indeed, a six-year-old child of average intelligence is aware that human actions are normatively ordered or regulated; and as he grows up under the guidance of adults, he learns more and more about this order. He finds that most of the actions dealing with men are expected to conform with moral norms and in fact usually do so. Most actions dealing with material objects regularly follow technical rules. Speech is phonetically, semantically, and grammatically ordered.

If the function of cultural sciences is to investigate the kind of order which has been for thousands of years a matter of common-sense knowledge, why did they develop so late? There must be something new in the scientific approach to this order which makes it essentially different from the common-sense approach. I thought that the origin of this new approach had to be traced before my hypothesis could be tested.

Such was the starting point of the present work. It would be very difficult and of little use to the reader to summarize here its total content. May the following hint as to its main conclusions suffice!

To explain the late origin of the scientific approach to culture we have to take into consideration the sequence in the evolution of new types of knowledge which historians have discovered. The development of cultural sciences was preceded by the development of natural sciences; the development of natural sciences was preceded by the development of philosophy. To find some explanation for this sequence, we went still further back, to the historical period which preceded the development of philosophy. And then we learned

---

[3] Florian Znaniecki, *Social Actions* (New York: Farrar, 1936).
[4] Talcott Parsons, *The Structure of Social Action* (New York: McGraw, 1937).

that the development of philosophy was an essential condition of the emergence of natural as well as of cultural sciences, and that the development of natural sciences was an essential condition of the emergence of cultural sciences.

But then, in surveying the later development of natural sciences, we noticed that their subsequent progress was conditioned by their growing independence from philosophy. And a survey of the later development of cultural sciences showed that their progress is conditioned by their growing independence, both from philosophy and from natural sciences. A brief study of some results of several sciences, each specializing in its own realm of culture— material technique, economy, art, literature, music—indicates that this independence is gained, and scientific progress is achieved in the very measure in which these sciences concentrate (just as sociology is now doing) on objective, comparative investigation of specific human actions and their relationships. This seemed to confirm our hypothesis.

Then the problem arose: Is there any connection between these sciences? The failure of all attempts to integrate them into one all-inclusive science of culture proves that their specialization is objectively justified and cannot be overcome. But an analysis of the connection between them and sociology leads to the conclusion that sociology, although it has also specialized, is the basic cultural science, just as physics is the basic natural science.

Order as Intentional Creation
of Conscious Agents

Popular conceptions of order

If we compare the various meanings of the word "order" and of the words in other Western languages etymologically derived from the Latin *ordo*, we find that most (though not all) of these meanings imply that order is something that human agents introduce among the objects of their activities.[1] Translators and lexicographers who seek for equivalents of this word in languages which have not adopted the Latin terminology select words which have the same implication.[2]

The wide use in common speech of the word "order" and of its equivalents with the same meaning suggests that the idea it symbolizes is not a product of philosophic or scientific development, but a result of that common-sense reflection about practical activity which historically preceded systematic philosophy and science.

Order in this popular sense is a positively evaluative concept. It is judged "good," from the point of view of the agents who create it, either for its own sake or because it helps achieve some of their purposes. It is implicitly or explicitly contrasted with disorder, a negatively evaluative concept, which may mean either disturbance of an existing order or absence of order where it ought to exist.

Take a few familiar examples. A room is in order when all the objects it contains have been intentionally selected and arranged according to a certain pattern, each object occupying a definite position in relation to other objects. The arrangement depends upon the purpose for which the room is to be used and the nature of the objects available for this purpose. Disorder means devi-

[1] Here we use the term "agent" in the indefinite sense of "any X who acts." Later (Chapter 7), we shall limit the application of this noun and define more exactly what we mean by the verb "to act."

[2] Out of the sixteen meanings of the word "order" listed in *Webster's Universal Dictionary* (Cleveland: World Syndicate Publishing Co., 1937), fourteen have this connotation, while one symbolizes a biological and one a mathematical concept.

ation from the pattern, due to the presence of objects which ought not to be there, or the absence of objects which ought to be there, or disturbance of the regular spatial arrangement. There is a specific kind of order for a Mongolian *yurta* and Eskimo *igloo*; a Polynesian men's house; a Western middle-class bedroom, kitchen, living room, dining room; a workshop; a store; a restaurant; a church; a court room; a lecture hall; an art museum; a public library. Obviously, the pattern of order for each kind of room differs in different cultures and changes in the course of history. The order of an American kitchen differs from that of a traditional Chinese kitchen; the arrangement of a modern department store differs from that of a medieval shop; the arrangement of furniture in a Louis XV salon was different from that of a late Victorian reception room.

A garden is in order when each plant or species is growing where it has been purposely planted or preserved; on the other hand, weeds growing among the cultivated plants and insect pests eating leaves, flowers, or roots mean disorder. Here also the pattern of order may vary considerably, according to custom; the utilitarian order of a fruit orchard differs from that of a vegetable garden, and both differ from the aesthetic order of a combined park and flower garden. And how widely parks and gardens can vary may be seen by comparing the French, English, Persian, and Japanese patterns.

Another type of order, sometimes verging on the spatial arrangement of objects, is that of interconnected parts of an artificially constructed whole. A complex object which possesses this type of order can be successfully used for certain practical purposes. Disorder interferes with its use; it may mean that some essential parts are missing or spoiled, or that something is included which disturbs the connection between essential parts, or that the arrangement of the parts deviates from the pattern necessary to make the whole useful. A kitchen stove, a suit of clothes, a boat, a building, a machine is supposed to possess such an order.

Still another type of intended order is that of moving objects. It is both spatial and temporal, involving either a prearranged succession of places through which a certain object must pass, or a prearranged succession of objects passing through a certain place, or both. Such an arrangement may serve various practical purposes, and disorder (in the sense of disturbance of such an arrangement or lack of an arrangement when it is expected) interferes with the achievement of these purposes. This order is exemplified, with various degrees of complexity, by the movement of a plow in a field, the sailing of a boat, the grinding of flour in a water mill, the progression of objects along an assembly line in a factory, scheduled transportation of goods by railroads, regulated motor traffic in urban centers.

The objects which an agent arranges in space and moves in a certain succession may be human bodies. We are familiar with many examples of such arrangements of human bodies, to which the term "order" may be applied: In a dining room during a ceremonial dinner, guests are seated in a certain prearranged order; a company of soldiers stands at attention in serried ranks on command of an officer; in a church, a school, a court, individuals are placed in accordance with a definite spatial pattern; in an opera house during a public performance, every member of the audience has a seat appointed in advance and is supposed to stay in that seat; at a royal reception, guests stand and move in a definite order of precedence; participants in a religious procession move in an orderly series along a designated route at a uniform speed. The general pattern of order for political or religious purposes is established by a tradition, sometimes centuries old, and it is applied in each particular case by a master of ceremonies or other special agent. Those who participate in the reception or the procession are informed of their places in the order and are expected to stay or move when and where the pattern requires it. Every deviation is viewed as a disturbance of order and negatively valued by the agents who have made the arrangements.

Somewhat different from this kind of order is the purposive direction of the physical behavior of human beings in the handling of inanimate objects. In a factory there is not only an orderly arrangement of things, stationary or moving, but an order of physical behavior among workers; it describes workers as "hands," performing the kinds of movements which, according to the division of labor planned by technologists and managers, are needed for the technical mass production of certain goods. Disorder means any outward behavior of workers which disturbs this prearranged combination of technical performances. Likewise, the order of movement of motor cars along roads and streets is maintained only if and insofar as their drivers, whose hands and feet control the machinery, follow certain regulations.

In other cases, the concept of order includes both physical and symbolic behavior. The chairman calls a meeting "to order," thus requesting that from then on the persons attending the meeting will behave and speak only in accordance with well-recognized rules. The order which a teacher introduces among the pupils of a class consists in their doing whatever, according to the teaching-learning pattern, they are expected to do at a given time—listen to the teacher, look at what the teacher shows them, answer questions, read, write. Disorder is whatever they do which interferes with this order; for instance, fighting, quarreling, talking instead of listening, playing instead of studying.

While in these instances order is connected with a spatial arrangement of human bodies and a temporal succession of human behavior which the ordering agent can observe, in other instances it consists in having certain human beings behave according to certain rules whenever they encounter specific situations in any place at any time, whether the ordering agent observes them or not. Disorder means any behavior which conflicts with these rules.

One of the most inclusive conceptions of order in this sense is denoted by the well-known term "legal order." As viewed by the agents who tend to control by law the behavior of human beings living in a certain territory, it is an order instituted and maintained by these agents themselves—the legislators who promulgate laws, the judges who apply them in particular cases, the executive officers who exact conformity with them—who together constitute a collective agency called "government." The government determines in advance how specific categories of human beings under its control ought to behave and/or ought not to behave in certain kinds of situations defined in advance. Order means conformity with law; disorder, transgression of law. From the standpoint of governmental agents, order is good because it is needed for the realization of certain purposes; disorder, bad because it interferes with their realization. Therefore, according to governmental agents, legal order is usually good and disorder bad for the people who are subjected to it, inasmuch as one of the main purposes of the government in establishing legal order is collective security, without which the people cannot satisfy their basic needs regularly. Similarly, the order of the schoolroom is good for the pupils, the order of motor traffic good for the drivers and the cars, the order of household furniture good for the furniture and the home.

Difference between popular and scientific ideas of order

In comparing these various examples of order, we notice that all of them have one fundamental implication in common. The agent who produces order is not conceived as a participant in the order produced by him; the order includes the objects which he experiences and upon which he acts, but not himself. This is, of course, taken for granted when his objects are nonhuman: The housewife is not a part of the orderly arrangement of things in her living room or kitchen; the gardener not a part of the botanical order of the garden which he cultivates; the builder of a boat or a house, not a part of the structural order of the boat or house which he builds. But the implicit assumption remains the same even when the objects upon which the agent acts are human: The teacher, the master of ceremonies, the commander of a military company, the manager of labor, the legislator, the judge, while functioning as maker and guardian of order, is not a participant in the orderly behavior of the pupils, or of the people joining a parade, or of the soldiers drilling in formation, or of the citizens who are governed by law. Obviously, he may include himself among the objects of his activity: A master of ceremonies, having arranged a parade, may himself take part in it; a legislator, having promulgated a law, may become subject to it himself as a citizen. But this is not considered essential to his function; while dealing with the objects of his activity, he acts unreflectively, sometimes reflectively, as if he were a creator of order and, as such, outside and above his creation.

This popular conception is not altogether invalid. Undeniably, the kind of order exemplified above is real, in the sense that it can be observed. We may even agree that human agents create it, if creating means producing something new which did not exist before within the range of human experience. But in the creative process as empirically known, no human agent creates order out of absolute chaos.

Philosophy and science have developed conceptions of order different from this popular conception. According to most philosophic and scientific theories, the possibility of a human agent's creating and maintaining what is called "order" in popular language depends on the existence of other kinds of order.

Thus, a theory of *natural order* has been developed by philosophers of nature and physical and biological scientists. This order is conceived as existing independently of human agents; human organisms are included as specific parts of it, and all human activities which deal with natural objects are supposed to be dependent upon this order.

Another theory is concerned with *logical order* (including the order of mathematics). According to many logicians and mathematicians, this is also independent of any human agency; man merely discovers it. And man as conscious agent cannot produce order unless his activity is rational, guided by thinking which conforms with the principles of logic.

The conception of *social order* used in modern sociology differs from the popular conception. While we must postpone its definition, we should state at this point that according to sociological theory no single individual or group —chairman, teacher, or government—can introduce a new order into a collectivity (a meeting, a class, or the people of a state) unless some order already exists among the participants of that collectivity.

Such theoretic conceptions of order are nonevaluative. They do not contrast the goodness of order with the badness of disorder, but are mere assumptions of investigators who are trying to discover what kind of order, if any, exists in a specific field of research, independently of their feelings and desires.

But these several theories of order are late historical products. Nowadays, of course, the conception of natural order is fully and consistently developed and known to many people who use the word "order" in the popular sense. Thus, every scientifically trained horticulturist knows that the possibility of making a well-ordered garden depends upon the existence of an objective, permanent order in the structure and functioning of plants, the chemistry of the soil and the air, the physics of light and heat, the movements of the earth within the solar system. But even this knowledge is of relatively recent origin and limited usage. The scientific conception of cultural order is not yet fully developed and is seldom consistently used.

There is considerable evidence that the idea which originally dominated human thinking and still dominates the thinking of the majority of mankind is that *all* order is an intentional creation of conscious agents. We find this idea prevalent in nearly all nonliterate cultures which have been studied by anthropologists and ethnologists and in most written documents from earlier historical periods. It would be a lifelong task to investigate thoroughly its multiple and various expressions. And yet without some knowledge of its past and present application, it is impossible to understand the origin of modern scientific thinking. Such knowledge is especially important for the present and future of cultural sciences, inasmuch as the persistent influence of this age-old idea has been the main obstacle in the way of their development. We shall try, therefore, to outline briefly those typical manifestations of this idea which seem most significant for the history of the scientific approach to culture.

Basic implications of primitive practical thinking

The idea that all order is an intentional creation of conscious agents is rooted in a still broader, more inclusive assumption: belief in the original causative power of the will of conscious agents in general. This belief sometimes goes so far as to ascribe to desire—not actively manifested, not verbally expressed, perhaps not even conscious—power to produce the desired effect. For instance, wishing somebody's death may bring about his death; an evil eye may unconsciously cause evil;[3] coveting a neighbor's property may be considered as bad as stealing it.[4] When an agent acts upon objects of his experience with the intention of producing certain changes and the changes he intends to produce actually occur, it is taken for granted that all the changes are effects of which his active will is the primary, determining cause. The assumption is the same whether his objects are inanimate or animate, unconscious or conscious, whether his action involves the use of physical instruments or is only a meaningful symbolic expression of his will—a command, a prohibition, a request, a promise, a threat, an advice. It is the same whether the changes in his objects are physical changes in position, in external appearance, in composition and structure, or symbolic responses, or later facts of presumably conscious behavior in predefined situations.

At first implicit and unreflective, this assumption becomes explicit in the primitive reflection of agents themselves, who remember their past actions and anticipate their future actions, and in the reflection of practical thinkers, who as potential agents compare the actions performed by others and reach such

[3] Lucien Lévy-Bruhl, *La Mentalité primitive* (Paris, 1922), pp. 392-404.
[4] Cf. the Tenth Commandment.

common-sense generalizations about their effectiveness as are expressed, for instance, in popular proverbs and maxims.

This common, uncritical reflection is concerned only with changes which follow actions and are judged to be desirable or undesirable from the point of view of the agent; the occurrence of desirable changes is conceived as success, the occurrence of undesirable changes as failure. Since the agent intended to produce desirable changes, success merely confirms his belief in the causative force of his action; it needs no explanation and does not raise any problem unless it is exceptional, greater than the success normally achieved by similar actions. In such a case, primitive thinking assumes that some other causative force must have been added to that which the agent put into his action. Failure, on the contrary, always raises a problem, unless the action was abnormal, so different from other actions which have been found successful that it can be assumed to have been devoid of causative force. If it was normal and nonetheless failed, this indicates to primitive thinkers that some other causative power conflicted with that which the agent put into his action.[5] Consequently, agents and practical thinkers who take the point of view of agents problematize failures much oftener than successes. The great majority of problems about which members of nonliterate societies explicitly reflect, especially those which are solved by resorting to mystical explanations, are raised in connection with failures or undesirable events in general. To this very day, especially in the social field, a problem as defined in practical thinking, even in works devoted to the guidance of practical agents, commonly implies something undesirable, conflicting with the normal.

Such a causative force, extraneous to the agent's will and resulting in either exceptional success or unexpected failure of his action, is evaluated positively or negatively as good or bad from the point of view of the agent's purpose; and evaluation is apt to be accompanied by an unreflective or reflective supposition that the effect of this extraneous force upon the agent's purpose was intentional, that there was some causative power analogous to that of the agent's own will which helped or hindered him. This supposition seems obvious and easily becomes rationalized when an agent's exceptional success or unexpected failure can be ascribed to the causative power of intentional activities, good or bad, of other human agents with whom he is in social contact. We are familiar with such explanations, especially of failures. Many a parent who fails to make his child behave well ascribes this failure either to the bad will of the child or to the demoralizing influence of some other child or adult. Many a college professor explains his failures by the badness of the students, while many a student ascribes his failure to the badness of the faculty. A person who fails to gain or maintain status in a community explains it by

[5] Lévy-Bruhl, op. cit., pp. 353-405; Raoul Allier, The Mind of the Savage, trans. by Fred Rothwell (London, 1929), passim.

malicious gossip; a politician ascribes his failure to machinations of his opponents; competitors are guilty in a businessman's failure. During an economic crisis, various types of human agents—speculators, bankers, merchants, industrialists, government officials, political party leaders—are sure to be accused of having caused the crisis.[6] And almost every kind of unexpected unsatisfactory change in the life of a collectivity may be ascribed to foreign influences; Hitler's accusation that Jews, communists, and foreign powers caused all the troubles of the German people is a typical example.

It is a well-known fact, however, that belief in causative powers intentionally helping or hindering a human agent in achieving his purposes is not limited to observable, or presumably observable, actions of other human agents who, like himself, pursue their own purposes and in so doing influence favorably or unfavorably the results of his actions. Even when an agent deals with non-human objects, he may be inclined to explain exceptional success or unexpected failure by the causative power of some hidden agency whose actions he cannot observe, but infers from their apparent results. This explanation underlies most of the mystical[7] beliefs prevalent in preliterate and earlier historical cultures. Nor has it yet disappeared from modern Western cultures. It is generally considered, by students of culture, to be a survival; but, for a survival, it shows unusual vitality.[8]

A number of recent studies of children indicate that children develop mystical beliefs of their own without any noticeable influence of cultural tradition.[9] This suggests the hypothesis that such beliefs represent an extension of early social experiences of the child. In infancy and early childhood, most objects of the child's experience are controlled by adults whose causative power—often mysterious, unforeseen, and apparently almost unlimited—can be stirred into action, favorable or unfavorable, by various manifestations of the child's attitudes. Therefore, when left to himself in contact with nonhuman objects, the child continues to assume the existence of causative forces similar to those of adults, capable of controlling those objects and of being influenced by the expression of his attitudes.

In any case, whether this hypothesis can be validated or not, mystical forces in nature or beyond nature which are believed to cause exceptional success or

[6] In a study of the unemployed carried on in 1936-39, the Polish Sociological Institute collected more than 300 autobiographies of unemployed persons and interviewed the members of nearly 1,000 families. The great majority of these accused various kinds of economic and political *agents* of causing the depression.

[7] We use the term "mystical" in this wide sense, following Lévy-Bruhl in his work *Les Fonctions mentales dans les sociétés inférieures* (Paris, 1910). Whatever the weaknesses of Lévy-Bruhl's theories, his material remains valuable.

[8] Cf., e.g., Allier, *op. cit.*, chap. IV, pp. 120-60.

[9] E.g., Jean Piaget, *The Child's Conception of Physical Causality* (New York: Harcourt, 1930); Stefan Blachowski, "The Magical Behavior of Children in Relation to School," *Am. Jour. Psych.*, Vol. 50 (1937).

unexpected failure are generally conceived as analogous to those active tendencies which an agent experiences in his social interaction with human individuals or groups. Because of this analogy, older religionists have called all mystical agencies *anthropomorphic*. We suggest instead the term *sociomorphic*. For the term "anthropomorphic" suggests a belief in personal active beings, whereas not all mystical agencies are personal. *Mana* is an impersonal force; so is *fate*. And yet mana and fate are not like physical forces; their activity is directed, destined in advance to produce desirable or undesirable effects. They are analogous to certain social agencies which are not experienced as personal. As Durkheim has emphasized, even overemphasized, in his works, the social group as a collective agency is one of the most important sources of mystical beliefs, and the impersonal pressure of group sanctions is often felt by the individual as a more powerful force than the personal influence of another individual.[10]

Primitive conception of the relation between the cultural and the natural order

This extension of the idea of causative force as an intentionally active force conditions in two ways the primitive conception of order. Most human actions, especially in preliterate collectivities, are culturally patterned, follow certain folkways. Folkways make collective life orderly, give it regularity and predictability. Actions which conform with the pattern are positively valued as right, normal; their performance is considered necessary for the maintenance of the established order, and the agents who perform them are thus contributing to its maintenance. Actions which deviate from the pattern (beyond a certain range of permissible variations) are wrong, abnormal, destructive; and agents who perform them disturb collective order. Thus, every action by itself is a causative force which affects, positively or negatively, the orderly life of a collectivity.

On the other hand, the persistence of a pattern indicates that the actions which conform with it are usually judged to have been successful, whether they dealt with natural objects or with human beings. From the point of view of an anthropologist like Sumner, this success is explicable by the fact that the folkway in question has evolved by a trial-and-error process in adaptation to a pre-existing natural order,[11] but this is not always the view of the people who follow the folkway. When they reflect about the relationship between folkways and nature, they often manifest the belief that it is the order of

---

[10] Émile Durkheim, *Elementary Forms of Religious Life*, trans. by Joseph W. Swain (London, 1915).

[11] A brief summary of this view is contained in William G. Sumner and Albert G. Keller, *The Science of Society*, I (New Haven: Yale University Press, 1927), 31-33. See criticism by Florian Znaniecki, "Social Organization and Institutions" in *Twentieth Century Sociology*, eds. Gurvitch and Moore (New York: Philosophical Library, 1945), pp. 191-92.

nature which has been adapted to folkways or at least that the adaptation is mutual.

This idea finds an explicit, significant expression in myths which explain the origin of order. In many of these myths, the same powerful beings are initiators of cultural patterns and also of a natural order which makes these patterns effective. Nature is ordered for the service of man, provided man's actions conform with the patterns which have been imparted to him.

A few examples will illustrate this point. In the mythologies of most Australian tribes, the totemic ancestors who initiate the social organization of moieties and clans create a natural order to fit this organization; they classify natural objects by clans and moieties, giving each clan or moiety a power of control over the objects which belong to it and teaching the human ancestors of the clan ways to use this power.[12] The great gods of Dahomey, after creating nature, saw that man was helpless and "made the earth habitable for man," endowing him with instruments and techniques necessary to control nature.[13]

Human magic

Whoever discusses magic must take into consideration the general conception of magic formulated by Sir James Frazer in his great work *The Golden Bough*. He distinguishes between "practical magic" and "theoretic magic." The latter involves a theory of nature by which magical activities are guided. Magic "assumes that in nature one event follows another necessarily and invariably without the intervention of any spiritual or personal agency. Thus, its fundamental conception is identical with that of modern science; underlying the whole system is a faith, implicit but real and firm, in the order and uniformity of nature."[14]

But the relation between theoretic magic and practical magic differs from that between modern science and modern techniques or "arts," as Frazer calls them. Nowadays scientific generalizations precede technical activities. Technique is the practical application of theory, whereas magic is primarily a specific kind of action which human agents either perform themselves or ascribe to other agents, human or nonhuman. Comparative reflection about such actions does lead to certain generalizations concerning their effectiveness. These generalizations, however, do not constitute a theory of nature, for they

[12] See Durkheim, *op. cit.*; Baldwin Spencer and F. J. Gillen, *The Native Tribes of Central Australia* (London, 1899). A somewhat different totemic myth is analyzed by W. Lloyd Warner, *A Black Civilization* (New York: Harper, 1937), pp. 371-411. Here the disorder of nature has been occasioned by the bad conduct of totemic beings, but from them also comes the ritual which can counteract this disorder and make nature conform with human needs.

[13] Melville J. Herskovits, *Dahomey*, II (New York: J. J. Augustin, 1938), 101-28.

[14] James George Frazer, *The Golden Bough*, 3d ed., Part I, Vol. I (New York: Macmillan, 1935), p. 220.

are mostly mystical, in the sense that they assume the existence of hidden causative powers which intentionally influence natural objects and can be intentionally influenced by other causative powers, including the causative power of the magician's own will. The very essence of practical magic consists in an interference of the magician's personal agency with the natural order. This interference may disturb the usual order of natural events or reestablish an order which some other agency has disturbed or even create a new order. Undoubtedly, the magician's own action to be effective must conform with a certain pattern, follow a certain order of its own; but this is a specific order, very different from the uniformity of nature.

All varieties of magical actions have in common one basic characteristic: They include explicit, symbolic expressions of the agent's will. These expressions must be clear and unequivocal, so as to prevent any misunderstanding of his intentions on the part of those agencies which he is trying to control. If he gives a verbal command, as he usually does, it must be expressed exactly in accordance with an established formula. Verbal commands are often supplemented by a ritualistic imitation of the events which are meant to occur—imitative magic. This makes the command more obvious and compelling. Occasionally the ritualistic imitation alone is sufficient to make the agent's intention clear.

When the magician, to produce changes in an object, uses as instrument a detached part of this object or some other object which was, but is no longer, connected with it (contagious magic), there is indeed an underlying belief that the original connection is not completely broken, but to some degree mysteriously subsists: for instance, that hair or nail parings preserve some connection with the body even after they have been cut, or that the personal property of an individual is still connected with him even after it has been lost or given away. But this connection is not sufficient to make a change in the one object produce a change in the other by natural causation. The hair or nail parings may rot without affecting the body from which they have been cut. A lost personal ornament may be accidentally destroyed without any physical injury to its owner. But if a magician takes hold of the hair or of the ornament and uses it in performing a rite intended to injure the individual with whom it was originally connected, it makes the rite more effective, because it helps direct the mystical power which the magician controls toward the intended victim.[15]

Of course, the practical magician did not distinguish clearly between mystical causation and natural causation. A medicine man in curing sickness often combined magical rites and natural remedies, ascribing causative power indiscriminately to both. He was primarily a man of action, not a thinker; and, as Paul Radin points out, even in primitive societies there is a difference be-

[15] See, for data, *ibid.*, II, 170, 399-424, 494-538.

tween the two. The man of action does not theorize about the natural order; he is interested primarily in practical results. He accepts the power of deities and magical rites "as aids for the proper functioning of a series of traditionally connected individual and social events."[16]

This confusion between mystical causation and natural causation persisted among inventors and scientists with practical interests throughout ancient and medieval history, as Lynn Thorndike conclusively shows.[17] But it does not indicate that magic and science share a similar basic conception of natural order. The bond between magic and science during this period was *experimental search for new practical results*. The medieval alchemist seeking for the philosopher's stone or the elixir of life combined magical attempts to influence natural processes, by compelling the mystical powers which controlled them to do what he wanted, with scientific attempts to control natural processes by other natural processes. This is the difference which Francis Bacon had in mind when he formulated his famous slogan, "Nature does not obey unless it is followed." The word "obey" (*obtemperat*) was not a mere figure of speech in his time; it expressed the point of view of the magician who literally commanded natural phenomena to behave according to his will.

The mystical agencies which the magician tries to influence by the manifestation of his will are of various kinds. According to Lévy-Bruhl, they can be summarily ranged into three categories . . . : the spirits of the dead; the spirits—taking this word in the widest sense—which animate natural objects, animals, plants, inanimate beings (rivers, rocks, sea, mountains, artifacts, etc.) ; and finally charms and spells coming from the actions of sorcerers.[18] In any case, they have the capacity of telic intentional activity which can help the magician achieve success or cause his failure and can be made to act as he wants them to act, if he is powerful enough.

The difference between evil magic (black magic) used to raise disorder and good magic (white magic) used to defend order against the disturbance of evil magic or to re-establish it after it has been disturbed is fundamentally a matter of social function rather than of magical technique. The good magician protects the natural order from disturbance for the benefit of the group and its members, inasmuch as this order is essential for collective and individual success. The evil magician in disturbing order cuts against the interest of the group and of its members. The distinction is, of course, relative; in conflicts between groups, what is good magic from the point of view of one group is evil magic from the point of view of the other.[19]

[16] Paul Radin, *Primitive Man as a Philosopher* (New York: Appleton, 1927), p. 23.
[17] Lynn Thorndike, *History of Magic and Experimental Science*, Vols. I-IV (New York: Macmillan, 1923-34).
[18] Lévy-Bruhl, *La Mentalité primitive*, p. 51.
[19] Henri Hubert and Marcel Mauss, "Préface," *Mélanges d'histoire des religions* (Paris, 1909).

Comparative reflection about actions indicates that the appeal to magic can fail. This does not mean that magic as such has proved ineffective, only that the particular magical action performed by the particular agent, whether its purpose was socially good or socially bad, had less causative force than the action of some other agent whose intention conflicted with this purpose. There is always a struggle between agents of order and agents of disorder, human and nonhuman; and the agents with greater causative power are bound to win in the end, to impose their will upon agents who have less power. Where a weak agent fails, a sufficiently powerful one will succeed. The difference may be personal or ritualistic or both. Some agents, men or spirits, have an inherent power which others lack; their power may be so great as to radiate from them without any explicit ritualistic performance. On the other hand, certain ritualistic patterns of magical action are much more effective than others, because through them the magician can enlist the cooperation of other powerful agencies against common antagonistic powers. In most nonliterate collectivities, only a few individuals—experienced old men, shamans or "doctors" trained by their predecessors, sorcerers initiated into secret societies —know the most effective ritual, for it would be dangerous to let ordinary members use it; any error, any deviation from the pattern, might turn the powers which the ritual invokes against the performer and perhaps injure his whole group.

In view of the interdependence between the cultural order of collective life as expressed in folkways and the order of nature, the function of guarding the first against transgressions of members of the collectivity and the second against nonhuman agencies of disorder or evil magicians were closely connected. Thus, in Australia the same old men who, through regular magical performances, prevented the order of nature from being disturbed had also the function of preserving cultural order within the tribe and the clan. Later, the two functions together became most fully developed in the role of the sacred king.[20] This change, so significant for the history of cultural thought, should be viewed in connection with another important change—the progressive substitution of gods for men as the supreme magicians who by expressing their will could control the order of nature as no human magicians were able to do.

The magical powers of gods

Development of the belief in gods as personal beings with magical powers superior to all human powers undermined the very foundations of human magic. But, far from upsetting the earlier ideas of the regularity of natural

---

[20] Frazer, op. cit., I, 332 ff., and Vol. II. See also Géza Róheim, Animism, Magic and the Divine King (London, 1930), chap. IV, pp. 203-310. We may ignore Róheim's Freudian explanations.

events, as Frazer claims, this development gave the conception of a natural order greater stability and consistency, in the very measure in which the powers ascribed to gods increased and became eventually centered in one highest god.

Of course, the development of this belief was rather slow. In many earlier religions, the will of the gods could be controlled by exceptionally powerful spells of human magicians. Furthermore, since there were conflicts among the gods just as among men, divine magic, like human magic, could be used to disturb order as well as to maintain order; and some divine beings, like "black" magicians, were mainly agents of evil.[21] And no sharp dividing line originally separated human magicians, who lived only through the ordinary life span of a generation, from gods incarnated in human bodies, who passed from body to body through many generations; or from gods with superhuman bodies of indefinite, though not infinite, duration; or from the eternal, spiritual gods without bodies. Yet certain significant differences grew up in the course of history. Whereas a magician with a human body, living in the same natural environment as other men, was susceptible to influences which might deprive him of his power or destroy his body, a god with a superhuman body could escape most of these influences; and a purely spiritual god was entirely inaccessible to them. Moreover, most of the actions of a human magician could be observed by other men, but a god could keep his actions shrouded in mystery. This meant that men could not always judge whether a god was successful or not; unknown to them, he might be working for a purpose beyond their understanding, which would be disclosed only in the final, triumphant result.

But the most important difference was that between men and those gods who were the original creators of natural order. Living human magicians, even the best and most powerful, were usually only continuators of an ordering process which had been initiated before they were born by agents who were better and more powerful than they; that is, by their divine ancestors or other gods. Even when the order was actively maintained by living magicians, even when they had to defend it continuously against the agents of disorder who were always trying to destroy it, such activities were not original; they merely reproduced the activities of the first creators. Their activities were, of course, indispensable whenever the first creators disappeared or withdrew from the empirical world after transmitting their wisdom and power to human successors. But as religious beliefs developed, the original divine creators came to be considered as permanently active in maintaining their supreme authority over the order they had created; then human magicians became

---

[21] See François Lenormant, *Chaldean Magic, Its Origin and Development*, trans. from the French (London, 1877).

sacred priests, with delegated powers, helpers of the gods, divinely guided and controlled.

Finally, the powers attributed to the gods became illimited, and they assumed full and exclusive responsibility for the maintenance of the order of nature. As a result, interference with the order decreased; human magicians could do little either to help or to hinder the gods. The chief function of the priest was not to guard the order of nature directly by his magical power but to propitiate the gods and by religious cultus[22] to induce them to make nature continually behave in a way beneficent to man. Though superhuman powers of evil were still active and "black" human magicians sought their help, the divine creators and guardians of the natural order were fully competent to keep them from disturbing this order. If they did not do so, if they permitted disorder to triumph for a time, it was a penalty for the wickedness of men who had neglected or offended the gods. After men had expiated their guilt, the gods reinstated the order. Normally, however, so long as men took care to propitiate the gods by regular cultus and did their best to avoid offending them, gods would not allow the order they had created to be disturbed. And so long as the order of nature remained stable, it was for men to use it to their own advantage.

Sacred kings as guardians of order

Frazer's famous theory of the king emphasizes mainly, almost exclusively, the magico-religious aspect of the role of king, rather neglecting the political aspect as ruler and war lord. It is true that in some cases the king was too sacred a person to engage in secular activities, and consequently the functions of political ruler and war lord were performed by somebody else. But in many other cases known from historical and anthropological research, the kings combined in their persons sacredness with political power, and this is what made their roles so influential historically.

Originally, it seems, the king was a most powerful human magician who controlled everything that was practically significant for his subjects. He was the guardian of the entire natural order within the area of his kingdom. He controlled the weather; he protected his people against sickness and death; he caused desirable plants, animals, and human beings to multiply and grow; he prevented or counteracted the multiplication and growth of noxious plants and insects, dangerous animals and humans; he strengthened his own warriors and weakened the enemy's. He did all this partly by his personal magical power and the exclusive use of certain secret rites, but partly also by enlist-

---

[22] We use the term "cultus" in the specific sense of ritualistic active propitiation of divine beings, intended to achieve definite desirable reactions of those beings; "cult" in the more general sense of any kind of "worship" or collective "admiration of superior beings," including men, which may be unregulated and have no definite purpose.

ing the cooperation of other agencies of order—minor "white" magicians among his subjects and good mystical powers, such as ancestral spirits and helpful forces animating natural objects. At the same time it was his function as ruler to maintain an order among his subjects that was good for all of them. We shall call this kind of order *moral*. The king fulfilled this function by making all his subjects conform with established customs and mores and counteracting nonconformity; for nonconformity was bad, both because it had a disorganizing effect upon the collective life of the people and because it disturbed the order of nature upon which this life depended.

Since, however, religious beliefs were also relatively developed in those cultures in which the functions of the king in an organized collectivity were definitely standardized and regulated, the magical power of the king was in part at least derived from the superior magical power of a god. The king might be the temporary incarnation of a god who had existed and acted before he entered the king's body and would continue to exist and act after he left it. Sometimes, indeed, the god was only partly present in the king and, while animating his body, continued to exist and act above the realm of mankind. Or the king might be a descendant of the god, with divine nature and mystical power, but with a mortal human body and obviously inferior to and dependent upon the god from whom he descended. Or he might be a new minor god, raised to the level of the deities by some greater god. In any case, even though he did control nature, this control was due not to the causative power of his actions as a man, but to the divine essence inherent in him. And he could lose his essence and become purely human: The god incarnated in him might leave his body, or his will might conflict with that of his divine ancestor, or the great god who deified him might push him back to the human level. All this could happen because of his human frailty; and if it happened, he could no longer control nature for the benefit of his subjects.

Gradually the king became less and less of a magician and more and more of a priest; he might still retain some inner power which enabled him to control certain natural events by his own acts, but in the main he had to rely on the willingness of divine creators to guard actively the order of nature against evil powers. And when the direct responsibility for maintaining the natural order passed entirely to the gods, the function of king, so far as the natural world was concerned, became exclusively that of high priest, supreme mediator between his subjects and the gods. The natural order necessary for the prosperity of his people depended on his ability to gain the good will of the gods in their behalf. If natural conditions within the realm of his kingdom were favorable, this meant that he had been successful, and the gods were well disposed toward him and his subjects; notable disturbances in the order of nature proved that he either provoked the anger of the gods or at least failed to propitiate them. But even this responsibility became gradually delegated, at least in part, to organized religious groups guided by a professional priesthood.

No such decrease in power and shifting of responsibility occurred in the function of king as ruler of men and guardian of moral order; he still enforced general conformity of the people over whom he ruled with definite patterns of right behavior in definite situations. Even if the moral order was originally introduced by the gods, it was the task of the king to maintain it and to prevent or repress all disorder among his subjects. The gods might help him in this task by punishing his subjects for nonconformity or rewarding them for conformity, through interference with the natural conditions on which their welfare depended. But essentially the task was his, and he was responsible before men and gods for the behavior of his people. A famous instance of this responsibility was the traditional role of the Emperor of China. Moral order within his empire was inseparably connected with the mystical order of nature and was an essential condition of its normal functioning.[23] An emperor's failure to maintain moral order affected nature as well as human lives; and as a consequence of his failure he and his descendants lost the support of mystical powers as well as the right to demand obedience from his subjects. This is how a change of dynasty was justified.

Indeed, in the course of history an even more important social function evolved from the original function of the king. For, although the natural order, once created by the gods, generally remained the same except for temporary disturbances, the moral order of which kings were in charge was constantly changing, as politically organized collectivities grew in size, developed distinct cultures, and expanded their intercourse with other collectivities. Moreover, when written historical records supplemented verbal tradition and enabled men of learning to trace the history of their collectivities back through the centuries, comparison between the past and the present brought an increasing consciousness of social change. If changes were evaluated positively, if they appeared to result in a new order which was considered better than the old one, their authorship was ascribed to the creative ability and power of some exceptional individual. And a king, by the very nature of his role, seemed best qualified for such a great achievement.

The creator of moral order among a mass of people must obviously be sup-

[23] "The Chinese always believed in a universal natural order existing in the heart of man as well as in the physical universe. There is an interaction between the natural order of the universe and that of the moral world. . . . Through the Chinese history the bad sovereign is precisely the one who by his misconduct troubles the universe." Jean Escarra, *Encycl. of Social Sci.*, V, 250.

The mystical order of nature was manifested in the divinely instituted and maintained order of heaven. "Chinese astronomy was closely connected with Chinese state religion . . . based on the conception that between earthly and heavenly events, viewed spatially and temporally, a perfect agreement existed. The Emperor was the 'Son of Heaven.'" Ernst Zinner, *Die Geschichte der Sternkunde* (Berlin, 1931), pp. 201-02.

posed to have supreme authority over these people so as to make them follow his guidance and obey his command—the more so, the newer the order, the more it differs from traditional patterns. His authority must be primarily moral, founded on a general belief in his personal superiority over everybody else and a faith in his ability to create successfully an order that will be good for those who follow and obey him. But it is well if he has also the power of physical coercion to deal with enemies and rebels. Kings satisfied these conditions, inasmuch as they were sovereign rulers with no human ruler above them; their sacredness gave them moral authority and their military status as leaders of warriors enabled them to exert physical coercion.

Consequently, most of the creators of moral order whose names are preserved in legend and history were kings; but, of course, only the most famous kings had this supreme achievement ascribed to them. On the other hand, we find creators who originally had only moral authority (superior individuals, divine, or divinely inspired), who promulgated the principles of a new order. Some of them became rulers later and ordered the lives of their subjects in accordance with these principles, while others left this task to rulers who followed their moral guidance. In a few cases a war lord who became king after gaining supreme military power constructed a new order, thus acquiring moral authority and prestige.

Creators of moral order as political heroes

Although some oral tradition has been preserved in folklore concerning creators of new moral order, most of our material is written. It consists of inscriptions on monuments; sacred books; epic, lyric, and dramatic poetry; chronicles; biographies written by followers and worshipers; many historical works, for historians only quite recently discarded belief in great men as absolute creators;[24] and publications of contemporary writers propagating faith in creative leaders among the masses.

Some of the creators whose names are transmitted in literature are purely mythical persons: Gilgamesh of Babylonia, Minos of Crete, Fu-hi of China, Manu the lawgiver in India, King Arthur of England, Lech of Poland, etc. Others are men who probably or even certainly did live, but whose personalities and achievements are largely legendary: Sargon of Agade (Babylon), Menes of Egypt, David and Solomon, Numa Pompilius. Most of those, however, whose names are familiar from history are personalities whose more or less authentic biographies are connected with historically ascertained processes of social organization and reorganization. A few are world-known figures of the twentieth century.

But whatever the historical evidence or lack of evidence concerning their

---

[24] See Thomas Carlyle, *On Heroes and Hero Worship*; and Ralph W. Emerson, *Representative Men*.

personalities and performances, if considered from the point of view of the kind of thinking which accepts their creative achievements as real and evaluates them positively, they belong to the general class which in French is called "héros civilisateurs," in English "culture heroes." This same class includes the mystical, the legendary, and the historical persons supposed to have initiated mankind into various material techniques, as well as the founders of religious systems. The term "hero" originally denoted a divine or semidivine personality who lived for a time among men; later it was extended to great men of the past, and finally to great men still alive.[25] A personality is a hero if he is an object of collective cult, as symbolic representative of the highest common values of a social group.[26] We call "political heroes," as distinct from other heroes, those personalities that are objects of collective cult as sovereign creators of a new moral order by political methods (with or without military force).

A few examples of political heroes drawn from various cultures and various historical periods will show the essential uniformity and persistence of this conception.

Take, first, the creators of new states. Their achievement is unification of human collectivities with no common order or a wrong order under a supreme authority which imposes a common right order upon all of them.

Sometimes the same hero begins and completes the task; sometimes the first hero is succeeded by another or even by two or three others who expand the state he created, strengthen it, and perfect its order. Most heroes in creating new states use military force. They are conquerors, or leaders in organized defense against a common enemy, or liberators of the people from foreign oppression. Sometimes, however, only peaceful methods are used when the inhabitants of a country want their lives to be ordered by a sovereign ruler.

Thus, Sargon I of Babylon, Menes of Egypt, Assur-nazir-pal of Assyria, Cyrus, Alexander, and the first Incas were mainly conquering heroes; Genghis Khan, and Tamerlane were exclusively so. Charlemagne, according to French tradition, was both a conqueror and a defender; the latter function is emphasized in the *Chansons de Geste*. Alfred the Great is extolled primarily as a defender. The builders of western Slav states were considered mainly as defenders against Teutonic expansion; thus Mieszko, the first historical ruler of Poland, was primarily a defender, but his son and successor, Boleslav I, a conqueror. Though liberating heroes are found at various historical periods, they have become especially popular in modern times (e.g., Washington, Bolivar, Pilsudski).

Most instructive, perhaps, as a source of information about the old concep-

---

[25] "Heroes and Hero Worship," *Encycl. of Rel. and Ethics*, VI (1914), 642-60; Gottfried Salomon, "Hero Worship," *Encycl. of Social Sci.*, VII, 336-38.

[26] Stefan Czarnowski, *Le Culte des héros* (Paris, 1919).

tion of moral order as the creative product of rulers, are the legends and stories of state builders who were invited to perform this task either because the people wanted order or because priests or prophets thought that the people needed the kind of order which only a ruler could create. A highly significant legend is contained in the work of the first Russian chronicler and historian, Nestor. According to him, the people of Russia sent to the Varangians (an old Norse group) a delegation which said, "Our land is great and plentiful, but there is no order in it. Come reign and rule over us." And three Varangian brothers, Riurik, Sineus, and Truvor, in response to this request came with their followers.[27]

The stories of Saul and David furnish good illustrations of state builders who started to perform this task at the initiative and under the sanction of religious leaders. Later historical examples are the war lords or competitors for secular power in the sixth and seventh centuries whom the Western Church made into sacred kings, hoping that they would succeed in creating and maintaining lasting order within certain areas after the inclusive Roman order had broken down.

Another familiar type of political hero is one who creates or perpetuates order within a state already in existence after a period of disorder. During such a period the popular demand for order is particularly manifest, and popular worship of the hero who seems to satisfy this demand develops most easily. The only king of Poland called "great" was Casimir III, who certainly was not a military hero (he ceded Silesia to Austria and left Pomerania to the Teutonic Knights), but whose reign was marked by inner peace and prosperity after a long period of dissension and poverty. Henry IV was exalted for ending the long inner conflicts within France. Louis XIV was considered by his admirers a great unifier and organizer, who made France the political and cultural center of Europe. Frederick the Great transformed the weak Prussia into a conquering power. Bismarck was the hero who not only welded many states into one German Empire, but modernized the inner order of Prussia. Napoleon, though primarily a military hero, was generally accepted by the French people as a maker of new order after the disorder of a decaying monarchy had been followed by a period of revolutionary terror; indeed, the "Code Napoléon" survived his downfall for a hundred years. A similar demand of the French people for an order-making ruler made Louis Napoleon their emperor. Recently, Mussolini and Kemal Pasha were heroized on similar grounds. Unfortunately for his heroic status, Mussolini later tried to become a conqueror and empire builder. Highly interesting is the fact that two periods

---

[27] A popular Russian revolutionary poem which circulated about fifty years ago (I do not know the author) summarized the history of the Russian rulers in a number of stanzas, each ending with the refrain "and still there is no order." Only two rulers were ironically referred to as real lovers and efficient makers of order: Ivan the Terrible and Peter the Great.

in English history, notable for political order and economic prosperity after periods of disturbance, were symbolized by the names of queens—the nearest approach, since the legendary Semiramis, which women have made to the role of order-making heroines, outside of Catherine the Great of Russia.

The greatest political heroes, however, are those whose achievements are not limited to the construction or reorganization of particular states among other states, but are intended to influence all mankind. They are creators of an order which is believed to include or expected to include all the peoples of the world as the world is conceived at the time, or at least all the peoples who are worthy to participate in it. Such a hero is above kings; if kings have any place in the order which he creates, it is only as subordinates or vicarious rulers of minor parts of the world—especially peripheral territories—and they all owe allegiance and obedience to the hero. Some emperors of China might be included in this category inasmuch as China was at one time the Central Empire and its order the only good and true moral order in the universe. However, this conception was more fully and explicitly developed in the West and reached its culmination in our own time.

Creators of a world order

Alexander the Great may perhaps be considered the first world hero in Western history, even though his attempt to unify all the states of the known world into a coherent whole was not completed, and whatever unity he did create broke down after his death. The idea of a world order was a product of philosophical theory, not of practical political thought. But it did acquire a practical significance with the growth of the Roman Empire and became associated with the worship of Roman political heroes.

Already Polybius conceived the Rome of the second century B.C. as a world state in formation and pointed out that because of this he was the first man who could write a universal history instead of (like his predecessors) histories of particular states and their interrelations. A century later the Roman state expanded still further; and the belief gradually developed that Roman order was practically a world order, that only under Roman rule was universal peace possible and only under Roman law could universal justice be attained. And with this belief there grew a popular cult of individual emperors as heroes to whose creative powers the maintenance, expansion, and development of this world order was due.

The first of these heroes was Caesar, who spread Roman domination to the western limits of the habitable world and who started to rebuild Roman unity and peace after a long period of political divisions and civil wars. The same kind of heroic achievement was expected of his successors individually, each of whom adopted Caesar's name, together with the term "imperator," indicating that order was maintained, expanded, perfected in a triumphant struggle against the forces of disorder, whether they arose inside or outside the Empire. The expectation became expressed in religious cult—typical hero cult. Disappointments with particular emperors did not destroy the popular faith, for the idea that a sacred ruler could lose his power had an old tradition, going back to prehistoric kings. In the course of time more and more idealized dead Caesar-Emperors who had been successful up to the end of their earthly lives were added to the list: Augustus, Vespasian, Antoninus Pius, Marcus Aurelius, "the beloved of all peoples," Septimus Severus, Alexander Severus, and others.[28]

After the partition of the Empire, the cult of emperors decreased. However, Justinian was one of the great heroes, mainly because of his legislative achievements. But the later Eastern emperors were mostly shadows of the original world heroes. The revival of the role of Caesar-Emperor in western Europe was not a complete return to the Roman ideal of a creator of world order, not so much because of the competing status of the Byzantine emperor as because the new conception differed from that of imperial Rome. While the Roman order was one, the true order of the Christian world was dual, religious and political. The first was sacred, created by God, maintained and expanded by the Church under the leadership of the Pope as earthly representative of God; the second was secular, which the Emperor could create, maintain, and expand, but only if empowered by God through the medium of the Church and if acting in harmony with the Church.

Still, some Western emperors became in legend and literature independent builders of a political world order. Although Charles the Great in the French tradition of the eleventh and twelfth centuries was a French hero, he became a world hero as Caesar (Kaiser) in German tradition. Frederick Barbarossa was an even more popular hero in German folklore. Thus, the ideal of one universal political order under a supreme monarch persisted and found expression in political writing, such as Dante's *Monarchia*. Along with it went the hope that some day a political hero or a succession of political heroes would appear and create this order. When a famous military conqueror and political organizer arose, some of his admirers expressed the hope that he was the one destined to unify mankind under one order or at least to initiate this creative achievement. Charles V, Louis XIV, and Napoleon had such admirers.

Nowhere, perhaps, was this hope so markedly expressed as in Russia after Peter the Great. Russian rulers had no religious competition, for they controlled the Church; they were the only ones in modern times who combined the two titles derived from ancient Rome: Caesar (Tsar) and Imperator. As Caesar the Russian ruler was the father of his people; as Imperator he was

[28] Cf. *The Cambridge Ancient History*, Vol. XI, *The Imperial Peace*. The extension of the cult from dead to living emperors was apparently initiated by Domitian, who enforced his own worship as "Dominus et Deus" (p. 41).

the triumphant victor over foreign enemies, and the rapid expansion of the Empire led to the expectation that eventually all mankind would be brought under his rule. As a Russian poet wrote a century and a half ago, the time must come when every man will be able proudly to say, "Maybe I am a slave—but a slave of the Tsar of the universe."[29]

In our times, several persons have seemed to their followers even during their lives to be supreme political heroes, each the creator of an order destined to become a world order.

It is uncertain whether Hirohito, the Emperor of Japan, should be included among them. The traditional role of the Mikado goes back to the old one of divine king, supreme guardian of order among his divinely chosen subjects. Although he and his people were supposed to be unique, absolutely superior to the rest of mankind, there was no idea of his actually becoming the ruler of mankind, for there was no conception of a world order. Only during the last half century, under the influence of Western political thought, this idea developed, became explicitly formulated, and began to be put into action after the invasion of Manchuria. The expansion of Japan was conceived as the creation of a new universal order progressively extended over Asia and intended finally to cover the rest of the world. Since the whole process was carried on in the name of the living Mikado, presumably by his will and under his sovereign guidance, the living Mikado became exalted as the supreme creator of the new order. Little emphasis was, however, placed on any exceptional ability of his as a great man; since every Mikado is divine by descent, his greatness is above all human greatness; only among his helpers do differences in ability and energy seem important.

Much more significant for the history of social thought is Hitler's rise to the status of a political world hero. He was not at first explicitly conceived as a creator of world order, but as a national culture hero, a liberator, unifier, reformer, organizer of all people of German descent and culture, including the millions of Germans who lived outside of Germany, most of them under foreign rule. According to him and his followers, Germany itself was not free, but controlled by foreign powers; its people were impoverished, weakened, divided among themselves, dominated by politicians who were either egoistic fools or servants of Jewish Marxism; their culture was deteriorating, the purity of their racial stock becoming contaminated. Hitler created a *Weltanschauung* which included a conception of the "mission of the German people upon earth" and an ideal of German racial purity, cultural greatness, and social unity. For the realization of this ideal, he created the Nazi Party

---

[29] I read this poem in secondary school in Warsaw under Russian domination, but I have forgotten the name of the poet. It certainly was not Pushkin, however much he exalted certain tsars (Peter the Great and Alexander I) and Russian imperialism in general.

and with its help obtained control of the German State. The state was to him "not an end but a means, a presupposition for the formation of a superior human culture, but not its cause. The latter lies exclusively in the existence of a race capable of culture."[30]

As early as 1923, this function of a national hero was ascribed to him. "His fire spread from him upon his listeners and planted a strong faith again in their hearts after the break-down of all previous ideas. Crowds of despairing people found in him a support for their lives, and men who were seeking for a leader of the German people looked more and more hopefully upon the *Man in München.* . . . We can say already today that the name Hitler has acquired a mystical sound and not only for us. . . . This name goes as a symbol over the entire world. He is hated and beloved like everything great. The honor of Germany, social justice, the freedom of the entire German people are leading motives of the Man. . . . Victory will be ours, because at the head of the German will to live stands *one man.* . . ."[31]

Ten years later this is how Goebbels described Hitler's achievement: "Like one man, all Germany is rising. Millions in the East and the West, in the North and the South are stretching their hands across the borders and forming a union which can never more be destroyed. In this solemn hour, they lift their hearts up to the Man who has roused them, brought them together, united them, fused them into one nation again."[32]

However, this was only the first step. Hitler in *Mein Kampf* anticipated a further development. The German people are Aryans, and Aryans are the only race capable of creating a truly great culture. They have always used inferior peoples as "technical instruments" in the service of this culture. "The Aryan conquered lower races and regulated their practical activities under his order, at his will, and for his ends. But, while he thus made them perform a useful, even if a difficult activity, he not only spared the lives of his subjects, but gave them perhaps a lot that was better than their previous so-called freedom."[33] Such is still the mission of the German people upon the earth. If the German people had been sufficiently solidary in the past, "the German Reich today would probably be master of the earthly sphere. . . ."[34] The result would be "a peace, supported not by the handwaving of tearful, pacifist, complaining women (*Klageweiber*), but founded by the victorious sword of a *Herrenvolk* that reduces the world to the service of a superior culture." The supreme pur-

[30] Adolph Hitler, *Mein Kampf*, 60th ed. (Munich, 1933), p. 431.

[31] Alfred Rosenberg, "Deutschlands Führer," *Völkischer Beobachter*, zum 34 Geburtstag des Führers am 20 April, 1923.

[32] Joseph Goebbels, "*Hitler über Deutschland*, Rundfunkreportage aus Königsberg zum Tage der erwachenden Nation am 4 März, 1933," in *Signale der neuen Zeit*, 2d ed. (Munich, 1934), p. 112.

[33] Hitler, *op. cit.*, p. 324.

[34] *Ibid.*, p. 438.

pose of the German state is "not only to unify and protect all the Germans, but slowly and surely to lead them up to the dominant position."[35]

Also highly significant, though different, has been the evolution of the role of Stalin, who followed Marx and Lenin as the third great hero-creator of the world order called "communism."

Unlike older types of moral order, communism as a world order *in statu nascendi* was originally conceived not as the intentional creation of conscious agents, but as a result of historical necessity determined by material forces. And yet Marx after his death became for his intellectual and practical followers a hero who promulgated the first ideal principles of this new order—a combination of prophet and legislator, a Buddha and a Manu, though a purely historical person, acting by his own human genius not by divine inspiration. The few principles he promulgated are absolutely valid; his opponents and critics are spokesmen of evil who want to perpetuate disorder and injustice.

Lenin gained followers as the thinker who developed further the "true" principles of Marxian communism, in opposition to those thinkers who deviated from the teaching of the master and falsified his ideal; this ideal is now often called "Marxism-Leninism." After the October Revolution of 1917 Lenin became recognized as the leading man of action and gradually was exalted (especially after his death) as the greatest revolutionary hero in history, who actually substituted the new good order for an evil, decadent order in the largest country of the world. For such an achievement it was necessary to overcome the resistance of adherents to the old regime and to impose the new order upon a hundred and fifty million people who were not ready for it.

This required dictatorial power. It is interesting to note how in the course of this process the Marxian idea of "dictatorship of the proletariat" became first interpreted as dictatorship of the Communist Party acting in the interest of the proletariat and later, in response to the age-old demand for an individual creator, was impersonated in the leader of the party. This impersonation was not quite completed during Lenin's lifetime, but only after Stalin took over the leadership of the party. However great Lenin's achievements were, he had no time to consolidate the new order, still less to extend it beyond Russia. Its extension to the whole world was expected to come when other peoples would follow the Russian example under their own leaders.

Stalin began as Lenin's successor, continuing his creative activity, developing, perfecting, stabilizing the new order. In less than ten years, he achieved heroic status in this role. To quote Henri Barbusse, one of his admirers:

These thoughtful parades which last for hours, and the enthusiasm which is reflected by the crowd massed tier upon tier in the stands erected before the red, crenellated wall of the Kremlin, form a vortex of muttering and roaring centred around a single point. The clamour assumes a human form: "Stalin!".

[35] *Ibid.*, p. 439.

. . . That man is the centre, the heart of everything that radiates from Moscow on the surrounding world. His portrait, either in the form of sculpture or as a drawing, or as a photograph, is to be found everywhere throughout the Soviet continent, like that of Lenin and beside that of Lenin. There is hardly a corner of any factory, military barracks, office or shop window in which it does not appear on a red background, between a list of striking socialist statistics (a sort of anti-religious ikon) and the emblem of the crossed hammer and sickle. Latterly, a poster of enormous dimensions has been put up on the walls, all over Russia and the Soviet Republics, representing the superimposed profiles of two dead men and one living: Karl Marx, Lenin and Stalin. And we may multiply these a thousandfold; for there are not many rooms, whether occupied by working men or by intellectuals, in which Stalin does not figure.

Whether you love or hate this nation which occupies one-sixth of the world's surface, that is the man who is at the head of it. And in this country, if the cobbles in the streets could talk, they would say: Stalin.[36]

Gradually, however, his role expanded beyond that of Lenin. For, although the revolution was officially considered to be unfinished so long as some counterrevolutionary activities remained unrepressed, as a matter of fact the forces of reaction presumably still rampant in Russia had ceased to be seriously dangerous, except when used by enemy powers who wanted to destroy the new order. The real threat came from the hostile environment of capitalistic nations. According to this belief, what Russia needed was not so much a revolutionary leader as a hero who, besides his main function as builder of a communistic society, would also act as protector of his people against foreign enemies. This was the old function of the tsars who, however ineffective they may have been as "fathers" of their subjects, however unjust the order of which they were the guardians, nonetheless up to the beginning of this century usually triumphed over external foes not merely by defending the Empire, but by extending it and subjecting dangerous foreigners to their domination.

Stalin assumed this function of the tsars. First, the peoples of Russia were taught to mistrust all foreign powers as actual or potential enemies and to avoid all contacts with outsiders. Next, preparation for defense against foreign aggression became a highly important task, second only to the development and stabilization of the new order; and Stalin was recognized as the leader in control of this task, especially after it was apparently proved that not all military leaders were to be trusted. Without waiting to be attacked, Russian armies reconquered nearly all the foreign countries formerly conquered by the tsars which had regained independence after the fall of the old regime. When the expected aggression did come, Stalin became the supreme and incomparable defending hero. And after successful defense, he extended his control over several foreign countries which the tsars had never controlled,

[36] *Stalin. A New World Seen Through One Man,* trans. by V. Holland (New York: Macmillan, 1935).

and subjugated a large part of the aggressors' land so as to eliminate all danger of future aggression.

And he is doing all this not only as the ruler of Russia and of its people; his function as heir of the tsars is merging with his highest function—that of creator of the communistic world order. Unlike Lenin, he does not wait for this order to be introduced into other countries by their own revolutionary leaders, but introduces it through the medium of chosen foreign assistants, helping them eliminate opponents (landlords, capitalists, reactionaries, fascists) who obstruct the process. Since communism is supposed to be the best possible order, created for the benefit of the inhabitants of those countries, they are expected to exalt him as their great benefactor, just as the peoples of Russia have exalted him.

Incontrovertibility of the dogma of the political hero

These various instances, especially those of Hitler and Stalin, indicate how belief in creators of moral order, just as belief in creators of natural order, persists notwithstanding the development of inductive, scientific thinking. Once accepted, it cannot be invalidated in the eyes of the believer by factual evidence, for the believer can always explain away to his own satisfaction any facts that appear to disagree with it. When it is rejected, this is not because it conflicts with scientific knowledge but with some contrary belief. Of course, the same individual who is worshiped as a creator by his adherents may be hated as a destroyer by his opponents; but the evil power which is ascribed to him by his opponents is often as great as the good power with which his adherents endow him.

So long as the hero is considered successful and seems to produce an order which he and his followers judge desirable, the believers' faith in his creative power remains unshaken; and if he achieves something unexpected, overcomes apparently insuperable obstacles and produces unforeseen positive results, the faith in him is strengthened, and even unbelievers may be converted. The significance of such an achievement in the social field is similar to that of a miracle performed in the natural field by a prophet who claims supernatural powers. Problems are raised only by failures, and there are several old and easy ways of solving such problems without disturbing faith in the creative power of the hero.

First, the hero is wiser and more far-seeing than others, but does not always disclose his plans. What appears at the moment to be a failure to the ignorant, the stupid, the shortsighted, may be really the best if not the only way to unexpected success. In war and in politics, the hero may intentionally mislead his opponents into thinking that he has committed a mistake. Or else he may test the loyalty of his adherents by seeming errors. The faithful must trust their hero, be always aware that his wisdom is above their understanding, and refrain from criticizing that which they do not understand.

Second, the hero cannot organize large masses of the people from a distance, by immediate psychic control, or compel them to behave permanently in an orderly way, or protect them against evil influences, even though he often is endowed with the power of hypnotic control over the minds of those who meet him face-to-face and listen to him. He needs loyal assistants who will absolutely obey his commands, who can be delegated with some of his authority, and who can be entrusted with the realization of specific parts of the total order he has planned. Their task is to make smaller groups of the people under him behave as he wants them to behave.

Within the limits of their appointed tasks, such assistants are also makers of moral order, though not original creators. It is their superior who makes them order makers, enlightens them as to their functions, and gives them the power to perform these functions. They are responsible to their superior for the behavior of their subordinates. If the assistants succeed in making the subordinates behave as the superior wants, the original merit for their success goes to their superior, and it is for their superior to grant them a share of this merit. If they fail, the fault is their own, for the superior could never fail in their place; and in appointing them, the superior gave them in knowledge and power all that they needed to succeed.

Such an assumption by the superior of primary merit for all successful performances of his subordinates, while putting upon the subordinates all the responsibility for their failures, is not merely an arbitrary expression of the personal ambition of superiors. It satisfies the popular need for hero worship and is indispensable for the preservation of the unshaken authority of the hero. The creator of order cannot be responsible for disorder. This is a very old and general principle. It is perhaps most clearly manifested in the Japanese tradition of obligatory suicide of any subordinate—from the immediate subordinates of the Emperor on down—who fails to fulfill the orders of his superior. Hitler became and remained the supreme hero and creator of the new order only so long as responsibility for all failures to introduce and maintain order was put upon subordinates who could be removed from their posts. Stalin's wisdom and power as builder of the new political and economic order remain unchallenged because subordinate officials of the party machine have been held responsible for all defects and deviations in the functioning of the machine, and because all economic deficiencies and failures are ascribed not to him but to planners, organizers, and managers of economic production. Successful subordinates are openly praised and given honorific awards or promotions; Stalin was particularly lavish in praising military commanders during the war. But the very fact that public praise came or was supposed to come from the supreme hero indicates that the primary merit was his, and it was for him to decide to whom a share of this merit was to be granted and how large the share was to be.

In such a complex moral order as that of a modern totalitarian regime, with a long hierarchical ladder of superordinates and subordinates, a similar division of positive and negative responsibility is found on every level of the ladder. All leaders, heads, or managers at a given level are responsible to their superordinate leader for the behavior of all those over whom they have been given authority; but each of them, while letting his superior assume the primary merit for his success, tries to shift the demerit for his failure to his subordinate leaders. In short, while the supreme leader is exclusively an active creator and the mass of the people exclusively passive objects which are being ordered, all intermediate leaders are both passive objects ordered by their superiors and creative agents who give orders to their inferiors.

Even under this system, however, if failures are important and frequent, a superior—even a supreme creative hero—may be blamed for having delegated authority to an assistant incompetent of performing his function. But there is a well-known way of justifying the hero. Even an incompetent assistant, if he loyally tries to obey the hero, will promote order, though his work may be imperfect and have to be supplemented and corrected. An essential difference exists between imperfect order and disturbance of order; though it may not be noticeable at once, it will manifest itself eventually. Serious and unexpected disturbances indicate that some agency is at work which intends to foment disorder, some force of evil trying to destroy the good which the hero is creating. When the failure of an assistant can be traced to willful disobedience, to conscious transgression of rules promulgated by supreme authority, it means that he is disloyal, an agent of destructive forces, a traitor.

This principle has been applied in all dictatorial regimes; Hitler's elimination of traitors in 1934 is a well-known example. But probably never has its application been so consistent as in Russia after the Communist Party gained complete control and Stalin rose to the role of the supreme political hero. Once all defendants of the old regime had been eliminated and organized opposition to the ruling group broken down, treason within the ruling group was the only serious threat, apart from the permanent danger of foreign invasion. Any unexpected and notable failure in technical production might be due to sabotage; any deviation from the rules of the political order sanctioned by Stalin as supreme creator might be traced to the secret influence of anticommunistic, especially Fascist, agencies. Elimination of individual saboteurs and disloyal officials proceeded continuously, with occasional purges, such as the purge of 1937, removing all convicted traitors as well as many suspected and potential traitors. And the accusation and condemnation of important traitors was widely publicized to exalt still further the hero, showing the contrast between him and the traitors and proving to the masses that those who oppose the hero are really enemies of the people, secret agents of evil.

Explanation of the hero's failures by the treason of his followers helps us understand why some creators of order have remained heroes in legend and history, even though they were ultimately overthrown and their order destroyed. Of course, their downfall might have been directly due to the power of their enemies; but, as proved by their earlier victories, their enemies would have been unable to defeat them without the help of traitors. When the posthumous cult of Napoleon developed, his defeat was ascribed to the treason of his allies, some of his marshals, and certain of his ministers of state (Fouché and Talleyrand). We can be sure that the cult of Mussolini and especially that of Hitler will continue and that their worshipers will consider treason one of the factors of their ultimate fall.

Finally, the failure of a creator of social order may be explained by the moral weakness or wickedness of the people whose conduct he wanted to regulate. This is the easiest explanation; and it can be resorted to by the followers of a political hero or of any prophet or reformer. Prophets of Israel who failed to influence the people condemned the wickedness of the people; yet they became heroes whose words have been preserved for posterity. For the followers of a prophet have been converted from wickedness to goodness; they are the select few to whom his condemnation does not apply, and to them he is a hero whose greatness is not impaired by his failure to convert the wicked majority. To this day may be found many such select groups, sacred and secular, each with its own hero who is prevented from creating order in his society or in the world at large only by the innate badness or acquired depravity of the human species, which makes the agents of evil more influential than the agents of good.

Objective Order as a Condition
of Successful Activity

The relation between magic, religion, and technology

Our brief survey of the old and persistent idea that order of every kind is created and maintained by the will of some conscious agent raises the question: In cultures dominated by this type of thinking, how could the conception of a factual order of phenomena existing independently of the will of creators and guardians ever have evolved?

In trying to answer this question, we find that it should be subdivided. For the persistence of faith in human creators of moral order, even after human individuals ceased to be considered capable of creating or maintaining an order of *nature* by the power of their will, indicates that the conception of an independent order among natural objects developed more rapidly and effectively than the conception of an independent order among human actions. There must have been two historical processes, both of which need explanation. We shall begin with the first.

It is generally recognized, of course, that even the most primitive peoples must have had a knowledge of the regularities of nature sufficiently objective and valid to guide their material techniques. But if this knowledge was inextricably mixed with and dominated by magical and religious beliefs, how did it ever become separated and freed from those beliefs and eventually organized into more or less coherent theories? It could not have been by testing the effectiveness of magical and religious methods in comparison with technical methods, and rejecting the former while preserving the latter; for, as we have already seen, magical and religious beliefs were and still are unaffected by such tests. To this very day, the majority of technical workers throughout the world preserve faith in the practical effectiveness of religion, and a considerable proportion of them still keep some faith in the effectiveness of magic. To them it is not a matter of choice between technique on the one hand and magical ritual or religious propitiation on the other hand: They use both.

Most investigators of magic and religion leave this problem unsolved. Thus Frazer, whose wealth of factual information in this field of research is probably greater than that of any other investigator, simply states: "From the earliest times man has been engaged in a search for general rules whereby to turn the order of natural phenomenon to his own advantage, and in the long search he has scraped together a great hoard of such maxims, some of them golden and some of them merely dross. The true or golden rules constitute the body of applied science which we call the arts; the false are magic.[1]

But this true-false dichotomy does not eliminate by transcendental necessity the false from human thinking. Men did not become aware that some of their judgments were "true" and others "false" until they discovered that there was a logical contradiction between them. And the discovery that there is a basic logical contradiction between magical judgments on the one hand and judgments of applied science on the other hand came very late—indeed, not until systematic philosophy of nature developed.

Moreover, the question is not merely why belief in the effectiveness of magical performances and the validity of magical doctrines weakened, while belief in the effectiveness of material techniques and the validity of technological generalizations strengthened. Even more challenging is the vast expansion of material techniques and technological knowledge which preceded by many centuries the emergence of natural philosophy and science. And here we notice that cultures in which organized religion dominated magic, and priests controlled the magicians, were also those which had the most developed technology; take Egypt, Babylonia, China, India, Peru, Europe during the Middle Ages. Whereas cultures where magical performances predominate over religious cultus have always been and still are also technically backward. This certainly does not conform at all with the famous assertion of Frazer: "In so far as religion assumes the world to be directed by conscious agents who may be turned from their purpose by persuasion, it stands in fundamental antagonism to magic as well as to science."[2]

If religion conflicts with magic, it is not because magic assumes that "the processes of nature are rigid and invariable," while religion implies an "elasticity or variability of nature," but because magicians, instead of leaving the control of nature to the gods, try to "deflect by their operations" the course of events determined by divine will. Whereas no such conflict appears between religion and natural, nonmagical techniques, so long as technicians do not interfere with the divine order.

We think that the key to the whole problem lies in the practical differentiation and separation of two kinds of human activity which deal with natural

[1] Frazer, *The Golden Bough*, I, 50.
[2] *Ibid.*, p. 224.

objects. This separation is mentioned and described in many monographic studies of nonliterate cultures; and the French school of sociology has generalized their results by distinguishing two categories or realms of primitive activity: the *sacred* and the *profane*. The term "profane" must be understood as "devoid of magical or religious significance"; it is not (as sometimes used in common speech) equivalent to "impure," i.e., endowed with negative magico-religious power.

The realm of the profane

Inasmuch as the kind of thinking which leads to magic and religion originates in practical problems of unexpected failure or unusual success, so long as such problems are not raised or anticipated, life goes on undisturbed by mystical speculation. In every society, day after day, people carry on familiar activities, following traditional patterns without resorting continually to magical ritual or religious propitiation. The many minor practical problems which arise in the course of these activities are viewed as purely technical, capable of being solved by the use of adequate tools and proper skill. Magical and religious performances are generally reserved for special periods, usually preceding or following commonplace activities.

Thus, before starting a specific activity, such as hunting, fishing, producing a weapon, a rug, a boat, a house, cultivating a garden plot or a field, an individual or collective rite is performed to bring success with the aid of good powers and to prevent failure by keeping evil powers away. After the technical activity is ended, another magico-religious rite may be performed to insure the desirability of its aftereffects. Group ceremonies also take place at regular intervals to make their participants successful and safe in whatever activities they will undertake after the ceremony or to neutralize whatever evil influences may have affected them before the ceremony. Such are family rites and prayers, morning and evening; weekly ceremonies corresponding to phases of the moon; monthly ceremonies between moon cycles; seasonal and New Year ceremonies.

The ceremonial activities are sacred; the technical activities between the ceremonies are profane, ordinary, commonplace. The whole time during which sacred activities are performed is sacred time; no ordinary technical activities are then permitted, for they would make the rites and prayers ineffective or even harmful.[3]

This division between the sacred and the profane is still clearer when not

[3] "Étude sommaire de la représentation du temps dans la religion et la magie," Hubert and Mauss, *Mélanges d'histoire des religions*, pp. 189-229; Webster Hutton, *Rest Days* (New York: Macmillan, 1910); "Festivals and Fasts," *Encycl. of Rel. and Ethics*, V (1912), 835-94.

only special times but special holy places are reserved for sacred activities: totemic wells, holy woods, rocks, mountains, graves, altars, chapels or corners in family homes, temples. Most sacred activities, or at least the important ones, are supposed to be performed in or near such holy places, and no profane activity should be carried on there. In all other spaces, once they have been made safe from evil powers, commonplace activities may go on undisturbed.[4]

Another factor separating still further the sacred from the profane is the use of special consecrated implements for the former. The material, shape, and color of a sacred implement, as well as the methods of using it, are strictly regulated and controlled, for its effectiveness depends on its inner sacredness; and this is conditional upon the complete conformity of its nature and usage with the traditional pattern. Technical instruments, which lack this sacredness anyway, are permitted to vary within limits, and it does not matter so much how they are used.

But the most important influence which has resulted in a growing contrast between the sacred and the profane components of practical life has been the development of a professional class of holy persons specializing in magical and religious activity and thought. Such specialists cannot perform ordinary technical actions which secular people devoid of sacredness carry on, for this might profane their holy essence and make them lose their power, besides diverting their time, attention, and energy from their main function, incomparably more valuable to society than anything they could accomplish in the technical field.[5] On the other hand, technical workers cannot carry on by themselves important magical or religious activities, since this would be not only ineffective but dangerous. They must leave to holy specialists the task of controlling magically the evil powers of nature and propitiating the gods; all they are expected to do is to participate in collective ceremonies under the guidance of specialists.

Consequently, within the general framework of magico-religious thinking there has always been a field left for the purely technological thinking which compared human actions in terms of their technical efficiency. And this field expanded as greater power came to be ascribed to the divine creators and guardians of the natural order. In the most developed religions, powerful gods—and only gods—could give men complete security against agents of

[4] John R. McCulloch, "Temples," *Encycl. of Rel. and Ethics*, XII (1922), 237-46 (brief, but good summary).

[5] Many such prohibitions are expressed in *Sacred Books of the East*, ed. Max Müller; e.g., "Let him treat Brahmanas who tend cattle, those who live by trade, those who are artisans, actors, servants . . . like Sudras" (Vol. XIV, *Bandhayana*, I, 5, No. 24); "The [pursuit of] agriculture impedes [the study of] Veda" (*ibid.*, p. 10); agriculture is forbidden to Buddhist monks (Vol. XIII, p. 33; Vol. XIX, p. 296).

See also Frazer, *op. cit.*, Vol. II, *passim*, about taboos to which kings-priests are subjected to prevent the profanation of their sacredness.

disorder, be they human "black" magicians or supernatural spirits of evil. And insofar as men were assured that gods would not allow destructive agents to disturb the order of nature, their success or failure seemed to depend exclusively on their own knowledge of natural phenomena and their skill in handling them.

Main sources of technological reflection

The most obvious and permanent source of the technological thinking which compared human activities in terms of their technical efficiency was the need of training the young in material techniques. Even if such training was not considered of itself sufficient to insure future success, it was an indispensable condition of success, and much of it usually preceded the initiation of the young generation into magical and religious beliefs and practices. Training the young and estimating their progress required some generalizations concerning the empirical characteristics of objects included in technical performances and the succession of empirical changes which these objects underwent in the course of these performances.[6]

Comparison between the technical performances of adult agents under presumably similar conditions is another source of empirical generalization. For instance, Malinowski described magical rituals presumed to stimulate the growth of vegetables in Trobriand gardens and to keep evil influences away. The benefits of these rituals extended to all the gardens, and yet some gardeners were more successful than others. While occasionally these differences might be ascribed to magico-religious causes, yet usually, by common consensus, they were explained by observable differences in the amount of work which individual gardeners put into the cultivation of their plots and the degree of skill and common-sense knowledge which they possessed. There was considerable rivalry for prestige among them, but the basis of prestige was not superior magical power, only superior technical ability.[7]

Even more marked is the relative importance of technical skill and secular knowledge as against magical power and sacred knowledge in specialized handicrafts dealing with inanimate objects. While certain crafts originally were reserved for those who possessed some magical powers, yet differences in experience, training, and information were always recognized. Increasing specialization in craftsmanship, which involved long periods of apprenticeship and eventually led to the organization of craftsmen's guilds, enlarged

[6] A vast amount of material about the technical training of children in tribal communities and rural folk communities is contained in ethnographic literature, but very few comparative studies have ever been published. We may mention Nathan Miller, *The Child in Primitive Society* (New York: Brentano's, 1928); Wilfrid D. Hambly and Charles Hose, *Origins of Education among Primitive Peoples* (London, 1926).

[7] Bronislaw Malinowski, *Coral Gardens and Their Magic*, 2 vols. (London, 1935).

considerably the field of purely technological reflection.[8] Usually guilds had secret lore which only members shared, and some of this lore was magical; but much of it concerned technical methods of production. And with the development of religious cultus, traditional magical lore either lost its importance or (as in the Middle Ages) was banned by the religious authorities, with the result that magic ceased to be used by guild members who submitted to the control of the church and continued to be used only by individual nonconformists and by secret associations.[9]

Religion, indeed, had a large part in the functioning of ancient and medieval guilds. Participation in religious ceremonies of the city or the church was considered indispensable for the normal existence of the individual craftsman and for the continued duration of his association. But the influence of these religious activities was not explicitly connected with specific techniques of the craft. They affected the total life of the individual and the group, not any particular technical performance of theirs. Once the good will of heroes, saints, or divinities was gained and the interference of evil powers warded off with the help of the sacred virtue and knowledge of priests, craftsmen assumed full responsibility for the effectiveness of their technical skill and the validity of their technological knowledge.[10]

In agriculture, this partial liberation of technique from magic and religion was slower, mainly because the intended final results of agricultural activities were not immediately observable (as were the products of handicraft), but

[8] Probably one of the reasons for this emphasis on technical efficiency was the need for military weapons. In republican Rome, out of ten collegia of artisans, those were the most privileged which produced arms. See Etienne M. Saint-Léon, *Histoire des corporations et des métiers* (Paris, 1909). We do not know whether any magical rites were used by them, but in any case victory in war depended primarily, if not exclusively, on religious cultus of the gods.

[9] There have been many, though seldom consistent or effective, attempts of prominent church leaders to distinguish between natural techniques and magic in alchemy and medicine. The fact that various virtues and powers were sometimes ascribed to things which seem to modern scientists survivals of early superstitions did not make the technical operations based on these beliefs magical, so long as the alchemist, pharmacist, or doctor did not rely on the alleged mystical power of some unknown will or on that of demons. See Lynn Thorndike, *History of Magic and Experimental Science*, Vols. III and IV.

[10] Historical evidence shows that in the late Middle Ages the separation of technique and religion in craft guilds (as distinct from the earlier religious fraternities) became very complex. The guild as a purely secular group exerted complete control over profane activities: the technical preparation of apprentices as well as the use of proper tools and the application of well-adapted processes of manufacture (Saint-Léon, *op. cit.*, pp. 87 ff., 148); Lujo Brentano, *On the History and Development of Gilds* (London, 1870).

On the other hand, the priesthood exerted complete control over the participation of group members in sacred activities. Profane technical work was entirely prohibited on Sundays, holy days, Saturday afternoons, and on the eves of important holy days (Brentano, *op. cit.*, p. 69; Saint-Léon, *op. cit.*, pp. 140-43).

only after a long period of waiting, during which various kinds of forces beyond the farmer's technical control might affect them favorably or unfavorably. Consequently, even in Western civilizations as late as the nineteenth century some old folk-magic survived in isolated rural communities,[11] and in nearly all rural communities religious ceremonies and prayers intended to bring divine blessing were used to supplement technical activities.[12]

But they were not substituted for technical activities. While hard work, skill, and knowledge were not sufficient to insure success and to prevent failure, no magic, no religious propitiation, could make a lazy, unskilled, or ignorant person a successful farmer. Divine agencies simply would not act for the benefit of the inefficient. "Gods helped those who helped themselves," for only such deserved divine help. And if sometimes gods did not help them either, there was always some reason; e.g., a penalty for personal or collective sins, which might not have been committed during the process of farming, but at some other time. And if the reason was unknown to men, this did not mean that there was none, for divine thinking was often above human understanding. In any case, the primary task of the farmer was to use the best technological knowledge and the best technical skill, according to the standards recognized in his community, and to hope and pray for divine assistance.[13]

Results of technological reflection

Technological knowledge due to comparative reflection about technical activities includes three types of generalizations.

First of all, the success or failure of a technical action was found to depend on the technician's knowledge of the empirical nature of the objects which he used as materials and as instruments of his activity. Such knowledge was an agglomerated product of the results of past observation and was expressed in taxonomic generalizations implying the existence of an objective order of similarities and differences characteristic of logical classes and subclasses.

Such a classification sometimes cut across a magico-religious classification of objects, as when under the totemic system certain kinds of animals, certain

---

[11] Materials in Frazer, *op. cit.*

[12] A classical example from China: The "son of Heaven," before farm husbandry starts every year, prays to God for a good year; later, on a propitious day, he plows three furrows, followed by ministers and feudal princes, *Sacred Books of China. The Liki* (*Sacred Books of the East*, Vol. XXVII). Over 60 pages of this book are devoted to sacred governmental ceremonies.

For an interesting example from present-day Europe, see Clement Simon Mihanovich, "Religious Folklore in the Poljica Region of Dalmatia," *Jour. of Am. Folklore* (July-September, 1948).

[13] E.g., James N. Williams, *Our Rural Heritage* (New York: Knopf, 1925), p. 36.

kinds of plants, and certain inanimate objects were classed together with members of a certain clan on the basis of a mystical affinity between them and the clan;[14] or when objects, however diverse empirically, were viewed as belonging together because they were under the tutelage and control of the same divinity. But this simply meant that a technician had to take the magico-religious category into consideration as well as the natural class. It might limit the range or importance of technological generalizations, but did not make them invalid. Even now, practical and scientific classifications do not always coincide; e.g., when a farmer classifies as weeds all the plants growing in his fields for which he has no use, or when chemical compounds sold by a pharmacist for medical purposes are classed as drugs, while chemical compounds sold by a grocer for nourishment are groceries.

Of course, so long as magico-religious thinking persisted, there was always a possibility that a particular object, seemingly belonging to an empirical class already known, possessed some hidden force, not apparent to observation, which influenced positively or negatively the technician's activity. What seemed to be an animal of a certain natural species might prove to be a supernatural being; an ordinary tree might be the seat of a spirit; a stone, a piece of metal might be the possession of a god; a weapon, a tool, a boat might have been blessed or cursed by a powerful magician. But the existence of such a mystical property inherent in a particular object did not invalidate technological knowledge about the natural properties characteristic of the empirical class to which this object belonged. If a technician who was ignorant of the nature of his objects failed, while those who knew their nature succeeded, he could hardly explain his failure away merely by asserting that his objects must have been mystically different from theirs.

These taxonomic generalizations about the nature of objects handled by technicians were supplemented by generalizations concerning the changes which occurred in them during technical actions. As such actions grew in length and complexity, thinkers who compared them analyzed their performance into sequences of factual changes. Craftsmen and craftswomen in teaching and learning, in competing for recognition of superior achievements, and especially in modifying established patterns, observed every change of objects in relation to preceding and following changes; with technical specialization and the formation of craftsmen's guilds, hundreds of diverse technical processes were thus analyzed. The discovery of regularities in sequence of elementary changes led to *causal* generalizations about natural facts. Even if the primary cause of the total technical performance was still the active will of the craftsman, yet each elementary change in an object could be causally explained by some observable preceding change in the same or another object.

[14] Cf. Émile Durkheim and Marcel Mauss, "De quelques formes primitives de classification," *L'Année sociologique*, Vol. VI (1901-02).

Whether this preceding change had happened independently of the craftsman or was initiated by him, once it occurred, its effect was bound to follow in the natural course of events, whether desired or undesired. Though human or divine magicians could divert this natural course of events by the causative power of their will, yet their interference was unusual; and if it occurred, it did not invalidate conclusions of technologists that observable changes of objects normally followed a causal order, just as the observable nature of objects normally conformed with a taxonomic order.

A third type of natural order, gradually discovered, was that of interdependence between the parts of a whole. The craftsman himself produced this kind of order when constructing a complex whole like a tent or a house, but he also found it existing independently of him. The most easily observable and therefore the earliest observed was the spatial order. The primitive geometer found it when outlining the limits of an area for camp or garden, subdividing it, tracing directions, and measuring distances from a given center. The primitive astronomer went further than this, since he observed not only the spatial patterns in the relative position of stars but—what was even more important for him—the primary regularities in the daily movement of the heavenly sphere and the secondary regularities in the movement of the sun, the moon, and the planets.

Originally this spatial order was pervaded by magico-religious powers and susceptible to magico-religious influences. Geometrical areas, lines, points, directions on the surface of the earth either were originally endowed with various degrees of positive or negative sacredness or could be consecrated or desecrated by men or by gods at the request of men. The sky, the heavenly bodies were either divine or controlled by gods, and radiated sacred powers; by propitiating gods, men could influence in some measure their arrangement and their movements. In short, if things located in space or moving in space constituted a system, it was because a magico-religious connection existed between them.

Nonetheless, even though man could occasionally influence this order, he was normally dependent upon it and had to investigate it for his utilitarian purposes. This investigation led gradually to mathematical and astronomical generalizations, which during many centuries were used for magico-religious guidance and prediction. Geometrical figures and measurements were applied for purposes of geomancy to ascertain what spots, areas, and directions were propitious or unpropitious for cultivation, the erection of buildings, roadmaking, etc.[15] Astronomical observations and calculations served to establish a calendar primarily for the regulation of holidays and to predict the influence

---

[15] Typically in China. Cf. Marcel Granet, *La Civilisation Chinoise* and *La Pensée Chinoise* (Paris, 1929 and 1934).

of heavenly bodies upon the future of human individuals and collectivities.[16] Even abstract numbers had such a magical significance. The survival of astrology and numerology in Western societies to this very day indicates how strong and persistent this magical application of mathematics is. But mathematics could also be used and became increasingly used for strictly technical purposes, such as architectural planning, agricultural planning, irrigation, weighing and numbering materials and products, etc.

A different idea of interdependence between the parts of a whole emerged from the observation of living organisms. Primitive artists, in their drawings, paintings, and sculptures of plants, animals, and human bodies, clearly manifested their awareness of this organic order as viewed from the outside; and technical workers, dissecting plants and animals and using their parts for various practical purposes, obviously acquired considerable knowledge of their inner structure. It is hardly surprising, however, that in view of the anatomical complexity of multicellular organisms, objective generalizations about the structural and functional order of living organisms were relatively slow to develop.

For another reason, theoretic generalization about the inner order of physical and chemical systems was also rather late to emerge. Generalization about physical systems had to be preceded by invention, for only within an engine regularly moving—whether driven by man power, animal power, water or wind power—could the structural and functional interdependence of parts be easily observed; and most of the regularly running engines required the use of wheels, which were not invented earlier than 5,000 years ago. Generalization about chemical systems could develop only in consequence of reflection about chemical analysis and synthesis, and this probably did not begin until the invention of bronze. The very fact that mechanical and chemical inventions were human products made it difficult for early reflection to conceive that there existed physical and chemical systems with an inner natural order of interdependence between their elements which was not created by the inventors, but which nonetheless conditioned the effectiveness of their inventions.

Thus, purely theoretic methodical knowledge about the order of nature emerged from a vast multiplicity of technological generalizations, which differed in different cultures and in every culture were divided among various branches of material techniques. Later we shall discuss briefly, in Chapter 6, how a systematic, coherent science of nature emerged out of this unsystematic,

[16] Some historians have noticed how much astrology has contributed to the progress of astronomy. Thus, Guillaume Bigourdan, *L'Astronomie* (Paris, 1911), has a chapter "Astrologie: son influence capitale sur le développement de l'astronomie." Incidentally, he quotes Kepler, "how small would be the number of scientists devoting themselves to astronomy if men did not expect to read future events in the sky" (although Kepler wrote it at the beginning of the seventeenth century). See also Lynn Thorndike, *op. cit.*, Vol. I. This is an interesting problem for the sociology of knowledge.

logically incoherent plurality of specialized technologies. An important point for our problem, however, as we shall see presently, in Chapter 3, is that the process of unification and systematization was originally carried on not by inductive reasoning from more specific premises to more general conclusions, but by deductive reasoning from universal premises, accepted *a priori*, to specific conclusions. This has affected the whole history of cultural thought, because the same *a priori* premises, which were applied to the domain of nature and there became eventually, if slowly, tested and modified by factual evidence, were as sweepingly extended to the entire domain of cultural phenomena, where it was impossible to test them because they bore no reference to empirical facts in this domain. To this very day, deductive reasoning from universal *a priori* premises, in the form of so-called scientific monism, interferes with the development of all inductive cultural sciences and especially of sociology.

Comparative thinking about social activities

Along with the evolution of technological reflection, another kind of comparative practical reflection evolved. It was concerned with the factual conditions upon which the success of social activities, i.e., activities dealing with human beings, depended. We notice a certain parallelism between these two evolutionary trends; and yet, as we shall see, the knowledge which resulted from practical social thinking could not compare in range, validity, and practical utility with technological knowledge about natural phenomena. Why?

We saw that activities dealing with nonhuman objects were divided into two realms, the sacred and the profane; technological reflection was restricted to the profane, the commonplace which raised no mystical problems, and developed as this realm expanded. Activities dealing with human beings also, though perhaps less clearly, fell into two divisions. One may be called "public," the other "private." Speaking briefly and rather superficially, public activities were those which affected the collective life of a social group, private actions were those which affected only individuals. Comparative social reflection was mostly restricted to the private realm.

The distinction between public and private did not coincide with that between sacred and profane. Many public activities were not sacred. Thus, public war was distinct from private fights, raids, head hunting, etc., and yet it has always been essentially a nonsacred, profane activity, just as collective hunting, fishing, or home building. Magical rites and religious ceremonies had to be performed by powerful magicians or priests of powerful gods before a war, so as to protect warriors against evil powers, and after the war, so as to purify them. Even holy wars, carried on to defend religion, to spread religion among unbelievers, or to destroy heretics, were not intrinsically holy but were made holy by priests or prophets, who dedicated warriors to the service of the gods, assured them of divine blessing, and brought the curse of the gods upon their enemies.

On the other hand, many private activities had a sacred character. The Romans explicitly distinguished between *sacra publica* and *sacra privata*. Magic and religion could be applied in relations between individuals. Thus, sexual intercourse was preceded or followed in many cultures by magical rituals intended to eliminate mystical dangers[17] and is still preceded (even in many modern cultures) by religious ceremonies which counteract its intrinsic impurity and make all the difference between marriage, which is right, and extramarital relations, which are wrong. Magic and religion were used by parents to make their children safe, by healers to help their patients recover, by witches and sorcerers to injure individual enemies, by hosts and guests for mutual security. Even when an individual intends to influence the behavior of another conscious individual by specifically social methods, without using any magical power, either his own or a god's, his action preserves some sacred significance, if it is intended to make the other individual behave in conformity with the order instituted or sanctioned by the gods. Thus, *religious* education of the young and *religious* conversion by persuasion of adult sinners are definitely not profane activities; yet there is often no clear dividing line between them and *moral* education of the young and *moral* reform of adult offenders, except where ideas of moral goodness and badness have become completely secularized.

The main difference between public and private activities which has affected the history of social thought is that the public activities were supposed to be ordered and controlled by rulers with supreme authority and unchallenged power over all members of the group, while the performance of private activities was left to ordinary human individuals acting on their own personal initiative. The contrast was clear when public activities were performed only at periodical tribal meetings under the guidance of high magicians and chiefs and had an essentially sacred character, while between these meetings interindividual activities went on without interference from tribal authorities, unless something occurred which was supposed to affect the welfare of the tribe as a whole, like a notable transgression of religious or moral prohibitions.

The contrast became radical with the development of states ruled by kings who combined the roles of high priests and war lords; it persisted even when, as in republics, the roles of rulers of states became partly secularized and subdivided among the many individuals functioning as members of the government. All the activities of royal subjects ordered by the king, or by those agents to whom he delegated directly or indirectly some of his authority, were public; whatever activities were not included in this order remained

[17] Cf. Alfred E. Crawley, *The Mystic Rose* (New York: Macmillan, 1927).

private, though they might at any time become a matter of concern to the king or his delegates if they affected the public order.

So long as the function of the king was that of supreme creator or guardian of public order, there was little opportunity for the development of any comparative objective reflection about him. Either he was successful in creating and maintaining public order—and this obviously meant that he knew all about it and did not need the guidance of any thinkers—or else he failed; and this meant that he had neither wisdom nor power and that some creative hero endowed with both should take his place. Kings, indeed, did use advisers, selecting them from among experienced specialists in public activity; but such advisers were regarded as assistants of the king, helping him build and maintain public order. Sometimes the assistant rather than the king was considered the real builder and even extolled as a hero, like Richelieu or Bismarck. The emergence of comparative investigation of public order by independent thinkers, who were neither rulers nor assistants of rulers but nonetheless tried to function as intellectual guides of rulers, is a late historical process which we shall discuss in our next chapter. Few rulers have followed such guidance.

As a matter of fact, the only kind of comparative investigation in the public domain which rulers have appreciated and stimulated when states became too large for anybody's direct observation has been geographical or statistical. Geographical surveys of state territories were made forty centuries ago; and statistical surveys, beginning with the enumeration of warriors, workers, slaves and peasants, domestic animals, houses, or agricultural and industrial products, were well developed in ancient Egypt and Babylon, and some documentary evidence of demographic statistics is found in the sacred books of other cultures. The character of this information is significant; for in a statistical survey, people (just as cattle or inanimate technical products) are not viewed as a united group of interacting members, but as an amorphous mass of passive objects of governmental activity. Out of this mass, statisticians chose and enumerated objects characterized by certain indices which made them fit for specific governmental actions: sex, age, social status, capacity for work, fitness for military service. To this very day, the current definition of the state as a combination of three components—territory, population, and government—preserves this old conception; government being the ordering agency, and population the amorphous passive mass of living beings which is being ordered.

Of course, a ruler needed more than a knowledge of the human masses which could be controlled by the causative power of his will. Inasmuch as he used auxiliary agents (assistants and delegates) to control the masses and to counteract the activities of hostile agents (political opponents, foreign rulers, perhaps traitors), he had to have some special knowledge about those agents, their abilities, their manifest tendencies, their hidden motives. Such knowledge did not necessarily include explicit generalizations. Indeed, successful kings and heroes were supposed to possess intuitive personal knowledge of the persons whom they selected and used as their helpers as well as of their individual enemies, while the lack of this intuitive knowledge often explained the failure of rulers who delegated power to bad or weak men or misunderstood the intentions of their enemies.

No psychological generalizations could take the place of such intuition; those who had it did not need psychological guidance, those who lacked it were beyond all help. Later, social thinkers who wrote for the guidance of rulers usually did include psychological advice meant to guide rulers in selecting their assistants and dealing with their enemies; but by then there already existed a considerable body of psychological knowledge agglomerated throughout thousands of years. The source of this knowledge can be clearly traced to comparative reflection about private social activities.

Moral conditioning of reflection about private social activities

Individuals who do not perform important public functions, whose social actions do not affect large groups, but only other individuals, unlike rulers or heroes, are not above criticism and advice from thinkers. They are mostly ordinary people, unequal in personal qualities, status, and influence, and often needing the intellectual guidance of wiser men who have done some comparative reflecting about human relations.

Such practical comparative reflecting appeared very early. Originally, it probably was done and still often is done by old and experienced men and women, spontaneously functioning as advisers of less experienced individual agents, telling them how to deal successfully with individuals who are the objects of their actions. Numerous maxims and proverbs contain the generalizations of those primitive sages.[18] Later, some thinkers specialized in this kind of advice by virtue of their professional roles. Thus, priests were often sages, and much of their social wisdom found expression in sacred books.[19] Eventually professional social thinking and advice became partly secularized by philosophers and psychologists.

There is an obvious difference between this practical reflection for the guidance of social agents dealing with human individuals and technological

[18] The persistence of this wisdom in civilized societies is well known. See *The Oxford Dictionary of English Proverbs*, compiled by William G. Smith (Oxford, 1935); and Le Roux de Lincy, *Le Livre des proverbes français* (Paris, 1859), with more irony than in English proverbs.

[19] We found social advice by wise religious men in the *Sacred Books of the East*, although not so much as we had expected. In the Bible, more such advice is contained in Proverbs than in any other part. It is often difficult, however, to separate practical advice concerning the most efficient ways of dealing with human beings, from theological and ethical norms.

reflection for the guidance of technical agents dealing with natural objects. Since in the latter kind of action only one human agent is involved, the technological thinker obviously takes his point of view; but because the object of a social action is also a human agent, the thinker who reflects about cases when two human agents simultaneously or alternatively act upon each other might take the standpoint of either of them. However, since his thinking is meant to guide a particular agent, to indicate how that agent can successfully achieve the results he intends to achieve, he will take the point of view of that individual in whose success he is primarily interested, and conceive the other individual as an object who should be made to react as the first agent intends him to react.

Generally speaking, practical social thinking as expressed in proverbs, maxims, and written generalizations is morally biased. Social thinkers usually take the side of those social agents who are morally right by the standards of the thinkers, not of those who are wrong; at least, very little advice to the wicked was socially preserved before the appearance of philosophic skepticism. Comparative social reflection is primarily intended to serve individuals who function as guardians of traditional mores or who wish to introduce into personal relations a moral order conceived by a god, a prophet, a social reformer.

So long as the thinker's ideas of right and wrong correspond to social patterns unquestioningly accepted by those whom he wishes to guide, his moral bias is unreflective. For instance, for thousands of years in patriarchal societies, social wisdom intended to guide parents in dealing with children took for granted the principle of paternal authority as the moral foundation of well-ordered family life. In societies with an organized priesthood, the agglomerated social wisdom transmitted by priests to priestly candidates for their guidance in dealing with laymen takes for granted the absolute validity of the moral standards and norms of which the priests are exponents and the right of the priests to control the behavior of laymen.

In complex and changing societies with conflicting interests and beliefs we find social thinkers on opposite sides with divergent ideas of right and wrong. Thus, even in early historical periods—along with practical wisdom meant to guide masters in controlling servants, priests in controlling laymen, nobles in handling commoners—there were a few popular proverbs, maxims, and tales advising servants how to influence masters, laymen how to act in relations with priests, peasants how to deal with nobles. While folklore and old-book wisdom are full of advice by men to men telling them how to deal with dangerous, recalcitrant, or rebellious females, there must have been considerable traditional wisdom guiding women in their relations with men; certainly high-class courtesans in antiquity, during the Renaissance, and in modern France were well instructed in masculine psychology. In recent times, wise women advising other women how to deal with males have become more numerous, probably more influential, and undoubtedly more original than the old-fashioned masculine advisers.

However, awareness of the existence of different standards of right and wrong in human relations did not eliminate moral bias. Thinkers representing opposite sides in social conflicts combined practical advice with ethical disputation. They tried to prove that their own ideas were ethically right and that the agents who followed their advice would promote moral order, while the ideas of their opponents were ethically wrong and if applied in practice would result in moral disorder. Such an attitude precluded any comparative investigation of the various kinds of moral order in human relations. That which is wrong cannot be compared with that which is right. If order means conformity with an absolutely valid moral pattern, any behavior which does not conform with that pattern is disorderly behavior. In short, moral conditioning of practical social wisdom tended to prevent the development of sociological generalizations about *social order* comparable to technological generalizations about natural order.

But it did not interfere with the development of psychological generalizations about human individuals as objects of social activity.

The origins and results of practical psychology ·

A social thinker usually assumes that social agents—parents, masters, priests—know what is morally good and what is morally wrong, what they and their social objects—children, servants, laymen—ought to do and ought not to do. He takes for granted that these agents have the necessary means to influence their objects. And yet he may question their ability to use these means effectively, to make their social objects behave as they ought to behave, and to prevent them from behaving as they ought not to behave. Good intentions and adequate means are not enough to achieve success in dealing with individual human beings, for they are sometimes apt to react differently than the agent wants them to react. Of course, the failure of a good agent to influence a human being in a desirable way may be explicable by the badness or wickedness of this being; as we mentioned before, such an explanation is quite often used to account for disturbances of moral order. But it cannot be used universally. For if a human being is judged unreservedly and incorrigibly wicked, nothing can be done except to cut him off from all social relations with normal people by excluding him from social life. This is an extreme measure, resorted to in only a small minority of cases: infants or adults possessed by evil mystical powers and secular criminals. Most human beings are sometimes good and sometimes bad, or good in some respects and bad in other respects, or good in relations with some people and bad in relations with other people; and they can become better or worse in the course of time. In nonethical terms, a human being may react to similar actions positively or negatively on different occasions, or react positively to one kind of actions by the same agent and negatively to a different kind, or react positively to one agent and negatively to another; his positive reactions may increase and his negative reactions decrease, or vice versa.

Therefore, success or failure in dealing with human individuals is found by thinkers to depend on the agent's ability to predict their reactions to specific actions of his. This ability is supposed to depend primarily on the agent's knowledge of the permanent psychological dispositions, characteristics, or traits of those human beings whose behavior he wants to control. Such knowledge is provided by thinkers who compare the behavior of human beings at different times and draw conclusions about their future behavior from their past behavior.

The practical origin and significance of psychological generalization is manifested, first of all, in the evaluative meaning of those terms which denote psychological characteristics or traits. To this very day, in every modern language, most of the adjectives used to characterize human individuals psychologically connote positive or negative valuations. This indicates that the behavior of human individuals denoted by such words has not been analyzed and compared according to theoretic standards of objective factual knowledge, but classified according to the standards of desirability or undesirability current in a given culture. Some of these adjectives which now appear to be neutral are in fact ambivalent, which indicates changing or dual standards of personal valuation, and almost every one of them has an antonym. The evaluative significance of each of such antonymous terms will be readily discovered if they are applied to different classes of human individuals. For instance, "bold" and "timid" in the abstract seem merely descriptive terms, but when applied to different categories, to men or to women, to businessmen or to unemployed workers, their ambivalence becomes obvious.

This example points to another old, widespread trend in psychological thinking which has not disappeared even in modern times. Most of the early psychological reflection and much of the reflection still current is concerned with specific classes of human individuals already distinguished not by previous psychological comparison, but by social status in relation to other individuals in a given society. Individuals of each class are ascribed psychological characteristics which are supposed to make them similar among themselves and different from individuals of other classes. Such a class may be further subdivided into psychological types with contrasting traits in addition to their basic common characteristics.

In every culture, we find people divided according to age and sex into at least seven classes: little children, young boys, young girls, adult men, adult women, old men, old women. Individuals belonging to one of these classes are supposed to possess common and distinctive psychological traits, though certain typical differences may be found within the class. Much of this is common-sense knowledge; yet the existence of explicit generalizations indicates that many social agents dealing with individuals of a certain class, especially a class different from their own, presumably need to be taught or reminded of this knowledge by its more competent bearers.

Even today, a considerable proportion of psychological generalizations concerns distinctive primary characteristics—intellectual, volitional, and emotional—as well as typical secondary differences of the lower-age classes, and are intended to guide parents and educators. Although these classes are predominantly defined in terms of chronological age, yet classification by social status still influences psychological research. Thus, preschool children, children in successive grades of primary school, high-school students, and college students are often investigated separately.[20] The psychology of women as distinct from the psychology of men still survives, and its practical significance is manifest whenever psychological generalizations are used to draw conclusions about the status of women—either defending or criticizing their traditional subjection to men.[21]

Cutting across classifications by age and sex, we find in many nonliterate societies a classification by clans or gentes. Individuals belonging to a clan or a gens are sometimes ascribed psychological traits which differentiate them from members of other clans or gentes and are presumed to be hereditary traits. This kind of psychological characterization of members of

[20] Of course, modern educational psychology is no longer based on evaluative generalizations, but constitutes an application of the agglomerated results of theoretic scientific research to practical educational problems. Still, it is sometimes difficult to eliminate the influence of the old evaluative approach.

[21] There are considerable differences in the psychological generalizations of men about women. Some generalizations contained in the *Sacred Books of the East*, in the Bible, in the works of early Christian Fathers indicate negative valuations of women in general. E.g., "Women are naturally wicked," *Sacred Books of the East*, XXV, 330. See Frazer, *Folklore in the Old Testament* (New York: Macmillan, 1923), for the misogynism of the author of the second story of creation. Usually, however, women are divided into two categories: women as wives and mothers, essentially good and seemingly devoid of sexual interest; and women dangerous to men—whores, wantons, adulteresses—who are all negatively valued and characterized essentially by their sexual interest. Later generalizations of secular wise men are not so simple. See, e.g., Pierre B. de Brantome, *Lives of Fair and Gallant Ladies*, where virtuous wives and mothers are taken for granted and not discussed; at the other extreme are "harlots, base at heart." The work is devoted to "high-spirited," "bold," "loving" ladies, by no means virtuous, but certainly positively valued. Very different is the work of William Alexander, *The History of Women*, 2 vols. (London, 1779), "composed only for the amusement and instruction of the Fair Sex." Besides much good advice, it contains generalizations about the characteristics of women at different historical periods, about the influence of education, and some rather critical comparative generalizations about the opinions of men concerning women.

The most radical classification of mankind by sex into two psychological categories, completely different in their whole inner essence, is that of Otto Weininger, *Sex and Character*, English translation (London–New York, 1918).

genetic groups also continues throughout history. For instance, members of every Scottish clan are supposed to have a distinctive psychology. Family histories and books of heraldry contain characterological generalizations about bearers of certain family names, and many recent works have tried to discover common and distinctive psychological features among the descendants of certain ancestors, so as to prove the importance of heredity.

In collectivities with a class hierarchy, where every class level includes individuals of both sexes and all ages, classes are supposed to differ in psychology as well as in status. Slaves have generally been considered to have a distinctive psychology; and in the Middle Ages, nobles and commoners were ascribed very different psychological characteristics, so much so that they were often supposed to have descended from different ancestors. In India, alleged psychological differences between the four traditional castes were sublimated in the famous myth according to which each caste originated in a different part of Brahma's body: Brahmans from his head as the seat of wisdom, Kshattriyas from his breast and arms as the sources of bravery, Vaisyas from his belly, Sudras from his legs.

Such generalizations persist in common-sense thinking, although by now psychological generalizations of lower-class thinkers about upper classes are as popular as those of upper-class thinkers about lower classes, if not more so. Generalizations about the psychology of the nobility by some ideologists of the French Revolution were as sweeping as those of the nobility about villains in the twelfth century; the psychology of the capitalist class, as described by proletarian thinkers, counterbalances the psychology of the masses, as characterized by the elite.

Since the middle of the nineteenth century, many psychologists have assumed the existence of class psychology and done some more or less— rather less—scientific investigation, starting from this assumption. By then, of course, it was well recognized that no psychological characteristic was exclusive, limited to one social class, and universally found among all individuals of this class; all that could be claimed was that the majority of individuals of a class possessed it or did not possess it. And this could be exactly ascertained by statistical methods. Niceforo's theory of the psychological inferiority of the lower classes; Galton's statistical findings in his *Hereditary Genius*, indicating that the majority of intellectually superior individuals came from the upper classes which formed a minority in English society; Woods's investigation of royal families, tending to prove that this highest social class contained a larger proportion of psychologically superior individuals than any other: these are instances of this approach.[22]

Another early and still familiar social category concerning which psy-

[22] Alfredo Niceforo, *Les Classes pauvres* (Paris, 1905); Francis Galton, *Hereditary Genius* (London, 1869); Frederick Adams Woods, *Mental and Moral Heredity in Royalty* (New York: Holt, 1906).

chological generalizations abound is that of outsiders ethnically different from participants in the collectivity to which the psychologizing thinkers belong. In many collectivities with few outside contacts, sweeping generalizations about all foreigners are still current, based on the behavior of visiting strangers. When contacts are relatively frequent, generalizations become more specific, applying to the members of particular ethnic groups who live in adjoining areas. Most tribal groups and folk-communities have traditional views about the psychology of other tribes or neighboring communities with different folk-cultures. With expanding communication and transportation, such generalizations are extended to large national collectivities. Compare, for instance, English generalizations about the Germans, the French, and the Spaniards, going back to the fifteenth century, with French generalizations about the English, the Germans, the Spaniards, and the Italians.

Migrations stimulated this kind of psychological thinking, both among migrants and among natives. Take the views of American pioneers and frontiersmen about the psychology of Amerindians generally and about certain Amerindian tribes specifically, of the British about East Indians, of the Boers about South African natives, of Western traders about the Chinese; and, reciprocally, the psychological conceptions of the Chinese concerning Westerners, of East Indians concerning Englishmen, of Amerindians concerning whites, of native white Americans concerning new immigrants. Generalizations of natives of various cultures about the psychology of Jews, who are considered foreign immigrants even after several centuries of residence, offer the best-known and most conspicuous examples.

Where cultural differences seemed more or less associated with visible differences in bodily appearance, psychological generalizations (mainly derived from culturally conditioned behavior) became correlated with biological generalizations. As a result, members of a foreign group were conceived as belonging to a race, an organic species whose basic psychological characteristics were hereditary and therefore changeless; only secondary traits responded to changes in culture.[23]

When anthropologists and, later, psychologists took over these popular conceptions, at first they made little effort to distinguish between the classifications of human individuals by their cultures and by their organic characteristics. Many anthropological monographs, after a preliminary survey of the geographic area in which a certain group lived, characterized the physical type of the people, continued with their psychological characterization

---

[23] Modern generalizations about racial psychology are now so familiar that we need not discuss them. Cf., for a brief survey, F. H. Hankins, *Demographic and Biological Contributions to Sociological Principles*, Part IV, "Racial Differences"; Barnes, Becker, and Becker, *Contemporary Social Theory* (New York: Appleton, 1940), pp. 296-307. For the history of racial conceptions see James Bryce, *Race Sentiment in History* (London, 1915).

(mainly based on their distinctive cultural patterns of conduct), and then proceeded to describe their culture in detail.[24] This confusion still persists. The term "race" is widely used in the United States in referring to the Jews, the Germans, the Italians, the French, the Swedes, the Poles, the Mexicans, the Chinese, with the implication that the individuals so designated form a logical class, combining specific cultural traits with specific biological traits. Much psychological thinking and some research is still carried on with the purpose of determining the typical psychology of the individuals of each race in this sense.

However, some efforts have been made to distinguish between the two kinds of classification. Thus, the French "psychologie des peuples," developed by G. Le Bon, Alfred Fouillée, and others, emphasizes cultural rather than biological subdivisions;[25] but present American studies of the psychology of American Negroes are necessarily concerned with the "Negro race" in the biological sense, since the descendants of imported African Negroes now participate in the same culture as the descendants of European white immigrants.

With growing functional specialization of individuals and groups, occupational classes became another well-known field of psychological generalizations. Farmers, warriors, craftsmen, and merchants were ascribed specific psychological traits conditioned by their occupations, and individuals engaged in other occupations had to know these in order to deal with them successfully. In occupations which were not altogether hereditary, and especially in those that were considered desirable and requiring considerable preparatory training, candidates selected for this training were expected to show at least potentially those psychological characteristics which were considered necessary for the effective performance of occupational functions. This enlarged the scope of the psychology of children and adolescents, and was the beginning of psychotechnics and occupational guidance.

The evaluative significance of psychological concepts, combined with the practical interest of psychological thinkers in specific social classes or groups, led to the well-known disagreements between psychologists representing socially conflicting points of view. In fact, most popular generalizations about the psychology of any class or group express the positive or negative

[24] As a typical example of this approach, we may mention Walter W. Skeat and Charles O. Bladgen, *Pagan Races in the Malay Peninsula*, 2 vols. (London, 1906).

[25] Gustave Le Bon, in his *Lois psychologiques de l'évolution des peuples*, is still influenced by biological racism. But Alfred Fouillée, in his *Esquisse psychologique des peuples européens*, 2d ed. (Paris, 1903), considers the cultural aspects, manifested in the history of peoples, as the main "dynamic elements" of their psychology. The most original attempt, however, to reach a conclusion about national character, based entirely on culture, is that of Richard Müller-Freienfels, *The German, His Psychology and Culture. An Inquiry into Folk Character*, trans. by Rolf Hoffmann (Los Angeles: The New Symposion Press, 1936).

prejudices of those agents whose point of view the thinkers have accepted: If the prejudice is positive, the class or group is ascribed with predominantly good, desirable, superior characteristics; if negative, its characteristics are predominantly bad, undesirable, inferior. And since prejudices vary and change, every popular psychological judgment is apt to be contradicted by other psychological judgments.

Classificatory generalizations about human individuals have been supplemented or modified by causal generalizations. After an individual has been defined as possessing certain psychological characteristics, so long as his behavior apparently manifests these characteristics, no additional psychological reflection is needed; it is just his nature so to behave. But if he unexpectedly does something which is not in accordance with his nature, which neither he nor other individuals of his type usually do, this raises a problem.

Of course, his original definition may have been erroneous. If the agent who defined him did not know him personally and ascribed to him certain characteristics only because he belonged to a social class or group in which these characteristics prevailed, he may be an exception. There are exceptional women with masculine psychological traits, and some men with feminine traits; foolish oldsters and wise youngsters; slaves with traits of freemen, and freemen with slavish traits; sinful priests and saintly laymen; miserly, cowardly, or disloyal nobles, and generous, brave, loyal commoners. But if an individual who has already in his past behavior manifested certain typical traits later behaves in a way which is not true to type, this can only mean that some special cause must have been active, affecting his disposition, making him act differently than he would otherwise have acted.

Such a cause may be designated by the term "motive," in the popular sense in which the word is widely used. When an obedient child disobeys or a disobedient child willingly obeys, when a modest maiden behaves immodestly or a wanton woman shows modesty, when a coward bravely faces danger or a courageous man runs from it, when a fool acts cleverly or a clever man foolishly, when a miser gives money away or a generous man behaves like a miser, when a lazy person spontaneously starts to work or a hard-working person loafs, there must be some motive to explain such atypical behavior.

Causal generalizations about the influence of motives partially cut across classificatory generalizations, inasmuch as individuals of different types may be influenced by similar motives. However, some individuals are found more susceptible to the influence of specific motives than others, and high susceptibility to a certain kind of motive is apt to be considered indicative of a certain psychological trait. But individuals who are easily swayed by various kinds of motives cannot be easily subdivided into definite classes. Consequently, in popular psychological thinking, relationships between classificatory generalizations on the one hand and causal generalizations on the other are neither clear nor consistent.[26]

Thus, when systematic theoretic thinking about the factual order of social reality began, all it found was an agglomeration of common-sense psychological knowledge about human individuals. While this knowledge was considered practically useful, it was much more limited in scope, much less definite, and less detailed than technological knowledge about natural reality. Furthermore, while the technological generalizations, developed in various fields of material technique, were unconnected but not contradictory, practical psychology was full of contradictions. Nevertheless, it became the foundation of theories which have endured for thousands of years. In a later chapter we shall briefly survey the theories which emerged from practical psychology. Only in relatively recent times has a new scientific approach to individual psychology gradually developed, and it has not yet eliminated the old approach.

[26] Perhaps one of the most interesting collections of practical psychological generalizations, based on an analysis of motives, is François de La Rochefoucault's *Réflexions ou sentences et maximes morales*, complete ed. (Paris, 1868): differences in nature are taken into consideration (as between men and women, wise men and fools, brave men and cowards), but most reflections are about the similarities of human motivation—not universal, but most frequent; and motives, like traits, are evaluated positively or negatively.

Metaphysical Theories of Universal Order

The beginnings of systematic philosophy

Philosophy, in the sense in which this word is used by historians, developed partly in continuation of and partly in opposition to the practical thinking which we have already discussed. Its original aim was to achieve a synthesis of all the essential knowledge hitherto agglomerated. Its problems originated in critical reflection about existing knowledge as judged by standards of logical consistency. Only logically consistent knowledge could be true, and the very possibility of logically consistent knowledge depended upon the existence of a coherent rational order among the objects of knowledge. This order could be discovered only by systematic theoretic thinking when guided by the principle of universal validity and therefore independent of the varying and changing practical interests and prejudices of individual thinkers.[1]

Such critical theoretic reflection originated in several advanced cultures, but was most fully developed in ancient Greece during the classical period. Its origin and growth have been explained by the many contacts of Greek colonies with diverse cultures in the Near East and by the variety of local and regional cultures within the Hellenic area. The knowledge agglomerated in these various cultures through thousands of years of theological, social, technological, and psychological thinking embodied so many divergent and

[1] The material for this chapter was derived partly from the works of philosophers and partly from histories of philosophy. To prove the validity of our generalizations by quotations from the works of philosophers is, obviously, far beyond the range of this brief outline. For the history of Greek philosophy, we used Eduard Zeller and Theodor Gomperz. The idea of the revolutionary significance of the Sophists is derived from George Grote. For the history of modern philosophy we find most useful Friedrich Ueberweg's *Geschichte der Philosophie,* as reworked and developed by his continuators (Vols. III, IV, and V, in their latest editions: 1911, 1923, and 1928). Here, as might be expected, much more space is devoted to German philosophy than to the philosophies of other nationalities, and some historical generalizations seem to be questionable; yet the authors most conscientiously try to be objective in summarizing the theories of particular authors, and no important philosopher of any nationality is omitted.

conflicting ideas of order that the Greek philosophers were unable to synthesize it.

In the first place, they found diverse religious conceptions of a natural order created by the will of the gods, as revealed to men in sacred traditions and books, and maintained by the gods against all agents of disorder. Greek gods differed from Egyptian, Phoenician, Babylonian, Assyrian, and Persian gods; and many radical contradictions arose between these religions, inasmuch as the gods of every religion took the part of their believers in conflicts with outsiders. And a god who was a creator and guardian of order according to his own priests might be a destructive spirit of evil, an agent of disorder, according to the priests of another god. Even within the world of Greek gods harmonious cooperation was lacking. Attempts to overcome these contradictions by building coherent theological systems were unsuccessful—Hesiod's, though it included only Greek gods in its cosmogony; and Pherecydes', though it applied an arbitrary allegorical interpretation to many myths. Philosophers, striving for logical consistency, were compelled to deny the existence of all the traditional gods, Greek and foreign, and to consider them anthropomorphic products of human imagination. But the conception of an order of nature, contrasted with disorder, did not disappear; on the contrary, gods were rejected precisely because the various kinds of order which theologians ascribed to them as creators and guardians proved incoherent, defective by logical standards, unsatisfactory according to the philosophic idea of perfection.

Second, a critical comparison of the conceptions of moral order found in different societies and manifested in the conduct of rulers, in legal enactments, in mores, also led to the discovery of irreconcilable discrepancies and conflicts. Not only were the various political structures of non-Hellenic kingdoms and empires incompatible with Hellenic standards, but the Greek cities themselves failed to show any uniform public order. Private mores also differed, even conflicted, for what was considered morally right in one society was often morally wrong in another. A philosopher aware of the logical inconsistency of these conceptions could no longer believe in superhuman political and moral heroes, original creators of an absolutely right order, or in kings as supreme guardians of divinely instituted order. Every order was obviously imperfect, marred by some disorder. But the very discovery of this imperfection implied the ideal of a logically perfect order.

Third, philosophers observed other disagreements between standards of right and wrong applied in various cultures. Greek thinkers were very much interested in poetry, music, and the plastic arts. The aesthetic standards applied in these realms of human activity obviously differed from the moral standards by which social activities were judged; and since artistic performances and their products were often evaluated positively by some judges and negatively by others, no universally accepted conception of aesthetic order could be discovered. But this did not preclude the possibility of finding an ideal of aesthetic perfection by which philosophers might judge all artistic performances. The same might be said of the technical activities, which were judged by utilitarian standards; participants in any culture usually considered their patterns of material technique the most efficient and useful. Could any universally applicable standards of technical perfection be discovered?

Of all the problems which philosophers had to face, the most important was that of relationship between the natural order and moral, aesthetic, utilitarian, and (in modern terms) "cultural" order in general. Natural order was explicitly recognized as entirely independent of human agents, but cultural order could be realized only by human agents. Were the two orders separate and unconnected, or was there a logical connection between them? And in either case, what was the connection between the one ideal order, natural or cultural, which philosophers postulated, and the multiplicity and diversity of factual orders, which technological thinkers observed among natural objects and which students of men discerned among human actions?

In trying to solve these problems, philosophers developed a conception of order which, though sometimes found in practical thinking concerning specific objects and complexes, was never before generalized. Every philosophic theory constitutes a system of logically interdependent concepts. Since this system is supposed to contain true knowledge of an objective rational order, it presupposes that the order itself must be essentially like its own logical structure; it must be, in short, an order of interdependence among the elements of a united, coherent *system*. An ideal order, natural or cultural, was thus conceived as the inner order of a perfectly rational system whose every element had a definite place in relation to other elements. All empirical factual order depended upon the existence of an objective systematic order; objects could be classified because they were elements of the same system; and processes were subjected to causal laws because they occurred within the same system.

As a matter of fact, Greek philosophy explicitly started with the postulate, initiated by theological speculation, that the entire universe is one harmonious whole—a *cosmos*. This postulate remains, even in our times, the basis of many metaphysical theories which aim at a logical synthesis of all "true" knowledge. Probably the boldest and most inclusive outline of a monistic philosophy of the universe—trying to take equally into consideration all kinds of order: natural and cultural, factual and ideal—was that of Heraclitus of Ephesus, but it was never fully developed. Most metaphysicians assumed one kind of systematic universal order as essential and derived from it by deduction the other kinds of order. Some, however, considered the natural and the cultural order as irreducible to each other, and yet maintained the postulate of a united universe: Either the two orders were really two aspects of the same rational system; or they belonged to two distinct, but functionally interconnected systems with a common foundation; or they were different manifestations of the same ultimate reality, the essence of which was super-rational, not accessible to logical reasoning but only to some kind of mystical intuition. Apart from the skeptics, who questioned the validity of knowledge in general, the possibility that there is no single coherent universe, but a multiplicity of systems and complexes with diverse orders of their own, partly and variously interconnected but not integrated into a systematic whole, has only in recent times received any attention.

We should not need to discuss here these metaphysical theories, were it not for their persistent influence, which has impeded and still often impedes the development of scientific thinking. The two great achievements of philosophy have been: First, the substitution of reason for divine revelation and for the practical success of human agents as supreme criterion of "truth"; second, the introduction of systematic universal generalizations in those realms of knowledge where only a multiplicity of unconnected or contradictory special generalizations formerly existed. But the weakness of most systematic philo-sophic theories, especially of metaphysical doctrines, has been that each aimed to attain absolute truth at once and claimed supreme final validity for itself; to support its claim, it had to reject as invalid all knowledge which was logically incompatible with it. Eventually, this rejected knowledge was incor-porated and systematized by some other philosophic theory, which in turn proclaimed itself supremely valid. The resulting conflict was irreconcilable by logical reasoning since, according to the principle of contradiction, the truth of one theory implied the falsity of the other, and vice versa. Such conflicts were gradually eliminated after the principle of scientific hypothesis —claiming only conditional validity and opening the way for new problems, new discoveries, and new hypotheses—was substituted for the principle of absolute and final truth; and this was also largely due to those modern philosophers who subjected all absolutistic claims to constructive criticism and helped develop scientific methodology. We shall see later that this sub-stitution of the hypothetical approach for the absolutistic approach has been much slower in the cultural than in the natural domain. It is still meeting considerable resistance from thinkers who are involved in the old philosophic controversies.

Materialistic metaphysics

The main original obstacle in the way of systematic philosophical thinking was, as we have seen, mystical belief in various conscious agents, some creative, others destructive, some maintaining order in nature, others disturbing this order. The simplest way to build a logically consistent theory of nature was to postulate a universal system of self-existing material objects and self-occurring physical processes, with an order independent of all conscious agencies. Theories based on this postulate are commonly designated as "materialistic." The term is rather inadequate, when applied to those modern philosophic theories which, though they exclude—like the older theories—all participation of conscious agencies from the natural system, no longer accept matter as absolute substance. Still the term may be preserved, inasmuch as modern naturalism does not reject the reality of material objects, though defining them as functional complexes rather than as substantial entities.

Now, such a philosophic theory of nature does not necessarily imply materialistic metaphysics, for it may be used without metaphysical speculation to guide physical sciences toward new problems and new discoveries. Or it may be part of a metaphysical doctrine which admits conscious agencies, but denies their interference with the natural order—e.g., Cartesianism or even some forms of deism. Materialistic metaphysics is a doctrine according to which every phenomenon, i.e., everything which is or can be experienced, is included within the material universe and determined by its order. Anything that is not logically compatible with this doctrine must be rejected as unreal, objectively nonexistent. The chief difficulty in the way of such a conception is to reduce all cultural order to the material order of nature by eliminating conscious agencies from human collectivities.

Of course, before reducing cultural order to natural order, materialism had to develop a logically consistent theory of the latter. This was not so easy, for the factual order of natural objects and processes as known from experience is not perfectly rational, cannot be logically synthesized. Philosophers had to postulate that behind this factual order there really is a conceptual order, a perfectly rational unity of the universal system of nature: Whatever disunity, divergence, or incoherence may be found among empirical data must be an illusion; any belief in the real existence of characteristics of objects or in the factual occurrence of processes which do not fit into the perfect conceptual order must be an erroneous opinion bound to be discredited by logical reasoning.

Even though, with increasing exactness of observations, philosophers came to recognize that factual relationships among empirical data only approximately, never fully, conformed with the perfection of the conceptual order; still the latter was the only order compatible with the requirements of logical reasoning. It had to be accepted as really existing, underlying the imperfection of observable facts; otherwise the whole theory of one natural universe would break down.

The only kind of conceptual order which could be thus postulated as inherent in the unified system of nature was that of mathematics. Every material object could be located in a certain space with reference to other objects. Thus, the development of astronomy and geometry led to the abstract conception of one universal, uniform, measurable space which included all material objects. Every material object could be viewed as a unit in an arithmetical sum, provided its qualitative difference from other units was ignored. And the simplest observable processes were movements of material units.

The logical systematization of geometrical and arithmetical concepts was already started in ancient Egypt and Babylonia. Greek thinkers continued and perfected it.[2] But mathematical generalizations, at the time systematic philosophy began, were relatively few—enough to postulate the existence of a perfect mathematical order behind the many imperfect and divergent factual orders, but not enough to reduce empirical classificatory and causal generalizations to mathematical regularities. They furnished a basis for materialistic metaphysics, but only a starting point for physical science.

The most conspicuous example of this limitation was the Eleatic philosophy which, in its search for logical consistency, conceived the universe as an absolutely perfect, indivisible, uniform, changeless geometrical whole, rejecting by mathematical reasoning all possibility of plurality, diversity, and change. Such a doctrine manifestly excluded scientific investigation of empirical facts. It was Democritus who laid the foundations for a philosophical conception of the material universe, the main premises of which could be used in scientific research. He accepted plurality, diversity, and change, but postulated that their real essence must be such as to make them reducible to a universal and permanent quantitative order. This precludes any idea of creation or destruction; the appearance of new objects or the disappearance of existing objects must be conceived merely as the connection or the separation of eternal, indestructible units. It precludes, further, all qualitative variations on which empirical classifications could be based. The units of which objects are composed must be not only indestructible, but devoid of qualities. Since no such units can be observed, they must be so small as to be inaccessible to human experience. These are *atoms*, indivisible components of the natural universe. Atoms differ among themselves, but all their differ-

[2] The Pythagorean theory was the first Greek attempt at such a systematization, though the Pythagoreans were certainly not materialists. "Pythagoras, one of the first who had faith in the order of the world, understood that it was necessary to explain by regular causes, by constant laws, the apparent irregularity of the phenomena of nature. . . . To him is due the principle, so universally admitted later during 2000 years, that the uniform circular movement is the most perfect of all. . . . He conceived the world as a sphere. The harmony of spheres is a famous part of the system of the Pythagoreans." According to Philolaus, "Numbers are the permanent cause of the order of the world. Unity is the principle of numbers and of all that exists," and it is identified with God. Cf. Bigourdan, *L'Astronomie*, pp. 47-51.

ences are reducible to differences in size, shape, and weight. Combinations of atoms differ endlessly, but only because atoms entering into combinations vary in number, in quantitative characteristics, and in the speed and direction of their movements. This theory makes untenable any assumption of disorder as an arbitrary interference or an unpredictable accident; whatever occurs is causally determined under the mechanical order of the universe and must be logically deducible from what has already occurred.

The heuristic application of these premises to empirical reality, in the form of hypotheses which could be tested by methodical observation, had to wait for the development of mathematics and experimental techniques. Their development eventually led to a substitution of the modern conception of the natural universe as an energetic system in the place of the old mechanistic conception. From the point of view of physical science, this change was of revolutionary importance. But if the new conception is used as a metaphysical doctrine, the issues it raises are essentially the same as at the time of Democritus.[3]

All these issues emerge as soon as philosophers attempt to include human collectivities in the material universe, with its mathematical order. They do this by conceiving human collectivities as nothing but agglomerations of organisms located in a spatial environment. Organisms are material realities, whether viewed as substantial mechanisms or as functional energetic systems. Each organism is in physical relationship with the material objects, including other organisms, which constitute its environment. The human collectivity is thus an integral part of the material universe; any phenomena that may be observed within it must be explicable in terms of the objective mathematical order of this universe.

Some thinkers have raised doubts whether such an approach is fully adequate not only for human collectivities, but for collectivities of other

---

[3] It must be remembered, of course, that materialistic metaphysics had no chance at all to develop during the Middle Ages and was revived only in the seventeenth century. The rapid growth of astronomy and physics, with their generalizations, extended to the entire material universe. The limitation of the known living beings to a tiny fragment of the universe; the proof of their complete dependence upon their anorganic environment; the reduction of mankind to only one of the numerous species of living beings: all this manifestly favored the materialistic doctrine of the essence of the universe as against the spiritualistic doctrine, which has no such empirical evidence to support it. It is hardly surprising that a thinker who wants to believe in one perfectly ordered universe and is unacquainted with modern philosophy, especially critical epistemology and methodology, is inclined to adopt materialistic monism rather than spiritualistic monism or dualism.

Unfortunately, there is no adequate history of modern materialism since Friedrich Lange's *Geschichte des Materialismus*, first published in 1866, Eng., trans. by Ernest C. Thomas (Boston: Houghton, 1881). Obviously, later materialists have introduced considerable innovations since Ludwig Büchner's famous *Kraft und Stoff*, though an English translation of the fifteenth edition of this work was published as late as 1891, under the title *Force and Matter or Principles of the Natural Order of the Universe*.

living organisms—animals, even plants. Bergson, for instance, explicitly rejected it on the ground that it conflicts with the factual evidence derived from observation of animal life. Here we are concerned only with the application of this approach to collective human life. In this field of investigation, materialists always were and still are confronted with a sequence of inescapable dilemmas; when they try to use the premises of materialism scientifically, they meet at every step factual evidence which conflicts with these premises. If they accept this evidence, their conclusions invalidate their metaphysics: if they reject it, their conclusions are invalidated by scientific standards.[4]

The dilemma of the conscious organism

The first, old and familiar, dilemma arises when the materialistic philosopher considers the fact that a human individual, taken separately, is empirically given as a conscious subject who experiences objects and whose behavior is motivated by his experiences. This is how human individuals have always appeared to observers and thinkers, judging from agglomerated psychological generalizations about them, and how they appear to the materialistic philosopher himself whenever they react to his movements or words. But these experiences of human individuals cannot be objectively real, for they do not conform with the mathematical order of the material universe: They are qualitative, they differ from individual to individual, their sequence does not follow physical laws. They must be subjective illusions or, to use a later term, "psychological epiphenomena." And the view of observers and thinkers that a human individual as a conscious subject is actively motivated by his experiences cannot be valid, for there is no place in the material universe for conscious motivation; such a view is an error based on appearance, not on reality, a survival of the old myth of the psyche as a spiritual entity. Individual experiences as subjective illusions must be explicable by the material nature of human beings and of their environment; in other words, by the structure and functioning of human organisms in relation to other objects as integral components of the universe. The impression that human individuals are actively motivated by their conscious experiences must be proved false by showing that all their behavior is really caused by physical stimuli to which their organisms are subjected.

But how can a quantitative universe, following physical laws, produce in human organisms an illusion of a multiplicity of qualitative objects and of sequences which conflict with physical laws? How can a material universe, containing no conscious motivation, produce an appearance of consciously

---

[4] The following survey of the main dilemmas of materialism is mostly, although not entirely, a summary of the criticisms to which material metaphysics has been subjected during the last hundred years, not only by philosophers, but by scientific methodologists.

motivated human subjects? It can, because materialistic metaphysics asserts that it does. This type of explanation, which recurs continually in the reasoning of materialists, recalls that of the medical candidate in Molière's *Le Malade Imaginaire*, who, when asked "Why does opium put patients to sleep?" answered: *"Habet virtutem dormitivam,"* it has dormitive power. Materialists have always agreed that it is the human organism which has this peculiar power of producing in human individuals the illusion of a pluralistic, qualitative, imperfectly ordered world and of making them appear as if they were consciously motivated, psychological subjects. Modern materialists, however, disagree with ancient materialists as to what part of the human organism is endowed with this capacity.

The explanation given by Democritus and his followers was quite naive. The human being was composed of two parts: a body, and a soul inside the body. The soul, like the body, was a material entity, a combination of atoms, but the atoms which composed it differed in shape and size from the atoms composing the body. Because of this distinct composition, the impact of external atoms produced in it the kind of effect which was manifested as sensory experience and resulted in apparently conscious behavior. Other ancient philosophers ascribed similar characteristics to various parts of the body itself.

With the development of biological science, this capacity of producing all kinds of psychological epiphenomena—perceptions, representations, feelings, volitions—came to be ascribed to the nervous system. Any doubts as to its capacity to produce them were removed by showing definite correlations between specific nervous processes and the occurrence of specific psychological epiphenomena. From a comparison of various animal species the conclusion was drawn that the wealth and complexity of these epiphenomena were correlated with the degree of development of their nervous systems. Under this theory the behavior of all organisms, including human organisms, in response to physical stimuli from their natural environment is theoretically accounted for without introducing consciousness as an active factor. Any apparent exception, any appearance that an individual's perceptions, representations, feelings, or volitions influence his activity can be dealt with by hypothetically assuming some hitherto unobserved combination of neural and muscular processes which will eventually explain both his behavior and the epiphenomenon of his perception, representation, feeling, or volition.

However, with the introduction into physical science of the concept of energy and the principle of conservation of energy, materialistic metaphysics became involved in a controversial issue. If the human organism as an energetic system uses the energy which it draws from the physical environment, is all of this energy used in physicochemical processes, resulting in outward behavior or in modification of the organism itself; or is some of it diverted into the production of psychological phenomena? If the former, then the occurrence of these psychological phenomena would be an inexplicable miracle, conflicting with scientific laws. If the latter, then psychological phenomena are not mere epiphenomena, subjective illusions; as specific forms of energy, they are objectively real components of the universe, to be recognized and investigated as such. Wilhelm Ostwald first promulgated the latter theory forty years ago.[5] It has been criticized by some philosophers of nature; but other philosophers, including George Lundberg, seem to accept it.[6] It has been neither proved nor disproved by scientific evidence, since exact measurement of the chemical and physical forms of energy used by the organism in neuromuscular processes is hardly possible by present techniques. But suppose that chemical and physical forms of energy can be measured, how could this psychological form of energy be measured? Obviously only in relation to the psychological energy manifested in the perceptions, representations, feelings, or volitions of other individuals with whom a given individual consciously interacts. Thus conscious agencies, originally

[5] Wilhelm Ostwald's basic doctrine is formulated repeatedly in several of his works, some of them translated with modifications into English and French. He is a monist who explicitly rejects the antithesis of materialism and spiritualism. See his *L'Énergie*, trans. by S. Philippi (Paris, 1911), p. 199. But his monism is based on the concept of energy, which is the "main concept" of "physical sciences" and becomes extended to "biological sciences," which include physiology, psychology, and sociology. "Through the age-long effect of the blunder committed by Plato in making a fundamental distinction between mental life and physical life, we experience the utmost difficulty in habituating ourselves to the thought of regular connection between the simplest physiological and the highest intellectual acts" (*Natural Philosophy*, trans. by Thomas Seltzer (New York: Holt, 1910), pp. 178-79). What is this connection? "Between psychological operations and mechanical operations there seem nearly the same similarities as between electrical operations and chemical operations. . . . In consequence of the property which phenomena of the first kind possess of transforming themselves under determined conditions and according to constant relations into phenomena of the second kind, and reciprocally, there is between these two groups of phenomena a bond [liaison] entirely determined and constant" (*L'Énergie*, pp. 200-01).

Ostwald's theory culminates in his "philosophy of values." He is much concerned with the progress of civilization, with education, stimulation of creative thought, and other problems of human values. See *Der Energetische Imperativ* (Leipzig, 1912). But even values must be reduced to physical processes. "Hitherto the concept of *value* (and the related concept of *end*, which represents a value projected into the future) had been found exclusively in the world of life [*sic*]. . . . The essential and fundamental progress beyond this point . . . is that I indicate the first source of the concept of value already in the *lifeless, the anorganic:* it is found in the *law of dissipation* [of energy]. All other attempted foundations of the concept of value, especially those which go back to . . . uncontrolled feelings, prove unreliable in contrast with this elementary analysis (*Die Philosophie der Werte* (Leipzig, 1913), p. 7).

We quote Ostwald as a typical example of what happens to a great natural scientist when he becomes a dogmatic metaphysician and rejects, ignores, or misinterprets all facts and theories which do not agree with his dogma.

[6] George A. Lundberg, *Foundations of Sociology* (New York: Macmillan, 1939), pp. 206-07. Lundberg, however, is not a materialistic metaphysician, but rather a radical epistemological and methodological naturalist.

banned by materialism, would be admitted, only disguised verbally. The dilemma is inescapable: Either the first principle of modern physical science must be contradicted, or the original premise of metaphysical materialism must be rejected.

Materialistic metaphysicians, however, seem either to be unaware of this dilemma or to ignore it consciously. Having to their own satisfaction explained the experiences and activities of the human individual by the responses of his organism to environmental stimuli, they investigate human collectivities as agglomerations of such organisms. But sooner or later they must take into consideration the origin of the stimuli to which an individual responds. And this gives rise to a new dilemma.

The dilemma of social behavior

An investigator of human individuals or collectivities finds that many of the stimuli to which an individual responds originate in the behavior of some other individual who stimulates him by using language or other symbols. The use of these symbols shows that the stimulating individual considers the one he stimulates to be a conscious subject, believes in the reality of the other's psychological life, and expects to influence his behavior not by affecting his organism physically, but by affecting his perceptions, representations, feelings, or volitions. The materialistic philosopher himself does this whenever he participates in a human collectivity, and he has to participate in it in order to live and philosophize. It matters not whether these beliefs and expectations are scientifically valid or not; they are empirical facts, practically significant, inasmuch as an individual behaves differently when he thinks he is dealing with another conscious human individual than when he thinks that he is dealing with a purely material object. In terms of the French philosopher Alfred Fouillée, his belief, whether true or false, is an "idea-force," which makes him act in a way he would not act without it.[7]

The significance of this belief is especially obvious when a human individual in acting upon another human individual takes the point of view of the other, in George Mead's terms, "assumes the role of the other," evaluates the other positively as a conscious being and is guided by "altruistic" considerations for the other's presumed beliefs, feelings, or volitions. For in such a case, his conduct in relation to this individual is contrary to his conduct in relation to a conscious being whom he evaluates negatively; and both kinds of conduct differ from his conduct in relation to nonhuman objects of his natural environment.

Probably this is why materialistic metaphysics has become associated with an egoistic interpretation of social behavior, a denial of the existence of altruistic conduct. If consideration for the beliefs, feelings, or volitions of

[7] Cf. Fouillée, *L'Évolutionnisme des idées-forces* (Paris, 1898).

others as conscious beings cannot really guide human behavior, if it is not an active force influencing relationships between human individuals, it must be a mere illusion and self-illusion, a by-product of real forces inherent in the organism. Inasmuch as the human organism is essentially like the organisms of other animal species and, like them, forms an integral part of the material universe, these forces must be fundamentally similar throughout the animal world, with only secondary differences between species. Thence the endless discussions of biological impulses, instincts, drives, etc.—those which human animals share with other animal species, and those which distinguish them from other animal species.

Ancient materialists, whose zoological knowledge was rather limited and who were concerned with human rather than with animal life, simplified the whole problem by reducing those biological forces to two categories: one manifested in human experience as search for pleasure, the other as avoidance of pain; the permanent predominance of pleasure over pain was termed "happiness." These concepts gave considerable leeway to interpretations of human conduct and enabled materialists to maintain the general principles of egoistic motivation of human activity and yet to explain, or explain away, the apparent existence of altruism. Most materialistic philosophers could not and would not avoid ethical controversies with other philosophers, and as participants in collective life did not want to reject altogether the moral standards and norms with which they actually conformed in their social conduct. A solution of these difficulties was sought in the diversity of individual experiences and interpretations of happiness. Some individuals were successful in their search for pleasure and avoidance of pain, while others failed. Though this depended partly upon environmental conditions, it depended also, perhaps even more, upon the individual's knowledge of the essence of happiness and upon his ability to organize his life in such a way as to gain under the given conditions all the pleasure that could be gained and to avoid all the pain that could be avoided. The successful pursuit of happiness became a matter of personal wisdom. According to Democritus, a wise individual found that truly ethical conduct was more conducive to happiness than unethical conduct; according to the Epicureans, ability to find pleasure in the happiness of others, especially of one's friends, increased one's own happiness.

This type of hedonistic philosophy, with its assumption that an individual's happiness depended on the individual himself as thinker and conscious agent, conflicted with the basic premises of materialistic metaphysics; indeed, it could be and was more consistently used by idealistic metaphysicians. Consequently, modern materialists dropped altogether the concepts of happiness and wisdom. If the human individual really is an organism and nothing more, pleasure and pain can be only subjective symptoms of those objective organic

processes which determine human conduct, not real motives conditioning purposive, intellectually planned human activities. The functions of every
organism are lastingly directed toward the satisfaction of its own biological
needs, such as the need of sex or food, the avoidance of danger. Man is an
animal whose needs can be satisfied only at the cost of other organisms;
this necessarily involves the human individual in struggles not only with other
species, but with other individuals of his own species. In its radical form,
this conclusion from materialistic premises was drawn by Thomas Hobbes and
summarized in his famous sentence: *Homo homini lupus.* Later, although not
so pregnantly formulated, the conception of interindividual struggle as basic
factor in human relationships remained a favorite with materialistic philosophers, especially since it seemed to receive some scientific support from the
Darwinian theory.

This doctrine, however, could not account for the existence of a legal and
economic order within human collectivities, in which the materialistic philosophers themselves participated. Physical struggles between men were more or
less effectively counteracted through criminal law, enforced by governmental
power; but human individuals satisfied one another's needs by mutual agreements under the sanction of the civil law. How could this kind of order have
emerged out of the original chaos of struggling human animals, and how can
it survive?

All explanations have had to resort to some kind of utilitarian reflection.
The "social contract" explanation initiated by ancient philosophers and
adopted by Hobbes implied that human individuals became guided by rational
considerations, realized that in their own egoistic interest they should submit
to the supreme power of a ruler who would repress violent struggles and en-
force contractual agreements. This explanation, which obviously contradicted
materialistic metaphysics, both because it revived the old ideas of rulers as
creators of order and because it introduced reasoning as an active force into
collective life, was dropped by later materialists. Another explanation, according to which social order developed gradually as a result of domination and
exploitation of the weak by the strong, was also started in antiquity and survived up to the beginning of this century, as exemplified by the popular book
of Le Dantec, *Egoism Basis of All Society.*[8] This also had to introduce utilitarian egoistic planning and conscious active control, which implied the
individual's ability to understand the psychology of others and to predict
their future reactions to his own actions.

Thus, either human egoists are rational social agents, guided by their
knowledge of the thoughts and motives of other egoists, and this is impossible,
since there is no place for such agents in the material universe; or the legal
and economic order of human collectivities does not exist, and this is impos-

[8] Felix A. Le Dantec, *L'Égoisme seule base de toute société* (Paris, 1911).

sible, since by ample empirical evidence the lives of participants in these collectivities, including the philosophers themselves, depend upon its existence. An apparent escape from this dilemma was provided by conceiving human collectivities as specific variations of what has been frequently termed *symbiotic* communities.

The dilemma of conditioning behavior

Studies of collectivities of animals and plants have proved that living together is essentially favorable to the survival of many a species, including the human species, insofar as in such a collectivity the behavior of some individual organisms has results that are useful for the satisfaction of biological needs of other organisms. Neither altruism nor utilitarian egoistic reasoning needs to be invoked to explain whatever order and solidarity is found in these symbiotic communities; individual organisms become adapted in the course of evolution to symbiotic existence, and respond accordingly to the behavior of other organisms.

Symbiosis does not eliminate struggle for survival; there is a natural selection within the collectivity, in the course of which organisms unfit for communal living become eliminated, and a struggle between collectivities, in the course of which the stronger and more coherent collectivities survive.

The application of this theory to human collectivities, however, has met with considerable difficulty. In a lower animal species the symbiotic order can be correlated with the hereditary biological nature of the organisms which constitute the species; it is essentially similar among all collectivities of the same species and persists so long as the composition of the collectivities remains biologically alike. All the collectivities formed by the same species of insects, birds, fishes, and quadrupeds have an essentially similar organization, which remains unchanged through many generations. But the social orders of human collectivities differ widely, and within the relatively short historical period have changed at an increasingly rapid rate. Attempts to explain differences in social order by biological differences in the racial composition of collectivities have been scientifically invalidated. Equally invalid are any explanations of rapid and radical changes in the social order of a human collectivity by changes in the hereditary nature of the organisms which compose it. If the biological composition of the Russian collectivity changed at all from 1916 to 1941, or that of the German collectivity from 1932 to 1944, it was an effect, not a cause, of the revolutionary changes in social order and of the partial elimination of those who opposed these changes.

The extension of materialistic doctrines to human collectivities is defended against this factual evidence by the modern theory of conditioned behavior. Even if the innate behavior mechanisms of the organisms which compose differently ordered collectivities, or the same collectivity when its order changes, are fundamentally similar, their behavior differs or changes because it is conditioned behavior, the secondary product of a biological process which was discovered by Pavlov and investigated by his disciples, under the term "conditioned reflex."

This, however, brings back in a new form the old problem of the social agent who tries to influence the behavior of others. Suppose we can explain biologically a living individual's behavior as conditioned by some other individual—a psychologist, a parent, a teacher, a propagandist, a leader, or a ruler. This still does not explain the activity of the conditioning individual. Generalizations based on the behavior of dogs or rats upon which the psychologist experiments are not applicable to the experimental activities of the psychologist himself; the process by which the infant under the influence of his mother acquires the habit of regular evacuation is very different from the activity of the mother who tries to make him acquire this habit.

Furthermore, a universal tendency manifested in conditioning the behavior of young human animals is teaching them to respond to symbols and to use symbols spontaneously in provoking responses from others; and the use of symbols, as we have seen, implies the conscious belief that the other individual is a conscious being. Thus, it is an empirically ascertainable phenomenon that those who condition human behavior do it so as to make the objects of their conditioning activity behave as if they themselves were conscious agents and as if other individuals were also conscious agents. In so doing, the conditioning individuals tend to make those whom they have conditioned into believing in conscious human agencies conform with certain patterns of social order, which can be maintained only if they and other participants in the given human collectivity share this belief and behave in accordance with it. And the most astonishing phenomenon is that those activities of conditioning individuals—parents, teachers, preachers, propagandists, leaders, or rulers—not only appear to be purposive, sometimes carefully planned, but are frequently effective to a considerable degree.

Thus, when materialistic philosophers attempt to explain the various and changing orders of relationship between individuals in a human collectivity in accordance with the theory of conditioned behavior, they have to face an overwhelming factual evidence which indicates that such an explanation is possible only under the hypothesis that individuals who already behave as conscious agents purposely and effectively condition others into behaving as conscious agents in interaction with other conscious agents. Either the existence of conscious agents must be accepted and the basic premises of materialistic metaphysics rejected, or the factual evidence has to be denied to save the materialistic dogma. Nor can materialists escape this dilemma by resorting to the reasoning of Molière's medical candidate and asserting that the development of conscious interaction between human individuals is due to the capacity of human organisms to produce conscious interaction; for such a capacity conflicts with the principle that the order of the universe precludes the production of anything but physical processes.

The dilemma of material technique

But this is not the end of the logical self-contradictions in which materialistic metaphysics becomes involved. Its postulate that a human collectivity as an agglomeration of organisms living in a natural environment is an integral part of the physical universe, whose relationships with its environment are reducible to natural laws, also meets factual evidence which is utterly incompatible with it.

In comparing human individuals and collectivities with individuals and collectivities of other species, as well as in comparing different human collectivities among themselves, thinkers have always been aware of the importance of material techniques, and this importance has been increasingly emphasized since the decline of magical beliefs. As we have seen, objective thinking about nature has evolved from a critical comparison of technical actions, which was and still is largely intended to guide technical agents in their control of natural objects and processes. This thinking presupposes that men are conscious agents who by modifying material reality can realize their purposes, although these purposes are, until realized, ideas which have no existence in the material world. Here the principle of creative agency, eliminated by philosophers from nature with the elimination of the gods, enters once more. Nor can it be rejected as a subjective illusion like magic, since technique is the very opposite of magic, in that the relation of cause and effect is not arbitrarily asserted, but can be objectively ascertained in its very process by scientific induction from observable facts. Nor can it be ignored on the ground that each observable fact is a sequence of certain movements of the agent's body and certain changes in the environment of the body; for it is the total purposive combination of these facts which constitutes a technical performance, in the course of which the agent's organism is used as a primary tool for the realization of his purpose.

Materialistic metaphysicians have been trying to overcome this difficulty by explaining causally the technical activity itself. The causal sequence does not begin with the idea of a purpose; this idea, if it appears, is a psychological epiphenomenon, utterly ineffective and entirely absent from the behavior of other animal species. The behavior of the organism causing changes in its environment is an effect of neuromuscular processes within the organism, and these in turn are effects of processes occurring in its environment. The seemingly telic character of the behavior of all animal organisms in relation to objects of their natural environment is a result of the adaptation of the various animal species, including the human species, to their environments.

Of course, there are notable differences between the adaptation of human organisms and that of other animal organisms. Democritus was the first to try to explain these differences. He asserted that man's technical superiority was due to his imitation of the most effective techniques used by other living beings, not only animals, but even plants.

Later materialists could substitute less naive explanations, thanks to the progress of biological science. The obvious and essential difference between the modifications of natural objects achieved by men, in comparison with other animals, is that, while some higher animals use tools besides their own organs, only man produces tools. The term "Homo faber" was invented to denote this characteristic of man. Evolution from the use of tools to the production of tools was evidently a long and gradual process. Materialistic metaphysics readily explained this process by the development of the central nervous system, without resorting to consciousness.

However, when applied to a comparative study of the material techniques used in various human collectivities at successive periods of time, this doctrine proves scientifically untenable. The past diversity of material techniques discovered by anthropologists cannot be explained by any specific biological differences between human races. At first, anthropogeography seemed to provide a satisfactory explanation; the differences between human techniques, just like those between the technical behavior of any other animal species, were due to differences in the natural environments to which human organisms became adapted. But the term "adaptation," as popularly used, denotes several different processes. The adaptation of an individual does not mean the same thing as the adaptation of a collectivity. A lasting collectivity of individuals belonging to a species may become adapted to its environment by acquiring certain hereditary organic traits or by evolving certain patterns of behavior that are transmitted from generation to generation by the teaching-and-learning process. The adaptation of human collectivities to their geographic environment is mostly of the latter type, increasingly so on higher stages of evolution. And transmission of technical patterns by teaching and learning obviously implies mental as well as physical interaction between conscious teachers and conscious learners.

Furthermore, the increasingly rapid development of material techniques has raised for materialists the insolvable problem of invention. So long as technical innovations could be ascribed to individual attempts to deal with changing natural conditions, they might be still interpreted as facts of organic adaptation to the natural environment. But many of the inventions which have emerged in the course of history are not explicable as reactions to changes occurring in the natural environment; they themselves initiated changes which would not have otherwise occurred. Such initiative implies imaginative anticipation of future changes, conscious planning of activities by which the imagined changes are to be achieved, and intentional performance of such activities. Even an invention which originates in an accidental discovery does not become an invention unless the individual becomes aware of the future possibilities which his discovery implies and planfully realizes these possibilities. Attempts to minimize the significance of individual inventions by showing that they are additions to or modifications of existing techniques only make the importance of conscious agencies in the total growth, multiplication, and diversification of material techniques more obvious, for they show the direct dependence of every invention not on natural conditions, but on past inventions.

Either materialistic metaphysicians have to ignore the entire development of material techniques—and this manifestly conflicts with the elementary standards of physical science on which materialists base their doctrine, since the objective order of material techniques is an order of physical facts and thus cannot be explained away as psychological epiphenomena—or else they accept it, in which case their materialistic premise leads to the absurd conclusion that nature, by definition devoid of conscious agencies, produces conscious agencies which control it.

The final dilemma of materialistic theory

Notwithstanding all these dilemmas, the faith of believers in the materialistic dogma still endures. What keeps this faith alive is hope; hope that the progress of science will eventually prove beyond all doubt the validity of materialism by solving all the problems which have not been solved hitherto. For the progress of science in general means to materialists the progress of physical science in particular, the science of the mathematical order of the material universe. Since physical science approximates more closely than any other the ideal of logical perfection, materialistic metaphysicians jump to the conclusion that the only way in which other sciences can approach this ideal is by becoming integral parts of physical science. Community of the logical standards and norms with which all scientific theories attempt to conform is confused with logical unity of scientific theories.

When shown that the problems giving rise to the dilemmas which we have listed are as insolvable as ever after centuries of progress in physical science, materialists are apt to answer that those problems are unscientific and therefore may be ignored, for science does not deal with insolvable problems. This is certainly true. But where did those insolvable problems originate? Obviously in the unproved and unprovable assertions of materialistic metaphysicians themselves. It is they who claim absolutely true knowledge of the ultimate real essence of all phenomena, deny *a priori* that anything can ever be found to exist within the range of human experience which is not reducible to this essence; and when faced with factual evidence to the contrary, instead of acknowledging as scientists do that their theory is inapplicable to such facts and that a different theoretic approach should be used, they persist in applying it and thus become involved in logical self-contradictions.

It is this unshakable faith of materialists in their own theory which is the ultimate undoing of materialistic metaphysics. According to them, it is the only true all-inclusive theory of the objective universe, for it is the only one which unifies all scientifically valid knowledge. All other theories are false, for they ascribe objective existence to subjective illusions and theoretic validity to irrational beliefs. But what does this only absolutely true theory say? That there is nothing in the universe which is not reducible to material reality, as defined by physical science. A theory symbolically expressed by men is really objectively nothing but a complex of physicochemical processes. It originates in processes which occur in the physical environment of an individual organism and stimulate its sensory organs; in consequence of such stimuli, other complicated processes go on, perhaps for a long time, in the central nervous system of this organism and eventually result in laryngo-oral muscular contractions, producing air waves of various length and frequency. Therefore, according to the materialistic theory, there can be no materialistic theory as logically systematized true knowledge about material reality; there is only material reality.

Let us assume, however, that a materialistic theory exists, distinct from material reality and from other theories as well. This is possible only if we postulate that human organisms are conscious, have experiences of material objects, and think about their experiences, i.e., compare them, generalize from them, systematize their generalizations. But according to materialism, this postulate is admissible only if conscious experiences and thoughts are mere subjective by-products of objective physicochemical processes, entirely determined by them, with no distinct and independent order of their own. If so, the materialistic theory is as subjective in its empirical content and meaning as other theories, and other theories are as necessary by-products of objective material processes as the materialistic theory. Its claims to superior validity cannot be defended on the ground that it expresses better the real relationships between the organism and its environment than any other theory; for, if all our experiences and thoughts are subjective epiphenomena, these conceptions of the organism and its environment have no more theoretic validity than any other conceptions. As Schopenhauer aptly said more than a century ago, the theoretic claims of materialistic metaphysics are as likely as the story of Baron Munchausen, who related how, when the horse he was riding got mired in a bog, he pulled both his horse and himself out of the bog by his own bootstraps.

Since the time of Schopenhauer the logical absurdity of materialism has become even more obvious, in consequence of the modern progress of scientific methodology and the sharp contrast between the hypothetical procedure of science and the dogmatic procedure of metaphysics. No scientist of nature, so long as he consistently seeks for an order of factual relationships between empirical data, is in danger of having to face Baron Munchausen's problem and use his own bootstraps. He will become involved in the dilemmas of materialism only if he ceases to function as a scientist and uses the results of his research not as a starting point for further research, but as a basis for speculation about the common essence of all empirical data. It is significant that the greater part of the materialistic speculation of recent times has been carried on by psychologists, sociologists, and economists, rather than by physicists, chemists, or biologists.

The persistent adherence of many otherwise critical thinkers to the materialistic dogma may be partly explained by their tendency to counteract the influence of another metaphysical doctrine which in various forms has dominated the intellectual life of the Western world for the last thousand years and frequently impeded the progress of objective scientific research. This doctrine is the very reverse of materialism, inasmuch as it asserts that the physical world of matter or energy has no real independent existence of its own, but is a product or by-product of conscious agencies which, as self-existing spiritual entities, constitute the ultimate essence of the universe.

The term "spiritualism" would most adequately denote the difference between this doctrine and the materialistic doctrine; but since this term has been rather discredited in common speech through its association with the old belief in the empirical manifestation of spirits, philosophers prefer to use the term "idealism," in contrast with materialism. But idealism does not necessarily involve any doctrine as to the ultimate essence of the universe; critical idealism explicitly rejects all such doctrines.[9] We shall, therefore, use the compound term *idealistic metaphysics* in opposition to materialistic metaphysics.[10] The controversy between these two metaphysical doctrines began in classical antiquity and continues to the present; it has always been stimulated by the uncritical assumption of the faithful adherents of each that the rejection of their doctrine necessarily implies the acceptance of the doctrine of their opponents. As the study of human collectivities has always been the main battlefield of the two metaphysics, their clashes have interfered and still interfere with scientific cooperation in this domain; for almost every problem

[9] Kant's *Critique of Pure Reason* may be considered the foundation of critical idealism. Among later representatives of this trend we may mention Thomas H. Green, Francis H. Bradley, Bernard Bosanquet, and George F. Stout.

[10] The distinction between the antithesis of materialism versus spiritualism as metaphysical doctrines, on the one hand, and that of sensualism versus idealistic rationalism as epistemological theories, on the other hand, has been drawn by Ernst Laas, *Idealismus und Positivismus* (Berlin, 1879).

which involves alternative hypotheses, instead of being solved by testing these hypotheses, is apt to be interpreted as a metaphysical issue.

The development of idealistic metaphysics

Idealism grew out of criticism of early naturalistic doctrines. This criticism was started by the Sophists, who were primarily interested in men rather than in nature. Comparative reflection about the diversity of mutually incompatible human beliefs and judgments, and the contradictions in which human reasoning became involved, led them to doubt the objective validity of human knowledge in general.

Existing theories concerning the natural universe seemed to justify this doubt. Every philosopher accepted as reliable those human experiences of natural phenomena which were compatible with his theory and rejected those which were not, while his theory itself was often incompatible with the theories of other philosophers. According to the Sophists, he was just an individual, like others; neither his experiences, as he interpreted them, nor those of any other philosopher could be accepted as the source of absolutely true knowledge of nature. Every theory was an individual's own conclusion from his own experiences, and his judgment of its validity was the only test of its validity which he applied. "Man is the measure of all things: of those which are, that they are; and of those which are not, that they are not."

This familiar phrase of Protagoras could still be interpreted as admitting at least relatively true knowledge. But Gorgias, in his work "About that which does not exist, or about nature," apparently went further. Three general statements which are ascribed to him indicate that he probably was a radical subjectivist. The first, "Nothing exists," suggests that no individual can be certain of anything but his own actual experiences; and since these are fleeting, changing, and inconsistent, nothing which they contain can be said to exist in the sense in which this word was used by materialistic philosophers. The second, "If anything existed, it could not be known"; this probably means that, if there were any objective, absolute reality, it would be inaccessible to the individual who had no other source of knowledge but his own experiences. The third, "If it were known, the knowledge could not be communicated to others" seems to imply that if any individual ever did experience objective reality, he could not share his experience with others, for everybody's experiences are exclusively his own.

If such was the reasoning of Gorgias, he did not go so far as certain modern subjectivists, the solipsists, who rejected not only all the reality which transcended their own experiences, but also the existence of other conscious individuals, since their own experience gave them no evidence of any conscious individuals but themselves. Gorgias' reference to "others" and the very title of his work apparently indicate that his criticism was limited to theories of nature as a self-existing reality and did not imply a rejection of the possibility of interindividual communication and agreement concerning social life. All the leading Sophists seem to have recognized some kind of order in human relationships, even if artificial rather than natural, which differed from collectivity to collectivity, changed from time to time, and allowed for different, even contradictory, interpretations.

The source of the idealistic trend was thus awareness that, while an individual thinker can criticize any theory of the natural order and any form of the social order, in so doing he necessarily admits that there are other thinkers besides himself; and that, however different from his own their experiences and thoughts may be, they can understand each other, at least enough to discover these differences. Whatever else may be questioned, the existence of a plurality of conscious human individuals, mutually aware of one another, is unquestionable. If there is a cosmos, an orderly universe, the key to its essence must be sought not in material nature, but in human consciousness.

What is the real essence of the conscious human individual? The answer to this question was found in the old concept of the psyche as a spiritual entity, distinct from the body and capable of existing independently of the body. With the development of social thought, the psyche became endowed, as we have seen, with those characteristics which agents ascribed to the human objects of their actions. Criticism of the belief in the reality of material nature, based on the subjectivity of individual experiences of natural objects, did not invalidate the belief in nonmaterial, spiritual entities. On the contrary, it strengthened this belief; for, if individual experiences had no existence in nature and yet could not be denied, if they were actually given to the individual and connected with preceding and following experiences in this individual's conscious life, the conclusion seemed obvious that they must exist in his psyche. The primary task of philosophy was, thus, to know the individual psyche, as the one entity whose real existence could not be doubted. And this knowledge the philosopher could obtain directly by investigating his own psyche, according to the famous slogan "Know thyself," which Socrates was said to have adopted from the Delphic oracle.

The first and self-evident result of this reflection was that the individual's psychic self was a repository of knowledge, a mind whose content was composed of ideas. Second, since each individual communicated with others and this communication affected their conscious lives, he as a psyche was a social being with inherent potentialities of acting upon other psyches and reacting to their actions. Third, as a repository of sensory experiences which composed his representations of nature, he was not passive but active, a maker, endowed with creative imagination; he created images of objects and organized sensory data according to these images.

Now, in each of these three capacities, as a knower, a social agent, and a maker, he found himself and others applying certain standards of validity to ideas, actions, creations, his own as well as those of other individuals. By conforming with these standards he could rise above the subjectivity of his own individual consciousness and become a participant in an objective order. All his ideas were validated or invalidated by standards of truth and error. True ideas constituted knowledge of objective reality, of that which was not a subjective illusion but which all individuals were bound to recognize as existing. All those ideas and only those were true which were not limited to the individual's own mind, but were components of a logically consistent universal system in which all individual minds participated if and insofar as they followed the principles of logical reasoning. There was thus a necessary coincidence, if not identity, between the validity of knowledge and the objective existence of that which was known. Only that, and all that, objectively existed which could be truly known; and only that, and all that, could be truly known which was rationally ordered in accordance with the standards of logical consistency. Hegel aptly summarized this old basic principle of idealistic metaphysics: "Everything real is rational, everything rational is real." And since all true knowledge had to be consistent and constitute *one* logical system, the real universe had to be coherent and constitute *one* rational system.

The conscious individual's social actions were validated or invalidated by ethical standards of right and wrong. These standards harmonized with the standards of truth and error. Ethically right actions were justified by logical reasoning, whereas ethically wrong actions implied logical error. Individuals whose actions conformed with ethical standards were participants in an ethical order that was objective, independent of any subjective impulses. This ethical order, just as the logical order, was one—universally valid and applicable to the actions of all conscious agents.

Finally, the conscious individual as a maker found the products of his creative imagination and those of others evaluated by aesthetic standards of purposeful harmony. These standards, like the standards of truth and goodness, were also universally valid. By following them, by organizing the data of his experience in accordance with them, the individual became a participant in an objective order of beauty. Deviations from purposeful harmony were subjective mistakes, indicating a particular individual's inability or unwillingness to create beauty and to understand beauty. The common universe of all conscious makers was essentially beautiful, just as it was essentially rational and good.

Such a universe, however, transcended the intellectual, moral, and aesthetic power of any one human individual. Even the best philosophers could not participate in it fully or perfectly; and precisely the best philosophers were most aware of their limitations. Like other human individuals, only more successfully, they were learning to conform with a universal order which existed before them and beyond them. And since this order implies logically perfect reasoning, ethically perfect activity, and aesthetically perfect creativeness, there must exist, transcending all human minds, a bearer of all Truth, Goodness, and Beauty, who is organizing the universe into one perfect system. Insofar as a conscious human individual follows the principles of universal order, he shares in the logical thinking, ethical activity, and aesthetic creativeness of this absolute Consciousness. The conception of the supreme Mind varies among idealistic metaphysicians from that of a personal God, a substantial spiritual Being, existing outside of the universe which he created and ordered, to that of a functional principle, an active Reason inherent in the universe.

The historical significance of idealistic metaphysics

Here we shall not criticize the various idealistic metaphysical theories which have developed since Plato;[11] for, unlike materialism, idealism, when faced with contradictory evidence, can always avoid self-contradiction by resorting to an interpretation of its doctrine which cannot be disproved, though incapable of proof.

Idealistic metaphysics meets no contradictory evidence in the domain of natural science. Kant showed that, according to standards of logical consistency, nature, as studied by science, should be conceived not as a self-existing absolute reality, transcending experience and reason, but as a product of reason, the organizer of experience. The progress of logic, mathematics, and physical science since his time has simplified and strengthened this theory by eliminating the dualism of space and time, the category of substance, the contrast between essence and accident, and the principle of causation. If all order in nature is reducible to mathematical order and if logical reasoning is identical with mathematical reasoning, then the natural universe as an orderly system is a product of mathematical reasoning, whether an original creation of one supreme thinker—God, the Mathematician—or a progressive creation of a universal impersonal Reason manifested in human thinking.

The difficulties of idealistic metaphysics, just as those of materialistic metaphysics, arise when it is applied to human collectivities. For then it has to face empirical evidence that the actual life of participants in these collectivities frequently conflicts with the absolute principles of truth, goodness, and beauty. Since that which conflicts with truth is false, that which conflicts with

[11] The only inclusive history of idealism that we know of is that of Otto Willmann, *Geschichte des Idealismus*, 3 vols. (Braunschweig, 1907). The author, however, contrasts genuine idealism, represented by Pythagoras, Plato, Aristotle, Augustine, the great scholastics, and those modern thinkers who follow the same principles, with spurious, "unechter," idealism, represented by Descartes, Spinoza, Leibnitz, and all those who "subjectify ideas" (III, 217).

good is evil, that which conflicts with beauty is destructive, the problem arises: How can a universe perfectly ordered by a supreme Mind contain so much that is false, evil, and destructive? How is it possible for human beings to disturb an order unconditionally binding all conscious beings?

The problem is not solved by the doctrine that the absolute order cannot be disturbed by human beings because the ideal universe includes only those human individuals who, by their own efforts or with the aid of God, conform with its order—the sages, the saints. For human collectivities include all kinds of individuals—wise and foolish, good and bad, creative and destructive—in continual interaction. The conclusion is inevitable that the ideal order is not absolute and universal; the empirical human world is a world of struggle between conflicting forces, be they personal—Ormazd and Ahriman, God and Satan—or impersonal, the rational purposive forces of spirit versus the irrational, purposeless forces of material nature. Such a conclusion obviously contradicts the basic premise of metaphysical idealism.

This conclusion, however, can be avoided by conceiving the idealistic order in such a way as to account for human nonconformity with standards of logical, ethical, aesthetic perfection. Nonconformity does not mean opposition to these standards, only imperfect conformity. All human individuals are potentially capable of logical thinking, ethical conduct, purposive production, but not of the same kind and not in the same degree; nor can their potentialities be fully developed without the cooperation of others. The full development of his own potentialities should be the personal goal of every individual; the full development of the potentialities of all participants in a collectivity should be the common goal of every collectivity. The task of the philosopher, by the light of his knowledge of supreme principles of truth, goodness, and beauty, is to discover the best possible order attainable by mankind and to promulgate his discovery as an ideal for the guidance of men.

Obviously, the validity of such an ideal cannot be tested by factual evidence, so long as it remains an ideal for the future with its possibilities still unrealized. However, one ideal can be compared with other ideals; and in the course of history many divergent ideals have been created by philosophers. The ideal of the Stoics differs from that of Plato; the ideal of Condorcet does not agree with that of St. Thomas; Hegel's ideal is irreconcilable with that of Kant, even if we view the ideology of German cultural and political imperialism as a distortion rather than a logical development of Hegelianism; the ideal of Nietzsche conflicts with that of Rousseau. Inasmuch as each of these ideals claims to be based on absolutely valid principles, idealism, having avoided the contradiction between universal order and human disorder, becomes involved in another issue, that of the relativity of order. Admitting that all men have some conception of order, accept some standards of truth, goodness, and beauty, comparative reflection indicates that these standards differ in different collectivities and change in the course of time. Since philosophers are only men, none of their conceptions of the ideal order is universally applicable; their standards of truth, goodness, and beauty are relative, valid only if accepted as such.

Some modern metaphysicians consider this issue as insolvable by human thinking. What is not absolutely valid is invalid; relativity is identical with subjectivity. Their point of view is like that expressed by Pascal in his famous sentence: "Vérité au deçà des Pyrénées, mensonge au-delà." And, like Pascal, they escape from philosophical criticism into theological dogmatism or from the uncertainty of reason into the certainty of mystical intuition. Both of these escapes imply resignation of the basic premises of metaphysical idealism.

But idealistic philosophers do not need to resort to these escapes. They can solve the problem of relativity, just as the problem of nonconformity, by referring the past and present to the future. The discovery of absolutely valid principles of the ideal order by human reason has not yet been achieved, but it will be achieved if men steadily and conscientiously strive for it. It is a long process, requiring the cooperation of many thinkers, and many different approaches must be tried. Every approach is limited, one-sided, subject to criticism, bound to be superseded by some other approach; but each is a step forward to the ultimate goal of absolute validity; each contributes something to the advancement of human thinking about the ideal order, though only the future will show how great are its contributions.

The historical significance of idealistic metaphysics is, thus, primarily practical. Insofar as its doctrines become ideals guiding human thoughts and actions, they exercise considerable influence upon the historical evolution of culture. But its contributions to theoretic knowledge are only indirect. Paradoxically, it has contributed to the development of natural sciences; by providing epistemological, logical, and methodological proofs of the invalidity of materialistic metaphysics, it helped scientific research in the realm of nature to gain independence from metaphysical absolutism. But in the realm of culture, in which idealistic philosophers are primarily concerned, their dominant interest in ideals rather than in facts has impeded scientific progress.

Attempts to reconcile the claims of materialistic and idealistic metaphysics

Soon after the antithesis of idealism versus materialism emerged, some Greek philosophers tried to integrate the two. The basis for this integration was the theory of Man. As an organism, he was a component of the material universe; as a conscious being, he was a participant in the ideal universe. Consequently, the two universes must be interconnected, not mutually exclusive.

Aristotle developed the most consistent synthetic metaphysical theory; it included what he considered the essence of both universes. He achieved this synthesis by assuming that the real order of nature was *telic*, like the ideal order of thoughts and actions. Later, metaphysical dualism evolved, familiar to all thinkers influenced by monotheism: There are two radically different universes, the natural and the spiritual, but they have a common origin, God, which transcends both. Hegel introduced the conception of a triple universe—an objective universe of material nature, a subjective psychological universe, and an objective spiritual (or cultural) universe, all three manifestations of the same Absolute. But, however different the attempts to integrate materialism and idealism, man was the center of the integration. We shall try to show in the next chapter that this conception of man, initiated by metaphysicians, but accepted by scientists, has been the chief medium through which metaphysical controversies have interfered with the development of sciences, especially cultural sciences.

Gradual separation of science from metaphysics

The development of scientific investigation, as distinct from both practical reflection and metaphysical reasoning, has been and is being studied by modern historians of science. In their studies, however, the term "science" is used with several different meanings.

Most historians, in using this term (especially in French and English), refer to the agglomerated results of research concerning natural objects and processes.[1] Originally limited to knowledge concerning inanimate nature—astronomy, physics, and chemistry—its meaning has become extended to results of research concerned with living organisms. The concept of science is thus made to include a certain domain of knowledge differentiated from the rest of knowledge by the character of the data which constitute its object matter.[2] But the same historians include under this concept also mathematics, which has no distinctive object matter, except perhaps Euclidean geometry, if space can be considered a specific datum of scientific investigation. Fur-

---

[1] This is, for instance, the content of one of the earliest historical works: William Whewell, *History of the Inductive Sciences, from the Earliest to the Present Time*, 3 vols. (London, 1837). Nearly a century later, Abel Rey's *La Science dans l'antiquité*, 2 vols. (Paris, 1930-33), deals with mathematics and natural sciences. William Cecil Dampier-Whetham's *A History of Science and its Relations with Philosophy and Religion* (Cambridge, 1929), explicitly defined science as "ordered knowledge of natural phenomena and the rational study of the relations between the concepts in which these phenomena are expressed" (p. xi).

[2] We use the term "object matter," instead of the more popular term "subject matter," to denote the data which are scientifically investigated, for the general assumption of scientific research is that the data upon which it bears exist even when they are not subjected to scientific investigation. We think that the term "subject matter" in the realm of knowledge should be used to denote the *content* of a scientific work, i.e., those experiences and observations which have been used by a scientist to draw certain theoretic conclusions about the data he has investigated. Thus, all animals and plants constitute the common object matter of biological investigations; the subject matter of Charles Darwin's *Origin of Species* contains the experiences and observations, his own and those of other scientists, upon which he based his conclusions.

thermore, historians sometimes use the word "science" as a proper name, designating a unique, all-inclusive whole, the one and only science, while elsewhere the same word appears as an abstract term, when, in studying separately the history of astronomy, physics, chemistry, biology, geology, they call each of them a science, thus implying that there is a general class which includes several particular sciences with specific differences among them.[3]

Much more significant from the point of view of the history of knowledge in general is another meaning of the term "science," which we are going to adopt here. According to it, a science is any dynamic system of growing knowledge, whatever its object matter, if it is characterized by certain *methods*. These methods differentiate scientific thinking from practical thinking, and from metaphysical thinking.

Scientific thinking differs from practical thinking in the theoretic objectivity of its problematization. The problem of the scientist, when functioning as a scientist, is not whether the data he investigates are good or bad, desirable or undesirable, by whatever standards of goodness or desirability they may be judged, but what order of relationships exists among them independently of his valuations and active tendencies. The solution of his theoretic problem may be intended to help solve a practical problem, his own or somebody else's; but the theoretic problem must be solved by strictly objective research, unprejudiced by practical considerations.

The difference between scientific thinking and metaphysical thinking lies in the relative use of deductive and inductive reasoning. Whereas metaphysicians postulate that the total universe must be an orderly system—the real essence of which can be discovered once and forever by logical deduction from absolutely certain premises, and that any results of inductive reasoning can be valid only if they agree with those premises—scientists reject this postulate. They proceed under the assumption that whatever order there may be within the realm of human knowledge can be discovered only gradually by inductive conclusions from empirical evidence; deduction serves only as an auxiliary method in formulating problems for inductive research and systematizing the results of this research.

In the course of their investigation, scientists are continually making discoveries, the results of which have proved irreducible to any metaphysical theory, however consistent and comprehensive. They have found many differ-

---

[3] E.g., Wilhelm Ostwald (see chap. III). George Sarton's *The Study of the History of Science* (Cambridge: Harvard University Press), 1936, refers to the *International Catalogue of Scientific Literature* and mentions that, at an international conference in London in 1896, "It was decided to divide science into seventeen branches" (p. 59), which include only mathematics and natural sciences. His own works (e.g., *Introduction to the History of Science*, 2 vols. (Baltimore: Williams & Wilkins, 1927-31)) bear in their titles the single noun "science" but in the text he sometimes speaks of different "sciences," sometimes of different "branches of science."

ent orders among empirical data; although they succeed in systematizing the knowledge gained and the knowledge sought about each of these orders during each particular period, any logical synthesis of all of them is unthinkable. Scientific research has to be carried on in many domains, and within every domain some order hitherto unknown may be discovered, necessitating further specialization. On the other hand, indeed, certain general categories of order have been found common to several domains, with the result that some systematic order has been established between sciences which were hitherto unconnected. Yet this does not eliminate the objective existence of specific, irreducible kinds of order which specialists must continue to investigate separately. The extension of chemical generalizations to living organisms does not reduce biology to chemistry; nor did the development of biology as a general science of living organisms interfere with the continued development of special sciences devoted to the investigation of certain classes of living organisms—e.g., ornithology, entomology, bacteriology—or of certain complexes of interdependent organisms, e.g., plant ecology.

In surveying the history of various sciences, we find that every science has developed gradually and that its development is characterized by an increasingly effective combination of empirical research, productive of new problems and new discoveries, with the logical systematization of these problems and discoveries. We find also that in every case this development was hampered in part by practical thinking which interfered with theoretic objectivity, and in part by metaphysical thinking which interfered with the consistent use of inductive methods. These obstacles proved especially difficult to overcome in studies of human collectivities. In our first two chapters we surveyed briefly the persistent influence of traditional practical thinking upon these studies; now we shall try to trace the persistent influence of metaphysical doctrines.

Even in the domain of nature, it took many centuries for science to free itself from metaphysics. Most of the early scientists were also metaphysicians and either investigated only those kinds of empirical order which they thought would confirm their metaphysical theories, or tried to prove that their discoveries were final and absolutely certain because they were consistent with the ultimate essence of the universe. Thus, the scientific work of Aristotle in zoology, with its emphasis upon the purposive character of all organic life, was influenced by his metaphysical theory of the telic order of the universe and used to confirm this theory. The scientific difference between Ptolemaic and Copernican astronomy became a nucleus of conflict between the metaphysical theory of a universe created for man, with the man-inhabited earth as a center, and a universe existing for and by itself, with the earth as a subordinate, insignificant component of a vast astronomical system. Galileo's discovery of the law of falling bodies, which invalidated the Aristotelian theory of bodies tending to assume their proper place in the spatial order according to their natural weight, became a controversial issue between adherents and opponents of the teleological metaphysics of Aristotle, as interpreted by medieval scholars. The whole history of chemistry up to the eighteenth century is pervaded with metaphysical speculations. Even in the nineteenth century the treatment of scientific problems concerning living organisms was still often influenced by metaphysical beliefs.

Nowadays, however, the liberation of natural sciences from metaphysics is almost completely achieved. While a scientist's conception of the essence of the universe may still stimulate him to seek for discoveries which he expects to agree with this conception or inhibit his search for discoveries which might be difficult to reconcile with it, metaphysical arguments are no longer used instead of factual evidence to validate or invalidate scientific discoveries.

Scientific theories are, indeed, still given metaphysical interpretations. Thus, the theory of organic evolution was interpreted by materialists as a convincing proof of the truth of their doctrine until Bergson turned the tables and used it as one of the foundations of his idealistic metaphysics. We mentioned above that the introduction of the functional concept of energy instead of the substantial concept of matter was welcomed by materialists as a way of avoiding the epistemological pitfalls of the old mechanistic doctrine; soon, however, idealists used the same concept to support the doctrine of a rational agency manifested in the functional order of the natural universe. But the very fact that the same scientific theory can be subjected to contradictory interpretations by metaphysicians of opposite schools indicates its independence from either school.

Metaphysical presuppositions, however, still influence scientific research in that entire domain which is now designated by the term "culture." Many students of culture are not even aware how deeply their thinking is affected by uncritically accepted dogmas. We have seen that in the age-old struggle between materialism and idealism, the total culture of human collectivities became inevitably involved. Any theory of the universe as an all-inclusive system had to explain the existence of various political structures, customs and mores, technical products, instruments and patterns, language, art, religion, even knowledge itself. However radically metaphysicians disagreed in their explanations, they all explicitly or implicitly accepted one general assumption: Since culture is produced by men, its existence must be explained by the ontological essence of men.

This assumption had the following main implications: First, that men are absolutely real beings, inasmuch as they are components of one absolutely real universe. Second, that the essence of human beings can be known with absolute certainty, inasmuch as the essence of the universe to which they belong can be known with absolute certainty. Third, that a human being—

whether his essence be material or spiritual, living body or conscious psyche —constitutes an orderly system, inasmuch as the universe of which he forms a part is an orderly system; or (in terms which are seldom employed now, but were quite popular not so long ago) he is a microcosm within the macrocosm.[4]

This ontological dogma of man is still uncritically accepted by many scientists in their general theories of culture, even though they may use inductive methods in their investigation of particular cultures. In defining man as ontological category, most of them refrain from speculations about the universe.[5] According to the prevalent view, human nature, or the essence of men as absolutely real entities, is manifested both in their organic existence and in their cultural products. Such a view presupposes the acceptance of some kind and degree of dualism. Man must be a biopsychological entity, a combination of living body and active psyche, to explain his participation in nature as well as his production of culture. While some students have resorted mainly to biological, others mainly to psychological explanations—a difference that has raised many controversies—none have consistently applied either materialistic metaphysics or idealistic metaphysics in their empirical studies. The ontological doctrine which underlies their attempts to create a general "science of culture" reducible to a "science of man"[6] is a compromise between the two main metaphysical doctrines.

Studies of cultures and theories of man before the nineteenth century

Greek and Roman travelers, geographers, historians, political thinkers, jurists, and philologists surveyed and described a vast number of cultural data and their relationships. In comparing their descriptions with those of contemporary investigators of natural data, we find that they were more biased by practical valuations; especially when describing the cultures in which they participated and were vitally interested, they seldom refrained from positive and negative estimates. Nevertheless, they did develop gradually a more objective approach and used it more or less consistently in observing foreign cultures and in explaining historical changes in their own cultures. We notice

[4] See Rudolf Hermann Lotze, *Mikrokosmos* (Leipzig, 1856-64). It contains the following parts: Vol. I, "The Body. The Soul. The Life"; Vol. II, "The Man. The Spirit. The Course of the World"; Vol. III, "The History. The Progress. The Connection between Things."

[5] Not all of them did. Thus, Adolf Bastian, the anthropologist, made the psychology of the human being the key of his "view of the world." Cf. *Der Mensch in der Geschichte. Zur Begründung einer psychologischen Weltanschauung*, 3 vols. (Leipzig, 1860).

[6] According to Ueberweg's *Geschichte der Philosophie*, V, 407, it was Hume who initiated the concept of "science of man" as the foundation of all science. "He made the dependence of metaphysics, of natural sciences, and of spiritual [=cultural] sciences upon the knowing subject into the central problem of philosophy." But Hume was an epistemologist, not an ontologist, and his conception of man as Subject differs from the conception of man as a Being on whom the modern "science of man" is based.

a striking progress in studies of foreign cultures from Herodotus to Strabo; Caesar's brief descriptions of Gallic tribes are almost entirely objective. Even thinkers who were mainly interested in practical problems often realized that their valuations would be more acceptable and their programs of action more apt to be carried out if preceded by objective research.[7] A considerable amount of objective investigation of legal systems and political changes underlies the ideological doctrines of Aristotle. Another special branch of study where objectivity reached a high level was that of military organization, inasmuch as military planners and leaders were aware that unbiased knowledge of facts was a condition of practical efficiency.[8] Greek philology, though originally intended to guide learners, speakers, and writers, in the Alexandrian period developed into a science almost up to modern standards of objectivity.

However, when investigators of cultural data conscientiously tried to be as objective as investigators of natural data, they encountered much greater difficulties than the latter in obtaining reliable factual evidence from which valid inductive conclusions could be drawn. The student of natural objects and processes could within certain limits rely entirely on his own observations; but the student of a culture, even when he participated in it himself, had also to take into consideration the observations of other participants. If the culture was foreign to him, he usually based his knowledge mainly, if not entirely, upon observations of others, symbolically expressed. Moreover, while nature seemed to change but slowly and scientists could repeatedly observe the same objects and similar processes, culture was changing rapidly during the period when Greek science developed. Especially striking were changes in social order due to wars and inner political struggles. Knowledge of the historical past was essential for the understanding of the present, and the historical past was irreversible and unrepeatable. To ascertain past facts, an investigator had to rely almost exclusively on the testimony, written or oral, of participants and witnesses. Greek historians realized the risks this involved, and they developed standards for judging the reliability of historical testimony and effective techniques for obtaining as reliable knowledge of past facts as was possible under the circumstances. Thucydides initiated this development, and Polybius completed it.

Even with a theoretically objective approach and reliable factual evidence, an investigator of cultural data finds the task of inductive research more difficult than an investigator of natural data, for there is less observable uniformity and regularity in culture than in nature. As studies in cultures in-

---

[7] Curiously, Walafrid Strabo justifies his "encyclopedic" *Geography* and the very objectivity of his descriptions by utilitarian reasons. "This book of mine should be generally useful—useful alike to the statesman and to the public at large," Bk. I, Pt. 2, p. 22.

[8] Polybius' description of the Roman Legion is perhaps the best sociological study of an organized social group written before the last part of the nineteenth century.

creased in thoroughness, more and more differences and unexpected variations appeared. Greek culture differed radically from barbarian cultures, which also differed widely among themselves; within Greek culture itself there were considerable differences in customs and mores, political organization, literature, art, even language. The spread of Greek culture during the Hellenistic period introduced some uniformity into a large area, but still left many foreign cultures outside of this area. The Roman Empire produced a uniform political organization, but brought Greeks and Romans into contact with many ethnic groups previously unknown and made Rome itself a center of interaction between diverse cultures. Furthermore, in every cultural field the cross-fertilization of cultures produced changes of which historians became increasingly aware. Because of this bewildering diversity, changeability, and complexity of cultures, we find in the classical period few generalizations methodically derived from inductive, comparative studies of cultural data and their relationships. Most generalizations either originated in or were supported by theories of human nature.

The ancient students of cultural phenomena accepted certain essential dispositions and capacities as inherent in all human beings and agreed that all cultures are essentially alike, inasmuch as they necessarily manifest these universal dispositions and capacities. Thus, all human beings seek to satisfy certain biological needs, such as the need for food and the need for physical safety, and all cultures are alike in that they contain instruments and techniques helping to satisfy these needs. The urge to procreation, involving sexual intercourse and parental care for children, is also inherent in human nature; consequently, all cultures are alike in that they contain some kind of family organization. Considerable disagreements, however, existed as to the other fundamental characteristics of human nature. Thus, sociability was considered by Aristotle and the Stoics an innate universal trait of human beings, which explained the general existence of social groups more inclusive than parental families; whereas Epicureans viewed the capacity of human beings to participate in such groups as acquired in reaction to certain disastrous consequences of unorganized social interaction. Other controversial problems arose in connection with human capacity for rational behavior. While all students of culture agreed that human beings sometimes behave rationally, sometimes irrationally, those influenced by idealism considered rational behavior a result of logical thinking and believed the capacity for logical thinking to be a universal, essential characteristic of human beings; whereas those who were under the influence of materialism considered rational behavior as a secondary result of man's adaptation to the objective order of nature. Opinions also differed as to what was rational. According to some theorists, behavior guided by belief in a divine order was the expression of a striving toward rationality, while according to others all religious beliefs were manifestations of human irrationality.

Whatever the universal, essential characteristics of human beings which were accepted as making all cultures similar in certain fundamental respects, significant differences in cultures called for some explanation. This was furnished by assuming that such differences either could be ascribed to specific original variations of human nature in general or were the results of secondary, acquired characteristics which combined to differentiate types and subtypes of human beings. Thus, cultural differences between ethnic groups were explained partly by the distinct hereditary traits of the people who composed those groups, partly by the characteristics acquired in adaptation to various geographic environments or in consequence of education. The first explanation was rooted in traditional ethnocentrism and gradually gave way to the second explanation as, first during the Hellenistic period and later (more fully) during the Roman period, the Mediterranean basin became a melting pot of widely different ethnic groups.[9]

The problem of cultural change had also to be taken into consideration. To explain the changes which occurred in cultures (although the nature of the people presumably did not change), historians resorted to psychological theories of motivation. Thus, if wars were not explicable by the innate pugnacity of mankind or of certain ethnic groups, each war had to be explained as caused by a certain combination of motives which activated the rulers of the states involved, the peoples of these states, or the controlling groups. A similar psychological analysis was used to explain political changes within a state, struggles of political factions and parties, revolutionary changes in the form of government, promulgation of new laws, etc. Changes in mores, if not explicable by the rise of lower classes presumably unfit by nature to keep up high moral standards, were explained by the influence of foreigners or the emergence of new motives in consequence of political or economic changes. Decadence of religion was caused by the changed psychology of priests who lost their beliefs and became motivated by secular interests.

The concept of motivation, as we saw in our survey of early psychology,[10] could lead to more sweeping generalizations than the concept of permanent traits of human nature; for it was easy to assume that all human beings were influenced by similar motives; any exceptions could be explained by claiming that the motive was not strong enough to counteract other motives active at the time. Such old generalizations, still current—as that every individual can be bought if the price offered is high enough; or that every individual will be tempted by power if power is to be gained and maintained without too

[9] Julius Jüntner, *Hellenen und Barbaren* (Leipzig, 1923), gives an interesting survey of these changing classifications of human beings and explanations of their differences.
[10] See Chapter 2.

much effort; or that every individual will yield to coercion to escape suffering if the suffering be strong enough—cannot be invalidated so long as other conflicting motives may be imputed to an individual who does not react to a given motive as expected. Consequently, explanations of cultural changes in terms of motives are even simpler and more universal than explanations of similarities and differences between cultures in terms of lasting human traits.

Of course, generalizations about cultures which were deduced from the essence of human beings required that, out of the vast wealth and complexity of a culture, only those components and aspects be selected as significant which could be interpreted as manifestations of universal human nature or some of its specific variations; everything else had to be left out or minimized as irrelevant. A typical instance of such selective interpretation is Tacitus' *Germania*. In the same way, generalizations about cultural changes required that changes be reduced to such facts as could be causally explained by the influence of certain general motives. Here we may mention Livy as a typical case.[11]

During the Middle Ages, attempts at a scientific approach to cultural data ceased almost entirely. Everything pertaining to man was either good or bad, which precluded theoretic objectivity altogether. Human nature was more directly known through divine revelation and inner conscience than through its empirical manifestations.[12]

While humanism revived the interest in culture as a human product, it was aesthetic, ethical, and political, rather than scientific, interest. For a long time the only significant attempt to develop an objective theory of culture, especially of social organization and its changes, modeled on classical examples and based on a general theory of human nature, was Machiavelli's, and even that was intended to serve political purposes.[13] The development of sciences of nature in the sixteenth and seventeenth centuries contributed almost nothing to the scientific approach to empirical cultural data. Scientists ignored history; historians ignored science. Francis Bacon never even attempted to apply the principles which he formulated in *Novum Organum* to the study of cultural phenomena; his *New Atlantis* contradicts them at every

[11] Titus Livius, *History of Rome*, trans. by George Baker, 6 vols. (Washington: Davis & Force, 1823). See especially Bks. VII, VIII, IX, and X.

[12] Some good descriptions of customs and mores in ethnically diverse European communities were made at that time, but no theoretic generalizations. Only some Arab thinkers, such as Ibn Khaldun, revived and followed Greek traditions; but they had no influence upon European thought in this realm of research. See Barnes and Becker, *Social Thought from Lore to Science*, I, 266-79, for an excellent summary of Ibn Khaldun's theories viewed in historical perspective.

[13] See "Discourses on the First Ten Books of Titus Livius" and "The Prince" in *The Historical, Political, and Diplomatic Writings of Niccolo Machiavelli*, trans. by Christian E. Detmold (Boston: J. R. Osgood and Co., 1882).

step. Hobbes manifests an astonishing ignorance of problems of cultural diversity and change.

In fact, although information about exotic cultures agglomerated rapidly from the end of the fifteenth century, in consequence of new discoveries and colonial expansion, and the growth of monarchical states attracted attention to the diversity of cultures within Europe, this broadening of the range of cultural knowledge had, for two centuries, little if any connection with the parallel development of natural sciences. It gave rise to the moral and religious relativism of Montaigne, to the political relativism of Bodin, and the intelléctual skepticism of Pascal; but not until the eighteenth century did the new conception of the world of culture begin to be connected with the new theories of the natural universe. The connecting link became again human nature, defined on the one hand by its hereditary biological characteristics, modified by geographical influences, and on the other hand by its inherent psychological traits, which result in cultural stability, and by the influence of specific motives, which result in cultural change.

But this approach, which in classical antiquity had seemed to work rather easily, proved increasingly difficult in modern times, as scientific discoveries in every field of knowledge expanded, and methods of scientific research and systematization became more exacting. Eighteenth-century theorists of culture, such as Vico, Locke, Hume, Montesquieu, Voltaire, Rousseau, Turgot, Herder, Condorcet, were still unaware of these difficulties; for, although at the beginning of the century sciences of nature stood above the level of Greek sciences, studies of culture did not reach the best classical standards until the second half of the century.

Since then, however, the ontological dogma of man as an entity with a dual essence—an organic material being among other material beings in the realm of physical nature, and a psychological being in the realm of culture—has been a permanent source of controversies. For the dogma demands a logically coherent theory of man, consistent with both the results of physico-biological research and the results of cultural research; and such a theory has proved incompatible with the principles of inductive science.

Main controversial issues in modern theories of man and culture

1. Biological versus psychological determinants of culture

The first controversy is between the view that culture is ultimately determined by man's biological nature and the view that culture is a product of the human psyche, inexplicable by human biology. Eventually, of course, this controversy leads back to conflicts between materialistic and idealistic metaphysics, if the essence of man is used as a key to the essence of the universe. But so long as it remains a scientific issue between two approaches to empirical data, it has to be solved by factual evidence. Ample factual evidence has been collected on both sides.

Evidence supporting the doctrine of the biological determination of culture has been gathered chiefly by investigators of "savages." Travelers who approached "savage" collectivities could easily observe their geographical location, the bodily appearance and outward behavior of the people, the visible products of their relatively simple material techniques; whereas it took a long time and considerable effort to become acquainted with their language, customs and mores, traditions, religious beliefs, etc. Thus, without any methodical reflection, descriptions of "savage" peoples as agglomerates of material human beings in their material environment usually anteceded and conditioned descriptions of cultures; and such is still frequently the case in anthropological monographs. Moreover, to the civilized observer these peoples seemed to represent the lowest, primitive stage of man's collective life, a direct expression of original human nature unmodified by agglomerated cultural achievements. The survival of this conception is manifested in the English and French usage of the term "primitives" and the German usage of the antithetic terms "Naturvölker" and "Kulturvölker."[14]

It was not difficult to develop an anthropology, a general "natural" science of man, so long as it was based only upon comparative studies of peoples whose simple cultures apparently manifested primitive dispositions and capacities deducible from their original biological nature. Differences between primitive collectivities could be explained partly by specific racial differences, whether existing from the very beginning of the genus *Homo* or developed later by inbreeding and natural selection, and partly by the influence of different geographic environments. Whatever was not reducible to these factors could be explained by the contacts and fusions of peoples either racially different or coming from different geographic areas.

Contrariwise, investigators of those contemporary higher cultures in which they participated and of historical cultures with written records were originally and chiefly interested in such cultural data as phonetically, semantically, and grammatically standardized languages, works of literature, aesthetically standardized works of creative art, moral and legal norms, religious doctrines expressed in sacred books, political systems and ideals, and philosophic theories. All such were mental products, irreducible to physicobiological objects and processes. Even technical culture appeared as rooted in ideas. Here was a vast agglomeration of factual evidence proving that culture was positively determined by the essence of the human psyche, even though man's biological nature and his material environment conditioned it negatively, limited the possibilities of its development.

---

[14] Such is the title of one of Vierkandt's books, though Vierkandt himself emphasizes the continuity of cultural evolution.

Nonetheless, the explanation of culture as a combined result of human biology and geographic influences has sometimes been extended from primitive to higher cultures; and, inversely, the explanation of culture as a mental product has been extended from higher to primitive cultures. This has led to epistemological disagreements where each side either explicitly proves the unreliability of the factual evidence on which its opponents rely or (more often) simply ignores it.

2. Individual entities versus collectivity

A second issue, cutting across the first, lies between the explanation of culture by the essence of man as a separate individual and its explanation by a superindividual system or synthesis of many men. The common ground for both explanations is the dependence of a culture on some lasting collectivity of human individuals. Under the ontological dogma that a man is an absolutely real entity, such a collectivity must be conceived as social, in the sense that it is not a sum of isolated entities but a combination of interacting entities. The problem is whether the social collectivity is reducible to an aggregate of interdependent human beings and its culture explicable by their similar essence, or whether it constitutes a comprehensive organized whole of which these individual beings are integral parts. In the latter case, its culture is explicable only by the nature of this whole.

Since both biology and psychology as inductive sciences investigate mainly individuals and take their existence as separate entities for granted, no matter how the connection between the individual organism and the individual psyche is conceived, students of culture as a human product who use the results of these sciences are inclined to favor the first solution of the problem. Under this conception, the main task of a scientific study, intended to explain the culture of the collectivity, is the search for general and decisive uniformities in the nature of the component individuals and for repetitions in the causative processes which occur in their lives.

To this very day, this individualistic ontological conception of collectivities is very influential. Theorists who consider man as essentially or primarily an organism view a collectivity as a lasting agglomeration of successive generations of individual organisms inhabiting a certain spatial area, a demographic aggregate. The originally vague generalizations about the composition of such an aggregate and the processes affecting its units became increasingly exact with the introduction of statistical mass studies. Initiated by Quételet and finally systematized by Stuart Dodd,[15] these studies of more or less lasting spatial agglomerations of human beings have become an inclusive, systematic science of everything pertaining to men which can be conceived as a mathematical total of uniform elementary indices—characteristics or

[15] Stuart Dodd, *Dimensions of Society* (New York: Macmillan, 1942).

processes abstracted from the human units living within a limited portion of uniform geometrical space during a limited section of uniform astronomical time.

When the emphasis is on individual psyche or mind rather than on individual organism, the collectivity is defined primarily with reference to its continuous duration rather than to its spatial location. It is circumscribed in terms of specific uniformities in thought and action which are transmitted from generation to generation and make the individuals included in the aggregate at any given time psychologically alike among themselves and psychologically different from individuals in other aggregates. This may be termed the ethnographic conception, as distinct from the demographic conception. Originally the term "ethnography" meant the study of peoples or ethnic collectivities circumscribed by language and eventually by other similar and distinctive cultural traits: customs and mores, religious beliefs and practices.[16]

There was, and still is, some confusion between acquired psychological uniformities which result from the transmission of culture traits and the innate psychological uniformities due to racial heredity. Inasmuch, however, as the same biological race includes peoples of different cultural inheritance, and people of similar cultural inheritance may include different racial stocks, the idea predominates that psychological uniformities among the human beings who compose an ethnic collectivity are mainly acquired habits. The process of transmission of culture traits resulting in such uniformities can be apparently explained by social interaction between individual psyches or minds. A very consistent theory of this process was developed by Gabriel Tarde in his *Laws of Imitation*. Tarde called the scientific study of these processes "sociology" or "inter-mental psychology." As a matter of fact, it gave a rather logical basis for ethnology as a generalizing science of ethnic collectivities, in distinction from ethnography as a descriptive science. Ethnologists have modified and perfected Tarde's theory, but its basic principles are still widely used, mostly without reference to their author. The later emphasis on the old discovery that few specific culture traits are limited to one ethnic collectivity, for almost any one of them may be accepted or imitated with modifications by individuals who in most respects follow the cultural inheritance of some other collectivity, seems to give a new validity to Tarde's conception.

The obvious weakness of this individualistic approach, both in its biological and in its psychological form, has been frequently pointed out by its

---

[16] According to the French use, the terms "ethnography" and "anthropology" are mutually supplementary. "The latter studies man mostly from the physical point of view, whereas the first considers him from the social point of view," *La Grande Encyclopédie*, XVI, 637-38.

opponents. Every culture includes complex diversities as well as simple uniformities, interdependence of qualitatively different and mutually supplementary components and processes as well as coexistence of similar traits and recurrence of similar processes. To solve this problem of integration of differentiated and interdependent cultural phenomena under the ontological dogma of the human being, the theory of an inclusive superindividual system of human beings (initiated by Plato) has been reintroduced. This theory, as we know, has several variants. Historically, the most important was the one anticipated by Comte and developed by Spencer. Both were originally physical scientists; both insisted on the use of the same principles of theoretic objectivity, factual evidence, and inductive method which were used in studies of nature; and both conceived all studies of culture as one science, systematically integrated, like physics or biology.

Comte gave this new science a program, a name, and a definite place among other sciences. It was to be "sociology," the science of society. A society had two aspects, just as an individual man. From the biological point of view, it was a demographic conglomerate of human beings living within a circumscribed geographical territory and composed of smaller conglomerates occupying particular areas within this territory. From the cultural point of view, society was an organized whole, including the entire conscious life of all the individuals who belonged to it, and consequently the total culture produced and maintained by all of them together. The science of man and the science of culture were intended to merge into a science of society.

Forty years passed before such a science could be constructed. By then, anthropology (as comparative study of primitive men in primitive collectivities) reached scientific status, and Spencer synthesized its results with comparative studies of contemporary and historical societies. This synthesis was made possible by his conception of evolution as passage from aggregate to system. The evolution of mankind began with unorganized aggregates of relatively homogeneous biopsychological units on the primitive, savage level and proceeded by the formation of societies as more and more inclusive, complex, organized systems of heterogeneous parts. Spencer's conception of society is thus more naturalistic than Comte's. Society in its biological aspect is more than a demographic conglomerate; it is a structurally coherent combination of differentiated and interdependent groups and classes inhabiting a territory. In its cultural aspect, it is an organization of institutions which serve to maintain the system as a whole. The two aspects are as inseparable and mutually supplementary as the anatomy and physiology of an organism.[17]

The comparison between society and an organism, which Spencer used only

[17] We shall discuss later the historical significance of Comte and Spencer, not as theorists of man, but as theorists of culture.

as a heuristically helpful analogy, has been used much more realistically by others who considered society as truly an organism, a biological system. Of all these social organicists, the most consistent was Jean Izoulet in his work *La Cité moderne*.[18] Association is a universal phenomenon in nature. It ranges from chemical compounds through Protozoa and Metazoa to Hyperzoa, politically organized biological systems of human animals. Association is accompanied by division of function, specialization, and coordination. The evolution of successive stages of association results in the development of many specific functions. The evolution of Metazoa has produced, among others, the function of animal sensation. Similarly, the evolution of Hyperzoa (societies, cities), not yet completed, is producing, among others, a new specific function—human reason.

While radical organicism is now rejected by social thinkers, the influence of Spencer's theory still pervades modern thinking, due mainly to his concept of institutions. Many sociologists still tend to conceive their science of society as a general science of culture and also as a science of man, who in his character of biological being is a unit of society as a demographic (or ecological) system and in his character of psychological being is a unit of society as a system of cultural institutions.[19] Many anthropologists, on the other hand, conceive their science of man both as a science of society and as a general science of culture, rooted in the socially institutionalized needs or interests of men.[20] The main difference between these points of view is that most sociologists who follow Spencer take into consideration the results of anthropological studies of lower societies, whereas most anthropologists have ignored until quite recently the results of sociological studies of higher societies; consequently, while anthropological materials grow, anthropological theories lag behind sociological theories.

In contrast with this conception of organized society as based upon, even though not reducible to man's biological essence, we find the concept of a spiritual synthesis of individual minds: "Volksgeist," "Volksseele," "Objektiver Geist," "âme collective," "esprit social," social mind, group mind, etc.[21]

[18] Jean Izoulet, *La Cité moderne* (Paris, 1895). The title was probably chosen in contrast to the famous work of Fustel de Coulanges *La Cité antique*, in which the ancient city is viewed as basically a religious organization.

[19] See William F. Ogburn and M. F. Nimkoff, *Sociology*, new ed. (Boston: Houghton, 1946).

[20] W. G. Sumner, A. G. Keller, and Georges Davy, *The Science of Society*, 4 vols. (New Haven: Yale University Press, 1927), the most inclusive synthesis of the results of this anthropological approach.

[21] This conception of collective spirit, soul, or mind as a synthesis of individual souls or minds and a producer of culture was in the main developed in Germany. It is difficult to say how much of this development was due to the influence of Hegel's metaphysical conception of an "Objective Spirit" manifested in culture and political organization and irreducible to individual consciousnesses. Most German thinkers, however, conceived the "folk psyche" as more or less similar to the individual psyche and extended

This superindividual soul or mind manifests itself in a culture; individual minds are included in it in the very measure in which they participate in this culture. The science of the collective mind under various terms bears various relations to the science of the individual mind. Sometimes the latter is supposed to deal only with those aspects of the individual mind which are below the cultural level, in which it does not essentially differ from animals. According to another theory, the social mind, just as the individual mind, is a dynamic organization of psychological elements: impressions, representations, emotions, volitions, etc.; but each element of the social mind is a synthesis of similar elements—representations, emotions, volitions, etc.—in the minds of the individual participants in collective life. In its most radical form, the theory of social mind implies a complete rejection of the independent existence of individual minds as continuous, coherent, organized entities, for continuity of consciousness requires retrospective memory of the past and purposive anticipation of the future, and these are exclusively products of the social mind.[22]

3. Determinism versus creativeness in the history of man and culture

The third issue, which cuts across both of the issues previously discussed, is raised whenever investigators pass from comparative studies of cultures such as they are, or were, at a particular moment of their duration to the study of their origin and change—or, to use the terminology initiated by Comte—from "social (and/or cultural) statics" to "social (and/or cultural) dynamics." The basic problem is whether cultural genesis and change are causally determined processes or creative processes. Any attempt to use both conceptions as alternative or supplementary heuristic hypotheses in particular cases under investigation is precluded by the ontological dogma of the human being. For inasmuch as all culture is a manifestation of the essence of man, the problem of the origin and change of any particular culture becomes a part of the more inclusive problem of the origin and change of

---

the term "psychology" to its study—first Moritz Lazarus and Heymann Steinthal in their publication *Zeitschrift für Völkerpsychologie und Sprachwissenschaft* (Leipzig, 1859), and finally Wilhelm Wundt in his ten-volume work *Völkerpsychologie*, latest ed. (Leipzig, 1912-27). Though to Wundt the consciousness of a human collectivity "is not a whole of a higher order, but simply a functional unity woven from the relevant aspects of the minds of its members" (Barnes and Becker, *op. cit.*, p. 883), yet the same general laws are applicable to it as to individual psychology.

Durkheim's theory of "conscience collective," on the contrary, is entirely different from individual psychology; however, unlike Hegel's "Objective Spirit," this "conscience" is not one metaphysical entity, but is composed of a multiplicity and diversity of "collective representations." The terms *Group Mind*, as used by William McDougall (London, 1920) and *The Social Mind*, as used by John Elof Boodin (New York: Macmillan, 1939) are limited to the common consciousness of organized groups.

[22] Such would be the logical conclusion from Maurice Halbwachs' *Les Cadres sociaux de la mémoire* and Charles Blondel's *Introduction à la psychologie collective*.

culture in general, inseparable from the problem of origin and change of the genus *Homo*.

If the total evolution of culture is a creative process, an irreversible, causally inexplicable growth of innovations, then the total evolution of mankind, as manifested in the evolution of culture, must be also a creative process, an irreversible, causally inexplicable growth of new traits and powers of human nature. But since man as maker of culture is the same indivisible entity as the human organism, this conclusion conflicts with the biological evidence, according to which the organic evolution of mankind is subjected to the same causal laws as all organic evolution. And if the evolution of mankind is causally determined, then by the same ontological principle the evolution of culture must be also causally determined and contain no creative innovations—a conclusion which conflicts with historical evidence, since none of the inexhaustible wealth of empirical data which compose the totality of our present cultures existed half a million years ago. The exclusive acceptance of one of these alternatives leads either to idealistic metaphysics as exemplified by the philosophy of Bergson, or to materialistic metaphysics.

Attempts to compromise follow the general assumption of a gradual passage of man and culture from determinism to creativeness. Culture at its initial stage is a result of man's adaptation to the influences of his natural environment; but as it agglomerates, it becomes increasingly a new factor influencing man and modifying his original nature. In the process of adapting himself to culture, he acquires the ability of making new additions to culture. When human beings are considered individually, this assumption leads to universal laws concerning the psychological evolution of human individuals under the combined impact of natural and cultural influences.[23] When human beings are viewed as included in societies, the assumption leads to universal laws of societal evolution under the combined impact of the existing natural environment and the agglomerated cultural products of the past.

Unfortunately, none of these laws seems to work. In the psychological evolution of human individuals, so many natural and cultural variables are involved that, whether we start with a selected set of presumably uniform natural factors or with a selected set of presumably uniform cultural influences, to every generalization many diverse exceptions will be found, each requiring a separate explanation. The same holds true of laws of societal evolution. Even Spencer was forced to confine his theory concerning the evolution of societies as wholes to a few avowedly approximate generalizations. His main work consisted of comparative generalizations about the

---

[23] This theory was initiated separately and independently by Johann G. Herder in his *Ideen zur Philosophie der Geschichte der Menschheit* and by M. J. A. N. Condorcet in his *Esquisse d'un tableau historique des progrès de l'esprit humain*.

evolution of institutions, abstracted from the total natural and cultural evolution of societies. Other attempts to discover general laws of societal evolution have been even more unsuccessful than Spencer's.[24]

As a consequence of all these controversies, quite a few modern scientists have adopted the principle of mutual tolerance. This is well manifested in joint publications to which scientists with different points of view contribute,[25] as well as in textbooks.[26] These scientists have become resigned to a multiplicity of one-sided approaches to the vast field of phenomena pertaining to man, admitting that each of these approaches has something more or less valid to contribute, provided its representatives are not too consistent logically and do not draw from their premises all the conclusions which those premises imply. The science of man viewed naturally and culturally, individually and collectively, biogenetically and historically, is an incoherent conglomerate of mutually incompatible theories.

The historians' revolt

During the second half of the last century, however, many thorough and conscientious investigators began to question the possibility of any generalization. The first to protest against the sweeping generalizations of philosophers and sociologists were the historians, especially when the field of historical research, for a long time almost confined to political history, expanded to include all domains of culture. Anthropologists, investigating lower cultures, followed the historians. And this skeptical trend is bound to grow with the growing wealth of factual information, so long as culture continues to be referred to human beings individually or collectively as ultimate realities, things-in-themselves, whose essence is manifested in cultural phenomena.

A historian who selects *a priori* as object matter of his investigation a durable human collectivity or society, whether defined geographically (like Mesopotamia, Assyria, Greece, Athens, the Roman Empire, the City of Rome, Germany, France) or ethnographically (the Sumerians, the Hittites,

---

[24] E.g., Franklin H. Giddings, *The Principles of Sociology* (New York: Macmillan, 1896); Lester F. Ward, *Dynamic Sociology*, 2d ed. (New York: Appleton, 1910), especially Vol. I, chaps. III to VII, "Cosmical Principles underlying Social Phenomena," and Vol. II, chap. VIII; Leonard T. Hobhouse, *Social Development* (New York: Holt, 1924).

[25] E.g., *General Anthropology*, ed. Franz Boas (Boston: Heath, 1938); *The Science of Man in the World Crisis*, ed. Ralph Linton (New York: Columbia University Press, 1945); *Personality in Nature, Society, and Culture*, eds. Clyde Kluckhohn and Henry A. Murray (New York: Knopf, 1948).

[26] E.g., Edwin A. Kirkpatrick, *The Science of Man in the Making* (New York: Harcourt, 1932); Ralph Linton, *The Study of Man* (New York: Appleton, 1936); Ogburn and Nimkoff, *op. cit.* Here are two explicit statements from the latter work: "Social life is best explained, not by group activities alone or even by culture as a whole, but by the interaction of the four factors of heredity, geographical environment, the group, and culture" (p. iii); "This book is about a remarkable creature called 'man'" (p. 3).

the Persians, the Phoenicians, the Israelites, the Etruscans, the Latins, the Hellenes, the Gauls, the Germans, the Franks) or by a combination of both, is bound to take into consideration everything pertaining to this collectivity or society during a certain period of time—its demographic composition and its changes, its environmental conditions and their changes, its relationships with other collectivities and their changes, the totality of cultural patterns and their changes. He has to assume that these phenomena are somehow interdependent and constitute one dynamic complex, since all of them are included in the organic and mental life of the same interacting and continuous human conglomerate, and every one of them influences the others and is influenced by them. The only standard of selection he can use is the relative importance of a phenomenon, judged by the degree of influence it has, directly or indirectly, upon the total life of the collectivity; and there is no objective way of separating this influence from the influence of other phenomena.

The historian's task, therefore, is to reconstruct this complex as exactly as he can, to achieve a synthesis of all phenomena which appear influential.[27] Though many phenomena found in this complex at a given time are lasting or repeatable, and may be compared with phenomena found in other collectivities at certain times, the complex in its entirety is unique and irreversibly changing. Neither can a similar total combination of similar natural or cultural phenomena be found in the same collectivity before or after the given period nor in any other collectivity during any period. And comparison of specific phenomena abstracted from their total historical complexes is deceptive, for apparently similar phenomena have a different significance in the total lives of different collectivities or in the life of the same collectivity at different periods.

The ideal of historical research conditioned by the ontology of man is thus not a development of logically coherent taxonomic and causal generalizations, but an inclusive synthesis of all the partial syntheses, a thorough survey of the entire history of mankind as a unique dynamic combination of many unique historical complexes. How distant and difficult this ideal appears to modern historians, as compared with philosophers of history and sociological theorists of evolution, is indicated by the series of works planned and published by French historians under the title *Évolution de l'Humanité*: seventy-six volumes have appeared to date, and probably many more will be published.

Less known, though much older, is the trend which tends to eliminate psychological generalizations about human individuals, just as the trend to

[27] Charles Langlois and Charles Seignobos, *Introduction aux études historiques* (Paris, 1905), pp. 202-03, give a taxonomy of six classes and nineteen subclasses with a number of subdivisions.

historical synthesis tends to preclude sociological generalizations about human collectivities. Biographers have always emphasized the uniqueness of the individuals whose lives they describe, at first chiefly because they selected for description "great men," individuals who were already considered exceptional, incomparable, in popular tradition or contemporary public opinion. But this selection did not altogether preclude comparison and generalization; for "great men," though not to be classed with ordinary human beings, still were supposed to constitute a logical class with subclasses: military heroes, creators of political order, prophets, saints, poets, artists, sages, and inventors. This classification still survives, though other terms, such as "genius" or "leader," have been substituted for "great man."

As the reliability and wealth of factual materials collected by biographers increased and their standards of theoretic validity improved, doubts were raised concerning the possibility of generalizing, first about famous individuals, then about any human individuals. Even the life history of a human organism in the light of detailed and thorough investigation of heredity and environmental influences showed a much greater degree of irreducible individual variants than was believed to exist when biological knowledge was less exact. The total evolution of an individual's cultural life became increasingly difficult to compare with that of any other individual, as concrete description, *ex post facto* in temporal sequence, became substituted for stereotyped selection of facts judged significant *a priori*, and a history of the cultural milieu in which the individual participated was combined with a detailed autobiographical record of his participation. If a biographer tries to combine (as he is bound to do if he follows the dogma of the indivisible human being) the biological and the cultural life history of a particular individual, the total historical complex of interdependent phenomena relevant to this individual, none of which can be abstracted from the whole, prohibits all taxonomic and causal generalization whatsoever.

It is not surprising, therefore, if some methodologists of history concluded that the human being had to be known in his uniqueness and that he could not be so known by any kind of scientific analysis, only by an intuitional synthesis which, starting from the concrete phenomenal content of his personality, reached direct understanding of its ultimate individual essence.[28]

Elimination of man from the realm of science

This challenge of historians to taxonomic and causal generalization in the cultural domain cannot be answered by any of the familiar scientific approaches mentioned above, since none of them can be conclusively

[28] This was the main foundation of Wilhelm Dilthey's famous antithesis between natural sciences and "Geisteswissenschaften." The latter are based on "insight," "direct understanding," first of the human personality, then of social life and culture in its humanistic meaning.

validated because of its irremediable conflict with the contrary approach.[29] Inasmuch, however, as the common root of such conflicting generalizations as well as of the rejection of all of them by consistent and conscientious historians is the ontological dogma of man, the elimination of this dogma might remove these obstructions to scientific progress.

It is not so easy, however, to eliminate a dogma which controls completely the common-sense thinking of human individuals about other individuals and themselves, inheres in most metaphysical systems, and has for twenty-four centuries dominated scientific systematization of the conclusions drawn from inductive study of cultures. The only way to do it is to maintain consistently the same principles of agnosticism with regard to the essence of man which modern science maintains with regard to the essence of the universe. Inductive science knows and can know no more what man as a whole really is than what the universe as a whole really is. Theories of the macrocosm have long since been excluded from the realm of science and left to metaphysics; it is high time that theories of the human microcosm be also relegated to the metaphysical domain.

Actually, there has been during the last hundred years a steadily growing number of inductive studies of human phenomena, in the sense of phenomena pertaining to men as conscious agents, independent of any ontological doctrines as to the essence of human beings. Most of these studies have been made by scientists who specialized in investigating certain categories of cultural phenomena: languages, religions, myths and rituals, material techniques, products of art and literature, customs and mores, patterns of social organization. Moreover, many psychologists carrying on monographic research on

[29] Historico-critical studies of historiography, such as those of Edward Fueter, Harry E. Barnes, James T. Shotwell, and James W. Thompson, indicate that the progress of historical methods has already eliminated some of these issues. In the first place, all forms of naturalistic determinism, which explains human actions causally by various combinations of human biology and geography, have been invalidated by historians. Second, although there is still a tendency among some historians and methodologists to explain human actions by universal psychological traits of human nature, to assume that actions of "long-past generations and distant peoples" are "only different manifestations of the same permanent psychological and spiritual foundations" (Ernst Bernheim, *Lehrbuch der historischen Methode* (Leipzig, 1908), p. 193), yet most historians realize that, instead of trying to understand unfamiliar actions of foreign peoples by imputing to them a psychological essence like the historian's own, it is much better to investigate thoroughly the cultural patterns which these actions follow. Third, the distinction between history and philosophy of history is becoming clarified, though some methodologists consider the two disciplines mutually helpful, e.g., Henri See, *Science et philosophie de l'histoire* (Paris, 1928).

Comparative generalizations about collectivities in their total cultures are now being left to philosophers. The problem which remains controversial is what generalizations can be drawn by abstracting certain specific phenomena from the total culture and comparing them with other, apparently similar phenomena found in different collectivities. Can historians do it, or must it be left to other scientists?

specific kinds of psychological phenomena have also refrained from theorizing about man. But the development of such studies has met and is still meeting considerable objections in *epistemological* controversies about the essence of scientific knowledge.

For it is found that inductive investigation of phenomena pertaining to men as conscious agents differs from inductive investigation of natural phenomena, both in the selection and definition of its data and in its conclusions concerning the factual order of relationships among these data. And inasmuch as inductive knowledge of natural phenomena, especially as developed in physics, is considered a model, both as to the reliability of its empirical evidence and the validity of its theoretic conclusions, the problem is raised: Can any knowledge which differs from inductive knowledge of natural phenomena be truly scientific, empirically reliable, and theoretically valid? And to solve this problem many of those who deny, as well as those who affirm, the scientific character of inductive studies of human phenomena resort to philosophic speculation concerning the reliability of empirical evidence as such and the validity of inductive conclusions as such.

Data of Human Experience

The scientist's experience as an epistemological problem

Epistemological controversies concerning scientific knowledge about everything which pertains to men as conscious agents—cultural products, social interaction, psychological processes—have a common source. Scientific knowledge presupposes scientists who as human individuals experience that which they investigate. In other words, a scientist is actually conscious of certain phenomena, i.e., certain data and certain facts (relationships between data) as they appear to him in the course of his investigation. Moreover, he is not only conscious but active; his investigation consists in the performance of various activities, mainly intellectual, but partly physical, bearing upon the data of his experience. He selects from among an unlimited multiplicity and variety of data those which seem to him relevant to some problem which he wants to solve; he observes factual relationships between the data selected; he often experimentally produces facts to be observed; he abstracts and generalizes; he expresses symbolically his generalizations and communicates them to other scientists; he learns what other scientists have done, and tests their conclusions by his own observation; he participates in attempts to systematize these generalizations into theories; eventually, he questions a theory and raises a new problem.

Now, astronomers, physicists, chemists, and biologists who specialize in investigating natural phenomena in order to solve problems and develop theories that have no direct reference to men take themselves for granted as conscious active thinkers. They are concerned exclusively with the empirical reliability of their particular experiences, observations, and experiments, and with the logical validity of their abstractions, generalizations, and systematizations. But a scientist whose problems and theories refer to men cannot leave himself altogether out of his investigation. For, if he experiences, observes, acts, and thinks, so do other men; if whatever pertains to others is empirical data to him, so whatever pertains to him is empirical data to others.

Of course, most men are not scientists; but the scientist is not exclusively a scientist either. His scientific function forms only a part of his human life. The possibility for men who function as scientists to reach by inductive methods scientific knowledge about anything which pertains to men in general depends upon the possibility of finding in their own experience, as well as in that of others, reliable empirical evidence concerning others as well as themselves.

Thousands of scientists for many generations have been searching for such evidence in various specialized divisions of this vast domain. In every such division, the search has resulted in the progressive definition and solution of a continually expanding range of new problems and in a slow but undeniable improvement in methods of investigation and standards of systematization. Students of knowledge, viewing all sciences in historical perspective, recognize the obstacles in the path of sciences concerned with human phenomena, appreciate the progress which has already been achieved, and realize that further progress in every one of these sciences must be difficult and will be possible only with the steady cooperation of numerous scientists.

But there are theorists of knowledge who lack this historical perspective. Their conception of valid knowledge is not derived from the factual evolution, past and present, of the different divisions of inductive research which bear upon various kinds of empirical data. Instead, they start with an absolute philosophic norm of what valid knowledge of empirical data ought to be and determine *a priori*, once and forever, what kind of data should be used as evidence in scientific investigation and what kind of results this investigation should achieve. Some of their epistemological doctrines are accepted by investigators of human phenomena who want to escape a slow and difficult search for reliable evidence in their domain of knowledge. Two opposite ways of escape have apparently been open to them.

Sensory experience as the only basis of valid knowledge

The first way leads to a complete rejection of all empirical evidence except that which, according to epistemologists, is recognized as reliable by scientists of nature. This way has proved particularly tempting to sociologists, since sociology, which was originally intended to be an all-inclusive science of everything pertaining to man, has become involved in the various difficulties with which investigators of specific human phenomena have to struggle. Several epistemological doctrines apparently allow sociologists to avoid such difficulties, if they refuse to consider any problems that cannot be solved by the use of the same kind of evidence which is used to solve the problems of natural sciences. Differences between these doctrines are merely secondary. Their common premise is the assertion that only data of *sensory experience* can be used for scientific purposes. Two main reasons are given for this assertion. First, sensory experience has an objective foundation; it is a reaction or response of the human organism, which is scientifically known, to external physical processes or environmental stimuli, which are also scientifically known. Second, the rapid progress of physical and biological sciences is due to the fact that all their theories are based on the evidence of sensory experience.

The modern epistemologists who developed this general theory were careful to avoid the old pitfall of materialistic metaphysics, since, like the physical scientists, they took for granted human thinking in general and scientific thinking in particular. Instead of trying to explain it away by reducing it to biophysical processes (as some of their more dogmatic followers do), they adopted the point of view of metaphysical agnosticism as the only one compatible with the scientific approach to inductive research. Nevertheless, they cannot avoid logical contradictions, except at the cost of their fundamental premise.

The most popular of these epistemologies is that formulated by Karl Pearson in his rather superficial, but stimulating essay, "Grammar of Science."[1] All human experience originates in "sense impressions" which, when transmitted from sensory organs to the brain, are stored in the brain as "sense impresses." Being limited to the organism itself, sense impresses give us no direct knowledge about the objective essence of the external world;[2] all our knowledge is derived by inference from our sense impresses. Inferences can be logically valid or invalid. Logically valid inferences are primarily those of physical science; they lead us to discover similarities of combinations and regularities of sequences among the vast multiplicity and complexity of sense impresses. By using the results and the methods of physical science, we have gradually progressed to a biological science of organisms, including human organisms, as receptacles of sense impresses.

This epistemology precludes in principle all objective search for empirical evidence concerning cultural phenomena (except technical products and processes) or concerning other human individuals as conscious agents, inasmuch as these are not sense impresses, only inferences from sense impresses, and inference is not experience. Thus, Pearson views religious myths or moral standards not as empirical phenomena to be investigated scientifically, but as inferences to be criticized in comparison with those of physical and biological sciences. Then most of them have to be rejected as scientifically invalid.[3] As to the general inference about the existence of other experiencing and thinking human individuals, though not certain, it can be accepted as

---

[1] Karl Pearson, "Grammar of Science" (London, 1895).

[2] "How close can we actually get to this supposed world outside ourselves? Just as near, but no nearer than the brain terminals of the sensory nerves." (*Ibid.*, p. 74.)

[3] *Ibid.*, pp. 63-64.

probable.[4] Obviously, if such an approach to cultural data and to facts of communication and interaction between human individuals were consistently maintained, the results would be entirely devoid of scientific significance. However, few, if any, adherents of this doctrine use it consistently during actual research in the cultural domain; they rightly prefer conceptual confusion to complete barrenness.[5]

The thinkers who accept this doctrine, including Pearson himself, have become involved in a vicious circle. Their original theory of sensory experience was inferred from their biological knowledge of the human organism; and biological knowledge of the human organism, like all scientific knowledge, is according to their theory inferred from sensory experience. The only way out of this circle is to recognize that our knowledge of sensory experience does not have to be deduced from biology, but has an independent source of its own. This source can be only psychological reflection about the sensory experiences of human individuals by these individuals themselves. In other words, the doctrine that only sensory experience can furnish reliable empirical evidence, and that the only valid inferences from this evidence are those of physical science and of other sciences derived from the latter, must be tested by psychology. And this is where the doctrine meets its most radical opponent.

Self-consciousness as the only basis of valid knowledge

The second way of escape from methodical difficulties has been taken by quite a few sociologists, cultural anthropologists, and especially students of various divisions of what is commonly called "spiritual" culture: religion, literature, art, music, ethical and political ideas, etc. It is provided by the epistemological doctrine according to which all the reliable evidence about everything pertaining to man (including man's function as natural scientist) is provided by man's direct experience of his own mental life.

Adherents of this doctrine also try to avoid metaphysics. They do not follow the reasoning of Descartes, who from "I think" concludes "therefore I am," meaning by "I" a substantial, spiritual, imperfect being, and from the imperfect and limited essence of this being draws conclusions as to the existence of God as perfect and absolute spiritual Being. Nor do they reason, like Fichte, that, insofar as thoughts and actions of any particular human "I" follow logical laws and ethical principles which transcend his individual experience, he must be a participant in the thoughts and actions of a universal, all-inclusive "I." They accept as self-evident two ancient premises: First, that all the content of empirical data is derived from individual experience; second, that

[4] *Ibid.*, pp. 59-61.
[5] See Pearson's studies of folklore, which was his "hobby"; George Lundberg, Mirra Komarovsky, and Mary A. McInerny, *Leisure; A Suburban Study* (New York: Columbia University Press, 1934).

all knowledge about empirical data is a product of individual thinking. They conclude that nothing can be truly known about anything the individual experiences which he cannot discover by investigating himself as an experiencing and active subject. For such an investigation shows that all the data of his experiences are integrated in his mind, not in the sense of a metaphysical substance, but as a dynamic, functional combination of conscious processes; no datum can be isolated from the stream of his consciousness as something existing outside of his mind. Whatever order there may be among these data he finds to be his own product; he is directly, immediately aware of himself as the producer of this order, whose thoughts, volitions, and feelings synthesize and organize the data of his experience.[6]

Some epistemologists have carried this doctrine to its logical limit—solipsism.[7] The individual thinker who accepts it unconditionally is led to the final conclusion that he has no empirical evidence and no logical reason to recognize the existence of anything or anybody but himself as an experiencing and thinking subject. However, solipsism is barren. Once accepted, nothing remains to be done; all philosophic and scientific problems are solved. It is not even necessary to prove to others that solipsism is true. Consequently, most adherents of this doctrine do not deny the validity of an individual thinker's belief that the other human individuals of whom he is aware are not only data of his own inner experience but conscious and active subjects existing outside his mind. This does not yet solve the epistemological problem whether he has any valid knowledge about them. He implicitly assumes that they have minds; but how can he discover whether and in what respects their minds are like his own or different from his own? Here many epistemologists resort to intuition or "sympathetic understanding."[8] They claim that an

[6] This conception in modern times began with German romantic individualists: Friedrich von Schlegel (1772-1829), Novalis (1772-1801). It was fully developed by Jakob F. Fries (1773-1843): "The object may be outside of me or in me, but the knowledge is inside of me, and thus I must observe it within myself" (Ueberweg, IV). Among French thinkers, Maine de Biran and Pierre Royer-Collard had similar epistemological conceptions.

[7] The two most systematic types of solipsism in modern times are the "Immanenz theorie" of Wilhelm Schuppe, *Erkenntnisstheoretische Logik* (several editions between 1882 and 1910), and the "epistemological solipsism" of Richard von Schubert-Soldern. According to Schuppe, there are no objects outside of consciousness, only consciousness itself together with all its contents. All empirical contents are contents of the conscious ego. The ego, which is spaceless, contains space. It is possible to conclude that other men exist, but it is impossible to experience them. Schubert-Soldern does not recognize the ego as container—he calls that conception "metaphysical solipsism"—only as an experience of the process of consciousness. It is impossible to go beyond the content of consciousness; any "inferences" about reality are merely extensions of consciousness.

[8] For a good critical analysis of various modern conceptions of intuition, see K. W. Wild, *Intuition* (Cambridge, 1938). The best-known work on "sympathetic understanding" is Max Scheler's *Wesen und Formen der Sympathie* (Halle, 1922). Willard W. Spencer's *Our Knowledge of Other Minds* (New Haven: Yale University Press, 1930) deals with this problem from a strictly scientific point of view.

individual can have the same kind of consciousness of the mental life of others as he has of his own mental life; he can intuitively understand their minds even when they differ from his own. Not all individuals are equally capable of such intuitive knowledge of others nor can its validity be proved by logical reasoning. But there are other proofs, such as mutual sympathetic understanding between two individuals who intuitively know each other's minds almost as well as each knows his own mind, and agreement between two individuals in their intuitive understanding of a third individual's mind.

Thus, the doctrine that the only reliable and valid knowledge is the individual's knowledge of his own mind can avoid solipsism by asserting that an individual's investigation of his own mental life by himself may be compared with investigations by other individuals of their own mental lives. The result is introspective psychology as all-inclusive science of individual consciousness, the foundation of all human knowledge. No other science has any reliable empirical evidence upon which it can base its conclusions or any way of validating those conclusions. For no particular experience of an individual gives evidence of the existence of anything outside of his own mind. Insofar as the individual can synthetize many of his experiences into coherent complexes, he believes that these experiences, taken together, correspond to an objective reality; but it is impossible to test this belief scientifically. For the facts which the scientist investigates are only psychological facts, abstract relationships between his own experiences; the principles of logic which he uses in drawing conclusions from these facts are only psychological regularities of individual thinking. Insofar as he unifies and organizes his thoughts into a systematic theory, he assumes that his theory corresponds to some objective order; but the truth of this assumption can never be proved.

The influence of this epistemological doctrine upon inductive research in the realm of natural science has been only indirect. The reduction of logic as objective standard of scientific validity to the psychology of individual thinking contributed to the development of pragmatism, which in turn contributed to the tendency to evaluate physical and biological research by its practical rather than by its theoretic significance. In studies concerning cultural phenomena, however, the doctrine of individual consciousness as all-inclusive container of empirical data gave apparent justification to certain old popular trends and strengthened some new trends.

We have seen that psychological explanations of similarities and differences between cultures originated in classical antiquity and continue to this day. Biographies of "great men" emphasizing their uniqueness and originality, especially under the influence of romantic individualism, led to the conviction that the only way of understanding cultural creations was by identifying oneself psychologically with the creators, living over their conscious lives, reproducing in one's own consciousness (through sympathetic understanding or intuition) their visions, imaginations, feelings, volitions, and thoughts, and organizing them as the creators did.

The psychological approach to culture, if not to nature, was further favored by the growth of psychopathology. For, inasmuch as the experiences of an abnormal individual deviated from the factual evidence accepted by others and his thinking failed to conform to the rules followed by others, his conscious life appeared to be altogether subjective, not a part of any objective world, but a self-contained process which could be described and explained only in psychological terms. Furthermore, some psychopathologists saw an essential analogy between insanity and genius, that is, between deviation from normality and cultural creativeness.[9] Most of them were inclined to view the difference between the psychologically abnormal and the psychologically normal as a difference in degree, and many believed that the study of the abnormal helped to understand the normal.

But the most important of all the psychological trends began when the concept of the unconscious was introduced. This concept made possible a psychological explanation of culture and social relationships, even when methodical reflective observation of the individual's conscious life gave no factual basis for such an explanation. And when even the concept of the individual unconscious seemed insufficient, the postulate of a racial unconscious was used as the last resort.

The problem of psychology as a science

Thus, we have two epistemological doctrines radically opposed to each other, each of which justifies its claims by arguments derived from psychology. This obviously raises doubts about the validity of psychology as a study of individual consciousness by the conscious individual himself. Such doubts have been voiced in recent times both by radical behaviorists, who deny that any reliable factual evidence can be gained about individual consciousness and limit themselves entirely to biologically observable facts of outward behavior of individual organisms, and by logicians who, following Husserl, insist that conclusions drawn from an individual's reflection about his conscious life are purely subjective and have no objective logical validity whatever. Nor is such skepticism surprising in view of the diversity of concepts which have been symbolized by the term "psychology" and of the dependence of many psychological theories on popular stereotypes, metaphysical theories of the universe, and ontological theories of man. Nevertheless, if we view in historical perspective the development of inductive research carried on by

---

[9] This theory was most explicitly formulated by Paul Radestock, *Genie und Wahnsinn* (Breslau, 1884), but popularized by Cesare Lombroso, *The Man of Genius*, 3d English ed. (London, 1912). Of course, most of the psychological conceptions of genius emphasize superiority rather than abnormality.

various psychological schools during the last century and a half, we find a slow but steady growth of psychology as a science, which proceeds by increasingly exact methodical investigation of a certain category of phenomena, just like any other science. The schools differ chiefly not as to the type of factual evidence, but as to the problems which they are trying to solve. In the course of the twentieth century, scientific psychology has expanded in several directions far beyond its original realm. We shall discuss this expansion later. Now, however, we are concerned with its original realm, which still provides the necessary basis for its new divisions.[10]

As psychology became a science, it ceased to speculate about the essence and reliability of human experience in general. It concentrated on a study of *relationships between particular experiences of particular individuals during their actual occurrence.* Each experience of a particular individual lasts for only a brief period of time and is preceded, accompanied, and followed by other experiences of the same individual. An experience in this sense is unrepeatable; the flux of experiences cannot turn back. My present experience of the tree beyond the window, of a telephone bell ringing, of my hand moving the pen across a sheet of paper, once passed, is gone forever. I may have many similar experiences in the future, but they will not be *the same.* Nor can any individual experience be actually shared with any other individual; even when you and I look at the same tree or listen to the same bell, my experience is not your experience.

Indubitably, observation of an individual's experiences must be carried on by the individual himself; but there is nothing introspective about it. The experience of seeing a tree, hearing a telephone bell or a thunderstorm, feeling hungry, or reading a letter does not occur inside the individual, whatever "inside" may mean. It occurs after some experience which preceded it, before some experience which follows it, and simultaneously with still other experiences. By observing this flux in his experiences, the individual does not gain any immediate knowledge about his own "self." The fact that in communicating his experience to others the individual uses the word "I"—"I see a tree," "I hear a bell," "I feel hungry"—and in asking somebody else about his experiences uses the word "you"—"Do you hear the bell?" or "Do you feel hungry?"—means only that he has been trained from childhood on to distinguish between his experiences and those of others.

Of course, in order to observe an experience of his own in the sense in which the term "observe" is used by scientists, he must "reflect" about it, that is, concentrate his attention upon it while it is going on and avoid having his attention diverted from the observation of this fluid process to the observation

[10] For the history of modern psychology before behaviorism developed, see James M. Baldwin, *History of Psychology,* Vol. II (New York: Putnam, 1913); and George S. Brett, *A History of Psychology,* Vol. III (London, 1912).

of the object which he is experiencing—the tree or the telephone bell. This is not easy, for our interest is always directed toward that which we are experiencing. Even when we do reflect about our experiences as they occur, we find that many experiences are too brief or change too rapidly to be adequately observed; their observation cannot be repeated, since the flux of experience is irreversible; and the very process of reflection frequently modifies the original experience, as when the observer reflects about his feelings or volitions. Therefore, only a trained psychologist can investigate by himself, without anybody else's cooperation, the flux of his own experiences. At the beginning of the nineteenth century, this was the main, if not the only, task of the scientific psychologist. However, when he published general conclusions based on his observations, even other psychologists often found it difficult to test them by observing their own experiences; and there was no adequate way of ascertaining whether they were applicable to the experiences of individuals who were not psychologists. Consequently, many controversies arose which were insolvable even by factual evidence.

Eventually, however, psychologists succeeded in overcoming these difficulties, and in the second half of the last century psychology was already started as an inductive, generalizing science of individual experiences as specifically psychological phenomena, and it has been steadily growing and improving. It has built up a systematic classification of these phenomena, based on their empirical content, and has reached many generalizations about the functional interdependence of elementary experiences, when combined into complexes, and about regularities in their temporal sequence. New hypotheses are being formulated and scientifically tested. Additional proof of the validity of these generalizations is furnished by the discovery of many significant correlations between certain regularities in the flux of individual experiences and certain regularities in the flux of physiological processes going on in individual organisms and observed by biological scientists.

We know that this development of psychology was made possible by the use of *experimental methods*. Wilhelm Wundt deserves credit as the psychologist who, though he did not initiate these methods, was the first to use them systematically and thoroughly as the main way of reaching inductive generalizations about individual experiences.[11] Now, experimental psychology is founded on the premise that actual individual experiences can be abstracted, but not isolated, from that which is being experienced. Every actual experience has not only an observable *content*, but a *meaning*. It refers to some-

---

[11] Wundt's psychological theory is well popularized in his *Outlines of Psychology*, trans. by Charles H. Judd, 3d ed. (Leipzig, 1907). His conception of the experimental method in psychology and a survey of the gradual development of this method is summarized in his *Logik*, III (Stuttgart, 1908), 162-225, "Aufgeben der Individualpsychologie."

thing which can be experienced at other times by the same individual, even if more or less differently each time, and which several individuals can experience simultaneously or successively, even if each experiences it in his own way. Every *empirical datum* is such a common center of reference and common source of more or less different experiences of several individuals. A tree, a thunderstorm, and a word are familiar examples of empirical data.

A psychologist can investigate comparatively the content of his own experiences only because he can refer successive experiences of his to the same datum. He can describe and communicate to others his own experiences, ask them to describe and communicate their experiences to him, compare his own experiences with those of others, and compare the experiences which several others have described by referring to some common datum which all of them experience and all of them identify as the same—the same tree, the same thunderstorm, the same word.

Originally, most psychological experiments consisted in making accessible to several "subjects" the same datum or the same complex (static or dynamic) of factually interconnected data and inducing them to communicate to the psychologist in some form or other their experiences of this datum or complex. Even though in recent times psychologists are more interested in individual behavior than in individual experiences, the basis of experimental human psychology remains the same. When the psychologist produces an experimental situation and investigates active responses of human individuals to this situation, the situation itself is composed of common empirical data accessible to the experience of the psychologist as well as to that of his subjects, and the ways in which they behave in response to it indicate how they experience it.

Although the psychologist has to use empirical data as a basis for comparative study of individual experiences, their similarities and differences, as well as their combinations and sequences, his task is not to investigate data as such. He does not draw from his own or anybody else's experiences of a tree any conclusions as to what the tree really is; he leaves that problem to the botanist. Of course, psychologists and botanists will agree that botanical knowledge of trees must be derived from actual experiences of trees by human individuals; but whose experiences, what kinds of experiences, what combinations of experiences botanists will use as reliable evidence from which valid conclusions about trees can be drawn are questions of botanical, not psychological, method.

Thus, psychology as a strictly inductive science of actual experiences gives no support whatever to any epistemology which tries to determine *a priori* what human experiences can be used as a basis of valid knowledge about the world of empirical data.

Sensory experiences and the sciences of natural phenomena

The doctrine that scientific knowledge about natural phenomena is valid because based on sensory experiences (sense impresses, sense impressions, sensations, sense perceptions, or however else they may be called) becomes irrevocably disproved when psychological evidence is combined with the historical evidence which the very development of sciences of nature provides.

In the first place, if experiences are classified by their content, according to the first principle of all inductive classification, no such logical class as sensory experiences in general will be found. We know that this term is applied to several classes, each of which separately includes experiences that appear similar in the light of psychological observation; but no similarity exists between these classes.

Thus, there is a definite class of visual experiences, colors and shapes which I see, though they vary widely in content from the simple experience of a colored spot or a dark line drawn upon a light surface, through more complex experiences of a clouded sky, or the foliage of a tree, or a moving automobile, or a dancing couple, to such highly complex experiences as that of a multicolored garden, or a street with moving automobiles, or a hall full of dancing couples.

Then, there is another definite class of auditive experiences, sounds which I hear, also varying from a loud clash of thunder to the barely perceptible hum of a fly, from the squeak of a tire to a fragment of classical music played by a symphony orchestra. But I cannot discover any similarity of empirical content between my auditive and my visual experiences. Simpler, but still diverse, are olfactory experiences; and these show no similarity whatever with the other two classes. Experiences of touch, more alike among themselves than experiences in the other three classes, cannot be compared with any of the others. Experiences of taste are seemingly comparable with olfactory experiences and with tactile experiences; but closer analysis shows that this is due to tasting being usually associated with smelling and touching.

What is the psychological reason for classifying together these otherwise incomparable kinds of experiences? In tracing back the history of psychological thought, we find that the main reason has been their association with the individual's experiences of his own body as empirical datum, the particular datum of which the individual is aware more frequently and persistently than he is of any other. Now, the individual's body is a *spatial* datum, which he can experience both from the outside, like other spatial data—see, touch, hear, and smell it—and from the inside, in a way in which no other datum can be experienced, as when he is aware of muscular tensions or feels pain. And he finds that the actual occurrence of his visual, tactile, auditive, olfactory, gustative experiences of other data is frequently correlated with the occurrence of certain experiences of his body. Briefly speaking, his body as spatial datum is to him the center of his actual experiences of other spatial data. This connection between an individual's actual awareness of his body and his actual awareness of external data was the original ground for the conception symbolized by such terms as "sense perception," "sensory experience," etc.

Early thinkers assumed that our experiences of our own bodies as well as of data external to our bodies gave us immediate knowledge of both. In the course of centuries, however, the progress of scientific psychology on the one hand, the progress of biological and physical sciences based on methodical investigation of individual bodies and their spatial environment on the other hand, has shown how little valid knowledge about these data could be gained from an individual's own actual experiences of them. The unreliability of the individual's inner experiences of his body as source of knowledge about this body has been familiar to physicians for forty centuries; the actual occurrence of an individual's experiences of spatial data outside his body has been found to be correlated with physiological processes in his nervous system about which he knew nothing, unless he was a physiologist; and the occurrence of these physiological processes has been found to be in turn correlated with the occurrence of physical processes in the spatial environment about which he could learn only from physical theory. Of course, physicians and biologists themselves successfully use their own sensory experiences, especially visual, tactile, and auditive, as empirical evidence in their investigation of spatial data; but they can do so only because they have developed objective standards by which they judge the reliability of this evidence and scientific methods by which unreliable evidence can be corrected.

However, conclusive, irrefutable proof of the invalidity of the dogma that sensory experiences are the only reliable basis of scientific knowledge is furnished by the very development of physical and biological science. This development would have been utterly impossible without the continual use of experiences which are not sensory as this term has been defined here.

Take, first, that familiar class of experiences popularly called "memories" or "remembrances," specifically those which refer to data that in the past were data of sensory experience, i.e., were included in the spatial complex which centered at the time in the individual's own body as experienced by himself. My present remembrance of a tree or of a ringing bell refers to a tree I saw or a bell I heard some time ago. But in the light of psychological observation, remembering a tree or a ringing bell is obviously an entirely different kind of experience from that of seeing a tree or hearing a bell. Nor is it connected with similar bodily experiences; I can remember a tree in the dark with my eyes shut, remember the ringing of a bell without that vague specific experience of my ears which accompanies the hearing of a loud sound. And even if, as occasionally happens, a vivid remembrance of something seen or heard makes me vaguely aware of my visual or auditive organs, the remembrance is independent of and unconnected with the present spatial environment of my body. Wherever I am now, I can remember a tree that I saw four thousand miles away or a tree which my memory cannot locate in any geographical space; I can also repeatedly and indefinitely experience in memory the fine tree that used to be in my neighbor's yard but has disappeared forever from the range of potential sensory experience, my own or anybody else's, having been cut and burned three years ago.

Here we are not concerned with any explanations, biological or psychological, of this possibility of remembering data which were experienced in the past as parts of the spatial environment of the individual's body, but are not experienced like that at the time when they are remembered and perhaps never can be so experienced any more. For whatever the explanation, the fact is that there could be no general physical or biological knowledge about empirical data, if we could not actually compare the content of our present sensory experience of a datum with the content of our present remembrance of the same and of other data, as experienced in the past.

Furthermore, we can not only experience in memory data of previous sensory experiences; we can also experience in anticipation, represent in advance, data of future sensory experiences; as in approaching a distant town I can anticipate many visual, auditive, and other experiences long before such experiences actually occur. This anticipatory representation is manifestly not a sensory experience, although its content is mostly derived from memories of the past. And it is an essential condition of scientific investigation, for it enables us to test conclusions about data based on past and present observation.

Another scientifically important type of nonsensory experience is commonly denoted by the term "imagination." We can imagine sensory data and combinations of data different from any we have experienced before. Although the content of such an imaginative experience can be psychologically analyzed into components each of which had its origin in some remembrance which in turn originated in some sensory experience, yet the total experience is more or less new. Such an imagined datum can become a datum of sensory experience if it is realized by action, as in technical inventions or scientific experiments. Or it may remain forever in the realm of imagination, like atoms as combinations of electrons, protons, and neutrons. Many scientists will agree that, although imaginative experiences are not sensory experiences, they constitute an essential condition of new discoveries concerning data of sensory experience.

Moreover, scientists have other experiences which do not contain any elements even indirectly derived from sensory experience. Abstract ideas or concepts such as matter, force, energy, function, though originally formed by inductive reasoning from concrete data given in sensory experience, once formed can be actually experienced without reference to any particular facts. Of course, they are symbolized by words; but the experience of a verbal symbol, spoken or written, is clearly and radically different from the experience of that which it symbolizes, whether it be a particular concrete datum or an abstract idea. Frequently in the development of science an abstract idea is formed first, and only then does the scientist seek for a word to symbolize it.

But there is an even more conclusive proof that the empirical evidence on which physical science is based is not reducible to sensory experience. Science is not a product of an absolute impersonal Reason which directly surveys and compares all the sensory experiences of scientists, but a coop-erative product of individual scientists, each of whom is aware of the experiences of others and compares their content with that of his own experiences, although the experiences of others are utterly inaccessible to his own sensory perception.

A physical or biological scientist, just like you or me, can see, touch, hear the movements of another human individual's body as an extensive datum among other extensive data in the spatial environment of his own body. This is all any one of us can know from sensory experience about anybody else. But each of us has many other experiences of others. While seeing a human individual's body and/or hearing his voice, I may become aware that he also sees my body and/or hears my voice. This is an actual experience of mine; and although it comes in consequence of my sensory experience or his movements or the sounds he emits, it is manifestly irre-ducible to the latter, for it consists in an imaginative reconstruction of what he sees or hears, derived from my own experiences (past or present) of my body and my voice. It is not a sensory, but a social experience. In a similar way, I become aware that he experiences other data in our common environ-ment and reconstructs his experiences in imagination by analogy with my own; furthermore, I realize that he is aware of my being aware of his experiences.

Thus and only thus, mutual symbolic communication, especially verbal communication, concerning our common data becomes possible. The very use of verbal sounds as symbols is irreducible to mere auditive experience of these sounds; it is a combination of mutual social experiences. It implies on my part not only a consciousness that the other individual hears the same sounds which I hear, both those which he emits and those which I emit, but that he is conscious of my hearing those sounds and also conscious of my consciousness of his hearing them. And since neither of us can share the auditive experiences of the other, use the other's ears as organs of his own hearing, each of us imaginatively reconstructs the auditive experiences of the other from his own experiences. Furthermore, these words as symbols refer to data which both of us do or can experience, but each in his own way; and if we want to reach any common conclusions about these data, we can do so only through an exchange of social experiences.

All these nonsensory social experiences of the experiences of others constitute an integral part of the empirical material which scientists use cooperatively in building their science. The validity of their conclusions about natural data depends not only on the reliability of their sensory experiences of these data, but also on the reliability of their social experiences of each other as conscious individuals.

Take a simple example. Suppose you and I are ornithologists. In roaming through a wood, I hear you say that you see a bird which you briefly describe. The meaning of your words not only makes me aware that you have had a visual experience, but indicates the content of this experience. Obviously I cannot see the bird as you see it through your eyes; I can only imagine what you see from your description of it, having seen birds myself in the past. My imaginative experience of your visual experience may or may not be followed by my own visual experience of the same bird. If it is, I can compare the content of what I imagine you see with what I actually see and communicate to you the results of my comparison; you, in turn, from my communication imagine what I see and compare this with what you actually see. Neither of us can know what the other's visual experience really is. Nevertheless, our conjectural, imaginative reconstructions of each other's visual experiences must have some reliability, for they enable us to reach certain common conclusions about the bird as our common datum which we could never reach otherwise.

Furthermore, it is indispensable for the development of science that a scientist be able to reconstruct in imagination the remembrances of others. Many sensory experiences cannot be symbolically described during their occurrence, only from memory. Even if others besides the scientist remember the same datum, they cannot directly compare their remembrances with his; they must reconstruct the content of his remembrance imaginatively from his description and compare this imaginative content with that of their own remembrance. If, as usually happens when a scientist finds something hitherto unobserved, he describes from memory a datum which others have not yet experienced, and they want to experience it or a similar datum in the future in order to test any conclusions he may have drawn about it, they will have to compare their observations not only with what he observed, not only with what he remembers, but with what they imagine he remembers. Obviously, their imaginative reconstruction of his remembrance must have some reliability; otherwise, their testing of his conclusions would be meaningless.

Going still further, scientists are made aware through symbolic communication of what other scientists have never observed, only imagined, and they construct in their own imaginations what they believe to be a reproduction of those original imaginative products. Such imagining of what somebody else has imagined would seem to be utterly worthless from the scientific point of view. And yet all physical scientists use visual symbols of such imaginary constructs as electric waves, which each of them has to imagine by himself, trusting without direct evidence that his imaginative experience is like that of others.

Finally, every scientist is made aware through symbolic communication that other scientists use abstract ideas, though he can only conjecture what these ideas mean to them. And yet his conjectures must have some reliability; otherwise, no scientific theory could be understood or accepted by other scientists. Of course, misunderstandings and disagreements between scientists do occur concerning the content of their ideas; but the very fact that such misunderstandings can be discovered and disagreements eliminated proves that ways exist for ascertaining the reliability of an individual's conjectures about the ideas of others.

A highly important point about these social experiences concerning the experiences of other scientists is that even after a scientist is dead and nobody can experience his body, others continue to experience, as if he were still alive, his perceptions, remembrances, imaginations, and ideas referring to natural data, provided he has left written records of them.

Thus, the development of sciences of nature demonstrates irrefutably that these sciences have been made possible only because (1) every individual scientist in investigating natural data uses besides his sensory experiences several kinds of nonsensory experiences of these data and draws his empirical material from his memories, anticipations, imaginations, abstract ideas; and (2) every individual scientist in addition to his own experiences of natural data uses as a source of knowledge about nature his nonsensory experiences of the experiences of other scientists as conscious individuals.

The fundamental difference between sciences of nature and the rest of human knowledge does not lie in any exclusive, privileged character of the empirical evidence which they use, but in the purpose for which this evidence is used. This purpose is to discover among empirical data an order entirely independent of human valuations and actions. Sciences of nature select for investigation only the data which can be conceived as located among other data in space, not in the particular, concrete, multiple spaces of sensory experience, with the bodies of experiencing individuals as centers, but in one universal, abstract, continuous space, mathematically defined.

The order they seek is an order of those factual relationships between spatial data which can be conceived as occurring during a definite section of a universal, continuous time, also mathematically defined with reference to universal space.

The individual mind and sciences of cultural phenomena

The epistemological doctrine according to which an individual's consciousness of his own mental life is the foundation of all knowledge becomes conclusively disproved by the development of scientific research in the domain of culture—that very domain from which it draws most of its arguments.

The individual mind of introspective psychologists, viewed historically, is really a residual conception. It has become a container for all the phenomena not used as sources of knowledge about nature because they are irrelevant to the problems with which natural sciences are concerned. Here belong all feelings and emotions from which natural scientists can draw no conclusions whatsoever about the data to which these experiences refer. The psychological fact that an individual's visual experience of a snake or his auditive experience of thunder is accompanied by fear can contribute nothing to the zoological knowledge of snakes or the physical knowledge of thunder. The physiologist knows that every occurrence of the emotion of fear as psychological phenomenon is correlated with physiological processes in the organism of the experiencing individual; however, what he knows about these processes is not derived from emotional experiences as such, but from nonemotional experiences of individual organisms as extensive objects which exist in the spatial-temporal framework.

Similarly, volitions are excluded as sources of knowledge about nature. Whether individuals wish to produce certain anticipated changes in their empirical data or to prevent anticipated changes from occurring is of no concern to the natural scientist. He investigates only observable changes of spatial data which may occur before, during, or after other observable changes of spatial data. There is no place in this temporal order of spatial changes for human will.

Moreover, while the natural scientist uses remembrances, anticipations, imaginative constructs concerning things and processes that presumably exist or occur in the spatial-temporal framework, he has no use for any remembrances, anticipations, imaginations concerning phenomena which cannot be definitely located in space in relation to other phenomena at a definite section of time. Dreams, daydreams, visions, mythical beliefs, and imaginative experiences of poets, painters, and musicians are beyond the range of investigation of natural scientists, because no regular factual relationships can be discovered between the data to which these experiences refer and other data which have already been included within the universal order of nature. Nor do natural scientists use in developing their sciences any abstract ideas— philosophic, psychological, social—which are not generalizations about the order of nature and can be neither proved nor disproved by methodical observation and comparison of spatial-temporal relationships between data.

Since men indubitably experience various phenomena which do not exist in nature, where do they exist? This problem is easily solved by meta- physicians who assume the existence of a spiritual world outside and above the material world. But a thinker who tries to avoid metaphysics cannot accept this solution. Instead he finds a solution in the conception of his own conscious and active self as a mind. Inasmuch as his mind, unlike his body, is not a spatial datum connected with other spatial data, it may be an extra- natural receptacle within which all those data of his experience are included that cannot be included in the natural universe.

The residual character of the individual mind explains the popularity of this conception among natural scientists. For it helps eliminate doubts and con- troversies which arise whenever the empirical evidence used as basis for their conclusions is later found unreliable, or the reasoning employed in draw- ing their conclusions is later judged erroneous, or the problems they attempted to solve are proved insolvable. The unreliable evidence, the erroneous con- clusions, the insolvable problems can be dumped into individual minds and branded as subjective, with no relevance whatever for scientific knowledge of the objective order of nature.

But a cultural scientist who investigates by inductive methods those phenomena which natural scientists exclude from the spatial-temporal uni- verse does not find them included in any individual mind. Indeed, the dis- tinction between data which are located in nature and those which are not has little bearing on his main problem. In contrast with the natural scientist, who seeks to discover an order among empirical data entirely independent of conscious human agents, the student of culture seeks to discover any order among empirical data which depends upon conscious human agents, is pro- duced, and is maintained by them. To perform this task he takes every empirical datum which he investigates with what we have called its *humanistic coefficient*, i.e., as it appears to those human individuals who experience it and use it. He can apply this coefficient both to data which natural scientists include in the physical world—a star, a mountain, a plant, an animal—and to those which they exclude from it—a religious myth, the fictitious plot of a novel, an ethical ideal. Furthermore, in applying the humanistic coefficient, an inductive student of culture does not accept the doctrine that his own active experience constitutes the main and most reliable source of knowledge about the data which he experiences. The investigators who are developing modern sciences of cultural data do not function as introspective psychologists, but as *historians*; and while their techniques for gathering evidence differ, depending on how near or how distant the past they investigate, their methodical approach is the same.[12]

A historian is fully aware that he cannot draw conclusions about a cultural datum from his own experience exclusively, for this datum was experienced and used by other human individuals before he became aware of it and began to study it. His task is to discover not what this datum is to him, but what it has been and perhaps still is to those others. And in the light of this approach it is utterly impossible to consider any such datum as contained in the minds of those individuals, for symbolic expressions and active performances of the latter furnish conclusive evidence that to each of them a cultural datum appears as something which exists independently of his current experience of it, something that has been and can be experienced and used by others as well as by himself—whether it does or does not exist in the natural universe.

A language, as investigated by philologists who consistently use the humanistic coefficient, is a typical complex of such cultural data. It is composed of words. Now, a word as experienced by those who use it cannot be located in the natural universe. The sequence of sounds emitted by any particular individual in pronouncing a word at a particular moment has, indeed, its place in the universal spatial-temporal framework. But a word is not experienced either by the speaker or by listeners who are familiar with it as a particular sequence of sounds occurring here and now. Nor does anyone consider it as a subjective mental phenomenon restricted to his own self. Rather, when a person uses a familiar word, it is a permanent meaningful common datum which he experiences and uses at the moment he pronounces it, but which he and others have experienced and used many times in the past and will experience and use many times in the future. The persons who hear him pronounce it and understand what it means are similarly aware that it is the identical word which they have been using and will be using. He as well as those others, if asked by the investigator, may remember that this word was used by their parents, now dead, and undoubtedly they expect that after their own deaths it will be used by their children. If they have traveled, they know that this same word is used by people who dwell at a considerable distance from their own dwelling place.

By communicating with a number of these individuals, a philologist can determine more exactly how long the word has been used and how wide the culture area is within which it is used. He can also classify it among several thousands or scores of thousands of words of the same language and find

---

[12] We are dealing here only with the historical approach to particular cultural products which constitute the concrete empirical material investigated by historians of various realms of culture. Historical studies of human actions will be discussed later.

the various patterned connections between it and other words. If each word were merely a multiplicity of individual psychological phenomena, there could be no philology as science of language. This does not mean, of course, that a comparative psychological study of individual linguistic experiences is scientifically useless. Such a study can disclose individual variations in the processes of learning and using a given language; but it already presupposes philological knowledge of the language itself as a complex of cultural data.

The same scientific approach is being used in modern studies of literature —one of the favorite fields of psychological interpretation. Since a work of literature, obviously irreducible to natural objects and processes, is a product of the imagination of an individual author, an adequate knowledge of this author's conscious life is needed to explain his product. But the author's conscious life is not an inner life, going on in his own consciousness. He is a participant in a culture shared by others, with whom he interacts. The data which he selects and uses as material in his work may be natural phenomena, cultural products, psychological facts, or social relationships. In any case, they are also experienced by other participants, although the content and meaning which a datum has for him may differ from the content and meaning which others commonly ascribe to it. The way in which he organizes these data and presents them symbolically in his work is not altogether unique; even though original, it represents some new variation of an aesthetic pattern which was gradually developed by his predecessors. The form of his presentation depends on the language he uses, though he may introduce some innovations into standardized arrangements of words and their current meanings, or perhaps occasionally create a new word. Even the feelings expressed in his work are by no means exclusively his own:

> The emotional pattern of the individual writer . . . is . . . socialized in the process of construction, and the individual artistic vision is a selection from potential elements; the emotional response of the readers . . . proceeds in an emotional milieu already socially conditioned.[13]

No adequate study of the psychology of an individual author is possible unless we already know the culture which he shared and the social life in which he participated. And a work of literature, once produced, becomes a common datum actively experienced in reproductive imagination by all its readers or, if a drama, by all those who see and hear it played.

The irreducibility of cultural data to either objective natural reality or subjective psychological phenomena is perhaps even more manifest in the realm of religion. No modern religionist would seriously discuss the question whether Zeus and Hera, Pallas-Athene, Aphrodite, Dionysos, Demeter and Persephone, Charon, the centaurs, and the cyclops really existed in the world of nature. It would be equally absurd to insist that nothing existed

[13] Max Lerner and Edwin Mines, "Literature" in *Encycl. of Social Sci.*, IX (1937), 525.

beyond the blocks of marble and patches of color found in Greek temples, plus certain marks engraved on walls and spots on parchments and papyri. Religionists have concluded from descriptions contained in Greek literature and from archeological remnants that these mythical beings existed as common data and common objects of active cultus among generations of Greeks. These conclusions are obviously not based on any psychological knowledge about the individual religious experiences of ancient Greeks, since we have no direct evidence of their experiences. On the contrary, psychologists who generalize about the religious experiences of ancient Greeks base their hypothetical generalizations on literary and archeological evidence about Greek gods and religious rites.

Consider, finally, abstract concepts. Here the doctrine of the individual mind—first as a substance, later as a closed functional system—was for centuries supposed to be the only solution of the conflict between nominalism and realism concerning general ideas. Nominalists, medieval and modern, asserted that general ideas do not exist at all, that they are only names, verbal symbols which refer to nothing more than particular data; whereas realists claimed that the general is prior to the particular, that general ideas exist by themselves in the objective universe and constitute its very essence. So-called "conceptualism" developed as a compromise doctrine. Conceptualists agree with nominalists that in the empirical world only particular common data exist; and yet thinkers can abstract characteristics common to many particular data and include these data in the same logical class. Abstract concepts of general classes exist, but only in the minds of the thinkers. This epistemological doctrine became explicitly or implicitly accepted by all philosophers and psychologists who assumed their knowledge of their own minds as true, however much they differed in their theories concerning the essence of the human mind, the relationships between the minds of particular human individuals, and the metaphysical connection or lack of connection between human minds and a divine or universal mind.

Here again an epistemological doctrine has been invalidated by historical research. Historians of philosophy have been studying methodically for nearly two centuries the abstract concepts used by philosophers; and, more recently, this methodical research has been extended to the abstract concepts which are not included in works of philosophers but are used by popular thinkers, ideological leaders, propagandists, and others. To a historian who does not function as a philosopher or try to judge the concepts of others as true or false, objective or subjective, but simply reconstructs their content and meaning from written records, an abstract concept is a cultural datum, just as a myth or the characters and plot of a novel. He finds that, although the abstract concept which he reconstructs was, indeed, produced by an individual thinker, it has been understood and used by other individuals who have either heard this thinker expound it or read about it in his writings, and it can be understood and used by anybody who hears him or reads his writings. From such historical evidence as discussions, polemics, and modifications of a concept by later thinkers who refer back to its originator, it is obvious that an abstract concept has been and can be identified by many individuals as a common datum of their experience and thought, even though they differ in their interpretation of its content and meaning.

Consequently, historians have been able to trace the origin and evolution of particular abstract concepts during certain historical periods, e.g., justice, virtue, natural law, soul, reason, will, matter, spirit, substance, function, sovereignty, nationalism, etc. In so doing, they did not need to study the psychology of the individual thinkers who contributed to the evolution of those concepts or of the teachers and learners through whom the concepts became widely known and shared by successive generations. What historians seek to discover is the kind of concrete data which a given abstract concept covers and its relationship to other concepts in a philosophic theory or a practical ideology.[14]

Duration and extension of cultural data

The impossibility of describing and explaining cultural data psychologically has been most consistently emphasized by the French sociologists of that cooperating group which has been popularly called the "school of Durkheim." Unfortunately, while rejecting the idea that cultural data were included in individual minds, some of them tried to conceive these data as included in some kind of mental receptacle—the collective mind or collective consciousness—as a synthesis of the minds of the individual participants in a society. Cultural data were accordingly called "collective representations," an expression suggesting representations of a particular collectivity in contrast with representations of a particular individual.

Although the French sociologists used these concepts mainly to counteract individualistic psychological methods in monographic studies, and (unlike some German theorists of "Volksgeist" and "Volksseele") did not try to develop any psychological theory of collective minds parallel to psychological theories of individual minds, nevertheless their doctrine of society has imposed certain methodologically unjustified limitations on cultural research.

First, by assuming that the individual is only a part and product of society and trying to explain all changes in collective life as determined exclusively by collective forces, sociologists have tended to neglect individual contributions to culture. While no human individual can create a cultural datum

---

[14] This approach has been increasingly used in philosophical dictionaries. Especially significant from this point of view is Rudolf Eisler's *Wörterbuch der philosophischen Begriffe, Historisch-Quellenmässig bearbeitet*, 4th ed., 3 vols. (Berlin, 1927-30).

"out of the depth of his own mind," all cultural data whose origin can be traced have grown as creative products of individual agents who use already existing data as material and add something new to their content and meaning which other agents can share.

How much or how little particular individuals contribute to the creative growth of cultural data depends on many factors, and we may agree with Durkheim and others that the most important among them are the attitudes toward innovation which are expressed by the groups in which these individuals participate. When groups oppose innovations, the growth of cultural data is apt to proceed by a slow agglomeration of small, mostly unintentional individual contributions, whose origins are difficult to trace. When innovations are socially allowed or even encouraged, the creative growth of cultural data is apt to be intentional; and every notable individual contribution can be historically ascertained. Compare, for instance, the growth of a folk dialect with the growth of a modern literary language through the agency of writers, grammarians, inventors of technical and scientific terms, authors of dictionaries; or the development of common-sense concepts in nonliterate communities with the development of philosophic and scientific concepts in classical antiquity and modern times. The difference, however, is not always so definite. Thus, although it is impossible to discover by what agglomerated individual contributions Greek mythology grew in prehistorical times, its development in the historical period can be ascribed to various creative contributions by well-known artists and poets.

On the other hand, many cultural data which have grown by creative contributions gradually decay, lose their content and meaning, and disappear finally from the realm of human experience. Their past existence can sometimes be ascertained and their content and meaning reconstructed by historians, ethnologists, and folklorists, especially if their content and meaning have been recorded in written symbols. Whenever the process of disappearance of a cultural datum can be reconstructed, it is found to be directly due to the fact that human individuals simply ceased to experience and use it. The cessation may have been the result of a sudden death of all the individuals who shared this datum or it may have resulted from a gradual decrease in the frequency with which human individuals experienced or used it.

We spoke of works of literature. Take, for instance, *Hamlet*. Since Shakespeare created that drama, it has existed as a common cultural datum for millions of human individuals, first in England, then in other countries, where sometimes it had to be translated into another language. During this period of its existence it has not remained changeless. It was interpreted by literary critics and played by actors in many different, often original ways, and these creative individual innovations have enriched its content and meaning for readers and theatergoers.

In contrast with this work, consider the many literary works, written and published in various languages, which sooner or later disappeared from the range of human experience, simply because human individuals ceased to read them. Even if some of them still exist in libraries, nobody is aware of their existence except the librarians who know their titles but not their contents. Occasionally a historian reads them for purposes of monographic research, resurrecting them for the benefit of other historians. Thus, individuals, not societies, are directly responsible for the continued existence of a literary work like *Hamlet* and for the disappearance of other literary works. No doubt, the individual reading of literary works is socially conditioned; but how it is conditioned is a problem which must be investigated in each particular case.

The use of the concept of society in studies of culture has another limitation. For a society, as conceived by many sociologists, is not only a synthesis of individual minds and therefore a kind of superindividual conscious container of cultural data; it is also a synthesis of individual bodies living within a certain geographically circumscribed portion of space during a certain section of astronomical time. This implies that the cultural data shared by the members of a society can be included in the universal framework of nature. Quite a few sociologists, not only those who accept the idea of a collective mind or collective consciousness but, even more, those who base their theories upon deductions from biological science, still conceive a society as a natural receptacle of culture. This conception is due to the obvious fact that the existence of a cultural datum, as something which many individuals experience and use, depends upon the biological existence of those individuals as living organisms, every one of which can be located at any given moment in some place on the surface of the earth during a certain time.

Evidently, cultural data do not exist in a timeless and spaceless world of Platonic ideas. Historians of culture always refer the phenomena which they study to certain historical periods and trace their origin to people who lived in certain geographic areas. The question arises, however, whether time and space have the same meaning for cultural scientists as they do for scientists of nature.

Some modern thinkers who have investigated the spatial-temporal framework used by physicists and astronomers came to the conclusion that this framework is an abstract mathematical construct which does not correspond to concrete human experience. Space and time have a very different significance for conscious human individuals in their active lives than they do in physical and astronomical theories. And insofar as historians of culture take the data they investigate with the humanistic coefficient and refer them to conscious human agents, their conception of space and time must differ from that of natural science.[15]

We cannot discuss in detail this difficult question from the epistemological point of view. We are concerned here only with problems of methodical approach to empirical data. Briefly, in the frame of reference used by physicists and astronomers the spatial order of natural data is primary and the temporal order of natural facts secondary, relative to space. (This is indicated by the modern concept of time as "fourth dimension.") But to the student of culture, time in the historical sense—i.e., as *duration* of one cultural datum as compared with the duration of other cultural data—is primary, while space in the geographical sense of terrestrial surface is secondary. For every cultural datum, as a product of conscious human agents, must be viewed by the historian not as it appears at any moment of astronomical time to any individual located in a certain place at this moment, but as it evolves in the dynamic, irreversible course of being experienced and used by a plurality of human individuals throughout its duration.

Geographic space is important for the historian only inasmuch as the changing content and meaning of a cultural datum depend on the number of individuals who experience and use it during a certain period, as well as on the degree of communication and cooperation between them, and inasmuch as these variables are conditioned in turn by the geographical distribution of these individuals. Since some cultural data are shared only by the relatively few individuals within small areas, while others are shared by the relatively many individuals distributed over large areas, it may be said that some data are experienced and used less, others more, or simply that they have a different extension. In the course of their duration the range of this extension can increase or decrease.

Thus, the extension of the French language has certainly increased since the sixteenth century, while the range of extension of the Basque language has probably decreased during the same period. And neither of these languages can be considered as coextensive with the French society geographically located in the territory of France, for the vast majority of inhabitants of France do not know any Basque, while the French language is used far beyond France: in Canada, in the French colonies, and quite often among the diplomatic and aristocratic sets of other countries. In general, no definite correlation can be found between the framework of space and time in which scientists of nature include natural data and the framework of historical

[15] An excellent historico-critical survey of various conceptions of space and time is that of P. Sorokin, *Socio-cultural Causation, Space, Time* (Durham, N. C.: Duke University Press, 1943). His own conception of sociocultural space, however, is a philosophic construct which has no reference to space as experienced by participants in culture; and his sociocultural time, though scientifically valuable, culminates in the metaphysical concept of eternity. Cf. Chapter 14 in this book.

duration and geographic extension in which cultural data are included. Take a few significant cases.

Trees constitute a familiar class of empirical data. But there are innumerable trees which for scientific purposes can be assumed to exist right now in the Amazonian basin or in the Siberian taiga, even though they may have never been observed by any human individual. On the other hand, a particular tree which, judging by botanical evidence, never could have existed in nature is the most famous of all trees. We refer to the Tree of Knowledge of Good and Evil from which Eve, at the instigation of a serpent, plucked the ominous fruit and shared it with Adam. This tree has been experienced and identified in imagination and thought by millions of individuals in the course of many generations. We cannot seriously entertain the theory that it is not an empirical datum common to all those people, but many millions of separate representations which exist only in the minds of particular individuals, disappearing as certain individuals die and appearing in the minds of their successors; for historians can identify it, define it, study its relationships with other cultural data—religious, aesthetic, linguistic, etc.—not by investigating the minds of believers (the vast majority of whom could not be investigated anyway), but by reconstructing its content and meaning from verbal descriptions and artistic representations. Nor can it be characterized as a collective representation existing in a particular society; for it began as a Babylonian myth, then became modified and incorporated into the sacred books of Hebrew society, and later spread with Christianity throughout Europe and finally throughout the world as a common datum of all those and only those individuals—to whatever society they belonged—who were converted to Christianity and accepted its traditional dogmas. And if we follow its history for centuries, we see how its content and meaning grew and changed through the numerous individual contributions of theologians, commentators, preachers of many denominations (some of whose sermons have been preserved), and artists (whose paintings of it still exist), until under the influence of modern criticism many members of religious groups ceased to believe that such a tree ever existed and conceived it as an allegory.

However, the fact that a datum actually exists or existed within the framework of nature does not prevent it from becoming also a cultural datum, a common center of imaginative experiences symbolically expressed by some individuals, accepted and reproduced by many others. But the duration and extension of this cultural datum does not correspond at all to the time and space within which the natural datum existed.

Take the "sacred city of Troy." In the nineteenth century, Schliemann and other archeologists proved that the Homeric poems referred to a city which really had existed in space and had been destroyed some time before these poems were composed. While the city existed as a natural datum, it was accessible to the active experience of only those people who inhabited the eastern part of the Mediterranean basin; and after its destruction it ceased to be accessible to human experience altogether. But the city of Troy as described in the *Iliad* and the *Odyssey* became a common cultural datum which was experienced throughout centuries and still continues to be experienced by all the individuals who hear or read these epics or their summaries, in the original or in translation. A historian of culture can investigate this cultural product; study the additions and changes introduced into its content and meaning by Greek tragedians, by Virgil in the *Aeneid*, and by some modern poets; discover its relationships with other cultural products; and survey the variations in its popularity and importance due to the increase or decrease of classical traditions in education, without having to test the validity of his conclusions by referring to what the city of Troy was in the natural world.[16]

While in the case of Troy the cultural datum has lasted much longer and been experienced much more extensively than the natural datum from which its content was originally derived, the reverse is true of many other common data of human experience. Probably the most instructive example is the datum generally identified as *the sun*.[17] We need not discuss what it is as a natural datum in the universal spatial-temporal framework, according to modern astronomy. The important point for our present problem is that by scientific evidence its existence in nature preceded by billions of years its existence as a datum of human experience and that it has been a center and a source of certain sensory experiences to nearly all the human individuals who have ever lived on the surface of the earth. They have always and everywhere experienced it as a shining disc, radiating light and heat, appearing above the horizon, slowly moving in a circular way across the sky for a shorter or longer time, disappearing under the horizon to reappear again sooner or later.

Throughout human history, the sun has been a nucleus around which slowly grew diverse combinations of myths, mystical beliefs, religious and magical rites, artistic symbolizations, metaphysical doctrines, astronomic and astrological concepts. While from the point of physical science only one sun exists as a natural reality independent of man, students of culture have found a number of complex cultural products which have little in common except that each of them derived its original content from the solar disc in the sky.

For instance, to some preliterate peoples the solar disc was an impersonal entity, endowed with great mystical power, which could be influenced by magicians and used for good or evil. To Peruvians, Egyptians, and early Greeks, it became a conscious and active divine being, but a different kind

---

[16] Cf., for a partial historical survey, M. K. Halevy, *Mythology and the Siege of Troy* (Philadelphia: G. Barrie, 1892).

[17] Cf. William T. Olcott, *Sun Lore in All Ages* (New York: Putnam, 1914); Louis H. Grey, George F. Moore, John R. McCulloch, *The Mythology of All Races*, 13 vols. (Boston: Marshall Jones Co., 1916-32), "Index," XIII, 403-05.

of being in each of these cultures. The development of the idea of purely spiritual divine beings without bodies resulted in conceptions of the sun as a visible instrument of invisible gods, eventually as the creation of an invisible god. To all believers in astrology, it was and still is one of the spheres which move circularly across a static background of configurations of stars, whose movements somehow mystically determine the life course of every human being. And we should not overlook the fact that the concept of the sun as an element of the Ptolemaic astronomical system was also a cultural product, as are all the modern concepts of the sun which have been current from Copernicus to Einstein.

Students of culture, using archeological and documentary evidence, have investigated or could investigate each of these "suns" as a common datum of the active experience of thousands or millions of individuals who have lived during a shorter or longer period of human history within a wider or narrower geographic area or scattered in smaller or larger groupings over all continents. To carry on such an investigation, the student of culture does not have to be a competent astronomer or physicist, since his problem is to find out not what the sun is in the natural universe, but what it is or has been to the people who share a certain cultural complex. This implies, of course, that he must refrain from judging any of these historical constructs as true or false, objective or subjective. In order to reconstruct such a complex, a student of culture does not need to analyze, any more than an astronomer does, the psychology of the particular individuals who share it. But once the complex has been reconstructed, psychological analysis can show how individuals learn to participate in it and how this participation affects their conscious lives.

Human individuals as cultural data

A man as a particular human individual, like everything else, can be scientifically investigated only as an empirical datum among other empirical data.[18] To avoid misunderstandings, it might be well to remember that the investigation of individual experiences, as carried on by modern scientific psychology, is *not* an investigation of the experiencing individual as such. And, anticipating later conclusions from modern developments of the comparative sciences of culture, it might be well if we stated right now that scientific investigation of human actions is not an investigation of the agents who perform them. As inductive scientists, we can know no more about men than about any other common data of human experience.

Like other empirical data, the data called "men" or "human individuals"

[18] Here we give no bibliographical references to studies of human individuals or groups as cultural or, more specifically, social phenomena, since these studies are carried on mostly by social psychologists and sociologists, whose scientific functions will be discussed later.

can be and have been approached from two different points of view. We are familiar with the naturalistic approach. From this point of view, a man is nothing but an organism, a natural object existing among other natural objects within the framework of universal space and functionally connected with other natural objects by processes which occur in universal time. The order of relationships between this organism and other natural objects is presumed to be as independent of the experiences, valuations, and tendencies of any conscious human agents as the order of relationships between a plant or a mineral and its natural environment. Anything pertaining to man as empirical datum which cannot be reduced to this order should be excluded from the realm of natural science, and is excluded by scientists who consistently apply this approach and do not speculate about the true essence of man.

The *cultural* approach to the human individual is relatively recent, more difficult, and less consistently used. In principle, it is the same as the cultural approach to language or mythology. A particular human individual is viewed primarily as he appears to other individuals who are repeatedly aware of him and identify him as a common datum of their respective experiences. Often, but not always, investigators find that he also is aware of himself; then, his own experiences of himself, if they can be ascertained by factual evidence, must be added to the experiences which others have of him. Every human individual is identified by others as a combination of conscious and active subject (psyche, spirit, mind) and an organic body. These two parts of his empirical content and the way in which they are supposed to be combined differ widely in different cultures. In most cultures, his identity as conscious and active subject is considered more essential than his bodily identity.

We should, following Park and Burgess, designate this compound datum by the general term "person," were it not that later on we shall have to use this term in a narrower sense. Let us, therefore, borrow from Cooley the word "image" or, more specifically, "human image," using it metaphorically, of course. The advantage of this metaphorical expression is the connotation that a human image, like other images, is a product of conscious agents and, like other such products, exists not in the natural world, but in the historical world of cultural data.

We begin with the human images which are explicitly known to be products of imagination, not real individuals, viz., fictitious personalities or characters in epics, dramas, and novels. What we said of other components of a literary work obviously applies also to these products. The author, however original, does not create a fictitious personality entirely out of his own spontaneous, culturally unconditioned experiences of other individuals, but uses certain patterns current in the culture in which he participates. From childhood, he has learned to follow various stereotypes in defining and evaluating others; and although in inventing his personalities, he modifies some of these stereotypes, combines some into a composite stereotype, and even tries to reject others, he cannot get rid of them altogether and, if he could, his readers would not understand his creation.

Fictitious personalities are often called "heroes" by critics and historians of literature. We shall, however, reserve the term "hero" to designate a human image which is not considered an invention by those who experience it, but is identified with a particular human individual supposed to have really existed, both as a body and as a conscious and active subject. We have already discussed the function ascribed to heroes as creators of order, and we have seen that from this point of view no sharp line divides human from divine creators. But the image of a hero usually differs from the image of a god in that the hero is represented as originally a human being among human beings, though superior to others in personal characteristics which are considered most desirable by those standards of valuation which admirers of the hero apply to other human individuals and themselves.

Now, most images of heroes, as of gods, developed gradually, growing by many individual contributions, few of which can be traced, unless preserved in writing. The production of such an image implies that some individuals, presumed to have been in direct social contact with the particular individual whom the image is supposed to represent, transmitted to others their experiences of him. The idealization of this image does not depend upon the reliability of these experiences, rather the contrary. It is easier to idealize the dead than the living, and to develop a perfect image of a legendary individual than of one about whose life there is considerable documentary evidence accessible to readers.

If the hero, though dead, is supposed to be spiritually alive in the "other world" and capable of influencing the earthly lives of men, his cultus, like the cultus of a god, includes requests for his assistance. For instance, a family ancestor, the legendary founder of a craft or a profession who is still supposed to be interested in the work of his successors, or a Christian saint is expected to help those who worship him.

But hero worship is not reducible to utilitarian motives. Most heroes are primarily, many exclusively, models of personal perfection for their worshipers. When St. Patrick became the national hero of Ireland, his image differed considerably from that of an orthodox Catholic saint, for he was also an impersonation of the most valuable traits which characterized pagan Irish heroes. Charlemagne, Roland, and Olivier, as described in the French *Chansons de Geste*, were no saints, but perfect images of feudal personalities; no prayers for help were offered to them. Jeanne d'Arc was a French national heroine long before she became canonized as a saint. The cult of George Washington and Abraham Lincoln as American national heroes includes no request for interference on their part with the present life of the American people. Monuments and celebrations in honor of soldiers who were killed in battle, especially the Unknown Soldier, are simply expressions of recognition and gratitude to heroes who by sacrificing their lives became models of national loyalty for the living.

Sometimes the image of a dead hero does not develop gradually, but is intentionally constructed and perpetuated in writing. For instance, Plato and Xenophon constructed somewhat different, but not conflicting, images of Socrates; thanks to them, especially to Plato, Socrates became and remained famous as an intellectual and moral hero for all educated people of Western civilization throughout twenty-three centuries.

Historical research based on documentary evidence has frequently proved that the human image of a dead hero is largely or almost entirely an idealized product of the imagination of his worshipers. This does not mean, however, that the historian discovers what the heroized individual "really was" as a human being. Documentary evidence can show only: First, that this individual did perform or did not perform in the course of his life certain actions; and second, how he was experienced and judged by his contemporaries. Furthermore, historical studies of the lives of dead heroes are by no means always carried on for purely scientific purposes. Historians often try to debunk a hero, because they reject the values which the hero impersonates in the eyes of his worshipers.

The cultural process of building up the image of a hero as a model of human perfection became in some cases intentionally hastened even in classical antiquity, so that an individual could become a hero during his life; the establishment of obligatory cultus of living Roman emperors is a good example. In modern times, with mass education, the press, and the radio, different, but even more rapid and effective methods have come into use. The planful construction of heroic images of Mussolini, Hitler, and Stalin, intended to make the masses accept their dictatorship, is familiar. And it is only a difference of degree between the human images of these heroes and the images produced by the public relations counselors of John D. Rockefeller, Calvin Coolidge, and many other less famous men.

In discussing heroes as impersonations of positively valued characteristics we must not forget human images of the opposite type—impersonations of evil. Sometimes we find two opposite images built up around the same individual, living or dead, like the mythical beings who were gods to unconverted pagans, but devils to Christian missionaries. Compare, for instance, the French image of Napoleon as a hero with the English image of Bonaparte as a villain. Somewhat less radical, but still evident, are differences between images of the same officeholder or candidate constructed by two struggling political parties.

Contrast the human image of F. D. Roosevelt as represented during his term of office by his faithful Democratic followers and the image of F. D. Roosevelt as viewed during the same period by stalwart Republicans.

Obviously, the human image of a hero, whether dead or alive, though referred by those who experience this image to an individual whose organism existed or still exists in the spatial-temporal framework of nature, can no more be included in this framework than a poem or a god. Nor is it reducible to a multiplicity of separate individual representations. The theory that it is the collective representation of a society does not cover all the facts, since as a common cultural datum such an image may last long after the society within which it originated has ceased to exist, e.g., the image of Socrates as an intellectual and moral hero or the image of Alexander, Caesar, St. Peter, St. John, or the archvillain Judas. Moreover, it can spread and be shared at the same time by peoples who belong to different societies, e.g., the image of an international hero like Woodrow Wilson in 1919-20 or F. D. Roosevelt in 1941-44.

Now, what is the difference between such a human image of a famous individual, an extraordinary man, which endures for centuries and is shared by millions of individuals who never met him or interacted with him, and the human image of an ordinary individual—a small-town businessman or his wife, a tribesman, a farmer, a college student—as experienced by those who have been interacting with him?

According to popular common sense, this difference is obvious. Such an ordinary individual is familiar to others from many face-to-face contacts and direct observation of his behavior. There is nothing imaginary about him; he is known as a real being. Some of the individuals who have observed him and interacted with him know more about him than others; he knows more about himself than others do; and even if some of this knowledge is erroneous, the truth may always become apparent after further observation.

This implies that in addition to sensory perceptions of an individual's body, the actions he performs are the main source of knowledge concerning him. We do not question here the possibility of observing, comparing, predicting human actions. We shall discuss this fundamental problem later. But, as we shall see from a study of actions, conclusions can be drawn only about actions. The popular belief that "what an individual does shows what he is" merely expresses the tendency of those who interact with a particular individual to construct an image of this individual based on their experiences and valuations of some of his actions. Once such an image has been constructed, certain actions of others bearing upon him are conditioned by that image.

For instance, teachers construct the image of an individual student, drawing conclusions about his characteristics primarily from such actions as oral or written answers to questions he is asked and papers he has written; and secondarily from what he has been doing while interacting with other students in class and in extracurricular groups. Since teachers define and evaluate all these actions according to certain standards of their own, the characteristics of the human image of the student which they construct are also evaluative. Subsequent actions of teachers bearing upon the student depend on this image. If the student finishes high school, schematic descriptions and valuations of his actions by his teachers are expressed in written symbols on the diploma he receives. If he wants to enter a college, administrative officials of this college reconstruct his image from the symbolic expressions of judgments of his teachers and decide whether he is fit or unfit to become a college student.

Some social psychologists and sociologists have gradually discovered during the last half century that all conceptions of human individuals, no matter by whom produced and accepted, are not theories to be tested as true or false, but empirical data to be investigated, and that such investigations require a study of the process in the course of which these conceptions develop. This approach has been most consistently applied to the individual's conception or image of himself. Baldwin, Cooley, and Mead found that this image develops gradually as the individual, in the course of interaction and symbolic communication with others, learns that he, both as a body and as a conscious and active subject, constitutes a common datum in the experiences of others and an object of their valuation and actions. His self, as he reflectively imagines and conceives it, is a reconstruction of the image of his self which others have communicated to him. Somewhat similar conclusions are implied by Adler's complexes and Freud's ego and superego. Such studies lead to the question: What is this image of the individual as viewed by others, from which his own image of his self is derived, and how has it been developed?

Sociologists have investigated various parts and aspects of this problem, and the general results of their investigations are well known. In analyzing the life history of a particular individual in his active relationships with others, we find a plurality of diverse, partly overlapping conceptions or images of this individual progressively formed by various social sets in which he participates from infancy to old age. Some of these images disappear, some become partly absorbed in later images. Consequently, his image of his self changes in the course of time; but it serves as a lasting nucleus, giving to the images constructed by others some degree of unity and continuity. It enables him to identify himself and helps others identify him as the same individual, however differently represented by different social sets and by himself at different periods of his life.

In short, a concrete, living human individual as common datum of human experience is a cultural product of many conscious agents, just as a mythical being or a hero. This product must be investigated not by biological or psychological, but by historical methods. Scientists who take a given human individual with the humanistic coefficient do not ask what he is to a biological or psychological observer, but what he is and has been to those human agents (including himself) who have experienced him, whether directly or indirectly, in the total course of his life; ascribed to him various characteristics; evaluated him by various standards; conceived him as belonging to various types and classes; and tried to shape his personality according to various models. Only after this history of the individual as a cultural product has been reconstructed up to a particular period of his life is it possible to solve scientifically psychological problems concerning his experiences of others or of himself during this period.

Human collectivities as cultural data

From the point of view of natural science, a human collectivity is not a distinct datum, but a complex of interconnected data—an aggregate of individual organisms which exist and move within a certain territory during a certain section of time, all functionally dependent on their geographic environment and in some respects functionally interdependent. But historians, cultural anthropologists, political scientists, and sociologists have found that it is impossible to explain many of the actions performed by individual participants in a collectivity without knowing what this collectivity is in their own experience; that factual relationships between individuals participating in different collectivities are often inexplicable, unless it is known how each of these collectivities appears to participants in the others; and that many changes occurring within a collectivity can be explained only if we know how its participants retrospectively conceive and evaluate it from its past, as they see it, and what they expect it to become in the future. In short, there is considerable evidence that many a collectivity is experienced by its participants and also by outsiders not as a mere aggregate of individuals, but as one concrete whole, identified by them as a common lasting datum which exists independently of any one of them.

A manifest symptom of independent existence of such a datum is the use of a name to identify it. The name may be derived from an individual's name, as when a clan or a tribe is named for its mythical or legendary ancestor, a religious order for its patron saint, a university for its founder. The name of a political collectivity may be the same as the name of the territory which it occupies—England, Italy, France, Poland—but the difference between its geographical and its social meaning is usually made clear by the context in which it is used. Even when the name of the collectivity is plural, e.g., Franks, Picts, Athenians, Romans, the plural form does not necessarily denote a mere plural of individuals. If the name is used through several generations and refers not only to the individuals living at a particular moment, but also to the dead and the unborn, this indicates that all those individuals together are viewed as constituting a continuous whole.

But names are not the only symbols for collectivities. The great multiplicity and variety of visual symbols is even more significant. Australian churingas, coats of arms of European noble families, symbols of craftsmen's guilds, animals, birds, plants, various combinations of colors for different cities and states, symbols of religious associations, of secret societies, of military regiments, of political parties, all serve to identify the collectivities symbolized as common and lasting data which exist independently of any individual's subjective experience; some of them may have existed long before any of the individuals who participate in them were born and may continue to exist long after all their present participants are dead.

Such a common conception of a particular collectivity as a whole, as including many individuals and existing independently of all individuals, is a cultural product, just like the image of a hero. Though it is seldom possible to trace the origin of conceptions of preliterate collectivities—clans, tribes, and secret societies—the development of such conceptions in historical periods can often be reconstructed from documentary evidence. We shall investigate this development in a later work, in connection with the formation of organized social groups. Now we wish merely to point out that sometimes the conception of a collectivity as a whole is formed long before the individuals, presumed to belong to it, begin to manifest any active interdependence and solidarity. They become effectively unified in the very measure in which they grow to believe in the existence of a collectivity which includes them and to act in accordance with this belief. Perhaps the most instructive example is the progressive unification of modern nationalities. The conception that all Italian people or all German people constitute an integral collectivity, united by a common historical past, a common contemporary culture, and common interests in the future, was initiated in each case by a few cultural leaders—poets, historians, and ideologists—and became increasingly influential as it spread among the intelligentsia, lower urban classes, and peasants; but it took centuries before its influence grew powerful enough to overcome political divisions.

On the other hand, even after a particular collectivity has ceased to exist in the realm of active social life, no agents being left to function as its participants, it may still survive as an imaginary and intellectual product in tradition and history, just as a myth, a poem, or a philosophic concept. And this product may influence the activity of participants in other collectivities; e.g., the influence of the Western Roman Empire as a historical datum persisted for a thousand years after its disintegration as a social system.

These conceptions of collectivities as wholes composed of many individuals gave rise to the well-known ontological controversy between social realists, who accepted these conceptions as true, and social atomists, who rejected them as false. Older theorists of the state (beginning with Plato) and modern theorists of society (beginning with Comte) attempted to integrate logically various conceptions of collectivities, especially those found among their contemporaries. They seldom took fully into consideration the fact that the same collectivity—be it a town, a state, a church, a political party, a factory, a school, a regiment, or a settlement of foreign immigrants—is apt to be differently conceived by its participants and by outsiders, by participants of different classes and occupations, by rulers and by subjects, by ideologists and by practical agents, by men and by women, by the old and by the young, by conformists and by rebels; or the fact that in the course of its duration its conceptions change, often radically. Moreover, they seldom realize the manifest contradictions which arise when conceptions of different collectivities which include the same individuals are compared. For instance, a state is conceived by jurists and governmental officials as including fully and completely all the individuals who permanently inhabit a given territory; but many of these individuals may belong to an international church which is conceived by them and by the clergy as also including fully and completely all of them, together with millions of individuals who inhabit the territories of other states.

During the last forty years, the sociological theory of a social group composed of individual members, not as biopsychological entities but as performers of specific roles, has provided a solution for these problems. Nonetheless, old theories, derived from popular conceptions of human collectivities as real objective wholes which contain total human beings, still survive, both in political science and in sociology. We shall have to give some attention to such theories in a later part of this book.

We can, however, discard definitely the contrary assumption according to which, because human collectivities are not what their participants believe them to be, they have no existence whatsoever. By the same principle, we would have to deny the existence of all products of creative imagination and conceptualization and ignore entirely all human actions which produce and use them. There would be no active religious cultus if there were no gods as cultural products shared by believers; no writing, printing, or publishing of books if the meaningful content of a book did not exist as a product of spiritual culture accessible to the experience of all readers. Just so, if collectivities did not exist as ideational constructs in the historical world of culture, there could be no active manifestations of individual loyalties to a tribe, a city, a state, a church, a cultural nationality, a social class, as a common superindividual reality—manifestations ranging from participation in a public ceremony to voluntary sacrifice of one's life. Nor would there be, on the other hand, active efforts tending to eliminate an enemy state without exterminating the people who inhabit its territory, or to put out of existence a pagan or heretical religious group by converting its members. As we shall see later on, whenever a relatively large number of individual agents carry on some relatively lasting organized cooperation, the conception of a superindividual collectivity to which all of them belong will be found to exist.

* * *

This brief survey of the empirical data which are being investigated by scientific specialists in various domains of inductive research clearly indicates that scientific knowledge in general, having gradually gained freedom from metaphysical speculations, is now becoming independent of conflicting epistemological doctrines. Anything that can be experienced by human individuals is an empirical datum and as such can be scientifically investigated; but no scientific investigation of any datum can determine what this datum really is. For the task of the scientist is not to define the true essence of the data he investigates, only to observe factual relationships among them and to discover whatever order exists in these relationships.

This task, however, has raised certain controversial issues about the *methods* of scientific research. In every science, some methical innovations were introduced during the last hundred years, especially during the twentieth century, and like most innovations resulted in controversies. But, while in physical and biological sciences, these controversies are usually solved by the scientists themselves, who test the application of different methods by comparing their results in terms of new discoveries; in sciences of culture (and also in psychology), the methodological disputes continue indefinitely. This is mainly due to the influence of those methodologists who believe that they know better than the research scientists what a truly scientific method ought to be. This belief is based on the assumption that, because certain methical principles are common to all sciences, the application of these principles in the course of investigation must be similar in all sciences. Starting with this assumption, methodologists construct a universal ideal of methodical perfection, tell scientists how to approach it, and judge the validity of every science according to the degree of its conformity or nonconformity with this ideal. Since the methodical progress in sciences of culture started later and has been more difficult than in sciences of nature, methodological authoritarians feel freer to criticize the work of cultural scientists and bolder in attempts to impose their ideals.

Natural Order Among Data

CHAPTER 6

The historical evolution of generalizations

Methodological controversies in the domain of cultural investigation refer mostly to *generalizations* about cultural phenomena. If judged by the theoretic objectivity, factual validity, and logical consistency of their generalizations, sciences of culture are still methodically inferior to sciences of nature. Since this inferiority cannot be explained by any epistemological doctrine which claims that cultural phenomena are inaccessible to scientific research, it must be due to some difference between these two domains of knowledge which made it more difficult for investigators to generalize about culture than about nature. The explanation of this difficulty has to be sought in the history of these generalizations.

We must remember that the development of theoretic knowledge was preceded by a much longer development of practical knowledge. When philosophers started their theoretic generalizations based on objective principles of logic, they found a vast multiplicity of generalizations, agglomerated products of thousands of years of practical reflection. Moreover, practical knowledge continued to develop independently for centuries after theoretic generalizations began to be substituted for practical generalizations, not only by philosophers but by scientific investigators. The entire development of human knowledge has been a dynamic, evolutionary process; although modern scientific knowledge represents the latest and most creative period of this process, its origins lie in the distant past.

We have emphasized hitherto the differences between practical knowledge and theoretic, scientific knowledge. The historical significance of these differences, however, will become clearer if we take into consideration certain basic *similarities* between the thinking of practical agents and the thinking of inductive scientists. Of course, we are not interested in activities which are unreflective, unaccompanied by conscious thinking.

First, a practical agent while he performs an action, just as a scientist when he carries on an investigation, has to select the data and the facts which he is going to use. Since the concrete empirical content of every datum differs in some respect from the empirical content of every other datum and every datum is a potentially inexhaustible source and center of diverse individual experiences which connect it with other data, in limiting his activity or his investigation to certain data and facts while excluding all the others, he is explicitly or implicitly guided by some principles of selection. These principles are derived from generalizations developed by his predecessors and transmitted to him in the course of learning. Most of the data within the range of his experience have already been classified according to more or less essential common and distinctive characteristics of their empirical content; more or less extensive regularities have been found among many of the facts accessible to his observation. He bases his selection upon these generalizations and limits his choice to data and facts, the essential nature of which is supposed to be already known and which he consequently expects to be relevant to his activity or his investigation.

Second, practical agents as well as scientists, in applying existing generalizations to particular data and facts which they use, are apt to find that the latter do not exactly conform with their expectations. Such nonconformity may be ignored and, if so, existing generalizations continue to guide subsequent activities or investigations. Sometimes, however, when expectations based on a generalization are not fulfilled, a practical agent as well as a scientist may become doubtful about the validity of the generalization. The doubt may be dispelled by connecting this generalization logically with some other existing generalization which is supposed to be absolutely certain. In such a case, the doubtful generalization either becomes accepted as true, the empirical evidence against it being explained away as irrelevant; or it is rejected as false, its previous claims to validity being branded as erroneous. But in other cases the doubt may give rise to a *problem* which cannot be solved by resorting to any existing generalization, only by new empirical evidence. And the solution of such a new problem results in a *new* generalization, which supplements, modifies, or supplants the old.

Now, the development of practical knowledge, the passage from practical knowledge to scientific knowledge, and the subsequent development of scientific knowledge are due entirely to the progressive emergence of new problems. Let us begin with a brief survey of the ways in which new problems emerge and become solved in the course of practical activity.

Evolution of practical generalizations

All empirical data with which a practical agent deals in the course of his activity are to him *values*, endowed with positive or negative significance of various kinds and degrees: pleasant or painful, useful or harmful, safe or dangerous, good or bad, benevolent or malevolent, sacred or impure, beautiful or ugly, etc. When he chooses some data as objects of his activity, that part of their empirical content is essential to him which at the time appears as positively or negatively significant. And inasmuch as in acting he tends to influence the objects of his activity by producing or preventing certain changes, those factual relationships between any datum he uses and other empirical data are important to him which help or hinder the production or prevention of those intended changes.

When discussing practical conceptions of order (Chapters 1 and 2), we pointed out that insofar as an agent consistently follows a pattern of activity established and transmitted to him by other agents and is guided by agglomerated results of past reflection, his selection of data is based on some taxonomic generalizations. He selects every datum by what he judges to be its identity with a particular datum previously used or its essential similarity to other data previously used in actions like the one he is performing. Thus, in hunting or fishing, he uses the same boat or the same weapon which has been used before, or a similar one, and tries to kill animals or catch fishes essentially similar to those which have been killed or caught before. In gardening, he chooses the identical plot which he or somebody else has cultivated in the past and by using the same or similar tools tries to raise plants not identical but similar to those which have been raised before. In a religious performance, he appeals to the same god to whom he and others have appealed before, uses either the same or similar sacred implements as have been used before, and tries to provoke a response similar to responses which he and others appear to have provoked before. Whether he selects the identical datum previously used or data similar to those previously used, in any case, he bases his selection on some accepted classification of data according to those similarities and differences which are considered practically important for the performance of actions of the kind he intends to perform. A particular boat, even though differing in some respects from other boats, belongs to the same class in contrast, say, with the class of garden plots. The god of a monotheistic religion is unique, and yet as a value has certain practically essential characteristics which make him relatively similar to some other values, e.g., human heroes, in contrast with such values as inanimate technical objects.

Furthermore, in trying to enact or counteract changes in his selected data, the agent anticipates that a certain change in one datum will cause a certain change in another datum. For instance, the hunter anticipates that a certain movement of the string of an arrow will cause the arrow to fly, and that the penetration of a flying arrow into a certain part of an animal's body will cause the death of the animal. A sailor anticipates that a storm will cause his boat to sink, but that this effect can be counteracted by skilful manipulation of the boat. Such anticipations are based on the agglomerated results of previous reflection about factual relationships between certain kinds of changes which certain kinds of data undergo; they are applications to particular cases of causal generalizations.

However, all generalizations by which practical agents are guided have definite limitations. A practical classification of data is obviously conditioned by valuations of them as objects of activity. How an agent will classify a particular datum depends upon the significance which this datum as a value has for him when in the course of his action he connects it with other values. A datum is not the same kind of practical object to agents who use it in combination with different objects while performing differently patterned actions. A tree is a different kind of object to the old gardener who planted it and takes care of it, to the child who climbs it, to the young lover who carves on its bark the initials of his beloved, to the artist who paints it as a part of the landscape, to the motorist whose car nearly crashes into it, and to the lumberman who cuts it. Such various classifications of a datum as a value cannot be systematized.

The same holds true of practical causal generalizations. Causal generalizations about changes imply taxonomic generalizations about the data which are changing. A practical agent does not think of changes in general as abstract processes; he is only concerned with specific, practically important changes of those values which he is using. For instance, many kinds of material objects may be observed to move in space. But hunters, sailors, and herdsmen do not generalize about movements as such. A hunter using a bow and arrow applies whatever knowledge he has about relationships between specific movements of arrows, as causes, and deaths of animals at which arrows are aimed, as effects, and some auxiliary knowledge about other causes which may interfere with the intended effects: e.g., movements of hunted animals, stray winds which are apt to deflect arrows, and magical rites which make bows and arrows effective or ineffective. A sailor in a rowboat combines knowledge of relationships between specific movements of boats, as effects, and specific movements of oars, as causes, with his knowledge about movements of water and about winds, as causes, and movements of boats, as effects—perhaps adding to it some knowledge about the causative power of good or evil spirits who may help or hinder him in reaching the harbor. None of these causal generalizations interest the shepherd who controls the movements of his sheep with the help of his dog by entirely different techniques.

According to our hypothesis, every step in the development of practical knowledge begins with a new problem. Not many problems, however, which emerge in the course of practical actions lead to this development, for most of them, as practical thinkers conceive them, are not new. In our previous discussion of practical problems, we mentioned that they usually emerge in cases of unexpected failure, sometimes—though less frequently—in cases of unexpected success. A practical problem is, first of all, the *personal* problem of a particular agent: How can he correct or prevent in subsequent actions the kind of failure which he (or somebody else) has committed; or how can he achieve in subsequent actions the kind of success which he (or somebody else) has achieved? What such a personal problem means from the point of view of existing knowledge depends upon the explanation of failure or success. The prevalent explanation, as we have seen, is in terms of the causative power and/or wisdom of this particular agent as compared with other agents. When a traditional pattern has become firmly established, there are always supposed to be some agents who know how to perform successfully actions of this type and who are endowed with the causative power needed for this performance. If so, the kind of problem which a particular agent is trying to solve is considered by thinkers familiar with the established pattern as having been already solved, probably many times. Its emergence raises doubts about the wisdom and power of the agent, but no doubts about the practical effectiveness of the knowledge on which it is based. Children, students, laymen, unskilled workers, and ordinary citizens have many problems which are explained by their personal weakness or ignorance in comparison with adults, teachers, professionals, skilled workers, and political leaders. All such problems presumably can be solved either by acquiring the causative power and knowledge which those superior agents already possess or by enlisting their help and guidance.

Only when a practical thinker finds that even the wisest and most powerful agents are unable to solve a certain problem is he apt to redefine such a problem. Instead of conceiving his failure as rooted in individual ignorance, he may ascribe it to some deficiency of the established pattern with which all agents performing actions of a certain kind tend to conform. It becomes then an impersonal problem and a new problem in the sense that, so far as he knows, it has never before been solved. The only way it can be solved is by initiating a change in the existing pattern, which will make the performances of all the agents who will follow his initiative more effective than the performances of those who conform with the traditional pattern. In short, the solution of a new, impersonal practical problem is provided by *invention*.

We are using the term "invention" to denote only conscious innovations which originate in critical reflection about past actions and are intended to guide future actions. We do not include under this concept a mere deviation from an instinctive or habitual pattern which succeeds when the latter fails. When a rat, after many attempts, finds a way out of a maze, this is not an invention. When Ariadne in the famous myth, knowing that all who had entered the Labyrinth were lost, advised Theseus to carry a spool of thread, one end of which was attached to the entrance, so that he could find his way back, this was an invention. An invention occasionally does start with some unintended, accidental deviation which occurs during the performance of an action; but this does not change the established pattern, unless the results of this action are compared with those of past actions, and the consequences of the regular use of this deviation in future actions are predicted.

Inasmuch as an invention in this sense implies a challenge to the authority of those agents who maintain the established pattern, its general acceptance always meets some resistance, as is well known to all historians of inventions. How this resistance becomes eventually overcome is a sociological problem which we shall investigate in a later work. The point right now is that the degree of resistance seems to depend upon several factors: the power and prestige of the agents who function as guardians of the established pattern, and the significance of the change which the inventor introduces. A challenge to the authority of priests or public rulers is more effectively resisted than a challenge to the authority of secular craftsmen or private experts on customs and mores. Established patterns of social organization are usually considered more significant for the preservation of order than established patterns of material techniques. And what seem to be major innovations meet more resistance than apparently minor innovations. The combination of these factors helps explain why innovations have been agglomerating mainly in the realm of material culture and why this agglomeration has proceeded slowly, by a sequence of minor changes or changes which seemed minor at the time, though they may later have proved to be of major historical importance as the original sources of many other inventions.[1]

Every invention implies some addition to existing practical knowledge, both taxonomic and causal. An inventor includes among the objects of his activity some data different from those which were included by his predecessors; for instance, he uses materials or instruments which were not

[1] Beginning with the second quarter of the last century, many histories of inventions have been published. Unlike histories of the sciences, however, most of them lack systematization. A curious example is *A History of Inventions, Discoveries and Origins*, by John Beckmann, trans. by William Johnston, 4th ed., 2 vols. (London, 1846). Inventions from the beginning of the eighteenth to the beginning of the nineteenth century are listed in the following order: Italian bookkeeping, odometer, machine for noting down music, refining gold and silver, cold or dry gilding, tulips, canary birds, I, 1-34.

Some later works are better, e.g., Louis Figuier, *Les Merveilles de la science, ou Description populaire des inventions modernes*, 4 vols. in 4° (Paris, 1868-70). Otis T. Mason's *The Origins of Invention. A Study of Industry among Primitive Peoples* (London, 1901), classifies techniques as most cultural anthropologists do; but the sequence of inventions through which these techniques developed is, of course, purely conjectural. Only recently have attempts been made to discover a continuity in historical trends. Cf. William F. Ogburn, *Social Change with Respect to Culture and Original Nature* (New York: B. W. Huebsch, 1922); S. Colum Gilfillan, *The Sociology of Invention* (Chicago: Follett Publishing Co., 1935); Robert J. Forbes, *Man the Maker* (New York: Schuman, 1950).

previously used, or produces something new, different from any previous product. This means that in selecting data he applies more or less new standards or classifies some of them differently than they were classified before. If by initiating a new technique he enacts or counteracts changes similar to those which agents employing the old technique have tried but failed to enact or counteract, the old generalizations concerning the causes of such changes become modified. And if he achieves by his new technique new changes considered more valuable than those which agents employing the old technique ever tried to achieve, he introduces an entirely new causal generalization.

For instance, the long sequence of inventions which led to the development of horticulture and agriculture, long before the beginnings of botany as a theoretic science, was accompanied by multiple, increasingly complex classifications of plants previously unclassified, unnoticed, or even nonexistent. The appearance of new kinds of tools resulted in generalizations about the materials from which these tools were made, their shape, size, etc. Many new generalizations evolved about soil, weather, quadrupeds, birds, and insects, depending on their supposed usefulness or harmfulness to the gardener or the farmer. Along with these came new generalizations about the causes which make plants of various species grow, or interfere with their growth, or bring their destruction; about the effects of special kinds of technical processes, such as digging, plowing, sowing, weeding, harvesting, fertilizing, etc.

The evolution of practical chemical generalizations is an instructive example. They were originally generalizations about the techniques which were considered effective for obtaining definite results.[2] The works of some classical writers—Theophrastus of Eresus, Vitruvius, Dioscorides, Pliny the Elder—and recipes found in papyri, intended to guide workers, indicate how vast was the multiplicity and variety of such techniques, cumulative results of the inventions which had been made throughout thousands of years in the culture areas accessible to Greek and Roman thinkers. Some generalizations include classifications of presumably basic substances and describe how they may be obtained in a "pure" state. Such substances are metals, especially gold and silver, salt, distilled oils, animal fats, vinegar, tannin, starch, and pigments. Most generalizations, however, refer to ways of making certain valuable products from these substances—making alloys, soldering metals, imitating precious metals, dyeing wool, producing medicines for curing the sick, etc. Classifications of these products were not based on their comparative chemical analysis, but on the purposes for which they

[2] Cf. John M. Stillman, *The History of Early Chemistry* (New York: Appleton, 1924), chap. I, "The Practical Chemistry of the Ancients" and chap. II, "Earliest Chemical Manuscripts."

were intended to be used. Special works were written, discussing the products so classified and the ways of producing them. Thus, Theophrastus wrote a treatise *Concerning Odors*, which dealt with the production of perfumes and unguents; the work of Dioscorides was almost entirely devoted to *Materia Medica*.

Such practical classifications of products and regulative generalizations about techniques continued throughout the Middle Ages and persist even now, cutting across the theoretic generalizations of scientific chemistry.[3] Thus, many books have been published concerning effective ways of making the products classified as metallic alloys, fertilizers, dyes, paints, perfumes, drugs, and wines—not to mention cookbooks.

Nevertheless, in the course of history, practical generalizations used in inventions have become increasingly dependent upon strictly theoretic generalizations developed independently of practical purposes. A modern inventor usually applies to practical problems certain results of objective, nonevaluative scientific research; and frequently he finds that to achieve his practical purpose he must carry on some additional objective research which leads beyond the range of his original problem.

The evolution of scientific generalizations about data

How does theoretic knowledge, free from evaluations, evolve out of practical knowledge?

It evolves in consequence of comparisons between practical generalizations and criticism of them by standards of logical consistency. Thinkers who in comparing practical generalizations find that the same data are differently conceived by agents who use them in different kinds of actions and that practical conceptions of causal relationships between changes differ, depending on what changes agents try to enact or counteract, are apt to problematize the validity of these generalizations. Such comparisons have been stimulated, on the one hand, by the growth of inventions and, on the other hand, by contacts between cultures which include different practical patterns. Both processes, by bringing to the attention of observers and thinkers the wide divergence of specific practical generalizations, contributed to the evolution of theoretic knowledge in classical antiquity as well as in modern times.

The obvious way of solving problems of logical inconsistency between practical generalizations about data and their changes is to abstract these data from the actions in which they are used and to discover some order

[3] See, e.g., Sir William A. Tilden, *Chemical Discoveries and Inventions in the Twentieth Century* (London, n.d.), chap. XXI, "Production of Dyes"; chap. XXII, "Drugs"; chap. XXIII, "Perfumes and Essential Oils"; chap. XXIV, "Vegetable Fiber and Cellulose"; and chap. XV, "Explosives."

among them which is not affected by the diversity and incompatibility of their practical valuations. In discussing the development of metaphysics, we noticed that it was intended to solve all such problems once and forever. By logical reasoning, the metaphysician tried to discover the absolute order of the entire universe as a rationally coherent system. Any generalizations which conflicted with such a theory of a rational universal order were false. In its extreme form, as represented by the Eleatic school, this principle led to the elimination of all practical knowledge: Since it was logically inconsistent, it had to be false. In less radical metaphysical theories, practical generalizations, though never entirely true, were estimated according to their approach to truth. A practical classification of data was theoretically acceptable in the measure in which it conformed with the ontological essence of data as elements of the universal system; a practical causal generalization was valid in the measure in which it agreed with the universal causal order.

The evolution of inductive science, as we know, proceeded differently. Instead of trying to make all knowledge logically consistent, the scientist, when starting an investigation, limited his task to the solution of a specific problem raised by the lack of logical consistency between certain existing generalizations when applied to particular empirical data or facts, and subjected these data or facts to a more thorough study. His problem was solved if he discovered among these data or facts some order hitherto unknown and, on the basis of this discovery, substituted for previous generalizations a new generalization which proved more valid when tested by empirical evidence. This procedure continued to be used whenever the extension of a theoretic generalization to data or facts, which had not previously been investigated, raised doubts about its validity. Search for an order hitherto unknown became, thus, a source of scientific problematization. The development of scientific knowledge progressed by new discoveries rather than by new inventions, although later discoveries were often made possible only by inventions which enabled scientists to observe phenomena hitherto inaccessible to observation.

The history of this development helps us understand why scientific knowledge about nature emerged earlier and progressed more rapidly than scientific knowledge about culture. This cannot be explained, as some metaphysicians have believed and still believe, by a uniform order inherent in the natural universe which enables scientists to reach increasingly extensive quantitative generalizations, and which eventually will result in an all-inclusive mathematical theory of nature. For the development of natural sciences has proceeded in two ways. Along with the progressive discovery of quantitative laws goes a progressive discovery of previously unknown varieties of natural phenomena which are qualitatively different from and irreducible to other varieties. The natural universe known to modern scientists is much richer and more widely diversified qualitatively than the universe known to Greek scientists; its study, therefore, requires greater specialization. Nor is this superiority of natural sciences explicable by the popular epistemological doctrine that natural phenomena are objective, because they can be scientifically observed and their observation tested by factual evidence, whereas cultural phenomena are subjective, inaccessible to scientific observation and testing. Though reliable evidence about cultural phenomena is, indeed, often more difficult to obtain than reliable evidence about natural phenomena (cf. Chapter 4), yet, as we have seen (Chapter 5), cultural data are objective, irreducible to anybody's subjective experience. As we shall see later on, there are two mutually supplementary sources of knowledge about cultural phenomena which together enable scientists to reach valid generalizations.

The explanation of the historical priority of natural sciences must be sought in the *very conception of empirical phenomena* which scientists originally substituted for practical, as well as for metaphysical, conceptions in carrying on inductive research. This conception proved to be heuristically successful, when applied to comparative studies of all kinds of natural phenomena, but it could not be so effectively applied to cultural phenomena. We shall try to give here a brief analysis of this conception. To avoid misunderstanding, we should point out that we shall not discuss *scientific theories*, only a presumably common *methodical approach* which natural scientists use in problematizing existing theories, reaching new hypotheses, and testing them.[4]

Since the growth of practical knowledge by way of inventions was most effective in the realm of material techniques and, as we have seen (Chapter 2), a partial separation of technology from magic and religion already existed in early culture and increased with the development of religion, the early attempts to introduce an objective, nonevaluative approach into comparative studies of those empirical phenomena with which technicians were

[4] It seems presumptuous on my part, since I am not a natural scientist, to make any general statements about natural sciences. In self-defense, I would like to point out that the methodical principles by which scientific research in the domain of nature is guided, have been investigated for a long time by methodologists, and that the generalizations here contained are primarily derived from their works. Now, scientific methodology is a joint product of the scientists who develop certain methods in the course of their research and of the philosophers who compare these methods. Some famous philosophers of science never did any scientific work, e.g., Francis Bacon; but some of them also functioned as scientists, e.g., Wilhelm Wundt. On the other hand, most scientists never philosophize about methods; but some do, e.g., Henri Poincaré. I owe whatever knowledge I may have about the methods of natural sciences mainly, though not exclusively, to John Stuart Mill, Ernest and Adrian Naville, Wilhelm Wundt, Henri Poincaré, Émile Meyerson, Frederick Barry, and Morris Cohen.

dealing met less resistance and were more successful than attempts to investigate objectively other kinds of phenomena.

Now, generalizations by which technicians are guided consist, first of all, in classifications of the data which they use. When scientists began to question the early classifications because they varied, depending on the purposes which the technicians were trying to realize, their first and main task was to find *a new basis of taxonomic generalizations*, by seeking to discover similarities and differences between data which were not dependent upon their practical valuations. Slowly and gradually they found that, though it is possible to take each particular natural datum separately and compare it with other natural data, also taken separately and according to their empirical characteristics, no consistent taxonomic generalizations can be reached by this method; for every datum has numerous, diverse characteristics, each of which makes it similar to data which may differ from it in other respects, so that eventually each may be included under many logically unrelated, overlapping classes. Nor can this difficulty be solved by the ontological doctrine according to which, underlying these empirical similarities and differences, certain ultimate essential properties exist by which natural data can be classified. Scientists have learned to reject the assumption that an empirical datum can be defined as a self-existing object, an entity independent of other objects. Instead, they work under the heuristic principle that every datum is connected by many factual relationships with other data, be they similar or different; he begins his investigation by observing these relationships in particular cases and seeks to discover some objective order among them. As a result of this approach, *every datum becomes conceived either as one of several interdependent components of an orderly system or as an orderly system of interdependent components or as both a system and a component of a more comprehensive system.*

This investigation proceeds by analysis or by synthesis, eventually supplementing one of these methods by the other. The analytic method, best exemplified in biological sciences, starts with the assumption that a certain empirical datum, e.g., a particular animal or plant, is really a combination of anatomically interconnected components; it distinguishes each of these components from others and tries to discover those physiological relationships between them which integrate them functionally into a living organism. Further analysis discovers that these components are themselves systems, though less complex than the organism as a whole. The synthetic method starts with the assumption that certain empirical data, each of which is given separately, are really interconnected components of one orderly system; it tries to reconstruct this system theoretically by observing what factual relationships of interdependence exist between these data. This is, for instance, how the solar system has been slowly reconstructed. Both methods are combined in experimental physics and chemistry, where theoretic analysis and synthesis are supplemented and tested by technical analysis of existing systems and technical construction of new systems.

Classification of data as systems or components of systems obviously implies that every particular empirical system can be scientifically defined and compared with other particular systems also scientifically defined. Such scientific definition of a particular system is possible only if and insofar as this system constitutes in some respects a distinct, separate whole and can be investigated in abstraction from the infinite wealth and complexity of the empirical universe. Its composition has to be limited: Each datum which it includes as a component must be identifiable and distinguishable from all other data of human experience, unlimited in number and diversity, which are not its components. Its inner order must be limited to certain distinctive, observable relationships of interdependence among the data which compose it, to the exclusion of all other relationships, unlimited in number and variety, which may be found between these data and other data of human experience.

To denote these essential conditions, which a particular system must fulfill to be scientifically definable and comparable with other systems, we need a specific term; for the general term "system" has several different meanings. We have discussed its metaphysical meaning, according to which the entire empirical universe is one logically consistent system. Many scientists who are not metaphysicians use it to denote a general category of order common to many particular systems. Thus, the physical universe often was, and still is, called a "system," only because the laws of physics are applicable to many, presumably to all, empirical combinations of spatial data. The expression "capitalistic system" is frequently used to denote an abstract economic pattern common to many diverse economic systems, each separately functioning under private ownership—banks, stores, factories, mines, farms, etc.—as if all of them were somehow integral components of one orderly system in accordance with Bastiat's ideal of "Economic Harmony." But we are concerned here with *particular* empirical systems, e.g., chemical compounds, living organisms, each of which can be included under a general class, if and insofar as it is similar to other particular systems in its composition and in the order of relationships between its components; obviously, however, this does not mean that all the systems of a certain logical class together constitute one system.

A term has been used by methodologists of natural sciences to denote such systems, the term "closed system." It was applied particularly to mechanical and thermodynamic systems. Years ago we borrowed this term and tried to apply it to social systems; but this application was misunderstood by social scientists, since closed system, as defined in physics, means a system isolated from external influences. Of course, no absolutely closed system in this sense exists in the empirical world; the term symbolizes merely the abstract concept of a common and distinctive structural pattern. But experimentators can construct relatively closed systems which approximate this pattern sufficiently to make scientific generalizations possible, though some of their generalizations may become partly invalidated by new developments in physical science.[5] From the very first, however, the concept of closed system, as used in physics, was obviously inapplicable in the realm of biology, since the very existence of living organisms depends upon their continuous connection with their environment. While a relatively closed physical or chemical system does not take in any new components during the course of its duration, this is obviously not true of a living organism viewed in the total course of its growth, nor yet, as we shall see later, of a cultural system. We shall adopt, therefore, the term *limited system* to denote any particular combination of particular interdependent components with an inner order of its own.

The substitution of scientific classifications of data as systems and as components of systems for the evaluative classification of data as objects by their empirical content and practical significance has affected *causal* generalizations. The concept of cause-effect relationship proved inapplicable to those processes occurring within a system which together constitute its inner dynamic order. In studying the movement of planets within the solar system or the combination of physiological processes within living organisms, it is impossible to prove that any one of them is the cause of which another is an effect. The principle of causation can be applied only to those cases in which a system undergoes a change which is not explicable by its own dynamic order. Such a change has to be explained and can be explained only as an effect of some change which occurred outside of the system. A comparative study of the effects of certain external changes upon systems of certain general classes—physical, chemical, or biological—has led not only to increasingly exact causal generalizations, but also to generalizations concerning the *functional dependence* of certain systems upon certain external conditions, e.g., the functional dependence of living organisms upon geophysical conditions.

Finally, the methodical progress of scientific studies of systems has led to the development of *genetic* theories which represent a relatively new kind of scientific generalization. Empirically limited systems are not eternal; they begin to exist at a certain time. This raises the problem of explaining their origin. Metaphysical explanations in terms of the creative will of

[5] See Albert Einstein and Leopold Infeld, *The Evolution of Physics* (New York: Simon & Schuster, 1938), pp. 52-54.

supernatural agents as primary cause or in terms of an accidental convergence of separate elements (Democritus and the Epicureans) have been rejected as unsupported by factual evidence. A comparative study of the specific factual origin of systems of a well-defined class, e.g., animals, plants, or chemical compounds, shows that the processes of formation of these systems regularly occur under definite conditions and manifest a definite similarity. Furthermore, as research bearing upon the past discloses the gradual appearance in the course of time of many new classes of systems, e.g., new animal species which did not exist before, scientists investigate comparatively the origin of these classes.

There seems to be considerable historical evidence that important advances in all natural sciences, at least until the beginning of the twentieth century, were mostly due to inductive studies of empirical data conceived as limited systems or components of systems. It is obviously not our task to investigate the evolution of natural sciences; this has been done and is being done by specialists. We shall mention only some well-known trends in this evolution which help us understand the difference between the approach used by natural scientists and the approach later developed by cultural scientists.

Examples of generalizations about limited systems in natural sciences[6]

The history of zoology and botany, recently and partially integrated into biology, gives the most conclusive evidence of this heuristic conception of empirical data as limited systems.[7] A living organism exists in the empirical world independently of the investigator; it is obviously limited in space, is accessible to direct observation, and usually lasts long enough to be adequately observed. Moreover, the diversity of living organisms is manifestly much greater than that of any other category of natural data; consequently, some systematic classification is indispensable, and any discovery of a previously unobserved variation is apt to raise a taxonomic problem. Here we shall refer mostly to the history of zoology, which became an independent objective science earlier than botany.

[6] A number of valuable historical works were published during the nineteenth and twentieth centuries dealing with the development of special natural sciences: astronomy, physics, chemistry, zoology, botany, and biology. Most of these works are sufficiently popular to be understood by nonspecialists. The content of this section is derived from some of the twentieth-century publications in these realms. We are omitting here altogether the history of mathematics, which is not a natural science in the sense of a science investigating natural data inductively, as well as histories of geology, geography, oceanography, where the concept of a limited system is seldom applied.

A vast amount of historical material is contained in biographies of natural scientists. We shall use some of it in our next chapter and in a later work on *Social Roles*.

[7] This survey is mainly based on *The History of Biology* by Nils Erik Nordenskiöld, trans. by L. B. Eyre (New York: Tudor, 1936).

The substitution of a theoretic classification of organisms, founded on objective comparative observation, for practical classification, based primarily on the usefulness (or harmfulness) of animals and plants to human agents, began under the influence of philosophy. Aristotle was the pioneer, the first to develop a general zoological theory. This included a classification of animals by four different characteristics: their ways of living, their actions, their habits, and their bodily parts—the last the most important—as well as a rather superficial study of their reproduction and a dogmatic doctrine of their evolution from lower to higher forms. His immediate successors did not achieve much methodical advance in the taxonomy of animals. Pliny the Elder in his *Natural History* gave an encyclopedic survey of the various animals described by other writers, but without any systematic order; and his work remained the supreme authority during the Middle Ages and early Renaissance. No scientific zoological research was carried on until the sixteenth century, and it remained for a long time almost exclusively descriptive. General works on animals, like Konrad Gesner's *Historia animalium*, although more reliable and critical than Pliny's, were still encyclopedic; Gesner lists animal forms with common Latin names in alphabetical order. Nils Nordenskiöld terms this kind of work "zoography" (*op. cit.*, Chap. XIII). Indeed, no systematic taxonomy was possible without a comparative anatomy, based not only on external, but on internal anatomical characteristics. While human anatomy, essential for surgical purposes, began in antiquity and, notwithstanding the persistent opposition against dissection of cadavers, reached full development in the first half of the sixteenth century (Andreas Vesalius), no such practical interest stimulated anatomical analysis of animals. Severino started it in the first half of the seventeenth century; he introduces his work *Zootonia Democritea* "with a defense of the comparative study of the anatomy of different animals. . . . He [Severino] finds it best to begin the study of anatomy with animals, as they often have simpler and more easily accessible organization than man, with whom, moreover, animal dissection offers interesting possibilities of comparison" (Nordenskiöld, p. 107).

In the following century, George de Buffon's *Histoire naturelle*, complete works, 54 vols. (Paris, 1749-1804), contained fourteen volumes devoted to quadrupeds and eighteen volumes to birds, with a comparative anatomical analysis by his collaborator Daubenton. At the beginning of the nineteenth century, Cuvier reached a systematic taxonomy of animals which remained influential for a long time; it was based on a sufficiently thorough anatomical research to enable him to initiate the progressive growth of paleontology, which reconstructs extinct classes from fossil bones. After the invention of the microscope, the development of cytology and microbiology resulted in a discovery of the whole category of monocellular organisms comparable to the cells which compose polycellular organisms.

Generalizations about the effects of external influences upon organisms, especially human organisms, had begun in prehistoric times, but they referred almost exclusively to the presumed causes of sickness and death and the presumed curative effects of various medicines; seldom, if ever, were they tested by a comparative observation of the processes occurring within organisms. Scientific causal generalizations were not possible until an investigation of the interdependent physiological functions within living organisms and a realization of their dependence upon the natural environment developed. Such an investigation was obviously much more difficult than the study of anatomy and morphology; it may be said to have begun with Harvey's discovery of the circulation of the blood; and not until the first quarter of the nineteenth century was a systematic work of physiology written (by Rudolphi). Ontogenetic theories, based on comparative studies of heredity, started in the first half of the nineteenth century. And only by using the theoretic results of previous taxonomic, functional, causal, and ontogenetic research could biologists formulate general scientific theories of organic evolution.

In the course of this history, experiments were increasingly used, first to test the causal explanations of specific changes within organisms of certain classes, later to test physiological, ontogenetic, and finally phylogenetic hypotheses; and many hypotheses resulted in new theories. Although in consequence of experimental research a static classification of organisms, based on their morphological and physiological similarities and differences, is no longer the foundation of all causal, functional, and phylogenetic theories, and new theories of life are beginning to emerge, yet even the biologist who questions the validity of established taxonomies has to carry on his research by studying comparatively particular organisms, simple or complex, as limited systems in the course of their duration.

Nor has modern biochemistry invalidated this heuristic conception. The progress of chemistry has contributed much to the progress of biology; but, although it has been proved that living organisms include the same chemical elements which are included in many anorganic systems, this similarity of composition does not eliminate the obvious empirical difference between a chemical compound, however complex, and a mammal or even an amoeba.

And, because of this obvious difference, the evolution of scientific chemistry proceeded differently from that of biology. Material substances as empirical data appeared much less complicated, less diverse, and easier to classify than animals or plants; their quality did not depend on their size, and most of them could be arbitrarily divided and subdivided into parts; technicians could produce many of them artificially.

The concept of elements as simple, uniform, permanent, universal substances of which all the diverse and changing empirical substances were composed was, as we know, introduced by the early metaphysicians who tried to explain the entire universe as emerging from one material essence. Empedocles combined different conceptions of the original matter into his famous theory of four elements—earth, water, air, and fire—which lasted for more than twenty centuries. All other empirical substances, however they differed, had to be various combinations of some or all of these four elements, though it was impossible to prove it by factual evidence. Eventually, throughout the Middle Ages, different theories evolved and were finally systematized by Paracelsus, who tried to prove by rudimentary experiments the theory of three primary elements (*tria prima*) contained in all material things: sulphur, mercury, and salt.

However, not until the seventeenth century did the methodical, experimental search for chemical elements begin, guided by the definition of Robert Boyle, according to which an element is a substance which resists analysis. This implied the heuristic principle that every empirical substance which has not yet proved to be an element by reliable factual evidence must be hypothetically considered a compound, an integrated combination of elements, and subjected to thorough experimental analysis. Analysis means purposive decomposition of a compound, which can be achieved by subjecting it to certain extraneous influences. The results of experimental analysis are validated by experimental synthesis, whenever the same kinds of elements brought together under definite conditions produce the same kind of compound. Thus, every material datum can be classified, together with other data, either as a certain element or as a system composed of certain elements.[8]

In the course of three hundred years, more than eighty different elements have been discovered, most of the known compounds analyzed and classified, and numerous new compounds synthetically produced. Much of this development, however, was achieved only after, toward the end of the eighteenth century, increasingly exact quantitative studies of the phenomena of chemical combinations were started and, later, a conception of elements and their relationships within chemical systems was adopted which provided a general hypothetical explanation of observable factual regularities. This was the atomic theory propounded by Dalton, which assumes that each element consists of minute separate particles, all alike in size, weight, and chemical properties, and that, when a chemical combination takes place between any two or more elements to form a compound, a definite and limited number of the particles of one kind are intimately associated with a definite and limited number of another kind. Later investigation showed that in every

[8] Stillman, *op. cit.,* pp. 320 ff.

case the associated atoms occupy in space relative positions toward one another which are definite, and that the properties of the body are connected with and dependent on the configuration of the resulting mass, which is called a molecule.[9]

Eventually elements became classified not only qualitatively, but quantitatively by their atomic weight, first by Mendeléyev,[10] and compounds classified not only qualitatively by the elements of which they are composed, but quantitatively according to the number of elements which their molecules presumably include.[11] Although the atoms and their spatial arrangement in molecules were merely conceptual constructs, not observable phenomena, their heuristic significance was unquestionable, since their intellectual use in comparative studies of empirical phenomena led to new discoveries which, when applied in practice, resulted in many new inventions.

Through this evolution, chemistry came to be increasingly dependent upon physics, especially for the explanation of dynamic changes in chemical systems under the impact of physical forces and, lately, of changes in elements.[12] The physical conception of atoms as energetic systems may prove even more productive heuristically than the conception of atoms as indivisible particles.[13] Nevertheless, the empirical phenomena with which chemists deal in experimental research still remain material data, located in laboratories, observable with or without the need of special instruments, classifiable either as elements or as systems of elements which are undergoing observable changes. And, as Wundt points out, in chemistry *inductive* methods are more fully and thoroughly used than in any other natural science.[14]

The evolution of physics differed from the evolution of biology, as well as from that of chemistry, for two reasons. In the first place, it started with the study of technical systems constructed to produce definite changes in natural data; and investigators sought primarily to reach generalizations not about their composition, since this was known, but about functional relationships between their components, as well as causal explanations of changes which occurred in their functioning under external influences. Thus, "the origin of mechanics is to be found in the attempts made to explain the mode of action of the various instruments and machines invented by man for the purpose of performing work, and to explain the phenomena of mo-

[9] Tilden, *op. cit.*, pp. 123-24.
[10] *Ibid.*, pp. 125 ff.
[11] *Ibid.*, chap. XII, "Architecture of Molecules," pp. 213-28.
[12] Wilhelm Wundt, "Die Logik der Chemie," in *Logik,* II (Stuttgart, 1907), 489-538.
[13] Cf. A. Frederick Collins, *The March of Chemistry* (Philadelphia: Lippincott, 1936), chap. I.
[14] Wundt, *op. cit.*, p. 490.

tion."[15] Second, throughout its history, physics was subjected to the influence of mathematics, and physicists concentrated upon such functional and causal relationships about which exact quantitative generalizations could be reached.

The evolution from practical to theoretic generalizations, however, required a comparative analysis of technical systems which served very different practical purposes; and scientific tests of these generalizations were achieved by constructing systems for strictly experimental purposes. Archimedes, famous for having used such objective comparative analysis and experimentation in his studies of static relations between components of a mechanical system (*On Plane Equilibria* and *On Floating Bodies*), is supposed to be one of the first who applied mathematical principles to his generalizations. Such studies were not resumed until the beginning of the sixteenth century, by Leonardo da Vinci, Simon Stevinus, and others. Experimental studies and measurements of dynamic relations between several components of a mechanical system, as manifested in their motions, did not start until the beginning of the seventeenth century (Galileo, Huygens, and others); their results culminated in Newton's theory. Technical instruments intended to produce light or to use sunlight for various practical purposes or to improve vision are very old; but scientific generalizations about light —reflection, refraction, and polarization—were not reached until studies of changes in light began to be carried on within closed spatial areas by means of selected technical implements (plates, crystals, prisms, and lenses), by Snell, Bartolini, Huygens, Newton, and others. The discovery of the finite velocity of light required astronomical observation; but an observatory is, after all, also a limited technical system, into which light coming from celestial sources is admitted under definite experimental conditions. Scientific generalizations about electricity and magnetism did not develop fully until limited electromagnetic systems were invented and used for experimental purposes by Gray, Canton, Cavendish, Volta, Davy, Oersted, Ampère, and Faraday. The energetic theory of heat was evolved and proved after thermodynamic systems began to be constructed by Davy, Canton, Gay-Lussac, Mayer, Joule, Sadi-Carnot, Kelvin, and Clausius.[16]

Now, the laws based on comparative analysis of functionally interdependent processes and causally explicable changes occurring within experimental systems are presumed to be applicable to natural systems existing independently of the experimenter, under the condition that they be essentially like the model systems constructed by the experimentator in their composition, structure, and functional order. However, according to the new

[15] H. Buckley, *A Short History of Physics* (London, 1927), p. 23.
[16] See Buckley, *op. cit.*, concerning the scientific contributions mentioned above; Florian Cajori, *A History of Physics* (New York: Macmillan, 1899); Henry Crew, *The Rise of Modern Physics* (Baltimore: Williams & Wilkins, 1935).

trends in physical theory, this condition, though it may be empirically approximated, is never fulfilled. The substitution of the concept of *field* for that of system, the elimination of the dualism of matter and energy underlying every experiment in which stable material objects must be used to study energetic processes, and finally the theory of relativity indicate that the physical order of the universe is not reducible to that category of order which is based on the conception of limited systems.[17] Nevertheless, without this conception modern physics could never have developed, for only by subjecting generalizations derived from this conception to quantitative tests of unprecedented exactness did physics discover previously unknown relationships between natural phenomena.

Indubitably, the reconstruction of the solar system is the best-known achievement of astronomers; it took about four thousand years to complete. The main obstacle, of course, was the geocentric conception of the universe, based on overwhelming empirical evidence. The movement of the stars seemed to fit very well into this conception. Only the complexity and apparent irregularity of the movements of planets made their inclusion into this orderly universe difficult. "The Chaldeans . . . compared the planets to capricious rams who escaped from the herd of stars to pasture at the will of their vagabond humor."[18] It was the will of the gods, limiting their movements to the range of the zodiac, which gave them whatever regularity they had; and the purpose of the gods was to inform men of events to come or perhaps to control these events.

After two thousand years or so, with the development of Greek philosophy and mathematics and the elimination of gods from the material world, we had a metaphysical theory of one universal system of moving spheres, with the earthly sphere as the center. This system, like all metaphysical systems, had to be logically perfect; consequently, a complex plurality of spherical movements of planets within the stellar sphere had to be devised. The attempt of Aristarchus to develop a heliocentric theory instead of a geocentric theory was rejected because it interfered with this established, logically consistent, though complicated, doctrine. The revolution that began with Copernicus and ended with Newton was much more than the elimination of geocentrism; it was the elimination of the absolute unity and perfection of the universe. The solar system became just one limited system within the universe, with an inner order representative of a general class which included all dynamic mechanical systems, whatever their size and complexity. This raised problems of the existence of other astronomical systems and of

[17] Cf. Einstein and Infeld, *op. cit.*; and Carl T. Chase, *Frontiers of Science* (New York: Van Nostrand, 1936).

[18] Bigourdan, *L'Astronomie*, pp. 17-26.

the causal and functional relations between them, as well as of their origin.[19]

Thus, whatever the future of the natural sciences may be—and, if anyone can predict it, I certainly cannot—there seems to be no doubt that their past and, for the most part, their present development is primarily due to the comparative analysis of empirical data defined as limited systems or elements of systems.

The problem of generalizations in the domain of culture

The scientific knowledge of data and facts which evolved from practical knowledge achieved objectivity and logical consistency because and insofar as it eliminated human valuations from its domain. Classifications of data as systems or components of systems are entirely independent of the practical significance of these data. For instance, the definition of a genus of animals or plants and its subdivision into species, based upon similarities and differences of their anatomical composition, structure, and physiological organization, is not affected by any judgments of hunters, breeders, gardeners, farmers, or lumbermen as to the usefulness or harmfulness of some of these animals or plants. Chemical classifications of materials as specific synthetic components of specific elements remain true, whatever the positive or negative valuations of some of these compounds or elements by engineers, pharmacists, or agriculturalists, who judge them with reference to certain practical purposes. Scientific laws of relationships between changes of these data are unaffected by any tendencies of practical agents to enact some of these changes as desirable or to counteract others as undesirable.

Consequently, all sciences which have developed by this process of redefining data in terms of an objective order of interdependence are sciences of nature. The scientists who contributed to their development gradually, but inevitably, had to exclude cultural data from the range of their research, since cultural data as human products cannot be defined without taking into consideration their significance as values for human agents. With the progress of scientific methods, it became increasingly evident that no logically consistent, objective generalizations in the domain of culture can be reached by the same approach as in the domain of nature, i.e., by analyzing and comparing particular data abstracted from the actions of those conscious agents who produce them and use them.

And yet there have been for many centuries systematic generalizations about values which often achieve a considerable degree of logical consistency, and the progress of science did not eliminate them. The substitution of

[19] Cf. Ernst Zinner, *Geschichte der Sternkunde* (Berlin, 1931). An instructive work. Unfortunately, the author divides the whole history of astronomy according to ethnic groups and treats the entire modern astronomy as a historical development of "die Sternkunde der Germanen."

theoretic for practical knowledge does not solve all practical problems. There still remain problems of the relative importance of the many different values which human agents are using and producing for the total active life of individuals and collectivities and for mankind as a whole. These problems are dealt with by what has been called in recent times the *philosophy of values*, with such specialized subdivisions as ethics, aesthetics, political and legal philosophy, philosophy of religion, and such synthetic disciplines as philosophy of history and general philosophy of culture.[20] Obviously, the method which the philosophy of values uses to solve its problems differs fundamentally from the method of inductive science. Instead of investigating the factual order of relations between data, the philosophy of values seeks to establish some universal standards of valuation which would be applicable to all human values, or at least to all values of a certain category, and enables the philosopher to construct a systematic hierarchy of values for the guidance of human agents.

We do not deny here the importance of the function which philosophers of values try to perform or the possibility of performing this function adequately. On the contrary, we believe that at this period of human history it is perhaps the most urgent of all the functions which thinkers can perform, though perhaps more difficult now than ever before, requiring an unusually broad historical knowledge of human values and a rare mastery of philosophic methods. But to realize any philosophical ideal, nonevaluative scientific knowledge of culture is indispensable; and the development of this knowledge has been impeded by unnecessary controversies between scientists and philosophers.

So long as theoretic thinking was still partly influenced by practical thinking, there was no clear distinction between scientific study of data and facts and philosophic standardization of values. Only after science gained complete freedom from practical considerations did such distinctions become possible. Kant was perhaps the first to establish this distinction clearly and consistently. And since in Kant's time only natural sciences had achieved theoretic objectivity, he limited the application of scientific methods to the study of nature. Kant saw two kinds of universal order, both products of reason, but irreducible to each other: the theoretic order of scientific laws applicable to natural phenomena, and the practical order of moral norms applicable to men as conscious agents. He recognized, indeed, a link between the two, but it was not an extension of the nonevaluative scientific approach to human valuations and actions; on the contrary, it was an extension of

---

[20] A historical survey of philosophic conceptions of values was written by me in Polish, *The Problem of Values in Philosophy* (Warsaw, 1910). So far as we know, the first systematic work under the title "Philosophy of Values" was that of Hugo Münsterberg, *Philosophie der Werte* (Leipzig, 1908). It includes, besides the disciplines here mentioned, also logic, epistemology, and metaphysics.

the evaluative approach to natural data in the form of aesthetic judgments.

Quite a few philosophers and scientists to this day accept that division and thus explicitly or implicitly exclude the possibility of applying scientific methods to the study of culture, believing that the world of culture is a world of values and that methodical reflection about values must be evaluative. For instance, when Morris Cohen in his well-known work *Reason and Nature* passed from the methodological discussion of natural sciences to the discussion of social studies, he introduced the evaluative approach.[21] Bertrand Russell applies the principle of scientific objectivity to mathematics and physics, but drops it entirely in his philosophic works dealing with social phenomena.

This point of view has penetrated deeply into popular and semipopular thinking. George Lundberg, in analyzing attitudes of United States senators toward social science, expressed during discussion of the bill to establish a National Science Foundation, shows that one of the main reasons given for excluding the section of the bill designed to make its provisions applicable also to social science was that the realm of data to which the term "social science" refers cannot be defined and investigated objectively. Social science, in the opinion of many senators, is not really science but (as Lundberg summarizes this opinion) a "nondescript category consisting mainly of reformist and propagandist ideologies and isms."[22]

Some philosophers of values and some natural scientists, however, try to overcome this distinction between the realm of nature as the exclusive domain of objective scientific method and the realm of culture as the exclusive domain of evaluative philosophic method by claiming the absolute supremacy of their own method in both realms and rejecting all the claims to validity of the other method. Some philosophers consider natural science itself as a human value and deny the very existence of scientific objectivity. On the other hand, some natural scientists consider the entire realm of culture, including philosophy, as an integral part of nature and deny the very existence of any kind of order among human values as such.

The reasoning of those philosophers of values about natural science is quite convincing up to a certain point. No doubt, scientific theories are cultural products of scientists as conscious human agents; and like other cultural products, they are values to the agents who produce them and use them. The philosopher is justified in evaluating them comparatively in relation to other human values, including them in some systematic hierarchy of values, and trying to prove by some universal standards that they should

[21] Morris Cohen, *Reason and Nature* (New York: Harcourt, 1931), Book III, "Reason in Social Science."

[22] George Lundberg, "The Senate Ponders Social Science," *Scientific Monthly* (May, 1947).

be subordinated to some other values, more important for mankind as a whole—as in the recent emphasis on the need of making physics serve constructive rather than destructive purposes.

But if the philosopher applies to scientific theories the humanistic co-efficient, as historians of culture do in studying all cultural products, he will find that these theories, considered from the point of view of scientists themselves, differ in certain essential respects from other cultural products as viewed by those who produce them and use them. First, a scientific theory is to the scientist an ideational product of reflection about data; unlike a technical product, it is not included among the data which it uses as material and cannot in any way modify these data, though some technical agent may be guided by it in planning and producing realistically a new invention. Second, a scientific theory as viewed by the scientist differs from other ideational products, such as works of theology, of moral, political, educational, or aesthetic philosophy (also sometimes called "theories") in that it does not include any valuations by the producer of the data to which it refers, only of scientific theories themselves.

Inasmuch as the scientist seeks to discover some order which actually exists among the data he investigates and is aware from critical comparison of practical generalizations that any valuations of these data on his part is apt to interfere with such discoveries, one of the basic standards by which scientists estimate the validity of scientific theories is their nonevaluative content, in other words, their theoretic objectivity. These judgments are not affected by the fact that once a discovery of an existing order is made, it can be used by practical agents in planning and attempting to realize a more or less different order which, by their practical standards of valuation, is preferable to the order which scientists have discovered.

The most conclusive proof, however, of the essential difference between the theoretic activities of inductive scientists and practical activities is that scientists have often succeeded in diverting the latter from practical to strictly theoretic purposes. We refer to the development of technical ex-perimentation subordinated to objective research in the domain of natural sciences. The analysis and the synthesis which result in the discovery of natural systems are primarily intellectual activities; but beyond a certain stage they have to be assisted by the invention of new technical instruments and operations especially devised to enable investigators to experience data which were previously not experienced and to observe facts hitherto un-observed—such as the telescope and the microscope. Many practically use-less physical systems are constructed in laboratories for theoretic purposes, in search for physical laws. By increasingly exact operations of measure-ment, differences and changes are discovered which were previously un-noticed or neglected as irrelevant by practical thinkers, though presumed to be important for scientific comparison and generalization. Of course, many technical instruments and operations which scientists use for theoretic purposes were originally invented for practical purposes; the thermodynamic engine is a case to the point. But even in such cases their diversion to theoretic usage required some new modifications.

Thus, the denial by philosophers that scientific thinkers are objective (in the sense in which scientists use this term) is contradicted by the study of valuations applied to science as a cultural product in comparison with other cultural products. And comparative study of standards of valuation is an essential condition of philosophic systematization of human values.

We shall postpone the discussion of some recent sociological theories of knowledge which assert that science can never be objective, because scientists as participants in various cultures and social structures are inevitably influenced in their scientific thinking by practical interests. We take the liberty, however, of expressing here our opinion that this assumption not only conflicts with philosophic reasoning, but is contradicted by sociological evidence.

We turn now to those natural scientists who deny the existence of any order among cultural data which is not reducible to the order of nature. Unless they are materialists and have become involved in the vicious circle of materialistic metaphysics, they will not deny that cultural data are values to human agents and that their valuations can influence objective reality. Instead, they try to reduce values to combinations of two categories of natural phenomena. A value is defined as a natural datum *plus* a psychological process which the experience of this datum causes in the human individual. While this process is usually denoted by psychological terms, such as "feeling" or "emotion," it is conceived as a natural process conditioned by the biological structure and functioning of the human organism.

This approach to values, however, led to problems which proved scientifically insolvable. It seemed to work as long as both the data which human individuals evaluate and the human individuals themselves were defined and classified as natural systems, and the regularities which were found in psychobiological processes of valuation could be ascribed to causal dependence or functional interdependence between changes in those systems. For instance, the naturalistic conception of values was approximately applicable to cases where human organisms, distinguished by sex, age, or other natural characteristics, regularly manifested a very different kind of feeling or emotion, when stimulated by unorganic objects or plants or animals or other human individuals of a certain natural class. But it did not work among human individuals who did not essentially differ as organisms in their natural characteristics when some, in experiencing objects of a certain natural class, regularly manifested one kind of feeling or emotion, while others, in experiencing objects of the same class, regularly manifested a very different kind of feeling or emotion. And it was still more obviously inapplicable to cases when the data which human individuals experienced were not definable as natural systems, e.g., gods, mythical events, products of fiction, abstract ideas; and nonetheless many of these individuals, experiencing such data, regularly manifested one kind of psychological process, while many others manifested psychological processes of a different kind— all this notwithstanding any similarities or differences which a scientific observer might find in studying those individuals as organic systems.

When comparative studies of cultures developed, more and more similarities and differences between human valuations were discovered which proved inexplicable by the inductive methods of natural science. As the cultures of particular collectivities grow in wealth and complexity of data, as the experiences of cultural data by particular individuals expand from the time of their birth onward, factual regularities of valuations increasingly conflict with naturalistic theories. Since they are regularities, not merely irregular deviations from causal or functional laws of nature, they indicate the existence of some factual order in the world of human values different from the natural order, but also discoverable only by inductive methods. The discovery of this order, however, required a new problematization in the domain of cultural studies, and this emerged rather slowly.

Idiography and typology in studies of cultural data

In surveying the approach to cultural data developed by historians of culture, we have found that an investigator who has access to products of human activities and understands symbolic expressions of human experiences can identify and describe a cultural datum in its historical duration and extension as common datum of many conscious human agents. If he consistently applies the humanistic coefficient, views a cultural datum not as it appears to him, but as it was and is experienced and evaluated by those human agents who produced it and used it, his investigation will be scientifically objective in the sense that it will not be affected by his own practical valuations.

This approach, however, prevents the historian from generalizing about cultural data by the same methods which natural scientists so effectively use in their domain of research, since he cannot overcome the original inconsistency of practical generalizations by abstracting data from human actions and comparing them in terms of an order of relationships entirely independent of human valuations.

An investigator who studies cultural data as historical products has, thus, to describe every particular datum not as a unit of a general class, but as something unique, taking into consideration as much of the entire wealth of its content and meaning as he can. This idiographic emphasis in historical studies of particular cultural data must be clearly distinguished from the scientifically impossible efforts to reconstruct total human collectivities or societies as both natural and cultural complexes which we have discussed in Chapter 4. A humanist who studies in historical perspective Sophocles' *Antigone*, the Parthenon, Virgil's *Aeneid*, the Cathedral of Notre Dame, Dante's *Divine Comedy*, Michael Angelo's "Last Judgment," Descartes' *Discourse on Method*, Beethoven's *Ninth Symphony*, or Byron's *Don Juan* identifies and describes each of these data as distinguishable from all others because of its own content and meaning, not because he incorporates it as an integral part into the infinitely complex natural and cultural whole called Greek, Roman, Italian, French, Austrian, or English society, even though, to understand what it was and is as a common datum of human experience, he must have some knowledge of the cultural background from which it emerged.

The more thorough and objective a historian is in investigating particular cultural data as historical products, the more difficult it is for him to generalize. For, inasmuch as the same datum is differently experienced and evaluated by the various agents to whom it is given, how can the historian decide which of these experiences and valuations are more and which are less important logically, by what part or aspect of its empirical content and meaning this datum should be defined and classified in comparison with other data? Take the realm of religion. It is not even always easy to decide whether a particular cultural product should be subsumed under the general category of religious data. A painting or sculpture of a Greek or Roman god was probably a religious datum when produced in classical antiquity, but became an aesthetic datum to artists of the Renaissance. Should Lenin, as experienced and evaluated after his death by the Russian people, be classified as a religious or a social datum?

And within the category of religious data different or even conflicting definitions and classifications are possible, depending on whose point of view the historian takes. For instance, Greek gods are primarily defined by mythologists according to those characteristics which most Greek believers seem to have unanimously ascribed to them; and yet the mythologist must take into consideration: first, the fact that many a deity was at the same time differently conceived and evaluated by people in different culture areas or by inhabitants of different city-states; second, that all these conceptions and evaluations were changing in the course of time. Christian churches, denominations, and sects have different, sometimes conflicting, ontological and ethnical conceptions of God, Jesus, Mary, the angels, devils, prophets, apostles, saints, and sinners. And how can a mythologist draw comparative generalizations which would include in the same logical class particular Greek, Christian, Egyptian, Hindu, Mexican, and Peruvian religious beings?[23]

Actually, the only kind of comparative generalization about cultural data that has been made and can be made is typological, not taxonomic. A particular datum—a god, a hero, a work of art or literature—selected and defined by what appears to be the most essential part of its content and meaning, serves as a model for defining other data as more or less similar to it. This

[23] The difficulty of reaching comparative generalizations about mythical beings is clearly manifested in various attempts of famous mythologists to develop a systematic theory of myths. Thus, F. Max Müller, *Contributions to the Science of Mythology*, 2 vols. (London, 1897), starts with the study of the Veda and bases his conclusion "with regard to the origin of mythology in general" on the meaning of names given in Vedic books to mythical beings. These names indicate agents who produce important natural phenomena (pp. 112-14). Names with the same meanings can be found in other "Aryan" languages. Thus, all myths can be classified according to natural phenomena. Müller pays little attention to the mythologies of nonliterate peoples.

Alexander S. Murray, *Manual of Mythology* (New York: Scribner, 1897), seeks for and finds some similar beliefs in the mythologies of all "Indo-Germanic races, from the Ganges to Iceland," assuming that, since their mythologies had a common origin, they remain essentially alike. On the other hand, he also states that "everywhere there existed among men the same sensitiveness to the phenomena of nature and the same readiness and power of imagining invisible beings" (p. 20); and he implicitly assumes that, because of this universal uniformity of human feelings and imagination, there must be an essential uniformity in all mythologies.

Andrew Lang, *Custom and Myth* (London, 1904), also postulates an essential similarity of human nature as a basis for comparative generalizations about mythologies. "Similar conditions of mind produce similar practices, apart from identity of race or borrowing of ideas and matters" (p. 24); his basis for classifying myths is not the classification of natural phenomena, but the classification of human needs. "The myths, like the arrowheads, resemble each other because they were originally framed to meet the same needs out of the same material" (pp. 24-25). His works, however, contain only monographic studies.

Ernest A. Gardner, "Mythology," *Encycl. of Rel. and Ethics*, Vol. IX, conceives the main subject of mythology to be mythical stories rather than mythical beings. He gives two classifications of myths: by the content of the ideas they express (twelve classes), and by their origin (seven classes).

Gradually the progress of historical and ethnological studies compelled mythologists to resign their ambition of developing a systematic general science of mythology. One of the most prolific mythologists, Salomon Reinach, *Cultes, mythes et religions*, 3 vols. (Paris, 1912, 1923, 1928), limited his work almost entirely to descriptive studies of a multiplicity of particular myths. Most instructive is the statement of William S. Fox, the author of "Greek and Roman Mythology," Vol. I of the collective work mentioned before, *The Mythology of All Races:*

"The author's purpose is to present the myths of Greece and Rome as vehicles of religious thought. . . . The system of interpretation to be followed is at best the comparative method. The entire stress, however, will not be laid upon the similarities or parallel instances; much emphasis will be placed upon differences. . . . In handling the legends singly, the following features will be noted: the peculiar cast of the conception, the names and epithets of the gods and heroes and the several forms of their symbols, the various versions of the myth, and the traditional interpretation of antiquity; but the utmost caution will be taken to avoid basing conclusions on any one of these features in isolation from the others. Finally, it will constantly be borne in mind that a myth is after all a process and not a finished product" (pp. lix-lx).

kind of comparison has been widely, though not always reflectively and systematically, used in comparing mythical beings of different religions, in generalizing about works of art and literature in different periods and cultures, in defining words in dictionaries, and especially in generalizing about human beings as social data.

Inasmuch, however, as any particular datum can be selected and defined so as to serve as a model for defining other data, the multiplicity and variety of typological generalizations is theoretically unlimited. Consequently, every such generalization can overlap many others. And since cultural data are values to human agents, either positive or negative, for every typological generalization an antithetic generalization can be formed.

Typological generalizations about human individuals as empirical data are perhaps the most familiar and instructive examples. We have seen that every individual as an object of action is mainly, though not exclusively, experienced by the agent as a psychological entity, a conscious being. Viewed in historical perspective, such a being is a cultural datum, like any other cultural datum differently defined and evaluated in the course of its duration by the various agents who use it in their actions.

All practical generalizations about human individuals as objects of actions are essentially evaluative, positively or negatively. We have discussed such generalizations, expressed in various stereotypes (Chapter 2), and found that they inevitably conflict, for those who accept them are either positively or negatively prejudiced toward individuals whom they include under a certain class.

Now, when psychology as an objective science began to develop, psychologists dropped such stereotypes. But they have not been able to substitute any exact and consistent taxonomy of human individuals as conscious beings, psychological entities, inasmuch as an individual's total conscious life, unlike his organism, is not a system which includes only a limited number and diversity of interdependent components with an inner structural and functional order of its own. The multiplicity and variety of experiences which constitute the content of his lifelong stream of consciousness are unlimited, interconnected with experiences of others, and their relations widely diverse and continually changing. Every human individual in his total conscious life is unique in the sense that, although he belongs to the general logical class of human individuals, it is impossible to subsume him under one and only one subclass.

Consequently, those psychologists who continued to be interested in studying human individuals as psychological wholes, had to resort to typology. They compared individuals in terms of diverse typical combinations of characteristics or traits, each manifested in various degrees by many individuals. This dates from classical antiquity when two entirely unconnected typologies developed: a sociopsychological typology, exemplified by the "Characters" of Theophrastus, and the famous biopsychological typology (initiated by Hippocrates and popularized by Galen) of four temperaments, sanguine, choleric, phlegmatic, and melancholic. The second typology was too simple and inclusive, having no subdivisions to cover the numerous practically significant individual variations; it lasted long, but did not develop further.

Recent substitutes, such as Kretschmer's,[24] have also remained unproductive, whereas sociopsychological typologies have grown and expanded, as is well shown in the *Characterology* of Utitz.[25] As generalizations, their wellknown weakness is their multiple overlapping. Every individual who by certain criteria is considered as belonging to a certain type, when analyzed psychologically is found to possess not only characteristics included in this type, but many characteristics which he shares with individuals who by other criteria are considered as belonging to entirely different types. For instance, he may be a more or less typical introvert or extrovert, in Jung's sense. In either case, he may have had an inferiority complex, in Adler's sense, and have developed one of several typical ways of compensating for it. Whichever of these types he represents, he may be also a more or less typical Frenchman or Englishman, i.e., possess a combination of characteristics acquired by those who have been consistently and exclusively brought up to participate in French or English national culture. He may also share a set of characteristics common to faithful Catholics or Methodists or religious skeptics. He may be also a more or less typical small farmer or tailor or university professor.

We do not deny the validity of typological generalizations, provided they are based on objective investigation, not on evaluative judgments of the

[24] Ernst Kretschmer, *Körperbau und Charakter* (Berlin, 1925).

[25] We refer here not only to Emil Utitz's own work *Charakterologie* (Charlottenburg, 1925), but especially to the *Jahrbuch der Charakterologie* which he edited (Berlin, 1924-29). It includes contributions of many characterologists, among others a number of monographic studies of famous personalities, e.g., Gogol, Nietzsche, Kant, Loyola, etc. It is perhaps not so generally known that John Stuart Mill was the first to promulgate methodological principles which according to him would lead to the development of what he called "Ethology, or the Science of the Formation of Character," *Logic* (London, 1843), Book VI, chap. V: "Mankind has not one universal character, but there exist universal [psychological] laws of the formation of character." He included in his examples different national characters—French, English, Italian— and characters of "different classes of society." Perhaps the best historico-critical survey of nearly all different approaches to human character is Paul Helwig's *Charakterologie* (Leipzig, 1936). His basic premise is that "Characterology does not aim to describe character in particular. This is what biography and poetry are doing. Characterology aims to make the particular understandable by proceeding from the general" (p. 15). Though recognizing the positive contributions of various typological theories, he states that: "No typology can exclude, supplement or supplant other typologies already outlined or to be outlined" (p. 73).

typologist.[26] But they are not scientific substitutes for taxonomic classifications; since they cannot be logically systematized, they either supplement classifications already developed or raise problems which eventually lead to new taxonomic, causal, functional, or genetic hypotheses. Thus, a zoologist who has discovered what he presumes to be a new species "constructs a type" (in Howard Becker's terms)[27] combining those common characteristics which most clearly distinguish this species from all others. Perhaps no single animal has all these distinctive characteristics fully developed. But insofar as differences between particular animals can be considered differences in degree of approximation to the common type constructed by the zoologist, all of them can be included within the species as a logical class.

On the other hand, a zoologist who studies the fauna of an arctic or a tropical region may find that animals of several genera possess in various degrees certain typical common characteristics (e.g., color), which animals of the same genera who live in other areas lack. This raises the problem of how these characteristics were acquired, and leads to certain hypotheses of causal and/or functional relationship between animals and the climatic conditions in which they live.

Typological generalizations about human individuals as conscious beings, objects of human experiences and actions, also raise important problems. How is it that the same individual can be included under so many different, logically unconnected types? Obviously, his conscious life as a whole is not systematically ordered. But it cannot be entirely chaotic; otherwise no typical similarities between him and other individuals could be found. The solution of this problem is provided by cultural sciences, especially sociology. He is an *active participant* in a number of different systems, each similar to other systems in which many, but never all, individuals participate. His typical similarities to certain other individuals are mainly due to his participation in systems of the same logical class as the systems in which they participate.

During the last fifty years psychologists have become increasingly aware of these problems and gradually developed a new methodical approach to human individuals, viewing them not as conscious beings, concrete empirical data, but as *agents*. While typological comparison still prevails in studies of abnormal or pathological cases, investigators of normal persons are increasingly concerned with comparative investigation of individual actions and at-

[26] Strong logical arguments in favor of the concept of type, especially its heuristic usefulness, are presented by Carl G. Hempel and Paul Oppenheim, *Der Typusbegriff im Lichte der neueren Logik* (Leiden, 1936).

[27] Cf. Howard Becker, "Constructive Typology in the Social Sciences" in *Contemporary Social Theory*, eds. Barnes, Becker, and Becker (New York: Appleton, 1940); and Howard Becker, "Interpretive Sociology and Constructive Typology" in *Twentieth Century Sociology*, eds. Georges Gurvitch and Wilbert E. Moore (New York: Philosophical Library, 1945).

titudes. The main purpose of this investigation is to predict how an individual will act under definite conditions. Such prediction is considered practically useful to authoritative agents—educators, employers and managers in various branches of industry and trade, and military organizers—who choose individuals for certain social roles, as well as to individuals themselves in their choice of future social roles.[28] This is a specific manifestation of a general trend manifested in the whole domain of cultural sciences.

Passage from the study of cultural data to the study of human actions

During the last hundred years, many cultural scientists engaged in inductive research, instead of merely describing and comparing cultural data as human values, have proceeded to investigate and compare *human actions* in which these values are used. Of course, practical generalizations about actions are as old as attempts to regulate them. But an objective approach to actions began only when Greek historians started to describe particular past actions and used for this description the most reliable testimonies of the agents and witnesses they could find. And not until modern times was a systematic comparative analysis of actions gradually introduced into the various sciences of culture. This led to inductive generalizations and constitutes one of the most important innovations in the whole history of human thought.

Even a superficial survey of the evolution of some sciences of culture indicates that their methodical progress is correlated with this growing emphasis on the study of human actions rather than on the study of cultural values abstracted from the actions in which they are used. The development of economics is a familiar example. The original practical approach to economic data always consisted and still consists in comparative estimation and gradation of economic values as such, judged by their utility. The use of money, providing an apparently universal standard of measurement of economic values, gave this practical approach an illusory objectivity and validity, seemingly analogous to that of quantitative methods in natural sciences. Even after the relativity of the monetary standard was conclusively proved, certain economic philosophers still tried to find some absolute principles by which economic values could be graded, e.g., the amount of labor required for the production of a value or the urgency of the need which a value served to satisfy. Economics became an objective theoretic science only when and insofar as it ceased to consider economic values in the abstract and concentrated upon the investigation of the actions which deal with these values—technical

---

[28] The practical significance of this approach is manifested in an early general outline by Katherine M. H. Blackford and Arthur Newcomb, *Analyzing Character. The New Science of Judging Men, Misfits in Business, the Home and Social Life* (New York: Review of Reviews Co., 1916). As we shall see in a later work, it is the sociological taxonomy of the social roles performed by an individual in the course of his life which makes a theoretic typology of social personalities possible.

actions (characterized as production, transportation, and consumption) and exchange as specific economic activity. Many economists, indeed, still do not distinguish clearly and methodically theoretic problems from practical problems; and some economic theories are still based on deduction from *a priori* definitions of economic activity (demand and supply) rather than on inductive analysis and comparison of observed actions. But these deficiencies indicate only that the science of economics has not yet succeeded in overcoming completely the difficulties with which all sciences of culture have been struggling; its progress since the middle of the eighteenth century is undeniable and especially striking in view of the tremendous growth in the multiplicity, complexity, and diversity of economic phenomena and the increasing rapidity of their changes.

Linguistics is another cultural science whose development in recent times is closely connected with inductive, objective investigation of the activities of speaking and writing, instead of the older study of words with their content and meaning authoritatively defined and evaluated by phonetical, grammatical, and semantical standards. While the older approach still persists and must persist in dictionaries and textbooks for the benefit of learners who want to understand a language, as used by a certain collectivity at a certain period, and to use it in accordance with the standards which that collectivity considers binding, scientists have recognized the relativity of these standards and the impossibility of reaching any generalizations about words which would be applicable to all the usages of these words in various collectivities at various historical periods. By viewing language not as a static complex of verbal entities, but as a dynamic multiplicity of actions and reactions of human agents, the linguists have opened up a vast and previously untouched field of scientific research. In analyzing and comparing the cultural patterns which these actions follow as well as individual deviations from these patterns, and in studying functional relations between these actions and other culturally patterned actions, linguists have made discoveries and have formulated and tested theoretic hypotheses which were unthinkable a hundred years ago.

A similar revolution is going on in studies of religion. It is true that many historians still consider their main task to be the preparation of exhaustive catalogues of mythical beings and events in various religions, and they continue old controversies concerning the significance of these myths. But the scientific unproductivity of this approach has become increasingly clear since the middle of the last century, as the attention of religionists turned from descriptive mythology, abstracted from the active life of believers, to comparative investigation of religious actions, individual and collective. Although their investigations sometimes led to hypotheses which became invalidated in the light of later discoveries, and even today some religionists are inclined to make sweeping generalizations on insufficient evidence, the essential point is that these generalizations can be tested by inductive research.

Another important cultural domain, where the passage from a study of practical objects to a study of actions has changed the whole scientific approach, is that of material techniques. The old method of collecting and classifying artifacts seemed above reproach, according to epistemological and logical principles. An artifact can obviously be seen, touched, measured, and analyzed into its component parts; relations between these parts can be objectively studied; and every observable characteristic of a given artifact can be compared, for purposes of classification, with characteristics of other artifacts.

Thus, the arrangement of artifacts in museums was originally, and sometimes still is, based upon this kind of comparison. This approach, however, is no longer considered scientifically satisfactory by anthropologists who want to know not what artifacts are to the collectors or visitors in a museum, but what they are to those agents who produce them and use them. The only adequate source of this knowledge is observation of their production and usage. Such observation includes, of course, spatial objects and processes. But the observer has also to investigate the standards by which an agent selects and evaluates the results to be attained, the materials and instruments he uses, and the sequence of changes in materials and instruments by which he expects to attain this result. However, the methodical progress achieved by anthropologists in their studies of the techniques found in nonliterate and folk cultures has not yet been extended to studies of modern industrial techniques, where the evaluative approach in terms of a utilitarian philosophy interferes with scientific objectivity.

In our last chapter we shall discuss the progress of sociology due to methodical and comparative investigation of social actions, i.e., actions in which the main objects are human individuals or collectivities.

Human Actions

What is a human action?

The general tendency of scientists of culture to investigate human actions presupposes that objective, inductive generalizing knowledge about human actions can be attained and systematized, whether these actions deal with material things, verbal symbols, mythical entities, conscious human beings, or any other empirical data. The development of this knowledge, however, has met some difficulties and raised methodological controversies which still persist.

We speak of methodological controversies, not of epistemological issues. The entire historical growth of practical knowledge (from which, as we have seen, scientific knowledge emerged) shows conclusively that human actions are accessible to the experience and reflection of the agents themselves as well as to others who observe them. Otherwise, it would be impossible for practical thinkers to know how the data used in an action appear and what they mean to the agent; it would be impossible to compare the content and meaning of data used by different agents and to draw practical generalizations which many individual agents can accept and follow. The epistemological doctrine which claims that the essence of an action can be known only to the agent, because he alone has immediate consciousness of his activity as an inner force determining what he is doing, is as irrelevant to the scientific study of actions as the contrary doctrine which claims that only observers of the behavior of human organisms can truly know what human actions really are. In the light of a general history of culture, especially of the history of knowledge as outlined previously, both doctrines are absurd.

The task of the scientist in every case is to derive from the agent's own experiences of a particular action of his, as well as from the experiences of the same action by others, reliable evidence which will permit him to define this action objectively, without using evaluative judgments or becoming involved in practical problems, and to compare it with other actions of the same kind, also objectively defined on the basis of reliable evidence, so as to reach valid theoretic generalizations.

Before discussing the methods which cultural scientists have used in performing this task, we must give a preliminary heuristic definition of the concept which we symbolize by the term "human action."

The verb "to act" (*agere*) and its derivatives—to react, action, reaction, agent, reagent, etc.—have been used by physical scientists to denote a certain category of cause-effect relationships. We can ignore this usage altogether, since physical scientists borrowed these words from popular language, where they originally referred to practical operations or performances of men; their extension to physical processes had from the beginning scientifically unjustifiable, anthropomorphic connotations. We see no justification, either, for using these terms, as they have often been used, to denote a certain category of processes of causal-functional relationships which scientific observers know to occur between an individual organism and its environment, even when the individual organism is not aware of them. Fortunately, the term "behavior" has been already partly substituted by biologists for the terms "action" and "reaction."

We shall therefore apply the term "action" only to *conscious* performances, i.e., those in the course of which the agent, the x who acts (whoever he may be), experiences the data included in his performance, and is aware of the changes which he is producing. Everybody knows, of course, that it is impossible to draw a dividing line between unconscious organic behavior and conscious actions; ontogenetically and phylogenetically, the former precedes the latter; and the evolution of active consciousness is gradual. But it is perfectly legitimate to limit the extension of the term "action" to those performances which can be proved conscious by factual evidence. Thus limited, the term might be applied not only to performances of human agents known to be conscious from symbolic communication, but to various performances of higher animals which, according to competent zoologists, are conscious.[1] Since, however, we are not concerned now with the active performances of animals and do not feel competent to judge how conscious they are, we wish to make it clear that we shall investigate here only human actions in the sense of conscious performances of human agents.

And, inasmuch as we do not want to become involved in controversies concerning the unconscious (in the psychological sense), our limitation of the term "action" to conscious performances is not intended to imply either rejection or acceptance of unconscious motivations, drives, and impulses, which make human agents act as they do. When we speak of an action as conscious,

[1] Besides exact studies of the behavior of animals by experimental scientists, interesting descriptions, though less exact, have been written by trainers of animals in circuses and especially by observers of wild animals in their habitats.

all we mean is that, while the agent is performing it, his performance affects the data of *his own present experience* as they are given to him. It is perfectly possible that, while aware of these data and of the changes he is producing, he is entirely unaware why he does what he is doing; or that, after having performed an action, he forgets it altogether. If he can be made to remember it by any psychological methods, this is an obvious and sufficient proof that, when he performed it, he was conscious.

But there is still another terminological difficulty. Theorists of conscious performances or operations of human agents use three terms with a common derivation: "act," "action," and "activity." What we need, first of all, is a general term which will cover all the particular and diverse performances or operations, each of which includes a complex of data that the particular agent selects and modifies while he acts. Should each particular operation or performance be called an "act" or an "action"?

We remained undecided for a long time. There were precedents for both usages. French thinkers seem to prefer the term *acte*. But the noun "act" has seldom been used in English scientific literature in this sense. It has, moreover, several other meanings which are apt to produce confusion, e.g., in theatrical language and in legal terminology. In the latter, it mostly refers to the final recorded results of past active performances of legislators or judges. Whereas what we want is a term to designate an active performance in its total course, while it is going on; and this is just what the word "action" suggests. The only objection against this usage is that many authors—especially French, but also English and American—have used it in a different sense; instead of referring to "an action" in the singular and "actions" in the plural as particular concrete units of a logical class, they refer to "action" in general, abstracted from the empirical data which are being selected and modified in the course of a particular operation or active performance. We reserve the term "activity" to denote this abstract process.

To illustrate what we mean by an action or, more explicitly, a conscious human action, we may refer to some of the specific active performances which have been investigated by students of culture. Here are a few of them:

Hunting wild game. Catching fish. Hoeing a garden. Transplanting rice. Harvesting wheat. Baking a cake. Eating a cake. Making a barrel of wine. Drinking a glass of wine. Making an iron plow. Weaving a rug. Making a piece of furniture. Buying a piece of furniture. Building a house. Performing privately a magical rite. Praying to a god. Performing a public religious ceremony. Greeting a friend. Visiting a neighbor. Entertaining a visitor. Curing a sick person. Asking a girl to promise herself in marriage. Killing the lover of one's wife. Attacking an enemy regiment. Writing a poem. Reciting a poem. Painting a landscape. Criticizing a painting. Composing a symphony. Playing a symphony.

These actions differ considerably in several respects. Perhaps the most familiar are differences depending on the kind of values with which the agents deal: Actions which produce material objects differ from those which tend to influence mythical beings; actions which bear upon men differ from those which create or re-create aesthetic values. On such differences is based the specialization of cultural sciences, and we shall discuss them later. But there are other differences which may be observed among actions, irrespective of the kind of objects with which they deal.

First, some of the actions mentioned above are relatively brief and simple, like drinking a glass of wine, buying a piece of furniture, greeting a friend, killing an enemy. Others last for a rather long time and are complex. The total performance of such an action as building a house or composing a symphony requires a prolonged combination of many simpler performances. We shall call the simplest of the latter *elementary* actions. The term "elementary" implies that such a simple action cannot be broken up into still simpler actions.

For instance, laying a brick is an elementary action included in the complex action of building a house. Yet, to perform this action, the bricklayer has to choose several definite objects—a brick, a place on the wall where the brick will be laid, a trowel, some mortar—and initiate a certain orderly sequence of distinct changes in the spatial location of these objects. His action cannot be broken up, for instance, into particular movements which can be interchanged, for the objects he uses and the sequence of changes he initiates are interdependent; if any one of them is omitted, this particular brick will not be laid in this particular place or its position in relation to other bricks permanently settled.

Another well-known difference has been overemphasized in recent times, especially by some sociologists, as a basic difference by which all actions must be subdivided into two mutually exclusive categories. Some of the specific actions mentioned above are performed each by one individual, others require the cooperation of several individuals acting together. This is, for instance, the difference between a private magical rite or a personal prayer and a public religious ceremony, between an individual attack on a rival in peacetime and a military group's attack on an enemy group in war, between the composition of a symphony to be played by an orchestra and the rendition of the symphony by an orchestra. The term "social action" has been used to denote actions performed collectively by a number of individuals.[2] This usage is rooted in the nineteenth-century antithesis between individual

[2] Such is the definition of this term in the *Dictionary of Sociology*, ed. Harry P. Fairchild (New York: Philosophical Library, 1944). The author completely ignores the only two sociological books hitherto published which bear this term in their titles: Florian Znaniecki, *Social Actions* (New York: Farrar, 1936); and Talcott Parsons, *The Structure of Social Action* (New York: McGraw, 1937).

and society, which has been invalidated by such sociologists as Cooley, Simmel, and Mead. If we accepted it, we would have to put into one general class such actions as hunting, fishing, building a house, saying a prayer, curing a sick person, shooting an enemy airplane, when performed by individuals; and into another, antithetic general class, such actions as hunting by a group of hunters, cooperative fishing by several fishermen, building a house by several carpenters and bricklayers, saying the same prayer together by a congregation, curing a sick person by several doctors and nurses in a cooperative hospital, shooting an enemy airplane by an antiaircraft battery. The transplanting of rice by the owner of a field together with his neighbors would have to be considered essentially similar to an attack carried on by a military company against an enemy company and essentially different from the transplanting of rice by the owner alone.

The absurdity of this classification becomes even more obvious when we find that in the course of cultural evolution almost every kind of action originally performed by one individual can change into an action performed collectively by several individuals. We shall, therefore, use the term "social actions" to denote all actions and only those in which the main objects that the agents tend to influence are conscious human individuals or collectivities, whether those actions are performed individually or collectively. Of course, as we shall see in detail later on, an action collectively performed—be it technical, religious, aesthetic, or social—requires certain auxiliary social actions between the individuals who participate in it.

However different the actions listed above may be, certain basic similarities between them justify their inclusion under one logical class. First, each of them has a beginning and an end; its duration is limited. It may have been and probably was preceded by other actions of the same agent or of other agents which produced the conditions necessary for its performance. To make hunting possible, the necessary weapons had to be made. Rice cannot be transplanted unless it has been planted some time before. Baking a cake or weaving a rug presupposes previous actions which produced the materials and instruments used by the baker or the weaver. A private religious prayer implies that certain beliefs and practices developed by his predecessors have been imparted to the individual who prays; a public ceremony presupposes many previous actions—building a temple, making the sacred implements used in the ceremony, transmission of the ritual, gathering of the congregation, etc. An elementary action included in the total complex action of building a house, such as laying a particular brick, is made possible only by a combination of many previous elementary actions. And the total action of building a house had to be also preceded by many actions—baking bricks, making tools, preparing lumber, etc. Each action, in turn, usually contributes to the preparation of the conditions necessary for the performance of another or several other actions. The action of making a piece of furniture produces the most essential, though not the only, condition of the action of buying this piece. Composing a symphony prepares the most indispensable, though not the only, condition needed for the action of playing the symphony by an orchestra. Building a house is essential for the subsequent action of a family's moving into the house.

Nevertheless, whatever the connection between a particular action and subsequent actions, no particular action can last indefinitely. Although (as we shall see presently) it is not easy to determine when an action begins—indeed, this is one of the major difficulties in methodical studies of actions—it is relatively easy to find when an action ends or, more exactly, when it is considered completed by the agent himself and by observers.

When we say that an action lasts from its beginning to its end, this implies a certain continuity. This continuity is not the same as the continuity of abstract astronomical time. Some actions are, indeed, carried on through a certain length of time without noticeable interruption, not only relatively simple actions like praying, greeting a friend, or reciting a short poem, but even some very complex collective actions like playing a symphony or producing an airplane in an industrial factory that functions day and night. But many relatively complex actions, individual or collective, can be interrupted for a certain period of time and resumed after the interruption without losing their identity and continuity, as if the interruption had never occurred. Weaving an Indian or a Persian rug by an individual weaver takes many months. It is interrupted every night when the weaver sleeps and frequently in daytime, when he or she has to perform various other actions. And yet it is the same complex action; every part of the performance after an interruption is a continuation of past performances and will be continued by future performances.[3]

Another common and distinctive characteristic of all actions has been already discussed in our analysis of practical thinking. Every action deals with a limited number of selected data, each of which is experienced by the agent as a value. In a simple action, these values are few. Greeting a friend includes the friend as a social value, some meaningful words which constitute the greeting, the friend's response as experienced by the speaker. Drinking a glass of wine includes the wine; the drinker's hand, which carries the glass to his lips; his mouth; his tongue and throat, which are pleasantly stimulated by the wine. In a complex action many values are involved, some different, some similar. Building a house includes the land on which it is

[3] This continuity of concrete duration, different from and partly independent of the continuity of abstract time, is analogous to the continuity of memory which has been studied by some philosophers (e.g., Henri Bergson, *Matière et mémoire*) and by some sociologists (e.g., Maurice Halbwachs, *Les Cadres sociaux de la mémoire*).

built; the more or less detailed representation of the house as it will be when the performance is completed, and as it becomes gradually materialized in the course of the performance; the thousands of stones, bricks, and pieces of wood; the number of different tools; and the hands of the builders. In any case, however, each of these values can be identified and distinguished from the unlimited multiplicity and diversity of data which are not included in the action.

Furthermore, in the course of the action every value included in it becomes factually connected with some other values; its empirical content and meaning become in some way modified by these connections. What is done or will be done to any value depends directly or indirectly on what was done or is done to other values, and vice versa. The continuity of the action from its beginning to its completion presupposes a certain dynamic order of interdependence between specific changes which the values included in it undergo during its performance.

In view of these fundamental similarities, we can state hypothetically that *every human action is a limited, dynamic system of interdependent, changing values.* If this is so, it follows that human actions can be investigated scientifically by the same methods which are used in the investigation of limited natural systems.

We presume that our heuristic definition of human actions as limited dynamic systems of values is applicable to complex as well as to simple actions. This assumption may raise certain doubts. It seems as if a complex action should be conceived as an organized system of elementary actions rather than as a system of values. As a matter of fact, it is both. At this time, however, we cannot discuss the problem of systematic order between actions. It is a difficult problem, indeed, and we shall give considerable attention to it later on. We shall find that there are many different systems of actions, some of which can be considered single, complex, or limited actions, as here defined, whereas others cannot.

In the examples to which we referred in the foregoing, elementary actions are organized and combined into a complex action only because they all deal directly or indirectly with the same central or dominant value (or set of values) to which the other values included in them are subordinated. It is this dominant value which gives such a complex action its unity; and its continuity is due to the progressive integration of all changes of values into a definite final change of this dominant value. Thus, in a complex action of religious cultus the god is the lasting dominant value; and active modifications of all other values—sacred words, sacred implements, sacrificial animals, plants, or inanimate materials—are integrated for the attainment of one final result, i.e., producing a positive reaction of the god, beneficent to the participants in the cultus. In the complex action of building a house, the representation of the future house is the dominant value, and all changes in other values produced in the course of elementary actions are integrated for the final change of this imaginative representation into a material reality. The symphony as a whole, an aesthetic system of sounds, is the dominant value both in the complex individual action of the composer who produces it and in the collective action of the orchestra which plays it.

Assuming that our heuristic definition of human actions proves true, the problem arises whether any universal and distinctive inner order characterizes all these systems.

Teleological and deterministic theories of action

While thinkers have reflected about actions for thousands of years, most of their thinking has been influenced by practical judgments, and the persistent influence of such judgments still frequently interferes with objective scientific investigation. As we have seen, practical thinkers characterize and compare human actions by the results which agents try to achieve and judge them by success or failure in achieving these results. Since practical generalizations about actions have been mostly developed by thinkers for the guidance of agents, they usually contain explicit or implicit definitions of results which agents ought to achieve and formulations of rules which agents must follow in order to achieve these results. Such conceptions of actions were and are extensively used by teachers in training learners; by rulers, leaders, planners, and organizers in guiding the actions of their subordinates, as in bureaucratic, military, industrial, and economic management; and by experts writing for the benefit of any readers who may want their guidance.

The universal principle of these practical generalizations about actions is that, before an action is started, its final result should be defined and the objects and processes necessary for the attainment of this result chosen. The action to be performed is ideationally constructed as a *telic* system, a combination of *means* for the attainment of a certain *end*. Thinking about the action ought to precede its performance and really does precede it when it is done by the adviser on behalf of the agent. When the agent accepts the advice, this implies, from the adviser's point of view, that he also thinks before acting, although his thinking mainly reproduces the thinking of the adviser. His task as an agent is then to realize in fact the telic system already ideationally constructed.

This view of actions by practical thinkers, who advise agents in advance how to achieve results defined in advance, has conditioned for centuries the theories of actions developed by philosophers and students of culture. An action in general is conceived as teleologically organized; it begins after the agent has decided what end to attain and what means to use, proceeds by using the means, and results in the attainment of the end. Its performance requires a combination of two causal sequences. The agent's decision to attain a certain end is the cause of the use of certain means, the *causa finalis*. The use of the means is the cause of the attainment of the end, the *causa efficiens*. Since such a conception implies a separation of the ideational, subjective, or mental process of thinking about the future action and the realistic, objective, usually physical process of performing the action, metaphysicians raised and discussed for centuries the problem: How can this ideational, subjective, mental process cause a realistic, objective, physical process?

However, until recent times philosophers and students of culture failed to realize that the teleological approach to actions, however useful practically, may be scientifically defective. For this approach makes a comparative study of actions apparently easy. Actions can be classified according to their ends. An observer of somebody else's action, who knows what end the agent has decided to attain, can predict the course of that action; every one who observes its course can infer from the means the agent uses what end he has decided to attain. And the observation of many actions, especially those included in modern technical and economic organization, seems to furnish incontrovertible evidence that the telic order, as ideationally planned, coincides with the telic order as realistically effected, provided the planning is logically consistent and based on adequate knowledge.

Of course, theorists have not failed to observe that many human actions lack this telic order; indeed, the very need of expert advice and teaching is due to the existence and even prevalence of such actions. But instead of questioning the theoretic validity of the teleological approach, its adherents have simply classified human actions under two categories: those which conform with the telic order and those which do not. The former are sometimes termed "logical," in the sense that the thinking which preceded and guided their performance follows the principles of logic; sometimes "rational," in the sense that the performance itself is rationally ordered. The latter are termed "nonlogical," "illogical," "nonrational," "irrational." This classification, which goes back at least to Socrates, is still accepted by many twentieth-century thinkers. Sometimes a distinction is made between illogical or irrational actions, i.e., those which are intended to be telic, and are expected to attain certain ends, but because of defective thinking, inadequate knowledge, or some other factor cannot attain these ends; and nonlogical or nonrational actions, i.e., those which are not intended to be telic.

In any case, the contrast between actions which are logical or rational and those which are not implies that the theorist functions as judge of the presence or absence of a logical or rational order in the actions which he investigates, just as in teaching-learning relations the teacher is the judge of the conformity or nonconformity of the learner's actions with the telic order. And just as to the teacher, nonconformity of the learner with the teacher's judgments is a symptom of individual immaturity, a defect that can be corrected by further teaching; so to the student of culture who classifies human actions by the principle of teleological rationality, nonconformity with this principle is the symptom of a low level of culture, the manifestation of a prelogical way of thinking. And if in a given culture certain kinds of actions (especially actions of material technique) become more rational than other kinds, the latter are regarded as lagging behind the former.

Inasmuch as the course of an action which is not rational cannot be explained by the agent's decision to attain a logically well-defined end by the use of means known in advance to be necessary for this attainment, scientists who adhere to the teleological theory try to explain the defectiveness of such an action by resorting to some force inherent in the agent's mind which interferes with his logical thinking. This familiar explanation is used by critics of other people's actions who are puzzled as to why those others, notwithstanding the fact that they can think, do not act as the critics believe rational beings ought to act. Deviations from the telic order are ascribed to the influence of such subjective factors as impulses, emotions, unconscious wishes, which agents are unable to control by objective, logical thinking. Perhaps the most comprehensive use of this kind of explanation is that of Pareto, who, having classified actions as "logical" and "nonlogical," devotes nearly fifteen-hundred pages to a survey of many kinds of nonlogical actions and by comparative analysis discovers not only the basic psychological forces which explain their logical defectiveness, but also the main ways of secondary rationalization by which this logical defectiveness is camouflaged.[4]

But deviations from the telic order are not the only difficulties which the teleological theory of actions has to face. Not less important are those numerous and diverse active performances which apparently conform with the telic order and yet are certainly not guided by logical thinking.

We refer to active performances of animals. When judged by the same teleological standards as those by which technical performances of human agents are judged, many of them manifest to the observer a telic order as effective, as nearly rational as that of some of the best-planned human actions and appear superior to many human actions which critics classify as irrational. Individual performances of birds building nests, of spiders weaving webs, and, even more, the complex collective performances of beavers, bees, ants, and termites often appear directed toward definite ends

[4] Vilfredo Pareto, *Traité de sociologie général* (Paris, 1917), Secs. 150-51, pp. 66-67. A rather positive, though critical, analysis of the theory of Pareto is contained in Parsons' work mentioned before; a strongly negative "Estimate of Pareto" is that of Ellsworth Faris, *The Nature of Human Nature* (New York: McGraw, 1937).

which are to be attained by the orderly use of certain selected means. To an observer who from past observation anticipates the final result of such a performance, knows the environmental conditions in which the animal lives and the capacity of the animal's body to change some of these conditions by certain movements, it seems as if the animal also anticipated this final result before beginning to act and reflectively planned to produce through the instrumentality of its body those and only those changes in its environment which in their total sequence are necessary and sufficient to achieve this result. Yet such an assumption was invalidated long ago by comparative scientific research. The seeming rationality of the actions of animals is certainly not a product of the logical thinking of the animals themselves. It is due to the reasoning of those observers who apply the same teleological conception to the actions of animals as to those of human agents. And since this conception has been proved invalid when applied to animal actions with an organization similar to that of human actions, how can its application to human actions be valid?

The problem is not solved by the theory that the telic organization of actions may be the result of two very different forces: intelligence, which makes human actions telic, or instinct, which makes animal actions telic. For, while intelligence is accessible to observation, instinct is not. The term "intelligence" refers to such phenomena, among others, as reflective judgments about actions—be they past, present, or future, the agent's own or somebody else's—judgments empirically manifested not in the performance of actions to which they refer, but in symbolic expressions. These phenomena, as we shall see later in detail, can be investigated apart from the investigation of actions, and hypotheses concerning their influence upon human actions can be inductively tested. But the term "instinct" originally referred to an unobservable causative power which thinkers postulated to explain what appears to them an otherwise inexplicable similarity between animal and human actions. Unless we accept Bergson's epistemological doctrine that animal instinct is the precursor and source of human intuition, which can be immediately known and symbolically communicated to others, the explanation of animal actions by instinct adds nothing at all to what is already known from observation of these actions. Of course, there is no reason why this term should not be used in a purely descriptive sense, to denote certain common characteristics of observable performances of animals, provided those who use it refrain from anthropomorphic interpretation of these characteristics.

When we question the validity of the teleological theory of actions, we do not have to accept as alternative the theory of naturalistic determinism, according to which every action is a process causally determined by other processes which have occurred in the natural environment of the agent and/or in the agent as a natural being. Since we are not investigating animal actions here, we may let the zoologists decide whether the deterministic theory is heuristically adequate to solve all the problems which observation of animal actions raises. So far as human actions are concerned, application of this theory is primarily based on the observation of simple, elementary actions which approximate originally unconscious organic behavior, in that similar changes in an individual's environment and/or in his organism are regularly followed by similar active performances on his part. Such a performance appears to be a process causally explicable by the process which preceded it; in familiar terms, it can be defined as a specific response to a specific stimulus.

But empirical evidence derived both from the experience of the agent, symbolically expressed, and from the observation of others shows that, the more complex a particular action, the more obviously inapplicable to its performance this deterministic theory. Take the total action of weaving a rug or making a cabinet. When we have analyzed such a complex action into elementary actions, before trying to explain *why* the agent at any particular time performs a particular action, we must find out *what he is doing* at this time to the data with which he deals. And then we discover that, though dependent on the past, what he is doing is not causally determined by the past, but directed toward the future. The specific changes which he introduces into the instruments and materials he is using have been made possible by previous changes which he has already achieved; but in introducing these present changes he anticipates that subsequent actions of his will depend on the results of his actions and is guided by this anticipation. And the total action of weaving the rug or making the cabinet is more than a mere sequence of separate elementary actions; it is a dynamic combination of elementary actions, all organized with reference to the future, guided by the expectation that all their fragmentary results will become synthesized in one anticipated final product. Any attempt to apply to such a complex action the principle of causal determinism would have to explain not only why each elementary action includes (out of an unlimited variety of possible changes) only such changes of data as are expected to produce the definite conditions necessary for the performance of a definite subsequent action, but also why in the total course of the complex action only those elementary actions are performed (out of an unlimited diversity of possible actions) which all together result in the realization of such a complicated and yet technically and aesthetically united product as the rug or the cabinet.

Since none of these problems concerning elementary actions as parts of a complex action—not to speak of the problem of the total complex action —can be solved by finding a single cause of which a given active performance is the direct effect, determinists necessarily resort to the principle of multiple indirect causation. They attempt to explain an individual's particular action as an effect of a combination of many causal processes which occurred in the near or distant past of the individual as a biopsychological being, subjected to environmental influences. Such an attempt, if conscientiously carried on, leads to an unlimited multiplicity of causes, none of which can be ignored, for without it this particular individual at this particular time under the given particular conditions might not have performed the particular action he did in the way he did. The entire past history of the individual and of the environment in which he has hitherto lived would have to be known to give an adequate causal explanation of any conscious action of his as observed by himself and others. The methodical impossibility of having the principle of causal determinism applied to human actions in general is even more manifest in the studies of collective actions, for here the life histories of all participating individuals and their environments would have to be studied. Ultimately, the consistent use of this principle would require adequate knowledge of the whole history of mankind and its natural environment.

The dynamic course of creative actions

The common methical deficiency of both the teleological and the deterministic theory of human actions is that neither of them is derived from comparative inductive studies of actions. Each is based on an *a priori* postulate—the postulate of conscious will to reach an end as primary cause or the postulate of multiple naturalistic causation—and seeks only for data and facts which seem relevant from the point of view of this postulate. For inductive studies of actions, using both the evidence of the agent's experience and that of other observers, are not easy; nearly everything which teleological and deterministic theorists take for granted must be problematized. If a conscious human action is a dynamic system of values, it must be studied in the course of its duration. It cannot be fully defined by its composition and structure at any particular moment; it is an evolving system, a system in becoming, which exists only so long as it evolves; once its evolution is completed, it ceases to exist. This evolution consists in a progressive selection and inclusion of values which become its components and in progressive initiation and functional organization of the factual relationships by which these values are modified. We may express this briefly by stating that *an action in its total course manifests a gradual formation of a purpose which becomes gradually realized as it is being formed.*

The word "purpose," as commonly used, is not very adequate for the concept we want to symbolize, inasmuch as in current speech little distinction is made between its meaning and that of the word "end"; but it is the best available, short of inventing a new one.

We may distinguish the concepts symbolized by these terms by stating, first, that the purpose includes both the end in the sense of the anticipated final result of the action which the agent expects to achieve and the means in the sense of the anticipated changes in existing data by which he expects to achieve it. The methodical justification for eliminating the distinction between end and means is that—as some theorists noticed long ago—in the course of an action what appears as a means when viewed with reference to a more distant future may appear as an end when viewed with reference to a nearer future; and, vice versa, what appeared as an end when its attainment is relatively distant may appear as a means for some more distant end as its attainment approaches. Furthermore, as Wilhelm Wundt pointed out in his principles of "heterogony of ends" and "transformation of means," in the course of cultural evolution similar means come to be used for different ends, and the attainment of similar ends comes to be sought by different means.[5] Thus, the teleological classification of actions by ends has always been of doubtful validity scientifically.

Second, we conceive the purpose of an action as continuously evolving and continuously functioning while it evolves, from the moment the agent begins to select the data to be included in his action up to the time when he ceases to modify these data. By the time he has decided what to do and how to do it, his action has been already on the way; and as it goes on, his decisions will continue to function and become more and more definite after every step toward its realization. There is no dividing line between ideational planning of an action and realistic performance of this action. Either the agent who plans an action realizes this plan in subsequent performance, in which case his planning was an integral part of the total course of the action; or else the agent who plans leaves the realization of his plan to somebody else, in which case (as, e.g., in modern industry) the planning itself is a distinct, complete action dealing with imaginative representations and abstract ideas and expressed in symbols. Reproductive interpretation and progressive realization of the representations and ideas systematized and symbolized by the planner is an entirely different action, collectively performed, a technical action dealing with material objects. Between the two, as a connecting link, lies the social action (or sequence of actions) of a managing individual or group who influence the technical agents into accepting the plan and being guided by it in their actual collective performance.

This progressive formation of the purpose in the very course of the action is most clearly manifested in those human actions which consciously tend to produce *new values*, i.e., values which did not exist before in human experience. Producing a poem, a painting, or a musical composition which is not a mere copy of an existing original; inventing a new technical instrument; expressing symbolically and communicating to others a mystical representation of a divine being or a sacred event different from those included

[5] Wilhelm Wundt, *Logik*, III, 281; and *Völkerpsychologie, passim.*

in existing religions; exploring a natural field in search of objects hitherto inaccessible to human experience; formulating a new hypothesis based on the discovery of a factual order hitherto unknown: These are typical examples of such actions, familiar to every historian of culture.

We may call such actions *creative*. They are of primary importance to cultural scientists, since all culture (viewed historically) has been created by human agents. No culture existed a million years ago. If, in the light of archeological evidence, we compare our culture with the culture of any prehistorical period, we find that it shows a great increase in wealth and complexity and that many, perhaps most, of the present cultural products are new, different in content and meaning from anything that existed in early times. There is no sense whatever in the denial of some theorists of culture that the growth of culture is creative—unless these theorists deny the very existence of cultural data, which implies the denial of the very existence of their own theories. And the factual evidence of cultural creativeness manifestly contradicts the doctrine that all human actions are causally determined, though it does not prevent the search for specific causal relationships between actions as systems.

We hardly need to mention that, when we call an action creative, we never mean that it creates something out of nothing. No such absolute creativeness has ever been observed. Human creativeness consists in producing data which have never before been identified and experienced by conscious human agents from a combination of data, each of which has been already identified and experienced by conscious human agents. And when we speak of culture as created by human agents, we do not mean that the total growth of culture is one continuous course of creative evolution with an inner dynamic order, in the sense in which Bergson uses this term. We find no factual evidence of a universal creative power which directs this growth. As everybody nowadays knows only too well, many human actions are not productive, but destructive, and, as we mentioned before, many cultural data decay and disappear from human experience, simply because human agents cease to experience and use them. But the fact that culture has grown in spite of destruction and decay provides an additional proof of the wide extension and continuous duration of human creativeness.

We have considerable factual material concerning creative actions in autobiographies, memoirs, letters, diaries of poets, painters, sculptors, musical composers, social reformers, philosophers, explorers, scientists, and in biographies written by their collaborators, followers, and admirers. Though much of this material is unreliable, because subjectively biased, and the total course of a creative action is seldom fully described, yet by comparing many descriptions certain general conclusions can be reached.

We have already discussed, in connection with the historical development of knowledge, two kinds of contributions to culture: new technical inventions and new scientific generalizations. Both are products of human actions which can be termed "creative." These actions have been observed, analyzed, and described, not very thoroughly, but sufficiently to reconstruct tentatively their course. However widely they may differ in certain respects, their course seems to follow a common general pattern. Each of these actions includes considerable thinking not determined by the past, but directed toward the future, and each manifests a continuity of purpose throughout its performance. But none of them conforms with the teleological theory, for the total purpose is not ready and defined in advance before its realization; it develops in the very course of its realization.

In descriptions of these creative actions, we find at least four stages frequently recorded by the agents or/and the observers. The first stage may be characterized as the emergence of an interest in some data of the agent's experience—concrete natural objects or cultural products, abstract ideas, or both. Viewed in reference to later stages, it is already a preliminary, reflective, or unreflective selection of some values which appear important to the agent. The second stage, which we emphasized in our previous discussion, is an increasingly clear awareness of some unnoticed problem, practical or theoretic, involving these data. The third stage is characterized by an increasingly consistent selection and usage of instruments and methods by which the problem is expected to be solved. The fourth stage is the formation of a new cultural product—technical object or system or scientific theory—which constitutes the final solution of the problem.[6]

A similar pattern is found in the course of other creative actions. A painter becomes interested in a landscape or a human figure; a lyrical poet has some emotional personal experiences; a dramatist notices some interesting facts of social interaction between people. Such an interest may eventually lead to awareness of an unsolved aesthetic problem, e.g., the painter finds in a

[6] Besides descriptions of particular inventions and discoveries in biographies, autobiographies, and histories of techniques and sciences, many generalizing works concerning these two kinds of creative actions have been published. These works, however, differ considerably in content. Nearly all of them contain comparative generalizations about the very process of creative activity: e.g., Jacques Piraud, *Invention* (Paris, 1928); Frédéric Paulhan, *Psychologie de l'invention* (Paris, 1930); Gaston Bouthoul, *L'Invention* (Paris, 1936) (including under this term technical inventions, scientific discoveries, and what he calls "moral inventions"); Sir Richard Gregory, *Discovery* (New York: Macmillan, 1929); Austin L. Porterfield, *Creative Factors in Scientific Research* (Durham, N. C.: Duke University Press, 1941).

Other authors try to explain, in addition, the origin of the important discoveries and inventions of particular individuals by a comparative study of their life histories. Alphonse de Candolle, *Histoire des sciences et des savants depuis deux siècles* (1885), started this kind of study and reached certain generalizations, some of which were later reached, probably independently, by Wilhelm Ostwald, *Grosse Männer*, 2d ed. (Leipzig, 1910).

landscape or a human figure a combination of colors or shapes which (so far as he knows) has never yet been presented in a painting; the poet becomes aware that such emotional experiences as his have never yet been adequately expressed in a lyric; the dramatist that such social situations as he observes have never been dramatized. The problem is how to give aesthetic presentation of those data. Or the painter or the poet may develop an interest in some works of his predecessors and become aware of hitherto unnoticed deficiencies or hitherto unnoticed perfections in their aesthetic pattern; the problem is how to substitute a new pattern free of these deficiencies or to revive the perfections of the old pattern. An aesthetic problem can be solved only by producing a new work of art; and this requires an increasingly well-organized selection and methodical use of instruments—canvas, pencil, paints, brushes, and knife, in the case of the painter; words in the case of the poet—by which the data constituting the original material of the artist's experience become gradually synthesized into an aesthetic system potentially accessible to anybody's experience (direct or indirect) which did not exist before.[7]

These four stages of creative action which we find in comparing autobiographical and biographical records do not always follow exactly the temporal sequence outlined in the foregoing; they often overlap. Thus, the emergence of the interest of an inventor in some technical objects, of a scientist in some theoretic concepts or concrete data, of a painter in a landscape, of a dramatist in a social situation may be due to his awareness of an unsolved technical, theoretic, aesthetic problem. Or the awareness of a hitherto unsolved problem may come only after a technician has already begun to apply established techniques, which previously were effective, to some material objects, and finds them unexpectedly ineffective; or after a scientist has already applied an existing theory to some empirical data and unexpectedly discovers that they do not fit into it; or after a painter has started to paint a landscape and sees that he is omitting something aesthetically significant.

Consistent use of instruments and methods for solving a problem may begin before the problem has been exactly defined and may result in a new definition. Thus, a scientist sometimes begins by applying to certain data more

---

[7] Studies of creativeness in art and literature are usually less objective and systematic than comparative studies of technical inventions and scientific discoveries—probably because in these realms of culture most students function as critics and aesthetic philosophers rather than as theoretic investigators; their emphasis on the uniqueness of artistic products interferes with generalization about the actions which produce them. There are, however, quite a few significant, though rather sweeping, psychological theories about artistic creativeness. Thus, Gabriel Séailles, *Essai sur le génie dans l'art* (Paris, 1902), considers what he calls "genius" as a general characteristic of human thought: "Genius is human; there are differences in degree, not differences in nature. . . . Thought is a continuation of life . . . it is a creation. . . . To understand genius, this creative power must be studied in all its degrees, under all its forms . . ." (pp. viii-ix).

exact methods of investigation than those hitherto applied. Only after find-ing new facts can he problematize some previous generalizations. A lyrical poet may start (as Poe claimed he did in writing "The Raven") with purely formal techniques of rhythm, rhyme, or refrain, and only later gradually decide what the emotional content of his poem will be. Or else the purposeful choice and use of definite instruments and methods may begin only after several unsuccessful attempts to solve the problem by trial-and-error tech-niques, as happens to many an inventor or artist. And the final solution of the problem may come before it was expected; a painter sometimes does not finish his painting as he intended, but stops when he suddenly finds that he has achieved an original aesthetic effect. Or, as the solution of the problem approaches, new problems may unexpectedly arise and lead to a reorganiza-tion of the action. All these, however, are secondary variations which do not obliterate the general pattern of creative action.

It is manifestly impossible to divide this total course of progressive forma-tion and realization of a purpose into two parts: a mental, inner, subjective process of thinking before acting and an outward, objective process of per-forming the action. For this would mean, first, that whenever a product of ideational culture has been created by the agent and already exists as a datum of his own experience but is not yet shared by others, we would have to con-sider the whole course of its production not as a real active performance, but as planning a future performance, which will begin only when he starts to communicate its content and meaning symbolically to others. Thus, a poem which has not yet been published or recited before an audience, a musical composition which has not yet been played (e.g., Beethoven's com-positions during the later part of his life when he was deaf), a philosophic or scientific theory which the theorist has not yet communicated to other philosophers or scientists would be classified as unreal, devoid of objective existence, and would acquire reality only when others became aware of it.

Second, whenever the agent, after introducing some observable changes into the objects of his action, stops before completing his performance, starts a different performance, perhaps stops again and begins to act differently, we would have to consider each of these performances as a separate action, ignoring altogether the fact that these stops and new starts manifest a con-tinuity of thinking while acting and contribute to a progressive formation and clarification of his purpose by helping him discover the way in which it can be realized. When a painter again and again repaints certain parts of his land-scape or portrait, when an inventor tries, one after another, various tech-niques, when a scientist successively carries on several different experiments, this does not mean that he is continually changing his goal and using new means to attain this goal, but that he is continually discovering new pos-sibilities of realizing a purpose which, at first indefinite and unpredictable, becomes more and more definite and predictable as some of these possibilities are tested and eliminated, until finally one stands the test.

Creative actions as representative of a general type

The existence of a similar dynamic pattern of creative actions in various realms of culture has been recognized by quite a few investigators, though their conceptions of this pattern differ considerably. Compare, for instance, the attempt of a psychologist like C. Spearman to analyze creativeness as a psychological process and to formulate a few very simple general laws, qualitative and quantitative, with the comparative study of creativeness as a cultural process by a theorist of culture like Sorokin.[8]

The majority of theorists of creativeness have been greatly influenced by the popular idea, deeply rooted in the old cult of heroes, according to which such creative actions as are described in biographies of famous men belong to a separate class, not to be compared with the rest of human actions; for these men are "great" men, endowed with a creative power usually called "genius" which "common," "ordinary" men do not possess.[9] From this point of view, studies of creative actions are inseparably connected with studies of creative men as superior human beings, and investigations become involved in several controversial issues.

The main issue is that of the relative importance of innate biopsychological factors and sociocultural factors in the origin of individual creativeness.[10] Those who accept the innate superiority of genius disagree, however, as to whether it is a superiority of degree or of essential nature.[11] Furthermore, psychologists, trying to reach generalizations about creative personalities, have to find a middle way between the strictly individualistic approach to the

[8] Cf. Charles E. Spearman, *Creative Mind* (New York: Appleton, 1931), chaps. III and IV; and Pitirim Sorokin, *Society, Culture and Personality* (New York: Harper, 1946), chaps. 35, 36, and 37.

[9] There have been partial attempts to trace the history of this idea in some cultures, e.g., Edgar Zilsel, *Die Entstehung des Geniebegriffes* (Tubingen, 1926); Hans Thüme, *Beiträge zur Geschichte des Geniebegriffes in England* (Halle, 1927); but, so far as we know, no general history of the origin and evolution of the concept of "genius" has been written.

[10] The importance of the first was overemphasized, for example, by Francis Galton, *Hereditary Genius*, and Théodule Ribot, *L'Imagination créatrice*. The more recent studies of genius by Lewis M. Terman and his followers were also based on the assumption of the predominance of innate mental superiority; see, e.g., Catherine M. Cox, *The Early Mental Traits of Three Hundred Geniuses*, Vol. II of *Studies of Genius*, ed. Terman (Stanford, Calif.: Stanford University Press, 1926). Whereas Alfred Odin, *Genèse des grands hommes* (Paris, 1893); John Fiske; and Lester Ward ascribed to "nurture" greater importance than to "nature."

[11] Terman, well known for his measurements of intelligence, represents the first theory; a typical representative of the second is Nathaniel D. M. Hirsch, who in his work, *Genius and Creative Intelligence* (Cambridge, Mass.: Sci-Art Publishers, 1931), formulates the conclusion: "The genius differs *in kind* from the species man" (p. 298).

creator as a unique, incomparable personality and the generalizing approach which seeks to discover basic similarities between great men and other personalities.[12] Finally, the problem raised by Radestock and Lombroso as to the connection between genius and insanity has to be solved.[13]

We must discard or postpone all of these issues, since we are not dealing here with total human personalities, only with human actions as limited, dynamic systems. And, contrary to the popular assumption, we find a great multiplicity of actions which, when viewed in their total course, are comparable with those to which creators owe their fame, even though their results add little or even nothing to the historical growth of culture.

The actions which result in well-known contributions to cultural growth are similar, as we have seen, because and insofar as the conscious purpose of each of the agents who make such contributions is to produce something that will be new, valuable, and important not only to himself but to all those who may use his product. In realizing this purpose, he is aware that to have his product recognized as original, different from past products, he must be acquainted with the latter; that to have his product accepted as valuable, he must know the standards by which such products are evaluated; and that his product will be considered important in the measure in which it helps other agents solve their problems. But creative actions, guided by these principles, merely represent the most explicit, systematic, and conscious development of a widely spread dynamic way of acting which only in recent times has begun to be investigated. We might say that they constitute an "ideal type" which an increasing number of other actions tend to approximate. We borrow the term "ideal type" from Max Weber, though we disagree with his theory that the most important ideal type from the point of view of cultural history, especially modern history, is that of *rational* actions in the teleological sense.

Innumerable individual products never become recognized as contributions to a culture, either because few active participants in this culture become aware of them or because those who are aware reject or neglect them. Probably millions of youngsters write poems; uncounted thousands of adults write short stories, novels, or dramatic works which are never published. Many of them are presented to authoritative judges and rejected because they do not contain any aesthetically significant innovations; many others are rejected because, even though they do contain something new, they deviate from aesthetic standards which the judges accept. Some of the authors, however, eventually achieve prominence, though not always in literature, and

[12] Cf. Henri Joly, *Psychologie des grands hommes* (Paris, 1912).
[13] The doctrine that the genius is a psychopathic personality has been quite conclusively invalidated by such prominent psychiatrists as Antoine Rémond and Paul Voivenel, *Le Génie littéraire* (Paris, 1913).

leave autobiographic records of their unsuccessful literary activities. Quite a few teachers of literature have observed attempts at literary production by their students. From their reminiscences and observations it appears that the total course of producing a poem or a novel which is judged as non-original or aesthetically defective does not essentially differ from the total course of producing an original and aesthetically valuable poem or novel.[14] For, unless the author is a conscious plagiarist, when selecting and synthesizing the content of his work, he usually believes that whatever seems new to him will be new to others, without realizing that almost everything he expresses or describes is similar to something which other authors have already expressed or described; and he usually expects that his work, when completed, will be aesthetically valuable, because he is insufficiently acquainted with contemporary standards or insufficiently self-critical.

Plastic art is another realm of culture where recent investigation has shown that actions resulting in cultural products are essentially alike in their dynamic course, though their products differ considerably in the degree of originality, aesthetic worth (as estimated by others), and eventual importance. Many teachers of art have reached the conclusion that artistic talent is very general in late childhood and adolescence. I have discussed this problem in detail with several teachers of art of different nationalities: Polish, English, and American. According to their independent estimates, more than half of their pupils manifested some degree of incipient artistic talent, which in the great majority of cases failed to develop, mainly because other interests pushed aesthetic interests into the background, but partly because our predominant educational methods repress originality except in childish play. In any case, the actions of these talented youngsters in pure and applied art are like the creative actions of prominent artists, though they show less technical skill, less conscious striving for originality, and of course less knowledge and understanding of what originality means in relation to the artistic products of the past.[15]

In the realm of material technique, comparative investigation has proved that the pattern of those technical actions which result in inventions is also very widespread. In modern industry not only is there a rapidly growing number of inventions that are considered sufficiently original and important to be patented, i.e., publicly recognized, but an even larger number of minor

[14] See, e.g., "Creative Expression through Literature," in *Creative Expression. The Development of Children in Art, Music and Dramatics,* eds. Gertrude Hartman and Ann Shumaker, for the Progressive Education Association (New York: Day, 1932), pp. 141-252; and R. W. Babcock, R. D. Horn, and T. H. English, *Creative Writing for College Students* (New York: American Book, 1938).

[15] Cf. "Creative Expression through Art," *op. cit.,* pp. 13-66; also some plans and observations, Josephine Murray and Effie Bathurst, *Creative Ways for Children's Programs* (New York: Silver Burdett, 1938).

inventions, initiating only relatively small modifications in some specialized technical field, which are nevertheless used in private production, and further-more an unknown but probably also large number of inventions (some of them very original) which are ignored as technically or economically useless. We learn about these inventive actions which have little or no influence on subsequent development of material culture chiefly from the autobiogra-phies or biographies of their inventors. Almost every well-known inventor made, besides the inventions which became recognized and used, some minor technical innovations which gained little or no recognition, and occasionally a major invention which, though new, was rejected as useless. Quite a few life histories of craftsmen describe inventions which they used in their special occupational activities; some, though not all of them, were adopted by others. Inventing—often original, but usually unsuccessful—was and is an avocation of individuals who perform various professional roles. Factual evidence indicates that the course of these forgotten inventive actions was like the course of actions which led to famous results. And, ever since Pestalozzi, growing encouragement and systematic observation of the tech-nical interests and the voluntary technical actions of children and adolescents have proved that these actions, if not authoritatively guided and controlled by teachers but performed independently, are often as dynamic, though less in-clusive and less organized, as those of adult creative inventors; occasionally, as a matter of fact, their results are really original and practically important.

In the realm of knowledge, the life histories of scientists show that the course of an investigation may be essentially similar, whether it results in new and important additions to knowledge or merely confirms a previous generalization or leads to new conclusions which are either rejected as invalid or ignored as devoid of scientific significance. Some records of the first, un-successful efforts of scientists who subsequently achieved prominence indicate that the differences between their later and their earlier results were due to a broader and more thorough knowledge of the agglomerated results of previous investigations or improved methods in selecting data, observing facts, drawing and testing conclusions; but the total dynamic actions were alike, including inseparably the progressive definition of the problem and the gradual approach to its solution.

For many years I have attempted to induce my students—undergraduates as well as graduates—to function not as passive learners, but as active scien-tists seeking new discoveries. In consultation with every student in each course, I have tried to ascertain the student's main field of interest within the range of the course. It was usually possible to find some section of this field, as yet unexplored or inadequately explored by sociologists, or to raise doubts about the validity of certain theoretic conclusions reached by previous inves-tigators. In either case, I suggested to the student that there might be some problem still unsolved which he could try to solve. If the student was willing to try, he was advised to look in sociological literature for theories, if any, bearing upon this section of his field of interest and to survey possible sources of factual material. Then he was expected either to define his problem more or less exactly (preferably in class) and discuss possible ways of solving it; or else, if he had reached a stage of confusion, found himself unable to define his problem, and did not know what to do, it was suggested that he should describe and explain how he had reached that stage. In the latter case, after the problem was finally clarified, subsequent results of investigation were usually more original.

My attempts to stimulate independent research have been more or less successful in at least half of the cases; and, when successful, the total course of the student's intellectual performance manifested the same type of creative thinking as that of any prominent scientist, even though (because of limitations of time and opportunity) his materials were necessarily more limited, his investigation less methodically organized, his conclusions more doubtful. Even with these limitations and imperfections, in my opinion, at least 25 per cent of the monographs written by my former students constituted real, even if relatively small, contributions to sociology; and most of them will be utilized and quoted in later works. When I could not induce students to function as scientists, this failure could rarely be explained by their inability to think independently. In most cases, students either were unwilling to devote enough time and effort to research of their own or else showed a tendency to avoid all problems for which no ready and certain solution could be found, a tendency which is frequently developed and stabilized by our prevalent educational pattern, with its examinations and grades.

This relatively wide range of actions which in every realm of culture consciously aim to produce something new and valuable seems to be quite recent in cultural history. Nevertheless, it indicates that creativeness is not an exclusive power of a small minority of great men. Every conscious human agent capable of performing an action can introduce innovations into empirical data. Usually these innovations are too insignificant to be recognized as such or are not considered valuable enough to be used by others; consequently, they soon disappear from the historical world of human experience. This is what happens to nearly all innovations which children and adolescents produce in dealing with the data accessible to their active experience.

Moreover, even in modern societies, where cultural creativeness is gaining wider acceptance than ever before, innovation is still much oftener prevented or repressed than stimulated. Instead, the vast majority of actions are supposed to follow a course which can be fully predicted as soon as they start.

These are the actions on which the teleological theory on the one hand, and the deterministic theory on the other hand are based.

Imitative and habitual actions

Human actions become approximately telic, i.e., achieve the kind of results which their agents define in advance, in the measure in which these actions purposely copy or reproduce previous actions of other agents.

It is difficult, however, to draw a sharp dividing line between reproductive actions and original creative actions. This difficulty is well illustrated in the biographies and autobiographies of actors, singers, concert musicians, and orchestra conductors. Their actions, as compared with those of dramatists and composers, appear as reproductive rather than originally creative. The actor does not create a new dramatic role nor does the singer or conductor produce a new musical composition; the range of any innovations he may introduce is limited. And yet the total course of the action, beginning from the moment when the actor (for whatever reason) becomes interested in a particular role or the conductor in a particular composition up to the final public performance of the role or the final public rendering of the composition, manifests the same progressive evolution and gradual realization of the purpose as the action of the dramatist or the composer. The actor, when he decides to perform a role, or the conductor, when he decides to direct a composition played by the orchestra under his guidance, cannot know in advance how he will finally do it. His decision means that he undertakes a problem, often a very difficult problem. What is the best way of performing this role or directing the playing of this composition? And he can solve this problem only gradually, step by step, by anticipating the next step, thinking of several future possibilities, excluding some, selecting others, until he finds the way which appears to him the best possible way, according to his aesthetic standards.

Although the actor or the conductor does not produce a new role or composition, his reproduction is creative insofar as it adds something new to the content and meaning of the product of the dramatist or composer. This becomes obvious if we compare such an action with that of an actor or musician who in playing a role or a composition *imitates* the reproductive performance of some other actor or musician.

The term "imitation" as used by students of culture[16]—primarily by

---

[16] In recent times imitative actions have also been investigated by psychologists. They usually start and sometimes end with a study of the simplest and least conscious forms of imitation found in the performances of children at an early age. Then the main problem of psychologists is to ascertain the process of emergence of purposive imitation from manifestations of instinctive drives or responses to stimuli. Paul Guillaume, *L'Imitation chez l'enfant* (Paris, 1925), gives a rather good comparative analysis of this process. He begins with what, according to him, can be indiscriminately termed

Gabriel Tarde—means that the imitator not only intends to produce a result similar to that originally produced by somebody else, but tries to reproduce the total course of the original action. Indeed, many imitators are less concerned with the final product than with the performance itself. Tarde's distinction between logical and nonlogical imitation is partly based upon the difference between instances in which individuals imitate the actions of others, mainly because they judge the products of the latter valuable, and those in which they imitate the actions of others, mainly because they consider those others superior to themselves and take them as their models. In every case, however, the imitator who knows the result of the action of his model and has observed the performance which led to this result can define in advance the end of his own action and select in advance the means by which he expects to attain his end. But even such an action, which is consciously intended to be imitative, does not become telic except after a period of *learning*. And learning by conscious imitation, as distinct from conditioning, is a purposive, dynamic activity. Its duration depends on several factors, especially the complexity of the action which the learner imitates and its novelty from the point of view of his previous active experience.[17]

Imitation, of course, presupposes a positive interest in somebody else's action which the individual has observed, remembered, or imagined. Such an interest, however, does not always result in imitation. The interested indi-

---

either "instinct" or "reflex," which is "every innate reaction to a stimulus of internal or external origin" (pp. 1-2). He ends with "complete imitation," which is "accompanied by the consciousness of imitating, after a notion has been formed of the resemblance of the ego to other men and of the equivalence of their actions" (p. 137).

[17] In the history of psychology, the concept of "learning" has been given many different, often conflicting meanings, depending largely upon various ontological conceptions of human nature. Cf. Boyd H. Bode, *How We Learn* (Boston: Heath, 1940), and John M. Fletcher, *Psychology in Education* (New York: Doubleday, 1934), chaps. V ff. Without becoming involved in any ontological issues, we wish to limit the meaning of the term to a definite category of phenomena. First, we see no reason whatever for including in the same concept (as Watson and Thorndike have done) the physiological processes of building up new conditioned reflexes, which have been observed by experimental studies of animal behavior, and processes of purposive learning to perform new conscious actions. Second, if the term "learning" is limited to conscious processes, it should not include memorizing, since the latter (though a condition of learning how to perform new actions) by no means always results in the performance of actions. Third, the action which an agent has learned to perform may or may not be repeated hereafter; only if often repeated does it become habitual. Thus, learning does not mean acquiring new habits. Fourth, although learning completely controlled by teachers and spontaneous learning without teachers differ considerably, nonetheless, whatever the difference, the learner is never a passive object, but always an agent, whether the action he learns be selected by him or by the teacher. What is important is that the more spontaneous his learning, the nearer it approaches creativeness. Cf., e.g., Fletcher, *op. cit.*; Harold S. Tuttle, *A Social Basis of Education* (New York: Crowell, 1934); Nathaniel Cantor, *Dynamics of Learning* (Buffalo, N. Y.: Foster & Stewart, 1946).

vidual may have no intention really to perform an action like the one in which he was interested, but may merely reproduce it ideationally by identifying himself with the agent, viewing the values with which the agent deals and the changes which the agent initiates as he believes the agent views them. Such ideational reproduction may be called "vicarious participation" in somebody else's action. This is what an admirer of a painting who is not a painter does when he remembers or imagines how the painter produced it, or what enthusiastic spectators at a football game do when they observe the performance of the players.

Imitation actually occurs only when the vicarious participant really attempts to perform a second action which he expects to be similar to the one in which he is interested. As his performance proceeds, the imitator usually finds that his expectation is not being fulfilled, that the course of his action deviates from that which he is trying to imitate, and that the result toward which it leads is unlike the original result which he intended to reproduce.

Such is the typical first experience of every conscious learner, unless he is guided by a teacher who controls his whole performance. If after his first failure he starts again an imitative attempt, he problematizes his task from the point of view of his own active experience, judged in comparison with the presumed active experience of the other agent who has become his model. So long as he is learning, his purpose is to make every step of his total performance conform with that of his model; for, although in choosing the action he tried to imitate he explicitly or implicitly decided what kind of end he wanted to attain and believed he knew by what means it could be attained, he is now aware that he still does not quite know how to realize these means or to attain this end.

Only after his learning has been completed (with or without the aid of a teacher) can he perform this kind of action without having to do in the course of his performance the kind of thinking he did while learning. His only problem then is the initial problem, whether to perform this kind of action at a particular time under the given conditions. Once he solves this problem positively and decides to do what he knows will have to be done in order to achieve the final result as defined in advance, his purpose is settled and he does not expect to face any other problem. Even then, however, new problems are apt to emerge if some new factors unexpectedly interfere with his performance; he may then have to think again and modify his purpose.

As we have seen, the deterministic theory is based on the observation of actions which seem explicable and predictable as caused by processes which occur among the data of the agent's experience but are not initiated by him. Now, actions—conscious human actions—approach this type in the very measure in which the agent repeatedly performs without unexpected interference a certain kind of action which he may have learned by imitation or performed spontaneously at first. Repetition leads to the formation of a *habit*. A habitual action differs from a telic action in that it is not consciously problematized. Having repeatedly decided to perform under given conditions an action similar to one which he had performed in the past under apparently similar conditions, the agent is led by the recurrence of similar conditions to start a similar action with less and less initial reflection. Eventually, a habitual action can be conceived as an unreflective response to a stimulus. But unreflective does not mean unconscious. For, if anything interferes with the habitual performance, the agent shows that he was conscious of what he was doing by becoming aware that he is facing an unexpected problem, and his action changes from unreflective to reflective.

*   *   *

Thus, in the light of empirical evidence derived from the observation of conscious human actions, it appears that creative actions, reproductive (imitative) actions, and habitual actions differ mainly in the formation of their purposes. At one limit we find creative actions, in which the purpose continues to evolve until the action is completed. At the other limit, we observe habitual actions, in which the purpose is formed at the very moment when the action starts. In between these limits fall imitative actions, in which stabilization of the purpose is achieved during the first part of the action and the purpose remains unchanged during its realization. Or, stated in other terms, the first part of a creative action consists in gradually defining a problem which does not become fully solved until the end; in an imitative action, the problem is given at the very beginning, and the first part of the action consists in determining what will be its solution; in a habitual action, the problem and its solution became defined while the habit was being formed, and this definition continues to be implicitly accepted and followed.

Of course, these are differences in degree, not in specie; creative actions, imitative actions, and habitual actions are characteristic *types*, not separate *classes*. The reason why we choose creative actions as the most representative type of human actions, and characterize the other two types by comparing them with this main type, is that comparative analysis of creative actions as dynamic systems provides the best foundation for distinguishing clearly conscious human actions as a general category of cultural phenomena from organic behavior as a natural phenomenon. When biologists wanted to establish a clear distinction between organic and unorganic phenomena, they also chose the most developed organic systems (the higher animals), the most obviously irreducible to mere combinations of chemical compounds and physical processes, as ideal types of the first category.

What is the connection between our typology of human actions in general and systematic taxonomy, i.e., division of actions into classes and subclasses according to similarities and differences which are considered more essential than those between our three types, or any other types for that matter? We must postpone the answer to this question. Meanwhile, to illustrate the distinction between types and classes, we appeal to common sense. Take two kinds of actions: writing poems and making mechanical tools. The difference between the two is much more obvious than the difference between writing an original poem and writing an imitation of somebody else's poem, or making for the first time a tool which was invented by the maker and making for the nth time a tool invented by somebody else.

The question of destructive actions

We have based our heuristic conception of actions primarily on the analysis of creative actions and their comparison with imitative and habitual actions. But how about those actions which constitute the very antithesis of creative actions in that, instead of purposely producing new values which did not exist hitherto, they purposely destroy existing values and deliberately eliminate them from the world of human experience? Such actions may be termed "destructive." This term does not apply to actions in the course of production, especially in the technical field, which often require a partial destruction of the values which are being used as material. The difference lies in the fact that values which are destroyed without being used are *negative* values from the point of view of the agent. Exterminating animals or plants which are considered not only useless, but harmful; killing human enemies; destroying material products which enemies use in aggressive or defensive struggle; eliminating any cultural products which are regarded as evil, impure, dangerous, or obstructive: These are familiar examples of deliberately destructive actions.

We shall analyze and compare some of them later, especially those which are connected with intergroup conflicts. We shall see that, however much they may differ from those actions which we have surveyed, their analysis does not affect our conclusions as to the dynamic course of conscious human actions. At first glance, destruction is simple, as compared with production. Killing a man is obviously simpler than curing him if he is sick, and incomparably simpler than the long sequence of widely diverse particular actions involved in raising and acculturating him from infancy to maturity. During the last war, many a church, library, and museum which took years to create was almost instantly destroyed. Since the atomic bomb has been invented, one individual can destroy in a few minutes a city which many thousands of men gradually built in the course of several centuries.

Probably because of this apparent simplicity, the principle of causal determinism has frequently been applied to destructive actions. Thus, certain social Darwinists who apply the biological theory of "struggle for existence" to interhuman relationships have tried to explain the destructive human actions which are common in warfare as innate antagonistic reaction to specific behavior of other human beings. Even now, the causes of war are being sought in such processes as population pressure, competitive struggle for the means of existence, etc.

Whereas, if we investigate a deliberately destructive action in its total course, we shall find that it is by no means simple. The action of killing a man or destroying a material object by the use of physical instruments represents usually only one step, though perhaps the decisive one, toward the solution of some problem which may have been gradually defined long before and may not be finally solved until long after. Sometimes, indeed, an individual kills another in physical fight without any previous anticipation or intention; in such a case, killing may be definable as a simple reaction to the behavior of the other individual and explained psychobiologically. However, whenever the conscious purpose to kill a man is formed before an actual physical fight begins, or is realized without a physical fight, the formation of the purpose involves various positive values which the agent believes to be harmed or endangered by the existence of the other man. It is thus impossible to explain or to predict the action of killing without making an investigation of these values and of the origin of the agent's belief in a connection between them and the other man; for there are many different problems for which homicide seems to individual agents to offer a complete or partial solution. This is well known to criminologists, especially to those who have investigated comparatively homicidal actions in culturally different societies and culturally different groups or classes within the same society. And an adequate survey of the formation of the conscious purpose which precedes and accompanies intergroup warfare will show that killing enemies and destroying their cultural products is expected to provide at least a partial solution of problems—often very old problems—which involve not merely individual values, but common values of the group as a whole.

*   *   *

Let us summarize the hypothetic results of our comparative survey of actions in the sense of conscious human actions. We include under this term only those performances which imply that the agents who perform them experience, select, and evaluate the data involved in their actions, and initiate factual relationships between them to produce anticipated changes in their content. An action is, thus, a dynamic system of changing values which should be investigated in its total course. When so investigated, it proves to consist in the formation of a purpose and its realization. Whatever its purpose, and no matter when it is formed, its realization cannot be separated from its formation. The formation of the purpose directs the course of its realization. This is what all human actions have in common.

Now, in view of the progress that has been achieved by sciences of culture in systematic studies of human actions, we postulate that all actions as limited systems can be analyzed and compared, like organic, chemical, or physical systems, and that from their comparative analysis taxonomic generalizations can be made upon which other scientific generalizations—causal, functional, genetic—depend. We shall devote five chapters to a critical study of the methods used in generalizing about actions. Before proceeding with this study, however, it may be useful to take into consideration two serious difficulties which investigators have to face when they try to compare actions of any kind whatsoever.

Active Tendencies

The problem of unfinished actions

We have postulated that an action as a dynamic system of changing values should be investigated in its total course, until it is completed, and that such investigations enable cultural scientists to reach comparative generalizations about actions. But many an action which was expected to be completed never becomes completed. Its purpose begins to be realized, but the course of its realization unexpectedly stops. How can we generalize about such unfinished actions?

A seemingly easy solution of this problem has been provided by those students of actions who use such psychological concepts as "wish," "desire," "volition," "urge," and classify together actions which apparently aim to satisfy similar wishes, desires, volitions, urges, whether their aims are attained or not. We do not question the usefulness of these concepts for psychology as the comparative science of individual experiences; but when applied to actions as systems of values which form the common data of human experience, they have proved methodically inadequate.[1]

A wish or desire is implicitly conceived, if not explicitly defined, as a subjective phenomenon included in the individual's stream of experiences, distinct and separated from objective reality. Its existence can be ascertained, even when it does not result in an action. It may be directly identified by the individual's psychological reflection or, if the individual is unaware of it, may be indirectly deduced by psychoanalytic methods from symbolic expressions. And when it is followed by an active performance, it is presumed to remain subjectively the same, whatever the objective character of this performance. Consequently, very different actions may be interpreted as manifestations of similar wishes or desires.

[1] We omit here the problem of connection between human wishes, desires, volitions, etc., as psychological phenomena and biological processes, for it belongs rather to the theory of motivation.

Such a conception has two manifest weaknesses. On the one hand, it is inapplicable to collective actions, since there is no factual evidence of the existence of collective wishes or desires as psychological phenomena. On the other hand, it leads to sweeping classificatory generalizations about individual actions which differ, depending on what kinds of wishes, desires, volitions, etc., the theorists consider basic. Compare, for instance, McDougall's generalizations about actions (based on his theory of instincts in the sense of innate desires) [2] with the generalizations of Freud and his followers (based on the theory of the libido); Pareto's classification of basic residues; and the theory of four main desires first formulated and used in *The Polish Peasant* by Thomas and Znaniecki to interpret the actions of participants in primary groups, later renamed "wishes" and widely applied (with important changes) in social psychology by Thomas and others.[3]

We think that such methodical deficiencies can be avoided by using the concept of *active tendency* in the sense of "tendency to realize the purpose of an action."[4]

An active tendency does not precede or cause an action. It is inherent in the action, manifested in the progressive realization of its purpose as this purpose is formed. It is not a separate, distinct empirical phenomenon directly accessible to psychological observation. Its existence can be ascertained only by its function, and its function can be discovered by observing changes in the factual relationships between values and in their empirical content which the agent initiates as the action proceeds.

From this point of view, a wish in the psychological sense is merely an incipient tendency, which may or may not develop into a fully active tendency. It represents that initial stage of an action when the agent becomes interested in some values and aware of a problem, but has as yet no definite purpose to be realized. Frequently, such an incipient tendency never becomes an active tendency; and, even when it does, we cannot tell in advance what kind of active tendency it will be. For instance, many a boy reading so-called comics becomes interested in some fictitious hero. This interest may or may not be accompanied by a wish to learn what the hero will do next. Such a wish may or may not develop into the manifest active tendency to read subsequent installments. But if this interest in the hero is connected with

[2] Ellsworth Faris, *op. cit.*, chap. VI, "Are Instincts Data or Hypotheses?" mentions the number of instincts listed by the following authors: James, 26; Angell, 13; Edward Thorndike, 40 or more; McDougall, 15; Trotter, 4; Ames, 2; Freud, Young, Le Bon, 1 each (pp. 61-73).

[3] The "desire for power" was dropped, and the "wish for response" introduced. See the criticism of Herbert Blumer in his "An Appraisal of Thomas and Znaniecki's *The Polish Peasant in Europe and America,* Bulletin 44 (New York: Social Science Research Council, 1939).

[4] I first used this concept in *The Laws of Social Psychology* (Chicago: University of Chicago Press, 1925), but redefined it in the light of later research.

an interest in the boy's own self, it is apt to be accompanied by the wish that he were the hero. If well aware that this wish can never be gratified, he does nothing. But if he has vague hopes that at least a partial gratification may be possible at some time in the future, the wish may be followed by day-dreaming, an imaginary enactment of his role as a hero in various situations. The daydreaming may remain secret, or the products of his imagination may be orally communicated to others; perhaps later, oral storytelling will change into writing stories. Or else, if the boy is a leader of a gang, he may induce the gang to re-enact in play some of the stories, with himself as the hero. In any case, we cannot draw from a psychological comparison of wishes or desires any generalizations about active tendencies; on the contrary, only by investigating the active tendencies empirically manifested and tracing them back to their origins can generalizations about wishes as incipient tendencies be drawn.

In some respects, the concept of tendency is analogous to that of physical force; and it helps us to apply quantitative methods to human actions and their relationships, just as the concept of force has helped us to apply quantitative methods to relationships between natural processes. However, the analogy is only partial; no principle analogous to that of transformation of energy can be applied to active tendencies. Since tendencies are manifested only in the course of actions, and actions are not natural processes, but cultural systems, each with a limited historical duration, we have no scientifically valid reason for assuming that the tendency manifested in a particular action existed before in some other form or that after an action has been completed the tendency which was manifest in it will continue to exist in some other form.

This does not mean that no general similarities exist between tendencies and no genetic connections between past and present tendencies; but such similarities and connections do not imply any essential *identity* of tendencies underlying their empirical differences. To clarify this point and at the same time to eliminate any confusion between the concept of active tendency and such concepts as "wish," "desire," "volition," "urge," let us look at the Freudian theory. According to this theory, the sexual libido is the most influential psychological force, continuously functioning, essentially the same, but undergoing various transformations and manifesting itself in a great diversity of actions—hedonistic actions bearing upon the individual's own body, social actions bearing upon other human individuals, artistic actions, religious actions, etc.[5] No doubt a particular person or persons of the other sex

[5] The analogy between the physical concept of energy and that of the Freudian libido as psychological energy which can be transferred into various active forces is inherent in Freud's theory of civilization. See Sigmund Freud, *Civilization and its Discontents*, trans. by Joan Rivière (London, 1939), pp. 62-63. Perhaps the most explicit brief

or of the same sex or even the individual's own body may be to the individual a more or less lasting value which, when experienced, usually becomes an object of emotional interest. Sometimes, however, the individual remains satisfied with this emotional experience of his sexual values, without any wish for sensory satisfaction. And even when he has such a wish, it sometimes finds expression only in dreams or daydreaming, imaginative representations of actions which he may never realistically try to perform. Only when his wish is followed by the formation of a more or less definite purpose to obtain some kind and degree of sensory sexual satisfaction and an attempt is made to realize this purpose can we speak of an active sexual tendency. Actions which manifest such tendencies—heterosexual, homosexual, autosexual— have been analyzed, compared, and classified, though not always very thoroughly, and a considerable literature about them has sprung up. But some of these studies have included many other kinds of actions, the purposes of which are entirely different: hedonistic actions, tending to obtain sensory satisfaction from food and drink; the vast diversity of technical actions, tending to produce material objects; various social actions, individual and collective, the objects of which have no sexual meaning to the agents; various magical and religious actions which do not include any sexual values; actions of plastic art and literature, devoid of sexual contents. The theory that the tendencies manifested in such actions are variations of tendencies originally manifested in sexual actions obviously conflicts with scientifically reliable factual evidence.

Even when actions do include sexual values, they may tend to realize purposes which are not sexual. The purpose which a lyrical poet tends to realize in composing a poem with an erotic content is to compose the poem; this tendency as empirically manifested is obviously different from the tendency to obtain sensory sexual satisfaction and obviously similar to the tendency to write a lyrical poem exalting a military hero or a victor in the Olympic games. An artist who paints a nude from a living model is probably interested sexually in women, perhaps even in this particular model, but painting a woman is much more like painting a landscape than like having sexual

---

and popular statement is that of Martin W. Pack, *The Meaning of Psychoanalysis* (New York: Knopf, 1931), "Libido: 'The dynamic expression of the sexual instinct or the energy of that instinct which deals with all that is included in the word "love." It comprises not only sexual love but self-love, love for parents and children, friendship, love for humanity in general as well as attachment to concrete objects and abstract ideas'" (p. 271).

Edwin B. Holt in *The Freudian Wish* (New York: Holt, 1915), also identifies the wish with "energy." However, he thinks it is best "not to hypotheticate . . . any such thing as 'psychic energy,' but look rather for the energy so expanded in the nervous system" (p. 4).

Jacob L. Moreno gives a good criticism of this concept in *Psychodrama*, Vol. I (New York: Beacon House, 1946).

intercourse with a woman. Nor can we prove that writing erotic poetry or painting a nude is a vicarious substitute for sexual intercourse, resorted to by individuals whose sexual desires have been inhibited; certainly neither Ovid nor Rubens showed any signs of inhibition of sexual desires in their relations with women.[6]

This leaves still unsolved such genetic problems as whether a particular individual's interests in certain aesthetic, religious, social values did or did not evolve from his sexual interests. In either case, how did he learn to perform the specific actions which deal with these values? To solve these problems, a very thorough, nonprejudiced, factual knowledge of the individual's total life history is required.

Once we ascertain from observation and communication, after an action has begun to be performed, what its tendency is and what kind of purpose the agent is trying to realize, we can predict conditionally the future course of this action. We base this prediction upon comparative studies of actions, not upon any classification of human instincts, desires, wishes, urges, as psychological phenomena. When we compare the course of an action which has begun to be performed with the known course of an action which has been completed, and when we find that in both cases the agents became interested in certain data which they experienced and evaluated similarly and started to introduce similar changes into these data, we assume that the tendencies of these actions are alike and conclude that the action which has begun to be performed will pursue a similar course and achieve similar results as the action which has been completed. We have called the heuristic principle on which this conclusion is based the *principle of achievement*.[7]

In applying this principle to a comparative study of actions, we must realize that all similarities are relative. No two actions are absolutely similar: They always differ in some respects. The range of variations is at a minimum in unreflected habitual actions, at a maximum in highly original creative actions, with imitative actions falling in between. Collective actions which repeatedly follow a planned model—as in mass production in mechanized industry—vary less, say, than the productive actions of individual craftsmen who also follow the same model. But under the general premise that actions can be classified, differences between particular actions of the same class do not prevent us from assuming and testing the assumption that, once the tendency of an action has been manifested at some stage of the latter, its sub-

[6] There are quite a few works applying the Freudian theory to literature and art. Cf., e.g., Otto Rank, *Der Künstler* (1907); Charles Baudouin, *Psychoanalysis and Aesthetics*, trans. by Eden and Cedar Paul (New York: Dodd, 1924), applied specifically to Émile Verhaeren, the Belgian poet; René Laforgue, *The Defeat of Baudelaire, A Psycho-Analytical Study of the Neurosis of Charles Baudelaire*, trans. by Herbert Agar and Virginia Woolf (London, 1932).

[7] Florian Znaniecki, *The Method of Sociology* (New York: Farrar, 1934), pp. 68-69.

sequent functioning and final achievement can be conditionally predicted, provided the range of variations which this class includes be taken into account.

When an agent manifests a tendency to create a new value within a certain realm of culture, different from the values which he or other agents have produced before, in predicting the subsequent course of his action we must anticipate that this course will include some innovations which cannot be predicted on the basis of our knowledge of previous actions. But since the agent's tendency to create a new value implies that he is acquainted with the products of his predecessors in the same realm of culture and that its achievement requires methodical use of specific materials and instruments, the differences between the course of his action and those of his predecessors are limited; and we can predict within what limits his unpredictable innovations will occur. For instance, from historical evidence we know that there were definite limits for innovations beyond which Greek tragedians or sculptors of the fifth century B.C., Byzantine painters, French architects of the twelfth century, Italian painters of the *quattrocento*, German poets of the *Sturm und Drang* period, eighteenth-century physicists or astronomers, nineteenth-century composers of symphonies did not intend to go. And, if we have studied comparatively recent creative actions in the respective realms of culture—after discovering what problem a painter, a dramatist, an inventor, an astronomer, a biologist tends to solve—we can predict what kind of dynamic, but definable general pattern his action will follow, with more or less significant variations.

Obstacles impeding the completion of actions

Suppose now that, contrary to our prediction, an action stops before its completion. This does not invalidate our definition of its active tendency, provided the definition was based on sufficient factual evidence; nor does it prevent us from classifying it with other actions which manifest similar tendencies and become completed. It shows, however, that our prediction (like all the predictions which scientists make) was valid only under the condition that no unforeseen factor interfere with the future course of the action. If the action unexpectedly stops, this indicates that there is some obstacle which impedes the achievement of its tendency. We must therefore try to discover the obstacle.

On the basis of a comparative study of many uncompleted actions, we have reached the conclusion that an action stops if the materials or instruments which the agent intended to use for the realization of its purpose prove inaccessible to him or unfit for this use. We find, however, a wide range of variations in the nature of such obstacles and their effects upon particular actions. Thus, since the neuromuscular system of the individual's organism is the primary, indispensable instrument of all his actions, all his performances are immediately stopped by his death; and at any time particular performances may be stopped by some specific change in his neuromuscular system. But an action which an individual starts to perform, though interrupted by his death, may be continued and completed by somebody else. A physical ailment—cold, "flu," indigestion—may be sufficient to stop one individual's performance of a work that he has started, while another individual, also ailing, may nonetheless continue to perform the same kind of work. One wounded soldier stops fighting, while another, similarly wounded, continues to fight. A boy may feel too sick to go to school, but not too sick to participate in an outdoor group game.

Other familiar obstacles which prevent the achievement of a tendency are technical. Actions, whether individual or collective, which include natural materials and cultural instruments are stopped if the agents find that some of the materials or instruments they need are unavailable or have become apparently useless for the purposes of those actions. Here also considerable differences between actions may be found. Some farmers in the Dust Bowl stopped farming after a year or two of drought, while others persisted until the drought ended. Reconstruction of the material culture destroyed during the last war often proceeded, notwithstanding obstacles which would appear insuperable in normal times, as exemplified by European peasants returning to their ruined villages, rebuilding them, and starting agriculture in spite of lack of adequate tools, seed, and domestic animals. In the realm of economics, an action which relies on money as a necessary instrument is impeded if the agent loses some of the money he intended to use; but, while some businessmen become quickly discouraged by financial losses, others try again and again in spite of financial difficulties.

Terms like "will power" and "strong will" have been used to denote the psychological characteristics of individuals who overcome obstacles which others are too powerless, too weak, to overcome. But, while the concept of will as a lasting psychological force which individuals possess in various degrees may be useful for the typology of human personalities, it is of no use for the comparative study of human actions. In the first place, it cannot account for certain differences between the active performances of the same individual. An individual who is prevented from completing one kind of action by obstacles which to other agents seem easy to overcome may complete a different kind of action, in spite of obstacles which others deem difficult to overcome. Second, it is not applicable to collective actions, since modern sociologists have invalidated the idea that human collectivities are endowed with "will" as a permanent psychological force comparable to individual will. Finally, as popularly used, it covers not only an individual's capacity to realize the purposes of his actions by overcoming obstacles, but also his resistance to the influences which affect the very purposes of his actions; and this, as we shall see, is an entirely different matter.

Therefore, we suggest that the concept of *persistency of tendencies* be used in comparing the effects of obstacles upon the realization of the purposes of actions. A tendency which continues to function, although the course of its achievement is impeded by an unexpected obstacle, is more persistent than a tendency which ceases to function under the impact of a similar obstacle. Of course, the persistency of a tendency does not imply that the purpose of the act will be finally realized, only that there is some probability—be it great or small—of its realization, so long as active attempts are made to overcome obstacles, e.g., to obtain other materials or instruments as substitutes for those which appear unavailable, or to find a way of using those which appear useless.

The concept of persistency of tendencies, as here defined, implies quantitative differences and raises the problem of scientific measurement of such differences. This problem is difficult, and its difficulties should not be underrated; but it cannot be said to be insolvable. We shall not attempt to solve it here, but only mention certain possibilities of its solution.

The first and rather familiar measurable difference in the persistency of tendencies is difference in the length of time which agents spend in trying to overcome obstacles. Obviously, this difference is significant only in comparing actions with similar purposes, since the length of time required to complete actions with different purposes, even when they are not impeded, can vary widely. It usually takes an hour or two to cook a dinner, and several months to plant and harvest a crop; but many years of research may be needed to solve an important scientific problem. Moreover, we must remember that the historical duration of an action does not imply that its performance is continuous in time. Almost every long-lasting action is performed with interruptions.

Second, to measure the persistency of tendencies, a method must be found of measuring the degree to which specific obstacles impede the realization of specific purposes. This has been done more or less exactly in some studies of biological and physical obstacles. The degree in which certain diseases or injuries impede the performance of certain actions has been estimated by physicians. Quantitative methods have been used in estimating the degree to which geographical obstacles, viewed with reference to available means of transportation, impede trade or military aggression. Such studies can be eventually extended to obstacles arising from cultural conditions.

In any case, in comparing the persistency of tendencies manifested in particular active performances, we do not have to go beyond an analysis of each of these actions separately as a limited system. The essential problem is *how* a certain unexpected obstacle affects the course of an action, and it can be solved without investigating the cause of this obstacle. The conditions which made the realization of a purpose difficult or impossible may have existed already when the purpose was being formed, only the agent was not aware of them. Columbus was unaware of the existence of the American continent, which made it impossible for him to reach Asia by sailing westward. Of course, when the realization of a purpose is impeded by some change which has occurred in the values included in the action, an investigator will usually try to discover the cause of the change, e.g., find what biological processes have incapacitated an individual's organs, what physical processes have caused the deterioration or destruction of technical instruments which an agent needed, what economic processes have caused the loss of a business-man's money. But even when the cause of the change remains unknown, its effect upon the realization of a particular purpose can be ascertained.

The problem of changing purposes

A different and more difficult problem which investigators of actions have to face arises when an action, though not stopped, becomes diverted from its course by a change of purpose. Instead of the original purpose which began to be realized, a different purpose becomes finally realized.

This is where the question of relationships between actions comes in. An action as a system of values, though limited, is not isolated; some of the values which it includes may be also included in a different action performed by the same agent or another agent. What is done to such values in the course of one of these actions affects, in some way and in some measure, the course of the other, depending upon the connection between the purposes of the actions. The realization of one of these purposes may help or hinder in various degrees the realization of the other purpose. If the agent is conscious of the relationship between the action he is performing and some other action, this consciousness influences the purpose which he is tending to realize.

Students of action have been for a long time aware of such relationships. Psychologists have problematized mainly relationships between actions of the same individual agent, while sociologists have concentrated on the problem of the influence which the actions of one agent have upon the actions of another. Unfortunately, as we shall see, many investigators in both sciences have applied rather indiscriminately the principle of causation; instead of using it only to explain changes in actions, they have used it to explain actions. Consequently, they fail to distinguish clearly the two very different kinds of relationships between actions: *functional relationships* and *causal relationships*.

This difference may be briefly characterized as follows: If an agent at the time he starts an action expects that its course will be affected by the course of another action, the formation of his purpose becomes adapted to these expectations and, as the purposes of both actions proceed toward their realization, they are functionally interdependent, though one of them may be more dependent, the other less so. Thus, a businessman's actions of buying and selling are functionally interdependent, so are the technical and the intellectual actions of an experimental scientist. Every case of active cooperation between individuals is an instance of functional interdependence between their actions. But should an agent who actively tends to realize a purpose already formed become unexpectedly aware that some other action is interfering with this realization, the purpose of his action undergoes a change; instead of the original purpose, he tends to realize a more or less different purpose. Such a change can be considered an effect of which the other action is the cause.

We shall later devote considerable attention to problems of functional relationships between actions. Now we have to survey critically causal explanations used by psychologists and sociologists, so as to eliminate those which are heuristically defective.

Causal relationships between actions of the same individual

We begin with psychological attempts to solve problems of relationships between actions of the same individual by applying the old concept of *motive*. This concept, as we know, is primarily intended to explain actions. Every action is supposed to have some motive behind it without which it would not be performed. A motive is, thus, that which makes an agent perform a certain action.[8] It is difficult to draw a clear distinction between a motive, a wish, or a desire, on the one hand, a goal or end, on the other hand; indeed, we might say that motive usually represents a synthesis of both wish and goal.

However, thinkers who try to explain actions by motives acknowledge that the motive which causes a certain action to be performed is not always known to others or even to the agent himself. If he acted as he was expected to act under the given conditions and as others would presumably act under similar conditions, his motive is supposed to be explicit: He really wanted or desired to attain the end he did attain, or at least tried to attain it and no other. No one doubts that an individual who after many hours of fasting eats a large meal is motivated by hunger; one who runs away from danger is motivated by fear; one who induces a woman to have sexual intercourse with him is motivated by libido.

Often, however, an agent performs an action which was not expected or which others would not have performed under similar conditions. This means

---

[8] As Paul T. Young explicitly states in the introduction to his general biopsychological study, *Motivation of Human and Animal Behavior* (Ann Arbor, Mich.: University of Michigan Press, 1933): "The central problem [of this book] is *the determination of behavior in man and animal.* From the start to the finish we have asked: 'What determines or motivates?'"

that he must have had some other, "real" motive, different from the "apparent" motive, which made him act as he did; or perhaps his action was caused by a combination of the apparent motive with several other motives which were not apparent. Thus, when a politician does a service to a rival whom he has hitherto consistently tried to harm, the latter wonders whether he is really motivated by altruism or by a desire to make friends, or whether some other, hidden motive lies behind his action. When a young man who has been successful with attractive girls manifests erotic interest in a wealthy girl whom all his friends consider sexually unattractive, they presume that his real motive is not erotic, but economic.

The main heuristic weakness of the theory of motives lies in the explicit or implicit assumption that we know what an individual would not do, if he were *not* urged by a certain motive. Such an assumption is usually based not on scientific research, but on popular theories of human nature in general or of specific variants of human nature (cf. Chapter 2). The source of this weakness must be sought in the very origin of judgments about motives. As C. Wright Mills has pointed out, these judgments, whether expressed by the agent himself or by others, are mostly evaluative; they serve to justify or condemn past actions and to influence future actions.[9]

Of course, with the progress of psychology the imputation of motives has become more objective and methodical and may be useful for psychological research. But it does not contribute much to a comparative study of actions. For, if we take into consideration all the motives, conscious and unconscious, recently emerging or deeply rooted in an individual's past, we come to the conclusion that similar actions of different individuals, or even of the same individual at different periods of his life, may be caused by various motives or various combinations of diverse motives.[10] This precludes any valid causal

[9] C. Wright Mills, "Situated Actions and Vocabularies of Motives," *Am. Sociol. Rev.,* Vol. V, No. 6 (December, 1940), pp. 904-13. This approach to the study of motives, as explicitly defined by the people who reflect about actions, has been fully developed by Kenneth Burke, who considers linguistic statements as the key to the understanding of motives. See *A Grammar of Motives* (New York: Prentice, 1945) and *A Rhetoric of Motives* (New York: Prentice, 1950). Though we may doubt the validity of generalizations about *motives* based on such evidence, there is no doubt that Burke has made very important and original contributions to the comparative study of symbolically expressed *attitudes*.

[10] For the multiplicity of "drives" or "motivating factors" and their diverse combinations "in any situation," see Young, *op. cit.*; Leonard T. Troland, *The Fundments of Human Motivation* (New York: Van Nostrand, 1928), especially chap. XXI, "Complexes and their Complexity," pp. 368-97.

George A. Coe, *The Motives of Men* (New York: Scribner, 1930), after surveying various psychological and biological theories, concludes that in investigating motives, one must take into consideration "the great range and diversity of human motivation, the great plasticity of it (that is, the indefinitely many possibilities . . . for the same individual) and the organic character of it (that is, the capacity for action from the standpoint of a desired whole)," p. 84.

generalizations. And, like the classification of actions by wishes or desires, the explanation of actions by motives is altogether inapplicable to collective actions.

If investigators reject these scientifically unproductive attempts to find primary and secondary causes of specific human actions and limit their research to the study of observable relationships between actions, they may be able to reach increasingly exact inductive generalizations which can be tested by factual evidence. And here again the concept of *active tendency* will be necessary. For, since actions have a limited duration, an action can influence the course of another only while both of them are being performed, though one may have started recently, while the other may be already nearing its completion; one may be long-lasting and the other short-lasting, or one may be temporarily interrupted, while the performance of the other goes on without interruption. This principle is as obvious as in the causal relationship between changes in two natural systems, which is possible only while both systems exist. To ascertain such an influence, the tendencies of both actions, as well as their factual connection through some common values, must be empirically manifested.

Take some of the typical cases in which students of motives are interested. A wealthy lady of the leisure class donates a fund to a charitable association; a captain of industry establishes an institute for scientific research; a businessman, having already received definite values or services from somebody else, gives to the other the values or services which he had promised to give under contractual agreement. In observing these actions, we cannot deny in the face of the empirical evidence that the purpose which the charitable donor tends to realize is to help the poor, through the medium of social workers, that the purpose which the captain of industry tends to realize is to promote scientific research, that the purpose which the businessman tends to realize is to fulfill his contractual obligations. This empirical evidence could be questioned only if some other evidence showed that the agent was surreptitiously doing something intended to prevent the realization of his explicit purpose. Otherwise, the problem is not whether the tendency is real, but whether it is the same tendency which the agent manifested when he began to deal with the values included in his action, or whether it is a different tendency.

In the first case, there is no causal problem, no scientific reason for trying to explain the action by some ulterior motive. Just as we cannot deny the existence of a tendency which is empirically manifested, we cannot impute the causative power which made the agent perform this action to the existence of some hidden tendency which was not empirically manifested at the time when the action we are studying was being performed. In the latter case, a causal problem does arise: What caused this *change* of tendency? The problem will be solved if we find sufficient empirical evidence to prove that the original purpose of the action we are investigating did undergo a change under the influence of some other action which was being performed at the time.

Let us illustrate these two possibilities. First, suppose we find that the lady, long before giving money to the charitable organization, had manifested an altruistic interest in the poor, made some attempts to help them, and finally decided that the most effective way to do so was to provide social workers with the necessary funds. Then her donation was simply the final stage in the realization of a purpose which developed gradually. We know what is essential about her action. We may, indeed, want to go further back in her personal life history and trace the genesis of her interest and of her acceptance of the specific pattern of social relations according to which the rich are supposed to treat the poor as objects of charity. But genetic research is not a search for causes.

We may find, however, that the lady had manifested no interest in the poor and originally intended to go on enlarging her fortune or to spend most of her income on luxuries, but that she was competing not very successfully with other ladies for social prestige. Now we may hypothetically assume that the diversion of her money from the original economic or hedonistic purpose to an altruistic purpose was a result of the influence of her tendency to be recognized as personally superior to her rivals, especially if she took care that her donation should be widely publicized.

Second, if we try to ascertain what the captain of industry was doing before he founded the research institute, it is possible (though not very probable) that he was interested in science as an amateur, learned that some important problems could not be solved without long and costly research, and decided to provide the materials and instruments necessary for their solution. If so, the purpose of his action needs no causal explanation, though the origin of his scientific interests does constitute a genetic problem. But factual evidence may show that, before diverting his money from its original economic purpose to the foundation of the institute, he wanted to improve his credit and thought that such a conspicuous economically unproductive use of a rather large sum would serve this purpose; or, perhaps, that the institute was primarily intended to promote inventions needed for the expansion of the industry he controlled.

Our third example raises controversial issues which have been widely discussed. Contractual agreements, as we know, have vastly multipled in the course of history. Sir Henry Maine[11] and later De Greef[12] conceived the passage from obligations based upon status (the socially determined position

---

[11] Sir Henry Maine, *Ancient Law* (London, 1891).
[12] Guillaume J. de Greef, *Structure générale des sociétés* (Brussels, 1908).

of individuals in society) to obligations voluntarily assumed by contract as the most important trend in social evolution. Under the postulate that every human action must have a motive, two problems have been raised: What motives caused two individuals to make a contractual agreement; and what motive causes an individual to fulfill his contractual obligations, even after he has received all the values or services which the other party had agreed to give him, and whatever he gives in return will be a loss to him?

The first problem is obviously a sociological one, since it involves interdependence between actions of two individuals. As Durkheim showed in his *Division of Labor in Society,* voluntary contractual agreements are inexplicable by individual psychology, but form parts of a certain type of social organization (though his explanation of the origin of this organization may be questioned). We shall, therefore, postpone the discussion of this problem until later.

As to the second problem, various psychological solutions have been proposed, seldom based on an adequate comparative analysis of particular cases. Under our postulate that the principle of causation is not applicable to actions as such, only to changes of actions, the fact that an agent who made a contract acted as he had obliged himself to act raises no problem, unless we find that from the very first he intended to realize a purpose which conflicted with the one he verbally expressed. Otherwise, in making a contractual agreement he already manifested the tendency to perform the action he promised, under the condition that the other agent first perform another action defined in the contract. This condition having been fulfilled, his tendency naturally proceeds toward its achievement. Only if we find that his action was diverted from the intended course by a change of purpose do we face the problem of explaining this change. Thus, he may have decided that he was not bound to keep his promise because in his opinion the other party did not conform with the contractual agreement, e.g., gave him services or goods much less valuable than he had expected. Or he may try to evade or postpone the fulfillment of his obligation because he has become aware of an unexpected opportunity to use the values he promised to give in some other way more profitable to himself.

And yet, in spite of such a change, it may happen that he finally does what he obliged himself to do. This means that the change of his original purpose has been subsequently counteracted by some new influence. Thus, he may have decided after reflection that maintaining his credit in the future would be more valuable to him than any present gain; if a religious man, he may have thought that keeping his promises, even at a loss, would be meritorious in the eyes of God. He may have been influenced by a threat of the other party to sue him or by some new inducement offered to him. Of course, to discover and to explain such changes is obviously a difficult task, especially since the investigator must usually obtain much of the information he needs from communications made by the agent, and such information, even when available, is often unreliable. But full awareness of difficulties is an advantage from the scientific point of view, for it prevents the investigator from drawing conclusions without sufficient factual evidence.

Causal relationships between actions of different individuals

Let us now consider briefly some aspects of the problem of causal relationships between actions of different agents. This problem was already implicit in the foregoing discussion of individual actions, for as examples we selected typical cases to which the concept of motive has been widely applied; for various reasons, modern students of motives have been mainly investigating actions in which the individual is aware of others as objects of his actions and as agents whose actions are apt to affect his values. But the problem of the significance which an individual's actions have for other agents cannot be solved by studying these actions psychologically as integral parts of the total course of his conscious life.

Relationships between actions of different agents have been investigated mostly by sociologists, and later we shall take into consideration various sociological approaches to this task. But right now we have to discuss the general question: How can the principle of causation be applied in studies of these relationships? This principle is frequently used in the form of an explicit or implicit postulate that a certain action of one human agent can be the primary cause of the performance or nonperformance of a certain action by another human agent.

Originally it is founded on the practical experience of an individual agent to whom a conscious human individual is a social object and who, by using definite instruments and methods, tends to produce a definite reaction of this object. If the result of his action appears to him to be the kind of reaction which he intended to produce, he judges by common-sense reasoning that his action was the cause of this reaction. Of course, the intended reaction may consist not in the social object's doing something the agent wanted him to do, but in refraining from doing something which the agent did not want him to do.

Such reasoning is most common among agents who are supposed to control the behavior of others: parents dealing with children, teachers dealing with pupils, rulers dealing with subjects, managers dealing with workers, etc. It is usually accompanied by the belief that effective control by others is the cause of individual conformity with social rules; that, without it, individuals would not perform actions which social rules require and would perform actions which social rules prohibit. This belief goes back to the old idea that individuals ought to be subjected to authoritative control of those agents who create and maintain social order; otherwise, disorder would result. Such normative connotation is still frequently found in works of legal, political, and educational thinkers. It survives in some theories of social control as the essential factor of an individual's conformity with cultural patterns, although Ross and others who adopted this term emphasize the causative power of *social groups* rather than of controlling individuals in producing such conformity. We shall survey these theories later, in connection with the problem of functional relationships between actions.

To prevent any misunderstanding of the present discussion, we repeat again that we are dealing here only with *conscious human actions*, as defined above. We do not deny that specific outward behavior of one individual organism as a biological system can be the cause of specific behavior of another individual organism as a biological system; we deny only that a specific conscious action of one human agent can be the cause of a specific conscious action of another human agent.

The methodical weakness of the latter postulate becomes apparent when from particular cases of individual reactions to individual actions causal generalizations are drawn, for reactions of several social objects to similar social actions may differ considerably. Even the same social object may react differently to similar actions of the same agent at different times or to similar actions of several agents at any time. On the other hand, several social objects who reacted differently to one kind of actions may react similarly to another kind of actions or even to the same kind of actions at a different time. We need not give examples. Every individual tending to control repeatedly the behavior of a number of individuals is familiar with such differences and similarities. To explain them, the assumption has been made for centuries that the reactions which social actions produce vary, depending on the psychological nature of the objects of these actions. But inasmuch as conscious human individuals when viewed psychologically, unlike biological organisms, do not constitute limited systems of structurally and functionally integrated components, this assumption cannot be scientifically tested.

Fortunately, it becomes altogether unnecessary if, instead of postulating that the performance or nonperformance of actions can be caused by the actions of others, we postulate only that *changes* in actions can be caused by the actions of others. When in investigating an individual's conscious reaction to the action of somebody else we use the humanistic coefficient, that is, take into consideration the reacting individual's own point of view, we find that to explain this reaction we do not need to study the psychological nature of this individual or to trace back the evolution of his total personality. All we have to do is to discover what values of his are being affected by the action of the other agent and how he was tending to use those values when the other agent interfered. A conscious individual is not a passive object that cannot act unless stimulated by somebody else. He is an agent who, in the course of his active life, becomes positively or negatively interested in many diverse values which come into the range of his experience and who spontaneously tends to perform many different actions dealing with these values. Though any one of his actions may be interrupted for a longer or shorter time, this does not break the continuity of its duration so long as his tendency persists and again becomes actively manifested after such an interruption. And although some of his tendencies may remain during a certain period at an incipient stage, latent or subconscious, nevertheless they are potentially dynamic and can become actualized, if some new experiences of his lead to the formation of definite purposes.

An individual does not consciously react to anybody else's action unless he becomes aware that this action does affect some values which are significant to him at the time when it is being performed. Millions of citizens, even in a democracy, do not react at all to most actions of legislative groups embodied in new laws, because they are unaware of any connection between those actions and their own active interests and tendencies. When an individual does react, his reaction indicates that his original tendency, bearing upon certain values of his experience, has changed under the impact of the other agent's action. But his reaction is not determined by what the other agent wants him to do; it depends upon what *he* tended to do before the other acted and what influence from his point of view the action of the other has upon the achievement of this active tendency of his. Often, indeed, an individual reacts to actions of others who do not attempt to produce any reactions in him and who may even be unaware of his existence, but inadvertently do something which helps or hinders the realization of some of his purposes.

Consequently, methodical investigation of causal relationships between actions of different agents must follow the same procedure as methodical investigation of causal relationships between natural systems. This begins by seeking for causes of certain observable changes and, after having reached a causal generalization, tests this generalization by ascertaining whether the factual occurrence of the hypothetical cause is regularly followed by the factual occurrence of the hypothetical effect. Instead of starting with actions of agents who attempt to control the actions of others, taking their causative power for granted and seeking for their effects, the investigator must start by studying observable changes in the course of actions as dynamic systems and seek to discover which, if any, of these changes can be explained as effects of actions which some other agents have performed. After having reached a causal hypothesis, he should test it, if possible, by reversing the procedure.

This means, first of all, that the popular explanation of individual conformity with social requirements as a product of controlling agents must be completely revised. When a child, a student, a church member, a worker acts as he "ought to" act, according to the judgment of his father, his teacher, his minister, or his supervisor, this fact by itself gives no basis whatsoever for the assumption that his action was caused by the active control of the father, the teacher, the minister, or the supervisor. Even when we find that, while performing his action, he intended to gain some positive response from his superior, this simply means that the superior and the expected response were among the values included in his action. It was, thus, he who actually tried to influence his superior and not his superior who tried to influence him. Unless we find sufficient evidence that he first intended to act differently and that his original purpose changed, his action raises no causal problem. If we do find such evidence, we have to ascertain what other action caused this change. It may, indeed, have been some action of his superior. But it may have been an action of somebody else—another child, a friend, a fellow worker, a rival, or his best girl. If we find no evidence that somebody else did something which diverted his action from its intended course, we have to seek for some other spontaneous tendency of his own which modified his original purpose. We need more information either about his original tendency or about the cause of its change. If we cannot find any, we must simply acknowledge that this particular problem cannot be solved for lack of adequate empirical material and should not substitute conjecture for hypothesis.

On the other hand, when children, students, and citizens do not perform actions prohibited by parents, teachers, and legislators, this fact by itself does not warrant the assumption that the lack of deviation is due to the control of prohibitive agents with the aid of negative sanctions, unless we find that the children, the students, and the citizens really tended to perform a prohibited action and that some action of a controlling agent interfered. Thus, the enactment of criminal laws has no observable influence upon the vast majority of actions performed by citizens, simply because most citizens seldom tend to perform the kind of actions which criminal laws prohibit; even a professional criminal tends to perform in the course of his life only relatively few legally prohibited actions.

When we do find that the realization of the purpose of a prohibited action has been prevented by somebody's interference, it is not enough to ascertain that because of this interference the agent did *not* do what he tended to do. The investigator must also find out whether in consequence of this interference the original tendency simply ceased to function because its achievement was obstructed by some obstacles which the controlling agent introduced into its course or whether it changed into another active tendency; and, if so, what one? For instance, physical coercion may be effective, indeed, in preventing the completion of a prohibited action, but it frequently leads not to a cessation of the latter but to open or latent active revolt against the agent who has used it.

Finally, an objective investigator must apply the same procedure to a study of changes in the actions of agents who try to control the actions of others. The original purpose which a parent, a teacher, a minister, a military commander, or an industrial manager tends to realize when acting upon a child, a student, a church member, a soldier, or a worker undergoes a change if in the course of its realization he finds that the other individual reacts differently than he expected him to react. Such a change of purpose must be considered an effect of which the unexpected action of the other individual is the cause.[13]

This procedure is being more and more widely used in such realms of research as criminology, sociology of law, and political sociology. We may mention as an example its use in the studies of educational interaction initiated by John Dewey and carried on by his continuators. Investigators have attempted to ascertain by inductive methods what the main interests and active tendencies of educands are at various periods of their lives, how these interests and tendencies are affected by specific actions of educators and, finally, how active tendencies of educators are affected by reactions of educands. Quite a few of the conclusions reached were tested by various experiments, and the results of this research have been applied in educational practice.

Of course, they are not sufficient to guide educational planning, since education is a long and extremely complex process of multiple interaction purposely organized to guide the development of a personality; consequently, planning must be based not only upon studies of the causal relationships between particular actions of educands and educators, but upon comparative genetic studies of this development.

Causal relationships between actions of collective agents

Hitherto we have been surveying the problem of causal explanation of changes in the purposes of individual actions under the influence of other actions. The concept of tendency which enables us to compare actions at various stages of their performance helps us to discover this influence and draw hypothetic generalizations, and at the same time prevents causal conjectures which are not based on factual evidence.

This procedure can be extended to collective actions. The original tendency manifested in actions which a fraternal group, a religious group, a political group, an industrial group, a corporation, or a labor union is performing may undergo an unexpected change; instead of the purpose which was being realized, a more or less different purpose becomes finally realized. We shall be able to explain this change—of course, only hypothetically—if we find either that the same group initiated another action, and that the purpose of

[13] We applied this method to such changes and drew some causal hypotheses in *The Laws of Social Psychology*.

the first became modified in adaptation to the purpose of the second, or that another group was doing something which affected values included in the action which we are investigating; and the group which was performing this action changed its course in reaction to the action of the other group. For instance, a political party preparing for an electoral campaign may change its program because its members have become interested in the solution of a new domestic or international problem. When a labor union which was organizing for a strike, or a corporation which was preparing a lockout, changes its purpose and manifests a tendency to reach an agreement with the other group, this change may prove to be the effect of a new action initiated by the other group or, perhaps, of the active interference of a governmental agency.

Finally, there is no reason why this procedure should not be used in studying causal relationships between individual actions, on the one hand, and collective actions, on the other hand. It would enable sociologists to substitute inductive generalizations, based on a comparative analysis of changes in actions, for two conflicting *a priori* doctrines: The old doctrine which ascribes to some individuals, especially rulers and leaders, an almost unlimited capacity to influence by their actions the collective actions of groups subjected to their rule or leadership; and the more recent doctrine, according to which every individual, even a ruler or a leader, is a product of the collectivity to which he belongs, and whatever he does is merely a reaction to collective tendencies.

The requirement to test by observation every assumption as to the causal relationships between one action and another is not the only advantage of using the procedure outlined above. Another advantage, at least as important, is that, if consistently applied, it will eventually enable students of culture to apply exact *quantitative* methods in investigating these relationships.

Although an action as a dynamic system of values is obviously irreducible to quantitative categories, yet, if we find adequate scales for grading changes which occur in the course of specific actions and ascertain that these changes are effects of another specific action, it will be possible to measure objectively and exactly the relative power of active tendencies (not of agents) to influence other active tendencies.

Quantitative terms implying such power, which are current in popular language, are obviously unscientific; even psychologists and social scientists sometimes use them without adequate theoretic justification. Psychological motives are called "strong" or "weak," according to their imputed influence upon individual activity, and individuals or groups are characterized as more or less "influential" or "powerful" socially. The term "social forces," with its explicit or implicit quantitative connotation, is used to explain all kinds of changes in collective life. Though quite a few attempts have been made to measure these presumed quantitative differences, they are seldom based on an exact quantitative comparison of the effects which tendencies manifested in certain actions have upon tendencies manifested in other actions.

*   *   *

However, the use of the concept of active tendency, in comparing actions which are stopped with actions which are completed and in explaining changes of purpose in the course of actions by the influence of other actions, is only auxiliary to the main task of scientific investigation of actions. As we mentioned at the beginning of this chapter, it is intended to help investigators overcome certain difficulties in comparative research.

The possibility of predicting conditionally the future course of an action soon after it has begun implies that this action belongs to the same general class which is already known and that we can ascertain, from observable manifestations of its active tendency, the class to which it belongs. In other words, this possibility presupposes a systematic classification of the actions which have been completed; the concept of active tendency simply enables us to extend this classification hypothetically to actions which are still at an early stage of their performance, even to those which have been definitely stopped and never will be completed. The implication is similar to that in zoological and botanical studies of organisms in early stages of their growth. A botanist can predict conditionally the future growth of a plant from a seed, or at least from observation of the initial stage of its growth, because he can ascertain to what already known class the seed or the sprouting plant belongs. A zoologist can tell, in investigating an embryo, into what kind of animal that embryo would have grown, because he can ascertain to what known animal genus and species this embryo belongs.

The possibility of drawing qualitative and eventually quantitative generalizations about changes in the purposes of actions occurring under the influence of other actions presupposes not only that the actions which are changing, as well as the actions which cause these changes, can be classified, but also that we can compare such causal relationships with functional relationships between actions. Indeed, as we shall see later, the study of functional relationships is the primary task of scientific research; causal explanation of changes, the secondary task.

Here, again, there is an analogy between studies of actions and studies of living organisms. The regular functional relationships between certain organisms and their environment must be known before any causal generalizations about the effects of certain environmental changes upon these organisms can be drawn.

Human Attitudes

The conception of attitudes as psychological phenomena

When in the preceding chapter we analyzed and compared presumably typical examples of various kinds of actions, we postulated that, by investigating similarities and differences between human actions, scientists can reach valid taxonomic generalizations about them. But the two old types of generalizations—teleological (based upon presumably universal human reason) and volitional (based upon presumably universal active forces inherent in human beings), e.g., instincts, drives, desires, behavior mechanisms—are obviously inadequate. Indeed, both of them were already undermined at the beginning of this century, chiefly as a result of ethnological and historical discoveries of the great diversity of actions performed by participants in various cultures. Investigators familiar with these discoveries became increasingly convinced that studies of actions should begin not with a search for universal psychological characteristics, but with comparative studies of cultures; for uniformities and differences which individuals manifest in their actions can be traced back to the different cultural influences to which they have been subjected.

To serve this new approach a new heuristic concept was introduced, chiefly at the initiative of William I. Thomas: the concept of *attitude*.[1] The study of attitudes was intended to connect theory of culture—or, more specifically, sociology—with individual psychology. From the very first, however, this study was carried on mainly for psychological purposes. The concept of attitudes was used chiefly in "social psychology" as a subdivision of general psychology of human individuals. In this sense, an attitude is a combination of intellectual, emotional, and volitional processes. It implies an individual's

---

[1] We do not mean to say that Thomas was the first to use this concept. Daniel D. Droba, by surveying the indices of textbooks, found that it was first used by Giddings in 1898, next by Judd in 1907. Cf. "The Nature of Attitudes," *Jour. of Social Psych.*, IV (1933), 444-63. But the sociocultural approach to attitudes was primarily due to Thomas. See Ellsworth Faris, "The Concept of Social Attitudes," in *Social Attitudes*, ed. Kimball Young (New York: Holt, 1931), pp. 3-16.

experience of a certain object or class of objects, a feeling which accompanies this experience, and a disposition or tendency to act in a certain way in dealing with this object or class of objects.[2] Inasmuch as the attitudes found in different collectivities vary, depending on the cultures of these collectivities and on individual participation in the cultures, rather than on natural characteristics of the objects to which they refer or on biological characteristics of individual participants, they are not innate, but acquired in the process of acculturation of these individuals.

The psychological approach to attitudes obviously had to take for granted the existence of cultures. Cultures had to be known to explain attitudes. Consequently, another general heuristic concept was needed to be applied to all cultural phenomena and connected with the concept of attitudes as psychological phenomena.

Before collaborating with W. I. Thomas, I had been using for several years the concept of "values" in this sense, as the basic concept of a general philosophy of culture.[3] The world of culture is a world of values; and values are primary data of human experience, irreducible to any natural categories. With the agreement of Thomas, I tried to synthesize this theory of values with his theory of attitudes. If attitudes have to be defined with reference to values found in a given collectivity, the meaning of these values to participants in this collectivity has to be ascertained by studying their attitudes. Cultural changes and psychological changes both have to be explained by causal interaction between values and attitudes.

This attempted synthesis, however, did not work so well as was expected, chiefly because it did not quite succeed in overcoming the traditional dichotomy between inner, subjective psychological processes and outer, objective reality. We still treated attitudes as subjective tendencies to act, and our generalizations about them as well as our attempts to explain actions were, as Blumer showed, methodically defective. Since then, studies of attitudes have become much more exact, but the majority of them are not intended to contribute to the knowledge of culture, only to the knowledge of psychology.[4]

[2] There has been some disagreement as to the relative importance of the emotional and the volitional components of attitudes. Cf. Peter A. Bertocci, "Sentiments and Attitudes," *Jour. of Social Psych.*, II (1940), 245-59.

[3] Florian Znaniecki, *The Problem of Values in Philosophy* (Warsaw, 1910); *Humanism and Knowledge* (Warsaw, 1912); and several articles (1909-14), all in Polish.

[4] We do not question the significance of these contributions. We agree especially with the statement of Allan Fromme, according to whom the main importance of studies of attitudes from the psychological point of view is that they have succeeded in overcoming the "naïve stimulus-response psychology." Thanks to them, the psychologist "is a student not only of behavior, but of potential behavior as well. The latter, of course, is the realm of inner life. . . . And just as the explanation of behavior is facilitated by the knowledge of one's inner life, so in the same way subjective states become more intelligible in the light of one's knowledge of behavior." See "On the Use of Certain Qualitative Methods of Attitude Research," *Jour. of Social Psych.*, XIII (1941), 429-59.

Take the many comparative surveys carried on during the last twenty-five years by social psychologists who wanted to discover how individual participants in a certain collectivity, or a certain category of individuals, evaluate a particular common datum of their experience (e.g., a particular person, association, or institution), or data which they include as units under the same logical class (e.g., people of a certain race or religion). At first, most of these studies were limited to surveys of the statistical distribution of positive valuations on the one hand, negative valuations on the other hand; and some of them (such as the public opinion surveys of attitudes of potential voters toward political candidates) still are so limited.

Eventually, however, such attitudes became graded on a scale ranging from maximum of positiveness through indifference to maximum of negativeness. The only basis for such gradation is the assumption that it is possible to ascertain and measure the *emotional intensity of the feelings for or against* a certain value which accompany individual experiences of the latter. This is a strictly psychological task, and psychologists are well aware of its difficulty. We do not deny its possibility, nor do we ignore the methodical progress achieved in surveying and grading attitudes in this psychological sense. The point is that the results of these studies have only an indirect bearing upon sciences of culture. Measurements of attitudes as feelings are measurements of personal characteristics. Individuals are the units which are compared and graded on the scale. The important difference between these comparisons and older comparisons which led to various typological classifications is that the individuals whose attitudes are measured are not viewed as self-existing entities, but as participants in a culture. Insofar, however, as the investigator measures only the intensity of positive or negative feelings toward certain components of a culture, individuals are investigated as merely passive participants. Their emotional attitudes as such do not affect the objects of these attitudes. Indeed, only when we assume that a given component of culture is already known and definable as a constant, do qualitative and quantitative generalizations about individual emotional responses to experiences of this component become possible.

Psychological generalizations become more difficult if individuals are conceived not only as passive, but as potentially active participants in a given culture. For then comparative surveys of psychological attitudes must include not only individual feelings, but volitional dispositions—urges, desires, wishes, wants, etc.[5] And an investigator who tries to ascertain how individuals are disposed to act, when dealing with a particular datum or data of a certain class which they all evaluate positively or negatively, finds that such disposi-

---

[5] Several selected bibliographies of these and other studies of attitudes have been published at intervals. Cf. the "Selected Bibliography" of Ellsworth Faris, *op. cit.*; Daniel Day, "Methods in Attitudes Research," *Am. Sociol. Rev.*, V (1940), 395-410; Quinn McNemar, "Opinion-Attitude Methodology," *Psychological Bulletin*, Vol. XLIII, No. 4 (1946), pp. 289-369.

tions may differ from individual to individual and change in the course of time. For instance, among individuals who evaluate negatively persons of a certain race, some may show no disposition to act at all, while others often differ considerably in what they want to do.

Investigators of attitudes have tried more or less successfully to overcome these difficulties by assuming a psychological correlation between feelings and volitions and devising a scale of attitudes which combines a gradation of positive and negative feelings toward certain data with a gradation of volitional dispositions to act for or against these data. The scale devised by Thurstone and Chave is a well-known example.[6] An important work where such a combined scale of feelings and volitions has been consistently applied is *Personality in the Depression* by Rundquist and Sletto.[7] Measurements of morale during the war were made also by the use of scales of this type.

Even the best of these studies, however, left unsolved the problem of relationships between attitudes and actions. No definite conclusions about actions could be derived from such studies. Even individual actions could not be adequately predicted or explained merely on the basis of psychological knowledge of the emotional and volitional processes which preceded their performance; and any attempt to predict or explain collective actions by feelings and volitions of individual participants in these actions was bound to be a failure. For, in approaching actions from the psychological point of view, the investigator had to take into account the objective conditions under which these actions were performed. Such conditions were both natural and cultural, varying independently of each other, and both varying independently of subjective psychological variables.[8]

Consequently, the original expectation that studies of attitudes would replace the discarded *a priori* theories of universal psychological traits of human nature and help generalize about actions was not fulfilled. Early attempts to

[6] L. L. Thurstone and E. J. Chave, *The Measurement of Attitudes* (Chicago: University of Chicago Press, 1929).

[7] Edward A. Rundquist and Raymond F. Sletto, *Personality in the Depression* (Minneapolis: University of Minnesota Press, 1936).

[8] Already Thurstone and Chave explicitly stated: "The measurement of attitudes expressed by a man's opinion does not necessarily mean the prediction of what he will do," *op. cit.,* p. 9. See also Richard LaPiere, "Attitudes vs. Actions," *Social Forces,* XIII (1934), 230-37, and especially Ellsworth Faris, *The Nature of Human Nature* (New York: McGraw, 1937), Part II, "Conduct and Attitudes."

See Read Bain, "An Attitude on Attitude Research," *Am. Jour. of Sociology,* XXVIII, 74-99. As a Pearsonian epistemologist, he rejects entirely the possibility of investigating attitudes as psychological phenomena distinct from "actual behavior." Nonetheless, in the collective work, *The American Soldier,* Samuel A. Stouffer *et al.* (Princeton, N. J.: Princeton University Press, 1950), 4 vols., when studies of attitudes by questionnaires were shown to have been followed up by later studies of "behavior," statistically significant correlations were frequently found, indicating that there is a connection between certain kinds of symbolically expressed attitudes and certain kinds of actions. We shall devote our next two chapters to the problem of what this connection is.

classify attitudes psychologically had to be discarded in the light of later research. As Albig pointed out in 1939, a classification of all attitudes has proved impossible.[9]

In view of all these difficulties, I was inclined, like quite a few other sociologists, to leave the concept of attitude entirely to psychologists, since it appeared of no use in studies of culture. However, when we survey the numerous investigations in which this concept has been applied, the operations performed by investigators, and the factual material which they have collected, we find that the term "attitude" has a dual meaning. While, on the one hand, it denotes those psychological phenomena which we have discussed above; on the other hand, it designates also an important category of cultural phenomena which psychologists in the course of their research use as empirical material for their conclusions, but which are irreducible to psychological processes.

In order to ascertain what these cultural phenomena are, we shall begin with a comparative survey of *situations*. The concept of situation, as we know, has been frequently used in connection with the concept of attitude. Apparently the original meaning of the word "attitude," as "a position of the body suited to a certain action, a physical preparation by position for action,"[10] implied that this position was connected with a certain situation in which the living being was involved. Bernard explicitly defined an attitude as "the set of the organism toward the object or situation to which an adjustment is called for."[11] When the psychological conception of attitude was substituted for this biological conception, the problem of connection between the two became more complicated. There have been quite a few systematic attempts to combine studies of attitudes with studies of situations.[12] In those attempts, situations are usually assumed to exist independently of the agents who are involved in them; an investigator can and should observe and analyze a situation objectively from his own point of view, not from that of the agent. The assumption is explicit when an attitude is termed a "response" or "reaction" to a situation, and implicit when the investigator first describes and compares situations and then studies the attitudes of those who are aware of these situations. The situation as conceived by the investigator is often popularly called the "real" situation.

This approach may be adequate in studies of bodily situations of animals; but if extended to culturally conditioned human attitudes, it represents an-

[9] John William Albig, *Public Opinion* (New York: McGraw, 1939), pp. 172-79.
[10] *Ibid.*, p. 173.
[11] Luther L. Bernard, *Introduction to Social Psychology* (New York: Holt, 1926), p. 246.
[12] Probably the most important is Muzafer Sherif and Hadley Cantril, *The Psychology of the Ego-Involvements* (New York: Wiley, 1947). The authors are mainly concerned with social situations as they appear to the participating individuals, and consequently avoid the methodological difficulties here mentioned.

other survival of the old and persistent separation between internal psychological processes and external reality. We shall try to avoid this separation by applying consistently to situations the humanistic coefficient. We postulate that every situation must be studied by the investigator as it is experienced by the particular human individual who is conscious of it. To prevent confusion, we suggest that a distinction be made between situations in this sense and objective *conditions* under which human individuals live and act. An individual, in dealing with a certain situation, may fail to include conditions which, if included, would modify radically his conception of the situation; and he frequently does include data which are not a part of objective conditions.

For instance, a deposit of metal, coal, or petroleum under the surface of a geographical area is not a part of any situation for the people living in that area or even for the experts who consider how to improve the economic life of the people, so long as none of them are aware of its existence; and when they do become aware and include this phenomenon in their situation, it may acquire many different, often unpredictable meanings in their active experience. An approaching hurricane or a pending earthquake which will destroy a town does not constitute a situation or a part of a situation for the inhabitants of this town, so long as they do not anticipate it. On the other hand, ghosts of the dead haunting a place and powerful spirits dwelling in a river or on a mountain are important components of many situations for inhabitants of the neighborhood who believe in them, though they obviously are not parts of the natural conditions under which these inhabitants live and act.

Attitudes as definitions of situations by agents

Let us begin with a brief survey of the situations of which human agents become conscious at some time in the course of their actions.

An agent's consciousness of a situation implies some kind and degree of *reflection*, i.e., deliberate thinking. Consequently, it is not a universal phenomenon found in all actions. Of course, during every conscious human action some practical thinking goes on about the values which the agent is using and the changes he tends to initiate; by such thinking, the purpose of the action is formed. But if the agent proceeds to realize this purpose as soon as it is formed, he does not separate his thinking about values and changes from his utilization of these values and his initiation of changes. Only when an agent consciously postpones, interrupts, or stops the realization of his purpose in order to reflect about the practical problems he is facing does such deliberate thinking become, during this time in his own experience, separated from his effective performance, especially when the latter requires the use of his muscular organs. While reflecting, he does not try to introduce any changes into empirical reality as given to him. Generally, his reflection consists in surveying the values which appear practically important to him and certain factual relationships between them; anticipating the possibilities, positive or negative, which these factual relationships may involve; and considering what should be done to actualize the positive possibilities and/or to prevent the actualization of the negative possibilities. This combination of interrelated values, with its inherent possibilities to be actualized or prevented, constitutes the situation with which the agent at the end of his reflection believes he has to deal.

Such a conception of a situation, reached by the agent after reflection, has been termed *definition of the situation*. We do not know who first coined this term. It was occasionally used in *The Polish Peasant* and much more extensively in the comparative study of typical patterns of *Primitive Behavior* by Thomas. It is true that the word "definition" is given by logicians and semanticists a connotation which seems too rationalistic for such usage. But there is nothing in its etymology that need prevent its being used beyond the realm of logic and semantics, provided we are aware that "defining a situation" refers to a type of thinking different from that referred to by the expression "defining a concept" or "defining a word." The common aspect of these definitions is that they all require reflection as an ideational activity which may or may not be connected with realistic activities. People can act without defining situations, and they can define situations without acting. They can also speak without defining the words they use, and define in dictionaries words which they do not use themselves. They can even reason without defining the concepts included in their reasoning or, as historians of philosophy and science often do, define concepts which others use and yet not use them in their own reasoning.

We shall describe briefly a few typical examples of definitions of situations made by agents themselves. Such definitions are no doubt familiar to our readers from biographical or autobiographical records or perhaps from their own personal experiences and observations.[13]

Take, first, a few instances in which an agent reflects about the situation as it appears to him at the beginning of his action. A farmer who intends to harvest a crop goes out to look at the field on which the crop is growing, judges that it is ripe enough to be harvested, reflects about the condition of his machine or tools, and wonders if the weather is going to change. A carpenter who has been hired by the owner of a cottage to repair it surveys the defects that have to be repaired; reflects about the nature, availability, and cost of necessary materials; estimates the time he will have to spend; considers the relative urgency of this task as compared with other tasks which he may have to perform; and calculates how much his labor is worth. An artist who

[13] The problem of group situations, i.e., situations as they appear to the members of a group, will be discussed later.

intends to paint a landscape surveys the combination of visual data within an area which appears aesthetically significant to him, anticipates the possibility of producing a painting which will express this combination in a way which will enable others to visualize it and understand its aesthetic significance, and considers by what techniques such a painting can be produced. A retail merchant reflects about the demand for certain goods in his community, surveys the supply in his store, anticipates that it may soon be exhausted, and considers how to prevent this possibility by obtaining more goods.

In these examples, the situation, as defined by the agent, includes most of the values and facts which are practically significant to him at the time, and this original reflection seems decisive for the later course of the action. By the time he has fully surveyed the situation, his purpose is nearly formed; its subsequent realization appears to fit into the telic framework of deciding in advance about the end and the means and then starting to realize the end by a realization of the means. Perhaps the persistence of the teleological theory of actions is due to the practical intellectualism of the thinkers who developed and supported this theory. Probably most of them, when functioning as agents, have usually reflected rather thoroughly and inclusively about situations at the initial stage of their actions, at least of those which they considered important. We must not forget, however, that some definitions of situations do not initiate, but impede actions. The carpenter, after surveying the situation, may not repair the cottage, because he judges the task too difficult or thinks that it would take too long and would interfere with some other obligations of his or because the owner does not offer him enough pay. A politician who would like to be elected to a lucrative office may decide not to run, after surveying the situation, because he has no chance of winning.

The same kind of reflection frequently occurs later, when the realization of the purpose is interrupted. The carpenter, at the end of a day's work or before starting his work again on the following day, is apt to survey the results achieved, the actual shape and relationship of the materials on which he has been working, and the tools he has been using, in view of the possibility that the materials in their present shape may not fit together as parts of the projected whole, the tools may not be in good condition, or perhaps some new tool may be needed. A painter, a musical composer, a poet, if his action has been interrupted, is apt to review critically the present stage of his painting, composition, or poem, considering the possibility that, if he keeps the results achieved unchanged and continues to follow the same pattern, his work may not be up to his own aesthetic standards or those of his potential critics or public.

Insofar as the results of the agent's reflection about the situation he is facing at a later stage of his action appear to confirm his previous valuations and anticipations, his reflection merely supplements, develops, and clarifies the original purpose of his action. This purpose becomes more explicit and detailed in view of its partial realization. But it is a different matter if, and insofar as, the situation he defines appears to conflict with his previous valuations and expectations. For this means that he has included in the new situation values which were not original components of his action, or facts which were not expected to affect its course. He becomes conscious of facing a new practical problem, not merely a new step toward the solution of the original problem.

The carpenter who started to repair a cottage falls sick and cannot go on. The merchant finds that the products he wanted for his store are unobtainable because of war shortages, or that new products have appeared on the market on which he can make more profit. A critical observer tells a painter or a dramatist that the outline of his work which he thought to be original is an imitation; or a movie producer tells an author that the drama he has outlined cannot be produced, because it is too original to be understood and appreciated by the movie-going masses. However the agent defines the new situation, this definition is as significant as his initial definition. His action may stop or its purpose may change, depending on what the new positive or negative values mean to him with reference to the values with which he was originally dealing and on how the new facts affect his belief in the possibility of realizing his original purpose.

Furthermore, at the final stage of an action performed, when the agent ceases to act because he assumes that he has realized his purpose, we often find that his belief is based on a reflective survey of the situation as he experiences it at the time, and that it is his definition of this final situation which ends his action. This definition is seldom based on an objective comparison of the result as given with the result as it was anticipated at the beginning of the action. Such a comparison would be impossible when the original anticipation was relatively vague and left a considerable range of possibilities to be defined later, as in many creative actions, especially in the realm of art and literature. But even in carefully planned actions, where the anticipation of final results is relatively definite and detailed, when the agent judges that the action is finished, he is concerned with the present and the future rather than with the past.

This can often be observed when the action is long and complex. For instance, in a graduate seminar under my leadership in 1928-29, about twenty students investigated a variety of planned social actions collectively performed. In every case, there was sufficient reliable evidence as to the original plan and the final result, and some reliable evidence about the actual course of its realization. In not a single case was the result as originally planned, and in not a single case did we find any evidence that the agents, whether they judged their actions as successful or unsuccessful, objectively compared their final results with their original plans. We did not have any cases—there are not many as yet—in which the action was planned by social scientists as a scientific experiment and subjected to methodical investigation.

Usually the agent's conclusion that his action is finished is based on a comparison of the results of his action with the results of other actions which have followed similar patterns. Specific actions of craftsmen, gardeners, and farmers are judged as finished according to certain common criteria which are applied to their results. A technical action of a medieval weaver was judged completed by the established criterion, whenever a definite length of cloth of a definite breadth and quality was woven; such a piece of cloth could then be sold. A farmer's action of plowing a field or harvesting a crop is judged completed by the same criterion by which other actions with similar technical patterns are judged completed. Every school of art has definite criteria for the stage at which a painting is considered finished.

By no means all definitions of situations by agents presuppose so much deliberative thinking as those mentioned above. Many of them are products of relatively brief reflection, especially as agents often reproduce in the course of their actions definitions of situations which they learned from others—a fact of considerable importance, as we shall see later. Moreover, definitions vary greatly in degree of inclusiveness and complexity, depending on the range of values in which the agent is interested and on the number and diversity of facts of which he is aware.

Let us return now to the general concept of attitudes as abstractly defined by theorists. We find two different conceptions. According to the original conception, an attitude is a "preparation for action." According to a later conception, it is "an incompleted or suspended or inhibited act."[14] Both conceptions imply that an attitude appears in consequence of a situation in which the agent has become involved. Nevertheless, it seems impossible to reconcile them, so long as situations are viewed as existing independently of the agent; for, according to one, a situation causes the agent to prepare for action, but according to the other, it causes his action to become "incompleted or suspended or inhibited." The two processes are obviously different and cannot be included under the same concept.

The only way to reconcile these two conceptions is to take situations with their humanistic coefficients, as defined by the agents themselves. The first conception would then cover cases in which the agent defines a situation at the beginning of an action as well as those in which a later definition causes the purposes of his action to change. The second conception would be applicable to cases in which an agent, after reflecting about a situation, stops temporarily or permanently the realization of his purpose. If the concept of attitude in the

[14] Cf. Luther L. Bernard, "Attitudes and the Redirection of Behavior," in *Social Attitudes*, ed. Kimball Young (New York: Holt, 1931), p. 46.

sense of "the attitude of an agent" is to be preserved, it must be used as co-extensive with the concept of definition of a situation by the agent. Of course, if used in this sense, it is applicable only to conscious attitudes of human agents, not to attitudes of animals. This is why we have entitled this chapter "Human Attitudes."

A human agent's attitude in this sense has a cultural and a psychological aspect which are inseparable: It is a *psychocultural phenomenon*. The definition of a situation is a cultural phenomenon, just as the definition of a concept or a hypothesis or the representation of a fictitious person. The situation as defined includes common data of human experience, observed present facts and anticipated future facts; the definer's selection and evaluation of these data, his observation and anticipation of facts, and his judgment of their desirability or undesirability are culturally conditioned and may be shared by others. Since this definition occurs when the definer is actively interested in the data and facts about which he reflects, it forms a part of his own conscious life. If an investigator has enough empirical evidence to analyze the total psychological course of defining a situation, he will find that this course shows the combination of intellectual, emotional, and volitional processes which is generally considered characteristic of an attitude as a psychological phenomenon. As in the typical examples mentioned above, whenever considerable reflection is involved, intellectual processes predominate; and yet, inasmuch as the data about which the agent reflects are values to him, there are also feelings of various degrees of intensity. Moreover, since the possibilities inherent in the situation constitute a practical problem, its definition is accompanied by volitional processes, even when these volitions become for some reason inhibited. Whenever relatively little reflection is involved, the definition of the situation is predominantly influenced by emotions and/or volitions of the agent.

It may be said that the psychological processes involved in defining a situation are too many and diverse for all of them together to be termed "*an* attitude." Thus, Thomas and I, in describing a situation, spoke of "attitudes" in the plural as components of it.[15] Nonetheless, since these psychological processes lead to *one* definition, a synthesis of all the values and facts of the agent's present practical experience which seem significant to him at the time, they may be viewed as one complex attitude, an integration of several simpler attitudes.

Now, we must emphasize that phenomena of this kind cannot be comparatively studied in abstraction from actions, for, viewed objectively, they are integral components of actions as dynamic systems of values. Although the situation, once defined, appears to the agent as given at a particular static

[15] Cf. our complex characterization of a situation in *The Polish Peasant* as a combination of conditions, attitudes, and a definition, I (New York: Knopf, 1927), 68.

cross section of his active performance, its definition is an intellectual activity, in the course of which the purpose of his action is tentatively formed before the agent begins to realize it; or modified and made more explicit when its realization is interrupted; or dropped as impossible to realize when its realization is impeded by seemingly insuperable obstacles; or changed into a different purpose; or judged to be already realized. Nor can the psychological aspects of this phenomenon be ascertained without a study of the total action, for an individual's experiences, ideas, feelings, and volitions change, depending on what he has already done and what he expects to do or not to do. Therefore, *a study of the attitudes manifested by agents in defining situations at various stages of their actions is not a separate scientific task: It forms a part of the study of actions.*

Students of attitudes, however, have included under this concept another kind of phenomena which, unlike those discussed above, are not integral parts of actions and can be successfully investigated on the basis of empirical evidence which is not derived from a comparative study of actions in their total course. These phenomena are symbolic expressions, mainly verbal statements (oral or written) made by individuals who expect them to be experienced and understood by others. During the last twenty-five years, investigators have collected and used as empirical material many millions of such statements, most of them recorded oral answers to interviews or written answers to questionnaires.

What is the scientific significance of this empirical material?

Symbolic manifestations of attitudes

Every symbolic expression made by an individual who expects others to experience and understand it is intended to communicate to others his experience of the phenomena to which the symbols refer. Since we are concerned here with the use which cultural scientists make of such expressions, we shall take into consideration mainly (though not exclusively) symbolic expressions which assume the form of verbal statements, oral or written; for the meaning of the symbols which compose these statements is usually more explicit and can be better ascertained than that of nonverbal symbols.

Now, we find that most scientists make a fundamental distinction between two kinds of verbal statements: Those in which the authors communicate to listeners or readers results of their *observations* of certain phenomena, and those in which they communicate their *valuations* of certain phenomena.

The first kind of communication may be used by scientists as second-hand evidence concerning the phenomena to which it refers or as an inductive conclusion from the observation of these phenomena, if and insofar as it stands the methodical tests which scientists apply to their own observations and conclusions. The second kind of communication can be used without any reservations, but only as empirical phenomena to be scientifically investigated.

Methodical use of the first kind of communication is, of course, the basis of cooperation between scientists, who thus communicate to each other their observations and conclusions. In natural sciences by now, only observations and conclusions of individuals trained in scientific research are accepted by scientists, and even these may be subjected to methodical doubt. In sciences of culture, however, scientists must still use knowledge symbolically expressed by individuals who are not scientifically trained, and one of their main difficulties is to test this knowledge. For instance, as we mentioned before (Chapter 4), historians, who are interested primarily in data and facts which are not accessible to present observation and consequently must rely upon information derived from recorded statements of contemporary observers, have developed during twenty-five centuries efficient methods of testing the reliability of the empirical evidence contained in descriptive statements and the validity of the general conclusions reached by their authors. They have found it necessary to discard as theoretically invalid most of the taxonomic and nearly all the causal generalizations of past writers and to eliminate many descriptive statements as unreliable. Nevertheless, a considerable proportion of the latter has proved sufficiently reliable to be used as a source of information about data and facts, especially if combined with statements of other authors referring to the same data and facts or to the same complexes of data and facts.[16]

Investigators of contemporary cultures, especially ethnologists and sociologists, if they use similar criteria as historians, also find it possible to discover in descriptive statements, oral or written, reliable sources of information; their task is even easier than that of historians, since they can usually draw on other contemporary sources for supplementary or corroborative evidence. Such is the case in studies of nonliterate cultures,[17] modern community studies, and statistical surveys. We have found, after many years of comparative analysis, that the reliability or unreliability of descriptive statements contained in autobiographies can be ascertained in most cases, and that the proportion of reliable statements is usually much larger than we had originally expected. Of course, in every autobiography many facts are omitted which may be important for the investigator.

Psychologists have also used such statements, not (like historians and ethnologists) as sources of knowledge about cultural data and social events which the authors have observed, but only to gain information concerning

---

[16] Cf. Louis Gottschalk, "The Historian and the Historical Document" in *The Use of Personal Documents in History, Anthropology and Sociology* (New York: Social Science Research Council, 1945), Bulletin 53.

[17] Cf. Clyde Kluckhohn, "The Personal Document in Anthropological Science," *ibid.*

actual experiences of their "subjects." An experimental psychologist who investigates experiences of colors or shapes, or feelings of sensory pain or pleasure, or a psychoanalyst who studies reminiscences, dreams, wishes, fears of his subjects, relies upon the description of these experiences which the subjects communicate to him. Psychologists, like other scientists, have developed rather effective methods of testing the reliability of such factual information imparted to them by their subjects, even when the latter are not trained in observing, analyzing, and comparing their own experiences.

A psychological student of attitudes, following other psychologists, sometimes uses similar factual statements of his subjects as a source of information about their experiences, e.g., when he asks a subject whether he likes or dislikes a particular person or people of a certain race. Usually, however, students of attitudes collect different kinds of statements as empirical material. Thus, when a scientific investigator inquires whether a presidential candidate is fit or unfit for this important office or whether members of a certain race should or should not be admitted to American citizenship, he does not expect his subjects to furnish him reliable factual knowledge about this candidate or this race or to communicate to him the results of their psychological reflection about their own feelings and volitions. What he does want is an expression of their evaluative judgment about this candidate in particular or people of this race in general.

And when another investigator asks his subjects to express agreement or disagreement with such judgments as "Most people can be trusted," "In making plans for the future, parents should be given first consideration," "The government should not attempt to limit profits," "A high-school education is worth all the time and effort it requires,"[18] he does not expect that the subjects will give him objective descriptions of their own psychological processes. Eventually, from a synthetic survey of answers to such questions, the investigator himself may draw some psychological conclusions about his subjects. But whatever his conclusions, these answers stand for what they empirically are: manifestations of agreement or disagreement with definite evaluative judgments about certain kinds of data and certain kinds of facts, present, past, or future, in which these subjects are presumably interested.

Sometimes such statements are studied comparatively as manifestations of the attitudes of those who express them. And this is rather puzzling, since many of them do not show those characteristics which, according to the theorists who connect attitudes with actions, all attitudes possess. For instance, the statements of most of the Americans who expressed approval or disapproval of the domestic policies of the Nazi regime several years before the war had no reference to their own actions; some of them judged that the American Government ought to do something about it, but many stated clearly

[18] Rundquist and Sletto, *op. cit.*, pp. 24-27, questions 24, 25, 26, and 48.

that neither the government nor the American people should interfere in any way with the domestic affairs of foreign countries. Similarly, individuals who, after completing high school, express positive or negative valuations of a high-school education are not "preparing for action" nor are their attitudes "incompleted, suspended, or inhibited" actions.

And yet, if we survey the meaning of these evaluative statements, we find some justification for including them under the general concept of attitude. All of them express symbolically definitions of situations, although these symbolic expressions are often vague, incomplete, and oversimplified. However—and this is important—relatively few of these symbolically expressed definitions explicitly refer to situations which the definers themselves are facing in the course of the actions they are performing at the time. Some of them refer to situations which the definers believe they will or may face in future actions; these may be called *prospective* definitions. Some refer to situations which the definers faced in their past actions; we may call them *retrospective* definitions. Many of them refer to other people's situations, present, past, or future; these are the most important from the point of view of sciences of culture, and we shall call them *vicarious* definitions.

Attitudes as definitions of situations by speakers and writers

We shall begin with a brief survey of the main types of statements which investigators of attitudes and students of public opinion planfully induce selected samples of individual subjects to make. Such inducement obviously requires social communication between the investigator and his subjects. Inasmuch as the statements made by subjects are symbolic responses to statements made by investigators, their meaning cannot be ascertained unless we know what the investigators said or wrote when trying to provoke such responses. Therefore, in comparing objectively the kind of empirical material which students of attitudes as well as students of public opinion have collected, we must consider their own statements as an integral part of the material. When we do take them into consideration, we find that most of them already include partial definitions of situations which the individuals who respond to them are expected to supplement. And every statement of this type made by an investigator has a parallel in other statements made by people who are not investigators, but active participants in social life and culture.

First of all, a student of attitudes or of public opinion has to select certain data before requesting individuals to express judgments about them. This means that he considers these data as practically significant to participants in the collectivity to which his subjects belong. His selection may be and sometimes is a manifestation of his own practical interests, due to his conception of certain situations in which these individuals and the collectivity as a whole are involved. He may find, however, that other participants whom he questions show no interest whatever in the data which he has selected; some of them may even be unaware of their existence.

Suppose, for instance, that before World War I an "internationally minded" American, interested in the conflicts between cultural nationalities that were going on in various borderland areas (Bosnia, Dalmatia, Slovakia, the Sudetic Mountains, Silesia) as having a possible bearing on the foreign policy of the United States, had asked a sample of American citizens what their opinion was about these conflicts. He would have found that most of his subjects were not at all interested, and many of them did not even know that such areas and such conflicts existed.

When, however, the investigator's selection is based on previous observation which indicates that certain data are in fact considered practically significant by participants themselves, the purpose of his investigation is not to find out whether they share or do not share his own attitudes, but to discover by asking questions what their attitudes are—in other words, what kind of practical significance they ascribe to these data. Since the elementary universal difference in practical significance is between data which are evaluated positively and those which are evaluated negatively, most investigators try to obtain answers expressing either positive or negative valuations of the data which they have selected; quite a few of them ask for nothing more.

Take, for instance, those questionnaires in which investigators inquire only how individuals characterize and evaluate such a datum of their experience as a famous public person (Coolidge, F. D. Roosevelt, Hitler, Stalin, MacArthur) or an impersonal institution (high-school education, income tax, Taft-Hartley labor law) or an organized group (Roman Catholic Church, Communist Party, Great Britain, Soviet Russia) or people of a certain race or nationality (Negroes, Mexicans, Chinese, Germans). The investigator often asks for rather detailed judgments about various positive or negative characteristics which his subjects ascribe to this person, institution, group, race, or nationality, but stops there. Can such evaluative judgments be considered in any sense "definitions of situations," if neither the questioner nor the answerer explicitly refers to specific situations in which agents dealing with these data are involved?

We must go beyond the explicit meaning of these statements and determine their implications from the practical point of view. If the objects to which they refer really are practically significant to the authors (as the investigator assumes), this obviously means that they judge their existence as affecting or apt to affect in some way their own actions or those of others with which they are vicariously concerned. They are aware, however vaguely, of various situations including this person, this institution, this group, people of this race or nationality—situations in which they themselves or other agents were, are, or will be involved. The positive or negative valuation of this object implies a belief that any agent involved in a situation that includes it faces desirable or undesirable possibilities. And all situations of which this object is the main component are supposed in advance to be similar, at least as to the desirability or undesirability of their possibilities, however much they may differ in other respects. Such a supposition constitutes a *prejudice*—positive or negative—if by prejudice we understand not an *a priori* theoretic judgment, but a practical presumption.

The kind of social communication between an investigator and his subjects which problematizes the practical significance of certain data and results in assertions that these data are positively or negatively significant is obviously not a new invention of present-day investigators. Similar communications have been going on for many thousands of years in all human collectivities, whenever people converse about common data of their experience—natural objects and processes, technical products, particular persons or persons of a certain class, social groups, religious objects, works of art, etc. The very selection of these data as subjects of conversation implies the assumption that they are interesting to those who converse, i.e., practically significant as potential objects of actions; otherwise, the conversation about them would languish and stop. If the conversation continues, their significance becomes increasingly definite.

In conversations, individuals frequently refer to practical situations—past, present, or future—familiar to others in which such objects were, are, or will be included. Farmers talk about the weather, housewives about household equipment, gossipers about community members, and students about their teachers. Often they describe their own active experiences or repeat what they have heard or read about somebody else's active experiences with these objects. Such references are apt to be preceded, accompanied, or followed by positive or negative evaluative statements. Or evaluative statements about objects of common interest may be expressed without any explicit descriptions of situations including these objects. But even the simplest symbolic manifestations of a positive or negative valuation of an object—a gesture, a facial expression, an exclamation—suggest at least that this object or an object of this kind is to be sought or avoided, because situations which include it have some desirable or undesirable possibilities. There may be agreement or disagreement between the conversing individuals as to the positive or negative significance of the objects which they discuss; explicit individual valuations of either kind may also vary in degree, a variation which becomes clear when one object is judged to be better or worse than another. And any statement expressed in conversation may be in answer to a question.

Thus, a vast amount of empirical material of the kind that students of evaluative attitudes gather could be observed and investigated without any special technique, simply by participating in conversations and recording them. Quite a few participant observers of relatively small collectivities have gathered such material and used it scientifically. The only difficulty in using it is purely technical; it often requires a long time and considerable effort to gather as much material as is needed for the solution of any sociological problem. The questionnaire technique is one way of saving time and effort, though it has a disadvantage; it prevents the investigator from discovering attitudes which he did not anticipate when formulating his questions.

Recently, however, students of attitudes have decided that evaluative judgments of data alone do not give sufficient information about the meaning of the data as values to those who express such judgments. The main difficulties arise when such evaluative judgments are neither unreservedly positive nor unreservedly negative, but express limitations, reservations, or ambivalence. To solve these difficulties, investigators began to ask what individuals would do or what they thought should be done by somebody else in certain situations, centered around these values. The underlying assumption, tested and frequently validated by the answers received, was that the same datum could be positively evaluated in some situations, negatively in other situations, depending on other values which those situations contained. In formulating such a question, the investigator defines a situation explicitly, though only partly. He refers to other components of the situation, besides its main component, indicates its inherent possibilities, but lets his subject judge whether these possibilities are desirable or undesirable and what should be done about them in either case. In other words, he wants an evaluative judgment concerning actions which the situation requires. His question *plus* the answer constitutes a complete, even though only briefly expressed, definition of the situation. A typical example is the questionnaire of Bogardus in his social distance tests, asking subjects whether they are willing to admit members of various races to specific social relationships of various degrees of social proximity.[19]

Such verbal statements describing situations and asking others what they think should be done in these situations have been formulated for thousands of years, and many of them are being formulated all the time, even by people who are not investigators. In fact, they are for the most part made by individuals who seek *advice* from others whom they consider more competent judges of what they ought to do. Parents, grandparents, teachers, priests, physicians, social workers, lawyers, and deans of men and of women in colleges continually hear children, pupils, laymen, patients, clients, and students speak about situations centered around various values important to the speaker: natural phenomena, cultural products, the speaker's own body, his mind, his status in a group, God, other individuals of the same or opposite sex, economic possessions, etc. Columnists who specialize in discussing certain

[19] Emory S. Bogardus, *Immigration and Race Attitudes* (Boston: Heath, 1928).

kinds of practical problems receive many thousands of letters describing particular situations of the writers. In these conversations and letters, the components of a situation and its inherent possibilities are usually described with much more detail than in a questionnaire, but just as in the latter its definition is incomplete; it formulates a practical problem and expects to be completed by advice about how to solve this problem.

An obvious difference between statements formulated by students of attitudes and statements formulated by those who seek advice is that the situation to which an investigator refers is not one in which he is involved, but either that of the individual whom he questions or that of somebody else in whose action this individual is interested. Nevertheless, the investigator often speaks or writes as if he were asking advice not for his own benefit, but for the benefit of others. In a questionnaire, a statement of this kind, taken by itself, manifests an attitude of uncertainty about the right way of acting in a given situation. Such an attitude is highly significant when it implies an awareness of two or more divergent cultural patterns which agents might follow in dealing with certain values. In any case, when students of public opinion, who are primarily concerned with judgments about controversial issues, ask a sample of individual participants in a collectivity what they would do or what they think should be done in specific situations, they assume the existence of such divergent patterns in this collectivity and want to discover which of them these individuals will select.

Some questionnaires are modeled on another type of question concerning ways of dealing with situations, the examination question, asked by educators (in the most general sense of the term) in order to ascertain whether educands have learned what they were taught about the right ways of acting in definite situations. The difference between this type of question and the other type is that when an educator asks how a certain problem should be solved, he does not imply any uncertainty; he is absolutely certain what the right solution is,[20] and the educands know that he is.

Many investigators go even further. They include in questionnaires assertive statements about situations which, taken in themselves, do not require any answers; the subjects are asked merely to express agreement or disagreement. Such a statement gives a complete, though only briefly symbolized, definition of a specific situation or a general type of situations; the indi-

[20] This belief of vicarious definers has been the main source of the assumption that situations can be objectively defined by investigators, who can then proceed to study the subjective attitudes of those who are actually involved in these situations. Investigators who make this assumption are unaware that so long as they use their own evaluative judgments about data and facts in defining the situations which others face, instead of studying the evaluative judgments of those others, they do not function as scientists, but as vicarious participants; their definitions cannot be estimated by standards of truth and error in the scientific sense, but may be scientifically investigated, just like the definitions of others.

viduals to whom it is submitted for approval or disapproval can add nothing to it.

Again we find that such statements imitate in a simplified form an old and familiar type. They are like vicarious definitions of situations expressed by authoritative judges for the benefit of their listeners or readers. To this category belong judgments of educators, preachers, moralists, jurists, self-appointed economic and political advisers (especially public speakers and writers of editorials), family counselors, advisers to the lovelorn, social workers and teachers of social workers, and writers of books on etiquette. All of them say or write what should be done by certain agents or any agents who are facing, will face, or may face definite situations. Some of their judgments are given in answer to questions asked by others who seek advice. However, many of the authors who formulate them start with the assumption that their listeners or readers need advice, even when they do not ask for it, because they are not fully aware of the practical problems inherent in certain situations and do not know how their problems can be solved. The statement of such an authoritative judge implies that he knows what the situation which the agent faces "really is"; his vicarious definition of this situation is "true," and he expects the agent to accept it.

When, however, in his questionnaire an investigator formulates a judgment, the very fact that he asks his subjects to state whether they agree or disagree with it indicates that he does not consider it an authoritative judgment to be uncritically accepted. But even this has a parallel in conferences and discussions between judges.

Investigators sometimes ask still another type of question: whether certain actions performed in the past by certain agents were right or wrong. For instance, after the occupation of Germany in 1945, interviewers asked many Germans to express such judgments concerning various actions of Nazi leaders and officials. Of course, an interviewer did not expect to gain reliable historical information as to what Nazi leaders were really doing in the past, since the subjects whom he interviewed usually had very little direct objective knowledge of the performances of prominent Nazis. What he wanted to ascertain was what these past actions meant to his subjects at the time they were being interviewed, in other words, their present attitudes toward these actions. When we consider the total content and meaning of the interviewer's questions and of the answers given by his subjects, we find that, taken together, they refer more or less definitely to various situations with which Nazi leaders had been dealing. Either the interviewer or the interviewee mentioned the objects included in those situations, especially the human individuals and groups: members and sections of the Nazi Party, Germans of various classes who did not belong to the party, nonconformists, Jews, various German groups which the Nazi leaders tried to control (e.g., military groups, workers' groups, religious groups, cultural associations, educational circles, play groups), foreign states and cultural nationalities, enemy armies, war prisoners, populations of subjugated countries. These objects were conceived and evaluated from their own point of view by the authors of the statements which the interviewer collected, and every statement more or less clearly expressed its author's present estimate of what should have been done or should not have been done in certain situations which included these objects. In short, such a judgment constituted a vicarious, retrospective definition of the particular situation or the type of situation which a Nazi agent had to face; whether the author expressed a positive or a negative judgment of the agent's action depended upon his approval or disapproval of what *he believed* to be the agent's valuations of the objects included in the situation and the agent's estimation of the desirability or undesirability of certain ways of acting in this situation.

Here again the statements obtained by investigators are similar to statements which have been made and are being made by innumerable individuals who are not subjected to investigation. Explicit praise or blame, approval or disapproval, of past actions of others is a familiar and socially very important type of phenomena. The vast majority of such statements are made in private conversation, but many are formulated in public by authoritative judges. In 1946-47, when interviewers asked Germans to express their approval or disapproval of actions of Nazi leaders, the judges who functioned at the Nuremberg Trials were pronouncing or preparing authoritative judgments which evaluated some of these actions negatively as crimes. Their judgments were preceded by detailed descriptions based on reliable evidence of the total course of the actions to which they referred. But the judgments which condemned these actions differed essentially from these descriptions; for they expressed not historical knowledge of past events, but vicarious, retrospective definitions by judges of the situations with which those agents had dealt during the Nazi regime. According to the judges, in all situations including human individuals (with certain exceptions, as when agents had to defend themselves against aggression), these individuals ought to have been considered as positive values, and no performances deliberately intended to destroy or injure them should have been initiated. Insofar as the valuations and intentions which the Nazi agents manifested in their past actions conflicted with the present valuations and estimates of the judges, those actions were judged to have been wrong. Whether, in consequence of such judgments, the performers of past wrong actions should be subjected to active punishment raises another problem, which we shall not discuss here.

Occasionally, but not often, a student of attitudes tries to obtain from his subjects evaluative judgments about certain past actions of their own. How reliable their factual descriptions of these actions are, can be ascertained only by using methods similar to those of social scientists. But insofar as their evaluative judgments express present retrospective definitions of past situations, they can be taken as such, whatever the subject's purpose in expressing them. Thus, the subject may state that his action was right or wrong, because he did or did not know and evaluate adequately the objects with which he was dealing, was or was not aware of certain important facts, did or did not anticipate and estimate rightly the consequences of his own performance.

Finally, investigators (especially those who study attitudes of children) often include in their interviews or questionnaires imaginative descriptions of actions of fictitious agents and ask their subjects to state whether they are right or wrong; and, if so, why. This is modeled upon works of fiction, particularly those in which an author defines in detail situations in which the hero and the villain become involved, and shows how they act in these situations.

Conclusion

We have found that the processes of verbal communication which investigators of attitudes initiate between themselves and their subjects are selected and abbreviated samples of various kinds of symbolic communication which originally occur between participants in human collectivities at all historical periods.[21] By such processes some individuals communicate their own evaluative judgments symbolically to others, and those others respond symbolically. If we analyze comparatively instances of this original communication, which consists in a sequence of explicit and detailed verbal statements, we find that these statements contain characterizations and evaluations of certain data included in human actions and of some factual relationships between these data, formulations of practical problems which agents face in dealing with these data and facts, and decisions as to how these problems should be solved. In short, authors communicate to others their definitions of certain situations with which human agents are dealing.

Now, as we have seen, statements obtained by investigators of attitudes, viewed in connection with their own statements, also contain at least partial, symbolically expressed definitions of situations, usually brief and often vague, depending on the meaning of the symbols used. If such definitions are considered manifestations of attitudes of the individuals who express them, so should be those original, often much longer and more explicit statements upon which students of attitudes have modeled their interviews and questionnaires.

[21] A large amount of highly significant material concerning such symbolic communication is contained in the works of Kenneth Burke mentioned in the notes to the preceding chapter.

If the concept of attitude is thus extended beyond its present range of application, it will serve as an important heuristic instrument in studies of culture. Just as the concept of active tendency helps compare all kinds of actions, so should the concept of attitude prove helpful in comparing all kinds of definitions of situations, be they partial or complete, simple or complex, vague or explicit. We can apply it to authentic definitions by agents of their own situations, be they actual definitions of their present situations, prospective definitions of their future situations, or restrospective definitions of their past situations. What is even more important, it is applicable to all vicarious definitions of other people's situations, present, past, or future; provided, of course, we consider these definitions as manifestations of the attitudes of the definers and not as statements of theories of knowledge about the situations of others to which they refer. It can be applied even to definitions of imaginary situations faced by fictitious agents. And, finally, we can include under it, as students of attitudes have been doing, all kinds of symbolic responses to all kinds of definitions of situations by those to whom the latter are communicated, whether their responses manifest only acceptance or rejection of these definitions or include some additions or changes.

An attitude in this sense is given to the investigator as a *sociocultural* rather than as a psychocultural phenomenon, though it does have some psychological implications. Communication is a social process; the verbal symbols used are cultural products; their content and meaning are accessible to all who experience and understand them. Of course, the very use of these symbols by the author of a statement indicates that his statement was preceded and accompanied by certain psychological processes. A word referring to certain data or facts manifests his intellectual awareness of these data or facts. Many verbal symbols have emotional and/or volitional connotations; the individual who uses them manifests to others his feelings and volitions. Thus, his symbolic expression constitutes factual evidence that he has the kind of attitude which he expresses. We can compare it with other attitudes symbolically expressed by the same author at other times and by other authors using similar or different symbols. But what connection exists between the ideas, feelings, or volitions which he expressly manifested in his statement and other ideas, feelings, and volitions of his is another problem, which can be solved only by a thorough psychological investigation of the stream of his conscious life. Frequently it remains unsolved, either because the author is inaccessible to psychological observation or because, as in studies of public opinion, he is considered only a unit of a selected statistical group.

The difference is obvious between this usage of the term attitude and the other usage which we discussed in the preceding section. An attitude manifested by the agent in the course of his action and an attitude manifested by the author in a verbal statement are entirely distinct phenomena. While both are definitions of situations, the former, as we have seen, is the definition of a particular situation which the agent is facing at the particular moment of his active performance. It conditions his subsequent performance, forms an integral part of the action, and can be ascertained only by investigating the latter. Whereas verbally expressed definitions of situations, which have no direct bearing on present actions of their authors, can be investigated for what they are, without having to study the actions of those who are, were, or may be actually involved in such situations as the authors have defined. Even if the author does refer to his own actual situation (as when he asks advice), the fact that he communicates his definition to somebody else makes it accessible to investigation, without any need to study the active performance of the author. Moreover, verbal definitions of situations may remain accessible to investigators long after they have been expressed. An individual's oral statement referring to some situation can be remembered by others for years, though the attitude he manifested at the time may have changed radically. A written evaluative statement can remain accessible and understandable to students for centuries after the values to which it referred have lost all practical significance.

Two such different usages really demand some terminological distinction, but it is difficult to devise adequate terms. We thought of applying to attitudes of the second kind the adjective "social," inasmuch as they are shared by social communication. However, the term "social attitude" has already been used with two other, different meanings. Most investigators use it as synonymous with *collective* attitudes shared by a social group, as distinct from individual attitudes, insofar as the latter differ from those which the group shares; but we do not care to help perpetuate this old antithesis of "social" versus "individual." Others (myself included) would prefer to call "social" only attitudes toward human individuals and groups, thus distinguishing them from religious attitudes, aesthetic attitudes, economic attitudes, etc., which refer to nonhuman categories of objects.

We, therefore, suggest that definitions of situations by agents in the course of their actions be termed "realistic attitudes," since they affect directly the performance of those actions; whereas definitions of situations by speakers and writers might be termed "ideational attitudes," since they affect directly not the actions to which they refer, but thinking about actions, and can be indefinitely experienced as ideas, even by those who never apply them in practice.

We shall try to show in the next chapter that comparative investigation of ideational attitudes is an indispensable task for all students of culture, for it opens the only road to scientific generalizations about human actions.

Standards and Norms

Consensus

In surveying the content and meaning of verbal statements which are being investigated as manifestations of attitudes, we found that the authors of these statements are communicating to other persons their definitions of situations with which human agents deal. Thus, all such statements refer, explicitly or implicitly, to some actions which presumably were, are, or will be performed or at least considered possible. However, we have not yet taken fully into consideration the fact that defining symbolically a situation is in itself an action.

All speaking and writing is, of course, a distinctive kind of activity. A speaker or writer tends to achieve some purpose. The purposes of actions vary widely. The pronouncement of a magician is usually intended to influence directly natural objects and processes. A worshiper's prayer, addressed to a god, aims to make the god use his mystical power in favor of the worshiper. The immediate purpose of a poet is to produce a phonetically harmonious and aesthetically meaningful system of verbal symbols. The purpose of writing a diary or a memorandum is to help the author remember what he has observed, done, or decided to do.

When a speaker or writer expects to be heard or read by others, individually or collectively, and purposes thus to influence them, his performance can be included under the general class of social actions.[1] The individual or collectivity to whom his speech or writing is directed or addressed is to him a social object, and he tends to provoke a definite reaction or response of this object. We find also notable differences between the purposes of such actions. Many of them explicitly manifest tendencies to influence directly some active performances of those to whom they are addressed. Such is the purpose of a symbolic statement in the form of a command, threat, request, or promise,

[1] Cf. Florian Znaniecki, *Social Actions*, chap. III.

when the author of the statement refers to certain data and tends to make the individual or collectivity whom he addresses perform (or refrain from performing) a definite action bearing on these data. In such a case symbols are instruments used, together with other instruments (e.g., anticipated punishment or reward), to produce the required reaction.

But when the author symbolically communicates to others his evaluative judgments concerning certain data and activities, without asking them to do (or not to do) something to the data to which he refers, his explicit, immediate purpose is not to influence their actions, but their attitudes. He may, indeed, as an investigator does, ask others to respond by expressing symbolically their valuations; frequently, however, he does not even ask for this, although he may expect some spontaneous response on their part.

For the scientific study of attitudes, the most important of such symbolic actions of communication are those which result or are intended to result in consensus, i.e., mutual agreement between the communicants.[2] But first we must try to ascertain what agreement in general means to those who agree. Let us survey some typical instances of agreement sought and obtained.

Parents, teachers, preachers, gossiping guardians of community mores, political propagandists, civil and criminal judges, advisers on etiquette, editorial writers, and critics of literature and art, in manifesting their attitudes verbally, expect to have their listeners or readers agree with their judgments of certain values and ways of acting. Their expectations are usually based on past consensus. The judgments they express are seldom original; they mostly reproduce with slight modifications particular judgments or apply to particular situations general judgments which they have heard or read and with which they agreed. Children, pupils, listeners to gossip, church members, and audiences of political propagandists sometimes express their agreement immediately, sometimes manifest it later by communicating to others judgments similar to those which have been communicated to them. Readers often repeat the judgments of authors as manifestations of their own attitudes. Many autobiographers express attitudes which presumably agree with the judgments of their prospective readers.

Frequently, indeed, an individual expects to provoke disagreement on the part of those to whom he communicates his judgments or explicitly disagrees with judgments that somebody else communicates to him. But we usually find that he is relying on the agreement of some other individuals. A teacher who scolds bad pupils, a preacher who condemns unrepenting sinners, a politician who accuses the party in power of misrule, or a critic declaring the works

[2] The significance of sociological studies of consensus and the many new problems, theoretic and practical, which these studies raise were briefly, but excellently, presented by Louis Wirth in his "Presidential Address" at the 1947 meeting of the American Sociological Society. Cf. "Consensus and Mass Communication," *Am. Sociol. Rev.*, Vol. 13, No. 1 (February, 1948).

of art exhibited by a certain school aesthetically worthless is aware that he provokes the disagreement of those whom he blames; but he assumes that there was, is, or will be consensus of judgments between himself and good pupils, righteous participants in the religious community, members of his own party, or artists and connoisseurs whose aesthetic standards differ from those of the school he criticizes. When a youngster disagrees with judgments of his parents, this probably indicates that he has accepted judgments which have been communicated to him by somebody else—the leaders of the gang to which he belongs, perhaps a teacher or a writer. The missionary among heathens who criticizes their beliefs manifests his beliefs which he knows to be shared by all the faithful members of his own church.

Some exceptional individuals—prophets of a presumably new religion, philosophers formulating new ideals, romantic individualists, and cultural revolutionists demanding the re-evaluation of all values[3]—express judgments which are intended to be original and are explicitly meant to disagree with all the judgments hitherto expressed by other people. Even they, however, expect to gain converts and hope their judgment will be accepted sooner or later, though perhaps only by a few elect capable of understanding and appreciating them. Sometimes they may doubt whether their converts understand them, but this does not cause them to change their judgments; while those who have no converts—prophets "crying in the wilderness," isolated mystics —may rely on their God, the Supreme Being who has communicated to them the judgments which they express.[4]

Standards of values and norms of conduct

If we compare various instances of consensus—past or present, actual or anticipated, real or imaginary—between individuals who express judgments about values included in certain situations and ways of acting in these situations, the problem arises: What does such consensus indicate?

First, that the values to which the judgments refer are common data in the experience of all the individuals who agree, and that all these individuals are aware of practical situations which include these values as potential objects of activities. As a matter of fact, an explicit evaluative judgment of a certain object, when communicated to others, implies that the object— e.g., a certain person or group, a mythical being, a work of art—is con-

---

[3] Nietzsche's term: "Umwertung aller Werte."

[4] Hegel, who had many followers during his life, is supposed to have said before his death: "Only one man really understood me, and even he sometimes misunderstood me." Karl Christian Krause, a rather mystical philosopher who had few followers in Germany but, long after his death, became exalted by many enthusiastic admirers in Spain (cf. Barnes and Becker, *Social Thought from Lore to Science*, pp. 1108-16), allegedly said toward the end of his life: "Sometime ago, there were two who understood me: God and I. Now there is only God."

sidered to be the main value, the most important component of a number of situations, present or future, with which various agents are dealing or will deal. This is even more obvious when the judgment refers not to one particular object, but to a whole class of objects—e.g., persons of a certain race, or a certain kind of technical products. Agreement with such a judgment indicates that those who thus agree define and evaluate the object or class in accordance with this judgment. And when an evaluative judgment about an object (or a class of objects) is accompanied by a judgment according to which all situations including the object require a definite kind of activity, this implies that, although agents dealing with such situations could perform various kinds of activities, yet the kind that the judgment prescribes is the most desirable, if not the only desirable activity.

However, the fact that individuals agree with such judgments does not mean that their experiences of the objects and activities to which these judgments refer are alike. An important public official is a different being to leaders of his party and to ordinary citizens, to those who serve under him and to those who have never had any direct contact with him, even though in the opinion of all of them he may be the right person for the office he occupies. Positive judgments about mothers on Mother's Day or about fathers on Father's Day are agreed upon by children, adolescents, and adults whose family lives differ considerably in the present and have differed in the past. Negative judgments referring to people of a certain race or nationality may be accepted by individuals who have met some of these people under diverse conditions or never met any of them at all. A symphony generally recognized as valuable has widely diverse contents and meanings for teachers, for students, for historians of music, for a conductor, for members of the orchestra who play different parts of it, for individuals in the audience who have considerable musical training, and for those with little or none.

No less different are apt to be the individual experiences of active performances, their own or others', past, present, or future, which are required in certain situations, according to the judgments with which these individuals agree. While there may be consensus between teachers and students as to what and how students should learn, the activity of learning in general has, obviously, a very different meaning to students and to teachers. To a particular student, learning a certain subject means something different if he has already done it, than if he expects to do it in the future; and in the latter case the meaning of this expectation varies, depending on other actions which he expects to perform. When workers in a factory accept the judgments of managers that certain technical actions ought to be performed, these actions have a different meaning for managers and for workers; each is differently experienced by a worker who expects to perform it himself and by a worker who does not, by one who has been trained for physical labor and by one who has prepared for intellectual work, by one who is satisfied with his wages and by one who is not, by one who has friendly relations with his foreman or fellow workers and by one who is in conflict with them. Even the same worker has different attitudes toward his work when rested and when tired, when cheerful and when depressed because of some situation which may have nothing to do with his work.

The significance of consensus in judgments about values and activities between individuals whose experiences differ is most clearly manifested when authors promulgate such judgments with the purpose of preventing any such differences from producing disagreement. Prophets, priests, missionaries, educators, propagandists, guardians of mores, legislators, judges, social reformers, industrial planners and organizers, critics and teachers of art and literature, and authors of books on etiquette accept a universal, well-known principle, according to which the judgments which they express about certain values and ways of acting are *right*, while any judgments which disagree with theirs are *wrong*. Their evaluative judgments concerning certain objects are supposed to express not merely their own intellectual and emotional experiences, but *standards in accordance with which everybody ought to define and evaluate these objects*. Their judgments about the desirability or undesirability of certain ways of acting in situations which include these objects are supposed to express not merely their own volitions that something should be done or not done, but *norms of conduct which everybody ought to consider obligatory for any agents who deal with such situations*. In other words, the definitions of situations which they communicate to others are supposed to be more than manifestations of their present subjective attitudes, and are claimed by them to possess an *objective validity*. It is, of course, a different kind of validity from that which scientists claim for theoretic judgments, though the two have been confused for thousands of years and are purposely identified by quite a few philosophers of values.

Now, if others agree with such judgments, this indicates that they accept as objectively valid the standards of values and norms of conduct which the authors have formulated. While this acceptance does not eliminate differences between individual attitudes, yet by subjecting all these attitudes to common criteria of validity, it superimposes upon them what may well be called the same "ideal type," which all of them presumably approximate.

Take another familiar and significant example. During World War II, the majority of Americans who expressed their attitudes concerning this extremely complex social phenomenon, which affected in some way all their lives, agreed that the American nation as a whole ought to be the highest, the most important, social value for every citizen and that it was everybody's duty to do what he could to help the United States win the war. This common standard of values and norm of conduct, insofar as accepted, introduced some degree of similarity into a wide variety of attitudes found among individuals differentiated by sex; age; ethnic, regional, and local origin; military and civilian roles; class status; occupational function; political affiliation; and religion.

Furthermore, under this general standard and norm, applicable to all situations connected with the war, were included a number of more specific standards and norms which referred to various values and activities considered important to the nation at war. Thus, soldiers who risked their lives for the supreme common value were supposed to be more valuable, *ceteris paribus*, than civilians. To soldiers at the front, the military group to which they belonged was supposed to be, for the time being, more important than any other group except the nation. Physicians and nurses behind the front were expected to treat wounded soldiers as the most valuable human beings. Managers and workers were supposed to judge technical products needed by the military forces as relatively more important than other products. Agents who dealt with these values were considered in duty bound to follow certain well-defined norms.

On the other hand, conscious, explicit disagreement with such a standardizing or normative judgment usually indicates not merely that the attitudes of those who disagree differ from the attitudes of those who agree, but that the former reject the standard of values or norm of conduct accepted by the latter, because they believe it *conflicts* with some other standard or norm of conduct which they consider valid. When a number of visitors at an art exhibition explicitly disagree with positive valuations of cubist paintings by some artists and critics, this means not only that each of them individually does not like the paintings, but that in their opinion the aesthetic standards of those artists and critics are wrong, because they conflict with some other standard (or perhaps with several standards) by which these visitors had learned to judge paintings before the appearance of cubism. Conscious disagreement with the normative judgment that it was the duty of every American citizen to support the national war effort implied not merely unwillingness of the disagreeing individuals to do anything, but rejection of the validity of this judgment because it conflicted with some other judgment which these individuals considered valid.

Thus, conscientious religious objectors and secular pacifists, even though accepting the American nation as a positive value, considered that it ought to be subordinated to another positive value of supreme importance—God or mankind as a whole. The religious objectors claimed that killing men in war conflicted absolutely with the divine norm of universal brotherly love among men; while the secular pacifists thought that war impeded the unification of mankind, which ought to be achieved by peaceful methods. Occasionally, of course, disagreement with the norm of participation of American citizens in war was founded on acceptance of the standards and norms of German, Italian, or Japanese imperialism.

Ideological models of attitudes

In the preceding chapter we found that symbolical definitions by speakers and writers of situations which are not components of their own present actions, and functional definitions by agents of situations as integral parts of their actions are different phenomena, though both are considered manifestations of attitudes. Now, we must extend this distinction to standards of values and norms of conduct as ideological principles by which *thinking* about situations is supposed to be guided, and the realistic application of these standards and norms by agents in the very course of their actions.

These two principles have been frequently confused, partly because of the indiscriminate use of such terms as "right" and "wrong," "should" or "ought," and "should not" or "ought not." From the point of view of those who promulgate definite standards of values and norms of conduct, everybody "should recognize" them as valid and "should not deny their validity"; the attitudes of all who accept them are "right," the attitudes of all who reject them are "wrong." Also, inasmuch as the standards refer to objects with which human agents are dealing and the norms to activities bearing on these objects, every agent who deals with them "ought to act" in accordance with these norms and "ought not to act" in any way which conflicts with them; actions which conform are "right," actions which conflict are "wrong."

Consequently, many practical thinkers and even theorists often treat the application of standards and norms to attitudes and to actions as coincident or even identical. Thus, the current conception of legislation is that by promulgating certain rules, it regulates actions and makes people of a certain category perform under certain conditions actions of a certain class as defined by legislation, e.g., makes debtors pay their debts and parents send their children to school. A similar conception is applied by students of mores to ethical rules, by students of religion to rules of cultus. Ethnologists, in reconstructing standards of values and norms of conduct from statements of authoritative participants in a culture, often explicitly call these standards and norms "patterns of actions" or "patterns of conduct."[5]

[5] Some ethnologists (cf. Clyde Kluckhohn, "Patterning in Navaho Culture," in *Language, Culture and Personality. Essays in Memory of E. Sapir* (Menasha, Wis.)) distinguish between "ideal patterns" and "behavior patterns." But we are not discussing this kind of difference, unless the term "ideal pattern" means "pattern of ideas" (Sapir). Assuming that the general term "pattern" denotes a cultural uniformity of specific phenomena, basic differences between patterns do not denote differences in degree of uniformity, but differences between the phenomena which are patterned. A pattern of pottery is different from a pattern of women's dresses; each of them

Of course, those who formulate standardizing judgments about values and normative judgments about conduct frequently also intend to regulate other people's actions and (by whatever methods) to make agents who face situations including these values define them in accordance with these standards and act in accordance with these norms. Nor can there be any doubt that agents frequently are guided by such judgments in practice; and this makes the investigation of standards and norms essential for any scientific generalizations about actions. Yet acceptance of the validity of standards and norms is so different from practical application of them that a terminological distinction seems indispensable. We shall call definition of a situation which includes a standard of values and a norm of conduct a *model of attitudes* or, more specifically, an *ideological model of attitudes*. It is a model in the sense that it is supposed to serve as a perfect example of right thinking about the situation to which it refers. We shall borrow from cultural anthropologists the term *pattern of actions* or, more specifically, *realistic pattern of actions* to denote a common and distinctive inner order, due to the practical application of standards and norms, which makes certain actions alike and different from other actions.

There are several reasons why models of attitudes should never be identified with patterns of actions. First, as we have indicated, judgments expressing standards of values and norms of conduct are supposed to be considered valid not only by those who are actively involved in the situation to which they refer, but by everybody who is aware of such situations.

For instance, an ethical judgment prescribing how a child should evaluate his mother and act toward her is intended to be accepted as valid not only by every child, but also by the child's mother, father, siblings, grandparents, uncles and aunts, teachers, and the children and adults of other families in the same community. The standards and norms promulgated by legislators in a legal enactment which defines how employers and managers in industry should evaluate and act toward workers whom they employ are supposed to be accepted as valid not only by active employers and managers and by all who expect to become employers or managers, but by all workers, whether employed or not, and by those who are engaged in industry in any capacity, as well as by judges, attorneys, and administrative officials who are or might be involved in juridical controversies between management and labor, and by all citizens, even those who have no active share in industrial situations and never expect to have any. During the war, standards and norms referring

---

usually has a certain model, perfect type, ideal type which particular pottery or dresses approximate. Since attitudes and actions are two different categories of phenomena, a pattern of attitudes must be different from a pattern of actions. By introducing the term "ideological model of attitudes" and applying the term "pattern" to actions only, we try to avoid confusing the two.

to specific situations were supposed to be accepted not only by agents involved in the situation, but by all loyal citizens. Not only physicians and nurses, but all civilians, were expected to recognize that wounded soldiers had a greater right to medical aid than sick civilians. Not only managers and workers, but tradesmen and consumers, were expected to acknowledge the priority of technical products needed in war over other products. Thus, the range of applicability of standards and norms as models of attitudes is much wider than their range as rules of actions. Many more people are in duty bound to accept them as valid than there are people to act in conformity with them.

Second, from the point of view of those who promulgate standardizing and normative judgments, verbal denial of their validity may be by itself a greater wrong than active nonconformity with the standards and norms which they express. Thus, to priests who function as authoritative exponents of truths about the essence of the deity and of the divinely sanctioned norms of human conduct, an expression of disbelief in any of these truths, a denial of the validity of any of these norms, unless retracted, is an unpardonable sin, leading to exclusion of the sinner from the community of the faithful. From the point of view of the rulers of the U.S.S.R., explicit disagreement with any of the absolutely valid principles of Marxism-Leninism is a more serious offence than actual conduct which fails to conform with these principles as interpreted by the rulers. This is significantly manifested in methods used to deal with individuals who for some reason have become *personae non gratae*. It is always easy to find in their actions some deviations from norms imposed by the regime; but this is not enough. They are publicly accused of entertaining and expressing ideas which conflict with the Marxian ideology, and may be branded as "enemies of the people" who side with capitalism in the supreme class struggle.[6] In 1948 such an accusation was publicized against Tito.

Third, many normative judgments are negative, not positive; they explicitly state what *should not* be done in situations which include certain values. They do imply standards by which these values are to be judged, but the standards may be positive or negative; in neither case do the norms prescribe

---

[6] Many former citizens of Soviet Russia give examples of such condemnation for alleged denial or profanation of absolutely valid ideological models. For a few minor cases, see Victor Serge, *Russia, Twenty Years After,* trans. by Max Schachtman (New York: Hillman-Curl, Inc., 1937). Perhaps the most significant is the case of Trotsky and his followers. Although the original conflict between Trotsky and Stalin was chiefly a struggle for power within the Communist Party, yet eventually it became interpreted as an ideological conflict; then to be called a "Trotskyist" meant to be branded as a heretic and perhaps also as a traitor. Trotsky did not aim to create at once a new society and culture, but hoped that one would evolve gradually from the most important elements of the old cultures. Nor did he want communism to develop fully in an isolated Russia before spreading to other countries, but expected that its development would be independently carried on in all advanced countries.

what *should actually be* done to the values. Consequently, while they constitute ideological models of attitudes presumed to be accepted by everybody, they certainly do not contain any patterns of actions; an agent can perform a great variety of actions while refraining from the kind of action which he should not perform. The negative judgment "Thou shalt not kill" implies a positive standard of valuation of human lives in general; but a human agent can perform diverse actions dealing with another without killing him. The rule prohibiting sexual intercourse with everybody but a conjugal partner not only leaves open the possibility of widely diverse actions which an individual can perform with one of the opposite sex without transgressing the rule, but, though implying a standard of positive mutual valuation between a husband and a wife, contains no definite norms as to what should be the interaction between husband and wife.

Fourth, another reason why ideological models should be distinguished from realistic patterns of actions is that standards and norms are often explicitly accepted by individuals who seldom act or expect to act in conformity with them when they are supposed to do so. Age-old religions or moral ideologies may be verbally recognized as valid by participants in a collectivity long after they have lost their original influence upon actions.[7] On the other hand, when a new ideological model emerges, it may remain for a long time an ideal for its promoters, to be realized in the future, rather than a guiding principle of present actions. And some ideological principles of conduct—e.g., the Christian principle "Love thy neighbor as thyself"—have been for centuries considered universally binding by millions of individuals who are well aware that neither they nor others are expected to conform regularly with them.

Ideological systems

Investigators find many different models of attitudes in every culture. Some of them are unconnected, inasmuch as the situations to which they refer do not include any important common values. Thus, in American culture hardly any connection exists between models of attitudes toward art and models of attitudes toward politics.[8] Other models are connected but conflict, inasmuch as they cover situations including some common values which, according to one model, should be judged positive and according to the other negative; or an activity which should be considered right according to one model should be considered wrong according to the other. Such conflicts are familiar nowadays in democratic collectivities, where political,

---

[7] The same is often found in nonliterate communities. Such a divergence may indicate that a new ideological model is evolving. Cf. Ralph Linton, *The Study of Man*, p. 100.

[8] There was, however, a definite connection in Germany under the Nazi regime, when loyalty to the party required approval of certain works of art and disapproval of others.

legal, economic, educational, aesthetic, and religious controversies are freely and openly carried on.

In contrast with these conflicts, a plurality of special ideational models of attitudes may become subordinated to some general model and more or less consistently integrated into what may be termed an *ideological system* of standards and norms. It is a system in the sense that evaluative conceptions of various objects and normative conceptions of various activities are logically interdependent. It usually includes a hierarchy of values graded by importance.

Such systems have been found in nonliterate collectivities, though their integration seldom manifests consistent, inclusive, logical reflection explicitly and fully symbolized in verbal statements.[9] Cultural anthropologists are inclined to supplement such incomplete, unreflective integration by natives; they seek to synthesize logically not only standards and norms which refer to certain specific kinds of situations (technical, magico-religious, social, aesthetic, etc.), but all presumably influential ideological models found in a given culture. The *pattern of culture*, in the "ideal-typical" sense in which Ruth Benedict used this term, denotes the result of such a synthesis. Other terms have been introduced; thus, Gregory Bateson uses "cultural structure" as a collective term for the coherent logical scheme which may be constructed by the scientists, fitting together the various premises of the culture.[10]

Ideological systems are usually more explicit and coherent in literary cultures. Many theories of culture are in fact primarily based on studies of such systems; and even though we may question some of these theories, we must acknowledge that investigation of ideological systems is an indispensable task of cultural scientists. For comparative purposes we need here a good example of what we mean by an ideological system. We select therefore the ideological system of the medieval Roman Catholic Church and give a brief summary of its main components. We do so not only because such rich and reliable material concerning it is available, but also because it is one of the most inclusive and complex systems ever developed. Furthermore, its logical integration by St. Thomas Aquinas in his *Summa Theologica* is probably more consistent than that of any other system of similar inclusiveness and complexity. Finally, it possesses to an unusually high degree a common characteristic of many ideological systems—the characteristic of *permanence* which has raised very difficult and important problems for theorists of culture. From the point of view of its adherents, it is essentially the same now as it was seven hundred (or even twelve hundred) years ago; so much so that in summarizing some of its basic principles, as they were recognized in the

---

[9] Paul Radin did find a considerable degree of ideological systematization in some Amerindian communities. Cf. his *Primitive Man as Philosopher*, quoted in Chapter 1.
[10] Gregory Bateson, *Naven* (Cambridge, 1936), p. 25.

thirteenth century, we can use quotations from works published in the twentieth century.[11] Of course, our summary must be on a popular level, far below the level of professional theologians and scholars. Indeed, the system, when taught to laymen and even to the lower clergy, has to be considerably abbreviated and popularized.

The fundamental principle of Roman Catholic ideology is the recognition of God as the supreme value in every human situation. There is only one God. God should be conceived and evaluated by every man aware of His existence as "infinite in knowledge, in goodness, and in every other perfection; who created all things by His Omnipotence and governs them by His Providence. In this one God there are three distinct Persons: the Father, the Son, and the Holy Ghost, who are perfectly equal to each other."[12]

This conception of God as a Holy Trinity was above ordinary human understanding; laymen, in particular, were not supposed to ask for an explanation, but were required to accept it on faith as absolutely true. And the conception of the Holy Ghost, "who inspired the prophets and imparted faith to the hearts of men,"[13] remained vague to everybody but theologians and mystics, although a special holy day was devoted to His cultus; perhaps this was due to the lack of a symbolic representation which could appeal to popular imagination. The conception of God the Father was easier to popularize because of the familiar anthropomorphic symbolism; but, whether because of the prevalent social significance of paternal authority in Western Europe or because of the emphasis of the Church on sin and divine punishment, He seems to be for most believers the personification of severe justice and a Power whose activities are often unpredictable and incomprehensible to ordinary mortals. Most popular, of course, was—and is—the conception of the Son as merciful Saviour of mankind: "Jesus Christ, the Second Person of the Blessed Trinity, is perfect God and perfect Man. . . . He is God of the substance of the Father, begotten before time; and he is Man of the substance of his Mother, born in time. Out of love for us, and in order to rescue us from the miseries entailed upon us by the disobedience of our first parents, the Divine Word descended from heaven, and became Man in the womb of the Virgin Mary, by the operation of the Holy Ghost."[14]

The supreme importance of the One God to men was due not only to His

[11] If our survey were limited to these principles, we might use consistently the present tense, since they are recognized as absolutely valid by all the faithful living members of the Church. We use the past tense sometimes when we view them as historical products, for their contents, meanings, and relationships to other historical products were different in the late medieval period than they are now.

[12] James Cardinal Gibbons, *The Faith of Our Fathers*, 17th ed. (Baltimore: John Murphy Co., 1904), p. 1.

[13] Karl R. Hagenbach, *Compendium of the History of Doctrines*, trans. by Carl W. Buch, I (Edinburgh, 1850), 124-25.

[14] Gibbons, *op. cit.*, chap. I.

absolute power over human lives on earth, but also, even mainly, to the fact that the men created had immortal souls and were destined to exist for eternity in the supernatural, spiritual world. What this eternal existence of theirs would be, depended partly upon the free will with which their Creator had endowed them. If during their earthly life they chose the good way, conformed with the laws instituted by God and by men under divine sanction, they would be rewarded by eternal happiness; if, on the contrary, they chose the way of evil, sinned against "the laws of God," they would be condemned to eternal suffering. But, inasmuch as men in general were inclined to choose evil or easily yielded to temptation, if they prayed for help, God by His grace helped them to choose the good, and in dealing with sinners tempered justice by mercy and forgave their sins, if they repented.

There were many other holy beings of minor importance—angels and saints—all of them good and kind to well-intentioned men. Angels were mainly conceived as delegates of God to help and guard men against evil. Saints were heroes, models for men to venerate and imitate, as well as mediators, praying to God on behalf of men. The Virgin Mary, the divine Mother, was the most perfect, the most benevolent and influential of all saints. The conception of every angel or saint was, thus, clearly standardized. A dead person did not become a saint until canonized by the Church; after that, any individual who was aware of the saint's existence was bound to believe in his or her continued spiritual life in heaven and accept the definition and valuation of his or her personality as expressed by the Church.

In radical contrast to these positively standardized valuations of angels and saints were the negative standards applied to Satan and the minor devils, former angels who rebelled and were banished to hell.[15] People were bound to accept the existence of devils as authoritatively defined, to evaluate them negatively as evil, and to believe that they had the intention and power to harm men's earthly lives, and by tempting them into sin to lead them to eternal damnation; but their power, though greater than human power, was incomparably weaker than that of God.

For all kinds of situations which included God as supreme value or other holy beings as subordinate values, certain norms were formulated. Virtue consisted in regular conformity with these norms. The most important were the three theological virtues: faith, hope, and charity (in the specific sense of love of man for God). They included norms of mystical relations with God "as the supernatural End or destiny of man."[16] Although essentially internal and spiritual, they were meant to be manifested in outward conduct,

---

[15] We use the word "devil," rather than the earlier "demon," because it was more popular in the Middle Ages. Cf. Hagenbach, *op. cit.*, p. 525.

[16] John A. McHugh and Charles J. Callan, *Moral Theology* (New York: J. F. Wagher, 1929), I, 22.

primarily in religious cultus. The purpose of cultus was to help men establish and maintain such relations with God, either directly or with the aid of angels and saints. Ceremonial cultus was carried on mainly in churches, under the leadership of priests. All the values used during it had a sacred character, and the conduct of every participant, from the highest officiating priest to the humblest member of the congregation, was supposed to conform with special norms.

Numerous and diverse, but also well integrated, were the standards and norms referring to situations where living men were the main values. Men were, of course, more valuable than natural objects or secular cultural products. And the Roman Catholic Church, as an association of living men, is from the point of view of its faithful members the greatest, the most important earthly value. For the Church, since its foundation, has been in continuous contact with the supernatural, eternal association of saints and with God. It is a perpetual holy union instituted by Jesus Christ, organized by the Apostles under the primacy of Peter, to whom Jesus delegated the task, guided by the clergy under the primacy of the Popes as successors of Peter. Its authority in all matters of faith and morals is infallible, because derived directly from God. All Christians are supposed to accept the articles of faith promulgated by the Church and submit to the guidance of those in whom its authority is vested. Rejection of one or more of these articles is heresy; spurning the authority of one's spiritual superiors is schism.[17]

Whatever men do has some bearing, good or bad, direct or indirect, on their own lives, as well as on the lives of others, present or future, and is therefore subjected to definite moral norms. Men are bound to conform with these norms. Some moral duties are binding for all classes of men, and their regular performance is included under the concept of virtue. Four of them—prudence, justice, fortitude, and temperance—like the three theological virtues mentioned above "are also called cardinal virtues, because all the other moral virtues hinge upon them."[18]

Many special duties of particular classes of men are explicitly formulated, such as duties of members of domestic and civil society, of husbands and wives, of parents and children, of superiors and subjects.[19] The most inclusive of these are the duties of priests. The following popular statement from a famous authority shows how important, from the point of view of Catholic theologians, is the role of the priest entrusted with these duties:

The exalted dignity of the Priest is derived from the sublime function which he is charged to perform . . . he exercises powers not given even to angels.

[17] Gibbons, *op. cit.*, chap. II, "The Unity of the Church," and chap. III, "The Holiness of the Church."

[18] McHugh and Callan, *op. cit.*, I, 50.

[19] *Ibid.*, pp. 596-615.

The priest is the *ambassador of God*, appointed to vindicate His honor and to proclaim His glory. . . . Priests are also dispensers of His graces. . . . A Catholic priest . . . is a *King*, reigning not over unwilling subjects, but over the hearts and affections of his people. He is a *shepherd*, because he leads his flock into the delicious pastures of Sacraments and shelters them from the wolves that lay in wait for their souls. He is a *father*, because he breaks the bread of life to his spiritual children, whom he has begotten in Jesus Christ through the Gospel. He is a *judge* whose office is to pass sentence of pardon on self-accusing criminals. He is a *physician* because he heals their souls from the loathsome distempers of sin.[20]

In the various special realms of culture which include nonhuman earthly values, the standards and norms of medieval Catholicism were more or less exacting and systematic, depending upon the importance which the values involved had for men in their relations with God and with one another. Thus, economic activities were subjected to very definite norms—mainly norms of justice—inasmuch as the satisfaction of human needs depended on the conduct of those who produced, owned, or distributed the essential values. While intellectual and artistic values and actions had their own secular standards and norms, they were subordinated to religious ideational models. All philosophy, i.e., generalized and logically systematized knowledge, was expected to be subservient to theology, i.e., religious knowledge of God. Art was supposed to help make men piously inclined and morally good. Although no religious standards and norms were unconditionally applicable to the realm of material techniques, yet, if a technical agent wanted to avoid failure and to achieve success, he was advised to appeal for aid either directly to God or, more frequently, to a patron saint. Of course, the purpose of his actions had to be acceptable to the holy being whose assistance he invoked, and he could not expect a holy being to do for him what he was too ignorant or lazy to do for himself. In no situation whatever could a human agent invoke the aid of Satan. If he did, his action, whatever its purpose, became sinful.

Except for that definition of Satan and the minor devils, we shall not mention here any negatively standardized values and shall not summarize the systematic description of the varieties of wrong conduct which are included under the general concept of *sin*. Authoritative negative judgments about sins are, indeed, integral components not only of the Catholic ideology but of many other religious ideologies, and all believers are supposed to accept them as valid. They obviously differ in important respects from religiously and/or morally right conduct. And this raises the general problem of the significance of prohibitive rules which we shall discuss in a later chapter.

Before we proceed, however, we should mention another problem. When, after a brief definition of ideological systems in general, we selected a well-known religious system as a typical example, our selection may have sug-

[20] Gibbons, *op. cit.*, pp. 379-81.

gested the following questions: Are not religious ideologies essentially different from nonreligious, secular ideologies, which contain no reference whatever to a world of supernatural values and no norms of religious cultus? Does not the comparative study of religions constitute a separate cultural science, distinct from other cultural sciences, such as political science, economics, philology, theory of art, each of which has to deal with certain ideological systems within its own domain?

We do not deny the existence nor underrate the differences between religious and secular ideological systems, but we shall show that there are certain similarities underlying the differences and try to develop a common heuristic approach to these similarities.

Antithesis between stable order and change in theories of culture

To those who promulgate and accept definite standards of values and norms of conduct, these standards and norms appear to be essentially changeless, since they constitute models for all human thinking, present and future, about the values and ways of acting to which they refer. The validity of the judgments formulating such standards and norms is not affected by the flux of events; it is above time, just as the truth of theoretic judgments is above time. Once valid, they remain valid forever, even if the objects and facts to which they refer should cease to exist. *Fiat justitia, pereat mundus* (let justice be done, even if the world perish) is perhaps the most pregnant expression of this belief applied to ethical ideas.

A well-integrated ideological system is also assumed by its adherents to be changeless, because of the absolute validity of its main components. This assumption can persist indefinitely, even if the composition of the system undergoes some modifications. New judgments may be promulgated and incorporated into it, and some old judgments may be discarded; yet the system continues to be regarded as essentially unchanged. For the introduction of new standards and norms may be interpreted either as an explicit formulation of some ideational model which was already implicitly contained in the fundamental principles of the system, though not verbally expressed, or else as an application of its fundamental principles to new situations which its adherents have to face. Discarding old standards or norms may be justified on the ground that, although still valid, they are no longer needed for the guidance of human valuations and activities, because the situations to which they were applied do not exist any more.

The continued acceptance of the ideological system of the Roman Catholic Church by present theologians as essentially unchanged since the thirteenth century—and in its main theological and ethical doctrines since the seventh century—is a significant example, especially in view of the fact that quite a few important philosophic, legal, political, and economic innovations have been incorporated into it, and quite a few old conceptions have been dropped. Certain ethical ideologies, even without a theological foundation (such as the Confucian ideology), were considered to be unchanged for many centuries. Not so much permanence, however, is ascribed to legal ideological systems; for although a particular law, once promulgated, is considered binding until abrogated, and some laws were accepted as valid for centuries, yet a complex legal system can expand rapidly through many innovations, especially in modern times. Nevertheless, even here the main principles of a legal system are expected by those who consider them valid to remain unchanged indefinitely; all new laws are supposed to conform with these principles, unless a revolutionary change has occurred and an entirely different system takes the place of the old one. This expectation of permanence is especially obvious when a well-systematized inclusive legal code is promulgated by legislators. Thus, the main principles of the "Code Napoléon," the first code of French civil law, were expected to remain changeless and were unchanged for a century. Even when no codification exists, some fixed ideology is usually recognized as a guide for legislators and judges. Thus, the Constitution of the United States still provides the basic principles by which the validity of numerous and diverse new laws is being judged.

This assumption of the essential changelessness of an ideological system by those who believe that it is based upon absolute principles, coupled with the popular identification of models of attitudes with patterns of actions, has been the main source of the old and persistent antithesis between stable cultural order and cultural change, which is found in many religious, political, economic, and sociological theories, theories of culture in general, and ethnological studies of particular cultures.

Many theorists use this antithesis with an evaluative connotation. When the theorist himself considers an ideological system, already formed and accepted by a collectivity, as absolutely valid, it is of primary importance from his point of view that it remain unchanged and continue to be accepted by this collectivity as binding for human actions; for only thus can a normal, stable cultural order be maintained; changes in standards and norms then imply deterioration, passage from good to bad, from order to disorder, from organization to disorganization. This is how the changes going on in Roman intellectual and social life appeared to Cato the Elder, how orthodox Catholic theologians interpreted the changes introduced by Humanism and later by the Reformation, how religious scholars of most sects viewed the rapid secularization of Western cultures from the seventeenth century on. In our times, many a thinker hankers for the stability and order which his society or civilization in his opinion had at some period in the past and asserts that now it has become a "sick" society or a decaying civilization. A few thinkers even extend this conception to the whole present world and believe its rapidly growing changes are producing an increasing chaos.[21] However, not only theorists who wish to maintain or revive the ideological systems which they accept as valid, but even those who function as objective investigators frequently consider cultural order as essentially stable and contrast it with cultural change. The explanation lies in the fact that many of them investigate the products of ideational culture as given to them at the time of their investigation, abstracted from the actions of those who have produced them and used them.

To a thinker who understands the meaning of symbols and the connection between them, every product of ideational culture expressed in lasting symbols appears as an intrinsically changeless system of ideas, unless he views it in historical perspective. To a student of religion who reads and understands a sacred book, it does not matter whether it was written thirty centuries or thirty years ago, so long as he concentrates upon its content and is not concerned with problems of its historical origin and background, its interdependence with other ideational products, or the influence it has exercised upon human actions. A student of philosophy can reconstruct conceptually Aristotle's *Organon* or Kant's *Critique of Pure Reason* as if it had been published last year. To a student of literature, aesthetically integrated lyric poems, epics, dramas, "once produced do not change; this is why they can even be immortal, a privilege which living men do not share." [22] Every living historian of law who has access to the necessary documents and knows the language can study the Code of Napoleon after nearly a century and a half, the Code of Justinian after fourteen centuries, and the Code of Hammurabi after nearly forty centuries.

Moreover, written works are usually more accessible and easier to investigate than active performances; and insofar as the historical past is concerned, the evidence they present about ideological models of attitudes is much more reliable than the evidence about actions which is derived from descriptions of observers. Inasmuch as standards and norms, symbolically expressed, are intended to regulate actions, a theorist who investigates an ideological system implicitly or explicitly postulates—not without justification—that the active life of the collectivity where this system is accepted is ordered in accordance with its requirements (unless there is evidence to the contrary), taking for granted, of course, that many individual deviations and transgressions are apt to occur. So long, therefore, as the system apparently continues to be accepted without notable changes, the cultural order of the community is assumed to remain essentially changeless. If later a different ideological

---

[21] On the other hand, many believers in progress, from Comte to Hitler, and quite a few Marxians believed that the dissolution of the old stable order would result in the formation of a new order, much more perfect and consequently even more stable.

[22] Georges Dumesnil, *L'Âme et l'évolution de la littérature* (Paris, 1930), I, xxxiii.

system becomes explicitly substituted for the first, this means that a new cultural order has taken the place of the previous order. This is how political historians, economic historians, historians of religion, literature, or art divide the past of particular cultures into sequences of periods, each period marked by a relatively stable order and separated from the preceding and the succeeding period by a process of change.

Theorists, aiming at generalizations which should be applicable to many, if not all, collectivities, went still further. They reconstructed and synthesized systems expressed by ideologists, making them more consistent logically. Political thinkers, ever since classical antiquity, have been reconstructing, integrating, perfecting constitutional systems promulgated by legislators. Thus, the three constitutional systems reconstructed by Aristotle—monarchy, aristocracy, and polity (democracy)—were, from the point of view of logical consistency, the "ideal types," which existing political organizations only approximated. Economists, starting from the given economic ideologies of practical thinkers and leaders, which are seldom inherently consistent and sometimes partially conflicting, have constructed from them consistent general theories of the successive types of economic structure—e.g., pastoral, agricultural, and industrial (the latter with subdivisions), each relatively stable, but eventually changing into the next. This trend culminated in general historical philosophies of total cultures, each passing through successive stages —Vico's sequence of "age of gods," "age of heroes," "age of men"; Comte's "theological," "metaphysical," and "positive" stages; Sorokin's "ideational," "idealistic," and "sensate" cultures.

It is hardly surprising that ethnologists have usually ascribed an essential stability to the culture of nonliterate societies, since their first task, and often the only task they had time to perform, was to reconstruct and, if possible, to synthesize all the ideational models accepted as binding by participants in the collectivity they investigated. No written history enabled them to compare the present with the past; and whenever an ethnologist was able to follow the subsequent evolution of the collectivity he had investigated, or when somebody else studied it at a later time, it was usually found that this collectivity had in the meantime been subjected to the influence of Western civilization; thus, whatever changes had occurred in ideational models and actual conduct could be explained as due to this influence, which had disturbed the presumed original stability of its collective life. Only recently, with the development of archeology, the historical approach has been extended to nonliterate collectivities, and the conception of a long-lasting stability of their cultures has become doubtful.

It was Comte who first used the old contrast between stable order and change as a basis for dividing sociology, in the sense of a general science of culture, into two parts: "social statics," i.e., theory of "society" as an orderly cultural system at a given stage of its existence; and "social dynamics," i.e., theory of change (which he conceived as "progress") from an earlier to a later stage. This division has been explicitly or implicitly adopted by many sociologists, even if under different terms.[23] General theories and specific studies of "social structure," "institutional structure," "social order," "social organization," on the one hand, and of "social change," "cultural change," "social process," "social disorganization," on the other hand, are frequently considered as distinct parts of sociology and even published separately.[24]

In the natural sciences, it took centuries to eliminate this antithesis betweeen stability and change. Scientists only gradually discarded the old conception of a permanent substance in general, of heavenly bodies and the earth as essentially stable, of changeless organic species, and of irreducible elements of matter. They discovered that nothing is changeless in the world of nature; all stability is relative, depending on definite conditions. But they found that change is also relative; it is impossible to investigate changes without defining what is changing.

It is time, we believe, that cultural scientists followed this example. But they cannot use the same approach as physical scientists use when they substitute a complex dynamic, energetic system for a stone or a star as empirical datum, and leave to the psychologists the task of explaining why this datum is experienced by men as an essentially stable object. For a cultural scientist has to use the humanistic coefficient in defining the phenomena he investigates, and he then finds that the distinction between stability and change pervades all human thinking about cultural phenomena. When a religious ideology, an ethical doctrine, a philosophic theory, a poem, or a drama *appears changeless* to those who reconstruct it as a system of ideas,

[23] Comte's terminology was adopted by Sorokin in his *Society, Culture and Personality. Their Structure and Dynamics* (New York: Harper, 1947).

[24] See, e.g., Ernest T. Hiller, *Social Relations and Structures* (New York: Harper, 1947), especially chaps. 39 and 40; George P. Murdock, *Social Structure* (New York: Macmillan, 1949), limited almost entirely to "kinship systems," especially in "primitive societies"; Talcott Parsons, "The Professions and Social Structure. Age and Sex and Social Structure," *Essays in Sociological Theory* (Glencoe, Ill.: The Free Press, 1949), and also his conception of institutional structure as expounded in "The Position of Sociological Theory," *Am. Sociol. Rev.*, 13, 156-64. Parsons, indeed, connects "structure" with "function," but gives priority to the theory of structure.

Two well-known special works on change are William F. Ogburn, *Social Change* (New York, 1922); and F. Stuart Chapin, *Cultural Change* (New York: Century, 1928).

As to the theory of "social process," it was a "reaction against static theory . . . opposed to the conception of society as a structure." Its "core is . . . the notion of movement, change, flux . . . of society as a continual becoming." (Max Lerner, *Encycl. of Social Sci.*, XIV, 148.) It was most fully developed by Edward A. Ross in his *Principles of Sociology* (New York, 1920), where 35 processes are distinguished and described (Part IV), besides "preliminary socialization" (Part III). This work, however original and stimulating, shows clearly the impossibility of developing a sociological theory based on the classification of processes abstracted from systems.

this is a scientifically significant fact. It cannot be simply discarded as an illusion or an error, although it conflicts with historical evidence that the content and meaning which such a system has for those who use it inevitably change in the course of history.

We believe that this antithesis can be eliminated in various realms of cultural research by a different heuristic approach. Briefly and popularly speaking, this approach consists in combining studies of ideas with studies of actions, while consistently maintaining the distinction between them.

Although these two categories of phenomena can be and have been investigated separately, yet in the historical world of cultural reality they are inseparably connected; and the main task of all investigators is to discover and analyze their most important connections.

If this task is adequately performed, not only will the antithesis between cultural stability and cultural change be eliminated, but scientists will be able to overcome the present dualism of psychological typologies of human behavior, based on the study of actions apart from cultural products, and historico-ethnological typologies of cultures, based upon the study of cultural products apart from actions—neither capable of exact taxonomic and causal generalizations.

The connection between ideas and actions is, vaguely speaking, that of mutual influence. Here we shall briefly survey the influence of actions upon ideologies.

Evolution of ideological systems as ideals

Ideological models and systems as cultural products have duration and extension in the world of culture. Historians of religion and historians of law have tried to trace the origin of particular religions and legal systems, viewed them as existing during longer or shorter periods, located each of them at a particular period within more or less definite geographical areas, and investigated their spread from one area to another. More recently, ethnologists and sociologists have begun to study methodically the range of extension of contemporary models—moral standards and norms, customs, fashions, political and economic ideas. If it is true, as we have assumed, that ideologies in general are influenced by actions, we must also assume that this influence affects the course of their duration and the range of their extension. We begin with the first assumption.

Here we are faced with an interesting problem. Why is it that a historian views the religious ideology of ancient Egypt, the Code of Hammurabi, the "Laws of Manu," as something which existed in the past and does not exist any more, although, as we have seen, it is possible to reconstruct right now the main content and meaning of these systems? This view obviously differs from that of the student of literature, who considers literary masterpieces as immortal, and from that of the historian of knowledge, who judges Euclid's *Elements* a permanent contribution to the development of mathematics.

There is a reason for this difference of approach: Ideological models and systems, as a matter of fact, differ significantly in their purposes from other cultural products. The main purpose of a lyric poem, an epic, a painting, a musical composition, or a scientific theory as a cultural product is to comunicate to others the final results of the *producer's own past experience and activity*. Whereas the main purpose of a legal system or a religious ideology as a cultural product is to guide the *future experiences and activities of others*. Such is also the purpose of the work of an aesthete who promulgates standards by which poetry, painting, or music ought to be evaluated; and norms which poets, painters, or musicians ought to follow. The same individual may function as a producer and as a guide, e.g., when an artist teaches future artists to follow aesthetic models which he has adopted or initiated in his own work, or when a mystic describes his own religious experiences and also acts as a prophet, trying to guide the future religious experiences and activities of his converts. But the two functions are distinct. Such written works as the *Laws of Manu* or Boileau-Despréaux's *L'Art poétique*,[25] viewed simply as systems of ideas, cultural products of their authors, have existed and will exist as long as they can be read and understood; but when viewed as systems of standards and norms intended to guide future experiences and actions of others, they will exist only so long as other thinkers and agents accept them as valid and are willing to be guided by them.

Let us now survey from this point of view the influence of actions upon the duration of ideological models and systems, beginning with their first appearance. Since the invention of writing, as every historian of culture knows, numerous new ideological models have appeared in every realm of culture, and quite a few new inclusive ideological systems have evolved, different from those which existed before. Historians may disagree as to how new a particular model really was, especially in such realms as literature, art, mores, fashions, or how new an ideological system really was, especially when intended to be merely a revival of some old system, as in many sectarian doctrines. Certain historians are inclined to minimize innovations, to seek for antecedents of every product of human thinking. We are not concerned with such controversies. From the point of view of our present problem, the essential question is not how much a particular model or system differs from others in the light of typological comparison, but whether it was *judged*

---

[25] Nicolas Boileau-Despréaux's *Art of Poetry* was intended to be mainly a revival of Aristotelian aesthetic principles, "l'abrégé de l'idéal classique": Ferdinand Brunetière, *La Grande Encyclopédie*, Vol. VI.

to be different by its own adherents and adherents of the models or systems which existed at the time it appeared.

We may tentatively formulate a hypothesis which we shall try to define more specifically and apply more exactly in later research. It seems that new ideological models and systems are initiated and developed by thinkers who become aware of persistent active *conflicts* within or between human collectivities and who purposely tend to eliminate these conflicts. The models or systems they create are intended to be collectively accepted and effectively applied, with the result that harmony will be substituted for conflict. This purpose is clearly manifested when a thinker who has created or adopted a new model or system tries to function as a social leader, to gain followers, and with their aid or through their medium to influence participants in a collectivity to accept and be guided by the standards and norms the model or system includes. Until this is achieved, it is, from the point of view of its promoters, an *ideal* to be realized in the future, in contrast with present reality.

This heuristic hypothesis might be applied to the creation of any new models —new fashions, new styles of art, new methods of diagnosing and treating certain diseases, new standards and norms of interaction between teachers and pupils, etc. Inasmuch, however, as the problem of relationship between stability and change has arisen mainly from studies of long-lasting, complex ideological systems, we shall consider here the evolution of some of these systems.

First, take three systems which were never fully accepted or actively applied by the collectivities for which they were intended. Plato's conception of a harmoniously organized republic was for him an ideal that, when realized, should eliminate once and forever those conflicts within the Greek states of his time which, according to him, led to increasing disorganization and deterioration. The Stoical philosophy was meant to overcome both psychological conflicts between individual impulses and reason, and social conflicts between men. It was an ideal which would make harmonious personalities of all individuals who realized it in their own lives and at the same time introduce order into collective life. Comte's "religion of humanity," formulated in his *Système de Politique positive*, was similarly an ideal which, if and when generally accepted and applied, would overcome all political, economic, and religious conflicts; by making mankind as a whole the supreme human value and an object of normatively regulated cultus, it would produce a universal harmony.

Karl Mannheim called such a conception of a harmonious order, which does not yet exist anywhere but is expected to exist in the future, a "utopia," borrowing this term from Thomas More's famous work, in contrast with an "ideology," which corresponds to the existing order. This terminology has been adopted by quite a few theorists of culture.[26] We suggest that the term be limited to such works as More's *Utopia*, Bacon's *New Atlantis*, Campanella's *City of the Sun*, Harrington's *Oceana*, Butler's *Erewhon*, which differ significantly from ideals as here defined. These works were fictitious constructs of perfect systems which the authors did not try to realize in their own collectivities. None of these authors attempted to function himself as an active social leader or to gain active followers who would eventually change the existing social reality into the kind of new reality he described.

On the other hand, Plato's description of a perfect republic, the Stoics' psychological representation of the sage and their social conception of an order based on natural law, and even Comte's "religion of humanity" were meant to initiate a dynamic course of activity through which the new ideological system would be gradually accepted and progressively realized. Plato tried at first to have an existing state reorganized in accordance with his ideal; later, in his *Laws*, he outlined a program for the formation of a new city-state, which was not a mere utopia, in view of the fact that many new colonial city-states had actually been formed by the Greeks. Nor was the Platonic Academy exclusively devoted to pure theory; it remained under the influence of the Socratic conception, according to which the main function of the philosopher was that of a social leader, affecting through his followers practical morals and politics. Most of the Stoics considered themselves bound to strive for the realization of their social as well as their personal ideal.[27] And while Comte's theoretic conception of sociology as a positive science had little influence during his life, his practical ideal of a world society gained immediate acceptance and led organized groups of his followers to work for its realization.

Moreover, if an ideological system becomes a dynamic ideal, a guiding principle for actions tending to introduce a new order into some part of the cultural world, unlike a utopia, it must inevitably change, in view of the new problems which arise when its active promoters meet active opposition or when cooperation begins between promoters of ideals which differed

[26] Karl Mannheim, *Ideologie und Utopie*, 2d ed. (Bonn, 1930), trans. by Louis Wirth and Edward Shils (New York: Harcourt, 1936). Of course, the word "utopia" was used as a general term long before Mannheim. He ignored entirely the conception of Joyce O. Hertzler, *The History of Utopian Thought* (New York: Macmillan, 1923), which corresponds better to the original meaning of the word. In contrast with this meaning, he includes under his *Utopie* only those ideas "transcending the being" which "by counteracting the existing historical reality succeed in transforming it in the direction of their own representations" (p. 173). We cannot discuss here the significance of this work for the sociology of knowledge, which Wirth emphasizes in his introduction to the English translation.

[27] Already Zeno, in his *Politeia*, connected the individualistic ideal of the sage with the collectivistic ideal of a state which would embrace the whole and include every man as citizen. Some of his disciples even became politically active. But "at Rome Stoicism fell upon congenial soil; it was, in fact, the one philosophy congenial to the Roman type": Charles H. S. Davis, *Greek and Roman Stoicism* (Boston: Turner, 1903).

originally. Plato himself modified his original ideal, and all his ethical and political conceptions underwent many changes in the Academy after his death. The Stoical social ideal changed considerably when taken over by Roman thinkers;[28] Cicero, "the eclectic," contributed much to its evolution, which culminated in the conception of a future integration of all human collectivities into one harmonious cosmopolis. The followers of Comte did not leave his ideal unchanged; as a matter of fact, it was partially merged with other, different, ideals of world unity. Thus, in studying an ideal, we cannot limit ourselves to its original formulation; we must investigate it as it evolves in the course of its duration.

An ideal lasts as long as it has active promoters who are trying to have it collectively accepted and who believe that it can be realized, even if only in the distant future. Only when it loses active promoters and its realization appears altogether impossible does it cease to function as an ideal. This is what happened to the Platonic political ideal—never very influential—after the Roman conquest of Greece. The Stoical ideal, both personal and political, was much more influential, since it gained the support of many prominent Roman leaders, including Marcus Aurelius, the Stoical Emperor. Though never universally recognized or consistently applied, it persisted as a dynamic factor of Roman moral and political life until the domination of Christianity, the division of the Empire, and the fall of the Western Empire.[29] Modern ideologies of world unity which differ in detail but are based, like Comte's, on the conception of mankind as the supreme value of human actions and on the conviction that this unity cannot be achieved by violence, only by peaceful progress, continue to evolve and to function as ideals through the agency of various promoters who believe in the possibility of their future universal acceptance and realization.

Stabilization of ideals as dogmas

Quite a few ideological systems, however, which started as ideals initiated by creative thinkers and which were promoted at first only by small groups of social leaders and their followers, at a certain stage of historical evolution became accepted by relatively large collectivities; then the standards and norms which they included at this stage came to be considered binding for all participants. Take two well-known examples: the evolution of Christian ideology from the first century on, and the evolution of the socialist ideology from the first quarter of the nineteenth century up to the present.

The Christian ideological system began to evolve as an ethicotheological ideal; it was meant to overcome certain religious conflicts in doctrine and

[28] Cf. E. Vernon Arnold, *Roman Stoicism* (Cambridge, 1911); Robert M. Wenley, *Stoicism and Its Influence* (New York: Longmans, 1927).

[29] It did have, however, some ideological influence upon Christianity (Barnes and Becker, *op. cit.*, pp. 207-11) and was perhaps also somewhat influenced by it (William W. Capes, *Stoicism* (London, 1880)).

ritual as well as certain moral conflicts in social relations—class, economic, ethnic, and political conflicts.[30] The ideal was at first relatively simple, centered in the conception of God as benevolent father of all mankind, supreme object of human love, and emphasizing the universal brotherhood of men and consequently their duty of mutual love. It became, however, increasingly complicated in the course of its evolution as, with the spread of Christianity, numerous and diverse new conflicts emerged and had to be overcome. Christian groups came into conflict in doctrine and cultus with groups professing orthodox Judaism and with other religious groups of Eastern origin, as well as with representatives of the official religion of imperial Rome. Christian thinkers had to defend their ideology against metaphysical, ethical, political, and economic criticisms of Greek and Roman philosophers of various schools. And a number of new groups tried to integrate some components of the Christian ideology with widely different components of other religious ideologies. Later, even within a Christian group, conflicting interpretations of some components of its religious ideology might arise, as in the famous controversy as to the relation between the substance of Christ and the substance of God, whether it was homoousia, i.e., identity in substance, or homoiousia, i.e., essential likeness, but not identity in substance.[31]

It took about six centuries to overcome such conflicts between religious groups. This was achieved by a gradual selection of those components of various religious ideologies which could be interpreted in accordance with the theological principles accepted by the most influential leaders, rejecting all components which defied such interpretation and systematizing those selected into an inclusive, universal system by which all human thought and conduct could be guided. And this ideological evolution was accompanied by a social evolution, a progressive integration of many groups, old or newly formed, into a united, well-organized religious society which really accepted this inclusive ideological system.[32] Social integration proved less

[30] Many histories of Christianity in general have been written, and quite a few popular textbooks are available. We found the collective work *Histoire de l'Église*, eds. Augustin Fliche and Victor Martin (Paris, 1937-49) the most thorough and objective. We have used here the first six volumes, 1937-39. From the point of view of our present problem, quite valuable is Ernst Troelsch, *Die Soziallehre der christlichen Kirchen und Gruppen* (Tubingen, 1923).

[31] *Histoire de l'Église*, Vol. III. The popularity of this controversy was described by Gregory of Nazianzus. Cf. John F. Hurst, *Short History of the Christian Church* (New York, 1894), p. 53.

[32] The main theological conflicts were overcome during the Oecumenical Councils of A.D. 680-81 and 787: *Histoire de l'Église*, Vols. V and VI. On the final separation of the two churches, cf. Louis Bréhier, *Le Schisme oriental du XIᵉ siècle* (Paris, 1899). He ascribes it mainly to a "perpetual rivalry which always separated Greek countries from Latin countries" (p. 305).

successful than ideological integration; and in spite of the lack of fundamental theological conflicts between Greek Orthodoxy and Roman Catholicism, the Eastern and the Western Church became permanently separated.

In the course of this evolution there were attempts to *stabilize* the ideological system as formed at certain stages; but the appearance of new theological and ritualistic conflicts between and within Christian groups interfered
with this stabilization.

However, such conflicts subsided after the social unification of the Roman
Church in the West and of the Greek Orthodox Church in the East; the
validity of their sacred standards and norms remained unchallenged, except by
heretics who were excluded from either church; and their theological and
ethical ideology became finally stabilized. Even then, various conflicts between
secular philosophies started by scholars, especially in the West, still prevented
the inclusive integration and stabilization of all evaluative and normative
thinking of loyal church members. But the system of Thomas Aquinas achieved
such an integration and stabilization of theological, ethical, metaphysical,
legal, and political doctrines.

Now, what did the stabilization of this ideological system, after a long
period of evolution, mean to its adherents? It meant that all the controversial
issues which divided thinkers and leaders had presumably been overcome
forever. Past ideals were either rejected or, if accepted, became *dogmas*.
While ideals change, since those who attempt to have them realized continually
meet new problems in the course of their attempts, dogmas do not change,
for they provide in advance a ready solution for all the problems which their
adherents may have to face.

But how can an evolving ideological system become stabilized as a system
of dogmas? The factual stabilization of the medieval religious system provides
an answer. It has been a cooperative achievement of the clergy who assumed
and maintained authoritarian guidance and control of all attitudes of church
members which were considered religiously significant. The primary dynamic
factor of this stabilization was—and still is—organized education: education
of successive generations of priests, who are taught for years by older priests
to understand and accept as absolutely valid and changeless the entire
dogmatic system; education of laymen by priests who transmit the basic principles of this system as absolutely valid and changeless to successive generations of children and who later repeatedly remind every living member of
the church in sermons, confessions, or private admonitions of the absolute
validity of these principles and explain to him how to apply the standards and
norms included in the system to any situations which he may face in the
course of his life. The second dynamic factor of stabilization (not so effective
in the long run) is active, organized repression of ideational innovations,
whether initiated by church members or accepted from outsiders, if they seem

to conflict with the established ideology. The repressive methods that have been used are well known; they ranged from persuasion through various kinds of moral and physical compulsion up to exclusion of the dissenter from the church, and even to death.

When these methods failed, conflict was overcome by a modification or reinterpretation of some components of the ideology. This is what happened when the results of modern scientific research in astronomy, physics, geology, biology conflicted with doctrines explicity formulated in the Bible concerning the order of nature and its origin. The presumably final solution of these conflicts was reached when leading Catholic thinkers established a distinction between the two realms of knowledge: In the realm of theology, metaphysics, and ethics, the knowledge revealed by God and promulgated by the church is composed of absolute truths, none of which can be invalidated by human experience or reason alone; but secular knowledge, reached by human science, is composed of hypotheses, every one of which either has been or can be invalidated.

If we survey the history of that modern secular ideology which is designated by the general term of "socialism," we find that it did not evolve out of any one ideal, but out of several different ideals more or less independently initiated by various thinkers—Saint-Simon, Fourier, Louis Blanc, William Thompson, Proudhon, Robert Owen.[33] These men were interested in common problems—how to eliminate class conflicts based on private property and to liberate the working class from the oppression and exploitation of landowners and capitalists, but the solutions they offered were different. Of all their ideals, the one initiated by Proudhon and Marx, developed under the name of communism by Marx with the aid of Engels, became the most consistent, inclusive, and influential. Yet this has not remained unchanged; from it a number of divergent ideals evolved, each including some components derived from other ideologies and each supported by a different group.[34] Among these variants, one has reached a stabilization at least equal to that of medieval

---

[33] A short, but good, historical survey of socialist ideals is Harry W. Laidler's *A History of Socialist Thought* (New York: Crowell, 1927). See also Max Beer, *A History of British Socialism*, 2 vols. (London, 1919-20). Maurice Bourguin, *Les Systèmes socialistes et l'évolution économique* (Paris, 1907), attempted to classify "the great variety" of socialist systems according to: (1) the ownership and control of means of production (by the state, the community, or the cooperative association); (2) the mode of estimating values (by units of labor or by supply and demand); and (3) the mode of distribution, depending on the ownership of the products. L. Garriguet, *L'Évolution actuelle du socialisme en France* (Paris, 1912), considers "revolutionary syndicalism" to be a new type.

[34] Take, for instance, the deviations from Marxism initiated by Ferdinand Lassalle; the minor deviations by Bebel, Liebknecht, and Kautsky; the liberal *Evolutionary Socialism* of Edward Bernstein, trans. by E. C. Harvey (New York, 1909); the democratic Fabian Socialism under the ideological leadership of Sidney Webb; and the split of the Russian Socialist Party into Bolsheviks and Mensheviks.

Roman Catholicism, and this stabilization is inseparably connected with the totalitarian organization of Soviet Russia. Marxism-Leninism, with some additions by Stalin, has become an absolutely incontrovertible dogmatic system with ideational models for every realm of culture—metaphysics, economics, politics, ethics, law, history, ethnology, literature, plastic arts, music, and even natural science (as exemplified by the recent authoritative decision concerning genetics).

Here again stabilization is manifestly due to organized collective activity as a dynamic force.[35] Unconditional adherence to this system implies, of course, continued explicit consensus of the ruling group as to the validity of its dogmas, agreement to make their acceptance obligatory, and regular elimination of all dissenters from the group. For years this system has been ac-

[35] There is a vast amount of material concerning the activities intended to integrate the communist ideology and stabilize it by having it accepted as absolutely valid by all the people in Soviet Russia. A very instructive work dealing with the early period, from 1918 to 1926, is René Fülop-Miller's *Geist und Gesicht des Bolschevismus* (Vienna-Zurich, 1926), with 602 illustrations. The author analyzes the foundations of social philosophy: exaltation of the "collective man," the "mass," combined with a cult of the "great personality"; naturalistic metaphysics, combined with dialectical epistemology; popular manifestations of various components of the ideology in architecture, decoration, sculpture, painting, theater; "theatralization of life" (demonstrations, festivals of music and song, movies—as yet, not popular poetry or novels). He is concerned only with these realms of culture and omits ordinary propaganda. The last part gives an outline of the "new education," which the author considers as radically conflicting with the ideal formulated by Trotsky of "raising the average of mankind to the level of an Aristotle, a Goethe or a Marx" (p. 290). Whereas, "the Bolshevik education . . . aims at nothing else, but the rapid formation of an expendable army, an eternally subordinate 'ecclesia militans' of agitators and bureaucrats" (p. 425).

Some books have been written more recently about Soviet education: e.g., Lucy Wilson, *The New Schools in New Russia* (New Haven: Yale University Press, 1928); Samuel N. Harper, *Civic Training in Soviet Russia* (Chicago: University of Chicago Press, 1929); Nicholas Hans and Sergius Hessen, *Educational Policy in Soviet Russia* (London, 1930). A comparative survey of them clearly indicates a change from the early ideal to a completely integrated dogmatic system. The final result of this stabilization and integration is excellently summarized by George S. Counts in his "Introduction" to a translation of some school texts by Yesipov and Goncharov, published under the title *"I want to be like Stalin"* (New York: Day, 1947): "In the first place, education in the Soviet Union is essentially . . . social in purpose . . ." (p. 13). "In the second place . . . [it] is extremely broad in scope. . . . In addition to that system which embraces a vast network of institutions from the nursery school and kindergarten through the elementary and secondary schools and various vocational, technical and professional schools of different grades to the universities and scientific institutes and academies, it includes . . . all organized agencies capable of enlightening and moulding the minds, both young and old . . . the family, the collective farm, the cooperative, the society of Young Pioneers, the League of Young Communists, the labor unions, the organs of government and the Red Army, the book press, the newspaper, the magazine, the radio, the bookshop, the theatre, the movie picture, literature, works of art, and all agencies of entertainment . . ." (pp. 15-16). "In the third place . . . [it] is essentially monolytic in control . . . actual control of this vast educational system . . . rests in the hands of the All-Union Communist Party and its central organs . . ." (p. 16).

tively taught as absolutely valid to children and adolescents by teachers, most of whom had been similarly educated. Their activities are supplemented, if necessary, by adult education. Furthermore, throughout their lives, adults are continually reminded of the validity of the system, its positive importance for all people, and the common obligation to support it. This ceaseless indoctrination is carried on by authoritative leaders of various organized groups, by preachers at meetings, and by popular writers. Periodical ceremonial celebrations, dramas, movies, operas, and concerts are usually accompanied by some references to the system and high appreciation of its models, often by condemnation of dissenters and transgressors. As far as possible, the Russian people are protected from external influences which might raise doubts as to the absolute validity of any communist dogma, by preventing them from becoming acquainted with conflicting ideologies. Since complete isolation from such influences cannot always be achieved, it is the special task of professional propagandists to present every conflicting ideology to the people in such a way as to make it appear incomparably inferior to the orthodox doctrine.

The other factor of stabilization—organized repression of unorthodox ideas—is more widely and effectively used by communist authorities in Russia than it ever was by the Roman Catholic clergy (except, perhaps, in Spain by the Inquisition). The communist authorities in Russia possess complete control of the State with its coercive power, whereas the clergy, however strong its political influence, never had such a monopoly.

Thus, both the evolution of ideological systems as ideals and their stabilization as dogmas depend on purposive actions—more specifically, *social actions*—of agents who explicitly aim to have people accept these systems and be guided by the standards of values and norms of conduct which they include. The results of such actions, in turn, apparently depend on cooperation between these agents and their function in the organized social groups existing within the collectivity in which they participate.

Expansion and recession of ideological models and systems

Our next task is to survey the influence of actions upon the extension of ideologies. As we mentioned in Chapter 5, every cultural datum—e.g., a word, a myth, a poem, a musical composition—has an extension in the sense that it is being experienced at any given time by a larger or smaller number of people who inhabit a certain geographic area or are scattered over many geographic areas. This is true also of ideological models and systems, since they belong to the general category of cultural data.

However, as we have seen, these models and systems differ from other data in that they are not only products of past activities but contain standards and norms intended to guide future activities; and from the point of view of cultural science, it is essential to know whether those who experience them also accept these standards and norms. Investigators have found that only in a small and isolated community, with a firmly established traditional culture, are standards of value and norms of conduct accepted by all participants who are aware of them. In a large collectivity which has many cultural contacts with the outside world not all the people who are aware of an ideological model or system accept its standards and norms; some reject them; others see no connection between the ideology and their own values and activities and are therefore unconcerned about its validity. For instance, right now most of the inhabitants of Western Europe and the United States—certainly those who are literate—are well aware of the communist ideology, whether they know much or little about it. Yet apparently those who disagree with it are much more numerous than those who agree, while an indefinite proportion manifest no positive or negative interest in it. Hereafter, in speaking of the extension of ideological models or systems as such, we shall consider only those people who explicitly accept them as valid.

Now, the extension of a given ideological model in this sense of the term can be compared with the extension of another, qualitatively different model, by using a common technique of measurement. Unlike the intensive measurement of the power of active tendencies, which requires a gradation of qualitative changes occurring in actions under the influence of other actions, the measurement of the extension of ideological models requires only statistical techniques. Having circumscribed a certain population, we can measure the extension of various models within this statistical universe by finding how large a proportion of the population accepts the validity of each model at the time when they are being investigated. The universe may be world-wide, may include all human individuals, or may be limited to those who are distinguished by certain indices—location in a territory, age, sex, status, occupation, membership in certain groups, etc. Verbal expression of acceptance is, of course, the primary evidence on which the investigator must rely, and students of public opinion are developing increasingly effective techniques to improve the reliability of this evidence.

However, measuring the extension of a given model at the time when the investigation is carried on is only the first necessary step toward the solution of a much more important problem in which modern investigators are interested: the problem of the increase or decrease of extension of a particular model in the course of its duration. We suggest that increase of extension be termed "expansion"; decrease, "recession." The range and rapidity of expansion or recession of a model can be measured by repeated statistical measurements of its extension at successive intervals. Furthermore, by measuring according to similar methods the range and rapidity of expansion or recession of several models within the same universe, scientifically significant connections between these processes may be found.

In recent times, a considerable amount of this kind of research has been carried on, mainly in the United States. The general problem with which most of the investigators are concerned is to ascertain the effect of specific activities which tend to make a growing number of people accept certain models or reject models which they had accepted before. Thus, many monographs have been written about the influence of organized education in changing specific attitudes of student populations in particular high schools or colleges—ethical, racial, sexual, and religious attitudes; valuations of foreign nations and cultures; morale during the war; etc. Investigators of public opinion have measured the expansion or recession of many different evaluative and normative judgments about social phenomena among selected samples of the population of the United States, under the impact of all kinds of oral and written propaganda and counterpropaganda. The expansion of new fashions in clothes, food, furniture, home decoration, architecture, gardens, etc., under the influence of advertizing, is being studied by practical economists. The measurements obtained indicate how widely and how rapidly the range of acceptance of the ideological model increases or decreases. The exactness of such measurements, however, depends not only on the use of adequate statistical methods and techniques for obtaining reliable data, but also on an exact definition of the model which the given population accepts. Thus, the expansion of models of fashion which are exactly defined can be more exactly measured than the expansion of the evaluative and normative judgments included in political propaganda, which are often vague, inconsistent, and connected with pseudo-factual information.

More difficult, of course, is the quantitative study of the expansion and recession of whole ideological systems. On the one hand, a complex ideological system, a product of considerable reflection by leading thinkers, can be understood in its totality by only a small minority of people. On the other hand, insofar as such a system is integrated, it would be an inadequate method to break it up into simpler ideological models and study the range of acceptance of each model separately. Nevertheless, it is possible to find in every ideological system a certain nucleus of standards and norms which are understandable to large masses of people after a minimum of education; their explicit acceptance means to authoritative leaders and to the people themselves unconditional acceptance of the system as a whole. For instance, right now acceptance by any individual of a dozen or so definite political, economic, and moral judgments is generally considered to mean that he accepts the total ideology of communism.

In any case, the problem of measuring the expansion and recession of ideological systems, however difficult, does not seem insolvable, if enough data are available. And it certainly is a problem of great theoretic as well as practical importance. What is popularly called a "conflict of cultures," originates in an expansion of certain ideological systems resulting in the recession of other ideological systems.

Take, for instance, the process of expansion and recession of religious ideologies during the last twelve centuries, which have affected the whole cultural evolution of mankind. Obviously, there is no possibility of measuring exactly these processes as they occurred in the more or less distant past. Nonetheless, some quantitative conclusions, however inexact and uncertain, can be drawn from the historical evidence.

Probably the most rapid expansion of any religious ideology (perhaps of any ideology before the present expansion of communism) was that of Islam from the beginning of the eighth to the end of the fifteenth century; only in Spain during the second half of this period did Islam recede. Inasmuch, however, as more historical material is available about the expansion of Christian ideologies in general and of the Roman Catholic ideology in particular, we shall again refer to the latter and mention some well-known processes in its history.[36]

We shall begin with that stage of its evolution when the central core of its doctrine had become stabilized, and the struggles with rival religious ideologies of Eastern origin, with the old Roman religion, and with conflicting Christian doctrines—such as Aryanism—had been won. In the course of its subsequent expansion, both within and outside the area of the original Western Empire, it met other religious systems, shared by rather large collectivities—Teutonic, Celtic, Slavonic, Prussian-Lithuanian—with standardized conceptions of divinities and ritualistic norms very different from those of Christian believers. All of them gradually receded, and some disappeared. By the end of the twelfth century, throughout Central and Western Europe only a few minorities had religious standards and norms more or less incompatible with those of the church—the Jews, some rebellious groups of heretics, isolated rural communities preserving their beliefs in the power of old pagan gods, small secret societies, some of which had a regular cult of Satan. Certain old standards and norms of Teutonic war lords which conflicted with those of Christian moralists were still maintained by military and political groups, but a considerable degree of compromise had been reached.

And then in the fifteenth century, two new dynamic trends started. On the one hand, Protestant ideologies evolved and expanded in Europe; consequently, the Roman Catholic ideology receded considerably in certain European countries. On the other hand, by the end of the century, Roman

---

[36] An excellent work devoted to this problem is Kenneth Scott Latourette's *A History of the Expansion of Christianity*, 7 vols. (New York: Harper, 1937-45).

Catholicism began to expand over other continents; and a similar expansion of Protestant ideologies began a century later.

In recent times, however, there seems to be more recession than expansion of religious ideologies in general, while the old struggles for converts between Christianity and Islam, Catholicism and Protestantism, have subsided. Instead, the world is full of conflicts between diverse secular ideologies struggling for expansion.[37] The opportunity for a comparative quantitative investigation of the expansion and recession of these ideologies is unprecedented, the factual material enormous; but well-known obstacles, political and economic, prevent us from gaining access to this material and utilizing it.

While emphasizing the importance of studying the expansion and recession of ideologies, we must point out that such studies constitute only a part of a more fundamental and complex scientific task. For the expansion of an ideological system is not a historical necessity; it is neither predestined by an absolute Reason or Will in control of human history nor determined by natural forces according to the dogma of dialectical materialism. Nor is it reducible to processes of mass psychology, explicable by "suggestion," "mental contagion," etc. When we investigate such an expansion, we find that it is a result of purposeful actions, individually initiated but collectively supported and continued. Most of the important advances in the expansion of Islam began by military conquest. The expansion of Christian ideological systems was due to apostles and missionaries who were supported by organized groups and who organized groups of converts for further expansion; rulers who decreed the acceptance of Christianity by their subjects; conquerors who imposed it upon the conquered (as in Spanish America); religious orders who spread it, sometimes by peaceful methods, sometimes by force (like the Knights of the Cross in Prussia and the Knights of the Sword in Latvia and Estonia).

The expansion of the communist ideology since the Bolshevist Revolution has been entirely carried out by organized groups. The groups either begin with military conquest, and impose their ideology upon the conquered by political coercion and compulsory indoctrination, or begin with indoctrination, and end with political coercion supported, if necessary, by military conquest. And we may notice that, so long as the expansion of an ideological system proceeds by peaceful methods, it remains an evolving, changing ideal;

[37] See, e.g., *European Ideologies. A Survey of 20th Century Political Ideas*, ed. by Feliks Gross, with an introduction by Robert M. MacIver (New York: Philosophical Library, 1948). The term "political ideas" rather oversimplifies the context of most ideological systems, and we notice some overlapping and some omissions where nationalism is concerned. However, the survey is instructive, although it covers only Europe, whereas some ideological systems of European origin have spread all over the world, and other quite different systems have emerged or are emerging on other continents.

but when coercive methods are resorted to by the groups which try to expand it, this usually means that it has become dogmatically stabilized.

The expansion of an ideological system, however, frequently meets resistance from adherents of a different system which conflicts with it, according to their opinion. This resistance may be passive, consisting in nonacceptance of the standards and norms of the expanding system. Or it may be active, manifested in organized opposition to the individuals and groups which try to have their system accepted, in which case, *ideological conflict* becomes *active social conflict*, which can range from peaceful competition for membership to violent struggle for mutual destruction. And when social conflict between groups grows in intensity, even minor differences between the ideologies which these groups represent may appear to them as fundamental, irreconcilable opposition.

Cultural Patterns and Systems of Actions

The principle of conformity and the classification of actions

We have now reached a most important and difficult general problem, one that has for some time engaged the attention of modern scientists in various realms of culture: the influence of ideas upon actions.

As we have seen, an ideological model of attitudes superimposes the same ideal type upon many diverse definitions of situations, since all those who accept a certain standard of values and a norm of conduct, in reflecting about any situation which includes such values, judge them in accordance with the standard and consider that in such a situation the norm should be actively followed.

Now, there is considerable and incontrovertible empirical evidence that many human actions really do conform with the requirements of ideological models. It is obvious that an action can conform with an ideological model only if the agent himself applies this model in defining his own present situation in the very course of this particular action. If he does, this means that, in selecting the objects of his action, he evaluates these objects in accordance with a definite standard and that, in anticipating his subsequent performance, he judges it in accordance with a definite norm. His evaluative and normative judgments become dynamic parts of his action, in that both of them together determine the formation of his purpose. And once the purpose is formed, his action proceeds toward its realization.

This is the only way in which ideological models can become actualized. Of course, the amount of reflection used to define a situation in accordance with a certain model may vary considerably. When agents merely imitate somebody else's action, they usually assume that the original agent effectively applied in practice certain valid knowledge about the values involved and the right way of dealing with such values; therefore, they simply follow his example without doing much thinking of their own, unless their imitation is a failure. And after an agent has repeatedly applied certain standards and norms in the course of his actions, reproducing such actions requires less and less reflection, unless some unexpected factors prevent their reproduction (cf. Chapter 7).

However, only those agents who have accepted an ideological model, no matter how they learned to accept it, can make their actions conform with this model. This seems perfectly obvious, yet it cannot be taken for granted. Indeed, quite a few thinkers have different conceptions of the relationship between ideological models and actions, e.g., believe that other agents can make an agent act in accordance with a model he does not accept. We therefore venture to suggest that the following heuristic principle be used in all studies of this relationship:

Agents who accept certain standards of values and norms of conduct as applicable to their actions tend to act in situations including these values as these norms require.

We shall call this the *principle of conformity*. It does not imply that such tendencies are necessarily achieved. Some obstacles may interfere with the realization of the purpose, or the purpose may undergo a change under the influence of some other action with a different purpose (cf. Chapter 8). Nor does it explain *why* agents apply ideological models to their actions; it only states what happens when they do.

Conformity with ideological models is a universal basis (though, as we shall see, not the only basis) for a *classification* of actions by practical thinkers, agents, or witnesses. Actions which apparently follow the same standards and norms, as accepted in a certain collectivity, are considered by participants in this collectivity to be essentially similar and are therefore classified together. In every language, many (though not all) verbs and verbal nouns referring to human actions symbolize such classifications. But they are so familiar that we often overlook their cultural implications. A word like "cooking," "hunting," "plowing," "harvesting," "buying," "selling," "painting," "singing," "writing" refers to actions presumed to be alike and different from other actions. Within each such general class, various subclasses may be distinguished. Thus, actions called "cooking" are classified according to the dishes cooked; actions called "hunting," according to the kind of game pursued and weapons used; and actions called "harvesting," according to the crops and techniques employed. Artistic painting is distinguished from house painting and is usually subclassified by the subjects painted, as in portrait painting, landscape painting, etc.; by the implements used, as in water colors, oils, etc.; or by the aesthetic style followed. Buying or selling is popularly subclassified according to the goods that are bought or sold; writing letters and writing poems are considered distinct subclasses of writing.

The cultural significance of these classifications becomes clearer when we notice the frequent use of evaluative judgments about such actions and/or the agents who perform them: people speaking of good cooking or singing and of bad cooking or singing, people saying that X is a better painter or writer than Y. This means, of course, that some ideological model exists, according to which the actions included under any of the classes can be judged.

Obviously such practical popular classifications cannot be uncritically accepted by scientists as foundations of systematic taxonomy; for, when subjected to the test of methodical research, they usually prove theoretically defective—by being inexact, by overlapping, by leaving out some important similarities or differences, etc. Many of these defects, however, can be corrected. Consequently, practical popular classifications have been successfully used for heuristic purposes, and will continue to be so used; no student of culture can ignore them. The concept of "pattern of actions," introduced by ethnologists, corresponds to such classifications of actions by participants in a collectivity according to their conformity with certain models; and it has certainly been scientifically productive. Only occasionally has some confusion crept in, as when the term is extended to uniformities of individual behavior in response to certain stimuli, even though the ethnologist finds no evidence that the individuals whose behavior appears similar to him have purposely tried to act as they believed they ought to act.

Even though the application of this concept in certain studies may be questionable, the validity of the general principle on which it is based can be thoroughly ascertained. When we analyze actions comparatively as dynamic systems of changing values, we find that actions which really tend to conform with a given ideological model are similar and can be objectively subsumed under the same class, inasmuch as they manifest a common and distinctive inner order in their composition and organization. The main values which they include are selected and defined by the same standards, and their purposes are formed in accordance with the same norms. We call this order *axionormative*. The term has been coined to indicate that the existence of such an order requires a joint application of standards of values *and* norms of conduct in the course of an action.

Of course, such a similarity in axionormative order between actions is not absolute, but relative, like the similarity in composition, anatomical structure, and physiological organization between animals of the same genus; it allows for many variations. Some of these variations are culturally patterned; they are due to secondary differences in the standardized values with which agents deal and in the normative methods which they use. These are analogous to variations between animal species within the same genus.

Other variations, however, are particular, not specific, like variations among individual animals of the same species. They are due to the differences of attitudes and of active tendencies of agents which either originated in their cultural past or are caused by present influences, cultural or natural. Many of these particular variations are considered normal, inasmuch as the situations with which agents deal are never exactly alike. Some of them, however, appear to those who judge them from the point of view of the ideological model as *deviations* from the standards and norms which the model contains. This does not necessarily imply, however, that such actions are not culturally patterned. Judges and agents are always aware that few actions are or can be expected to be perfectly right, according to the model. Yet this does not prevent them from including many imperfect actions in the same class as those which are perfect or nearly perfect, provided only that the agents accept the same standards and norms and tend to conform with them, even if their actions are obstructed or diverted from their course. Every cultural pattern of actions allows for a certain range of deviations from the model, wider or narrower, and the model may be more or less exacting. As we shall see, there is a fundamental difference between deviations which are judged permissible, though undesirable, and prohibited *transgressions*.

Examples of classified actions

To show how cultural classifications of actions proceed, we have selected three kinds of actions (already mentioned in Chapter 5) : I, cultus of divine beings; II, weaving rugs; III, curing sick persons. Our reason for this choice is that specialists in each of these realms of culture have applied certain distinctive methods in defining and solving their taxonomic problems.

In naming such actions, we are already using classificatory terms previously used by others. Each of these terms refers to a certain class of cultural data—divine beings, rugs, sick persons. And actions dealing with data of each class —cultus, weaving, curing—are presumed to be essentially similar among themselves and essentially different from actions dealing with data of the other classes.

This does not mean, however, that students of culture must first investigate, compare, and classify cultural data, and then use this classification as a basis for classifying actions. If such were the case, there could be no scientific taxonomy of actions. As we have found before, cultural data as such, abstracted from actions, cannot be systematically classified; only typological generalizations about them, each cutting across many others, are possible. As a matter of fact, a student of culture finds data already classified as *objects of activity* by practical thinkers who, having defined and evaluated such objects by certain standards, expect actions in which these objects are the main values, the most important components, to be alike, because they are supposed to follow definite norms. And, as we have seen, insofar as the agents themselves in dealing with such values do conform with these standards and norms, their actions really become what they are expected to be. Consequently, investigators are justified in classifying actions: first, by their objects, as conceived and evaluated by practical thinkers and agents; second, by the norms which they follow.[1]

There are certain culturally significant differences between divine beings as objects of cultus, rugs as objects of weaving, and human beings as patients, objects of curative or medical activity. From the point of view of the agents, divine beings as well as human beings are supposed to exist as real objects, independently of the agents; the agents merely aim to introduce certain changes into them. Whereas the very existence of a rug as a technical product depends on the weaver; when he begins to act, the future rug is to him only an imagined datum which does not become real until the action of weaving is completed. From the point of view of the investigator, the actual result of the weaver's action can be fully observed in every detail, the intended result of a curative action at least partly ascertained, but the intended result of religious cultus—the reaction of the deity—is manifestly inaccessible to observation.

I. Historians of religion, especially when investigating religions with highly developed ideological systems, usually give more attention to myths and theological dogmas than to active cultus.[2] Nevertheless, considerable material about cultus has been agglomerated. In every religion which includes standardized conceptions of divine beings as supernatural conscious individuals with power to influence human lives, such beings are the objects of actions whose purpose is to propitiate them, to make them use their power for the benefit of the agents, or to prevent them from harming the agents. Such actions are expected to follow definite norms. The term "cultus" is now generally used by religionists to denote such normatively regulated propitiatory performances.

The primary material which religionists use is contained in sacred literature. Students of contemporary religions, however, have supplemented this material by observing real performances of living believers, and their observations provide indisputable evidence of the prevalent conformity of active

[1] This is what I have done in including under one general class all social actions, i.e., those in which the main values are social objects, human individuals and collectivities as defined and evaluated by the agent, and in distinguishing them from other actions in which the main values are not human.

[2] A typical example is Goblet d'Alviella, *Croyances, Rites, Institutions*, 3 vols. (Paris, 1911). We notice it even in what seems to be the best collective attempt to develop a general comparative science of religion, namely, Pierre D. Chantepie de la Saussaye, *Lehrbuch der Religionsgeschichte*, 4th ed. by Alfred Bertholet and Edvard Lehmann (Tubingen, 1925). See, however, Reuben Levy, *An Introduction to the Sociology of Islam*, 2 vols. (London, 1930-33): Herbert Spencer's *Descriptive Sociology*, continued by his trustees, 2 vols. (London, 1930-33), where the practical application of theological doctrines is emphasized.

cultus with models which the believers accept. And although historians of religion find only a few, mostly fragmentary observations of active cultus as it was carried on by ancient Egyptians, Sumerians, Phoenicians, Greeks, Romans, Hindus, and Persians; nonetheless, there is enough indirect evidence to justify the assumption that their actions usually did conform with ideological models.

Religionists have met considerable difficulty in trying to reach consistent classificatory generalizations about cultus. It may be doubted whether a clear distinction can be drawn between religious cultus and magical ritual; for magical rites have sometimes been used not in propitiating, but in coercing gods and goddesses to do what human magicians wanted. And under the general class of cultus as propitiation, many widely diverse, specific patterns of religious actions are found. Even within the same religious system, norms of cultus differ, depending on the standards by which divine beings are defined and evaluated. In Vedic religion the cultus of Vishnu and of Siva followed different norms, as did the cultus of Horus, Set, and Isis in Egypt; of Baal and Astarte in Phoenicia; and of Apollo, Dionysos, Demeter, and Pallas Athene in Greece.

Private individual cultus differs from public cultus, and in the latter considerable variety is found. Actions of priests frequently follow different patterns than actions of their semisecular assistants; both usually differ from those of lay participants which often vary, depending on the sex, age, secular status, and group membership of the agents.

Certain actions performed during public cultus with the purpose of propitiating divine beings may be subsumed under some other category; thus, playing music, singing songs, and enacting dramas during public ceremonies in certain religions can be considered as aesthetic actions by musicologists or theorists of literature, and classified by them together with the aesthetic actions lacking religious purposes which are performed by participants in the same collectivity during secular festivals.

When a religionist goes beyond the historical study of one religion and attempts to reach a systematic classification of the numerous varieties of cultus found in many religions, his effort may seem hopeless at first. A historian who specializes in the investigation of a particular religion usually refrains from it altogether; for this religion, taken in its total wealth and complexity and viewed in the course of its duration, is to him historically unique. He is rightly skeptical of nineteenth-century attempts to establish a taxonomy of all religions; at best, some typological comparisons appear possible. And because he views his religion as an integral whole, he may doubt the validity of abstracting for comparative purposes any part of this whole, without taking fully into account the connections between this part and other parts.[3] How can we abstract and compare, say, ceremonial cultus in a nineteenth-century Tibetan temple with ceremonial cultus in an ancient Egyptian temple, without referring each of them to the total religious system of which it was a component? This is the kind of methodical doubt which some modern cultural anthropologists apply to all components of culture when they insist on the necessity of referring every pattern found in a particular culture to this total culture. If the doubts of the historians of particular religions were scientifically justified, obviously no comparative science of religious phenomena in general would be possible; if the doubts of cultural anthropologists were justified, such comparative sciences as linguistics, theory of art, theory of literature, economics, political science, and sociology would have no future.

As a matter of fact, however, quite a few religionists have succeeded in abstracting and comparing actions of cultus found in many collectivities with different religions. In so doing, they met another problem: that of the apparent antithesis between cultural patterns of actions. In general, when participants in one collectivity are aware that participants in another collectivity accept ideological models different from their own, they are often inclined to interpret those differences as contradictions. One collectivity may deny the reality of a divine being which the other considers real; a supernatural being whom one evaluates positively as benevolent, the other may evaluate negatively as malevolent; implements of cultus which one considers sacred, the other may consider impure; ritualistic performances which one judges to be right, the other may judge to be wrong. From the point of view of these collectivities, actions which follow either one of such contradictory models are the very antithesis of actions which follow the other model; and this obviously means that they cannot be included under the same logical class.

Religionists are not the only ones who find such antithetic classifications of actions; all cultural scientists are faced with this problem and do not always solve it adequately. The first step toward its solution is, of course, to investigate what participants in a collectivity actually do when they conform with their own ideological models. Then the question arises: Why do they classify the actions of those who do not conform with these models as antithetic to their own? Their classification should not be accepted as valid by investigators (though, unfortunately, it is quite often accepted); nor should it be

[3] Some students of religion, however, are rather optimistic. Take, e.g., Stanley A. Cook's statement in his *The Study of Religion* (London, 1914): "There is an evident similarity of beliefs and practices in spite of the equally noteworthy differences. . . . The fact that, despite the possibility of enormous variations in thoughts, studies in thought can be pursued at all and that thought is found to be orderly and along relatively few lines, brings us to realize a factor of which we are scarcely aware—the process of implicit selection" (pp. 19-20).

ignored, for it is a manifestation of certain active tendencies which can be very influential.

All those difficulties notwithstanding, religionists have drawn and continue to draw increasingly valid classificatory generalizations about cultus in collectivities with different religions; and some of them are now recognized as widely, if not universally, applicable.[4] We may refer by way of example to generalizations about sacrificial offerings, prayers, or mystical communion with divine beings through sacred food. Of course, the development of a systematic taxonomy of all kinds of religious actions is a long and arduous task, and we are not sure whether the approach used by religionists is quite adequate for this task.

II. The general concept of rug weaving was originally formed not as a result of comparative investigations, but mainly due to the practical interests of merchants, who classified and designated by this term material products which, however much they differed otherwise, had certain common characteristics important for trading. What is now called a "rug" is a textile product differing from other textile products in certain respects. It is a finished product, not mere material from which future products (such as clothes) are to be made; it has a certain decorative pattern of design and color which makes it aesthetically valuable for those who approve of it; its design is such that it is supposed to be indivisible, unlike a carpet which can be divided. The fact that different rugs were produced in many countries also attracted, first, the attention of merchants seeking to buy and import for sale rugs of previously unknown or little known varieties. Eventually, a comparative investigation of rug weaving was initiated for practical purposes, mostly by French, English, and American industrialists who selected and imitated (with modifications) chiefly those techniques originated by individual craftsmen which were found most effective for large-scale production. Finally, rug weaving began to be studied by historians of culture and investigators of contemporary cultures.

In modern popular literature, we find inclusive classifications of rugs primarily by territorial divisions, each with a geographical name. Rugs are classified as Oriental and Occidental,[5] and the Occidental, in turn, as European

[4] One of the most interesting attempts to develop a systematic general theory of religion is that of Georges Foucart, *La Méthode comparative dans l'histoire des religions* (Paris, 1909). "To treat, one after the other, the religions of particular ethnic groups is to make *histories of religions*, not one *History of Religions*" (p. 5). "Religious phenomena are manifestations of human activity. . . . The first point is to observe facts and to know how to isolate them from the multiple circumstances in which they are produced" (p. 9). "First of all, one must choose the religion whose evolution serves as a prototype to which one will be able to compare the others" (p. 14). He chooses Egyptian religion as a prototype and concentrates on the evolution of ritual, especially sacrifice.

[5] Rosa Belle Holt, *Rugs, Oriental and Occidental, Antique and Modern. A Handbook for Ready Reference* (Chicago: McClurg, 1928).

and American;[6] both Oriental and European are subdivided by countries. Cutting across this territorial classification is a rather vague temporal division into antique and modern. Now, we wish to discuss briefly this classification, for it is rather typical of an old and persistent approach to cultural phenomena which, though it has some factual foundation, has nonetheless resulted in much conceptual confusion.

Assuming that this classification is consistently based on the same logical principles as systematic scientific taxonomies, it apparently presupposes, first, that all rugs produced in such a large territory as the Orient (mainly Asia) or Europe have certain essential common characteristics which distinguish them from all other rugs in the world; second, that these characteristics are more essential than the common and distinctive characteristics of rugs produced in particular subdivisions of this territory, e.g., China, India, Central Asia, and Asia Minor as parts of the Orient; and Spain, France, England, Germany, and Poland as parts of Europe; and third, that rugs designated by the names of these smaller territories are subclasses of the general class of rugs designated by the name of the larger territory.

As a matter of fact, however, such general presuppositions can be easily invalidated. It is true, indeed, that rugs produced in particular areas during certain periods usually have some distinctive characteristics which enable a connoisseur who is familiar with all varieties of rugs to ascertain where and when they were produced. There are a number of these characteristics, each with many variations in raw material, design, color, knots, warp, weft, pile, border, sides, ends, textures, weave, length, and width.[7] But the relative importance of similarities and differences in these characteristics cannot be judged by the relative size of the territories within which they are found. Two kinds of rugs produced in different localities of the same country may differ more than each of them differs from specific rugs produced in some other countries. Modern rugs now produced in one continent may be like antique rugs which were produced in another continent. Viewed in the light of thorough comparative analysis, the popular classification of rugs by territories is a catalogue rather than a systematic taxonomy.

How did such a defective territorial classification originate, and why does it continue to be used? So far as rugs are concerned, it can probably be traced to practical considerations of the merchants importing rugs. Importers, for obvious reasons, were primarily concerned with geographical location, ways of transportation, and human ecology of the territories from which these rugs came.

[6] Cornelia Bateman Faraday, *European and American Carpets and Rugs* (Grand Rapids, Mich.: Dean-Hicks Co., 1929).

[7] Holt, *op. cit.*, chaps. II and III; Faraday, *op. cit.*, chaps. I-VII; Walter A. Hanley, *Oriental Rugs, Antique and Modern* (New York: Tudor, 1937), chap. VIII.

But there is a more general and, from the point of view of cultural sciences, much more significant reason for this kind of classification, which has been applied not only to rugs, but to many other cultural products. The key to the problem lies in the dual meaning of geographic names. Many such names have two connotations, spatial and cultural. They imply that all the people who live in an area with one geographical name share a common and distinctive culture. Thus, when students of rugs use such terms as "Chinese rugs," "Persian rugs," "Turkish rugs," and "Kurdistan rugs," they explicitly or implicitly mean that all rugs produced by inhabitants of the territory of China, Persia, Turkey, and Kurdistan are also components of Chinese, Persian, Turkish, and Kurdish culture.[8] These terms symbolize the old and persistent idea according to which cultures are coextensive with geographic territories. The territorial classification of rugs is a minor but significant example of the conceptual confusion resulting from this idea. Much more important confusions, due to this territorial approach to cultures, can be found in certain political, economic, anthropogeographic theories.

Quite a few modern investigators, however, instead of beginning with a general classification of rugs by territories, begin with the analysis of particular rugs and proceed by inductive methods. Such an investigator is fully aware that whatever similarities and differences he may find between particular rugs are due to the weavers who produce them. Therefore, he will either use whatever descriptions of these performances have been made by other observers or try to observe and compare the performances of weavers which resulted in definite products. Since observation requires the observer to be present in the locality in which the weaver is active, many observations have been made by travelers and technicians for purposes of imitation, and more recently by ethnologists.[9] However, the processes of production of the majority of rugs, especially those produced in a more or less distant past, have never been described by observers. And the investigator of rug weaving can seldom supplement this deficiency of factual descriptions by a study of written documents which express symbolically the standards and norms for rug weavers, since few such documents have been written, nearly all of them in recent times.

In this respect, the investigator is at a disadvantage in comparison with a historian of religion, who finds numerous standards and norms of cultus formulated in writing by prophets and priests. In another respect, however, his position is more advantageous (as we mentioned before). For the religionist can draw no conclusions about actions of cultus from a study of the intended

[8] E.g., Gordon B. Leitch, *Chinese Rugs* (New York: Dodd, 1928).
[9] Many monographs based on observation have been written by students of material cultures in tribal communities, especially Amerindian, and in European and Asiatic folk communities.

results of these actions, since they are inaccessible to observation; whereas a study of rugs as the lasting observable results of rug weaving and sometimes also of tools which were used in the process helps the investigator to draw hypothetic conclusions about the actions of weavers, and his hypotheses can be and often are tested by experimentation. Thus, a general methodical approach to rug weaving, whenever and wherever performed, has been developed; and its principles are fundamentally the same as those used by investigators of other actions.

In every collectivity where rugs are produced, rug weaving is considered by participants as a distinct class of actions. Rugs as final products are, of course, the main objects of these actions; they are characterized and evaluated by definite standards—aesthetic, utilitarian, sometimes also religious, as when the design of a rug symbolizes mystical beings or mythical events, or when rugs (e.g., prayer rugs in Mohammedan collectivities) are used as sacred implements of cultus. Auxiliary objects included in these actions— materials from which the rugs are woven and the tools which are used in weaving—are also supposed to be selected and evaluated in accordance with certain standards. And the cultural pattern obviously includes definite technical norms, sometimes also ritualistic norms, which the weaver is supposed to follow in the course of his work.

In large collectivities with complex cultures, several different cultural patterns of rug weaving may coexist; and in the course of time the predominant pattern may change. But in any case, when a craftsman, male or female, begins to think about weaving a rug, the formation of his purpose is usually determined by the cultural pattern which he has learned to accept. He defines in advance the kind of rug he means to produce, so as to make it valuable according to recognized standards. He selects textile materials, either already dyed or to be dyed, chooses the tools he will use as the pattern requires, and plans to follow recognized norms throughout the course of his production. If and insofar as his purpose becomes realized, the axionormative order of his action will be essentially similar to those of all actions, past, present, or future, of rug weavers who purposely conform with the same cultural pattern.

This similarity does not imply complete uniformity. The common standard by which rugs are evaluated in a given collectivity at a given time usually includes several distinctive but standardized variations in size, shape, texture, color, and design. It may also include standardized variations in materials or tools and corresponding differences in technical norms. This means that rug weaving in collectivities, as one culturally patterned class of actions, may include several culturally patterned subclasses.

Moreover, in some collectivities the acceptance of a cultural pattern does not preclude innovations by individual weavers.

There are many innovations in rug weaving which are of deep significance to the Eastern mind [*sic*], such for instance as a lock of human hair woven in as a love message . . . or a bead or two to guard against the evil eye. The irregularity of design, which may appear to be the result of accident or carelessness, is frequently the intentional work of some devout weaver to emphasize his belief that nothing but Allah is perfect.[10]

The range of individual innovations, however, may vary considerably in different cultures; innovations approved in one culture may be disapproved or altogether prohibited in another.

The Persians . . . being liberal Shiite Mohammedans, weave all sorts of figures of birds, animals, or men into their rugs, but the Turks, being conservative or Sunnite Mohammedans, never weave forms of living creatures or beings, as it is forbidden in the Koran for fear it might lead to idolatry.[11]

Any scientific classification of rug weaving must, thus, proceed by investigating, first of all, the cultural patterns followed in a particular collectivity at a certain time by weavers who consciously conform with common standards and norms. Only then can investigators compare them with cultural patterns followed by weavers in other collectivities located in more or less distant areas or in the same collectivity at other times, seek to discover similarities and differences among them, and attempt to explain such similarities and differences. The methods used in this research are familiar to historians of culture. Many similarities can be explained by diffusion of certain models from one collectivity to another. Many differences can be explained by the emergence of new models from old. In any case, classificatory generalizations about rug weaving in various collectivities at various times must be based not on a comparison of their static products, but on an investigation of dynamic trends of cultural expansion and innovation.

III. Here we can survey only briefly the classificatory generalizations about actions of curing the sick, for the patterns of these actions vary so much that it would take a whole chapter to give enough significant examples. We must therefore refer the reader to the books mentioned in the notes to this chapter, especially McKenzie's and Shryock's. Most of these actions, moreover, are components of certain social systems which require a thorough investigation,[12] and which we shall analyze and compare in a later work. What is essential from the point of view of our present study is that investigators of this category of actions are using a very different and scientifically more productive method of classification than investigators of the other two categories.

[10] G. Griffin Lewis, *The Mystery of the Oriental Rug* (Philadelphia: Lippincott, 1919), p. 18.

[11] *Ibid.*, p. 20.

[12] As Bernhard J. Stern has pointed out, "sociologists, social psychologists and economists have not taken full advantage of medicine as a field for fruitful research": *Society and Medical Progress* (Princeton, N. J.: Princeton University Press, 1941), p. 216.

Of course, axionormatively ordered actions of this kind are more widely spread and have been performed during a longer historical period than rug weaving; they probably began even earlier than cultus of personal deities. In every human collectivity ever studied by historians and ethnologists, evidence has been found that certain agents were trying to cure human beings defined as sick by following specific norms.

The cultural patterns of actions purposing to cure sick human beings involve: first, standardized positive valuation of these beings as social persons; second, standardized negative valuation of sickness in general as a process injurious to these persons; and third, a general norm which requires that the agents should effectively counteract sickness. Underlying this basic similarity, however, is a wide range of specific differences. Sick persons are differently conceived and evaluated, depending on age, sex, and other presumably important physical, mental, and even mystical characteristics, social status and function, and membership in certain groups. Various kinds of sickness or various diseases are distinguished, defined, estimated as more or less dangerous, often also causally explained. Various medicines and auxiliary instruments are recognized and evaluated by their presumed effectiveness in curing specific diseases. Agents who tend to cure sick persons are supposed to follow various special norms in diagnosing their patient's diseases, selecting effective medicines and instruments, and using adequate methods in their application.

We know from historical and ethnological studies how great the diversity of those specific standards and norms is in various collectivities[13] and how they change in the course of time within a particular collectivity. Ideological models of diagnosis and treatment which are based on the belief that all sickness is intentionally produced by human magicians and can be cured only by more powerful magicians differ from those in which sickness is ascribed to superhuman agents and can be cured only by superhuman agents when duly propitiated by priests; both of them differ radically from ideological models based on the theory that sickness is always an effect of natural causes and can be cured only by application of natural remedies. The first

[13] The diversity is greatest in nonliterate communities. Perhaps the most comprehensive survey of standardized definitions of sickness and norms of treatment in those communities is the work of O. von Hovorka and A. Kronfeld, *Vergleichende Volkmedizin*, 2 vols. (Stuttgart, 1908-09). Under *Volkmedizin* they include "old-time methods of curing and representations of sickness of the people, in contrast with the medical science and art of physicians" (p. xiv). Although most of the data are derived from European and Asiatic folk cultures, and many results of anthropological studies of tribal cultures are omitted, the wealth and variety of material is so great that the authors apparently find it impossible to develop any systematic comparison. Vol. I, "general part," is merely an alphabetical encyclopedia of "the causes, the essence and the cure of diseases." Vol. II, "special part," is a methodically defective classification of diseases (*Krankheiten*).

two beliefs are frequently found to coexist in various combinations; the third may coexist with the second, as when natural remedies, though necessary, are not believed to be sufficient to cure a dangerous disease without the help of a deity. Moreover, standards and norms may be not only different, but considered contradictory. Materials and techniques judged to be useful for curative purposes by adherents of one ideological model are apt to be judged harmful by adherents of another.

How can any systematic classification of the actions which conform with such widely diverse and even contradictory ideologies be achieved? A survey of historical and ethnological works dealing with medicine indicates a probable solution of this problem by the increasingly effective use of what can be termed the *evolutionary* approach.[14] This approach consists in a study of the gradual emergence and expansion of new classes of medical actions which follow the creation and acceptance of new ideological models, as well as the gradual recession and eventual disappearance of those old classes which conflict with the new. This evolution is one consequence of the general evolution of natural sciences; new ideological models of medicine are created by the technological application of new scientific discoveries.[15]

This approach was never used by students of rug weaving. It was originally applied to religions as wholes, rather than to specific patterns of religious actions, and was discarded by most religionists when this application proved invalid. Later we shall try to show that, if applied in accordance with the same methical principles which biologists are using in their realm, the evolutionary approach is indispensable for the development of coherent scientific theories of actions and systems of actions.

[14] Quite a few prominent historians of medicine used an approach similar to that of philosophers of history. Take, e.g., Pierre V. Renouard, *History of Medicine, from Its Origin to the Nineteenth Century*, trans. by Cornelius G. Comegys (Cincinnati: Moore, Wilstach, Keys & Co., 1856), who divides this history into three ages: "The first, the Foundation Age, commences with the infancy of society . . . and terminates . . . at the death of Galen. . . . Second . . . the Age of Transition . . . the art remains stationary or . . . retrogrades. . . . Third . . . the Age of Renovation . . . from the fifteenth century" (p. xx). Within these three ages, the author finds eight "secondary divisions" (pp. 15-17). Those ages were accepted as late as 1906 by Roswell Park, *An Epitome of the History of Medicine* (Philadelphia: Davis, 1897).

The evolutionary approach, initiated by Spencer, began to be applied to the history of medicine at the end of the nineteenth century. Of course, it required a systematic comparative study of medicine in the early stages of its evolution. Max Bartels, *Die Medizin der Naturvölker* (Leipzig, 1893), is perhaps the first methodical attempt at such a study. A rather important later work is Don McKenzie, *The Infancy of Medicine, an Enquiry into the Influence of Folklore upon the Evolution of Scientific Medicine* (London, 1927).

[15] Richard H. Shryock, *The Development of Modern Medicine, An Interpretation of the Social and Scientific Factors Involved* (Philadelphia: University of Pennsylvania Press, 1936), is methodically the best general survey of this evolutionary process.

The principle of functional interdependence and systems of actions

We have found considerable factual evidence, derived by scientists from several realms of culture, that human agents tend to conform with ideological models which they consider applicable to their own actions and that, when they do so, their actions as dynamic systems of values become axionormatively ordered. This axionormative order enables scientists to develop, even if only slowly and gradually, a systematic classification of human actions. But we have left still untouched two problems with which cultural scientists have been concerned for a long time: Why are most, if not all, the actions of participants in every collectivity required to follow definite cultural patterns? and Why do agents tend to act in accordance with these requirements? Several solutions have been offered. We may mention the two best known and most generally accepted. The first claims that conformity is required because the cultural patterns of actions—folkways, mores, institutions—followed in a given collectivity enable its participants to satisfy their basic needs under the given environmental conditions. The second claims that individual agents follow these patterns because they are subjected to influences which modify their innate drives, motives, or behavior mechanisms until conformity with social requirements becomes a habit.

These solutions are based on general theories of human nature. While we do not question the validity of such theories in the biopsychological realm of research, we doubt the assumption that explanations of culture or of individual participation in culture can be deduced from them.

We have no alternative universal solution of our own to offer. What we suggest, instead, is that an investigator, in dealing with these problems as with other problems concerning cultural phenomena, should begin by taking into consideration the point of view of the people whose attitudes and actions he investigates. He will find that these people have their own explanations. Indeed, the verbal formulation of an ideological system frequently contains an explanation why agents should conform with the specific model which the given system contains. Authoritative agents who function as educators, advisers, leaders, rulers often explain why they require conformity with certain standards and norms from those to whom their statements are addressed. Agents who describe their past actions or express anticipation of their future actions (spontaneously or in answer to questions) express in terms of ideological models why they acted as they did or intend to act as they anticipate. From comparative studies of such explanations, a general heuristic hypothesis can be drawn, to be confirmed by further research. It is the only hypothesis that enables us to solve another important problem with which modern scientists have been struggling, the problem of nonconformity.

We must remember that human actions as dynamic systems of values, though limited, are not isolated. We have discussed before the causal influences of actions upon other actions. What has been done or is being done to a value in the course of one action can affect the course of another action dealing with the same value, inasmuch as it may either help or hinder the realization of its purpose.

Now, practical thinkers and agents are not only fully aware of the influence which actions exert upon one another, but anticipate it and regulate it in advance in order to make certain kinds of actions mutually helpful and to prevent conflicts between their tendencies. As a consequence, actions which have certain values in common are culturally patterned in such a way that, if they regularly conform with those standards and norms with which they are required to conform, their respective purposes will be regularly realized. This is the general principle by which agents are guided when they consistently tend to follow definite cultural patterns. We call it the *principle of functional interdependence between actions*. When and insofar as culturally patterned actions dealing with the same value (or the same complex of values) are functionally interdependent, they become integrated in the course of their performance into an axionormatively organized, dynamic *system of actions*.

Let us tentatively apply these generalizations to two categories of actions: religious cultus and material technique. The reason why we choose these categories is that they differ radically in one respect. In material technique every assumption that certain culturally patterned actions mutually contribute to the realization of their respective purposes can be tested and proved or disproved by observing the results of these actions and ascertaining whether their purposes have been realized. But in religious cultus no such test is possible, since the dogmatic belief that cultus is effective if it conforms with ideological models can be neither proved nor disproved by observing their results. Nevertheless, not only are religious agents as well as technical agents guided by the idea that actions which regularly follow certain cultural patterns are functionally interdependent, but this idea has been even more influential as a factor of integration of actions in the realm of religion than in that of material technique.

Cultural systems of religious actions

In every religion with a well-developed, relatively coherent ideology, the common assumption of those who propound and accept this ideology is that regular conformity with its standards and norms lastingly benefits all the agents who participate in it, because what any one of them does has some positive influence upon other actions, his own or somebody else's.

We shall survey some of the consequences of this assumption, beginning with a brief comparative analysis of more or less complex religious actions performed by individual agents. When in a previous chapter we analyzed various actions as dynamic systems of values, we found that a complex action tending to realize a certain purpose includes many elementary actions organized in such a way that the purpose of each is formed with reference to one total purpose, and this total purpose becomes finally realized through the progressive realization of all these partial purposes. At that time, however, we had not yet investigated the problem of systematic taxonomy of actions; we only postulated that actions can be classified; and we made certain typological distinctions, such as between individual and collective actions, among creative, imitative, and habitual actions, and between productive and destructive actions.

Now we must take fully into consideration the fact that many complex actions which follow the same cultural pattern and manifest a similar axionormative order may be performed repeatedly not only by the same individual, but separately by many individuals, throughout a lengthy historical period.

In the realm of religion, this similarity is most striking and easily observable when actions conform with a definite, stabilized ritual. Take by way of example the kind of action—not very complex, but still including a few elementary components—which every one among the millions of faithful Moslems performs five time a day, when he turns toward Mecca, lays down a rug if the soil or floor is impure, kneels, says a short prayer, and bows so as to touch the earth with his forehead. Or the regular ritualistic cultus of *lares* and *penates* by the head of a family in ancient Rome. Or the daily morning and evening prayers of lay members of the Catholic Church (Pater Noster, Ave Maria, and Credo). Or the much longer and more complex obligatory daily prayers of the priests of any modern religion. Or regular celebrations of Communion (with or without assistants) by Protestant clergymen of those denominations which consider Communion to be the most important religious performance—celebrations differing somewhat between denominations, but essentially alike within each denomination.

When we analyze comparatively many performances of these complex ritualistic actions, we find that not only are the actions as wholes supposed to conform with certain basic standards and norms, but all elementary actions included in each of them are also usually expected to follow strictly definite patterns, with hardly any individual innovations. Some of these patterns, e.g., kneeling, using certain verbal symbols, may be applicable to elementary components of complex actions which differ in their total course. Others, such as using certain sacred implements or sacrificial offerings, are applicable only within complex actions of a specific variety. But, in any case, every complex ritualistic performance includes culturally patterned elementary rites of several classes, all of which are presumed to be functionally interdependent, since each is supposed to contribute to the realization of their total purpose.

Insofar as they follow their respective patterns, the whole performance becomes integrated into an axionormatively organized system of actions.

The principle underlying this requirement of conformity of every simple rite, as well as of every combination of rites, with a definite model is that ritualistic patterns have been devised either by a divine being himself or by his human representatives, so as to teach believers how to conceive and evaluate him and how to manifest their tendencies to propitiate him. Individual conformity with religious ritual thus presupposes considerable *learning*. Every elementary rite necessitates a special training, and systematic integration of these rites in the total course of a religious performance requires some ideational education. Complex actions of religious cultus performed by priests are learned gradually by candidates for priesthood under the guidance of priests, who learned them fully before they began to teach. Even less complex religious actions of laymen, such as saying daily prayers, require a thorough memorization of the words and sentences and some understanding of their significance.

However, even in highly ritualized religions, the regulation of elementary individual actions is not quite so rigid as it is in magic with its stabilized traditional patterns. For the magician deals with impersonal forces; an unintentional omission of an elementary action—a sentence, an imitative gesture—can make his whole performance ineffective; and any error, even if due to ignorance, may have detrimental effects. Whereas the object of cultus is a personal deity, who usually takes into account good intentions of the believer and may forgive accidental omissions and errors. Moreover, in some modern religions the individual's own experience of a mystical bond between him and the deity is becoming more important than conformity with ritualistic standards and norms. But this is another problem.

Further investigation of the relationship between religious actions discloses that functional interdependence is by no means limited to elementary rites included in a complex ritualistic performance which is being carried on by an individual believer. In the first place, a significant connection exists between the separate actions of cultus of the same deity performed many times in succession by the same individual. While every one of these actions taken by itself—every daily prayer, every sacrificial offering—has a beginning and an end and constitutes a complete whole, not a part of another, more complex action, yet all of them are in some degree functionally interdependent. Each of them is supposed to help the individual gain the good will of the deity, and each is also supposed to be necessary in order to maintain it. Their positive results accumulate in the course of the individual's life, but only under the condition that he does not cease to perform them every time they are required. These suppositions are clearly manifested in the personal valuation of individuals who consistently perform the actions required of them by their religious ideology. A truly pious person who has fulfilled regularly, perfectly, and for a long time his duties of cultus toward a deity is favored by the deity; but this favor will last only if he continues to fulfill his duties as long as he is able to do so.

There are, of course, differences of degree in the divine favor granted to individuals, depending on the relative importance and difficulty of their duties. A priest, a hermit, a monk, whose duties are very exacting, is gaining greater favor than an ordinary layman, who devotes much less time, thought, and energy to cultus.

Now, if and so long as an individual performs all the ritualistic actions which, according to his belief, he must perform in order to gain and maintain the good will of a deity, we can say that these consecutive actions of his become integrated into a system of indefinite duration. For, although each of them separately is a distinct dynamic system of elementary rites which lasts only while it is being performed, his conviction that such regular conformity with religious standards and norms makes the deity favorable to him gives a continuity and unity to the whole sequence of these actions.

Still more significant, from the point of view of the theory of religion, is the belief that individual actions which conform with ideological models benefit not only the individual himself, but others. How great these benefits are depends upon the relative sacredness of the individual. Sometimes others gain incomparably more from his religious activities than he gains from theirs. For instance, the presence of a holy person in a secular community is beneficial to the whole community, for he may divert divine ire provoked by sinners or induce the deity to help the weak and the ignorant. Remember that if the cities of Sodom and Gomorrah had had only ten righteous inhabitants, Jehovah would not have destroyed them. A resident saint, a hermit living in the neighborhood, even a visiting holy pilgrim brings blessings upon the community. And these religious benefits may remain quite one-sided; for, unless he assumes the responsibilities of a priest or a prophet, he does not need any religious cooperation from others. All the community can do and usually does is to offer him some material aid in satisfying his bodily needs. Even that may not be necessary. Monks and nuns in some economically self-sufficient religious orders, while striving most of the time for their own salvation, also regularly pray to God for the salvation of laymen—presumably with some success.

But an individual does not have to be an unusually holy person for his religious actions to be of some advantage to others. Thus, such actions of the master of a house, as offering sacrifices or addressing prayers to guardians of his home, his land, his domestic animals and useful plants, benefit not only the master himself, all residents of his house, and workers on his land, but also indirectly all his neighbors, inasmuch as they help keep evil powers away from the area; and the same principle applies to similar actions performed by every neighbor. The wider significance of domestic ritual is indicated by the history of early Roman religion. Janus, the protector of the household door; Vesta, the goddess of the hearth; and Juno, the goddess whose mystical power enabled a woman to become a mother—all once private divinities—became divinities of the city of Rome. Thus, out of domestic cultus, ceremonial public cultus developed.[16]

Rites performed by parents before the birth of a child, after his birth, and during his passage from childhood to adolescence benefit not only the child and the parents, but—by endowing the child with positive religious qualities—all those good people who in the future come in contact with him. Wedding rites are beneficial to the bride and groom, to the near relatives of both, and to their future children. Cultus of common ancestors by every individual head of a family who is a descendant helps maintain the unity of the gens for the benefit of all descendants.

The widely spread assumption that religious actions of particular individuals can benefit others, provided they conform with ritualistic standards and norms, has been the main principle underlying the development of ceremonial collective cultus carried on by congregations of believers. During such cultus, obligatory ritualistic performances of all the participants become functionally interdependent. Such cultuses are frequently found even in nonliterate communities. The most complex and most widely spread were, and still are, the religious ceremonies performed in agricultural communities every year on the dates which mark the beginning or the end of agriculturally important seasons. Sometimes all adult members, men and women, participate in these ceremonies under the guidance of wise and experienced religious leaders. Such a seasonal collective cultus is intended to gain help from the deities of plants and animals for the common welfare of all inhabitants.[17]

Better known are the ceremonial collective cultuses carried on in or near temples as religious centers during holy days, when professional priests are the main participants as well as the authoritative organizers. These cultuses, as we know, vary considerably in different religions, ancient and modern. And yet they have certain essential characteristics in common. As we mentioned before, some participants in a public ceremony specialize in ritualistic actions of definite patterns. The actions of those who function as priests are the most complex and the most highly ritualized. In urban religious centers on important holy days, several priests participate, usually under the leadership of a high priest, and their functions are partly differentiated.

Assistants preparing sacred implements for priests have also culturally

[16] Ludwig Deubner, "Die Römer," in Chantepie de la Saussaye, op. cit.
[17] See the material contained in Frazer's *Golden Bough*. In recent times much new material has been gathered by cultural anthropologists and folklorists.

patterned tasks. The functions of specialized singers and musicians obviously differ from the functions of other assistants. And yet all these different functions are interdependent and integrated into one coherent, well-organized dynamic system. When ordinary participants follow a leader—repeat a prayer, express confirmation of a prayer, take part in singing, march in a procession —their actions are manifestly dependent on the actions of the leader, but the leader's actions also depend upon theirs, for his purpose cannot be fully realized unless he is followed. Vicarious participation in a ritualistic action— i.e., witnessing a sacrifice—is sometimes necessary to make the whole congregation fully aware of its significance, though certain rites may be too sacred for laymen to witness.

Inasmuch as the total ceremonial cultus propitiates the deity, gains divine good will for the group as a whole, every participant benefits, not only by what he is doing, but by what all the others are doing. Though a layman benefits more by what a priest does than a priest by what a layman does, yet even the priest benefits by the actions of laymen, for it is his duty toward the deity to make every layman share in the cultus.

While a public religious ceremony as an organized system of individual actions has a limited duration—a few hours, at most a few days—it is not isolated, but functionally connected with other ceremonies, past and future. The positive effects of each of the seasonal rituals collectively performed in an agricultural community in the course of a year depend in some measure on the positive effects of the ritual which preceded it and of the ritual which follows it. And the repeated performance of similar rituals in the same sequence, year after year, is essential for the continuous welfare of the community and all its members.

The religious benefits of a public ceremonial cultus in a temple under priestly guidance are expected to continue after the ceremony has been completed, at least until the next ceremony is performed. Every participant, besides having obtained through his participation some aid of the deity which he needed, is supposed to have acquired some degree of purity and piety, which will make him act later in conformity with the standards and norms of his religion, to the benefit of his fellow believers with whom he will be in contact. And similar expectations apply to the total congregation. Not only did it gain help from the deity in some actual matters of common interest, but its religious solidarity has been strengthened. Regular participation of the inhabitants of an area in periodical public cultus of a common deity, collectively carried on in a common sacred center, is supposed to unite them into a permanent group with a harmonious religious life. If and so long as the members of such a group continue to believe in the same god and, in propitiating him, act in conformity with ritualistic standards and norms with which they are expected to conform, their actions contribute to the continuous worship of the god, which will last as long as the group lasts. All of them are functionally interconnected and in the total course of their repeated performances become integrated into a large dynamic system of indefinite duration, including numerous smaller systems of limited duration.

Such integration can extend beyond the religious group inhabiting a particular area. While many deities are supposed to dwell permanently in a certain locality, be accessible only to those who come to this locality, and have no power outside of a certain territory, in more developed religions a powerful god may dwell above the earth—like the sun—and be accessible to all men. In every area in which his believers live, a temple may be erected to him and ceremonial cultus regularly carried on. All these spatially centered systems of ritualistic actions then become parts of one superterritorial system, the duration of which does not depend any more on the continued existence of any particular local group of worshipers. The system may even be more comprehensive and include cultuses of several gods. Such was the case in Egypt when the various regional religious ideologies became in some measure united.

Egyptian gods . . . have ceaselessly, actively to maintain the order of the world in heaven and on earth; they must struggle against evil powers which assault them and, though always vanquished, always return to attack. For this struggle, they need a vigor ceaselessly renewed and growing. It is sacrifice which strengthens the god, just as abundant nourishment strengthens man. The more temples the faithful erect where he nourishes himself with immolated victims, the more of these living statues they consecrate to him which absorb nourishment, the more strength he will have for the performance of his role. Thus, sacrifice, without losing its naïvely material meaning, acquires a more sublime character: it serves to maintain the order of the world and the prosperity of Egypt.[18]

Cultural systems of technical actions

In discussing relationships between actions which deal with material values, we have to take into consideration the distinction which economists make between production and consumption. The term "consumption," however, has a specific connotation which makes it unsuitable from the point of view of our present problem. Let us rather speak of the use of products.

1. First, we must briefly survey technical production. This is the realm of the comparative science of material technique (or material culture). A vast amount of research has been done in this realm by ethnologists, historians, and investigators of contemporary technological development, and many of their results are familiar to everybody with secondary or even primary

[18] Foucart, *op. cit.*, pp. 111-12.

education.[19] Nevertheless, it may be well to state explicitly some of its basic cultural implications, just as we did in discussing religious cultus. We regret that in so doing we cannot avoid repetition. But the very fact that repetition is inevitable indicates that the same conceptual framework has to be applied to both realms of culture, and this is obviously significant from the scientific point of view.

We begin again with an analysis of complex actions performed by individuals, such as weaving rugs, making furniture, planting vegetables, sowing seed, cooking. Some of these actions start, but are never completed. Those that are completed always conform with definite standards and norms. Each of them is like many others, repeatedly performed by the same individual and/or other individuals, although every one differs slightly from every other, and a few occasionally manifest minor intentional innovations.

In analyzing these complex actions into the more numerous simple actions of which they are composed and comparing the latter, we find that they also follow, with relatively rare exceptions, definite cultural patterns. The actions of attaching threads of the warp to a loom may be similarly patterned, even though the rugs to be woven will differ considerably or though the total action of weaving is not meant to produce a rug, but a piece of cloth. The pattern of hoeing or plowing may be the same, though the soil is prepared for different seeds. However, the subsequent elementary actions—tying knots in the course of weaving, planting or sowing seeds—are apt to be more specific, their common pattern applicable only within complex actions of a certain limited class. But, just as in the case of religious rituals, all those elementary actions which are presumed to be necessary for the realization of the final purpose of the total culturally patterned action are meant to be functionally interdependent and become integrated into an axionormatively organized system.

An individual who intends to weave a culturally standardized rug, to make a table or a chair of a certain style, to cultivate effectively plants of a certain species, or to cook a certain dish must learn how to perform these elementary actions and how to integrate all of them in the total course of their performance, so as to achieve the intended final product. The more complex such a

[19] Because of the great diversity and growing complexity of technical systems, an adequate history of their evolution would require the cooperation of many specialists. As yet no such cooperation has been achieved, and a general comparative science of material techniques above the level of nonliterate cultures is still undeveloped. Most of the historical studies are mere outlines. See, e.g., Karl Bücher, *Industrial Evolution* (New York, 1901); Georges F. Renard, *L'Évolution industrielle* (Paris, 1912); Harry B. Smith, *Industrial History* (New York: Macmillan, 1923). Leon C. Marshall, *Industrial Society* (Chicago: University of Chicago Press, 1930), 3 vols., covers the organization of modern technical systems rather well in Vol. II; but, like most economists, he considers technical organization of production an integral part of a more inclusive economic order of which the open market is the functional center.

technical action, the longer it takes to learn. Girls learn rug weaving in childhood and continue to learn until they are married. The apprenticeship of a medieval craftsman usually lasted from five to seven years. A farmer's son in Central Europe had to spend many years helping his father before he was allowed to function as an independent farmer.

Functional interdependence began very early between culturally patterned productive actions performed by several individuals. In many primitive communities men hunt or fish together. Some productive domestic cooperation is found between husbands and wives, based on sexual specialization in certain techniques. But systematically organized collective production, in the course of which numerous participants regularly perform differentiated actions, seems to have evolved later than systematically organized collective cultus. A yearly Australian totemic celebration is unequaled, so far as the systematic organization is concerned, by any collective technical performance of members of the same tribe.[20]

Full development of functionally differentiated, systematically organized collective production was primarily connected with the development of architecture; and architecture originally developed whenever and wherever large buildings were erected as *public centers*—religious, military, political, recreational, economic. Such public centers have been and still are constructed in all historical societies.[21]

In such a collective performance as raising and decorating a temple, a royal palace, a city hall, a theater, a number of skilled specialists and semi-skilled assistants are involved: stonecutters, masons, tile makers, carpenters, joiners, metal workers, sculptors, painters. Only craftsmen adequately prepared for their functions are admitted as participants. All the actions of these participating specialists are expected to conform and, judging by their results, usually have conformed with the standards and norms recognized as binding by craftsmen of their specialty in the given society during the given historical period. Conformity is indispensable for two reasons. First, because every action of a craftsman has to adapt itself to a situation defined in advance

[20] This complex organization of collective religious performances may have been one of the reasons why Durkheim selected Australian totemism as a typical "elementary form of religious life." Later research modified somewhat the results of earlier studies; but the difference in complexity between magico-religious and technical cooperation was confirmed. See, e.g., in Baldwin Spencer and Francis J. Gillen, *The Arunta, A Study of a Stone Age People*, 2 vols. (London, 1927), a new, more complete and thorough edition of a part of their earlier work; the description of initiation, death, burial, and mourning ceremonies and dances, and of their material techniques.

[21] Historians of architecture are interested in architectural products rather than in the actions which produce them. Still, there are some historical studies which throw light upon the organization of such actions, especially those which deal with the function of the architect as "the chief who commands workers of different professions so as to insure good execution of a public or private edifice." *La Grande Encyclopédie*, Vol. III, "Architecte," pp. 680-89; "Architecture," pp. 689-741 (bibliography).

and purposely prepared by preceding actions, and in turn purposely prepares situations defined in advance for subsequent actions. Second, because the final product—a building with a definite technical structure and aesthetic style —was planned in advance, and the realization of the plan necessitated purposive, harmonious integration of culturally differentiated functions of various specialists.

Such an integration requires the social guidance of an authoritative professional leader, just as the integration of public ceremonial cultus requires the social guidance of a professional priest or a high priest. Some degree of individual innovation may be allowed during the last period of the performance, after the building has already been erected, especially to sculptors and painters, but not while it was being erected. Sometimes, indeed, the original plan may be changed after it has begun to be realized; but such a change, even though individually initiated, must be collectively accepted, for it makes a reorganization of the collective performance necessary.

The total system of actions in the course of which a public building is raised and decorated lasts for rather a long time; it usually takes several years to complete it, and a few medieval cathedrals have not yet been completed according to the original plans. But not until modern times did dynamic technical systems of unlimited duration develop, analogous to systems of continuous ritualistic cultus of the same deity by a united religious group living around a temple. Such an axionormatively organized system of technical production, which has no definite temporal limits (unless an unexpected change makes its duration impossible), is a modern factory producing continually a multiplicity of material products of a certain class—domestic utensils, farming implements, automobiles, etc. In a system of this kind, actions of all participants are directly or indirectly interdependent, and their regular conformity with definite cultural patterns is essential for the continuous functioning of the entire system.

We are familiar with the requirements of skill and knowledge which an individual must satisfy to be admitted and to remain as an active participant in such a system. These requirements vary, depending upon the relative influence which specific actions of one agent have upon the total course of collective production. The complex actions of a skilled worker affect this course more than the simple actions of an unskilled worker. The actions of a technical coordinator which integrate many diversely patterned actions of workers are still more influential. And, of course, the whole organization depends upon the authoritative social leadership of planners and managers.

Recently, the functional interdependence between technical actions has been extended beyond the range of a particular localized factory, just as many centuries ago the functional interdependence between actions of cultus became extended beyond the range of a localized religious group. Several factories now specialize in producing parts of a product which becomes synthesized in a central factory.[22] Thus, a superterritorial dynamic system of unlimited duration develops which includes several local systems, each also unlimited in time, though limited in composition.

2. We pass now to a brief survey of the relationship between technical production and the use of technical products. We shall limit this survey to individual production and use. Here we find two different kinds of relationship. First, an individual may produce material values for his own use; second, he may produce material values which others will use.

Sporadic production of a particular object which the producer uses later is of little importance for our present problem. We are concerned with regular production of certain material values which the producer regularly uses to satisfy his needs, as when a primitive hunter who produces his own hunting implements regularly kills game and feeds mostly on the game he has killed, or when a gardener subsists mainly on the plants he has cultivated. Regular production of such values makes possible the regular satisfaction of the producer's needs, and regular satisfaction of his needs makes regular production possible. Actions of producing and actions of using products are thus interdependent, and their continued sequence is necessary for the individual to maintain his life. There is a certain analogy between this continuity of actions of production and use and the continuity of ritualistic actions which a faithful believer considers necessary to maintain the good will of his god.

Of course, the material values an individual produces are seldom sufficient to satisfy all his needs for a lengthy period of time. An economically self-sufficient individual who, like Robinson Crusoe, makes his own living for several years by his own productive efforts, without the aid of others, is at least as rare as a holy mystic who gains and maintains the favor of his god without anybody else's assistance. Every active human individual throughout most of his life is a participant in a collectivity which shares a certain culture; and in every collectivity with a relatively developed material technique, most of the values which an individual uses have been produced by others; and most of the values which he produces are intended to be used by others.

Now, if in such a collectivity we survey the relationships between actions of individuals who produce certain values and actions of other individuals who use these values, we find that these relationships are culturally regulated, so

---

[22] Cf., e.g., Georges de Leener, *L'Organisation syndicale des chefs d'industrie* (Brussels, 1909); Vol. II, chap. IV, "L'Évolution industrielle du XIXe siècle," especially "Concentration industrielle verticale" and "Spécialisation des entreprises." Also George R. Carter, *The Tendency Toward Industrial Combinations* (London, 1913), especially "Vertical Combination" due to the fact that "every industry is connected with a number of other industries engaged upon processes anterior to, subsequent to, or subsidiary to the operation with which it is itself concerned. This forms a basis of integration" (p. 47).

as to make the actions of these two categories functionally interdependent. The product of a technical action is considered a common value of the producer and the user; as such, it is subjected to definite cultural standards. Both the action of the producer and the action of the user are supposed to conform with specific, though different, norms; and if they do conform with these norms, the purposes of both are expected to be realized. The producer is supposed to follow an established cultural pattern, so as to make his product fit to be used in a specific kind of action; otherwise, the product will be judged useless. On the other hand, if the product is judged fit for use in a specifically patterned action, it is supposed to be used as it was intended; otherwise, the performance of the producer will be considered wasted. Whether a product is judged fit or unfit for a certain use and whether, if fit, it is used rightly or wrongly depends on the technological patterns considered binding in the given collectivity for both producers and users. The production of a Navaho basket destined to be useful as a semisacred ritualistic implement must strictly follow a complex cultural pattern; and once produced in accordance with this pattern, it is expected to be used for the purpose for which it was made, not for any "impure" purposes.[23] The same basket, however, would be considered useless in an Indian community where baskets of a different kind are made in order to carry water or to cook food. A Prince Albert coat produced by a Saville Row master tailor was judged suitable to be worn by an English gentleman during semiformal social meetings, but was never supposed to be worn while playing cricket or hunting. The same coat would have been of no use to a Chinese mandarin.

Such functionally interdependent actions of separate individual agents, some of whom produce standardized values which others use, become, as we know, integrated into dynamic *systems of economic interaction* when values are exchanged by producers. Agents give specific values which they produce for use to others who do not produce them, and receive from others for their own use different values which they do not produce themselves. Such systems have no predetermined duration. Economic interaction between two agents may end after an exchange has been completed, or last for a long time if they regularly continue to exchange their products. And many individual agents can participate in an economic system, especially when exchange becomes indirect and merchants assume the function of middlemen, interacting separately with technical producers of values, on the one hand, and with users of those values, on the other hand. These systems have been expanding and becoming increasingly complex in consequence of the gradual substitution of collective mass production for individual production and the growing rapidity of trans-

[23] Harry Tschopik, Jr., "Navaho Basketry," *Am. Anthropologist*, Vol. 42, pp. 444-62.

portation and communication.[24] But functional interdependence between culturally patterned actions of those producing certain values and culturally
patterned actions of those using these values remains the basic principle of
dynamic economic systems, although with the continual invention of new
standardized products new norms of producing and new norms of using them
evolve. We need not devote more time to a discussion of these systems, since
this has been for two centuries the domain of economics as one of the special
cultural sciences. Whether economists are justified in including within their
realm, as they often do, other categories of cultural systems is a problem
which must be postponed.[25]

3. The third kind of relationship in the realm of material technique which
has not yet been investigated by cultural scientists is that between the various
actions which use the same material values. The possibilities of using any
material value—be it a field, a forest, an orchard, a house, a table, a telephone, a herd of wild or domestic animals—are necessarily limited. If several
agents use it, what one is doing may interfere with the actions of several
others, unless their actions are axionormatively ordered and mutually adapted

[24] It is significant, however, that this growth, expansion, and integration of economic
systems lagged behind the growth and expansion of religious systems. While world-wide
integrated religious systems (especially Roman Catholicism, but also Islam) developed
centuries ago, a world economy was not even conceived in the eighteenth century and
grew only slowly during the nineteenth. Cf. A. Sartorius von Waltershausen, *Die
Entstehung der Weltwirtschaft* (Jena, 1931).

[25] The problem is difficult in the light of the history of economic thought. First of all,
economic thinkers, like other thinkers in the realm of culture, were originally interested in practical problems which involved some ideological issues; this obviously
impeded, and still impedes, the development of economics as an objective science. Even
those who try to be objective do not always succeed in avoiding evaluative and normative judgments. See, e.g., Maurice Block, *Les Progrès de la science économique* (Paris,
1897); and Alfred Marshall, *Principles of Economics* (London, several editions).
Second, the central theoretic problem with which most economists, like many religionists
and students of art, have been concerned was to reach scientific generalizations about
values as such. The very term "value," as used by them, denotes not an empirical
datum which is evaluated, but a common characteristic of certain empirical data.
What they actually have achieved, beginning with the Austrian school and ending
with the neoclassicists, is measurement of *evaluative attitudes*. In this respect, they are
far ahead of other cultural scientists, mainly because quantitative differences and changes
of those attitudes which they measure are manifested in prices. But here, as in other
cultural sciences, studies of attitudes become fully significant only when connected
with studies of actions.
Now, the first main category of actions with which economists are concerned—
production—actually constitutes, as we mentioned before, a vast realm of research
requiring such a knowledge of the great diversity and complexity of material techniques
as no economist can be expected to possess. Consumption, meaning use of final
products for the satisfaction of human wants, though less complex, is also widely
diversified; and we do not know of any attempt to develop a general cultural science
of these actions, although some monographic studies of some specific varieties have
been made. Thus, by studying only actions of exchange economics as a special objective
science has been making real progress.

in such a way as to make the realization of their respective purposes possible. A good example of this kind of relationship, familiar to most Americans, is the use of public roads built and maintained by a city, a county, a state, or the United States.

A public road is obviously a common value of those who make it and of those who use it. Now, the very existence of public roads suggests that the movement of men and the transportation of material objects from one place to another within a given territory are considered desirable by those who build and maintain the roads. Originally, however, public roads were intended to serve the purposes of the ruling groups rather than of private individuals. They were built by governments primarily to achieve more effective political control and unification of the population within the state territories, and to help defend the frontiers of the state against foreign invasion. Such were, for instance, the main purposes for which Roman public roads were built, and in the late Middle Ages highways were mainly intended to unify kingdoms. Modern civil engineering, applying scientific techniques in building roads and bridges, evolved out of military engineering; and its original purpose, like that of military engineering, was to help the government in performing its functions. Even today, under the present regime in Soviet Russia, all movements of men and goods on public roads are intended to promote political and economic integration of the state under complete governmental control.[26]

We shall not attempt to explain why in the United States right now the use of public roads for the movement of men and the transportation of material things, not only by governmental agencies, but by private individuals, is considered valuable from the point of view of the territorially circumscribed society as a whole (city, county, state, United States).[27] The evidence is conclusive that it is so considered, especially since privately owned automobiles have become the most numerous and most frequently used means of transportation. Individual drivers use for purely private purposes roads and streets collectively built and maintained. New roads are being built and old roads and streets improved, with the explicit intention of facilitating and increas-

[26] Books and articles about public roads, written almost exclusively by technologists for technicians, ignore their social and cultural significance. We found a few exceptions: e.g., Hilaire Belloc, *The Road* (New York: Harper, 1925), brief and limited to England. Most of the historical surveys of the development of roads are parts of the history of transportation and rightly so, since the extension and improvement of roads is connected with the evolution of carriers. The history of transportation, however, is usually treated as a part of the history of commerce. See, e.g., William H. Boulton, *The Pageant of Transportation through the Ages* (London, 1931); Albert Steinberg, *Evolution and Economics of Transportation* (Toronto, 1930); Labert St. Claire, *Transportation* (New York: Dodd, 1933).

[27] Seymour Dunbar, *A History of Travel in America*, 4 vols. (Indianapolis, 1915), offers considerable valuable material bearing directly or indirectly on this problem.

ing motor traffic. Progressive improvement of automobiles is publicly appreciated as one of the great achievements of American industry.

We know, however, that use of public roads and streets by drivers of motor cars is conditional upon their conformity with numerous standards and norms. These standards and norms constitute a rather coherent ideological system (though some minor disagreements are found between the specific norms recognized as binding in different states). We mention only the most important of them. First, no motor car is supposed to be used unless it satisfies certain minimum technological standards which insure that the driver will be able to control it. Second, for every driver in every situation he may face in the course of his driving, living human bodies are the supreme values, which must be unconditionally safeguarded. There is a significant gradation of values for drivers. The bodies of others are expected to be more important to him than his own body; if he takes the risk of injuring somebody else's body, this is considered ethically wrong, but if he risks only his own body, his action is judged as intellectually defective. Other people's bodies, those of pedestrians and especially of children, are expected to be more carefully safeguarded than those of car drivers, mainly because children are more helpless and more easily injured. Less important, but still valuable, are the material possessions which may be destroyed or harmed by careless driving; and here again the driver is expected to be more careful of other people's possessions than of his own, as is shown by the legal responsibility attached to actions that are injurious to others.

These standards of values are connected with many specific norms of conduct. Most of the latter require definite technical actions: driving on the right side of the road, slowing down and limiting speed in certain areas, stopping at certain signs, waiting for another car or a pedestrian to cross an intersection, refraining from passing another car at crossroads or on hills, etc. Some norms also require that the driver signal his intention to others, indicating that he is going to stop, to turn right or left, to pass the car ahead, etc. The basic implicit premise of all these norms is that, inasmuch as a public road or street is continuously open to many agents and it is impossible to predict who will use a particular section of it at a particular time, the action of any agent who uses it at any time may affect and/or be affected by the action of some other agent. And the norms are planned under the assumption that, if all agents always conform with them, the totality of actions which constitute motor traffic within a certain territory will be axionormatively ordered in such a way as to achieve a maximum of technical effectiveness compatible with complete safety.

Such axionormative order among the technical actions of car drivers obviously does not mean that all these actions are functionally interdependent components of one technical system, like the technical actions of workers in a factory. Each driving agent pursues his own purpose of transporting himself and often some passengers and material objects to a certain destination; if he functions as a private person, as most drivers do, the realization of his purpose does not contribute anything positive to the realization of the purposes of other drivers who use the same roads. The order, insofar as agents conform with it, simply makes the realization of these separate and independent purposes possible by *preventing* certain actions injurious to the agents and to the instruments which they use.

But—and this is a phenomenon of primary importance to students of culture in general and sociologists in particular—to maintain this axionormative order among the technical actions of car drivers, a complex, integrated system of functionally interdependent *social actions* has been organized in every state, with subsystems in particular counties, cities, and villages. These actions, aiming mainly to control human individuals, include, first, promulgation and popularization of legal rules by legislative groups. Taken by themselves in their content and meaning, such rules express symbolically evaluative and normative attitudes of the legislators who define vicariously various situations for drivers. But viewed as to their form, they are commands of legislators as authoritative agents, intended to make others perform definite actions. Many are addressed to all drivers within the state as a class. They are supplemented by more specific commands which local authorities express on road signs and in traffic lights; these are addressed to the drivers who are using the particular roads and streets controlled by a smaller territorial group within the state. They are sometimes further supplemented by commands, expressed orally or in gestures, and addressed to individual drivers by the policemen regulating traffic. And when the drivers themselves, conforming with legal rules, give signals to others, they manifest demands that those others should also act in the given situations in accordance with the commonly recognized norms.

Other actions of legislative groups are intended to make the administrative agents acting on behalf of the government follow definite cultural patterns in dealing with car drivers as persons. Thus, certain administrative officials are expected to grant permission to drive motor cars on public roads only to individuals who have learned how to drive. This means that they must have acquired a necessary minimum of technical knowledge about cars and their movements, be physically trained in the actual handling of those implements by which movements of cars are controlled, and be psychologically trained to define and solve rapidly every situation they may have to face. Besides, they must know and accept all the standards and norms formulated by legislators. It is the duty of administrative officials to test the knowledge and training of every individual before granting him a license. Finally, as an essential part of this complex social system intended to make drivers conform with standards and norms of motor traffic, we find numerous and diverse axionormatively ordered, functionally interdependent actions intended to *counteract transgressions*. Counteracting transgressions, however, requires a special investigation.

Summary and problematic conclusions

Having found that cultural scientists can and do classify human actions on the basis of their factual conformity with the requirements of ideological models, we postulated that, if different actions dealing with the same values regularly tend to conform with definite models, their conformity implies that they are considered by the agents to be functionally interdependent, mutually helpful in achieving their respective tendencies. This postulate proved to be applicable to relationships between certain categories of culturally patterned actions in the realms of research of three cultural sciences—comparative theory of religion, technology in the sense of comparative theory of material techniques, and economics. In each of these realms we found that, when and insofar as functionally interdependent actions are regularly performed in accordance with their respective standards and norms, they become integrated in the course of their performance into dynamic, axionormatively organized systems of actions.

These systems vary considerably in size, complexity, and duration. Every one is qualitatively limited, inasmuch as only actions of definite cultural classes are included in it. Most of them are also quantitatively and temporarily limited. If, and insofar as, the purposes of all the actions which a system includes are subordinated in advance to a single final purpose expected to be realized after the total performance has been completed, the system as a whole is one more or less complex action, which ends as soon as the purpose has presumably been realized. Such is the case, as we have seen, when an individual worshiper or a group of worshipers starts and completes a particular ritualistic performance composed of a limited plurality of interdependent simpler rites; when an individual craftsman produces a particular rug, or a group of craftsmen builds a palace; when a merchant buys and sells a particular product or a limited collection of products. We have found, however, that many such numerically and temporarily limited systems, repeatedly performed, can be integrated into a much more comprehensive system without a single final purpose, but with a multiplicity of distinct, mutually supplementary purposes. Such a system has no numerical or temporal limit determined in advance. The number of ritualistic actions, individual or collective, repeatedly performed by religious believers in worshiping the same spiritual, superearthly deity may increase indefinitely as the religious ideology expands, or decrease as the religious ideology recedes.

Nor is the duration of this system limited in advance; it will last as long as there are believers who continue to function as worshipers. Actions of workers in a factory producing definite objects at a given time have numerical limits, but their number may increase if new techniques are introduced, or decrease during a depression. And there is no predetermined time limit inherent in the system, for the total course of production is never completed, though it may be interrupted or stopped permanently under the impact of some force external to the technical system as such. Trade in certain goods carried on by a commercial group can expand or recede territorially, increase or decrease numerically, and last indefinitely, without ceasing to be economically integrated and systematically organized, unless and until some external force interferes with its integration and continuation.

If we should investigate actions in other realms of culture, we should also find axionormatively organized systems of functionally interdependent actions which follow definite patterns. We mentioned before, the continuous systems of culturally patterned *social* actions tending to influence drivers of motor cars within a certain territory, so as to maintain an axionormative order among the technical actions which they perform.

The original *artistic* action of a musical composer or a poet is an organized system of simpler interdependent actions, all of which follow definite cultural patterns, though with a wider range of variations and innovations than those which the cultural patterns of religion, technique, or trade include. The creative performance of the composer or poet can be indefinitely re-created, reproduced, by musicians, declaimers, readers, if those who re-create it accept and follow the standards and norms which the creator applied in the course of his creation. And inasmuch as the composition or the poem is identified by all those who are aware of its existence as the same cultural product, and those who re-create it intend to maintain its existence as a common human value, their re-creative actions have a certain historical continuity.[28] In the realm of *science*, not only are particular complex scientific actions as limited systems reproduced by imitators and learners, but there is functional interdependence between various culturally patterned creative actions within the same science, which makes this science as a whole a more or less integrated, creative dynamic system of unlimited duration.

Thus, in every realm of culture, apparently the same two categories of axionormative order are found among human actions: the order of conformity of particular actions with definite standards and norms, which enables scientists to compare and classify actions; the order of functional interdependence between actions, which enables scientists to investigate the

[28] An objective generalizing science of literature, based on comparative studies of creative literary actions, as distinct from a history of literary works, began to develop at the end of the nineteenth century and is progressing slowly, but steadily. Cf. Max Lerner and Edwin Mines, Jr., "Literature," *Encycl. of Social Sci.*, Vol. IX (New York: Macmillan, 1937).

integration of many different actions into organized dynamic systems. This means that all cultural scientists, whatever their specialty, can use a common heuristic approach in trying to reach taxonomic and functional generalizations in their respective domains; and that their approach must be different from that which natural scientists are using, since obviously no axionormative order is observable in the natural universe. Even those who postulate that the whole order of nature is produced and maintained by a supreme thinker and agent for the realization of some absolute ideal must agree that this belief cannot be tested by observation.

Another important problem, however, must be taken into consideration. We have been discussing here only those human actions which conform with the requirements of ideological models. But how about actions which do not conform? Various kinds and degrees of nonconformity are found in all human collectivities and in every realm of culture. Students of culture have been concerned with these phenomena for thousands of years; special disciplines, such as criminology and psychopathology, are devoted to their investigation. Obviously no science of culture can omit them. The questions are, how can scientific generalizations about nonconforming actions be reached, and how can they be logically connected with generalizations based on the principle of conformity?

Disorganization of Cultural Systems

The puzzle of prohibitive generalizations about actions

Classification of actions by the standards and norms with which they conform has usually been, and still is, supplemented by another classification. Thinkers who promulgate ideological models for the guidance of others are aware, of course, that these others do not always act as they ought to act in the situations vicariously defined for them. Within certain limits, deviations from a model may be tolerated, so long as agents actually tend to conform with its requirements; but if agents manifest tendencies which apparently conflict with the standards and norms which they are required to follow, their deviating conduct is condemned. Authoritative ideologists usually assume the task of forestalling such condemned deviations by warning agents against them. This is what priests, prophets, moralists, legislators, political thinkers, military strategists, technologists, educational advisers, critics of art and literature, grammarians and lexicographers, and authors of etiquette books have been doing for thousands of years. The more important types of condemned deviations are defined in general terms, and their occurrence is prohibited by explicit rules. Prohibition is often accompanied by a prediction of the undesirable consequences which will follow every transgression of a prohibitive rule. As a result, almost every ideological system includes a division of actions into two antithetic categories: those which conform with the requirements of the system and those which do not conform with these requirements; and actions of each category are usually classified separately.

This classification seems even to predominate in relatively small traditional collectivities. In many primitive religions, classificatory generalizations about prohibited actions formulated in taboos are much more numerous, exact, and explicit than generalizations formally expressed in positive norms of religious conduct, which accounts for these religions being sometimes characterized by religionists as "tabooistic."[1] In comparing earlier and simpler societies with later and more complex societies, Durkheim points out that in the earlier and simpler societies law is almost exclusively criminal law.[2] But this predominance of negatively evaluated actions is found also in more developed societies. Thus, in the Egyptian Book of the Dead, the soul of every dead person is brought before Osiris, the supreme judge, and his assistants and forced to justify itself by stating in answer to their questions that it has *not* committed any of the long list of prohibited actions.[3] In the *Avesta* "the entire [book of] Vendidad can be viewed as a code of sins."[4]

In some ideologies an explicit formulation of prohibitive rules apparently serves to popularize the main principles of the system. In any case, a negative rule is easier to formulate in abstract terms than a positive ideological model. For instance, out of the Ten Commandments, which all adherents of Judaism and Christianity have to memorize, eight are prohibitive. The ideological principles of Buddhist ethics are popularly summarized in the simple form of five prohibitive rules: "Do not kill, Do not steal, Do not commit adultery, Do not tell a lie, Do not take intoxicating liquors."[5] Frequently, indeed, the formula is too inclusive and inexact, as in the commandment, "Thou shalt not kill." This fails to mention that the killing of certain kinds of people is not prohibited but even recommended; Jehovah himself helped the Israelites kill the inhabitants of Canaan during an invasion.

In most highly developed ideologies, however, positive as well as negative taxonomies are complex and well systematized, and the positive predominate. We have discussed the positive standards and norms of Roman Catholicism. All offenses against these standards and norms are categorized as sins. Sins are classified according to their importance into mortal and venial—the first with seven, the second with a rather indefinite number of subclasses.[6]

There exists another, partly overlapping classification into sins of commission (performance of actions which conflict with positive norms) and

[1] Cf. Edvard Lehmann in Chantepie de la Saussaye, *Lehrbuch der Religionsgeschichte*, pp. 122 ff.

[2] Émile Durkheim, *De la division du travail social* (Paris, 1902), chaps. II and III, pp. 35-118.

[3] George Foucart, *La Méthode comparative dans l'histoire des religions*, p. 172.

[4] Lehmann, *op. cit.*, p. 246.

[5] Shundo Tachibana, *The Ethics of Buddhism* (London, 1926), p. 59.

[6] See, e.g., John A. McHugh and Charles J. Callan, *Moral Theology, passim.* The general distinction between positive norms and prohibitive rules is formulated as follows: "laws are either affirmative (i.e., preceptive) or negative (i.e., prohibitive). An affirmative law obliges always, but not for every occasion; a negative law obliges always, and for every occasion."

sins of omission (nonperformance of actions which positive norms require). Very significant from this point of view are the modern legal ideologies developed in political societies. We find everywhere at least two distinct ideological systems: constitutional and civil law, including quite systematic classifications of the actions expected to conform with definite standards and norms; and criminal law, which includes prohibitive generalizations about offenses. Like sins, offenses are classified according to their importance into crimes and misdemeanors, with specific subclasses. Just as in religion, this classification covers not only performances of actions which conflict with norms, but nonperformance of specific actions required by the norms: nonattendance of children in schools, nonappearance in courts when summoned as a witness, failure to report income subjected to taxation, nonregistration of men liable for military duty, nonperformance by soldiers of actions ordered by commanding officers, etc.

Can these classifications of transgressions be scientifically tested and validated by comparative analysis, like classifications of actions which conform with definite standards and norms? Quite a few cultural scientists believe that they can, especially those criminologists who accept the system of criminal law maintained by their own society and assume that its generalizations were originally based on a comparative study of the actions therein classified as crimes.[7] No doubt some such studies have been carried on, and in recent times their results have occasionally been taken into consideration by legislators. Nevertheless, attempts—like that of Raffaele Garofalo—to discover some essential similarities between actions classified as crimes in all societies at all periods have completely failed.[8]

The reason for this failure is clear. All prohibitive rules define and classify actions as experienced and evaluated by those who promulgate the rules, from the point of view of the standards and norms which they consider binding. Since the agents who perform such prohibited actions *ex definitione* do not conform with these standards and norms, such a classification

[7] Jerome Hall, "Criminology," eds. Gurvitch and Moore, in *Twentieth Century Sociology* (New York: Philosophical Library, 1945).

[8] Raffaele Garofalo, *Criminology*, trans. by R. W. Millar (Boston: Little, 1914). The author recognizes that, in view of the vast diversity of actions characterized as crimes in various societies, "we are compelled to relinquish the idea of collecting a group of *facts* universally hated and punished." But "it by no means follows that the notion of the natural crime is impossible of achievement. To attain it, however, we must change method: we must lay aside the analysis of *facts* and undertake that of *sentiments*. Crime, in reality, is always a harmful action, but, at the same time, an action which wounds some one of the sentiments which, by common consent, are called the moral sense of a human aggregation" (p. 6). ". . . created, like all the other sentiments, by evolution, and transmitted from generation to generation. . . . But since the moral sense is a psychic activity, it may be subject to change and infirmity . . . may even become entirely lost" (p. 9).

by itself contains no information as to what the actions really are from the point of view of the agents themselves.

Frequently, as we know, an objective analysis of actions which are negatively evaluated and classified as wrong by adherents of one ideological system shows that they do conform with definite, though different, standards and norms (included in another ideological system) and are positively classified as right according to this conformity by the agents and by others who accept the other system. Thus, the erection in temples of painted or sculptured human figures as representations of holy beings is absolutely prohibited by orthodox Mohammedans, and branded as sinful idolatry by several Protestant sects; but these figures constitute important implements of religious cultus in Brahmanism, Chinese and Burmese Buddhism, Greek Orthodoxy, and Roman Catholicism. Polygamy, religiously and legally prohibited in modern Western societies, is not only permitted but positively valued in many others. In every large state certain groups accept ideological models according to which many actions classified by legislators as crimes are considered normal, even commendable. Such cultural patterns are found not only in groups which together constitute the so-called "criminal underworld"—professional thieves, gamblers, gangsters, vice rings, sets of corrupt politicians—but also in various minority groups with distinct cultures and in rebellious associations with ideologies opposed to those of the legislators. Revolutions often result in a reversal of previous classifications; some actions prohibited as crimes before a revolution become normatively required afterward, and vice versa.

Manifestly, wherever actions which adherents of one ideology evaluate negatively as conflicting with standards and norms which they consider binding are found to conform with different standards and norms which the agents themselves consider binding, the investigator must classify them on the basis of this conformity, together with other actions which follow similar cultural patterns. A scientific religionist obviously will not classify religious actions of Methodists by their conformity or nonconformity with the standards and norms of Roman Catholicism, nor the actions of Catholics by their conformity or nonconformity with the standards and norms of Methodism. An objective investigator of political organizations will not divide the political actions of Russian communists into two classes: those which conform and those which do not conform with the principles of American democracy. Nor will he classify the actions of adherents of American democracy according to their conformity or nonconformity with the principles of Marxism-Leninism-Stalinism.

Even when the actions prohibited by some ideological thinkers do not follow any standards and norms considered binding by adherents of some other ideology, their classification may vary and change. Actions similarly defined may be crimes in some states, but not in others. In nearly every state, when new criminal laws are promulgated, actions which were not crimes become crimes; and when old criminal laws are abrogated, actions which were crimes cease to be crimes.

Thus, considerable variations and changes are found in the classification of sexual actions. A curious example right now is sodomy, which is a severely punishable crime in some states of the Union, whereas in others it is no crime at all. Even more significant inconsistencies are observable in classification of the conduct of agents who have not been trained to accept and follow cultural patterns. In certain civilized societies, only a few centuries ago, noxious behavior of animals was sometimes defined as criminal and subjected to punishment.[9] In some tribal societies, "abnormal" behavior of small children, even of infants, was considered evil, and they had to be killed just like adult criminals, while in other tribes a child was not expected fully to conform until he became an active participant in adult culture. The myth that all infants were born bad because of the original sin of Adam and Eve, and were destined for damnation unless saved by the grace of God, had at least an indirect influence on criminal law in some states; after a child had reached the age when he understood the difference between good and evil (usually fixed at seven years), if he committed an action similar to that of an adult criminal, his action was classified as crime. The concept of juvenile delinquency was only recently introduced to distinguish transgressions of youths from transgressions of adults, and there is still no universal standard by which judges decide when childish misbehavior becomes juvenile delinquency or when juvenile delinquency becomes crime.

Another proof of the inconsistency of prohibitive classifications is the confusion between individual and collective transgressions. In many societies, when an individual member of a social group—a family, a clan, a village— commits a sin or a crime, all other members of the group are considered participants in this action. Sins of parents become also sins of their children and of their grandchildren, even though they may not yet have been born when the sins were committed. While this conception of the collective share in individual transgressions has receded in modern times, yet remnants of it still survive in some military groups; it was recently fully revived by the Nazis and partly revived by the Bolsheviks. On the other hand, when an organized group collectively acts in a way which conflicts with certain ideological principles, we find that adherents of these principles sometimes consider all members of the group guilty, sometimes a certain proportion of them, sometimes only a few, or even one particular individual.

[9] Cf. George Ives, *A History of Penal Methods* (New York: Stokes, n.d.), pp. 255-61; Carl L. von Bar and others, *A History of Continental Criminal Law*, trans. by T. S. Bell (Boston: Little, 1916), p. 151.

The final and most conclusive proof that generalizations expressed in prohibitive rules cannot be even tentatively accepted as valid classifications of human actions is the inclusion in these generalizations of the nonperformance of actions which ought to be performed: sins of omission in religious ideologies, and similar offenses defined by criminal law (such as nonpayment of certain taxes, nonappearance of certain witnesses in court or of enlisted men at military centers). How can the nonoccurrence of certain facts be included in the same general class as the occurrence of certain other facts?

One of the most puzzling problems in the history of cultural thought is the persistence of this age-old assumption of practical thinkers that all behavior or conduct which does not conform with the requirements of the ideological doctrine accepted by these thinkers has an essential similarity and is essentially different from conduct which conforms with these requirements.[10] After all, many authors who systematized such doctrines—theologians and moral, political, or legal philosophers—were and are good formal logicians. How could they fail to notice the logical defects of their theories?

In the first place, what was their reason for listing and explicitly condemning various kinds of conduct which conflict with certain standards and norms, since the very requirement that human conduct should conform with these standards and norms already implies that it should not conflict with them? Second, why were and are these thinkers unaware of the logical absurdity of including under the same class the performance of certain actions and the nonperformance of certain other actions? Third, how could they ignore the fact that their classifications of actions as sins, crimes, or vices are contradicted by other classifications, and that there are no universal objective tests of validity by which such contradictions can be eliminated?

These considerations lead us to doubt whether the negative generalizations about human conduct found in most ideological systems can be taken by cultural scientists for what they appear to be to listeners and readers, i.e., as *classifications* of the phenomena to which they refer. Perhaps they have some

[10] Some criminologists, aware of the contradictions and inconsistencies between definitions of prohibited actions, have substituted different generalizations for these vain attempts to find common characteristics of all crimes. Thus, Heinrich Oppenheimer in *The Rationale of Punishment* (London, 1913), clearly states: "There are no acts intrinsically criminal, no deeds that constitute offenses at all times and in all places. Indeed, the sole generic character of crime is that it is visited by punishment, and, by being made punishable, any course of conduct is converted into crime" (p. 2). His definition of punishment, however, is evaluative. Following, with some modifications, the theory of Westermarck, he defines punishment as follows: "Punishment is an evil inflicted upon a wrongdoer, as a wrongdoer, on behalf and at the discretion of the society, in its corporate capacity, of which he is a permanent or temporary member" (p. 4). Fear, not indignation, is the root emotion underlying punishment. The rationale of punishment is regard for the welfare of society (p. 10). While the theory is partly valid, like most psychological explanations of social phenomena, it ignores their cultural patterns.

significance which is not apparent when we judge them only from their symbolic expression. This supposition seems to be partly confirmed if we take into consideration certain statements which often—though not always—accompany the promulgation of prohibitive rules. Authors sometimes explain *why* the kind of conduct to which these rules refer must be negatively valued. Sometimes also they add normative statements explaining how this kind of conduct ought to be counteracted. And, in any case, the investigator can conclusively ascertain the full significance of these generalizations by studying their origin.

Transgressions as causes of cultural disorganization[11]

Let us begin with the heuristic hypothesis that generalizations expressed in prohibitive rules, though invalid if judged by standards of scientific taxonomy, are originally based upon certain *causal generalizations* which can be scientifically tested and at least partly validated.

To illustrate what this hypothesis means, some analogies from generalizations about natural phenomena may be helpful. The general term "poisons" is current in popular speech; farmers and gardeners use the general term "weeds" in referring to certain plants, and the term "pests" in referring to certain insects (sometimes also to certain birds and mammals). These terms are negatively evaluative; they imply that men should avoid poisons, that weeds should be destroyed, pests eliminated. Obviously, if the concepts symbolized by these terms are judged by the principles of scientific taxonomy, they are worthless. There is no logical class of poisons as chemical systems essentially similar among themselves and essentially different from other

[11] The term "cultural disorganization," which we use here, is obviously more inclusive than the popular term "social disorganization," which Thomas and I used in *The Polish Peasant* and which has been the subject matter of several important books (e.g., Mabel A. Elliot and Francis E. Merril, *Social Disorganization* (New York: Harper, 1934); Stuart A. Queen, Walter B. Bodenhafer, and Ernest B. Harper, *Social Organization and Disorganization* (New York: Crowell, 1935); and lately Robert E. L. Faris, *Social Disorganization* (New York: Ronald Press, 1948).

Social disorganization is defined by Robert E. L. Faris as "disruption of the functional relations among persons to a degree that interferes with the performance of the accepted task of the group" (p. 19). This is an excellent definition. As the author makes clear later, since "functional relations among persons" are culturally patterned, a group based on such relations is a distinct cultural system, and consequently social disorganization can be included under the concept of cultural disorganization. Indubitably also, when a nonsocial cultural system—technical, religious, aesthetic, intellectual—is maintained in existence by a socially integrated group, the social disorganization of the group results in a disorganization of this system. But the disorganization of a cultural system individually maintained does not imply any social disorganization. Furthermore, as we shall see, a cultural system maintained by a group can become disorganized under the impact of external influences, and yet such disorganization may lead to an increasing integration of functional relations between the members of the group.

systems, no distinct botanical class of weeds, no definite zoological class of pests.

But when we investigate the origin of these concepts, we find that they are not based on a comparative analysis of the data which they include. They originated in observations of definite changes which occurred in human organisms or cultivated plants and could be causally explained by the influence of other objects. It did not matter how different the latter were; the significant fact was that the effects of their influence were similar. Men died when their organisms absorbed certain chemicals; the growth of cultivated plants was impeded by the growth of other, unwanted plants; cultivated plants already grown were destroyed by insects or animals. From the practical point of view, the most essential characteristic of all poisons is that they usually cause men to die; the most essential characteristic of all weeds is that they impede the growth of cultivated plants; the most essential characteristic of all pests is that they destroy cultivated plants. Although scientists reject these practical classifications and substitute instead theoretic classifications of chemicals, plants, or insects based on comparative analysis, this does not mean that we must also reject those original causal generalizations, for, when tested, they may prove valid within certain limits and under certain conditions.

Similarly, when ideological thinkers generalize about transgressions of recognized standards and norms, they are not concerned with the objective characteristics of these transgressions, but with their presumed effects. And their fundamental assumption, as we shall try to show, is that all transgressions have a disorganizing influence upon that kind of systematic order among actions which depends upon their regular conformity with ideological models; they injure values important to conformists or otherwise interfere with the realization of their purposes. They have to be prohibited in advance and counteracted whenever they occur, not merely because they are intrinsically bad, antithetic to the good, but because, and insofar as, they are injurious to the good. A farmer does not treat uncultivated plants as weeds if they grow in the wilderness; he treats them as weeds only if they grow in his fields and interfere with his crops. A legislator or a judge does not treat as crimes actions performed by citizens of a foreign state, unless these actions are injurious to the values of fellow citizens which his government is supposed to protect, or disturb the legal order of his own state.[12]

Of course, not all disorganization of cultural systems is due to the conduct of human agents which conflicts with the requirements of ideological

[12] This is quite clearly exemplified by the Roman conception, according to which "*any act* in consequence of special circumstances could be regarded as criminally prejudicial to the interest of the state and be dealt with as such"; von Bar and others, *op. cit.*, p. 16.

models. Much of it is caused by natural processes which destroy values or impede the constructive activity of participants. But it is significant for our present problem that participants in a cultural system, as we have noticed before, are inclined to seek for some purposive actions as first causes of these natural processes. They may be ascribed to bad sorcerers or to evil spirits. According to Zoroastrian ideology, all destruction and disorganization is caused by Ahriman and his evil followers struggling against Ormazd and his good followers. Here, however, we are concerned only with the problem of ascertaining and testing the assumption of conformists that human transgressions have a disorganizing effect upon the orderly system in which these conformists participate.[13]

Take, first, a few typical examples of the effects which sins are supposed to have upon the orderly systems of functionally interdependent, culturally patterned religious actions. A serious sin performed by a faithful worshiper has a disorganizing effect upon his relations with the deity and may even deflect him permanently from the straight path of righteousness. Holy hermits and saints were aware of this danger and avoided even minor transgressions. Saint Anthony became famous mainly because of his effective resistance to temptations which no ordinary believer could have resisted. A single sacrilegious action committed by an individual in a temple may profane its sanctity and make it unfit for public cultus. A notorious sinner or foreign unbeliever should not be admitted to a public religious ceremony, for his presence might deprive the ceremony of its beneficent results, perhaps even arouse the ire of the deity against participants in the cultus. A notable deviation of an active participant, especially a leader or a priest, from the established ritual makes the ceremony ineffective. Nonparticipation of an active member in a ceremonial cultus in which he is obligated to participate impedes the performance of that part of the ceremony in which his share is essential, if not the whole ceremony. The unjustified absence of even an ordinary member with no important special function, though it does not disturb the ceremony, can have later disturbing effects, for if ignored by the group it may be repeated or perhaps imitated by other members; consequently, the deity might judge that the group was losing interest in the cultus, and its benefits would decrease or be lost. In any case, another consequence of such sins of omission would be certain. A member who arbitrarily refrains from participating in public cultus or neglects his duties of private cultus does not gain in purity and piety. Consequently, he is sure to become an active

[13] These examples are, of course, meant only to clarify our heuristic hypothesis, not to prove it. In our opinion, objective comparative studies of the effects of transgressions on all kinds of cultural systems would make an important, perhaps an indispensable, contribution to the development of cultural sciences.

sinner, if he is not one already; and active sinners are bearers of evil, serious dangers to all the faithful.

The latter belief, as we know, goes far back in the history of religion. Originally it seems to have been associated with the idea that evil forces inherent in a human being, just as in other objects, can magically contaminate all who are in contact with him, even without his doing anything. In religions with relatively developed cultus of divine beings, it has two main forms. The active transgressor of religious rules may be a sorcerer or a witch, an evil magician, or an active enemy of good people bent on doing harm to them. Or he may be an enemy of good gods, a rebel against divine authority. In the latter case, he is even more dangerous; for while good gods are always willing to help the faithful against evil sorcerers, the presence in the community of an enemy of god, if tolerated, is apt to bring a divine curse upon the whole community.

Of course, an investigator cannot test the truth of such assumptions as to the maleficent effects of sins upon the mystical relationship between men and gods; but he can observe the disorganizing effects which these assumptions have upon systems of culturally patterned actions performed by believers. The assumption that the temple has been profaned by a sacrilege disorganizes the regular sequence of public ceremonies; the presence of an excommunicated sinner or a foreign unbeliever, a marked transgression of norms by an active participant, when noticed by the congregation, disorganizes the collective ceremonial performance; and we know from historical evidence how the regular, orderly life of a faithful community can be disorganized by the discovery that one of its members is a witch or an enemy of god.

Transgressions of criminal law also are supposed to have, and frequently have in fact, disorganizing effects upon axionormatively ordered systems which legislators recognize and support. Killing a member of a collectivity who is considered socially valuable destroys all positive, legally approved social relations between him and others, and disturbs the functioning of various cultural systems in which he was actively participating. The more important he was as participant, the greater the disorganizing influence of his sudden death. This is why in many collectivities killing a lord was a worse crime than killing a serf, killing a priest worse than killing a layman, killing a military commander worse than killing a soldier, and killing a king, the worst crime of all. It does not explain, however, the distinction between murder as intentional killing and manslaughter as unintentional killing. This distinction did not emerge merely as a consequence of the progress of ethical standards concerning responsibility. When unintentional killing lost its early magico-religious implications, intentional killing came to be considered much more dangerous, because the killer by his conscious radical transgression of criminal law challenged the supreme authority of legislators and defied the power of those who enforced legal rules, and that might lead to repeated transgressions with a cumulative disorganizing effect upon public order.

The same principle underlies other prohibitive rules of criminal law. Over and above direct effects of particular transgressions is the cumulative disorganizing influence which repeated violations of law are supposed to have, and often really have, upon large systems of axionormatively ordered actions which governments organize and maintain. Any particular failure to report taxable income and pay the tax has only a minor effect upon the economic system of public finance; but if such conduct were repeatedly imitated by many citizens with taxable incomes, the whole system might become disorganized. A burglary, a theft, an embezzlement disturbs in some measure the functioning of a particular private economic system; but their multiplication disturbs the normal functioning of all law based upon the principle of private property, and this in turn results in a further multiplication of such crimes.

A particular transgression of a prohibitive rule by a car driver on a public road may disturb his own or somebody else's regular driving; and it is possible that it will result in serious damage to a car or even to a human body. When such transgressions multiply, investigations carried on within a state or a large city during such a period of time as a year or even only a month show that a number of people are killed, a much larger number injured, many cars and other material values destroyed or damaged. And since one of the collective functions systematically performed by legislators, administrative officials, and cooperating citizens is to regulate motor traffic on public roads in such a way as to prevent moving cars from injuring persons and property, these multiplied transgressions of rules by car drivers have a cumulative disorganizing effect upon the regular performance of this function.

Not many of the prohibitive rules formulated in criminal law are explicitly based on the idea that the conduct described in these rules should be forbidden because it has a disturbing effect on the agent's own orderly life rather than on the order of the collectivity in which he participates. Such old legal rules as those which include suicide or the use of animals as sexual objects under the category of crime are derived from religion. However, modern legislators are increasingly concerned with the problem of preventing or stopping personal disorganization or demoralization. Legal enactments prohibiting the use of narcotics or alcohol, forbidding children and adolescents to attend immoral plays or to frequent places where "bad" adults congregate, prohibiting truancy, etc., are obviously intended for the good of those to whom they are addressed, inasmuch as repeated transgressions of these rules would presumably have a demoralizing influence upon their personalities.

The disturbing effects of nonconformity are probably most obvious in technical production; perhaps for that very reason prohibitive generalizations in this realm are not so numerous, so explicitly formulated, or so highly evaluative as in religion or law. Nevertheless, we do find such generalizations in many collectivities. When individual craftsmanship was fully developed, as it was in medieval Europe, deviations from standards and norms included in the total cultural pattern of a complex technical performance were expected so long as the individual was an apprentice, a candidate for a craftsman's role. But the master who entrusted the apprentice with certain simple auxiliary functions was supposed to take care that his deviations did not noticeably affect the final product, and to correct his mistakes, if necessary. Of course, if the apprentice disobeyed the master, his disobedience was condemned, and rules were formulated by some guilds to counteract such transgressions. But when an apprentice became an independent craftsman, he was expected regularly to conform without further guidance with the standards and norms of his craft. Although these standards and norms allowed for some variations and minor deviations, certain major deviations were explicitly prohibited, such as the use of materials definitely inferior in quality to those which other craftsmen used or of technical methods which were obviously much less exact and thorough than those of recognized masters. The products of a craftsman who transgressed those prohibitive rules were less valuable than the standards of his craft required. When such transgressions multiplied, they had a disorganizing effect upon the economic system of relationships between craftsmen and their customers, and eventually lowered the social prestige of the craftsmen as a class. Consequently, guilds endeavored to control the performances of individual craftsmen so as to prevent such effects.

In modern systems of industrial production, with a strict division of labor, the range of permissible deviations is usually narrower than in individual craftsmanship, for what a worker does, affects not only the course of his own performance, but also the course of the collective performance. When a worker's particular action deviates markedly from the norm which he is expected to follow or when he does not perform an action which he is supposed to perform at a certain stage of collective production, such deviation or omission disturbs in some degree that part of the total system of functionally interdependent actions in which he and some other workers are participating. If his function is that of an unskilled worker, this particular disturbance may be slight and easily corrected by himself or by others. But if he is a skilled worker and his technical action is important in the sense that many other actions depend upon it, correcting the disorganizing effects of his transgression may require some special collective effort. If he repeatedly transgresses the technical norms which he is expected to follow, regular conformity becomes increasingly difficult for other workers whose actions depend upon his; and if a number of workers fail to perform regularly the functions that are entrusted to them, the whole industrial system may become at least temporarily disorganized.

We can refer only briefly to the disorganizing effects which transgressions are supposed to have, and often really have, upon other categories of axionormatively organized systems. Thus, a thinker's transgressions of logical standards and norms—popularly called errors—disturb the orderly system of rational thought which constitute together an integrated philosophic or scientific theory; sometimes important errors in general premises can make the whole system logically inconsistent. When a short poem, e.g., a sonnet, is supposed to follow a definite aesthetic pattern, a single verse conflicting with the standards and norms with which other verses conform disturbs the aesthetic unity of the poem. When an aesthetically harmonized musical composition is played, a brief sequence of discordant sounds may destroy the harmony of the whole. When a painter follows a certain style, the introduction of a color or a shape which does not fit into the stylistic pattern appears as a distortion of the aesthetic order of the total painting. And if we go beyond the range of a particular cultural system of actions—producing or reproducing a theory, a poem, a composition, a painting—and remember that, when many particular systems follow the same general cultural pattern, a certain unity and continuity exists among them, we can understand why to faithful adherents of any ideology repeated transgressions of its standards and norms by thinkers, poets, musicians, painters who follow different patterns appear as gradual disintegration and decay of the philosophy, the literature, the music, the art in question.

Collective actions conflicting with the requirements of certain ideological models have, of course, greater disorganizing effects upon systems which conform with these models than individual transgressions. A united heretical group disturbs the orthodox religious system more than a number of unorganized individual unbelievers. An integrated revolutionary association can disorganize an established political system much more effectively than a loose mass of individual rebels. And in any active conflict—military, economic, or intellectual—between organized separate groups, actions of one group which seriously injure some of the values of the other and disturb its regular functioning are interpreted by the other group as radical collective transgressions of absolutely valid standards and norms with which the first group ought to have conformed.

Scientific studies of the causal relationship between transgressions and disorganization of cultural systems have to overcome certain methodical difficulties.

First of all, it is essential to distinguish between an investigation of the effects of transgressions, and a search for their causes, such as is being carried on by modern criminologists.[14] There is some connection between the two kinds of research, for the origin of an individual's nonconformity with certain cultural patterns can often be traced back to the disorganization of collective systems in which he participated or to conflicts between their requirements.[15] But this is not a problem of changes in cultural systems, but only of the evolution of the individual's personality. To solve it, his life history must be investigated.

Second, as in all attempts to solve causal problems, the investigator has to begin not with presumed causes, but with presumed effects, and then test his hypothetic conclusions by proceeding from causes to effects. This means that he has to study, first, not transgressions as such, but the cultural system which is supposedly affected by them, ascertain the axionormative organization of this system, observe the changes in its functioning which require a causal explanation, and see whether they can be explained by the influence of transgressions.

Third, he must combine the humanistic approach with scientific objectivity. A transgression has to be viewed by the investigator as it is defined by participants in the system, for its disorganizing effect upon the system depends upon the importance which they ascribe to it. On the other hand, he must also find how actions (or omissions of actions) which participants in a given system consider transgressions appear to the agents themselves. For— as we mentioned before—he may discover that these actions tend, as a matter of fact, to conform with the requirements of some other ideology which the agents accept and follow. If so, his investigation may result in a causal hypothesis which will contribute to the solution of a general problem in which

---

[14] Objective search for the causes of criminal behavior, initiated by the so-called "positive school" of criminology, was, as we know, a turning point in the history of criminological thought; it substituted a scientific approach to the phenomena included under the concept of crime for the old moralistic approach. The task, of course, has proved difficult, and explanations of criminal behavior vary considerably. Thus, Enrico Ferri, following Cesare Lombroso, assumes the existence of an "anthropological criminal type" whose innate biopsychological nature is the primary cause of crime: "The social environment has its base in the biological factor." *Criminal Sociology*, trans. by Joseph I. Kelley and John Lisle (Boston: Little, 1919), p. 76.

Gabriel Tarde in his *La Criminalité comparée* (Paris, 1886) and *La Philosophie pénale* (Paris, 1890) considers social causes predominant: crime, like all social phenomena, is a result of imitation. Edwin H. Sutherland, *Principles of Criminology* (Philadelphia: Lippincott, 1939), also seeks for causes of criminal behavior in social processes; unlike Tarde, he does not explain it by imitation, but by association with those who commit crimes (pp. 4-8). Donald R. Taft, *Criminology* (New York: Macmillan, 1950), views crime as a product of the general culture of a society (pp. 226-46).

[15] See, e.g., Sutherland, *op. cit.*, "Social disorganization is the basic cause of systematic criminal behavior" (p. 8). Cf. Robert E. L. Faris, *op. cit.*, p. 51: "If, as Cooley stated, personality is the subjective aspect of culture, it is to be expected that in a disorganized society personality would tend to be heterogeneous, individuated, disintegrated and demoralized" (p. 51).

students of cultural change or social change have been interested for a long time: the problem of disorganization and eventual disappearance of specific organized cultural systems—religious, political, technical, economic, intellectual, aesthetic—under the impact of other organized systems.

Finally, in seeking for causal generalizations, we must remember that the effects of certain influences to which a system is subjected can be modified by the effects of some other influences. If a system of actions is affected by repeated transgressions, and no other factors interfere with the disorganizing process, it becomes rapidly and completely disintegrated. Usually, however, especially when a system is collectively maintained, its participants tend to counteract disorganization. This is being done in two ways: repressing transgressions harmful to the system, and developing positive contributions to the system. Although they are often used together, we shall consider them separately; for each, if predominantly used, has different results.

Penalizing transgressions[16]

We are familiar with the age-old method of repressing transgressions by punishment. The use of this method is frequently explained in psychological terms. The primary motive of inflicting punishment is supposed to be vengeance for a wrong done. Thus, Westermarck explains the origin of all punitive repression by individual desire for revenge—revenge for harm done to the individual himself or to others with whom he sympathizes; the satisfaction of this desire compensates him for the suffering which the transgressor inflicted.[17] The secondary motive is supposed to be a desire for safety from future harm, coupled with the belief that fear of retaliation will have a deterring effect upon potential transgressors.[18] We do not deny the existence of either of these desires. But, while they may explain particular spontaneous reactions of small collectivities to harmful actions which destroyed or injured important common values—human lives or material possessions or sacred objects—they leave unexplained the regular punitive repression of all prohibited behavior (including omissions as well as commissions) by participants in an axionormatively organized cultural system. Nor do these psychological explanations help us discover the influence which such regular repressions have upon the system.

The key to both problems is that punitive actions in all collectivities with

[16] I discussed this kind of activity in *Social Actions* (pp. 345-408 and 690-98). The present approach, however, is somewhat different.

[17] Edward A. Westermarck, *Origin and Development of the Moral Ideas* (London, 1908), Vol. I.

[18] Cf. Oppenheimer, *op. cit.*, Book I. A different psychological theory of the motivation of punishment has been developed by psychoanalysts. See, e.g., Theodore Reik, *The Unknown Murderer* (London, 1936).

well-developed ideological models are *culturally patterned*.[19] They are expected to defend a collective system against agents who disturb its order. They are specifically *social* actions. Their objects are obviously not transgressions as such; they do not deal with such phenomena as sin, crime, vice, error in the abstract, but with transgressors as "human beings"— sinners, criminals, vicious men, fools. According to the popular conception of human nature, the primary cause of the transgression is some innate or acquired trait, disposition, characteristic, or behavior complex inherent in the transgressor. Since a transgression not only injures those who are affected by it, but also violates the principles on which an orderly system of actions is based, it constitutes an *offense* on the part of the transgressor against all who consider these principles binding. Consequently, every participant in the system ought to evaluate negatively the transgressor as a violator and an offender, and thus uphold the validity of the principles and the dignity of those who conform with them.

But negative valuation is not enough. For so long as the transgressor's nature remains unchanged, he will be a violator and an offender; his sinful, criminal, vicious, foolish disposition will make him continually inclined to disturb the right order and to injure its adherents. It is therefore an active duty of those who support the order to repress his transgressions by eliminating their cause. This is what all kinds of punitive actions are intended to achieve.

Punishments vary, depending on the definition and valuation of transgressors as offenders by participants in a cultural system, as well as on the importance of the standards and norms which they violate and the harmful effects of their transgressions.

Thus, the worst offenders are usually outsiders, who are not admitted as participants into the system upon which their actions have a disorganizing

[19] Comparative studies of punishment in different societies during various historical periods inevitably lead to this conclusion. Most criminologists give considerable attention to comparative penology, particularly in modern societies. See especially John L. Gillin, *Criminology and Penology*, 3d ed. (New York: Appleton-Century, 1945); and *Taming the Criminal* (New York: Macmillan, 1933). We mentioned previously some works devoted mainly to comparative surveys of punishment. Other general works on the subject deserve attention, such as Maurice Parmelee, *The Principles of Anthropology and Sociology in Their Relation to Criminal Procedures* (New York: Macmillan, 1908); George Rushe and Otto Kirchheimer, *Punishment and Social Structure* (New York: Columbia University Press, 1939). On punishment in nonliterate societies, see e.g., Rudolf S. Steinmetz, *Ethnologische Studien zur ersten Entwicklung der Strafe* (Leyden, 1894); Bronislaw Malinowski, *Crime and Custom in Savage Society* (New York: Harcourt, 1926); William I. Thomas, *Primitive Behavior* (New York: McGraw, 1937), chap. XV. On changing cultural patterns of punishment in modern societies, see, e.g., Harry E. Barnes, *The Repression of Crime* (New York: Doran, 1926); Raymond Saleilles, *The Individualization of Punishment*, trans. by R. S. Jastrot (Boston: Little, Brown, 1911); Hermann Mannheim, *Criminal Justice and Social Reconstruction* (London, 1946), normative plans for the future, rather than a theoretic study.

effect. The oldest and most persistent method of dealing with them is to destroy them. It was applied by tribal communities to individual strangers who on entering into the tribal territory presumably brought with them some evil forces and whose conduct violated the principles of order upon which the cultural life of the tribe was based. A woman who witnessed a magico-religious ritual reserved for men and an infidel who was present during a mystical ceremony profaned the sacredness of the performance and had to be killed. Wherever a strict caste hierarchy exists, a low-caste individual who disturbs the order maintained by a high-caste group is killed as an offensive outsider.

The application of this method to a whole group of outsiders, or an alien group, is well known. Since in intergroup conflict the standards and norms which one group considers right are apparently violated by the other, the behavior of the latter is an offense against the former. The attitude is reciprocal, and as each group collectively reacts to the offense of the other, each becomes to the other an evil enemy, a dangerous enemy, insofar as its collective actions are injurious to the other group and have a disorganizing effect upon it. Eliminating the enemy group is then not only the most efficient method of protecting "our" group against danger, but the right method, for it upholds the absolute validity of the principles which the enemy has violated and prevents their further violation.

The alien group must be disintegrated so as to make its organized collective transgressions impossible; the disintegration of a hostile state, a heretical sect, or a revolutionary association offers a typical example. But disintegration of the group is not enough. According to popular belief, the real offenders are human beings, members of the offending group. They are the bearers of those evil forces that caused the collective transgressions; it is the evil inherent in them which must be destroyed, and the simplest way to achieve this is to destroy their lives.

The scale of destruction of alien offenders which authoritative members of a group consider necessary to safeguard their group from harm and to prevent further violations may differ considerably. Quite a few instances have been reported in historical and ethnological literature where all participants in an alien group, irrespective of sex and age, were considered actual or potential enemies to be exterminated. This seems to have occurred occasionally, though not often, in intertribal warfare. The most conspicuous examples described in historical documents are those in which ideological conflicts led to physical destruction; whether these descriptions are reliable or not as records of facts, they are significant as indications of attitudes. Take, e.g., the extermination of the whole population of Jericho, presumably sanctioned by Jehovah; the wholesale killing of inhabitants of Jerusalem by crusaders after taking the city; the mass extermination of the Albigenses.

The most significant of all is, of course, the extermination of Jews, children as well as adults, by the Nazis, not only because of its unprecedented scale, planfulness, and thoroughness, but also because it was so explicitly and consistently rationalized as essential for the restoration and preservation of the Aryan racial purity and of the greatness of German culture.

More frequent has been the destruction of all those and only those alien offenders who had actively participated in the collective conflict. In tribal wars and in wars between city-states, sometimes all the men of the conquered group were killed, and the women and children were enslaved. Also during clan feuds and large family feuds, only the men were considered enemies to be killed. In many religious struggles, only those infidels who refused to be converted were destroyed. Mass annihilation of class enemies is usually limited to those who manifest active opposition: Roman slaves who joined Spartacus, peasants who participated in revolts, French aristocrats who opposed the revolutionary government under Robespierre; Russians who opposed Bolshevism after the October Revolution.

In most wars, killing enemies is mainly limited to the period of violent struggle; however, after the struggle victors may select and eliminate prominent individual offenders who presumably initiated the war and in so doing violated basic principles of order which the victors consider binding. The execution of enemy leaders in ancient Rome who in starting war broke the pacts they had concluded and the trial and execution of "war criminals" after World War II are well-known examples. Any subsequent rebellion against conquerors is frequently repressed by killing the rebels, sometimes also—as under the Nazi regime—by killing hostages or exterminating whole communities which presumably gave support to the rebels.

It is probable that death penalties inflicted upon individual *participants* in a cultural system originated in this traditional killing of alien offenders.[20] Any individual who has committed a serious offense against his own group may be considered as having voluntarily alienated himself from the group. "Apostates, heretics, and witches differ from other sinners in that they try to harm the religious group to which they belonged and to profane its religious system *after* having secretly or openly severed their bonds with it."[21] The apostate does this by joining an infidel group, the heretic by sharing with other heretics false opinions that conflict with holy truths, the witch by cooperating with an evil mystical being who is an enemy of the faithful and of the god whom they worship. A traitor differs from other criminals in that he began by breaking all moral communion with his own

[20] This hypothesis, as Ferri points out (*op. cit.*, p. 313) may be traced back to Spencer. See his *Principles of Sociology*, Vol. II, chap. XIII, "Primitive Identity of Military Institutions with Institutions of Administering Justice."

[21] Florian Znaniecki, *Social Actions*, chap. XII, "Repression of Criminal Behavior," p. 388.

group and allying himself with an enemy group; he was thus an outsider when he committed the crime of acting against the group to which he originally belonged. When an individual is convicted of such a sin or crime and not only excluded from participation in the group but condemned to death, it is often explicitly stated that he is an ally of dangerous, hostile powers. This is easier to assume when the hostile powers are supernatural than when they are human; for in the latter case some evidence of treason is needed, but evidence of treasonable *intentions* may be held sufficient. For instance, in the Soviet Union, individuals condemned to death are usually branded either as political or military traitors, actively cooperating with foreign states against the Union or at least as adherents of capitalism and consequently enemies of the working class, willing to overthrow the communist order.

Even when a criminal who is not a traitor—e.g., a murderer of a private person—is condemned to death, we often find a tendency to consider him as somebody who not only transgressed legal rules, but broke his bonds with the society of law-abiding citizens and thus, by explicitly acting against the principles upon which the unity of this society is based, became a public enemy, a dangerous outsider. He definitely ceases to be considered a participant before he is executed. However, relatively few individual participants in a collective system who transgress its standards and norms are treated as destructive alien enemies, sufficiently dangerous to be killed. Generally two other punitive methods are used to counteract transgressions.

The simpler method is to exclude the offender permanently from participation. This is punishment insofar as it deprives him of all the benefits which participants share; moreover, it upholds the validity of the principles of order which he has violated, restores the offended dignity of those who maintain this order, and at the same time safeguards the system from the disorganizing influence of any future transgression of his.

Excluding a tribesman from his tribe or a citizen from an ancient city-state (like early Rome) usually implied that he was expelled from the tribal or state territory, could not use anything in this territory—not even fire or water—for the satisfaction of his needs, and could not obtain assistance from other members, for any contact with him would profane them; nor would tribal or city gods help him. He might be killed by foreigners or by magico-religious powers roaming outside the territory, but this was not the concern of those who had expelled him. Excommunication of an incorrigible sinner and rebel against religious authority excluded him from participation in the community of the faithful and deprived him of all the benefits in this and the other life which the faithful gained from the god whom they worshiped. He might, and probably already had, come under the power of Satan, who would make him suffer permanently after death; but obviously it was not the function of the faithful to inflict such a penalty upon him.

Banishment of criminals to distant lands, uninhabited or sparsely inhabited, e.g., English criminals to Australia in the middle of the nineteenth century,[22] Russian criminal and political offenders to Siberia from the end of the eighteenth century to this day,[23] was intended to eliminate them as causes of disorder in their native society. And it was punishment, since exile deprived them of all social and economic advantages which law-abiding members of their society presumably enjoyed. In Siberia quite a few exiles died during the tsarist regime and many more are now dying under the present regime, due to unfavorable climate and insufficient means of subsistence; but death was not the main purpose of the government which had exiled them. The government usually helped them keep alive, under the condition, however, that they should either bring wild land under cultivation or work for the state. Firing a lazy, incompetent, or disobedient worker deprives him of his wages and separates him from his fellow workers; but the management is not concerned about what happens to him later, unless indeed he should be branded as a criminal *saboteur* and subjected to further punishment.

Exclusion of a harmful offender, however, is not always considered sufficient, for he may still be dangerous or even become more dangerous if he joins an enemy group. Nor can collectivities afford to exclude permanently all transgressors. Rare, indeed, are participants who never transgress. "Even a saint sins at least seven times a day." Most transgressions are committed by individuals who in other situations actually conform with the requirements of the system. Although a transgression which violates the principles of order shows that there is something bad inherent in the transgressor, the fact that at other times he did conform shows that there is also something good inherent in him. What the adherents of order believe they ought to do is to repress permanently the specific disposition that is the cause of his offense by inflicting a penalty which will make him suffer. The greater his offense, the stronger the bad disposition which caused it, and the more painful the punishment needed to repress it. But after he has suffered the penalty, his offense has been expiated, the badness inherent in him has been destroyed, and he will again become a conformist.

[22] Cf. Ives, *op. cit.*
[23] About Siberian exiles under the tsarist regime, see George Kennan, *Siberia and the Exile System* (New York: Century, 1891); under the Bolshevik regime, see, e.g., *International Committee for Political Prisoners, Letters from Russian Prisons* (New York: Boni, 1925); Vladimir M. Zannzinov, *The Road to Oblivion* (New York: McBride, 1935); David Y. Dallin and Boris I. Nicolaevsky, *Forced Labor in Soviet Russia* (New Haven: Yale University Press, 1947), based on a vast amount of material, mainly autobiographical. Many thousands of unpublished documents are available.

Removal of the evil member of the offender's body was the most realistic way of eliminating his badness: Sexual offenders were castrated, blasphemers had their tongues torn out, thieves their fingers cut off. Scourging to drive evil passions out of the body; bread-and-water diet to repress the palate's cravings for pleasure; public humiliation, if pride was the chief source of the offense; and hard forced labor to counteract laziness are typical forms of a penance aiming to eliminate the cause of transgressions. Even the gods purified sinners by subjecting them to expiatory punishments, as is shown by the myth of purgatory, still surviving to this day. Purification was especially effective when the offender imposed the penalty upon himself, as many self-conscious sinners did, and still do. Advice to sinners or breakers of taboos, which tells them how to purify themselves by self-inflicted, painful ordeals, is often contained in sacred books. Another presumably effective way of eliminating evil impulses is to confess the sin or crime and voluntarily submit to the penalty which authoritative guardians of order impose. In any case, an offender who, after having suffered a penalty, recognizes that it was good for him, because it destroyed his evil disposition, is apt to refrain from such offenses hereafter.

Imprisonment as a penalty represents a combination of the three chief methods used to counteract offenses. The prisoner is temporarily excluded from participation in his community and treated as a potentially dangerous outsider; he is isolated physically and guarded so as to prevent him from doing harm by his own efforts or allying himself with a hostile group. At the same time he is subjected to punishment sufficiently severe and long-lasting to destroy his badness; only after this has been achieved can he be again admitted to active participation in his society.

The idea that the adherents of order must penalize transgressions is perhaps most explicit and most widely applied in the realm of education.[24] An educand—child or adolescent—is not yet a fully active participant in cultural systems, but merely a future participant, a candidate. Certain adult participants endowed with authority assume the function of educators, to prepare him gradually for full participation. At every stage of this preparation, he must be taught to perform specific culturally patterned actions and be trained not to act in any way which conflicts with established standards and norms. During this educational process he is made continually aware that what educators require him to do is right, and ought to be done; what they prohibit is wrong, and ought not to be done.

If in spite of this awareness the young educand performs a prohibited action or does not perform a required action, such a transgression is considered a violation of those standards and norms which educators have im-

[24] I dealt with this problem in my *Sociology of Education*, in Polish (Warsaw, 1928-30), 2 vols.

parted to him and an offense against the authority of educators (currently termed "disobedience"). His transgressions are usually not so disturbing to cultural order as similar transgressions of adults, since generally he has not yet begun to participate in collective systems maintained by adults or, if he has, his participation is relatively unimportant. But they do disturb the normal function of educators and are presumed to have a disorganizing effect upon the formation of the educand's personality. And—what is most important from the popular point of view—they manifest the existence of certain characteristics in the educand which may become increasingly dangerous as he becomes a more active participant. Consequently, according to the principle prevalent in most societies with well-developed educational systems, it is a duty of the educator to repress those characteristics by punishment— a duty toward both the culturally organized adult collectivity and the educand himself. Punishment is expected to make the educand conscious of the badness or foolishness inherent in him and to inhibit its active manifestations. If the educator is unwilling to perform this duty or lacks the necessary power, a higher authority, a guardian of public order, takes over the task.

Investigations of the influence which punishment has upon individual transgressors have been carried on in modern times by criminologists, penologists, psychopathologists. Originally their humanitarian interests made investigators challenge both the doctrine that transgressions are caused by inherent badness of transgressors and the corresponding doctrine that painful punishment has a corrective effect, inasmuch as it eliminates this badness by repressing its manifestations. Objective comparative research has invalidated the second as well as the first doctrine, showing that the psychological effect of punishment is as complex a problem as that of the etiology of individual transgressions, and that no simple universal solution of either is possible.

One of the most significant results of this research is the increasing use of the psychopathological approach in explaining transgressions and of psychiatric methods in dealing with transgressions. A transgressor who is defined as a mentally sick person is not to be judged as a guilty violator or offender, for he is unable to think and to act in accordance with cultural patterns. The duty of conformists is not to punish but to cure him or, if incurable, to safeguard society by excluding him from participation, without inflicting unnecessary suffering upon him.

The conception of a psychologically abnormal transgressor who cannot be held fully responsible for his conduct is not entirely new. An individual's deviations and minor transgressions have often been tolerated because of an idea that this individual, though not bad, was intellectually incapable of acting as normal conformists do. In some religious groups, a major transgression, if accompanied by a manifestation of intellectual abnormality, was ascribed not to the individual's own evil nature, but to some powerful evil spirit who had gained possession of him; in this case, what had to be done was not to punish the human being, but to exorcise the evil spirit. Such attitudes, however, were relatively rare and applied only to exceptional, not to ordinary transgressors. With the development of modern psychopathology, transgressors—especially juvenile delinquents—are being increasingly defined as more or less psychopathic, and many of them are being subjected to psychotherapy.[25] However doubtful the validity of some psychopathological explanations of transgressions in general and however uncertain the effectiveness of some psychiatric methods, their development has certainly modified many of the old ways of dealing with transgressors.

[25] There has been considerable disagreement between psychopathologists and sociologists as to the relative importance of psychological abnormality as a factor of criminality. Most of them, however, agree nowadays that both psychological abnormality and criminality are largely due to the social or, more generally, the cultural conditions in which individual personalities grow. Consequently, most of them favor humanitarian treatment of criminals and psychopathic individuals, though their conceptions of the relative effectiveness of individualistic psychiatry versus applied sociology differ.

Reorganization of Cultural Systems

Conservative reorganization

Although a vast amount of research has been devoted to the study of transgressors, the causes of their nonconformity, and the effects which punishment has upon them, another aspect of punitive repression—even more important for cultural sciences—has been rather neglected. If we investigate repressive actions from the point of view of the agents who perform them, we find that they have considerable influence upon cultural systems.

Punishment of transgressors, whether inflicted by the whole collectivity or by its representatives, is a manifestation and a confirmation of the common belief of participants in a cultural system that the principles on which this system is based are valid. Furthermore, it manifests and confirms their common assumption that acceptance of these principles and conformity with their requirements endow the righteous with a superiority which no transgressor can challenge. Whether the harm which the transgressor did can be remedied or not, his punishment is expected to restore the ideological foundations of the system and the dignity of its adherents. And whether punishment actually prevents or does not prevent future transgressions of the offender, it really seems to strengthen the conformity and solidarity of those who actively or vicariously share in inflicting the punishment. There are exceptions, as we shall see; but after these are taken into account, considerable evidence remains that repressing other people's transgressions makes repressors themselves more conformistic and thus contributes to the conservation of the systems in which they participate.[1]

Let us now consider briefly the problem of the influence which collective struggle against a foreign enemy group has on the solidarity of those who participate in the struggle, on their loyalty to the ideology of their own group, and on the rising requirements of conformity of all members of the group

[1] This is implicit in the basic concepts of society and culture developed by the French school of sociology—Durkheim, Bouglé, Lévy-Bruhl, Davy, Duguit, Gurvitch.

with the order which the enemy endangers. This problem has not yet been thoroughly investigated, but some tentative conclusions are possible.[2]

Conflicts between religious groups are perhaps the most significant in this respect. The faithful who struggle against a group of infidels have no doubt that their enemies are bad, since they deny divine truth, rebel against the authority of god and his human representatives, and lead the weak and ignorant into sin. If the conflict has been accompanied by violence and if the enemy has used or presumably will use force to interfere with worship, to destroy sacred objects, and especially to harm the faithful, his offenses must be punished by force. A holy war, in which all the faithful actually or vicariously ally themselves with the powers of Good against the powers of Evil, seems the only solution. In surveying holy wars—wars of Moslems against pagans and Christians, wars of Christians against pagans and Moslems, wars of Catholics against medieval heretics and Protestants, wars of Protestants against Catholics—we find that these wars were usually strong unifying factors in that, while they were being carried on, various nonreligious conflicts between fellow believers were at least temporarily suspended. Moreover, the faith of believers in the absolute validity of their religious ideology was strengthened, and it seems also that active conformity with the requirements of this ideology increased. For instance, if the Spanish branch of the Roman Catholic Church became more conservative than other branches and its conformity more strict and exacting, this may have been due to its long struggle against Islam, its later expulsion of Moors and Jews, its active opposition to all forms of Protestantism, and the compulsory conversion of millions of Indians after the conquest of Central and South America.

Struggles between modern national groups, in the sense of groups sharing common and distinctive secular literary cultures, furnish other instructive examples.[3] When a group with alien culture presumably tends to destroy or to lower "our" national culture, to disintegrate "our" group, to exploit "our people" economically, or to dominate them politically, it becomes a bad and dangerous foreign enemy, especially if it uses the military or administrative power of a state to realize its harmful purposes. Defense against such an enemy not only strengthens the solidarity of the national group, but leads to the exaltation of its own culture as supremely valuable. The growth of Polish and Italian solidarity during the nineteenth century was greatly advanced by such struggles against foreign national groups. The ideas of German unification and the exaltation of German culture began to spread after the Napoleonic invasion (cf. its explicit public formulation by Fichte) ; and more than

---

[2] We shall devote considerable attention to this problem in a later work.

[3] A preliminary outline of a general theory of these groups and of their relationships written by me has been published in a Spanish translation: *Las sociedades de cultura nacional y sus relaciones, Jornadas,* 24 (El Colegio de México, 1944).

a century later Hitler and his associates, in trying to promote German unification under their leadership, continually referred to the need of common defense against foreign enemies of the German people who wanted to destroy German culture.

On the other hand, when a national group already dominates or tends to dominate another nationality, any attempt at active resistance or rebellion by the latter arouses the righteous indignation of the former as a challenge to its superiority, which has to be vindicated. Effective suppression of such resistance or rebellion increases the social solidarity of the dominant group and its belief in the supreme validity of its culture. This is, for instance, how English and Russian national consciousness and unity slowly grew through the centuries by a long series of conquests and repressions of rebellious tendencies of the conquered peoples, and how the victorious war of 1870-71 confirmed the idea of German greatness. Eventually prophets appear who explicitly proclaim that it is the mission of the victorious nationality to impose its superior culture and authority upon other nationalities, and this mission is eagerly undertaken by many active members of the group.

In order to strengthen the solidarity of the group, belief in the validity of its ideology, and active conformity with its requirements, the struggle against an enemy group must seem to be successful or at least on the verge of success. The righteous should be victorious and triumphant, their enemies defeated and humiliated, although the struggle may be long-lasting, with many partial victories and partial defeats. The group is always inclined to minimize its defeats. Some groups manifest remarkable perseverance, sustained by the hope that an ultimate victory is bound to come, however many the temporary defeats that precede it. Religious groups are especially apt to cherish such hopes founded on divine revelation, direct or indirect. Thus the Jewish group was able to maintain its religious system through nineteen centuries of struggles and persecutions. And many a Christian group expects that at the end of the world mankind will witness its final triumph, for God will then explicitly confirm its belief that it is absolutely right and that all its opponents are wrong.

The perseverance of some modern national groups in their struggle against enemies is even more remarkable, since no mystical belief that the group will be victorious in the supernatural world can offset its manifest defeats in the empirical world. In the struggle of the Polish national group against Russians and Germans between 1792 and 1918, six military attempts to preserve or regain national independence occurred, five of which ended in complete defeat; the sixth, which proved victorious, appeared hopeless in the beginning to outside observers. The new, complete defeat in 1939 was followed by a seventh attempt, much more difficult than the preceding ones. Still more protracted was the Irish struggle for independence from England, carried on in spite of serious conflicts within the Irish group.

Since, in intergroup struggles, belief that "our" group is right and the enemy group wrong is based on faith in the absolute validity of the standards and norms which "we" accept and which the enemy violates, an intensified *conservatism* is the usual consequence of the struggle. By *conservatism* we mean the determination of group members to preserve the perfection of their system or to restore its original perfection if this has been disturbed. Thus, in orthodox Judaism all the norms and prohibitive rules formulated in the Torah have been preserved. Every Christian group in its struggles against other groups traces its ideology back to the original divine revelation and accuses enemy groups of violating the principles of this revelation. In struggles between national groups, each group exalts its cultural past and traces its greatness as far back as possible. More recently, there have appeared, however, other trends which we shall survey presently.

In contrast with a collective offense committed by an alien enemy group, a single offense committed by an individual outsider, however harmful, can be rather easily counteracted; the isolated outsider alone does not represent any lasting danger. But gradual penetration into a collectivity of a number of foreigners, strangers, whose cultural patterns differ from those of native participants is apt to be dangerous. Plato ascribed the disorganization of Greek cities mainly to such alien influences. This danger increases when the strangers begin to participate actively in cultural systems which the collectivity maintains, because their cultural differences are supposed to have disorganizing effects upon these systems. Faithful adherents of the original order unite in its defense by expelling strangers or at least prohibiting under penalties the entrance of new strangers, excluding the strangers already present from participation in important systems, and repressing as punishable transgressions any conduct of strangers which does not fully conform with the requirements of the right order. Indeed, all disturbances of the right order may be ascribed to foreign influences. We are familiar with these phenomena from the modern history of peaceful mass migrations (as distinct from forcible group invasions). Active collective repression of the disturbing influences of strangers is expected to restore the original order as it presumably was before the strangers disturbed it; actually, it makes the repressors more ethnocentric and more sure of the absolute validity of the order which they are restoring.

Exclusion of an offending participant from the system which his conduct disturbed has also a stabilizing influence upon conformists, inasmuch as they are thus reminded of the benefits which he has lost and which they continue to share. Condemnation of a citizen in ancient Rome to life-long banishment and absolute isolation, like excommunication of a church member, seems to have been accompanied by an explicit enumeration of all the rights of which he was forever deprived. Such is apparently also the meaning of a decision by a modern court that an offender be deprived of civil rights.

Inflicting punishment upon sinners increases the conformity and solidarity of the righteous, who are conscious that they act on the side of their god against the forces of evil. This is especially noticeable in those religious groups where the responsibility of repressing sins does not rest entirely with priests, but is shared by the whole faithful community. When for certain sins sinners are severely punished in public, not only does the number of these sins decrease, but the righteous tend to raise the requirements of righteousness, so that what were once deviations or minor transgressions, subjected only to blame, eventually become punishable sins. This is what occurred, for instance, in several Puritan communities in New England during the eighteenth century.

Other significant examples of the influence which punitive repressions have upon the conformity of repressors are found in nineteenth-century military groups. The task of judging transgressors and condemning them to punishment was performed by officers with the assistance of noncommissioned officers, although obviously the majority of transgressors were ordinary soldiers. Professional officers, commissioned and noncommissioned, became not only the exponents and supporters of conformity with established standards and norms, but strict conformists and perfectionists, tending to make the requirements of military discipline increasingly detailed and exacting.

Although in modern political societies punitive repression of crimes legally defined as such is seldom carried on collectively by ordinary group members, but is entrusted to judicial and administrative authorities, still all law-abiding citizens, if called upon, must cooperate with these authorities. Cooperation may be actual, as when members of a jury and witnesses cooperate with the judge or when private citizens join the police in hunting down an escaped criminal. Or it may be only vicarious, as when citizens manifest positive interest in the repressive actions of prosecutors and judges, or in condemnatory statements express their negative interest in criminals. In either case, by taking the side of legislators, judges, and law administrators against criminals, they reaffirm their acceptance of the legal principles of order, strengthen their common belief in their own dignity, not only as conformists but as guardians of order, and dissociate themselves from criminals as inferior beings. This has a more powerful deterring influence than any fear of punishment. It is especially manifest when criminality, or at least a certain kind of criminality, is considered typical of lower-class people, whereas guardianship of order is assumed to be a function of the upper classes. There may be crimes, indeed, which lower classes have no opportunity to commit, such as Edwin H. Sutherland's "white collar crime"; and, obviously, the belief that criminals are inferior beings has little deterring effect upon this kind of crime.[4] Of course, for citizens to act as guardians of legal order, the standards and norms promulgated by legislators and enforced by administrators and judges must harmonize with those of other currently accepted ideological systems—moral, religious, and economic. If they do agree, their enforcement contributes to the stabilization of these ideologies also. If they do not, ideological disagreements result in social conflicts between official guardians of the legal systems and guardians of those other systems.

The modern development of a psychopathological approach to nonconformity, though it modified to some degree the methods of dealing with transgressors, has not weakened the belief of conformists in the validity of the ideological models which they accept and follow or in their own superiority; on the contrary, it has often strengthened this belief. For, if transgressions are manifestations of psychological abnormality, feeble-mindedness, or mental sickness, this implies that conformists are normal, strong-minded, mentally healthy, and gives additional proof that the established order which they support is right. At most, the frequent occurrence of transgressions shows that the established order does not provide adequate methods of preparing individuals for participation and preventing personal crises; and it is the self-assumed task of psychologists and psychiatrists to supplement this deficiency. Insofar as they do, they function as guardians of the social order and contribute to its conservation.

Cooperative repression of revolutionary movements emerging within a society is probably most influential in strengthening the solidarity and increasing the conservatism of conformistic participants in those systems which revolutionists are presumably attempting to disintegrate. Since revolutionists avowedly intend to use violent methods in their rebellion against the exponents and guardians of established order, they are branded as dangerous enemies of all law-abiding, peaceful people. Those who cooperate against them in defense of order are usually inclined to consider any other nonconformists, critics of the order, or opponents of authority as at least potentially dangerous; for their conduct may encourage the revolutionists in their efforts to disorganize the normal functioning of existing systems and thus help to prepare the way for a future revolution. Consequently, deviations, innovations, reformatory movements which might otherwise be tolerated are apt to be repressed; the goal of conformists is return to normalcy, restoration of order such as it was before the danger of revolution appeared.

On the other hand, after a revolution has been successfully carried out and reorganization has begun, fear of a counterrevolution results in the elimination by victorious ex-revolutionists of all overt or covert adherents of the old order, and leads to rapid stabilization of the new order, increasing re-

[4] Edwin H. Sutherland, *White Collar Crime* (New York: Dryden Press, 1949).

quirements for conformity, repression of all opposition or criticism and, finally, a conservatism which impedes further changes.

Very significant, though not yet adequately studied, is the influence which punitive repression of juvenile transgressions by educators has upon the educators themselves and upon the systems for which they are preparing educands.[5] In general, educators—parents and other relatives, elders, teachers, initiators, priests—function as representatives of adult society, morally responsible to present participants in the cultural order for adequate preparation of educands as future participants. When it is a duty of educators to punish educands for offenses of omission as well as of commission, for not doing what they are required to do acording to established standards and norms, as well as for doing something which is prohibited, educators come to consider the order for which they are preparing educands as absolutely valid and permanent, sure to remain without change long after the educands have been prepared for it. A comparative survey of various educational systems, past and present, has led me to the conclusion that the educators who regularly inflict punishment on educands are among the most conservative supporters of the established cultural order.

Thus, active repression of transgressions by participants in culturally ordered systems really prevents the systems from becoming disintegrated. We use the term "conservative reorganization" to denote the two main aspects of this activity. It is conservative, inasmuch as conformistic agents tend to preserve intact those ideological standards and norms on the basis of which their realistic system of actions is organized. It is reorganization, inasmuch as these agents continually have to perform individual and collective actions which keep their system functioning, notwithstanding the disorganizing effects of repeated transgressions, and which would be unnecessary if no transgressions disturbed its order.

Creative reorganization

Another way of counteracting the disorganization of a cultural system is to expand its positive functions, to make it increasingly valuable to participants, and to introduce positive bonds between its participants and participants in other systems, thus substituting cooperation for conflict. This means that new common values, new cultural patterns of action, new relationships of functional interdependence are introduced. As a result, a new, more dynamic organization is developed. We use the term "creative reorganization" to denote this development.

Such creative reorganization is usually more difficult and more protracted than conservative reorganization. It requires the more or less reflective evolution of an ideal and its gradual realization, cooperatively carried on by active

[5] Cf. my work on *Sociology of Education* mentioned previously.

leaders and growing circles of their followers (cf. Chapter 10). It has frequently been and still is impeded, either by active opposition of participants in other systems who consider innovations dangerous to the order which they maintain, or by a revival of conservatism among the participants of the new system.

1. In the realm of religion, the historical trend toward creative reorganization is characterized, first of all, by a gradual substitution of the conception of essentially benevolent, protective deities who reward every good action and guide men to happiness for vengeful deities who eagerly detect every transgression and condemn transgressors to suffering.[6] However unscientific and exaggerated the famous statement of Lucretius, "Fear made the gods," many modern historians of religion and ethnologists have found that usually (though not always) the type of religious system with fear of god as the basic principle of conformity developed earlier than the type with love of god as the leading ideal. Compare the "Lord God" of Exodus with "God the Father" of the Gospels. While in the first type of religious system, prohibitive rules are much more numerous, strict, and binding; in the second, positive norms predominate. While in the first, every sin must be expiated by punishment; in the second, it can be compensated by "good deeds" in excess of the obligatory positive requirements with which all believers are supposed to conform. The culmination of the idea of the supreme benevolence of God and a complete rejection of God the Vengeful is found in those modern Western ideologies in which the existence of hell and even of a painful purgatory is explicitly denied and in which all human souls are destined for happiness, though only after undergoing positive preparation under divine guidance in this or the other world.

Along with this development goes another: allowance of minor variations in conduct, which makes possible the incorporation into a system of components derived from other systems. This was exemplified during the expansion of Christianity by the toleration of many customs and mores found in various ethnic groups, the transformation of pagan holidays and celebrations into Christian holy days and ceremonies, the identification of old heroes with saints or the endowment of saints with the characteristics of heroes.

Increasing recognition of individual innovations as potentially valuable makes religious systems more adaptable to changing cultural conditions. In systems with an organized priesthood, opportunities for such innovations are usually limited to priests, and every innovation must be approved by authoritative clergy. Whereas in most democratic systems every participant, at least

---

[6] Evidence about these trends can be found in the works on history of religion mentioned in the preceding chapter and in the histories of certain modern religious denominations. See especially, Ernst Troelsch, *Die Soziallehren der Christlichen Kirchen und Gruppen* (Tubingen, 1923).

in principle, on his own initiative can attempt to introduce innovations which the group is free to accept and to develop collectively. For instance, the development of new functions by such religious groups as the Unitarians and the Quakers has been achieved by democratic leadership and followership. Relatively recent attempts to create common ideological bonds between diverse, originally exclusive, and conflicting religious systems have usually failed in the realm of theology, but quite a few of them have been successful in the realm of ethics, with the result that some active cooperation in solving social problems is going on among Protestants, Catholics, and Jews.

Of course, these trends in the history of religious systems have been neither continuous nor universal. Partial or complete returns to the older conception of God the Vengeful, with accompanying emphasis on the repression of sins as the only effective way of preserving the divinely established order, have occurred many times in the past and still occur. Old conflicts continue and new conflicts appear between mutually exclusive religious groups, each of which considers the other as essentially wrong because its ideas and actions violate absolutely right, divinely instituted principles. But violent punishment of sinners by the righteous is decreasing; indeed, punishment is either left to God or to the legal authorities when sinners are considered to be also criminals. And holy wars have become relatively rare and unimportant in comparison with secular wars.

2. Very instructive are the modern trends toward creative reorganization of collective industrial systems, especially in view of the type of organization which evolved when machine industry took the place of individual craftsmanship, and participation of workers in many technical systems became almost completely dehumanized. When ownership of the means of production was assumed by individual capitalists, corporations, or authoritatively ruled states, an industrial system was usually planned and organized not as a system of axionormatively ordered human actions dealing with objects which were values to the agents, but as a system of multiple, interdependent physical or chemical changes in instruments and materials—the workers' bodies, especially their hands, being the primary instruments. The task of every worker, according to this plan, was to cause repeatedly certain specific changes, defined in advance, by specific movements of his hands. Workers had no share in the ownership of the machines or materials which they used or in the products; they could not influence in any way the formation of the technical purposes of collective production, as defined in the total plan; indeed, many of them knew very little about the plan.

Some degree of social cooperation between workers was, of course, indispensable; but this was not entrusted to the workers themselves, only to foremen or superintendents, who had complete authority over workers. Since the worker had no direct interest in the realization of the technical plan, and his task, though requiring considerable time and effort, precluded any spontaneity that would make it interesting (like play) for its own sake, he performed it only if and insofar as he was granted economic remuneration. And inasmuch as the remuneration had to be deducted from the economic gains of the owners of industry, and the worker's positive individual contribution to the total collective product was relatively small, the tendency of industrial owners was to reduce the remuneration to the minimum necessary to make him work. To be 'sure, when new inventions were introduced into an industrial system at the decision of the owners, technical processes had to be in some measure replanned and reorganized, and some habits of the workers changed by retraining; but the basic principles of the system remained unchanged.

As is well known, disorganization of industrial systems under these conditions occurs frequently. First, in consequence of economic competition (conflicts between economic systems on which the functioning of private industrial production depends), privately owned productive systems, unprofitable to their owners, become dissolved; and when such dissolutions multiply, a general economic depression results. Second, even when economic conditions necessary for the continued existence of an industrial system remain relatively favorable, purely technical disturbances are apt to interfere with its functioning. These disturbances are directly caused by the nonconformity of the physical performances of workers with technological requirements of planners.

This technical nonconformity may be ascribed to inadequate preparation of workers for their specific jobs, their physical or mental subnormality, their laziness or unwillingness to work, their carelessness (resulting in accidents injurious to materials, machines, or the bodies of workers), or to explicit rebellion, organized or unorganized, of workers against the domination of their superiors. In any case, industrial owners and managers tend to consider workers whose nonconformity has a disorganizing effect upon technical systems as guilty of transgressions which must be repressed in order to restore the normal functioning of the systems. Under private ownership without state control, transgressions are repressed by economic penalties, effective in the measure in which the voluntary supply of labor exceeds the demand, since then being fired may mean starvation. Under state control, all transgressions of workers can be repressed by punishment, economic or physical, even though demand may equal or exceed supply, for a powerful government can coerce workers to participate in an industrial system whenever production is considered desirable. Thus, in the eighteenth century, local governments often compelled all kinds of vagrants to work in factories; and in the nineteenth century collective rebellions of workers were usually repressed in most countries by the governments. Under the Nazi regime, conformity of workers in industries considered necessary for the state was compulsory; moreover, during the war, millions of workers were imported from conquered countries and compelled to work in German factories, mines, and farms.

Many ideologists have objected to this dehumanization of industrial systems, this complete reduction of active individual participation to the repeated performance of specific, mostly simple technical actions, strictly regulated and planned in advance with exclusive regard to *material results* and without any consideration for the agents who performed them. Some ideologists have advocated a return to medieval craftsmanship, seeing no way to humanize machine industry and believing that once man has become a slave of machines he cannot regain mastery. Others, however, have offered a different solution: It is not the technical system as such that has to be reorganized, but the *social system* of relationships between the agents who together keep the technical systems functioning. Various terms have been used to denote the programs for this reorganization: communism, socialism, cooperativism, syndicalism, collectivism. But the leading principles of these programs are the same, though they differ in method and scope of application. We suggest the term "socialization of production" to cover all these diverse programs.[7]

The first common and familiar principle is to have all active participants in a productive system share the ownership of all the objects with which their actions deal—the land on which the system is located, buildings, machines, materials, and products. This means that these objects become common values to all the agents, all assume responsibility for their effective use, and the benefits of collective production are shared by all.

The second is the principle of democracy, according to which social organization is based upon relationships of leadership and followership rather than upon domination and submission. This means that new problems relevant to the functioning of the system as a whole are solved not by arbitrary decisions of authoritative rulers, imposed upon subjects, but by mutual understanding and cooperation between planners and organizers accepted by the group as leaders and the other group members as voluntary followers. Thus, the system becomes more dynamic, especially when new inventions are introduced which require the replanning and reorganization of technical activities, since adequate understanding of a new plan by workers and their willingness to cooperate with leaders facilitate its realization and prevent resistance to changes. Moreover, in a democratic organization not only leaders but followers can offer new solutions of technical problems and make new inventions which may be introduced into the system with the cooperation of the group.

The third principle which overcomes the impersonal character of participation in large industrial systems is positive personal valuation of every indi-

---

[7] Some of the works on the development of socialist thought which were mentioned in Chapter 10—e.g., Laidler, Beer, Bourguin—contain materials on the practical application of these ideals.

vidual participant. It is manifested in the relative security of economic status granted to all participants, recognition of past achievement as meritorious, and continued opportunites offered for future achievements. Recognition of merit may take the form of economic or honorific awards granted for supererogatory achievements exceeding the normative requirements for all who perform similar functions, and also for long-lasting regular fulfillment of obligations. It is an old method used in various authoritarian groups, e.g., militaristic and bureaucratic, where the judges of merit were the ruling members, and merit was graded according to gradation of status. Its use in a democratically organized group differs from the former use in that recognition is granted by the group as a whole, and merit is graded not by the status of members, but by the relative importance of their factual contributions to the functioning of the group. Individuals who have manifested superior ability are offered an opportunity for future achievements in the form of promotion to more important roles. And individuals who have failed to perform their specific tasks are entrusted with different tasks more adapted to their personal abilities and interests, or are re-educated.

The ideal of socialization of production has had a growing influence upon the factual organization of technical systems. This influence is manifested in three historical trends. Its earliest manifestation was the organization of collective agricultural and/or industrial systems by various relatively small groups in countries with a predominant capitalist economy. Quite a few of these groups were religious or ethnic and attempted to achieve economic self-sufficiency; but this proved impossible in the long run except in a few isolated areas. Eventually, cooperative productive associations, specializing in making and marketing certain products, began to develop; they differ considerably in relative proportion of collective versus individual ownership of means of production.

From the second half of the nineteenth century on, as the ideal of socialization in some form or other spread in many countries among all classes of people, its principles began to influence directly or indirectly the active adherents of capitalist economy.[8] Partial reorganization in accordance with these

[8] In a later work we intend to use descriptions of paternalistic industrial organizations, with owners or managers functioning as wise and benevolent rulers who maintain complete control over workers, but are personally interested in their security and welfare. This role is similar to that of a lord who, under the influence of Christianity, benevolently aided and guided his serfs.

As to the impact of trade unions or labor unions upon the humanization of industry, we need only refer to a few well-known historical works: ed. John R. Commons, *Trade Unionism and Labor Problems* (Boston: Ginn, new ed., 1921); Sidney and Beatrice Webb, *The History of Trade Unionism* (London, 1894); *Industrial Democracy* (London, 1897), 2 vols.; Charles Gide, *Economie sociale: Les Institutions du progrès social* (Paris, 1912); Wilhelm Kulemann, *Die Berufsvereine*, Part I, "Geschichtliche Entwicklung der Berufsorganisationen Arbeitnehmer und Arbeitgeber aller Länder" (Jena, 1908), especially Vol. II.

principles has occurred and is occurring in many particular industrial systems owned and controlled by individual capitalists, private corporations, and public associations, sometimes at the initiative of owners and/or managers, more often in recent times under the pressure of labor unions. Many monographs have been published on this subject, showing that the principle of positive personal valuation of workers has been much more widely recognized and more effectively applied than either the principle of the workers' share in ownership or the principle of democratic relationships between workers and managers.

Most influential, of course, have been the well-known efforts of powerful socialist groups to reorganize the entire production in large politically circumscribed territories; their results are very significant from the point of view of theorists of culture.

The main difficulty which ideological planners and active organizers of collectively owned and democratically maintained industrial systems have been facing is how to develop continuous cooperation among all the numerous and diverse productive groups which compose a modern industrial society. Such cooperation is essential in order to satisfy adequately and regularly the wants of members of the society and to prevent the recurrence of such phenomena as poverty, dependency, nonemployment, depression, which are considered typical of capitalistic economy. Some socialists think that this cooperation should be achieved by the productive groups themselves. As a matter of fact, however, when socialism is introduced into a society at the initiation of a political government, with or without revolution, it is the government which assumes the task of coordinating production and distribution within the state. To perform this task in accordance with the principles of socialist ideology, governmental planning must be carried on by a cooperating group of creative technological and economic thinkers who are not only fully acquainted with actual problems, but aware that the development of production will raise new problems and require changes in their plans. Progressive realization of their plans should be achieved by initiating and organizing voluntary cooperation among leaders accepted by democratic productive groups rather than by coercive use of political power; moreover, in the total course of developing and coordinating production and distribution, consideration for human persons as social values should have priority over impersonal striving for technical efficiency. Obviously, such a complex and difficult function assumed by the government requires considerable creative reorganization of the government itself in order to change it from a ruling group into a leading group.[9]

[9] Part of this difficulty lies in efforts to develop cooperation between agricultural and industrial groups. Cf. Maurice Dobb, *Soviet Economic Development since 1917* (London, 1949), chap. VIII, "The Problem of Industrialization," and chap. IX, "The Agrarian Situation on Eve of the First Five-year Plan," pp. 177-229.

The history of Soviet Russia shows what happens when a new socialist government reverts to the old type of autocratic government and imposes its plans of total production by compulsory methods. When technical systems began to be reorganized after the Bolshevik Revolution, the three principles of socialist ideology mentioned previously were at first adopted.[10] But when the government secured absolute political control, the method of coercive rule was gradually substituted for the method of democratic leadership. The government increasingly monopolized the function of integrating all technically productive systems, not only in Soviet Russia but in the whole Union of Soviet Socialist Republics. To achieve this integration as rapidly as possible, the autonomy of particular industrial groups had to be curtailed. This was in apparent agreement with communist ideology as interpreted by the Bolsheviks: The means of production were not owned by the particular group of workers who actually used them, nor did the products belong to the group that produced them, but both means and products were the property of the whole communist society; it was the right and duty of the government which represented this society to regulate all production and distribute all products.[11] Nor was much democracy left within industrial groups. Industrial production was planned by the dominating governmental group; the particular industrial groups did not participate in the planning, but each group had to realize that part of the plan which was allotted to it.[12] The principle of positive valuation

[10] Nominally, of course, they continue to be accepted and have actually been applied in some measure, though their application changed considerably in the course of time and at any one time differed in various industries and various parts of the Soviet Union. For an optimistic survey of their application before the war, see Harry F. Ward, *In Place of Profit, Social Incentive in the Soviet Union* (New York: Scribner, 1933).

[11] "The Communists . . . constantly emphasize the doctrine that the industry of the country belongs to the workers as a whole and that any individual factory or any single industry is not the property of those who work therein." (The opposite doctrine was termed "syndicalism" and branded as dangerous.) "Because of this belief, the Communist government early nationalized the factories and took an increasingly large share of actual direction of production away from factory centers and lodged it with the Supreme Council of National Economy and with the State trusts," *Soviet Russia in the Second Decade. A Joint Survey by the Technical Staff of the First American Trade Union Delegation*, eds. Stuart Chase, Robert Dunn, and Rexford G. Tugwell (New York: Day, 1928).

Aron Yugoff, *Economic Trends in Soviet Russia*, trans. by Eden and Cedar Paul (London, 1930), mentions "two conflicting tendencies, the tendency toward centralization and that toward decentralization. For brief periods, at critical moments, decentralization gets the upper hand; but always, ere long, there has been a return to centralization" (p. 73). For an excellent analysis of the control exercised at this time over the total group of participants in a factory, see Alexander Vucinich, "The Structure of Factory Control in the Soviet Union," *Am. Sociol. Rev.*, April, 1950, Vol. XV, No. 2, pp. 179-86.

[12] The workers, however, or at least a certain proportion of them, participate in some measure in productive conferences, which influence the management of production within the limits imposed by the central government, although the final decision as to which, if any, suggestions of workers should be applied in practice rests with the manager.

of workers ceased to be generally applied,[13] partly because rapid development of industry for the future benefit of communist society as a whole became the supreme goal of rulers. And technical values assumed greater importance than living individual workers as social values, partly because of the general negative valuation of a large proportion of the Russian population as nonconformists, whose failure to follow the commands of rulers is considered denial of the principles of communism and consequently an offense against the authority of those who promulgate and maintain these principles. Thus, throughout the Soviet Union the satisfaction of the workers' present wants has been subordinated to the program of machine industrialization.[14]

Moreover, in order to hasten and expand the development of the technical production presumably necessary for the good of the Soviet Union, the government assumed the task of utilizing hitherto unexploited or insufficiently exploited natural resources in northeastern Europe and in Siberia. Since efficient and conformist workers were unwilling to move to such areas and, in any case, could not be spared from participation in the technical systems already developed, the labor needed for those enterprises was recruited by force from among nonconformists. It included ordinary criminals; political offenders who had proved to be disloyal or who were suspected of disloyalty to the regime; peasants resisting collectivization; industrial workers who had left their jobs without permission, who had not appeared regularly, or who had failed to perform adequately their appointed tasks; and managers of factories which produced less goods or goods of inferior quality than the government required. From 1939 on, such sources of labor rapidly increased. Millions of actual or potential foreign enemies—Poles, Lithuanians, Latvians, Estonians, Germans, Rumanians, Hungarians, Japanese—became accessible,

---

The origin and spread of the Stakhanow movement, "a movement to rationalize working methods that arise from the initiative of the workers themselves," when not abused by the government in order to raise repeatedly the minimum standard of output, is definitely democratic. Cf. Dobb, *op. cit.*, pp. 429 ff. As to some typical later abuses, see E. Strauss, *Soviet Russia* (London, 1941), pp. 281-83.

[13] Or, to state it more mildly, it has ceased to be generally applied as the supreme and most important standard. Its limited application is manifested, among others, in the main function of the trade unions. "The functions of the trade union were defined in part in the following terms at a meeting of the Trade Union Council in 1939: 'To help the workers improve their technical skill, to encourage socialist competition, to see that the workers do not get more sickness and disability benefits than they are entitled to,'" William H. Chamberlin, *The Russian Enigma* (New York: Scribner, 1944), pp. 171-72. Of course, the underlying idea is that the chief task of trade unions in capitalist countries—that of protecting the personal worth and welfare of workers—is unnecessary in communist Russia, since the whole communist system is based on the positive valuation of workers as a class. As a matter of fact, however, any particular worker is evaluated not as an individual, but as an active, useful, and loyal participant in communist society.

[14] This subordination became even more thorough when a large proportion of the machine industry was devoted to preparation for war.

as well as members of nationalities within the Soviet Union who during the war had manifested some rebellion against Russian domination—Ukrainians, White Ruthenians, Tartars of the Crimea, German settlers on the Volga, Uzbeks. Thus, all nonconformists who either had lost their rights as participants because of their transgressions or had no rights because they had never participated in the Soviet Union or had fought against it could nonetheless be useful to the communist society, if compelled under severe penalties to work for its benefit at the lowest possible cost to the government.[15]

However, voluntary cooperation of groups of workers for common productive purposes has not disappeared, though the organization and functioning of these groups is subjected to political domination. During the war, when defense against foreign invasion strengthened national solidarity, many such groups—industrial and agricultural—were observed.[16] They were, and still are, mostly composed of younger workers who from early childhood learned to accept political domination as necessary and desirable and to consider political rulers as benevolent heroes acting for the good of the people and protecting the people against enemies. Within this unshakable political frame, they have been trained for cooperative technical work. The particular industrial system in which they participate is a common value for all participants; honorific and economic awards are granted for supererogatory achievements, opportunities are offered for later advance to more important positions, and minor innovations are encouraged.[17]

3. We shall briefly mention here two other historical trends toward creative reorganization. One of them, probably the most effective of all and the best known, has been manifested during the last three centuries in the realm of scientific theory.

The postulate of classical thinkers, that a valid theory must be a logically consistent system of truths without any errors, presupposes that the system has been completed, that all the judgments it contains have been proved true, and that all false judgments have been eliminated from it. Under this postulate, if a new theoretic system was formed which was logically consistent but in-

[15] Cf. Dallin and Nicolaevsky, *op. cit.*

[16] The Nazi invasion of Poland and the large-scale destruction of Polish industry had similar aftereffects. From 1946 to 1950 an unprecedented, largely spontaneous cooperation of Polish workers was noticeable in the reconstruction and development of industries socialized by the communist regime.

[17] There is another, very important aspect of the social organization of industrial groups in the Soviet Union. "The life of the Russian worker centers around his factory . . . [the latter] is not looked upon as simply a dirty work place . . . one could spend practically a whole life in a Soviet factory and have one's social and generally cultural and artistic demands reasonably well satisfied . . . something is provided for every member of the family." Anna Louise Strong, "Worker's Life in Soviet Russia," published in *Soviet Russia in the Second Decade* (see fn. 11), p. 200. This is what some "company unions" in the United States have been trying to do in order to promote the loyalty of their workers to the company.

cluded judgments contradicting some judgments included in a previous system, one of these systems had to be rejected in its entirety as false. Such was the original issue between the astronomical and physical theories held by later medieval scholars and the new theories formed by creative scientists in the sixteenth and seventeenth centuries. The postulate is still widely used in teaching. Teachers usually transmit to learners only validated and systematized results of scientific research, and learners are trained to distinguish between objective truths contained in such systems and their own subjective errors.

But, if a modern scientific investigator applies a systematic theory to facts to which it has not been applied before, and finds that this application invalidates some generalization included in the theory, he does not think of eliminating the error or rejecting the theory as logically inconsistent. He merely concludes that the theory is not yet completed, that its components must be judged not as unconditionally valid truths or invalid errors, but as conditionally valid hypotheses. The theory then becomes problematized and leads to further research, new discoveries, new hypotheses, and new systematization.

The other, more inclusive and perhaps historically more important trend toward creative reorganization can be observed in the modern evolution of national cultures and of the societies which maintain them. While struggles between these societies still go on, mostly through the agency of economic, political, and military groups which support conservative ethnocentrism and negative valuation of foreign cultures, nevertheless, within almost every society, increasing effort is devoted by intellectual leaders and associations to new creative growth of its culture. In the course of this growth, the creative products of other cultural societies are used; gradually, purposive, cooperative cross-fertilization of cultures develops; and finally, the ideal of a supernational world culture as the common creative product of many nationalities begins to emerge. I have investigated this trend for many years and am trying to systematize the results of this investigation.

4. Whenever and wherever creative reorganization of collectively maintained cultural systems is substituted for conservative reorganization, sooner or later educational methods undergo a similar change. Educators eventually become aware that, though some degree of punitive repression may be necessary at early stages of the child's growth to supplement positive awards, continued use of penalties for nonconformity impedes the development of innovating tendencies; and, further, that continued submission to the domination of adults prevents development of leadership in children. Consequently, new methods are invented to prepare educands for participation in cultural systems where innovation is positively valued and social relationships between participants are democratic rather than autocratic. Comparative studies of this reorganization of educational systems and of its influence upon the later

participation of educands in other cultural systems began some thirty years ago, but as yet we find no adequate systematization of their results.

Summary and tentative conclusions

We raised the problem of scientific generalizations about actions which do not conform with cultural standards and norms. Numerous classifications of such actions are contained in prohibitive rules formulated by ideological thinkers, but we found that, when judged by the principles of scientific taxonomy, they are theoretically invalid. Ideological thinkers often include under the same general class actions which conflict with certain standards and norms and also failures to act in accordance with these standards and norms. Actions which conform with the requirements of one ideology may be prohibited by adherents of another as conflicting with its standards and norms. Actions which adherents of one ideology prohibit may be neither prohibited nor required by adherents of other ideologies.

There is, thus, no such logical category of phenomena as nonconformity in general, which could be investigated apart from conformistic conduct. Cultural scientists can only study transgressions of specific cultural requirements by agents whom adherents of a given ideology expect to conform with these requirements. Such transgressions are scientifically significant for students of axionormatively organized systems of actions; if and insofar as they have disorganizing effects upon the functioning of these systems, their effects can be objectively investigated, and eventually causal generalizations can be reached. This should enable scientists to explain why many cultural systems of actions—religious, technical, economic, aesthetic, intellectual, social—become disintegrated and disappear. Cultural scientists should not accept the theory advanced by some thinkers that the inner structure of every cultural system makes its eventual disintegration a necessity. Only a particular action planned to end as soon as its purpose is realized has a duration limited by its very organization. Whenever a system of functionally interdependent actions which is originally organized in such a way as to make it last indefinitely becomes disintegrated, this needs a causal explanation. Such an explanation is provided by the disorganizing influence of repeated transgressions by its participants and/or of actions performed by outsiders, nonparticipants, which conflict with its requirements and interfere with its functioning.

Especially significant scientifically are the tendencies of participants in a system to defend it against transgressors and to restore conformity with its axionormatic order—what we have termed conservative reorganization. For these tendencies strengthen the belief of conformists in the validity of their common ideology and increase their solidarity. This explains why certain cultural systems, though subjected to disorganizing influences, not only do not disintegrate but become even more closely integrated and preserve for a long time—sometimes for centuries—the main ideological principles on which their order is based.

In studies both of disorganization and of conservative reorganization the problem is raised: Can their hypothetic conclusions be tested by the use of exact quantitative methods? Criminal statistics have been used by some investigators under the assumption that criminality is a symptom of social disorganization and that the increase or decrease of the latter can be measured by the increase or decrease in the number of crimes. But the problem is not so simple. In view of the vast factual evidence, there can be no doubt that crimes, like other transgressions, are not mere symptoms but causes of disorganization. And disorganization itself is a sequence of changes which occur within an organized system. It can be measured only if we know the system, ascertain the changes which it undergoes, compare them with changes occurring in other systems, and devise a scale for grading them according to their relative importance, with final disintegration as the limit. Only then can quantitative generalizations about causal relations between multiplication of transgressions and increase of disorganization be made, and eventually the assumption can be tested that increase of disorganization has a reciprocal effect upon multiplication of transgressions.

As for the influence of organized repression of transgressions upon a cultural system, although sociologists long ago found that collective defense of group values against outsiders who endanger these values increases the loyalty of group members and the solidarity of the group, few methodical attempts have been made to measure this process. Some measurements of morale have been made, but they are almost exclusively measurements of attitudes and do not include any quantitative studies of the conformistic *actions* performed by participants in a system in trying to protect it from disorganizing influences. There seems to be no reason, however, why such research should not develop in the future, though it will probably be difficult to devise exact standards of measurement which will be both reliable and valid.

The study of creative reorganization of cultural systems of actions is of primary importance for the history of culture, for it opens the way to generalization about the appearance of *new varieties* of systems. In our brief survey of the evolution of ideals (Chapter 10), we made the hypothetic statement that new ideals are initiated by thinkers who become aware of persistent conflicts within or between human collectivities and believe that the realization of their ideals would substitute harmony for conflict. And this is what creative reorganization of cultural systems is intended to achieve.

Thus, new varieties of cultural systems of actions are not, as determinists assert, necessary effects of the multiple causative forces which preceded their appearance; nor are they, as some humanistic philosophers believe, scientifically inexplicable manifestations of creative will, human if not divine. Although new cultural systems emerge out of previous systems, their emergence is a creative process in the sense that, insofar as they are different from those from which they emerged, their composition and organization cannot be predicted in advance by any causal laws. On the other hand, when these creative processes are investigated in their total course, their results are explicable, provided the genetic rather than the causal approach is used. From comparative studies of such processes it may be possible to reach conclusions about the evolution of specific classes of cultural systems—religious, technical, economic, etc.—perhaps even to develop a general theory of *cultural evolution*, just as biologists are developing a general theory of organic evolution by means of comparative studies of the processes of emergence of new variants. The fact that first attempts to apply an evolutionary approach in studying the history of culture—especially the attempts of Spencer and Leonard T. Hobhouse—could not be scientifically validated does not mean that such an approach is impossible, only that the methods which those theorists used were defective.

Students of cultural phenomena should reject once and forever the doctrine initiated by nineteenth-century naturalistic philosophers, according to which it is impossible to develop theoretically valid sciences of culture as such, independent of natural sciences, because there is no distinct factual order in the world of culture irreducible to the order of the natural universe. Any investigator of cultural phenomena, whatever his specialty, provided he uses the universally recognized methodical principles which all theoretic scientists follow, can expect to find within his realm of culture four categories of dynamic factual order. These are, as we have seen, the order of *conformity* of particular actions as systems of values with cultural standards and norms; the order of *functional interdependence* within axionormatively organized systems of actions; the *causal* order of relationships between changes in actions and systems of actions and extraneous influences to which they are subjected; and the *genetic* order of emergence of new systems. If the investigator consistently limits his research to cultural phenomena and does not attempt to act also as a natural scientist—biologist, chemist, physicist, geologist, astronomer—he will be able to reach taxonomic, functional, causal, and genetic hypotheses which, though perhaps more doubtful and less exact than those of physical or even biological sciences, can be validated or invalidated *exclusively* by empirical evidence derived by him and other cultural scientists from the observation of *cultural* data and facts. This does not mean that he will not need the aid of natural scientists in solving some problems which cultural research alone must leave unsolved. Since the very existence of cultural systems obviously depends upon definite natural conditions, causes of cultural changes which cannot be explained by cultural influences must be sought in changes of those conditions.

The Function of Sociology
as Cultural Science

Specialization among cultural scientists

During the last two centuries, specialization has been steadily increasing among cultural scientists, just as among natural scientists, as a result of the enormous wealth of empirical material made available to all scientists. Historians and ethnologists have discovered or recovered cultural data and facts previously unobserved or forgotten, while innumerable and widely diversified new data and facts are continually emerging in the course of the creative growth of modern cultures. Obviously, no individual scientist can become acquainted with all this material.

Specialization proceeds mainly in two ways. Some investigators devote their efforts to the study of particular total cultures or civilizations developed and maintained during certain historical periods by collectivities inhabiting certain territories. Thus, we have specialists in the cultural history of ancient Egypt, Greece, Rome, medieval Western Europe, Italy, France, Germany, India, China, etc. Each specialist is acquainted with the results of studies of his predecessors, and each hopes to add something new to those results. As the amount of knowledge concerning any civilization increases, an individual investigator in order to make new additions may have to specialize still further, by limiting his research to a certain portion of the total historical period or to a certain area within the total territory. An ethnologist or cultural anthropologist, investigating smaller collectivities and simpler cultures through brief periods of their duration, does not have to specialize in one culture, but can cover in the course of his life quite a few particular cultures. Even here, however, we find individual investigators more and more inclined to specialize in cultures which are maintained by collectivities located within limited areas and which have certain characteristics in common.

The other familiar trend toward specialization is the one on which in preceding chapters we based the distinction between different realms of culture. It has resulted in the development of the following cultural sciences, already recognized as such, though not equally advanced: political science, more or less closely connected with the history and theory of law; economics; sociology; religionistics; linguistics, with its many subdivisions; comparative science of material techniques, also subdivided; inductive studies of knowledge; theory of literature; comparative studies of plastic arts; objective musicology. This differentiation is based on the assumption that the cultural phenomena included in each of these categories are essentially similar and essentially different from those included in the other categories. We found this assumption at least partly justified in comparing religious, technical, social, intellectual, artistic actions. According to this assumption, although particular cultural phenomena of each of these categories may be found in collectivities with many diverse cultures, past and present, yet for comparative purposes it is possible to abstract them from these total cultures and, while taking into consideration their historical differences, to reach scientifically valid generalizations about them.

These two trends toward specialization often overlap. For instance, a specialist in a particular total culture may add to the agglomerated knowledge about that culture by concentrating on one of the recognized categories of cultural phenomena which it includes—language, literature, art, religion, law, economic organization. On the other hand, a political scientist, economist, religionist, linguist, theorist of art frequently limits his investigation to the cultural phenomena of this category to be found in a particular territorial collectivity during a particular historical period.

Attempts to develop a general theory of culture

From the very beginning the specialization of historians and ethnographers aroused considerable opposition from philosophers, for the numerous and diverse new discoveries made by them in their respective fields constituted a challenge to metaphysical doctrines of a universal, perfectly consistent order regulating the entire history of mankind, past, present, and future. Philosophers met this challenge by attempting to integrate and systematize what they judged to be the most significant results of historical and ethnographic research.

It would take too long to criticize here the theories of such famous thinkers as Vico, Condorcet, Herder, Hegel, and their successors. Each of them tried to develop an inclusive theory of culture in general, based on studies of total particular cultures. Such a theory needed three kinds of generalization. First, it was necessary to prove that no particular culture was absolutely unique by discovering some essential similarities between it and other cultures, underlying their differences. Second, since each culture changes in the course of its duration, some generalizations about these changes were indispensable. Third, since the history of each culture is only a part of the total cultural history of mankind, some genetic connections had to be found between it and the other cultures which preceded and followed it.

The combination of these three tasks was difficult even in the eighteenth century and proved gradually impossible, as historical and ethnological knowledge about particular cultures steadily grew. Consequently, by the end of the nineteenth century they became separated. The search for similarities between total cultures led to the typological classifications initiated by some philosophers of history and lately developed by cultural anthropologists.[1] The search for regularities in changes of cultures resulted in several laws, such as those formulated by Spengler[2] and Toynbee.[3] The search for genetic connections between total cultures in the entire course of human history led to a partial revival of the old doctrine of the origin of later civilizations in an earlier common center, from which they presumably emerged through migration and diffusion.[4]

The gradual formation of separate sciences, each dealing with a distinct category of cultural phenomena abstracted from total historical cultures, was

[1] Heuristically the most valuable, but also the most complex (because including several partly overlapping types), is the typology of societies developed by Howard Becker. Cf. his latest collection of essays, *Through Values to Social Interpretation* (Durham, N. C.: Duke University Press, 1950).

[2] Oswald Spengler, *Der Untergang des Abendlandes*, 2 vols. (1920-22).

[3] Arnold J. Toynbee, *A Study of History* (Oxford, 1948), 4th impression, 5 vols.: "The intelligible fields of historical study are societies which have a greater extension in both space and time than national states or city-states or any other political communities" (Vol. I, pp. 44-45). Such societies are "indivisible wholes," "independent entities" (p. 45). They represent the same species, for each of them is united by a common civilization. Toynbee distinguishes twenty-one such societies: Egyptian, Andean, Sinic, Minoan, Sumerian, Mayan, Syrian, Indic, Hittite, Hellenic, Western, Orthodox Christian (in Russia), Orthodox Christian (main body), Far Eastern (Korea and Japan), Far Eastern (main body), Iranic, Arabic, Hindic, Mexican, Yucatean, and Babylonian (p. 133). They are different from "primitive societies" (pp. 177-78). The generalizations presumably applicable to all of them concern first their genesis, which is due in every case to the factor called "Challenge-and-Response"; the "Challenge" is a "Stimulus," of which there are several varieties (Vol. II). All of them undergo a process of "Growth" (Vol. III), "Breakdown" (Vol. IV), and "Final Disintegration" (Vol. V).

[4] The earlier theories of genetic connections are based on the idea of progress. The whole history of mankind is supposed to be a history of cultural progress, during which every civilization continues the progress achieved by preceding civilizations. The idea was first formulated, though from different points of view, by Turgot and by Condorcet, and it continues to influence quite a few popular historians of humanity. More recently, we find attempts to trace all cultures back to a common central area. Thus, Edmond Demolins, in *Comment la route crée le type social*, 2 vols. (Paris, 1901-03), assumes that all cultures originated in the area of the steppes—central Asia and oriental Europe—and evolved as the peoples slowly moved from this area in various directions along geographically different routes. Better known is the theory of Elliot Smith and his disciple W. I. Perry, expressed in a number of monographs, which traces the origin of all civilizations above the neolithic level back to ancient Egypt.

not opposed by philosophers. Indeed, philosophers initiated it, already in classical antiquity, by dividing philosophy itself into several branches—theory of knowledge (including logic), politics, ethics, aesthetics. An objective scientific approach to these realms of culture did not begin to supersede the original evaluative and normative approach until the nineteenth century. Serious objections to this kind of specialization arose only in the course of the twentieth century, and generally for practical rather than for theoretic reasons. When social leaders as well as scientists began to realize that in the world of culture, as in the world of nature, important practical problems could best be solved by applying the results of scientific research, it soon became clear that the solution of most of these problems required the cooperation of specialists in several sciences: political scientists, economists, sociologists, psychologists, sometimes religionists, linguists, ethnologists, and others, not to speak of cooperation between cultural and natural scientists. Moreover, educational preparation of a college or even a high-school student for participation in a modern collectivity requires some integration of the several disciplines taught to him in separate courses; and this also can be supplied only by cooperation among specialists.

Such cooperation, as we know, has been difficult to achieve. Specialists have been accused of ethnocentrism, that is, exaggerating the importance of their own disciplines, exalting the superiority of their own methods and the validity of their results, extending the realm of their research to data which other specialists consider exclusively their own. No doubt some ethnocentrism in this sense does exist. But it does not explain why—even when specialists are eager to cooperate, appreciate positively the work of other specialists, and do not impinge on each other's realms—the separate results of their research are seldom if ever systematically integrated. For instance, most books which include contributions of many specialists are more like encyclopedias than like systematic theories; recent regional studies, to which human geographers, students of material techniques, historians, ethnologists, linguists, political scientists, sociologists, religionists, and art students have contributed, also lack scientific integration.

The source of these difficulties does not lie in the attitudes of specialists toward other specialists; nor can the difficulties be eliminated by counteracting specialization. Efficient cooperation between specialists, whether for practical or for theoretic purposes, would require a methodical investigation of the *factual relationships* between the various categories of cultural phenomena which they are studying; and such an investigation has not yet been adequately carried on. We find, indeed, many sweeping generalizations about the historical influence which one category of cultural phenomena has had upon all the others, e.g., Comte's theory of the dominant influence of intellectual systems, technological and economic determinism in various forms,[5] and the theories of totalitarian political philosophers which assert the determining power of the state.[6] Such theories have usually been constructed *a priori* by thinkers to whom some one realm of culture appears as the most important, not only from the theoretic but from the ideological and practical point of view; and in trying to prove the validity of their theories, they select only facts which apparently confirm them.

There are, indeed, quite a few objective, inductive studies of relationships between one category of cultural phenomena—religion, economic organization, knowledge, technology, language, art, music—and another or several other categories. But as yet the only thorough and consistent effort to integrate *all* specialized nomothetic cultural science into a general theory of culture is that of Sorokin. Because of its important methodological implications, we shall give a brief analysis of it here.

Sorokin is the first cultural scientist to apply the same approach to every realm or, as he calls it, "compartment" of culture and to relationships between the cultural phenomena of different compartments. His basic concept is that of system. Although this concept has been used by specialists in various realms—students of philosophy and of science, economists, political theorists, sociologists—yet nobody before him, so far as we know, extended it to all categories of cultural phenomena. The number and diversity of particular cultural systems he includes in his investigation are unequalled. Moreover, his study covers systems ranging from the very simple to the very complex. He takes into account differences in their integration, ranging from congeries to highly organized systems, and compares their relative duration and the range of their extension. He emphasizes the need of studying changes in systems, those which are immanent and those which are caused by extraneous influences (though the evolution of new kinds of systems is neglected). And throughout this study the problem of relationships between the systems included in various realms of culture is taken fully into consideration. Generally these relationships are of two kinds: (1) logico-meaningful connections, those between contemporary systems belonging to different compartments—religion, philosophy, art, technique, economic organization, political organization (which taken together constitute a historical civilization); and (2) causal-functional relations between changes which occur within these different compartments.

---

[5] Many authors have reformulated and developed the theory of economic determinism initiated by Marx. One of the best of their works is Nikolai Bukharin's *Historical Materialism, A System of Sociology*, Eng. trans. (New York: International Publishers, 1925). Yet Bukharin later became *persona non grata* in Soviet Russia. However, the followers of Marx are not the only theorists of history who overemphasize the importance of economic factors.

[6] Heinrich von Treitschke and Othmar Spann exemplify this conception.

Sorokin's generalizations about specific systems and their relationships have been subjected to considerable criticism by specialists.[7] No doubt quite a few of these generalizations are scientifically defective, but these defects are of minor significance; for no methodologist or historian of science would expect that such an original attempt by an individual thinker to cover every realm of cultural phenomena to which many specialists have devoted their whole lives could be immediately and fully successful. It should be judged as a creative effort intended to open a new way for future intellectual progress. The question is: Does this way lead to the progressive formation of a general *science of culture*, in the sense in which the term "science" is used by investigators of natural as well as of cultural phenomena?

By the evidence of Sorokin's own theory, the answer is definitely negative. First, he considers that full knowledge of the cultural universe can be attained only by combining three methods: those of empiricism, rationalism, and mystical intuition.[8] While the first two methods are actually combined in various degrees in every science, the third has been unanimously rejected by all scientists. Second, his theory of cultural time (which can be scientifically validated so far as comparative studies of the relative historical duration of cultural systems are concerned) culminates in the concept of the *eternity* of certain logico-meaningful systems.[9] Obviously, there can be no scientific proof that any cultural system is eternal. Third, Sorokin's theory of cultural space, which can be also validated insofar as it is possible to prove that human experiences and ideas of space are culturally conditioned, leads to a conception which, though symbolized by the word "space," leaves out altogether those phenomena which this word designates. It enables him to

---

[7] Thus, my main objection, as a sociologist, to Sorokin's theory of social systems is that, according to him, social systems—such as the state, the family, a political party, or a university—are not cultural systems like language, science, religion, the fine arts, although they are integrally connected with the latter. Cf. *Social and Cultural Dynamics*, Vol. IV (New York: American Book, 1941), pp. 44-142. If he had applied the humanistic coefficient in his studies of social systems, he would have realized that a social group, as experienced and evaluated by its members, has the essential characteristics which he ascribes to other cultural systems. Most of the deficiencies of his sociological theory, as formulated in *Society, Culture and Personality* (New York: Harper, 1947), are due to his failure to use this approach.

[8] Cf. Sorokin, *Sociocultural Causation, Space, Time* (Durham, N. C.: Duke University Press, 1943), chap. V: ". . . sociocultural reality, including man as its creator, bearer and agent, is a *complex manifold*. It has its empirical aspects to be recognized and studied through *sensory perception*. . . . The logico-rational aspect . . . represented by all consistent systems of thought . . . is to be apprehended through the *discursive logic of human reason*. . . . Finally . . . [the] *supersensory, superrational, metalogical phase of sociocultural reality, including man himself, must be apprehended through the truth of faith*—that is, through a supersensory, superrational metalogical *act of 'intuition'* or mystic experience" (p. 228).

[9] "*Aeternitas* . . . the plane of time on which all the eternal validities, verities, pure meanings and pure values—even pure falsities—are located," *ibid.*, p. 215.

treat connections between contemporary cultural systems as if the world of culture possessed an extension of its own, hitherto entirely unknown, independent of, and different from the spatial extension of the empirical world.[10] Fourth, he introduces the concept of *supersystem* as a combination of cultural systems of all categories found in a certain collectivity during a certain historical period and presumably sharing certain essential characteristics. This concept enables him to superimpose, upon taxonomic, causal, and functional generalizations about specific cultural systems and their factual relationships, ideal-typical generalizations about total civilizations and deterministic generalizations about their changes. The result is a specific variant of the philosophy of history—a doctrine of "trendless fluctuations" of civilizations between the ideational and the sensate type.

These four conceptions are obviously necessary for Sorokin to develop his theory. This means that the theory transcends the limits of scientific research; its unity is based on scientifically unprovable metaphysical dogmas. In other words, it is not a general nomothetic science of cultural phenomena, but a synthetic philosophy of a superhuman cultural universe. As such, it is certainly superior to all philosophies of culture developed by his predecessors. Compare it, for instance, with the philosophy of Hegel and the neo-Hegelians, on the one hand, and with that of biological evolutionists, on the other hand. But the very fact that a thinker with such exceptionally wide knowledge of the results of special cultural sciences—theory of religion, theory of knowledge, theory of literature, theory of the plastic arts, musicology, technology, economics, sociology—could not achieve even a tentative systematization of these results without the use of idealistic metaphysics with theological implications indicates that the possibility of one general science of culture still remains as doubtful as ever.

The same may be said, of course, concerning the development of one systematic theory of nature. Up to now, all attempts to build such a theory have had to use materialistic metaphysics as a foundation. But, as we know, *physics* has become the basic science in natural research. Basic, however, does not mean all-inclusive. Its progress does not destroy the autonomy of other sciences—chemistry, astronomy, geology, biology—nor does it eliminate specialization, which is due not only to subjective limitations of scientists but to objective differences between natural systems irreducible to one

---

[10] "As any sociocultural phenomenon consists of three components—meanings, vehicles, and human agents—sociocultural space must be able to indicate the position of each of these components. . . . The position of meanings is determined where the place of the given meaning in the universe of meanings is determined. . . . Where is Bach's *Mass in B Minor* as a system of pure meanings located? Nowhere, so far as geometric space is concerned; in the 'field of music' as one of the systems of the fine arts. . . . The Christian credo is located in the 'field of religion'. . . . Napoleon's civil code, in 'the field of law' . . ." (pp. 122-24).

category. But, since it deals with universal conditions on which the existence of all natural systems depends, it promotes cooperation, both for the practical purpose of new inventions and for the theoretic purpose of new discoveries.

A similar trend started in the domain of culture toward the end of the nineteenth century, and sociology as a cultural science is now assuming in this domain a function methodically similar to that of physics in the domain of nature.

To trace the development of this function, we must go back to the original conception of sociology as the science of society. We omit here the naturalistic foundations of this science, since we discussed them in Chapter 4 and found that no systematic integration of biological studies of human collectivities as aggregates or systems of human animals and of studies of the cultures found in those collectivities has been achieved or ever can be achieved. Therefore, we shall limit our survey to the cultural aspect of the conception of society.

The conception of society as a cultural system

When Comte introduced the concept of sociology as a new science using the same objective approach and the same methods as the older sciences, he gave it a definite place in his classification of sciences. It was to be the sixth and last positive science, following biology, which followed chemistry. Just as the reason why biology functioned as a distinct science was the existence of living organisms as complex systems irreducible to combinations of their chemical components, so the reason why sociology as a distinct science had to be formed was the existence of societies as the most complex of all systems, irreducible to combinations of individual human organisms.

Comte's idea of society was rooted in the age-old political theory of the state as an integral whole incorporating completely the people who inhabit a definite territory and are organized under a government. But, under the influence of eighteenth-century historians, economists, and cultural philosophers, he expanded it to include the entire culture presumably shared by the participants in a state. His society is, thus, a cultural system maintained by the biologically continuous population living within a geographically circumscribed area. The people who belong to it are united not by natural, but by cultural bonds: common political structure, mores, technology, economic organization, language, religion, knowledge, and art. Those cultural activities are distinct but interdependent functions of society; consequently, sociology as the science of society is also the inclusive science of culture, and all the special cultural sciences are its components.

This conception was not the result of objective studies of relationships between cultural phenomena within particular societies; it was due to Comte's attempt to combine his new science with his theory of the three progressive stages through which total historical civilizations passed. The inclusion of the latter theory in his outline of sociology under the term "social dynamics" led to the long-lasting confusion between sociology and philosophy of history, which culminated in Paul Barth's identification of the two.[11]

This definition of sociology as the science of *society* conditioned *a priori* the approach to cultural phenomena of the sociologists who accepted it. They all agreed that societies are separate wholes, territorially located, including biological human beings on the one hand and cultures on the other hand; and all of them conceived the culture of a society as systematically integrated. They differed as to the relative importance to be ascribed to natural and cultural factors in this integration. For instance, among the social organicists who conceived the unity of society as similar to that of an organism, Izoulet, with his strictly biological theory of the genesis and structure of society, differed greatly from Schäffle and Worms, who ascribed its unity to conscious solidarity manifested in cultural functions.[12]

Spencer's sociological theory of culture is highly important in that his general evolutionary philosophy enabled him to treat social evolution as a continuation of organic evolution, yet irreducible to it. As social evolution reaches the stage when it becomes an evolution of institutions, his generalizations about it are increasingly based not on deductions from biology and biological psychology, but on cultural material derived from ethnology and history. Only the general concept of society remains as the common link between human biology and cultural theory. Since society to Spencer, as to Comte, is the only system over and above individual organisms, all cultural phenomena are included in a society as integral components. Sociology as the science of society is thus the general science of culture.

Spencer's approach, however, differs from Comte's in that in his theory of institutions he attempts to establish a definite connection between social organization as such and specific cultural phenomena. An institution is primarily a subdivision of the total organization of the society; domestic and political institutions are nothing but that. Some institutions, however, serve to maintain and develop specific classes of cultural phenomena. Thus, religion is maintained and developed by ecclesiastical institutions, i.e. organized religious associations, mostly controlled by the priesthood; music, art, literature, medicine, and science are maintained and developed by professional institutions. If we connect this concept of institutions with Spencer's basic premise,

[11] Paul Barth, *Die Philosophie der Geschichte als Soziologie*, 4th ed. (Leipzig, 1922).
[12] Albert G. F. Schäffle, *Bau und Leben des sozialen Körpers*, 7 vols. (1875-78). René Worms, in his *Organisme et société* (Paris, 1896), used a predominantly biological conception. But his theory changed considerably later; cf. his *Philosophie des sciences sociales*, 3 vols. (Paris, 1903-07).

that the essential characteristic of society as a system is cooperation, and with his theory of ethics, we conclude that the primary condition of all cultural evolution is the evolution of morally regulated interaction between individual participants in cooperating groups. Unfortunately, he did not consistently apply this conception. Later sociologists who adopted his term "institution" gave it a somewhat different meaning. They applied it to *religions* rather than to organized religious groups, and included under it art and science, instead of the professional functions of artists and scientists.[13]

The French sociologists who more or less explicitly recognized Durkheim as their leader accepted in principle the conception of society as a spatially located collectivity of human beings with a common integrated culture, but did not develop a systematic general theory of society, only a general methodical approach to the specific cultural phenomena which it includes.[14] This approach became altogether independent of biological premises,[15] except for Durkheim's early explanation of the division of labor by increasing density of the population (later almost ignored by his followers and by Durkheim himself) and some overemphasis on biogeographic factors in Mauss's concept of social morphology.[16] The unity of society is based on conscious solidarity among its members; its organization is founded on collectively recognized and supported norms, which regulate not only actions but experiences and representations of its members. From this point of view, all cultural phenomena are social, since all are subjected to collectively sanctioned rules. The first task of sociologists is, of course, to investigate those rules which are formally expressed in law, less formally in mores, and to study the ways in which conformity with them is collectively enforced.[17] Objective comparative studies of laws and of their enforcement in various societies during various historical periods have been carried on by Durk-

[13] Cf. Florian Znaniecki, "Social Organization and Institutions," eds. Gurvitch and Moore, in *Twentieth Century Sociology* (New York: Philosophical Library, 1945).

Talcott Parsons recently systematized, in his heuristic theory of the "institutional structure" of society, the strictly social conception of "institutions" initiated by Spencer. Cf. "The Position of Sociological Theory," *Am. Sociol. Rev.* (April, 1948), pp. 156-64.

[14] And yet, according to the basic premise of this school, there *must* be a unity of society, even though it may be a long time before a systematic, general science of society develops. As Lapie said: "On ne peut croire à la sociologie sans croire à l'unité des faits sociaux." *L'Année sociologique*, I (1896-97), 274.

[15] Cf. the sharp criticism of "biological sociology" by Bouglé in *L'Année sociologique*, I, (1896-97).

[16] "Divisions et proportions des divisions de la sociologie," *L'Année sociologique*, new series, II (1927), 98-173.

[17] In *L'Année sociologique*, the third section of critical reviews is devoted to "Sociologie juridique et morale." It includes, besides general theories of law and/or mores, property law, criminal law, studies of social and political organizations—among others, the local community, family, marriage. "Sociologie criminelle et statistique morale," in the sense of a sociological study of crimes and moral transgressions, constitutes a separate section.

heim,[18] Davy, Fauconnet, Duguit;[19] recently, Gurvitch gave a general systematic outline of sociology of law as a branch of sociology.[20] Lévy-Bruhl formulated a program for an objective, comparative science of the mores regulating interhuman relations;[21] but no systematization of studies of mores has been attempted.

But inasmuch as in all realms of culture specific representations and actions are collectively regulated, all of them must be investigated sociologically. In the course of this investigation some differences of approach developed. Thus, Durkheim's sociological conception of religion resulted in his well-known theory that religion as such does not constitute a separate and distinct cultural product. The antithesis between the sacred and the profane, found in all religions, is reducible to the antithesis between experiences and activities shared by a group as a whole and individual experiences and activities; gods are mere symbols of the group that worships them. This theory has been invalidated, but the dependence of religion as a distinct cultural product upon social organizations, already postulated by Spencer, proved valid.[22] Most original and historically important was the use of the sociological approach to knowledge, for it attempted to show that not merely particular theories, but basic logical principles and categories, are collective, i.e., social, products. Lévy-Bruhl tried to prove that the principles of identity and contradiction were unknown to primitive societies, and that the category of causation was not consistently used;[23] Durkheim showed that some early classifications of natural phenomena were not based on their similarities and differences, but on their presumed mystical connections with separate clans as subdivisions of a tribe;[24] Halbwachs tried to prove that memory, without which no

[18] This study forms a part of Durkheim's work *De la division du travail social.*

[19] Georges Davy, *La Foi jurée* (Paris, 1922); and Paul Fauconnet, *La Responsabilité* (Paris, 1925). Léon Duguit, however, though influenced by Durkheim in his theory of law, has been criticized for not accepting the concepts of "realité collective" and "conscience sociale" by Davy, *L'Année sociologique,* XII (1909-12), 364.

[20] Georges Gurvitch, *Sociology of Law* (New York: Philosophical Library, 1942).

[21] Lucien Lévy-Bruhl, *La Morale et la science des moeurs* (Paris, 1903).

[22] Sociology of religion was, from the very first, one of the branches of sociology in which Durkheim and his followers were most interested. If we survey, however, the content of the section "Sociologie religieuse," with its eleven subsections, in the "new series" of *L'Année sociologique* (started in 1925), we find that it includes critical reviews of all publications pertaining to religion. There is little in the reviews of these publications that would clarify the difference between sociology of religion and historical and ethnological studies of religions. Only in some of their generalizing works do members of this group use an original sociological approach: e.g., Hubert and Mauss, "Esquisse d'une théorie générale de la magie," *L'Année sociologique,* VII; or Stefan Czarnowski, *Le Culte des héros* (Paris, 1919).

[23] *Les Fonctions mentales dans les sociétés primitives* (Paris, 1923); *La Mentalité primitive* (Paris, 1925).

[24] Durkheim and Mauss, "De quelques formes primitives de classification," *L'Année sociologique,* Vol. VI (1901-02).

individual awareness of time is possible, is socially determined;[25] Czarnowski, that all conceptions of space were originally developed by social groups with certain magico-religious ideologies.[26] This theory was used by Granet in his studies of Chinese civilization.[27]

While the general postulate that knowledge, like religion, forms part of the total organized life of a society, which regulates all the thinking of its members, has been invalidated, yet enough evidence has been obtained concerning the dependence of knowledge upon social organization to start the development of sociology of knowledge as a branch of general sociology. The same may be said of the results of monographic research carried on by French sociologists concerning economic systems,[28] political systems,[29] and language.[30] The very progress of this research, however, has slowly undermined the conception of society as an integrated system within which all the culture shared by its members is included. In 1913, Durkheim and Mauss stated in *L'Année sociologique*:

> One of the rules which we follow here, while studying social phenomena in themselves and for themselves, is not to leave them in the air, but to refer them always to a human group that occupies a definite portion of space and is capable of being geographically represented. And it seems that the largest of all these groups, the one which includes within it all the others and consequently frames and embraces all the forms of social activity, is the one which constitutes the political society. . . .
>
> However, there are [social phenomena] which have no such clearly defined frames; they pass above political frontiers and extend over spaces which cannot be easily determined. . . .
>
> Political and juridical institutions, phenomena of social morphology, are parts of the constitution belonging to each people. On the contrary, myths, stories, money, trade, fine arts, techniques, instruments, languages, words, scientific knowledge, literary forms and ideals, all these travel. . . .
>
> There are not only isolated facts, but complex solidary systems which

[25] *Les Cadres sociaux de la mémoire* (Paris, 1925).

[26] "La Division de l'étendue," *Revue d'histoire des religions* (Paris, 1927).

[27] Marcel Granet, *La Civilisation Chinoise* (Paris, 1929); *La Pensée Chinoise* (Paris, 1931).

[28] Simiand, Mauss, and Halbwachs eventually led to the study of economic groups and classes.

[29] Celestin Bouglé, *Les Idées égalitaires* (Paris, 1899); *La Démocratie devant la science* (Paris, 1903).

[30] Antoine Meillet, Ferdinand Brunot, and Jacques Vendryes. The relation between linguistics and sociology is well characterized by Meillet as follows: "Without doubt, linguistic facts have an autonomy . . . a well-marked specificity. . . . But they develop in well-defined social groups in response to certain social needs. And it is useless to pretend to explain this development without describing these groups and without studying these needs." *L'Année sociologique*, new series, I (1925), 947.

Two other categories of cultural phenomena were included within the domain of sociology: technology and art. Some original work has been done by followers of Durkheim, especially Charles Lalo, in the realm of art, but not much in technology.

are not limited to a determined political organism. . . . To these systems of facts, which have their own unity, their own way of being, it is convenient to have a special name: the name *civilization* seems to us the most appropriate.

There was still another difficulty. The radical opposition of Durkheim and his followers to psychological individualism, especially as developed by Tarde, led to complete neglect of the function of the individual as innovator and imitator, leader and follower. Consequently, many cultural processes remained inexplicable which could have been explained if the factual evidence on which Tarde based his hypotheses had been taken fully into consideration. But that would have meant redefinition of the whole concept of society, since Tarde's generalizations were mostly independent of this concept.

American sociology began with the explicit or implicit acceptance of the theory of society initiated by Comte and developed by Spencer, but without the organismic analogy. A society was considered to be a territorially and demographically circumscribed collectivity with an integrated culture. This cultural integration was conceived by most sociologists as a system of differentiated but interdependent, collective functions or institutions, each of which serves to satisfy certain basic needs or interests of the people included in the society. General sociological theories were essentially theories of society in this sense, e.g., Ward's *Pure Sociology*, Small's *General Sociology*, Sumner and Keller's *Science of Society*. And even now this approach is still used by quite a few sociologists who are unwilling to relinquish the original ambition of the founders of their science and by those authors of sociological textbooks who want to help college students overcome the separatism of specialists by giving them some idea of the interdependence between various categories of cultural phenomena.

However, the rapid growth of inductive sociological research, instead of providing new proof of the validity of general theories of society as an inclusive cultural system, has resulted in a gradual limitation of the realm of sociology. Sociologists cannot compete with economists, students of material techniques, linguists, historians and theorists of literature, art, music, philosophy, and science in their respective realms. What they actually do is to specialize in the investigation of what have been termed "social relations" or "human relations" and of the human groups within or between which such relations exist. As a result of this specialization, general sociological theories have become much less inclusive.

This new trend in sociological theory cannot be traced back to any single source. The explicit program of sociology as a *special* science was first formulated and partly applied by Simmel,[31] later reformulated with some

[31] Georg Simmel, *Soziologie: Untersuchungen über die Formen der Vergesellschaftung* (Berlin, 1908), a collection of special studies.

changes and much more widely applied by von Wiese.[32] These authors definitely excluded from the realm of sociology the phenomena which other cultural scientists were already investigating. According to both, the first task of sociology is to study relations between individuals as elementary social phenomena, and then proceed to the study of more complex social systems. Simmel stopped with the comparative study of limited *social groups* composed of interacting, mutually conscious individuals; von Wiese went further and surveyed what he termed "abstract collectivities" composed of many smaller groups, such as the state and the church.[33] A somewhat similar approach was initiated independently by Cooley,[34] who began with the study of personal relations between individuals, continued with a survey of combinations of these relations in primary groups, and extended tentatively the realm of sociology to wider groups. Several other sociological theorists also gradually limited their generalizations to this category of phenomena.[35]

Sociologists who participate in this trend, even when they still use the term "society," give it a new meaning. Thus, according to MacIver: "Society . . . signifies the whole complex system of social relationships . . . in and through which we live. . . . And its structure is for ever changing."[36]

According to Hiller: "The subject of sociology is that of human relations. These relations are social because they consist of the conduct and inclinations of persons with reference to one another. . . . Social relations are discovered through a study of rules, standards, and usages prescribing conduct between persons. All such regulations . . . are a part of the culture of a given society."[37]

Not only do those authors define society in terms of specific phenomena called social relations or human relations rather than as a system including all categories of cultural phenomena, but they recognize the need of inductive research in order to discover how a particular society is organized, instead of assuming that the organization of all societies is essentially uniform and its

[32] Leopold von Wiese, *Allgemeine Soziologie:* Vol. I, *Beziehungslehre* (Munich, 1924); Vol. II, *Gebildelehre* (Munich, 1929). Howard Becker amplified and adapted this work to certain American trends, and it was published in English under the title *Systematic Sociology* (New York: Wiley, 1932).

[33] We must mention here also Max Weber, who ascribed to sociology the specific task of investigating social actions. He defined a social action as "an action carried on . . . with reference to the behavior of others and oriented toward the behavior of those others throughout its course," quoted in von Wiese-Becker, *op. cit.*, p. 894. Unlike von Wiese, however, Weber did not develop a general theory of facts of *interaction* between social agents.

[34] Charles Horton Cooley, *Human Nature and the Social Order* (New York: Scribner, 1902); and *Social Organization* (New York: Scribner, 1909).

[35] I did this in the *Introduction to Sociology* (Warsaw, 1922), in Polish.

[36] Robert M. MacIver, *Society: Its Structure and Changes* (New York: H. Long & Smith, Inc., 1931), pp. 9, 56.

[37] Ernest T. Hiller, *Social Relations and Structures* (New York: Harper, 1947), p. 2.

basic principles already known. In other words, society is becoming a heuristic concept for guidance toward future discoveries.[38]

This new conception of the task of sociology raises three important problems: (1) What are these presumably elementary phenomena, sometimes termed "human relations," sometimes "social relations," and what kind of order exists among them? (2) What is the connection between sociology and the established cultural sciences? (3) What is the connection between sociology and natural sciences?

Sociology as the science of order among social actions

Let us begin with a brief survey of the meaning of the term "human relations," which is apparently much more widely used than the term "social relations," judging from the number of publications which contain it in their titles.

We find, however, two very different conceptions of a human relation. It may be, and frequently is, conceived as a relation between "*human beings*" as biopsychological entities. It consists in any process, simple or complex, which occurs between them and affects directly or indirectly their biological functions or their psychological processes. It includes, among other things, those phenomena which human ecology, following the models of plant and animal ecology, investigates and which James A. Quinn has defined as "spatial and temporal relations between human beings as affected by the selective, distributive and accommodative forces of the environment."[39] According to this conception, human beings between whom a relation occurs need not even be conscious of each other. The lives of those human beings in New York who consume oranges produced in Florida or California or drink tea imported from Ceylon are in some measure affected by the behavior of the human beings who cultivate and gather oranges or tea leaves; yet most New Yorkers know very little about the latter in general and nothing at all about any one of them in particular, and vice versa. During depressions the lives of millions of human beings are affected by changes which have occurred in the lives of millions of others who are unknown to them.

The other concept symbolized by the term "human relations" is more specific and limited. It includes essentially the same phenomena as those

[38] For an excellent systematic survey of this and of other new trends in sociology up to 1931, and a "suggested organization of sociological theory in terms of its major concepts," see Earle Edward Eubank, *The Concepts of Sociology* (New York: Heath, 1932). Obviously, in this book I could not refer to all the important new contributions to sociological theory made since 1931. Many of them, up to 1945, are summarized in *Twentieth Century Sociology*, eds. Gurvitch and Moore (New York: Philosophical Library, 1945).

[39] James A. Quinn, "The Development of Human Ecology in Sociology," eds. Barnes, Becker, and Becker, in *Contemporary Social Theory* (New York: Appleton, 1940), p. 212.

included in the concept "social relations" as used by sociologists. This is the meaning which Hiller gives it in the paragraph previously quoted.[40] And in surveying some studies of so-called human relations, e.g., human relations in industry, we find that the meaning of this term is also almost identical with that of social relations in sociological works. As there seems to be no reason for this terminological duplication, to avoid confusion we shall drop the term "human relations" altogether and limit our analysis to *social* relations.

The simplest, elementary phenomenon which certain sociologists, e.g., Simmel, von Wiese, Hiller, denote by this term, is a single process of conscious intercourse between two individuals which affects both of them. The first essential condition of its occurrence is that both individuals be aware of each other. If neither is aware of the other, there obviously cannot be any conscious relation between them. If only one is aware of the other, as when A sees B walking on the street, but is not seen by B, this experience may affect some attitudes or tendencies of A, but it would not be called a social relation, since B is unaffected by it. Even when two individuals are aware of each other, this by itself is still not enough to produce a social relation between them. On a crowded street, many individuals see each other, but usually nothing occurs to make them mutually conscious of any influence exerted by one upon the other. The consciousness of such influence appears only when one of them, A, performs an action bearing upon the other, B, as a datum of his experience; for instance, when A tries to make B move out of his way or purposely opens a way for B to pass, asks B about the location of a street or a building, or attempts to start companionate conversation with B. Considered from B's point of view, A's action results in a situation of which A, as a datum of B's experience, is a component. B usually tends to do something in this situation; and whatever he does, both A and B are aware that A has done something practically significant to B and that it is practically significant to A how B will act under the influence of this action, or—briefly speaking—how he reacts to it.

Thus, when we investigate the simple, elementary phenomenon which certain sociologists call "social relation" from the point of view of the two individuals who participate in it, rather than from that of an observer, and analyze it as a combination of their experiences and active tendencies, we find that it is not really a relation between two individuals as such, but between their *actions*. We prefer, therefore, to call it an "interaction" rather than a "relation," for the word "relation" in common language connotes a more durable interdependence. Later we shall limit the term "social relation" to rather long-lasting axionormative *systems* of numerous actions performed by two interacting agents, each of whom is a durable positive value

[40] Hiller's conception of human or social relations is similar to that of von Wiese.

to the other (e.g., mother and child, husband and wife). Nevertheless, even a single interaction is definitely a social phenomenon, for its chief component is a *social action* of which one individual, as given to another, is the object and which tends to influence the latter, to provoke a reaction from him. This reaction may be also a social action in this sense, as when the second individual gives verbally the directions he has been asked to give or responds positively to the initial attempt of the first to start a conversation. Or it may be a technical action, as when, without trying to influence the first individual, he moves along the way which the former opened up for him; but even in this case, his action has been socially conditioned, since he is aware that the other intended to make him perform it.

If sociology is essentially the science of human or social relations, as experienced by those who participate in them, then the primary phenomena which sociologists have to investigate are social actions, just as the primary phenomena investigated by religionists, students of material technique, economists, and theorists of art are religious, technical, economic, artistic actions. In an earlier work, we tried to analyze and classify social actions as a distinct category. We included in this category all those and only those human actions (individual or collective) which have as main values other human individuals, experienced and conceived by the agents as living and conscious beings (or collectivities composed of such individuals), and which tend to produce some changes in these main values as social objects by using as instruments some data experienced by both of them.

As most historians, ethnologists, and sociologists well know, social actions, just like other kinds of actions, are axionormatively ordered insofar as they conform with definite cultural patterns, and they can be classified according to this order. The similarities and differences between them are primarily based on the standards by which their main objects are defined and evaluated, secondarily by the norms which they are supposed to follow. Of course, as in every realm of culture, actions which do not conform raise special problems.

We surveyed briefly in Chapter 10 one rather general cultural class of social actions—curing sick persons. Basically, all the objects of these actions are supposed to be positively valuable to the agents, though their valuation differs in degree and their definitions vary, depending upon their presumed sickness or disease. We noticed the great diversity of norms with which medical agents are expected to conform in various collectivities and saw how they change in the course of history. When investigating the problem of transgressions, we found that individuals who are judged to be transgressors are negatively evaluated by conformists according to certain standards and subjected to normatively regulated social actions, though their definitions and negative valuations differ in kind and degree, and the actions dealing with them vary accordingly.

Functionally interdependent social actions of different agents become integrated into axionormatively organized systems of various size, complexity, extension, and duration. Relatively simple are the systems of interdependent actions of two individuals who evaluate each other positively by standards which both accept, and who follow certain norms in acting upon each other. Take, for instance, companionate conversation carried on by two acquaintances in accordance with definite principles of etiquette, or the functionally inter-dependent sexual actions of a man and a woman each of whom tends to give maximum satisfaction to the other and to enjoy fully what the other does. Such a short-lasting system may be part of a long-lasting system—life-long companionship or enduring mutual love. Many such long-lasting systems of culturally patterned interactions between two individual agents have been investigated by sociologists and ethnologists, and the term social relations has usually been applied to them. Numerous works have been written about marriage, or conjugal relations, courtship relations, parent-child relations, kinship relations in general, relations of mutual aid and cooperation, relations between ruler and subject, employer and employee, teacher and pupil, leader and follower, etc.

Considerable research has also been done on the highly complex systems of interdependent social actions performed by the numerous individual agents who constitute together an organized social group. One class of the latter—military groups—began to be thoroughly studied in classical antiquity (Xenophon, Thucydides, Caesar, especially Polybius). Since then many other specific social groups have been investigated—legislative groups, administrative groups, political parties, craftsmen's guilds, professional groups, religious groups, clans, secret societies, lately labor unions, and various smaller, apparently less influential associations.[41]

Much less attention has been paid to social systems of the intermediary type—axionormatively ordered combinations of social relations between one individual and a number of others—e.g., a physician and his patients, a teacher and her pupils. Historians have made quite a few studies of such systems as relations between a prince and his courtiers, a military or political leader and his followers, a philosopher and his disciples, an artist and his

---

[41] Many sociologists consider that a comparative study of social groups constitutes the primary task of sociology. Cf. the statement of Charles A. Ellwood in *The Psychology of Human Society* (New York: Appleton, 1927): "It is the concrete group, rather than the abstract society, that is the primary datum of present-day sociology" (p. vi). Cf. Eubank, *op. cit.*: "The group is the pivotal concept of sociological theory" (p. 164). Every textbook of sociology contains a section on social groups. And yet, except for a few brief and superficial essays, not a single general systematic work on social groups has been published in any language.

patrons and admirers, the hostess of a salon and her guests.[42] But not until thirty years ago did sociologists begin to investigate these systems and apply to them the general concept of social role, and they still do not agree concerning the heuristic significance of this concept.

However questionable methodically and insignificant theoretically may be certain results of recent specialized sociological researches, there is no doubt that many sociologists who investigate social actions in the sense just defined, have found and will find within the realm of their investigation the same two basic categories of order which other cultural scientists discover in their respective realms—the order of conformity of actions with cultural patterns and the order of functional interdependence which integrates conformist actions into systems. Since these orders are axionormative, due to the acceptance and practical application by agents of ideological models, and axionormative order does not exist in the world of nature, sociology as a science of social actions is manifestly a cultural, not a natural, science.

The general term *social order* has been widely used to denote axionormative order among phenomena called "social." Cooley and other sociologists have used it in an objective, scientific sense. To quite a few thinkers, however, it symbolizes an ethical, rather than a scientific, concept. For instance, Edward L. Thorndike, the famous psychologist, in his book *Human Nature and the Social Order*[43] does not define social order at all, but apparently takes for granted that it means economic and legal organization, which should be studied not by scientific methods, but from the point of view of its goodness for man. Some French thinkers have given it a moralistic connotation, which probably led Gurvitch to suggest that it be altogether excluded from sociological theory.[44]

[42] Other, widely different examples of such studies might be mentioned, such as Frazer's investigation of the socioreligious functions of kings and priests, in his *Golden Bough*; Sombart's *Der Bourgeois*; several studies of medicine men and shamans in nonliterate societies; Léon Gautier, *La Chevalerie*, etc. Spencer's *Professional Institutions* was the first attempt to develop an evolutionary theory of one general class of these systems. A comparative analysis of a considerable diversity of them led me twenty-five years ago to the conclusion that all of them have certain common components: a set or circle of people with whom any particular individual interacts; an evaluative representation of him as a person by the circle and by himself; a definition of "rights" which his circle actively supports; and a definition of "duties" which he actively performs. In 1930, I borrowed from Park and Burgess the term "social role" to designate such dynamic systems of actions and have used it since in three books (two in Polish, one in English) and in several articles. Recently a general survey of the main logical classes of such systems was published by Hiller; but the author uses a static approach, and terms these classes "statuses," in the sense of "positions" in the "structure of society" (*op. cit.*, Part Six).

[43] Edward L. Thorndike, *Human Nature and the Social Order* (New York: Macmillan, 1940).

[44] Georges Gurvitch, "Social Control," eds. Gurvitch and Moore, in *Twentieth Century Sociology*, p. 247.

There is some reason for this confusion. If social order means *only* axionormative order, this implies that social phenomena which do not conform with established standards and norms have no order whatsoever, no regularity which would enable scientists to generalize about them; in short, that they belong under the general category of disorder as antithesis to order. This is as if biologists limited their search for natural order in their realm to anatomical structures and physiological functions of organisms and omitted the search for causal laws of relationship between organic changes and environmental influences as well as the search for regularities in the genesis of new species. Nonetheless, this term should be preserved in its objective, nonevaluative sense, for it has been helpful in distinguishing sociology from other sciences. But it should be extended so as to include those regularities of change occurring within social actions and systems which make causal generalization possible and those regularities in the genesis of new patterns and systems which may lead to evolutionary generalizations. In other words, sociologists must postulate that some kind of objective order exists among all social phenomena and discard altogether the concept of disorder and other analogous concepts.

As a matter of fact, many sociologists who specialize in investigating axionormatively ordered social actions and axionormatively organized systems of such actions have been searching for causal order in social change. Thus, quite a few attempts have been made to draw causal generalizations about the changes in social actions occurring in the course of their performance.[45] Many studies of changes in various kinds of systems of social actions, ranging in size and complexity from conjugal relations to governmental organizations, have been carried on and have resulted in causal hypotheses. We believe, therefore, that sociologists will soon cease to separate studies of social change in general from studies of social order in general.

The development of methodical genetic research has been somewhat impeded in recent times by the discredit attached to the concept of social evolution; but many historical studies have been made about the emergence of new social systems in the course of the last two centuries, and some sociologists are aware of the significance of these studies for sociology as a generalizing science.

The connection between sociology and other cultural sciences

While social actions, like all conscious human actions, are dynamic systems of values, yet the main values included in them differ essentially from those included in other categories of actions. This difference is of primary importance for the function of sociology as a cultural science.

[45] Most of them are included within the realm of social psychology. Cf. Florian Znaniecki, *The Laws of Social Psychology* (Chicago: University of Chicago Press, 1926); Lois B. Murphy and Gardner Murphy, *An Experimental Social Psychology* (New York: Harper, 1931); and many other works.

The primary value of any particular social action, as we have seen, is a human individual, experienced and conceived by the agent both as an object and as a conscious performer of actions. Anthropomorphic deities are similarly conceived, but their actions cannot be observed as human actions are. Many animals also appear similar to human beings in the experience of those who act upon them; but this is irrelevant to our present problem since, though the higher animals are indubitably conscious, any evidence that they can actually participate in human culture is indirect and inconclusive.

Now, a human individual is not only a lasting social object of many diverse attitudes and actions, but also an agent who in the course of time manifests many diverse attitudes and performs many actions dealing with various kinds of objects. Most of the actions which he performs, not only social but non-social—technical, religious, intellectual, aesthetic, etc.—influence directly or indirectly, positively or negatively, some actions of others; and those who act upon him are well aware of this. Consequently, the definition and evaluation of a human individual as a social object depend in considerable measure upon various kinds of actions which he has performed or is presumed to have performed in the past; and the predominant, if not the only, tendency of most social actions of which he is the object is to make him perform (or refrain from performing) in the future specific actions, not only social but nonsocial. This is, of course, not one-sided social control, but many-sided social influence, since every conscious individual in his turn, when he experiences others and acts upon them as social objects, manifests such evaluative attitudes and active tendencies. The same may be said, with some modifications, of organized social groups.

Social actions are thus cultural forces which influence the participation of human agents in every realm of culture. In our preceding chapters, we mentioned occasionally some manifestations of this influence. Let us survey them briefly.

In investigating the spread of ideological models of attitudes in a collectivity, we found that whatever the values and ways of acting to which these models refer—social, religious, technical, economic, aesthetic, etc.—their acceptance by participants in the collectivity is the result of specific social actions performed by those who tend to have these models generally accepted. These actions consist in communicating to others the standards and norms which the models include and inducing others to recognize them as valid. This is necessary, though not always sufficient, to have any model accepted. Without symbolic communication and persuasion, no consensus about the validity of standards and norms would be possible.

In surveying changes in ideological systems we noticed that, although those changes are initiated by thinkers who create new ideals, yet an ideal does not effectively modify an existing ideological system unless socially active leaders and their followers succeed in having it accepted and practically applied by influential social groups. And we saw that the stabilization of ideals into dogmas is achieved by social actions, individual and collective, of authoritative agents who tend to maintain an ideological system changeless by having it recognized as such by all present and future members of the groups which they dominate. When we discussed the expansion and recession of ideological systems, we found that both these processes are conditioned by social interaction between the adherents of different ideologies.

In our comparative analysis of culturally patterned actions performed by individuals, we included various kinds of actions, more or less complex, most of which were not social in the sense defined above. Private religious cultus, technical production of individual craftsmen, artistic performances of individual painters, sculptors, musicians, or poets, and intellectual actions of philosophers or scientists cannot be classified as social. When we passed to organized systems of specific actions performed by many individuals, we found that, though they differ from individual performances as to size, complexity, and duration, yet such differences do not justify their classification in a separate category, in contrast with individual actions, as some thinkers who identify "collective" with "social" have been doing.

Collective cultus of limited or unlimited duration is still religious, not social, activity; for the main common objects of all who participate in it are mythical beings, not living and active men. The collective construction of a building; the making, maintaining, and using of roads for motor traffic; and the continuous functioning of a factory or a mine are systems of interdependent technical actions, and must be studied by specialists in these realms. The playing of a symphony by an orchestra, just as the playing of a nocturne by an individual pianist, is obviously music, and has to be investigated by musicologists, not by sociologists. Even a collective economic system, although it requires interaction between human agents, includes as main values not men, but utilitarian products; and economists have drawn valid generalizations about such systems without investigating how producers, consumers, merchants, or bankers evaluate and act upon one another.

And yet we noticed that not only these collective systems of actions, but even the regular conformity of individual actions with cultural patterns depend upon social actions. Individuals do not automatically become participants in a collectively organized religious, technical, artistic, or even economic system; they must be actively admitted to participation, whether at their own initiative or at the initiative of others. The regular, continuous functioning of a collective system requires that deviations and transgressions which disturb this functioning be counteracted or prevented; and this, as we have seen, means *social* activity. When a collective system becomes creatively reorganized by introducing a new order, this reorganization requires continuous social cooperation between initiators of the new order as leaders and other participants as followers.

And, as every cultural scientist knows, before an individual can perform culturally patterned actions, even all alone, he must have learned how to perform them. Now, not all learning requires teaching. An individual who is already acquainted with certain cultural data and ways of acting can learn at his own initiative by observation and imitation how to perform an action unlike those he has performed before, or even a relatively new action somewhat different from any he has observed others performing. And yet he could not have originally learned to deal with any cultural data or acquired the ability to perform any culturally patterned action without being educated for a rather long period of time, for self-education is an outgrowth of education. And education consists of specifically social interaction between educators and educands. In any particular case, it consists of a sequence of culturally patterned social actions performed by an educator of which the educand is the main object, and of actions of the educand performed under the influence of the educator's actions.

Even when an individual has completed his education and performs culturally patterned nonsocial actions without anybody's guidance or cooperation, others are still interested in him and his performances; unless he lives in isolation, they are apt to manifest their interest by social actions bearing upon him. This is easily explicable when what he is doing is supposed to have some bearing on values with which the others deal. Thus, we found that private cultus is a matter of active interest to fellow believers who think that its regular performance by an individual worshiper propitiates their common deity and brings indirectly some blessing upon the whole congregation. In the realm of material technique, it is also easily understandable that, when trade developed, members of the various guilds became interested in the actions of their fellow craftsmen; and also that those who use technical products are interested in the actions of the producers, and vice versa.

But, in fact, this interest is found not only when actions of separate individuals are functionally interdependent. Ethnologists have noticed that, in many collectivities with traditional technological patterns, men who make hunting implements; women who make clothes, rugs, or domestic implements; potters, gardeners, male or female, who make any products not for sale but for their own use or the use of their families and so have nothing to gain or lose by the success or failure of others, nevertheless, manifest considerable interest in each other's performances. They compare and evaluate the products by the standards and norms of the craft. They subject the performers to social sanctions—positive for those who conform and negative for those who deviate—at least in the form of personal praise or blame.

Historians of art are familiar with the interest, positive or negative, which artists working in the same realm—painters, musicians, poets—show in one another's work, and which critics manifest in the works of all of them. This interest is not limited to art itself, but extends to artists as persons and leads to numerous social actions, individual and collective, ranging from private or public approval or disapproval to the formation of schools and associations which tend to maintain the conformity of artists with established standards and norms, or to induce young artists to follow new aesthetic patterns.

The purpose of this brief survey is to justify our heuristic postulate about the function of sociology in relation to other cultural sciences. We must remember that the very existence of culture ultimately depends on conscious and active human individuals. Cultural data are the common data of successive experiences of many individuals; they grow in the course of time as agglomerated products of individual agents and are being used in the course of time by numerous individual agents. Consequently, no cultural pattern can last, no cultural systems can survive, unless the unlimited diversity of changing individual experiences of cultural data is continually uniformalized by common standards; and the many different, often conflicting, actions of individuals simultaneously and successively dealing with these data are continually regulated and integrated by common norms. This cannot be achieved by anybody but the individuals themselves who regularly cooperate in developing, preserving, and applying those standards and norms. Such regular cooperation requires conscious social interaction between them, not arbitrary and accidental, but guided by common standards of mutual experience and understanding and by common norms of conduct.

This means that, whatever axionormative order may be found among nonsocial actions dealing with nonhuman objects—material things, meaningful symbols, mythical beings, fictitious products of creative imagination, aesthetic constructs of sensory perception, abstract ideas—is conditioned by an axionormative, dynamic social order of interaction between the individuals who perform those nonsocial actions. And, however different may be the cultural patterns and systems of actions dealing with such nonhuman objects, their continued existence depends on certain essential similarities in the social order.

These similarities enable sociologists to generalize about the common social foundations of all categories of cultural order.[46] The development of the concept of organized social groups or associations has already resulted in the discovery that the functioning of various cultural systems—religious, indus-

---

[46] Sociologists are gradually becoming aware that the importance of sociology for other cultural sciences *increases* in the very measure in which it *limits its task* to a comparative study of those social systems upon which the existence of every realm of culture depends. Compare the subdivisions of sociology found in *L'Année sociologique* with those in Barnes, Becker, and Becker, *op. cit.*, and later in Gurvitch and Moore, *op. cit.*

trial, economic, recently even scientific—found in collectivities with widely different cultures or civilizations, depends upon organized groups with an essentially similar social order (though, of course, with specific differences). The concept of social role, as a system of social relations between one individual and a number of others, is being applied to various kinds of culturally patterned performances of individual agents, in nonliterate as well as in literate collectivities (intellectual, artistic, technical, economic) ; and its application shows that the regularity and continuity of such performances depend upon the functioning of social systems of this general class.

I have tried to use the sociological approach in a comparative study of education. However wide the differences in cultures, past and present, in which individuals have been and are now being taught to participate, there are beyond all doubt certain universal similarities of social systems on which all educational processes depend: social relations between educators and educands, which become integrated into specific social roles as education grows in length and complexity; social groups of which the educand is expected to become a member and which tend to regulate his preparation for membership; and schools as a specific class of social groups. Consequently, it is possible to develop a general sociological theory of those social systems which condition individual acculturation.

Of course, studies of the social order among human actions were initiated in classical antiquity by political theorists. Their emphasis on practical problems interfered with scientific objectivity, and their tendency to consider the order of a state as all-inclusive often prevented them from noting the existence of other types of social order which are not reducible to political organization. These were the main reasons for the conflict which emerged in the nineteenth century between sociologists and political scientists, radically exemplified on the sociological side by Spencer's *Man versus the State,* and on the political side by Heinrich von Treitschke, Othmar Spann, and the totalitarian ideologists who completely rejected sociology. Such conflicts have subsided with the progress of scientific research, both among political scientists and among sociologists. Sociologists cannot deny the theoretic validity of many generalizations reached by political scientists, and political scientists no longer ignore the existence of many influential social systems, investigated by sociologists, which are not included in the structure of the state.

While sociologists no longer support the claim of Comte, Spencer, and their followers that political science is necessarily a part of sociology because the state is one of the institutions of society, yet it is highly probable that the results of theoretic research in the realm hitherto covered by political science (not the practical application of these results in political planning) will be gradually incorporated into sociology; for, evidently, the specific social systems which together compose the organization of a state can be classified together with the other social systems which sociologists are studying. Legislative groups, administrative groups, juridical groups, military groups, and political parties manifest some common, universal characteristics of all organized groups or associations. Social roles of individuals who perform specialized official functions in the government are comparable to the social roles of individuals whose functions are not official in the political sense of the term. Thus, in our opinion, sociology is definitely becoming the one and only science of social order, in the sense in which this term has been defined here.

But neither historians of culture nor cultural anthropologists are as yet willing to recognize sociology as the basic cultural science. According to them, in every civilization or culture, all categories of cultural phenomena—technical, social, economic, linguistic, magical, religious, intellectual, aesthetic, etc.—are interconnected and more or less integrated functionally; each depends on all the others, although in any particular culture one of them may be more influential than the others. Sociologists have to show not only that the continued existence of specific cultural systems depends upon axionormatively ordered social interaction, but also that the connections between specific cultural systems are not direct but indirect, mediated through social relations, and that whatever cultural integration may be found in a particular collectivity ultimately depends upon its social organization. We believe that comparative sociological analysis will prove the validity of these hypotheses.

Consider, by way of example, the connection between two important categories of cultural phenomena, religion and art. In investigating sociologically particular cases in which religious actions and artistic actions are connected, we find that in every case this connection is socially conditioned. It is due to the fact that the same individual performs two social roles: the role of a member in a religious group, and the role of an artist—sculptor, painter, musician. As an artist, recognized as such by other members of his religious group, he is expected to make special contributions to the common values of the group or to its collective cultus and is therefore granted special privileges by the group. Why certain artistic functions are positively valued by certain religious groups, but not by others, is a matter of different ideologies. If we trace such differences back to their historical origin, we shall probably find that the acceptance or rejection of specific artistic functions by a religious group was due to social factors—participation or nonparticipation of artists and patrons of art in the group during the period of its formation, cooperation or conflict between it and other groups which appreciated and supported art.

The combination of the role of artist and that of a member of a social group is also found in secular art; e.g., the painters and sculptors who contribute to the beauty of a city hall are usually members of the municipal group. Moreover, when artists are dependent upon patrons, the role of an artist functioning under the patronage of a high priest does not differ essentially from that of an artist patronized by a king, a dictator, or a millionaire, though the content of the creative work he is required to do may differ considerably.

As to the dependence of cultural integration in general upon social organization, we may mention, first, certain significant similarities and differences between so-called "preliterate" or "nonliterate" collectivities. Cultures maintained by well-organized, autonomous tribal groups seem to be better integrated than most folk cultures in the old sense of the term; i.e., those found in collectivities inhabiting areas under control of modern civilized states and lacking autonomous social organization. If, however, such a folk community has preserved some autonomy and is coherently organized, its culture remains rather well integrated, even though in the course of history many components which had no connection with its traditional patterns penetrated it. On the other hand, when intergroup conflicts frequently occur within a tribal collectivity, its culture does not seem to be functionally united. And the disintegration of tribal cultures under the impact of European colonial expansion apparently began in many cases with social disorganization.

However, more varied and more valid evidence in favor of the hypothesis that cultural integration depends on social organization can be found in the historical development of modern national cultures—Italian, French, Spanish, German, English, Swedish, Polish, Russian, American, Chinese, Japanese, etc. Each of these cultures includes a common literary language (which may be also a part of another culture, though with some differences) ; secular literature written in this language (epics, lyrics, drama, semi-fictitious and fictitious prose, history, biography, political and legal ideologies, general philosophy, eventually also products of cultural and natural sciences) ; all realms of art (architecture, painting, sculpture, music) ; systems of technical production; and economic systems. And each culture is viewed by its educated participants as well as by investigators as a unique, more or less integrated whole. Every national culture grows through centuries by the creative contributions of numerous individuals, although, as we have seen above, when social conflicts between nationalities are very active, creative tendencies are checked by national conservatism.

I have been investigating comparatively for many years not national cultures as such, a task beyond my competence, but the development of the social organization to which their growth and integration are due. It is impossible to summarize here the results of this investigation. The important point is that, however much these cultures differ, the development of social organization by the collectivities which create and maintain them was, and is, essentially the same. It began in various realms of culture with the emergence of social roles of creative leaders who gained followers and sponsors. And it continued with the progressive formation of social groups which promoted the organization, extension, and duration of various cultural systems. Throughout this development the common ideal of the individuals and the groups who participated in it was *social unification* of the millions of people who were supposed to share the same, age-old cultural heritage (and sometimes a common semi-mythical biological ancestry), although they were divided into diverse ethnic subgroups, separate states, social classes, and sometimes even conflicting religious groups. A fully developed and integrated literary culture, superimposed through education upon more or less diversified folk cultures, regional cultures, class cultures, and religious cultures was expected to become, and actually did become, a powerful bond of social solidarity—more powerful than political, economic, or even religious bonds. But this was achieved only through the continuous cooperation of increasingly numerous, diverse social groups which gradually became functionally united into an organized, highly complex society.

The connection between sociology and natural sciences

When we compare the conceptions of the human individual used by such cultural scientists as religionists or historians of literature, who consistently apply the humanistic coefficient to the phenomena they investigate, with the conception of the natural scientist, who does not use this coefficient at all, we do not find any logical connection between the two. From the point of view of cultural scientists, a religious prophet or a poet can be defined exclusively by what he experiences, thinks, and does as an active participant in the realm of culture. It is irrelevant for the theory of religion or of literature how this particular individual would appear to outside observers who know nothing about his conscious life and creative work. Indeed, most prophets and poets are dead and thus inaccessible to observation. But, from the point of view of the natural scientist, every human individual as a biological system is accessible to outside observers and definable by his anatomical structure and physiological functions. And since as an organism he is essentially like organisms of various animal genera, with only minor differences—indeed, there is much less difference between him and other mammals than, say, between other mammals and insects—his cultural experiences and actions have little bearing on his biological definition. Furthermore, while the culture in which conscious agents participate must be conceived by the cultural scientist as these agents experience it, the natural environment in which organisms live is conceived by the natural scientist as he and other natural scientists experience it. Consequently, a student of literature or religion can and usually does ignore the results of biological research, and a human biologist can and usually does ignore the results of research of historians and theorists of religion and of literature.

But this separatism does not apply to sociology. Since the sociologist investigates actions of which human individuals are the main objects, he must take into consideration some facts which human biologists investigate. For he finds that, from the point of view of those who act upon human individuals, these individuals are organisms as well as conscious agents; that actions to which they are subjected as well as their reactions to these actions vary, depending upon their biological characteristics (age, sex, bodily structure, state of health); and that social interaction is conditioned by the natural environment in which individuals live. On the other hand, human biologists, even though sometimes unwillingly, have to take into consideration some results of sociological research. For the environment of a human organism includes other human organisms, and their mutual adaptation involves so-called "symbolic behavior," or rather "symbolic interbehavior," which implies their mutual awareness as conscious agents and their purposive tendencies to influence one another—in short, the very facts which sociologists investigate.

However, in spite of certain doctrines of metaphysical dogmatists, the connection between sociology as a cultural science and biology as a natural science is not direct, but indirect. Two intermediate scientific disciplines connect them: psychology of human individuals, and demography of human collectivities.

1. Psychology can function as a connecting link between sociology and biology, because it is no longer a special nomothetic science of one category of phenomena. It investigates three distinct categories and seeks to discover functional relationships between them. The main category is the one which nineteenth-century psychologists started to investigate methodically, with the result that psychology changed from a plurality of different, often conflicting, ontological doctrines of the human individual as a spiritual and/or a material entity into an inductive science. These phenomena, as we mentioned before, are actual individual experiences appearing and disappearing in the course of time. Beginning with the psychologist's reflective observation and comparative analysis of the flux of his own experiences (which still remains essential as a standard of comparison), it extends to a study of the experiences of others as described by themselves in symbolic communication with the psychologist. In experimental psychology specific common data and facts are being selected and made accessible to the psychologist and to all those conscious subjects with whom he communicates, and comparison is limited to their experiences of these data and facts.

But, as we know, though such studies provide the basic material for psychological generalizations, modern psychology is not limited to them. Psychologists increasingly investigate not only how an individual experiences certain data or facts, but also how he behaves or acts when he experiences them. This has, first, a methodical purpose. Investigation of such behavior or activity provides the psychologist with an additional source of information about the subject's experiences. It not only supplements and tests his descriptions of his own experiences, which may be unreliable, but even supplants them when the subject's ability for symbolic communication is inadequate or nonexistent. Experimental studies of behavior or activity consist in producing definite situations for experimental subjects and observing how they solve these situations.

Second, such an extension of the realm of psychology links it with biological studies of animal behavior and with studies of culturally patterned human actions. Physiological psychology investigates the dependence of individual experiences and behavior upon physiological functions of the organism in relation to its physical environment, while social psychology studies the dependence of an individual's experiences, attitudes, and actions upon the social influences to which he is subjected by participants in the collectivity in which he lives.

The results of these studies are synthesized in the theory of the human individual as a personality to be investigated in the course of his life history. Inasmuch as the individual obviously begins to live as an organism long before he becomes a conscious cultural agent, theories of the personality usually start with human biology and proceed to physiological psychology; they then take into account the results of studies of those experiences and active tendencies which are not determined by the organism's relations with its natural environment, but are being learned through social interaction with other individuals, and finally incorporate information about the functioning of the individual as an active participant in culture.

This theory of the psychologists is still ontological, since the personality is conceived as a biopsychological or biosocial being, an inclusive whole. But it is more significant scientifically than the old static conception of this being as either a single material entity, a body, or a dual entity composed of body and mind; for it concentrates upon the gradual emergence of what is presumed to be a more or less integrated, dynamic combination of conscious attitudes and actions from a purely biological system. Gardner Murphy's *Personality* is the best example of this approach.[47]

The main scientific importance, however, of such thorough, objective, and conscientious studies is that they show how impossible it is to synthetize into one general theory of human personalities as a logical class two categories of order, each with a wide range of variations: the natural order of the individual organism, and the axionormative order of values and actions in which the individual as a conscious agent participates. Individual human organisms as biological systems differ; the natural environments in

[47] Gardner Murphy, *Personality* (New York: Harper, 1947).

which they live also vary considerably. Much greater, and irreducible to these differences, is the diversity of cultural patterns and systems in which individuals participate; for not only do the total cultures maintained by particular collectivities differ widely, but within each collectivity there are many different, culturally regulated functions which individuals perform in the course of their lives. If all these differential components of individual lives are taken into consideration, as they have to be by a student who postulates the existence of a total personality emerging from an organism which remains its permanent though changing foundation, then each personality as a whole is *unique*. This is what Gordon Allport emphasizes in his conception of the personality.[48] But if so, what is the scientific significance of synthetic psychological studies of particular personalities?

Their significance for natural sciences in general or for human biology in particular does not concern us here. Their significance for cultural sciences, especially sociology, will become clear, if we begin with the cultural rather than the natural approach. We are justified in so doing, for as a matter of fact the existence of culture is taken for granted by psychologists before they begin any studies of human personalities, and the entire course of these studies is socially conditioned.

We should not forget, in the first place, that the psychologist himself, if and when he starts with the assumption that the organism is the foundation of every human personality, functions as a participant in that vast and complex system of culturally patterned, functionally interdependent actions called "biology," which slowly evolved in the course of cultural history; and consequently, this naturalistic assumption of his is a cultural product. But—what is even more important for the results of his psychological research—as soon as he starts to investigate particular human individuals, he begins to function as one of the participants in the collectivity in which these individuals are located. Every individual whom he studies is a social value to other participants, even an infant, not yet a conscious and active participant. Even simple observation by the psychologist of this organism's outward behavior is usually observed by other participants and must seem to them to conform with recognized cultural patterns or at least not to transgress such patterns. As he proceeds to study the behavior of this organism in situations which require that the organism experience certain data and facts which the psychologist himself experiences, the psychologist's attitude toward his subject is like that of other active participants, e.g., parents, who conceive this human being not only as living, but as conscious. When the psychologist produces experimental situations for his subject to solve, he performs social actions in which his subject is the central value; and these actions are more or less like many culturally patterned

[48] Gordon Allport, *Personality: a Psychological Interpretation* (New York: Holt, 1937).

actions performed by other participants in the collectivity in dealing with the same individual. When the psychologist communicates verbally with his subject, both function as participants in a common cultural system of axio-normatively ordered actions called "language," which he and his subject learned during more or less long periods of socially ordered education. When the psychologist investigates the attitudes and actions of his subjects who are learning to participate or already fully participating in other kinds of cultural systems—social groups, material technique, religion, art, literature—he must know, either from active participation or from cultural investigation, what the axionormative order of those systems is. And all the time, whatever he does, he is himself a social object not only to all his subjects who are sufficiently conscious to be aware of him, but to other participants in the collectivity; and his actions are subjected to their judgments.

In short, unless John Watson's dream of a closed psychological laboratory including subjects completely isolated after birth from the outside world comes true, psychological research must be carried on within the cultural framework of a collectivity with a social order of which every action of the psychologist and every reaction of his subjects forms an integral component. Why not begin with the study of this cultural framework and the social order?

Such is the approach now used by those cultural anthropologists and sociologists who, while taking for granted that the functioning of the individual organism as a biological system is an essential condition of all individual participation in culture, yet want to ascertain by inductive research the relative importance of cultural and biological factors, especially in explaining differences between attitudes and actions of individual participants. Insofar as such differences affect the functioning of cultural systems, it is important to know how they originated.[49] Thus, among participants in a particular system there may be creative innovators and traditionalists, transgressors and conformists, leaders and followers, rulers and subjects. If we can trace the origin of these individual differences, it will help us explain why the system functions as it does. Moreover, in complex cultures, we find growing individual specialization, professional and occupational. We will understand better the evolution of this specialization and the differentiation of functions which specialists perform, if we can discover why some individuals specialize in one profession or occupation rather than in another.

Comparative studies of personal life histories provide factual material for the solution of these problems. Since, however, the problems to be solved are cultural, not biological, every investigation should begin with the study

[49] This is the main task which some modern social psychologists have undertaken. See Richard T. LaPiere and Paul R. Farnsworth, *Social Psychology* (New York: McGraw, 1949), especially Parts IV and V.

of the individual's cultural life history. But what is an individual's cultural life history? It is not simply a history of the development of his psychological personality as an entity in which all his subjective experiences, attitudes, and active tendencies are completely included. It is inseparable from the life histories of other participants in the same culture. The cultural data which he experiences are the same as those which others experience. His attitudes are interconnected with the attitudes of others and usually subjected to common ideological models. His active tendencies are interdependent with the tendencies of others and usually follow some common cultural pattern. His conscious life is an integral component of the culture in which he and others participate and cannot be abstracted from it.

But there is a *continuity* in the course of his cultural participation. It is not the continuity of mind (an unobservable construct of psychologists), but the continuity of an observable dynamic component of his life history. It is his continuous identification by others and by himself as the same lasting, though changing, object of many diverse actions performed in the past and expected to be performed in the future by a number of agents, and as the same lasting, conscious agent who performed many diverse actions in the past and is expected to perform them in the future. Although his own identification of his self develops under the influence of social interaction with others and is originally a reflection of their identification of him, yet, since his past experiences and later memories of the actions of which he was the object inevitably differ from those of others, his own representation of his continuous ego becomes increasingly different from that of others, especially if, as is often the case, the individual conceptions which others have of him vary considerably.[50]

Now, as we noticed before, the conceptions which other agents have of an individual's past actions and their anticipations as to his future actions influence their actions bearing upon him. On the other hand, the individual's own memory of the actions to which he was subjected, and of the actions he himself performed, conditions his anticipations of the future actions to which he will be subjected and of his own future actions. In short, his cultural past influences his cultural future—the more so, the longer and richer his past. To ascertain exactly this influence, the individual's life history should be studied, both as it appears to himself as participant in culture and as it appears to his fellow participants. In other words, both autobiographical and biographical materials are needed.

Within this cultural framework, all biological influences upon the individual's cultural participation can be included. As a general heuristic premise,

[50] The influence of this component has been thoroughly studied, though its importance is rather overemphasizd by Muzafer Sherif and Hadley Cantril, *The Psychology of Ego-Involvements* (New York: Wiley, 1947).

we might suggest that, whatever is inexplicable by the individual's cultural past—not only as an agent, but as an object of other people's actions—has to be explained by his biological disposition as his organism grew and changed in adaptation to changing environmental conditions. The question is, can such studies be combined so as to allow comparisons to be made, not between unique life histories in their total course but between specific components of individual life histories?

We believe that sociology provides the answer to this question in the concept of *social role* as a system of relations between one individual and several others. An individual's biological dispositions are *included in the cultural patterns* of many social roles. Thus, the social role of a child from the time of his birth includes, on the one hand, the duty of adults to provide for his organic needs, to respond to manifestations of his biological drives, to aid and guide his neuromuscular behavior, to reward biologically motivated behavior considered desirable, to repress or deflect behavior considered undesirable, and to stimulate the development of sensory and symbolic experiences. On the other hand, we find the growing expectation of adults that the child will react positively to their actions and will accept their communication of the idea that it is his duty to do so.

Thus, the biological influences affecting an individual's cultural life history do not have to be studied in abstraction from the cultural influences; they can be observed as they affect the course of particular social roles in which the individual is the main, but never the only, actor. Since in the course of his life the individual performs many social roles, each of which conditions what other people do to him and what he will do in some later roles, it may be said that his total personality from the sociological point of view is a dynamic historical synthesis of all his social roles.

2. When we designate "demography" as the second intermediate science between sociology and natural sciences, we give it a broader meaning than it usually has. We believe this is a good term to denote all studies of populations or total human collectivities inhabiting certain geographic areas during certain periods of time. Many demographers concentrate on statistical studies of the composition of the population. Human geographers are mostly concerned with relations between the population and the natural environment within which it lives. And human ecologists study the spatial distribution of this population within the area in consequence of the biological dependence of its human components upon the limited supplies of the environment. Yet it is the *population* which constitutes the common subject matter of all these specialists, and their work is mutually supplementary and interdependent.[51]

[51] The connection between statistical demography and anthropology was fully realized by Friedrich Ratzel, who devoted a large section of his famous work to what he called "Das statistische Bild der Menschheit," *Anthropogeographie*, II (Stuttgart, 1922), 95-260.

Their specialization is for purely practical reasons and has no objective, theoretic basis, as it has in the differentiation of the various cultural and of the various natural sciences.

Now, demographic studies of spatially located human collectivities, just as psychological studies of human individuals, explicitly or implictly start with obvious naturalistic premises. In order to survive, men must have a natural environment to which they can become biologically adapted and which will furnish them the necessary means for subsistence. Mankind, like any other genus, will last beyond the life span of a single generation only if new organisms are born and grow to maturity; and inasmuch as participants in a human collectivity, just as in an animal or plant collectivity, compete for the available means of subsistence, there must be some symbiosis between them for the collectivity to survive.

Since, obviously, no culture can last without human collectivities to maintain it, these three universal natural conditions for the existence of human collectivities are also universal essential conditions for the existence of cultures. Therefore, when the problem arises as to how to explain the differences between human collectivities and the changes within a collectivity, demographers usually try to solve it as far as possible by resorting to natural causes. This does not mean that all of them ignore cultural factors. According to geographic determinists, the significant differences between collectivities— their biological composition, the ways in which their needs are satisfied, their material culture, social organization, even ideational culture—are essentially due to differences in geographical environment; and their main changes are effects of natural environmental changes, especially of climate.[52] But most human geographers take into consideration the cultural variations between peoples living in similar environments, as well as those appearing in the same environment during successive historical periods, and the culturally initiated changes in the environment.[53] Although racial determinists claim that differences between collectivities are essentially due to hereditary differences in their biological composition and that the main changes are caused by racial mixtures or by positive or negative selection within the races, only a few of them ignore the influence of cultural innovation and diffusion. Malthus ascribed the most important changes in human collectivities to the natural law, according to which population tends to increase at a geometrical rate, whereas natural resources can increase at only an arithmetical rate; yet

[52] This approach is typically represented by Ellsworth Huntington and Sumner W. Cushing, *Principles of Human Geography* (New York: Wiley, 1921). According to their theory, there are three kinds of "elements of human geography": first, physical conditions—location, land forms, bodies of water, soil and minerals, climate; second, plants and animals; third, "human responses," which include all activities and their products, from food and drink to religion and art.

[53] Definitely so, Ratzel, *op. cit.*

neither Malthus nor the neo-Malthusians ignore the cultural factors which can affect both the rate of births and the rate of increase of resources. And human ecologists recognize that human ecology, as well as natural plant and animal ecology, is influenced by culture in general, especially by standards and norms of social order.[54] Furthermore, all naturalistic demographers include in their theories migrations, both as effects of natural demographic changes and as natural causes of other demographic changes; and many of them have taken into consideration certain cultural aspects of migration.

What is common to nearly all of them is the assumption that the investigator of territorially located collectivities should begin with the naturalistic approach; according to this, natural objects and processes observed by the investigator can be studied without considering the cultural data and facts experienced by the people themselves, until the investigator finds that he has to include some of them in order to explain certain natural processes.[55] He can take for granted the lasting geographic location of a population as a natural phenomenon and even explain it by migration as a natural process, unless and until he discovers that certain cultural factors conditioned this migration and settlement. As a naturalist, he can survey the flora and fauna found in the geographic environment of a collectivity until, in asking how it came to be there, he discovers that the existence of some species in this area is due to the technical culture of the population. The composition of the population, its continuity, and its changes can be studied from the strictly biological point of view, until it is found that in the course of history definite cultural standards and norms have affected and are affecting these biological phenomena, etc.[56]

---

[54] Cf. Quinn, *op. cit.* For some recent developments, see Thomas Robertson, *Human Ecology* (Glasgow, 1949); Amos H. Hawley, *Human Ecology* (New York: Ronald Press, 1950); and James A. Quinn, *Human Ecology* (New York: Prentice-Hall, 1950).

[55] There are exceptions, however. Jean Brunhes, *La Géographie humaine* (Paris, 1912), explicitly states: "Human geography . . . must be, first of all, *the geography of material human works*; it is also a geography of *human masses and races*, but only in the measure that these masses and races express their specific and differential modes of activity through material works" (p. 87).

[56] This was the typical approach of the founder of scientific statistical demography, Adolphe Quételet, in his *Physique sociale*, 2 vols. (Brussels, 1869); and it continues to predominate in "population studies," especially when investigators are primarily concerned with the practically important *effects* of population changes, rather than with their causes. An extreme manifestation of this attitude is a short book by Henri F. Secrétan, *La Population et les moeurs* (Paris, 1913). The author assumes that the increasing or decreasing "density of peoples" is an important factor of "historical crises." The transformations of "mores" during these changes are effects of population changes. He never asks whether the reverse may not be possible. Edward B. Reuter, in *Population Problems*, 2d ed. (Philadelphia: Lippincott, 1923), and Edward C. Hayes, in the editorial introduction to that book, emphatically consider population studies important, because population changes have a great influence upon the "welfare and permanence" of the social group; the study of their influence, rather than the explanation of these

The trouble is that under this naturalistic approach, widely diverse and complex cultural variables become included in studies of particular collectivities without yielding any adequate scientific generalizations about them which could serve as a basis for comparison between collectivities. Not only does each collectivity differ from others in the biological composition of its population and the nature of its geographic environment, but the cultural factors which affect the history of both differ even more. Each collectivity is as unique, when viewed in its natural and cultural history, as each human personality viewed in its biopsychological life history.

Suppose, now, that demographers reversed their procedure, began with the results of historical and ethnological studies of particular cultures, and then supplemented them with studies of the geographic environment, the biological composition, and the symbiosis of the peoples who maintain these cultures.[57] This would not conflict with the premise based on the indubitable results of natural sciences, that the existence of human collectivities as lasting natural complexes of organisms living together in definite natural environments and adapted to their environment is the essential condition of the existence of culture. But it would introduce another premise, also based on valid results of scientific research; that is, on studies of those human collectivities which are accessible to direct observation or about which reliable historical or prehistorical evidence is available: The premise that the existence of culture is the essential condition of their lasting existence as natural complexes in natural environments.

Demographers must realize that they are not the first to observe geographic areas, the populations which inhabit these areas, the environmental conditions under which these populations live, and the biological continuity of these populations, their symbiosis, and their migrations. The people themselves who compose these populations also observe such natural phenomena, though their observations differ from those of demographers, inasmuch as these phenomena are mainly of practical significance to them as objects of their valuations and actions.

First, as cultural scientists have discovered during the last thirty years, human experiences and conceptions of space, especially of geographic areas, are evaluative and culturally standardized, and most of them differ very much from the theoretically standardized conceptions of astronomers and geographers. It is not the geographer's conception, but that of the inhabitants, which primarily conditions the limits of the area they inhabit, its sub-

---

changes, is the primary task. Only recently have demographers turned their attention to those hitherto neglected problems. See Paul H. Landis, *Population Problems. A Cultural Interpretation* (New York: American Book, 1943), especially Part II, "Cultural Forces in Vital Processes."

[57] Such an approach was attempted by Ludwik Krzywicki, *Primitive Society and its Vital Statistics* (London, 1930).

division into parts, the purposes for which each part is used, the distribution of habitats, the admission or exclusion of outsiders, etc.

Second, the inhabitants themselves experience, define, and classify one another according to standards which also frequently differ from those of the demographer; and it is their definitions and classifications, not those of the demographer, which condition their interactions. Third, they are usually even more conscious of the biological continuity of the demographic collectivity to which they belong than the demographer, for their consciousness usually extends to a distant past and envisions a far future; moreover, since they evaluate this continuity by definite standards and regulate it by definite norms, their ideas condition sexual selection, rate of births, and survival of the young, though obviously only within the range of natural possibilities. Fourth, so far as environmental conditions are concerned, their knowledge, objectively judged, is probably less thorough than that of the geographer, but whatever they believe they know about geological formation, flora, fauna, soil, water, climate, etc., they actually use in conformity with their own cultural patterns. And when it comes to migration, the decisive factors are not only the technical means of territorial mobility, but the culturally standardized definitions and valuations of settled populations as well as of migrants concerning spatial areas, men as social objects, and natural conditions and resources.

In short, at no stage in demographic research can the investigator study a population and its environment as natural phenomena, in abstraction from the valuations and actions of those who compose this population and who have experienced these phenomena and dealt with them for many years, sometimes for centuries, before the demographer appeared. Of course, the demographer will be able to explain by his superior knowledge of natural conditions certain similarities, differences, and changes in the cultural order of the collectivities he investigates which would be otherwise inexplicable; but he must first know this order.

Can this approach help us draw better generalizations than the naturalistic approach, concerning the connection between natural and cultural factors in collectivities whose histories differ so widely? Here again sociology provides the concept of a common dynamic component which conditions the cultural and natural history of all collectivities. It is the concept of *social group*. Every inhabitable territory on the surface of the globe, every section of this territory is a possession of some social group, often a joint possession of several groups, and is subjected to its or their control. Nobody can live in any portion of space or even move across it without the explicit or implicit permission of the group which controls it or tends to gain control over it. The struggles between social groups for territories as common values are well-known factors of demographic changes. Every individual participant of a population is a member of several groups, and most of his relationships with other participants as well as with outsiders depend on the groups to which he and they belong. Utilization of natural resources and culturally initiated changes in the natural environment are usually regulated by social groups, and sometimes are carried on collectively by social groups. The biological continuity of the population depends on the continued duration of the various groups of which every newborn individual is expected to become a member as he grows up. Changes in the composition of the population through migration are usually initiated or impeded by social groups. Each of these groups deals with natural phenomena, and their functions depend upon what these phenomena are from the observer's point of view and how the group defines, evaluates, and uses them. By comparing the standards and norms of these groups, on the one hand, and the phenomena with which they deal, on the other hand, it is possible to ascertain which similarities, differences, and changes in their functions are due to cultural uniformities, variations, or innovations, and which can be explained by the natural conditions under which they function. And when new kinds of groups evolve, their evolution may be studied also by taking into consideration their cultural origin and the natural conditions under which they function.

Thus, by viewing the population of a given territory in the course of its duration as a dynamic complex of changing social groups, whether interacting or not with groups existing outside of this territory, demographers will be able to compare it with populations inhabiting other territories during the same period or the same territory during other periods, taking into consideration primarily the cultural and secondarily the natural factors which affect their continuous existence.

As a matter of fact, many agglomerated results of historical research can already be used for this purpose. For instance, the main trends in population shifts and environmental changes during the last two centuries within certain areas of the present United States can be investigated comparatively in the light of historical knowledge about specific social groups and their relationships: autochthonic ethnic groups, invading groups of colonists and later immigrant groups with diverse cultures, genetic groups, religious groups, growing and expanding political groups of various degrees of complexity and levels of integration, and especially the new industrial and economic groups continually evolving.

Practical Applications of Cultural Sciences

Difficulties in solving practical problems

In our survey of the development of scientific knowledge about culture, we did not take into account the practical applications of this knowledge. And yet, insofar as they affect the course of human lives, these applications are commonly considered to be even more important than the knowledge itself. Many cultural scientists, especially sociologists and social psychologists, devote most of their efforts to application of the results of theoretic research for the solution of practical problems in which other people are involved. And even those who specialize exclusively in scientific theory are aware that their conclusions will be evaluated by thinkers interested in practical problems, and by the public at large, according to their presumed usefulness to human individuals and collectivities. Consequently, any cultural scientist may be accused of being enclosed in an ivory tower, unless he can answer the challenging question: Knowledge for what?

A survey of all the significant attempts to apply in practice the results of scientific research in the domain of culture would be a long and strenuous task, even for a competent investigator—and I am not competent to perform it. But let me indulge in a few tentative generalizations.

One of the strongest arguments of the critics of cultural sciences who contrast them with natural sciences is their failure to provide adequate techniques by which the cultural life of mankind could be controlled. The development of natural sciences has enabled man to gain increasing control over nature, whereas the human world, the world of culture, seems to remain beyond his control. Right now, civilization is in danger of being destroyed by the use of new technical inventions, products of natural scientists and engineers, and cultural scientists are apparently powerless to prevent it.

Undoubtedly, the practical applications of cultural sciences are much less effective than those of natural sciences. But we believe that this is due to difficulties similar to those which have impeded the very development of cultural sciences, and that these difficulties are being gradually overcome.

All practical progress in any realm of human activity is due to innovations introduced for use in the future; their usefulness will depend upon the possibility of predicting their consequences. The advantage of scientific knowledge is that general conclusions from observation of the past provide a basis for predicting the future and for testing these predictions by new observations. Scientific experimentation is the best method of devising and applying such tests.

Now, there are obvious, fundamental differences between introducing innovations, predicting their results, and testing these predictions in the domain of nature and performing analogous functions in the domain of culture. In the first place, when a natural scientist carries on an experiment, he functions as a conscious agent entirely independent of the phenomena with which he deals. He is the maker of the experimental situation, not a part of it; the components of the situation are passive objects of his actions, and the results of his experiment depend entirely on what he is doing to them. Moreover, he can artificially produce a relatively closed system subjected only to such external influences as can be hypothetically predicted. Whereas a cultural scientist who tries to introduce an innovation intended to be used by others, a new standard of valuation and/or norm of conduct—whatever the attitudes and actions he wants to influence, whether religious, aesthetic, linguistic, economic, technical, hedonistic, intellectual, or social— must perform social actions bearing upon others. And since each of his subjects is a participant in a collectivity with many diverse cultural systems, he cannot isolate his experimental situation from external influences as effectively as a natural scientist can. If he carries on an experiment, it is first of all a social experiment. He deals with other human agents and is himself involved in the experimental situation as an object of attitudes and actions of those with whom he deals. The results of his experiment depend on the relations between his actions and those of his experimental subjects. Moreover, an experimentator who tries to find out how a new cultural pattern can be introduced must have some knowledge not only of social interaction, but of those specific cultural actions which he attempts to influence. Under such complicated conditions, it is obviously much more difficult to predict the results of his experiments or to discover why his prediction has proved invalid, if it has.

Nevertheless, many experiments have been carried on more or less successfully by sociologists, sometimes using the results of other cultural scientists to supplement sociological knowledge. Most experiments serve to test *causal* hypotheses which, if proved valid, are later used by practical agents. Experimentators perform specific actions expected to influence specific attitudes or tendencies of their subjects, and observe their reactions. Here belong, for instance, the majority of experimental studies of the reactions of children and students to actions of psychologists or teachers. The recent large-scale experimental studies of the reactions of certain classes of the public to economic advertizing and political propaganda through mass media of communication belong to this type. Of course, most of the causal hypotheses which these experiments test, and the tests themselves, are not based on exact comparative study of the effects which certain specific actions have upon active tendencies of particular individuals. Nonetheless, the results of these experiments are indubitably recognized as useful for practical purposes; consequently, they are gaining the increasing support of powerful individuals and groups.

Another kind of experiment, more recently developed and used mostly on a smaller scale, is the collective performance of common tasks by a group of experimental subjects at the initiative of the experimentator. Such experiments have been carried on by theorists of education in many kindergartens, not so many primary schools, fewer secondary schools, and very few colleges; however, extracurricular activities on all school levels are often treated by educational sociologists as experiments of the same type. Similar experiments have been started by social workers, rural sociologists, urban sociologists, students of cooperative movements. These experiments are obviously not applications or tests of causal hypotheses, but of hypotheses of functional interdependence between the actions of several agents on which the very existence of collectively maintained cultural systems depends.

Consequently, they are of fundamental importance, both from the theoretic and from the practical point of view. Certain significant conclusions have been reached. The development of new systems, whether similar to or different from the already existing ones, presupposes social cooperation between those who contribute to their formation. It has been proved that this development is effective in the measure in which the cooperation of participating individuals is a spontaneous manifestation of their own active tendencies rather than the effect of coercion exerted by controlling agents.

While tests of practical innovations introduced by scientists for experimental purposes are much more difficult in the realm of culture than in the realm of nature, in one respect cultural scientists have a certain advantage over natural scientists. Innovations are continually being introduced for practical purposes by human agents who are not scientists: political innovations by legislators, administrators, revolutionists; economic innovations by financiers, business managers, socioeconomic reformers; moral innovations by ethical idealists; religious innovations by prophets and priests; aesthetic innovations by plastic artists, poets, musical composers; and, of course, technical innovations created by scientists, but applied and spread by technical organizers and planners, industrial managers, governmental officials, military staffs, etc. Cultural scientists can treat such innovations *as if* they were experiments, predict hypothetically, on the basis of theoretic knowledge already developed, what their results will be if no unexpected external influences interfere with their course, and test these hypotheses by observing the results. This obviously requires that scientists should have the opportunity of investigating objectively each innovation from its very beginning through its subsequent course; and such opportunities are as yet seldom granted. Nonetheless, scientists frequently do obtain considerable information about the course of some innovations, attempt to predict their future, and try to explain why their predictions prove wrong (as they often do) by problematizing their original hypothesis and seeking to discover in what respects their knowledge was defective.

The second well-known difficulty which cultural scientists meet when they apply theoretic knowledge to practical problems is that such applications are apt to raise controversial issues of right and wrong. No such issues have to be faced by natural scientists while they are functioning as scientists; every technical invention is judged by pragmatic standards of efficiency, and any disagreements as to its efficiency can be solved by experimental methods. But an innovation in the domain of culture which affects human attitudes and actions—political, economic, moral, religious, aesthetic, hedonistic, educational—usually involves ideological controversies and leads to social conflicts.

Thus, when a cultural scientist has to solve a controversial practical problem, he must make a choice between different ideologies and find a solution which will be satisfactory from the point of view of the one he has chosen; then it will inevitably be opposed by those who disagree with his choice. Even the practical use of inventions made by natural scientists, insofar as it affects human lives, raises issues which have important cultural implications. We know that technical inventions which give the group that uses them advantages over other groups in economic competition or political struggle stimulate intergroup antagonism and sharpen social conflicts. The development of machine industry, leading to an aggressive expansion of Western capitalism, resulted in increasing conflicts, first between industrialized nations and technically backward peoples, later among the industrialized nations themselves. Military inventions have made wars increasingly destructive.

The prospect of applied sociology

Can cultural scientists ever overcome such conflicts, find common principles which could be applied by them to all cultural innovations and enable them to cooperate in practical applications of theoretic knowledge, as they are already cooperating in the advancement of theoretic knowledge? We believe that sociologists have developed such principles, partly under the influence of certain social philosophers, and are already using them on an increasingly large scale. These principles are based not on arbitrary evaluative and normative judgments of sociologists themselves, but on objective comparative study of social attitudes and actions.

In the first place, they found long ago that in every human community mutual positive valuation of individual participants and the performance by participants of actions which benefit others are generally considered much more satisfactory than negative mutual valuations and the performance of actions harmful to others. Consequently, when sociologists function as practical scientists within their communities and try to solve social problems which apparently cannot be solved without their guidance, they try to apply the results of sociology and social psychology in stimulating the development of positive social relations between individual participants and eliminating or preventing antagonistic interaction. This is what students of the family, social welfare workers, criminologists (especially those dealing with juvenile delinquency), rural sociologists, sociologists working in urban neighborhoods have been doing. We do not know of any practical sociologist tending to stimulate interindividual antagonism.

Second, in studying relationships between social groups, sociologists find that effective cooperation between groups for common or mutually supplementary purposes is usually considered satisfactory by members of these groups. Whereas an intergroup struggle which may be satisfactory from the point of view of members of the winning group is judged as unsatisfactory by members of the losing group. If the struggle lasts for a long time and culminates in mutual violence and destruction, it has effects on each group which its members consider harmful. Consequently, sociologists who investigate attitudes and active tendencies of cooperating groups and of groups involved in struggles generally try to invent methods by which intergroup cooperation could be developed and intergroup struggles eliminated and apply these methods in practice if they have the opportunity to do so. This is what they are doing, for instance, in dealing with relationships between racial or ethnic groups within a certain territory, or between managerial and labor groups. Seldom, if ever, do scientific sociologists nowadays try to stimulate conflicts between groups; for they dropped long ago the doctrine of social Darwinism, according to which intergroup struggles, however undesirable from the point of view of those who participate in them, are good for mankind because they make the fittest groups survive. Of course, once an intergroup struggle has started, sociologists may come to the hypothetic conclusion (whether scientifically valid or not) that the victory of one group (e.g., of the Germans in World War II) would have consequences more undesirable from the point of view of the vanquished or of outsiders who might be affected by it than the victory of the other group. In such a case sociologists might attempt to find ways of preventing such consequences. But usually seeking how to prevent or reduce intergroup struggles and to develop intergroup cooperation is nowadays one of the main problems of applied sociology.

This problem has reached world-wide proportions in recent times. But the sociologists who look for its possible solution find that similar problems on a narrower scale have been faced by social thinkers and agents for thousands of years and sometimes solved (though not always) by trial-and-error techniques. The accumulative consequence of these solutions has been a slow but general trend toward the progressive integration of smaller groups into increasingly larger groups. The most important manifestations of this trend have been the passage "from clans to empires" (which is the title of a history of ancient Egypt by Davy and Moret) ; the passage from secret magico-religious associations of two or three scores of men to religious groups as large as three hundred million; the passage from rural folk communities of several hundred people with a somewhat traditional culture to modern urbanized cultural nations of millions of people, each with a rich and complex literary culture of its own; the passage from small groups of a dozen or so economically interdependent individuals to vast fluid combinations of numerous functionally specialized, economically interdependent groups of producers, ranging in size up to a hundred thousand or even more persons. Throughout this history two different methods were used: coercive submission of weaker groups to the domination of a stronger group, mainly for the purpose of repressing conflicts, and voluntary unification of groups.

This age-old trend is nowadays definitely directed toward world unity, integration of all the large and influential social groups, however different their cultures and however diversified and specialized their functions. And here the question arises: If this trend continues and is not reversed, by which of the two methods will world unity be eventually achieved, by submission of all groups to the domination of one powerful group monopolizing the instruments of social control or by voluntary unification of all the groups functioning in the various realms of culture? In short, is mankind facing a static world empire or a dynamic world-wide association of functionally interdependent, cooperating groups?

Most sociologists seem to favor and, we believe, will increasingly favor the second method. This is not simply because they find that men generally prefer freedom to submission. Quite a few recent historical events indicate that, when freedom requires initiative and responsibility in solving problems, many men prefer the authoritative control which gives a ready solution of all such problems. But these events suggest another tentative conclusion: that authoritarian domination impedes initiative and originality; and considerable historical evidence supports this conclusion. Sociologists, like most cultural scientists, share a positive interest in the creative growth of culture; and since they also investigate the social conditions of individual participation in culture, they are aware that this growth depends upon development of the creative potentialities of human individuals in general and their training for voluntary cooperation in collective production of new values. This is the third main principle which, in our opinion, will increasingly guide sociologists in practical applications of their science.

Of course, the vital practical problems in any realm of culture cannot be solved by sociologists alone without the cooperation of other cultural scientists; but such cooperation will steadily increase as the theoretic importance of sociology as a basic science becomes generally recognized. However, this still leaves a fundamental difficulty, which even natural scientists are often unable to overcome. In order to introduce into a large human collectivity an innovation which will affect its future, the innovating individual or group must have considerable *social* prestige and power. Now, scientists may have social prestige, but seldom power. We recall that Plato, after discouraging experiences as adviser of rulers, saw only two ways for the realization of his ideal of a perfect republic: Either kings will be philosophers, or philosophers will become kings. Both ways are impossible nowadays. The social functions of rulers and leaders and the intellectual functions of men of knowledge are too specialized, too difficult, and too exacting for any individual to combine both effectively.

But kings are becoming gradually aware that they need philosophers. In recent times nearly every government—even the Nazi government—has used the help of specialists in various realms of culture as experts in legislation and executive planning. Some cultural scientists—as yet too few—are carrying on research for the United Nations. However, the practical problems which these scientists are expected to solve are usually selected and defined by rulers or ruling groups, not by the scientists themselves. And in most cases such quick results are demanded that there is little opportunity for original and thorough research.

In general, cultural scientists are esteemed by governmental agents much lower than natural scientists. This is, of course, partly due to those methodical difficulties mentioned before which make practical applications of the cultural sciences less effective and their results less easy to ascertain; but other obstacles interfere with the recognition of their usefulness. Many practical problems with which governmental agents deal are controversial and involve conflicts between political parties, bureaucratic groups, special interest groups who want different solutions and are unwilling to abide by any solutions worked out by independent scientists. And even when no such controversies arise, the men endowed with public authority—legislators, administrators, judges, military commanders—though usually aware of their ignorance of modern natural sciences, are often entirely unaware of their ignorance of cultural sciences—especially in the social realm—and are sure that because of their practical experience they can solve social problems better than the less experienced scientists.

Since all these difficulties are rooted in the organization of the social groups which compose a government, and in their relationships with other groups within the state and with governmental groups in other states, the task of overcoming such difficulties and gaining the cooperation of all groups for the solution of cultural problems can be performed only by the practical application of sociology as the science of social groups. We cannot say how and when this will be achieved, but we have some grounds for assuming that such an achievement is possible.

As a sociologist and a philosophical optimist, I like to imagine that sooner or later the solution of all important human problems will be entrusted to cultural scientists, and that sociologists will assume the task of ascertaining how innovations of specialists in various realms of culture (including the realms of natural sciences and of techniques) can be cooperatively used by social groups of practical agents for the best advantage of humanity. This does not mean that the future of mankind would be planned and controlled by sociologists, as Comte imagined, or that the human world would become not only socially united, but culturally uniform. It means rather that sociologists would function as intellectual leaders in the ceaseless course of differentiation and integration of social roles and social groups throughout the world. By performing this function, they would indirectly contribute to the continuous creative growth of new varieties of cultural systems and the enrichment and diversification of individual lives.

Index to Subjects

Quantitative methods in cultural sciences; *see* Measurement; Statistics

Questionnaires as empirical material about attitudes, 251-58

Recession of ideological systems, 290-94

Relationships
between actions
causal, 225-34
functional, 311-28
between natural and cultural data, 140-41
between various categories of cultural phenomena, 376-77

Relativity and idealistic metaphysics, 90-91

Religion, 22-26, 43-49, 134-35, 271-76, 300-03, 310-16

Religionists, theorists, 300-03

Religious
actions, 300-03
ideological systems, 271-76
systems of actions, 310-16

Reorganization of cultural systems
conservative, 353-59
creative, 359-72

Roads, 324-26

Rugs, 303-07

Science in general, characterized by theoretic objectivity and inductive method, 94
slowly liberated from metaphysics, 96-97

"Science of man," a combination of various controversial theories of man and culture, 110

Sciences, plurality and diversity of, 94
cultural, 183-400
intermediary, 400-11
natural, 159-72

Self, 118-19, 147

Self-consciousness, 118-19

Sensory experience, 116-18, 125-26

Sins, 331, 333-34

Situations, 241-43

Social actions
general definition, 389
axionormatively ordered, 389-90

Social actions—*Continued*
functionally integrated into axionormatively organized systems, 390-91

Social control, not a cause of action or inaction, but of changes in active tendencies, 23-33

Social integration, as main factor of all cultural integration, 398-400

Social order; *see Order*
ethical conception, 391
scientific conception, 387-92

Social statics versus social dynamics, 279-80

Social systems
groups, 390, 410-11
roles, 390-91, 406, 410-14
social relations, 390, 410-11

Socialist ideals, 288

Socialization of technical products as an ideal, 363-64
early attempts to realize, 364
influencing adherents of capitalistic economics, 364-65
applied by autocratic government of Russia, 366-68

Society
as an integration of social relationships, 385-86
as social integration of cultural phenomena which its members share, 382-84
as spatial receptacle of culture, 137-38
as system
cultural, 380-81
natural, 107
natural and cultural, 106, 385

Sociology
applied to practical problems, 415-19
connection of
with natural sciences, 400-11
with other cultural sciences, 393-400
as general science of culture, 380-84
as general science of man, 110
as science of order among human actions, 387-92
as special science of human relations, 385-86

Indices

Index to Names[1]

Abel, Theodore, viii
Adler, Alfred, 147, 181
Agar, Herbert, 220n
Ahriman, 338
Albig, John William, viii, 241
Alexander I, 35n
Alexander the Great, 31, 33, 146
Alexander Severus, 34
Alexander, William, 60n
Alfred the Great, 31
Allier, Raoul, 19, 20
Allport, Gordon, 403
Alviella, Goblet d', 300n
Ames, Edward S., 217n
Ampère, 170
Angell, J. R., 127
Angelo, Michael, 178
Anthony, Saint, 338
Antonius Pius, 34
Apollo, 301
Aquinas, Thomas, 271, 287
Archimedes, 170
Ariadne, 156
Aristarchus, 171
Aristotle, 89n, 91, 95, 96, 98, 99, 166, 278, 279, 289
Arnold, E. Vernon, 285n
Arthur, King, 30
Assur-nazir-pal, 31

Astarte, 301
Augustine, Saint, 89n
Augustus Caesar, 34

Baal, 301
Babcock, R. W., 206n
Bach, Johann Sebastian, 379n
Bacon, Francis, 24, 101, 284
Baker, George, 101n
Bain, Read, 240n
Baldwin, James M., 122n
Bar, Carl L. von, 334n
Barbusse, Henri, 37
Barnes, Harry E., 9n, 62n, 101n, 108n, 113n, 182n, 263n, 285n, 345n, 387n, 396n
Barry, Frederick, 161n
Bartels, Max, 309n
Barth, Paul, 381
Bateson, Gregory, 271
Bastian, Adolf, 97n
Bastiat, Frédéric, 163
Bathurst, Effie, 206n
Baudouin, Charles, 220n
Bebel, Ferdinand August, 288n
Becker, Frances B., 9n, 62n, 387n, 396n
Becker, Howard, 9n, 62n, 101n, 108n, 182, 263n, 285n, 375n, 386n, 387n, 396n

[1] Since we could not include in our brief survey of the development of sociology all the important contributions of contemporary sociologists, many well-known authors are not mentioned. Their works will be discussed in a later book.